THE BOOK ®

Citroën Berlingo & Peugeot Partner
Owners Workshop Manual

John S. Mead and A K Legg AAE MIMI

Models covered

(4281 - 3AQ1 - 400)

Citroen Berlingo Multispace & Van (inc. 'First') and Peugeot Partner Combi & Van (inc. 'Origin')
Petrol engines: 1.4 litre (1360cc) & 1.6 litre (1587cc)
Diesel engines: 1.6 litre (1560cc), 1.8 litre (1769cc), 1.9 litre (1868cc & 1905cc) & 2.0 litre (1997cc), inc. turbo

Does NOT cover models with 1.8 litre (1761cc) petrol engines
Does NOT cover new 'B9' model range introduced during 2008

© Haynes Publishing 2011

ABCDE
FGH

A book in the **Haynes Service and Repair Manual Series**

ISBN 978 0 85733 950 8

British Library Cataloguing in Publication Data
A catalogue record for this book is available from the British Library.

Printed in the USA

Haynes Publishing
Sparkford, Yeovil, Somerset BA22 7JJ, England

Haynes North America, Inc
861 Lawrence Drive, Newbury Park, California 91320, USA

Haynes Publishing Nordiska AB
Box 1504, 751 45 UPPSALA, Sverige

Contents

LIVING WITH YOUR CITROËN BERLINGO & PEUGEOT PARTNER

MAINTENANCE

Routine maintenance and servicing

Contents

Designed as a joint venture between Citroën and Peugeot, the Berlingo and Partner were introduced into the UK in 1996 as purpose-built Vans available in 600kg or 800kg payloads. To increase the appeal of the range, the Berlingo Multispace MPV was introduced in mid-1998. The Multispace is mechanically identical to the Van version but with the addition of rear seats, side windows and additional interior trim. Initially, all models were available only in three-door format, but in mid-1999, the option of a sliding side door on the right-hand side was added. The Peugeot MPV version, known as the Partner Combi, joined the model line-up for the 2001 model year, which also saw the introduction, on all models, of a second sliding side door for the left-hand side.

In the autumn of 2002, the entire range underwent a major facelift, with significant styling changes to the front bumpers, headlights, bonnet and front wings, together with numerous mechanical and electrical revisions.

During the production run a variety of petrol and diesels engines have been offered according to model and year of production. These include 1.4 litre (1360cc), and 1.6 litre (1587cc) petrol engines, and 1.8 litre (1769cc), 1.9 litre (1868cc &1905cc) and 2.0 litre (1997cc) diesel and turbo-diesel engines. A 1.8 litre (1761cc) petrol engine was also available for a limited period on early models, but is not covered in this manual. The engines are all of four-cylinder single- or double-overhead camshaft design and are versions of the well-proven units which have appeared in many Citroën and Peugeot vehicles over the years. All engines are fitted with a manual transmission as standard and are mounted transversely at the front of vehicle, with the transmission mounted on the left-hand end.

The front suspension is of the fully-independent MacPherson strut type, incorporating shock absorbers, coil springs and an anti-roll bar. The rear suspension is derived from the Peugeot 405 range and is of the semi-independent type with torsion bars and trailing arms. Rack-and-pinion steering gear is used with power assistance available on most models.

A wide range of standard and optional equipment is available within the range to suit most tastes, including power steering, central locking, engine immobiliser, electric windows, electric sunroof and airbags. An anti-lock braking system and air conditioning system are also available as options, or standard equipment on certain models.

Provided that regular servicing is carried out in accordance with the manufacturer's recommendations, the vehicle should prove reliable and very economical. The engine compartment is well-designed, and most of the items requiring frequent attention are easily accessible.

Your Owner's Manual

The aim of this manual is to help you get the best value from your vehicle. It can do so in several ways. It can help you decide what work must be done (even should you choose to get it done by a garage), provide information on routine maintenance and servicing, and give a logical course of action and diagnosis when random faults occur. However, it is hoped that you will use the manual by tackling the work yourself. On simpler jobs it may even be quicker than booking the vehicle into a garage and going there twice, to leave and collect it. Perhaps most important, a lot of money can be saved by avoiding the costs a garage must charge to cover its labour and overheads.

The manual has drawings and descriptions to show the function of the various components so that their layout can be understood. Tasks are described and photographed in a clear step-by-step sequence.

References to the 'left-hand' and 'right-hand' sides of the vehicle are always in the sense of when viewed by a person sat in the driver's seat, facing forwards.

Acknowledgements

Thanks are due to Draper Tools Limited, who provided some of the workshop tools, and to all those people at Sparkford who helped in the production of this Manual.

We take great pride in the accuracy of information given in this manual, but vehicle manufacturers make alterations and design changes during the production run of a particular vehicle of which they do not inform us. No liability can be accepted by the authors or publishers for loss, damage or injury caused by errors in, or omissions from, the information given.

Working on your car can be dangerous. This page shows just some of the potential risks and hazards, with the aim of creating a safety-conscious attitude.

General hazards

Scalding

• Don't remove the radiator or expansion tank cap while the engine is hot.
• Engine oil, transmission fluid or power steering fluid may also be dangerously hot if the engine has recently been running.

Burning

• Beware of burns from the exhaust system and from any part of the engine. Brake discs and drums can also be extremely hot immediately after use.

Crushing

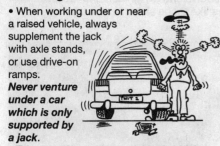

• When working under or near a raised vehicle, always supplement the jack with axle stands, or use drive-on ramps.
Never venture under a car which is only supported by a jack.
• Take care if loosening or tightening high-torque nuts when the vehicle is on stands. Initial loosening and final tightening should be done with the wheels on the ground.

Fire

• Fuel is highly flammable; fuel vapour is explosive.
• Don't let fuel spill onto a hot engine.
• Do not smoke or allow naked lights (including pilot lights) anywhere near a vehicle being worked on. Also beware of creating sparks (electrically or by use of tools).
• Fuel vapour is heavier than air, so don't work on the fuel system with the vehicle over an inspection pit.
• Another cause of fire is an electrical overload or short-circuit. Take care when repairing or modifying the vehicle wiring.
• Keep a fire extinguisher handy, of a type suitable for use on fuel and electrical fires.

Electric shock

• Ignition HT and Xenon headlight voltages can be dangerous, especially to people with heart problems or a pacemaker. Don't work on or near these systems with the engine running or the ignition switched on.

• Mains voltage is also dangerous. Make sure that any mains-operated equipment is correctly earthed. Mains power points should be protected by a residual current device (RCD) circuit breaker.

Fume or gas intoxication

• Exhaust fumes are poisonous; they can contain carbon monoxide, which is rapidly fatal if inhaled. Never run the engine in a confined space such as a garage with the doors shut.
• Fuel vapour is also poisonous, as are the vapours from some cleaning solvents and paint thinners.

Poisonous or irritant substances

• Avoid skin contact with battery acid and with any fuel, fluid or lubricant, especially antifreeze, brake hydraulic fluid and Diesel fuel. Don't syphon them by mouth. If such a substance is swallowed or gets into the eyes, seek medical advice.
• Prolonged contact with used engine oil can cause skin cancer. Wear gloves or use a barrier cream if necessary. Change out of oil-soaked clothes and do not keep oily rags in your pocket.
• Air conditioning refrigerant forms a poisonous gas if exposed to a naked flame (including a cigarette). It can also cause skin burns on contact.

Asbestos

• Asbestos dust can cause cancer if inhaled or swallowed. Asbestos may be found in gaskets and in brake and clutch linings. When dealing with such components it is safest to assume that they contain asbestos.

Special hazards

Hydrofluoric acid

• This extremely corrosive acid is formed when certain types of synthetic rubber, found in some O-rings, oil seals, fuel hoses etc, are exposed to temperatures above 4000C. The rubber changes into a charred or sticky substance containing the acid. *Once formed, the acid remains dangerous for years. If it gets onto the skin, it may be necessary to amputate the limb concerned*.
• When dealing with a vehicle which has suffered a fire, or with components salvaged from such a vehicle, wear protective gloves and discard them after use.

The battery

• Batteries contain sulphuric acid, which attacks clothing, eyes and skin. Take care when topping-up or carrying the battery.
• The hydrogen gas given off by the battery is highly explosive. Never cause a spark or allow a naked light nearby. Be careful when connecting and disconnecting battery chargers or jump leads.

Air bags

• Air bags can cause injury if they go off accidentally. Take care when removing the steering wheel and trim panels. Special storage instructions may apply.

Diesel injection equipment

• Diesel injection pumps supply fuel at very high pressure. Take care when working on the fuel injectors and fuel pipes.

 Warning: Never expose the hands, face or any other part of the body to injector spray; the fuel can penetrate the skin with potentially fatal results.

Remember...

DO

• Do use eye protection when using power tools, and when working under the vehicle.

• Do wear gloves or use barrier cream to protect your hands when necessary.

• Do get someone to check periodically that all is well when working alone on the vehicle.

• Do keep loose clothing and long hair well out of the way of moving mechanical parts.

• Do remove rings, wristwatch etc, before working on the vehicle – especially the electrical system.

• Do ensure that any lifting or jacking equipment has a safe working load rating adequate for the job.

DON'T

• Don't attempt to lift a heavy component which may be beyond your capability – get assistance.

• Don't rush to finish a job, or take unverified short cuts.

• Don't use ill-fitting tools which may slip and cause injury.

• Don't leave tools or parts lying around where someone can trip over them. Mop up oil and fuel spills at once.

• Don't allow children or pets to play in or near a vehicle being worked on.

The following pages are intended to help in dealing with common roadside emergencies and breakdowns. You will find more detailed fault finding information at the back of the manual, and repair information in the main chapters.

If your car won't start and the starter motor doesn't turn

☐ Open the bonnet and make sure that the battery terminals are clean and tight.
☐ Switch on the headlights and try to start the engine. If the headlights go very dim when you're trying to start, the battery is probably flat. Get out of trouble by jump starting (see next page) using a friend's car.

If your car won't start even though the starter motor turns as normal

☐ Is there fuel in the tank?
☐ Is there moisture on electrical components under the bonnet? Switch off the ignition, then wipe off any obvious dampness with a dry cloth. Spray a water-repellent aerosol product (WD-40 or equivalent) on ignition and fuel system electrical connectors like those shown in the photos.

A Check the security and condition of the battery connections.

B On petrol engines check that the ignition HT coil wiring connector is securely connected (1.4 litre petrol model shown).

C Also check the security of the wiring connectors at the various engine management sensors such as the coolant temperature sensor.

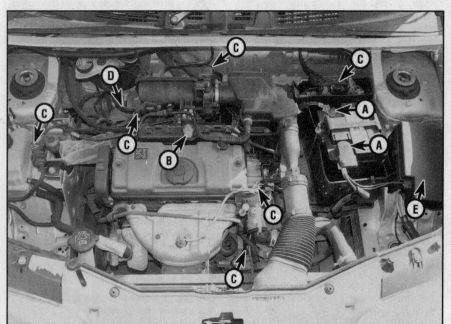

Check that all electrical connections are secure (with the ignition switched off) and spray them with a water-dispersant spray like WD-40 if you suspect a problem due to damp.

D Check that the alternator wiring connectors are securely connected.

E Check that all fuses are still in good condition and none have blown.

Jump starting

When jump-starting a car using a booster battery, observe the following precautions:

✔ Before connecting the booster battery, make sure that the ignition is switched off.

✔ Ensure that all electrical equipment (lights, heater, wipers, etc) is switched off.

✔ Take note of any special precautions printed on the battery case.

✔ Make sure that the booster battery is the same voltage as the discharged one in the vehicle.

✔ If the battery is being jump-started from the battery in another vehicle, the two vehicles MUST NOT TOUCH each other.

✔ Make sure that the transmission is in neutral (or PARK, in the case of automatic transmission).

 HAYNES HINT *Jump starting will get you out of trouble, but you must correct whatever made the battery go flat in the first place. There are three possibilities:*

1 *The battery has been drained by repeated attempts to start, or by leaving the lights on.*

2 *The charging system is not working properly (alternator drivebelt slack or broken, alternator wiring fault or alternator itself faulty).*

3 *The battery itself is at fault (electrolyte low, or battery worn out).*

1 Connect one end of the red jump lead to the positive (+) terminal of the flat battery

2 Connect the other end of the red lead to the positive (+) terminal of the booster battery.

3 Connect one end of the black jump lead to the negative (-) terminal of the booster battery

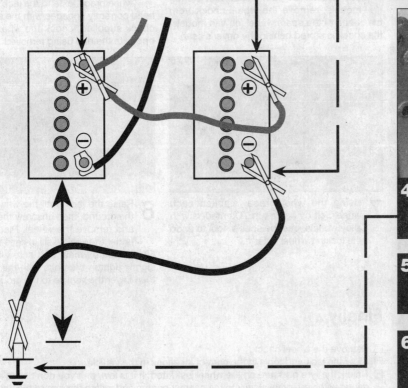

4 Connect the other end of the black jump lead to a bolt or bracket on the engine block, well away from the battery, on the vehicle to be started.

5 Make sure that the jump leads will not come into contact with the fan, drive-belts or other moving parts of the engine.

6 Start the engine using the booster battery and run it at idle speed. Switch on the lights, rear window demister and heater blower motor, then disconnect the jump leads in the reverse order of connection. Turn off the lights etc.

Wheel changing

Some of the details shown here will vary according to model. For instance, the location of the spare wheel and jack is not the same on all vehicles. However, the basic principles apply to all vehicles.

Warning: Do not change a wheel in a situation where you risk being hit by other traffic. On busy roads, try to stop in a lay-by or a gateway. Be wary of passing traffic while changing the wheel – it is easy to become distracted by the job in hand.

Preparation

☐ When a puncture occurs, stop as soon as it is safe to do so.
☐ Park on firm level ground, if possible, and well out of the way of other traffic.
☐ Use hazard warning lights if necessary.
☐ If you have one, use a warning triangle to alert other drivers of your presence.
☐ Apply the handbrake and engage first or reverse gear.
☐ Chock the wheel diagonally opposite the one being removed – a chock is provided in the tool kit for this purpose.
☐ If the ground is soft, use a flat piece of wood to spread the load under the jack.

Changing the wheel

1 The jack and wheelbrace are stored behind the driver's seat on Van models . . .

2 . . . and behind a cover panel on the rear right-hand side on Multispace and Combi models.

3 At the rear of the load area, lift up the floor covering and use the wheelbrace to lower the spare wheel cradle.

4 Disengage the cradle from the lifting hook and slide the spare wheel out from under the vehicle. On Multispace and Combi models, remove the wheel chock from the centre of the spare wheel (on Van models, the chock is stored behind the driver's seat).

5 Position the jack on firm ground below the reinforced area on the sill (indicated by a triangle – arrowed). Using the wheelbrace, extend the jack until the jack head correctly engages with the sill. Using the chock supplied, chock the wheel diagonally opposite the one being removed.

6 On models with steel wheels, remove the wheel trim/hub cap (as applicable).

7 Using the wheelbrace, slacken each wheel bolt by half a turn. On models with alloy wheels, use the special tool to undo the locking wheel nuts.

8 Raise the jack until the wheel is clear of the ground, then unscrew the wheel bolts and remove the wheel. Place the wheel under the vehicle sill in case the jack fails.
Fit the spare wheel and screw in the bolts. Lightly tighten the bolts with the wheelbrace, then lower the vehicle to the ground.

9 Securely tighten the wheel bolts in a diagonal sequence then refit the wheel trim/hub cap (as applicable).

Finally...

☐ Remove the wheel chock.
☐ Stow the jack and tools in the correct locations in the vehicle.
☐ Check the tyre pressure on the wheel just fitted. If it is low, or if you don't have a pressure gauge with you, drive slowly to the nearest garage and inflate the tyre to the right pressure.
☐ Have the damaged tyre or wheel repaired as soon as possible.

Identifying leaks

Puddles on the garage floor or drive, or obvious wetness under the bonnet or underneath the car, suggest a leak that needs investigating. It can sometimes be difficult to decide where the leak is coming from, especially if an engine undershield is fitted. Leaking oil or fluid can also be blown rearwards by the passage of air under the car, giving a false impression of where the problem lies.

 Warning: Most automotive oils and fluids are poisonous. Wash them off skin, and change out of contaminated clothing, without delay.

 The smell of a fluid leaking from the car may provide a clue to what's leaking. Some fluids are distinctively coloured. It may help to remove the engine undershield, clean the car carefully and to park it over some clean paper overnight as an aid to locating the source of the leak.
Remember that some leaks may only occur while the engine is running.

Sump oil

Engine oil may leak from the drain plug...

Oil from filter

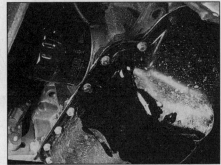

...or from the base of the oil filter.

Gearbox oil

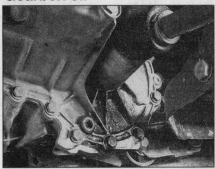

Gearbox oil can leak from the seals at the inboard ends of the driveshafts.

Antifreeze

Leaking antifreeze often leaves a crystalline deposit like this.

Brake fluid

A leak occurring at a wheel is almost certainly brake fluid.

Power steering fluid

Power steering fluid may leak from the pipe connectors on the steering rack.

Towing

When all else fails, you may find yourself having to get a tow home – or of course you may be helping somebody else. Long-distance recovery should only be done by a garage or breakdown service. For shorter distances, DIY towing using another car is easy enough, but observe the following points:

☐ Use a proper tow-rope – they are not expensive. The vehicle being towed must display an ON TOW sign in its rear window.
☐ Always turn the ignition key to the 'on' position when the vehicle is being towed, so that the steering lock is released, and that the direction indicator and brake lights will work.
☐ Only attach the tow-rope to the towing eye provided at the front or rear of the vehicle.
☐ Before being towed, release the handbrake and select neutral on the transmission.
☐ Note that greater-than-usual pedal pressure will be required to operate the brakes, since the vacuum servo unit is only operational with the engine running.

☐ On models with power steering, greater-than-usual steering effort will also be required.
☐ The driver of the vehicle being towed must keep the tow-rope taut at all times to avoid snatching.
☐ Make sure that both drivers know the route before setting off.
☐ Only drive at moderate speeds and keep the distance towed to a minimum. Drive smoothly and allow plenty of time for slowing down at junctions.

Introduction

There are some very simple checks which need only take a few minutes to carry out, but which could save you a lot of inconvenience and expense.

These *Weekly checks* require no great skill or special tools, and the small amount of time they take to perform could prove to be very well spent, for example:

☐ Keeping an eye on tyre condition and pressures, will not only help to stop them wearing out prematurely, but could also save your life.

☐ Many breakdowns are caused by electrical problems. Battery-related faults are particularly common, and a quick check on a regular basis will often prevent the majority of these.

☐ If your vehicle develops a brake fluid leak, the first time you might know about it is when your brakes don't work properly. Checking the level regularly will give advance warning of this kind of problem.

☐ If the oil or coolant levels run low, the cost of repairing any engine damage will be far greater than fixing the leak, for example.

Underbonnet check points

▶ 1.4 litre petrol engine (pre-September 2002)

A *Engine oil level dipstick*

B *Engine oil filler cap*

C *Coolant expansion tank*

D *Power steering fluid reservoir*

E *Brake fluid reservoir*

F *Washer fluid reservoir*

G *Battery*

▶ 1.6 litre petrol engine

A *Engine oil level dipstick*

B *Engine oil filler cap*

C *Coolant expansion tank*

D *Power steering fluid reservoir*

E *Brake fluid reservoir*

F *Washer fluid reservoir*

G *Battery*

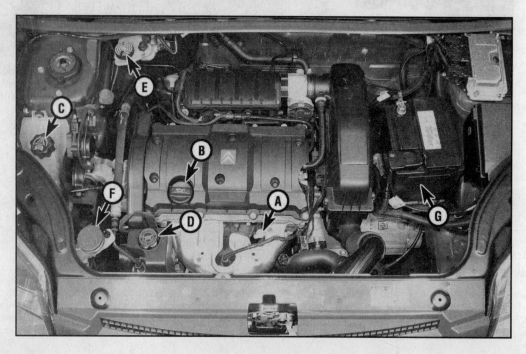

▶ **1.6 litre diesel engine**

A Engine oil level dipstick

B Engine oil filler cap

C Coolant expansion tank

D Power steering fluid reservoir

E Brake/clutch fluid reservoir

F Washer fluid reservoir

G Battery

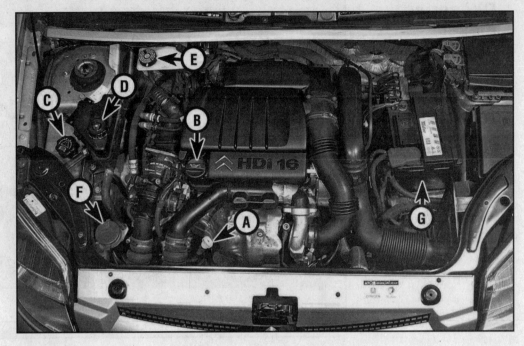

▶ **1.9 litre DW series diesel engine (pre-September 2002) – XUD series diesel similar**

A Engine oil level dipstick

B Engine oil filler cap

C Coolant expansion tank

D Power steering fluid reservoir

E Brake fluid reservoir

F Washer fluid reservoir

G Battery

▶ **1.9 litre DW series diesel engine (post-September 2002)**

A Engine oil level dipstick
B Engine oil filler cap
C Coolant expansion tank
D Power steering fluid reservoir
E Brake fluid reservoir
F Washer fluid reservoir
G Battery

▶ **2.0 litre DW series diesel engine (post-September 2002)**

A Engine oil level dipstick
B Engine oil filler cap
C Coolant expansion tank
D Power steering fluid reservoir
E Brake fluid reservoir
F Washer fluid reservoir
G Battery

Engine oil level

Before you start
✔ Make sure that your vehicle is on level ground.
✔ Check the oil level before the vehicle is driven, or at least 5 minutes after the engine has been switched off.

 HAYNES HiNT *If the oil is checked immediately after driving the vehicle, some of the oil will remain in the upper engine components, resulting in an inaccurate reading on the dipstick.*

The correct oil
Modern engines place great demands on their oil. It is very important that the correct oil for your vehicle is used (see *Lubricants and fluids*).

Car Care
● If you have to add oil frequently, you should check whether you have any oil leaks. Place some clean paper under the vehicle overnight, and check for stains in the morning. If there are no leaks, the engine may be burning oil.

● Always maintain the level between the upper and lower dipstick marks (see photo 3). If the level is too low, severe engine damage may occur. Oil seal failure may result if the engine is overfilled by adding too much oil.

1 The dipstick is often brightly coloured for easy identification. Withdraw the dipstick.

2 Using a clean rag or paper towel, wipe all the oil from the dipstick. Insert the clean dipstick into the tube as far as it will go, then withdraw it again.

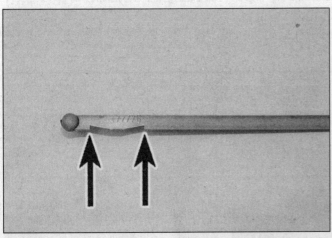

3 Note the oil level on the end of the dipstick, which should be between the upper (MAX) mark and lower (MIN) mark.

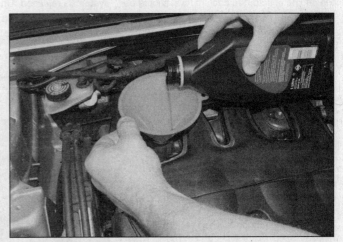

4 Oil is added through the filler cap. Unscrew the cap and top up the level; a funnel may help to reduce spillage. Add the oil slowly, checking the level on the dipstick often. Don't overfill (see *Car Care*).

Coolant level

⚠️ **Warning: DO NOT attempt to remove the expansion tank pressure cap when the engine is hot, as there is a very great risk of scalding. Do not leave open containers of coolant about, as it is poisonous.**

Car Care

● Adding coolant should not be necessary on a regular basis. If frequent topping-up is required, it is likely there is a leak. Check the radiator, all hoses and joint faces for signs of staining or wetness, and rectify as necessary.

● It is important that antifreeze is used in the cooling system all year round, not just during the winter months. Don't top-up with water alone, as the antifreeze will become too diluted.

1 The coolant level varies with engine temperature. On pre-September 2002 petrol models, the level is checked in the expansion tank, which is built into the right-hand side of the radiator. When the engine is cold, the coolant level should be between the MAX and MIN marks.

2 On pre-September 2002 diesel models, the expansion tank is located above the radiator, and the level can only be checked by removing the expansion tank cap (see step 4). When the engine is cold, the level is correct when it is just below the MAXI mark indicated on the side of the tank.

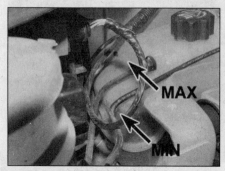

3 On all post-September 2002 petrol and diesel models, the level is checked in the expansion tank located on the right-hand side of the engine compartment. When the engine is cold, the coolant level should be between the MAX and MIN marks indicated on the side of the tank.

4 If topping-up is necessary, wait until the engine is cold then turn the expansion tank cap slowly anti-clockwise, and pause until any pressure remaining in the system is released. Unscrew the cap and lift off.

5 Add a 50/50 mixture of water and antifreeze to the expansion tank, until the coolant level is up to the MAX level mark. Refit the cap, turning it clockwise as far as it will go until it is secure.

Screen washer fluid level

Screenwash additives not only keep the windscreen clean during foul weather, they also prevent the washer system freezing in cold weather – which is when you are likely to need it most. Don't top-up using plain water as the screenwash will become too diluted, and will freeze during cold weather.
On no account use coolant antifreeze in the washer system – this could discolour or damage paintwork.

1 The washer fluid reservoir is located at the front right-hand side of the engine compartment. To check the fluid level, open the cap and look down the filler neck.

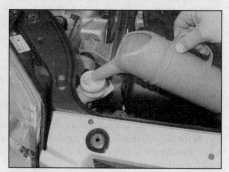

2 If topping-up is necessary, add water and a screenwash additive in the quantities recommended on the bottle.

Power steering fluid level

Before you start

✔ Park the vehicle on level ground.
✔ Set the steering wheel straight-ahead.
✔ The engine should be turned off.

HAYNES HINT *For the check to be accurate, the steering must not be turned once the engine has been stopped.*

Safety First!

● The need for frequent topping-up indicates a leak, which should be investigated immediately.

1 On pre-September 2002 models, the power steering fluid reservoir is located on the right-hand side of the engine compartment. The fluid level should be checked with the engine stopped. A translucent reservoir is fitted, with MAX and MIN markings on the reservoir.

2 The fluid level should be between the MAX and MIN marks. If topping-up is necessary, and before removing the cap, wipe the surrounding area so that dirt does not enter the reservoir.

3 Unscrew the cap, allowing the fluid to drain from the bottom of the cap as it is removed. Top up the fluid level to the MAX mark, using the specified type of fluid (do not overfill the reservoir), then refit and tighten the filler cap.

4 On post-September 2002 models, the power steering fluid reservoir is integral with the power steering pump, located at the front of the engine. With the engine stopped, wipe clean the area around the reservoir filler neck, and unscrew the filler cap from the reservoir.

5 Wipe all fluid from the cap dipstick with a clean rag. Refit the filler cap, then remove it again and note the fluid level on the dipstick. When the engine is cold the fluid level should be between the lower (ADD) mark and the middle (C) mark on the dipstick. If the engine is warm, the fluid level may be up to the upper (H) mark.

6 If the fluid level is on or below the lower (ADD) mark, top-up the fluid level to the middle (C) mark, using the specified type of fluid (do not overfill). When the level is correct, securely refit the filler cap.

Brake fluid level

Warning:
● Brake fluid can harm your eyes and damage painted surfaces, so use extreme caution when handling and pouring it.
● Do not use fluid that has been standing open for some time, as it absorbs moisture from the air, which can cause a dangerous loss of braking effectiveness.

 ● Make sure that your vehicle is on level ground.
● The fluid level in the reservoir will drop slightly as the brake pads and shoes wear down, but the fluid level must never be allowed to drop below the MIN mark.

Safety First!

● If the reservoir requires repeated topping-up this is an indication of a fluid leak somewhere in the system, which should be investigated immediately.

● If a leak is suspected, the vehicle should not be driven until the braking system has been checked. Never take any risks where brakes are concerned.

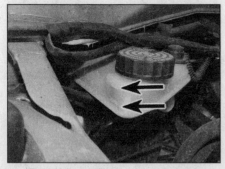

1 The MAX and MIN marks are indicated on the side of the reservoir, which is located on the front of the vacuum servo unit in the engine compartment. The fluid level must be kept between these two marks.

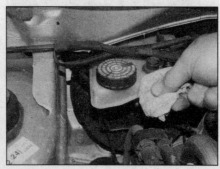

2 If topping-up is necessary, first wipe the area around the filler cap with a clean rag before removing the cap. When adding fluid, it's a good idea to inspect the reservoir. The system should be drained and refilled if dirt is seen in the fluid (see Chapter 9).

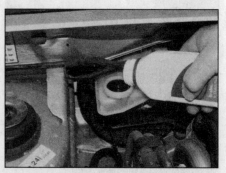

3 Carefully add fluid, avoiding spilling it on surrounding paintwork. Use only the specified hydraulic fluid; mixing different types of fluid can cause damage to the system and/or a loss of braking effectiveness. After filling to the correct level, refit the cap securely and wipe off any spilt fluid.

Wiper blades

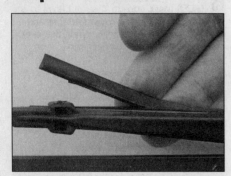

1 Check the condition of the wiper blades; if they are cracked or show any signs of deterioration, or if the glass swept area is smeared, renew them. Wiper blades should be renewed annually.

2 To remove a windscreen wiper blade, pull the arm fully away from the screen until it locks. Swivel the blade through 90°, then depress the locking clip at the base of the mounting block.

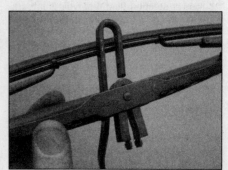

3 Move the blade down the arm to disengage the mounting block, then slide the blade from the arm. Don't forget to check the rear wiper blade(s) as well (where applicable).

Battery

Caution: Before carrying out any work on the vehicle battery, read the precautions given in 'Safety first!' at the start of this manual.

✔ Make sure that the battery tray is in good condition, and that the battery is secure. Corrosion on the tray and the battery itself can be removed with a solution of water and baking soda. Thoroughly rinse all cleaned areas with water. Any metal parts damaged by corrosion should be covered with a zinc-based primer, then painted.

✔ Periodically (approximately every three months), check the charge condition of the battery as described in Chapter 5A.

✔ If the battery is flat, and you need to jump start your vehicle, see *Roadside Repairs*.

HAYNES HiNT

Battery corrosion can be kept to a minimum by applying a layer of petroleum jelly to the clamps and terminals after they are reconnected.

1 The battery is located on the left-hand side of the engine compartment. The exterior of the battery should be inspected periodically for damage such as a cracked case or cover.

3 If corrosion (white, fluffy deposits) is evident, remove the cables from the battery terminals, clean them with a small wire brush, then refit them. Automotive stores sell a useful tool for cleaning the battery post . . .

2 Check the tightness of the battery cable clamps to ensure good electrical connections. You should not be able to move them. Also check each cable for cracks and frayed conductors.

4 . . . as well as the battery cable clamps.

Electrical systems

✔ Check all external lights and the horn. Refer to the appropriate Sections of Chapter 12 for details if any of the circuits are found to be inoperative.

✔ Visually check all accessible wiring connectors, harnesses and retaining clips for security, and for signs of chafing or damage.

HAYNES HiNT

If you need to check your brake lights and indicators unaided, back up to a wall or garage door and operate the lights. The reflected light should show if they are working properly.

1 If a single indicator light, brake light or headlight has failed, it is likely that a bulb has blown and will need to be renewed. Refer to Chapter 12 for details. If both brake lights have failed, it is possible that the brake/stop-light switch operated by the brake pedal has failed. Refer to Chapter 9 for details.

2 If more than one indicator light or tail light has failed it is likely that either a fuse has blown or that there is a fault in the circuit (see Chapter 12). The main fuses are located behind the cover in the facia on the driver's side . . .

3 . . . and in the fuse/relay box in the engine compartment. To renew a blown fuse, remove it, where applicable, using the plastic tool provided. Fit a new fuse of the same rating, available from vehicle accessory shops. It is important that you find the reason that the fuse blew (see *Electrical fault finding* in Chapter 12).

Tyre condition and pressure

It is very important that tyres are in good condition, and at the correct pressure - having a tyre failure at any speed is highly dangerous.

Tyre wear is influenced by driving style - harsh braking and acceleration, or fast cornering, will all produce more rapid tyre wear. As a general rule, the front tyres wear out faster than the rears. Interchanging the tyres from front to rear ("rotating" the tyres) may result in more even wear. However, if this is completely effective, you may have the expense of replacing all four tyres at once!

Remove any nails or stones embedded in the tread before they penetrate the tyre to cause deflation. If removal of a nail does reveal that the tyre has been punctured, refit the nail so that its point of penetration is marked. Then immediately change the wheel, and have the tyre repaired by a tyre dealer.

Regularly check the tyres for damage in the form of cuts or bulges, especially in the sidewalls. Periodically remove the wheels, and clean any dirt or mud from the inside and outside surfaces. Examine the wheel rims for signs of rusting, corrosion or other damage. Light alloy wheels are easily damaged by "kerbing" whilst parking; steel wheels may also become dented or buckled. A new wheel is very often the only way to overcome severe damage.

New tyres should be balanced when they are fitted, but it may become necessary to re-balance them as they wear, or if the balance weights fitted to the wheel rim should fall off. Unbalanced tyres will wear more quickly, as will the steering and suspension components. Wheel imbalance is normally signified by vibration, particularly at a certain speed (typically around 50 mph). If this vibration is felt only through the steering, then it is likely that just the front wheels need balancing. If, however, the vibration is felt through the whole car, the rear wheels could be out of balance. Wheel balancing should be carried out by a tyre dealer or garage.

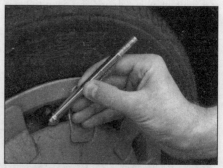

1 Tread Depth - visual check
The original tyres have tread wear safety bands (B), which will appear when the tread depth reaches approximately 1.6 mm. The band positions are indicated by a triangular mark on the tyre sidewall (A).

2 Tread Depth - manual check
Alternatively, tread wear can be monitored with a simple, inexpensive device known as a tread depth indicator gauge.

3 Tyre Pressure Check
Check the tyre pressures regularly with the tyres cold. Do not adjust the tyre pressures immediately after the vehicle has been used, or an inaccurate setting will result. Tyre pressures are shown on page 0•20.

Tyre tread wear patterns

Shoulder Wear

Underinflation (wear on both sides)
Under-inflation will cause overheating of the tyre, because the tyre will flex too much, and the tread will not sit correctly on the road surface. This will cause a loss of grip and excessive wear, not to mention the danger of sudden tyre failure due to heat build-up.
Check and adjust pressures
Incorrect wheel camber (wear on one side)
Repair or renew suspension parts
Hard cornering
Reduce speed!

Centre Wear

Overinflation
Over-inflation will cause rapid wear of the centre part of the tyre tread, coupled with reduced grip, harsher ride, and the danger of shock damage occurring in the tyre casing.
Check and adjust pressures

If you sometimes have to inflate your car's tyres to the higher pressures specified for maximum load or sustained high speed, don't forget to reduce the pressures to normal afterwards.

Uneven Wear

Front tyres may wear unevenly as a result of wheel misalignment. Most tyre dealers and garages can check and adjust the wheel alignment (or "tracking") for a modest charge.
Incorrect camber or castor
Repair or renew suspension parts
Malfunctioning suspension
Repair or renew suspension parts
Unbalanced wheel
Balance tyres
Incorrect toe setting
Adjust front wheel alignment
Note: *The feathered edge of the tread which typifies toe wear is best checked by feel.*

Lubricants and fluids

Engine:

Petrol . . . . Synthetic or semi-synthetic multigrade engine oil, viscosity SAE 5W-40, 10W-40 or 5W-30* to specification API SH/SJ and/or ACEA A3: ESSO ULTRA/ULTRON or TOTAL QUARTZ

Diesel . . . . Synthetic or semi-synthetic multigrade engine oil, viscosity SAE 5W-40, 10W-40 or 5W-30* to specification API CD and/or ACEA B3: ESSO ULTRA/ULTRON or TOTAL QUARTZ

Cooling system . . . . Mixture of monoethylene glycol based antifreeze (PROCOR TM 108, GLYSANTIN G33 or REVKOGEL 2000) and clean de-ionised water

Manual gearbox . . . . ESSO BV 75W-80W or TOTAL TRANSMISSION BV 75W-80

Power steering fluid reservoir . . . . ESSO ATF D or TOTAL FLUIDE AT42

Brake fluid reservoir . . . . Hydraulic fluid to SAE J1703, DOT 4

* SAE 5W-30 engine oil may only be used in vehicles manufactured from the 2000 model year onward.

Choosing your engine oil

Engines need oil, not only to lubricate moving parts and minimise wear, but also to maximise power output and to improve fuel economy.

HOW ENGINE OIL WORKS

• *Beating friction*

Without oil, the moving surfaces inside your engine will rub together, heat up and melt, quickly causing the engine to seize. Engine oil creates a film which separates these moving parts, preventing wear and heat build-up.

• *Cooling hot-spots*

Temperatures inside the engine can exceed 1000° C. The engine oil circulates and acts as a coolant, transferring heat from the hot-spots to the sump.

• *Cleaning the engine internally*

Good quality engine oils clean the inside of your engine, collecting and dispersing combustion deposits and controlling them until they are trapped by the oil filter or flushed out at oil change.

Note: It is illegal and anti-social to dump oil down the drain. To find the location of your local oil recycling bank, call 08708 506 506 or visit www.oilbankline.org.uk.

Note: *On later models, the tyre pressure recommendations are marked on a label attached to the edge of the driver's door, or on the driver's door pillar. The following pressures are included as a guide, and apply to original-equipment tyres. The pressures may vary if any other make or type of tyre is fitted; check with the tyre manufacturer or supplier for correct pressures if necessary.*

	Front	Rear
Van models (600kg payload)		
1.4 litre petrol:		
165/70 R14 89R tyres....................................	2.5 bar (36 psi)	3.2 bar (46 psi)
175/65 R14 90T tyres....................................	2.5 bar (36 psi)	2.9 bar (42 psi)
1.6 litre petrol:		
185/65 R15 88H tyres....................................	2.2 bar (32 psi)	2.2 bar 32 psi)
1.8 and 1.9 litre diesel:		
165/70 R14 85R tyres....................................	2.9 bar (42 psi)	3.2 bar (46 psi)
175/65 R14 90T tyres....................................	2.5 bar (36 psi)	2.9 bar (42 psi)
1.6 and 2.0 litre diesel:		
175/65 R14 90T tyres....................................	2.5 bar (36 psi)	2.9 bar (42 psi)
Van models (800kg payload)		
1.4 litre petrol:		
165/70 R14 89R tyres....................................	2.5 bar (36 psi)	3.7 bar (54 psi)
175/65 R14 90T tyres....................................	2.5 bar (36 psi)	3.3 bar (48 psi)
1.6 litre petrol:		
185/65 R15 88H tyres....................................	2.2 bar (32 psi)	2.2 bar (32 psi)
1.8 and 1.9 litre diesel:		
165/70 R14 89R tyres....................................	3.0 bar (44 psi)	3.7 bar (54 psi)
175/65 R14 90T tyres....................................	2.7 bar (39 psi)	3.3 bar (48 psi)
1.6 and 2.0 litre diesel:		
175/65 R14 90T tyres....................................	2.7 bar (39 psi)	3.3 bar (48 psi)
Multispace and Combi models		
1.4 litre petrol:		
175/65 R14 86T tyres:		
Normal use..	2.6 bar (38 psi)	2.6 bar (38 psi)
Fully laden...	2.6 bar (38 psi)	2.9 bar (42 psi)
175/70 R14 84T tyres:		
Normal use..	2.3 bar (33 psi)	2.2 bar (32 psi)
Fully laden...	2.3 bar (33 psi)	2.7 bar (39 psi)
1.6 litre petrol:		
185/65 R15 88H tyres:		
Normal use..	2.2 bar (32 psi)	2.2 bar (32 psi)
Fully laden...	2.5 bar (36 psi)	2.9 bar (42 psi)
1.8 and 1.9 litre diesel:		
175/65 R14 86T tyres:		
Normal use..	2.6 bar (38 psi)	2.6 bar (38 psi)
Fully laden...	2.6 bar (38 psi)	2.9 bar (42 psi)
175/70 R14 84T tyres:		
Normal use..	2.3 bar (33 psi)	2.2 bar (32 psi)
Fully laden...	2.5 bar (36 psi)	2.8 bar 41 psi)
1.6 and 2.0 litre diesel:		
175/70 R14 84T tyres:		
Normal use..	2.3 bar (33 psi)	2.2 bar (32 psi)
Fully laden...	2.3 bar (33 psi)	2.7 bar (39 psi)
185/65 R15 88H tyres:		
Normal use..	2.3 bar (33 psi)	2.3 bar (33 psi)
Fully laden...	2.3 bar (33 psi)	2.5 bar (36 psi)

Chapter 1 Part A:
Routine maintenance and servicing – petrol models

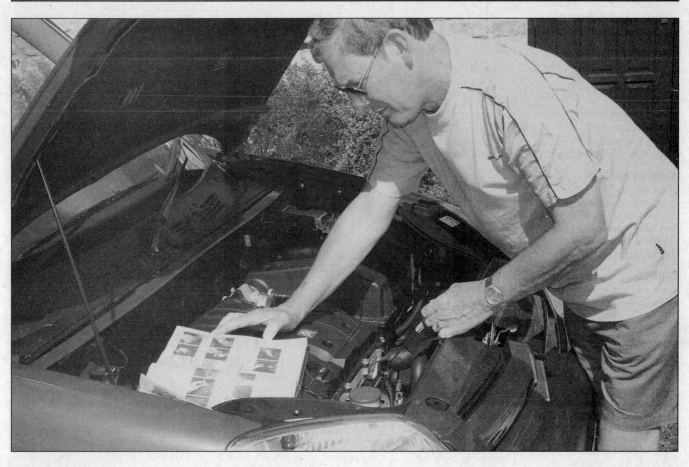

Contents

Degrees of difficulty

Easy, suitable for novice with little experience | **Fairly easy,** suitable for beginner with some experience | **Fairly difficult,** suitable for competent DIY mechanic | **Difficult,** suitable for experienced DIY mechanic | **Very difficult,** suitable for expert DIY or professional

Lubricants and fluids

Refer to *Weekly checks*

Capacities (approximate)

Engine oil (including filter)	3.2 litres
Difference between MAX and MIN dipstick marks.	1.5 litres

Cooling system

Pre-September 2002 models:	
Without air conditioning	6.5 litres
With air conditioning.	7.0 litres
September 2002 models onward.	8.0 litres
Transmission.	2.0 litres
Power-assisted steering	1.0 litre
Fuel tank	55.0 litres

Cooling system

Antifreeze mixture:	
50% antifreeze	Protection down to –35°C

Note: *Refer to antifreeze manufacturer for latest recommendations.*

Ignition system

Spark plugs:	
1.4 litre models:	
Pre-1999 models	Eyquem RFC52LSP or Bosch FR7LDC
1999 models onward	Eyquem RFN58LZ or Bosch FR7KDC
1.6 litre models.	Bosch FR7ME
Electrode gap.	0.9 mm

Brakes

Brake pad friction material minimum thickness.	2.0 mm
Brake shoe friction material minimum thickness	1.5 mm

Tyre pressures

See end of *Weekly checks*

Torque wrench settings

	Nm	lbf ft
Oil filter cover (later 1.4 and 1.6 litre engines)	25	18
Roadwheel bolts.	90	66
Spark plugs	25	18
Transmission filler/level plugs.	25	18

Note: *This maintenance schedule is a guide recommended by Haynes, for servicing your own vehicle. For the manufacturer's maintenance schedule, check with your local dealer.*

The maintenance intervals in this manual are provided with the assumption that you, not the dealer, will be carrying out the work. These are the minimum maintenance intervals recommended by us for vehicles driven daily. If you wish to keep your vehicle in peak condition at all times, you may wish to perform some of these procedures more often. We encourage frequent maintenance, because it enhances the efficiency, performance and resale value of your vehicle.

If the vehicle is driven in dusty areas, used to tow a trailer, or driven frequently at slow speeds (idling in traffic) or on short journeys, more frequent maintenance intervals are recommended.

When the vehicle is new, it should be serviced by a factory-authorised dealer service department, in order to preserve the factory warranty.

Every 250 miles (400 km) or weekly
☐ Refer to *Weekly checks*

Every 10 000 miles (15 000 km) or 12 months – whichever comes first
☐ Renew the engine oil and filter (Section 3)*.
☐ Check all underbonnet components for fluid leaks (Section 4).
☐ Check the condition of the driveshaft rubber gaiters (Section 5).
☐ Lubricate all hinges and locks (Section 6).
☐ Carry out a road test (Section 7).
☐ Reset the service interval indicator (Section 8).
***Note:** Peugeot/Citroën recommend the engine oil and filter are changed every 20 000 miles or two years. However, oil and filter changes are good for the engine and we recommend that the oil and filter are renewed at least once a year.*

Every 20 000 miles (30 000 km) or two years – whichever comes first
☐ Check the pollen filter (Section 9).
☐ Check the condition of the auxiliary drivebelt (Section 10).
☐ Check the condition of the front brake pads (Section 11).
☐ Check the condition of the rear brake shoes (Section 12).
☐ Check the operation of the handbrake (Section 13).
☐ Check the condition of the exhaust system (Section 14).
☐ Check the steering and suspension components (Section 15).

Every 40 000 miles (60 000 km)
☐ Renew the timing belt (Section 16).
Note: *Although the normal interval for timing belt renewal is 80 000 miles (120 000 km), it is strongly recommended that the interval is reduced to 40 000 miles (60 000 km), especially on vehicles which are subjected to intensive use, ie, mainly short journeys or a lot of stop-start driving. The actual belt renewal interval is therefore very much up to the individual owner, but bear in mind that severe engine damage will result if the belt breaks.*

Every 40 000 miles (60 000 km) or two years – whichever comes first
☐ Renew the brake fluid (Section 17).

Every 40 000 miles (60 000 km) or four years – whichever comes first
☐ Renew the spark plugs (Section 18).
☐ Renew the air cleaner filter element (Section 19).
☐ Renew the fuel filter (Section 20).
☐ Check the manual transmission oil level (Section 21).
☐ Check the exhaust emissions (Section 22).
☐ Renew the coolant (Section 23).

Every ten years
☐ Renew the airbags and seat belt pretensioners (Section 24).

Underbonnet view of a pre-September 2002 1.4 litre model

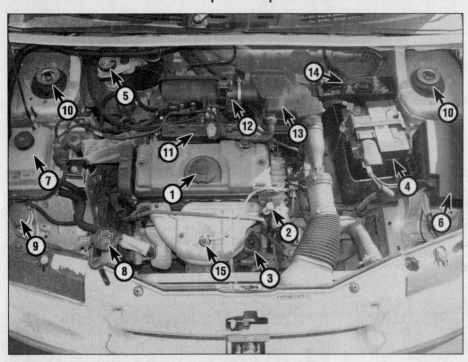

1 Engine oil filler cap
2 Engine oil dipstick
3 Engine oil filter
4 Battery
5 Master cylinder brake fluid
   reservoir
6 Fuse/relay box
7 Power steering fluid reservoir
8 Radiator filler cap
9 Windscreen/tailgate washer fluid
   reservoir
10 Suspension strut upper mounting
11 DIS ignition coil
12 Throttle housing
13 Air cleaner housing
14 Engine management system ECU
15 Lambda sensor

Underbonnet view of a 1.6 litre model

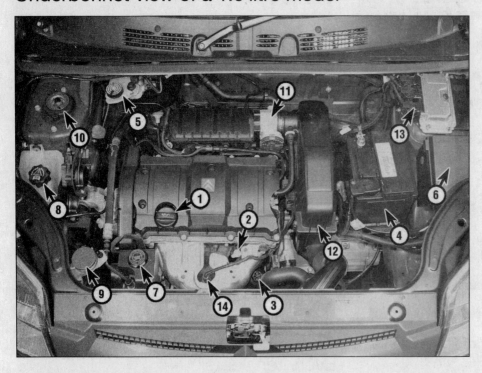

1 Engine oil filler cap
2 Engine oil dipstick
3 Engine oil filter
4 Battery
5 Master cylinder brake fluid
   reservoir
6 Fuse/relay box
7 Power steering pump fluid
   reservoir
8 Cooling system expansion tank
9 Windscreen/tailgate washer fluid
   reservoir
10 Suspension strut upper mounting
11 Throttle housing
12 Air cleaner housing
13 Engine management ECU
14 Lambda sensor

Front underbody view of a 1.6 litre model (1.4 litre similar)

1 Sump drain plug
2 Engine/transmission rear mounting
3 Exhaust front pipe/catalytic converter
4 Lambda sensor
5 Alternator
6 Radiator bottom hose
7 Clutch cable
8 Front suspension subframe
9 Front brake caliper
10 Front suspension lower arm
11 Track rod balljoint
12 Front anti-roll bar
13 Steering gear assembly

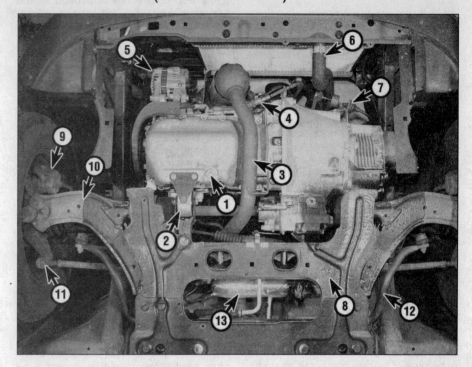

Rear underbody view

1 Spare wheel
2 Rear silencer
3 Fuel tank
4 Handbrake cable
5 Rear suspension torsion bar
6 Rear suspension tubular crossmember
7 Rear shock absorber
8 Rear suspension trailing arm

1 General information

This Chapter is designed to help the home mechanic maintain his/her vehicle for safety, economy, long life and peak performance.

The Chapter contains a master maintenance schedule, followed by Sections dealing specifically with each task in the schedule. Visual checks, adjustments, component renewal and other helpful items are included. Refer to the accompanying illustrations of the engine compartment and the underside of the vehicle for the locations of the various components.

Servicing your vehicle in accordance with the mileage/time maintenance schedule and the following Sections will provide a planned maintenance programme, which should result in a long and reliable service life. This is a comprehensive plan, so maintaining some items but not others at the specified service intervals, will not produce the same results.

As you service your vehicle, you will discover that many of the procedures can – and should – be grouped together, because of the particular procedure being performed, or because of the proximity of two otherwise-unrelated components to one another. For example, if the vehicle is raised for any reason, the exhaust can be inspected at the same time as the suspension and steering components.

The first step in this maintenance programme is to prepare yourself before the actual work begins. Read through all the Sections relevant to the work to be carried out, then make a list and gather all the parts and tools required. If a problem is encountered, seek advice from a parts specialist, or a dealer service department.

2 Routine maintenance

1 If, from the time the vehicle is new, the routine maintenance schedule is followed closely, and frequent checks are made of fluid levels and high-wear items, as suggested throughout this manual, the engine will be kept in relatively good running condition, and the need for additional work will be minimised.

2 It is possible that there will be times when the engine is running poorly due to the lack of regular maintenance. This is even more likely if a used vehicle, which has not received regular and frequent maintenance checks, is purchased. In such cases, additional work may need to be carried out, outside of the regular maintenance intervals.

3 If engine wear is suspected, a compression test (refer to relevant Part of Chapter 2) will provide valuable information regarding the overall performance of the main internal components. Such a test can be used as a basis to decide on the extent of the work to be carried out. If, for example, a test indicates serious internal engine wear, conventional maintenance as described in this Chapter will not greatly improve the performance of the engine, and may prove a waste of time and money, unless extensive overhaul work is carried out first.

4 The following series of operations are those most often required to improve the performance of a generally poor-running engine:

Primary operations

a) Clean, inspect and test the battery (See 'Weekly checks').
b) Check all the engine-related fluids (See 'Weekly checks').
c) Check the condition and tension of the auxiliary drivebelt (Section 10).
d) Renew the spark plugs (Section 18).
e) Check the condition of the air cleaner filter element, and renew if necessary (Section 19).
f) Renew the fuel filter (Section 20).
g) Check the condition of all hoses, and check for fluid leaks (Section 4).

5 If the above operations do not prove fully effective, carry out the following secondary operations:

Secondary operations

All items listed under *Primary operations*, plus the following:
a) Check the charging system (Chapter 5A).
b) Check the ignition system (Chapter 5B).
c) Check the fuel system (Chapter 4A).

Every 10 000 miles (15 000 km) or 12 months

3 Engine oil and filter renewal

Note: *A suitable square-section wrench may be required to undo the sump drain plug on some models. These wrenches can be obtained from most motor factors or your Peugeot/Citroën dealer.*

1 Frequent oil and filter changes are the most important preventative maintenance procedures which can be undertaken by the DIY owner. As engine oil ages, it becomes diluted and contaminated, which leads to premature engine wear.

2 Before starting this procedure, gather together all the necessary tools and materials. Also make sure that you have plenty of clean rags and newspapers handy, to mop-up any spills. Ideally, the engine oil should be warm, as it will drain better, and more built-up sludge will be removed with it. Take care, however, not to touch the exhaust or any other hot parts of the engine when working under the vehicle. To avoid any possibility of scalding, and to protect yourself from possible skin irritants and other harmful contaminants in used engine oils, it is advisable to wear gloves when carrying out this work. Access to the underside of the vehicle will be greatly improved if it can be raised on a lift, driven onto ramps, or jacked up and supported on axle stands (see *Jacking and vehicle support*). Whichever method is chosen, make sure that the vehicle remains level, or if it is at an angle, that the drain plug is at the lowest point.

3 Slacken the drain plug about half a turn; on some models, a square-section wrench may be needed to slacken the plug **(see illustration)**. Position the draining container under the drain plug, then remove the plug completely. If possible, try to keep the plug pressed into the sump while unscrewing it by hand the last couple of turns **(see Haynes Hint)**. Recover the sealing washer from the drain plug.

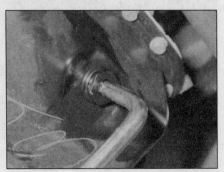

3.3 Slackening the sump drain plug with a square-section wrench

As the drain plug releases from the threads, move it away sharply so the stream of oil issuing from the sump runs into the container, not up your sleeve.

3.7 Cartridge type oil filter housing location (arrowed) – later models

3.8 Using an oil filter removal tool to slacken the canister type oil filter

3.11a Slacken and remove the filter cover . . .

4 Allow some time for the old oil to drain, noting that it may be necessary to reposition the container as the oil flow slows to a trickle.

5 After all the oil has drained, wipe off the drain plug with a clean rag, and fit a new sealing washer. Clean the area around the drain plug opening, and refit the plug. Tighten the plug securely.

6 Move the container into position under the oil filter, which is located on the front facing side of the cylinder block.

7 On early 1.4 litre models, the oil filter is of the disposable metal canister type screwed into the front of the cylinder block. However, on later 1.4 and all 1.6 litre models, the oil filter consists of a separate disposable cartridge contained in a plastic housing. The housing is located on the front of the cylinder block adjacent to the radiator hoses **(see illustration)**. Proceed as follows according to filter type.

Metal canister type filter

8 Using an oil filter removal tool if necessary, slacken the filter initially, then unscrew it by hand the rest of the way **(see illustration)**. Empty the oil in the old filter into the container. To ensure that the old filter is completely empty before disposal, puncture the filter dome in at least two places and allow any remaining oil to drain through the punctures and into the container.

9 Use a clean rag to remove all oil and dirt from the filter sealing area on the engine. Check the old filter to make sure that the rubber sealing ring hasn't stuck to the engine. If it has, carefully remove it.

10 Apply a light coating of clean engine oil to the sealing ring on the new filter, then screw it into position on the engine. Tighten the filter firmly by hand only – do not use any tools.

Disposable cartridge type filter

11 On these engines, the filter element is contained within a filter cover. Using a socket or spanner, slacken and remove the filter cover from above. Be prepared for fluid spillage, and recover the O-ring seal from the cover **(see illustrations)**.

12 Pull the filter element from the filter cover.

13 Use a clean rag to remove all oil, dirt and sludge from the inside and outside of the filter cover.

14 Insert the new filter element in to the cover, then apply a little clean engine oil to the new O-ring seal, and fit it to the filter cover **(see illustrations)**.

15 Refit the filter/cover to the housing and tighten the cover to the specified torque.

All engines

16 Remove the old oil and all tools from under the car. Lower the car to the ground (if applicable).

17 Remove the dipstick, then unscrew the oil filler cap from the cylinder head cover or oil filler/breather neck (as applicable). Fill the engine, using the correct grade and type of oil (see *Weekly checks*). An oil can spout or funnel may help to reduce spillage. Pour in half the specified quantity of oil first, then wait a few minutes for the oil to fall to the sump. Continue adding oil a small quantity at a time

until the level is up to the lower mark on the dipstick. Adding approximately 1.5 litres will bring the level up to the upper mark on the dipstick. Refit the filler cap.

18 Start the engine and run it for a few minutes; check for leaks around the oil filter seal and the sump drain plug. Note that there may be a delay of a few seconds before the oil pressure warning light goes out when the engine is first started, as the oil circulates through the engine oil galleries and the new oil filter before the pressure builds-up.

19 Switch off the engine, and wait a few minutes for the oil to settle in the sump once more. With the new oil circulated and the filter completely full, recheck the level on the dipstick, and add more oil as necessary.

20 Dispose of the used engine oil and filter safely, with reference to *General repair procedures* at the rear of this manual. Do not discard the old filter with domestic household waste. The facility for waste oil disposal provided by many local council refuse tips generally has a filter receptacle alongside.

---

4 Hose and fluid leak check

Cooling system

⚠ *Warning: Refer to the safety information given in 'Safety first!' and Chapter 3 before disturbing any of the cooling system components.*

3.11b . . . and recover the O-ring seal

3.14a Fit the new element into the cover . . .

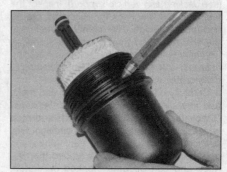

3.14b . . . and apply a little clean engine oil to the O-ring seal

A leak in the cooling system will usually show up as white- or rust-coloured deposits on the area adjoining the leak.

1 Carefully check the radiator and heater coolant hoses along their entire length. Renew any hose which is cracked, swollen or which shows signs of deterioration. Cracks will show up better if the hose is squeezed. Pay close attention to the clips that secure the hoses to the cooling system components. Hose clips that have been over-tightened can pinch and puncture hoses, resulting in cooling system leaks.

2 Inspect all the cooling system components (hoses, joint faces, etc) for leaks. Where any problems of this nature are found on system components, renew the component or gasket with reference to Chapter 3.

3 A leak from the cooling system will usually show up as white or rust-coloured deposits, on the area surrounding the leak **(see Haynes Hint)**.

Fuel

 Warning: Refer to the safety information given in 'Safety first!' and Chapter 4A before disturbing any of the fuel system components.

4 From within the engine compartment, check the security of all fuel pipe attachments and unions, and inspect the fuel pipes for kinks, chafing and deterioration.

5 To identify fuel leaks between the fuel tank and the engine bay, the vehicle should be raised and securely supported on axle stands (see *Jacking and vehicle support*). Inspect the fuel tank and filler neck for punctures, cracks and other damage. The connection between the filler neck and tank is especially critical. Sometimes a rubber filler neck or connecting hose will leak due to loose retaining clamps or deteriorated rubber.

6 Carefully check all rubber hoses and metal fuel lines leading away from the fuel tank. Check for loose connections, deteriorated hoses, kinked lines, and other damage. Pay particular attention to the vent pipes and hoses, which often loop up around the filler neck and can become blocked or kinked, making tank filling difficult. Follow the fuel supply and return lines to the front of the vehicle, carefully inspecting them all the way for signs of damage or corrosion. Renew damaged sections as necessary.

Engine oil

7 Inspect the area around the cylinder head cover, cylinder head, oil filter and sump joint faces. Bear in mind that, over a period of time, some very slight seepage from these areas is to be expected – what you are really looking for is any indication of a serious leak caused by gasket failure. Engine oil seeping from the base of the timing belt cover or the transmission bellhousing may be an indication of crankshaft or input shaft oil seal failure. Should a leak be found, renew the failed gasket or oil seal by referring to the appropriate Chapters in this manual.

Air conditioning refrigerant

 Warning: Refer to the safety information given in 'Safety first!' and Chapter 3, regarding the dangers of disturbing any of the air conditioning system components.

8 The air conditioning system is filled with a liquid refrigerant, which is retained under high pressure. If the air conditioning system is opened and depressurised without the aid of specialised equipment, the refrigerant will immediately turn into gas and escape into the atmosphere. If the liquid comes into contact with your skin, it can cause severe frostbite. In addition, the refrigerant contains substances which are environmentally damaging; for this reason, it should not be allowed to escape into the atmosphere.

9 Any suspected air conditioning system leaks should be immediately referred to a Peugeot/Citroën dealer or air conditioning specialist. Leakage will be shown up as a steady drop in the level of refrigerant in the system.

10 Note that water may drip from the condenser drain pipe, underneath the car, immediately after the air conditioning system has been in use. This is normal, and should not be cause for concern.

Brake fluid

 Warning: Refer to the safety information given in 'Safety first!' and Chapter 9, regarding the dangers of handling brake fluid.

11 With reference to Chapter 9, examine the area surrounding the brake pipe unions at the master cylinder for signs of leakage. Check the area around the base of fluid reservoir, for signs of leakage caused by seal failure. Also examine the brake pipe unions at the ABS hydraulic modulator (where applicable).

12 If fluid loss is evident, but the leak cannot be pinpointed in the engine bay, the front brake calipers, rear wheel cylinders and underbody brake lines and should be carefully checked with the vehicle raised and supported on axle stands. Leakage of fluid from the braking system is serious fault that must be rectified immediately.

13 Brake hydraulic fluid is a toxic substance with a watery consistency. New fluid is almost colourless, but it becomes darker with age and use.

Unidentified fluid leaks

14 If there are signs that a fluid of some description is leaking from the vehicle, but you cannot identify the type of fluid or its exact origin, park the vehicle overnight and slide a large piece of card underneath it. Providing that the card is positioned in roughly in the right location, even the smallest leak will show up on the card. Not only will this help you to pinpoint the exact location of the leak, it should be easier to identify the fluid from its colour. Bear in mind, though, that the leak may only be occurring when the engine is running!

Vacuum hoses

15 Although the braking system is hydraulically-operated, the brake servo unit amplifies the effort you apply at the brake pedal, by making use of the vacuum created in the inlet manifold. Vacuum is ported to the servo by means of a large-bore hose. Any leaks that develop in this hose will reduce the effectiveness of the braking system.

16 In addition, many of the underbonnet components, particularly the emission control components, are driven by vacuum supplied from the inlet manifold via narrow-bore hoses. A leak in a vacuum hose means that air is being drawn into the hose (rather than escaping from it) and this makes leakage very difficult to detect. One method is to use an old length of vacuum hose as a kind of stethoscope - hold one end close to (but not in) your ear and use the other end to probe the area around the suspected leak. When the end of the hose is directly over a vacuum leak, a hissing sound will be heard clearly through the hose. Care must be taken to avoid contacting hot or moving components, as the engine must be running, when testing in this manner. Renew any vacuum hoses that are found to be defective.

5 Driveshaft gaiter check

1 With the vehicle raised and securely supported on axle stands (see *Jacking and vehicle support*), turn the steering onto full lock, then slowly rotate the roadwheel. Inspect the condition of the outer constant velocity (CV) joint rubber gaiters, squeezing the gaiters to open out the folds **(see illustration)**. Check for signs of cracking, splits or deterioration of the rubber, which

5.1 Check the condition of the driveshaft gaiters (arrowed)

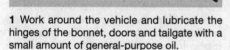

may allow the grease to escape, and lead to water and grit entry into the joint. Also check the security and condition of the retaining clips. Repeat these checks on the inner CV joints. If any damage or deterioration is found, the gaiters should be renewed (see Chapter 8).

2 At the same time, check the general condition of the CV joints themselves by first holding the driveshaft and attempting to rotate the wheel. Repeat this check by holding the inner joint and attempting to rotate the driveshaft. Any appreciable movement indicates wear in the joints, wear in the driveshaft splines, or a loose driveshaft retaining nut.

6 Hinge and lock lubrication

1 Work around the vehicle and lubricate the hinges of the bonnet, doors and tailgate with a small amount of general-purpose oil.

2 Lightly lubricate the bonnet release mechanism and exposed section of inner cable with a smear of grease.

3 Check carefully the security and operation of all hinges, latches and locks, adjusting them where required. Check the operation of the central locking system.

4 Check the condition and operation of the tailgate struts, renewing them if either is leaking or no longer able to support the tailgate securely when raised.

7 Road test

Instruments and electrical equipment

1 Check the operation of all instruments and electrical equipment.

2 Make sure that all instruments read correctly, and switch on all electrical equipment in turn to check it functions properly.

Steering and suspension

3 Drive the vehicle, and check that there are no unusual vibrations or noises.

4 Check for any abnormalities in the steering, suspension, handling or road 'feel'.

5 Check that the steering feels positive, with no excessive 'sloppiness', or roughness, and check for any suspension noises when cornering, or when driving over bumps.

Drivetrain

6 Check the performance of the engine, clutch, transmission and driveshafts.

7 Listen for any unusual noises from the engine, clutch and transmission.

8 Make sure the engine idles smoothly, and that there is no hesitation when accelerating.

9 Check that the clutch action is smooth and progressive, that the drive is taken up smoothly, and that the pedal travel is not excessive. Also listen for any noises when the clutch pedal is depressed.

10 Check that all gears can be engaged smoothly, without noise, and that the gear lever action is smooth and not vague or 'notchy'.

11 Listen for a metallic clicking sound from the front of the vehicle, as the vehicle is driven slowly in a circle with the steering on full lock. Carry out this check in both directions. If a clicking noise is heard, this generally indicates lack of lubrication or wear in a driveshaft outer constant velocity joint (see Chapter 8).

Braking system

12 Make sure that the vehicle does not pull to one side when braking, and that the wheels do not lock when braking hard.

13 Check that there is no vibration through the steering when braking.

14 Check that the handbrake operates correctly, without excessive movement of the lever, and that it holds the vehicle on a slope.

15 Test the operation of the brake servo unit as follows. With the engine off, depress the footbrake four or five times to exhaust the vacuum. Start the engine, holding the brake pedal depressed. As the engine starts, there should be a noticeable 'give' in the brake pedal as vacuum builds-up. Allow the engine to run for at least two minutes, and then switch it off. If the brake pedal is depressed now, it should be possible to detect a hiss from the servo as the pedal is depressed. After about four or five applications, no further hissing should be heard, and the pedal should feel considerably firmer.

8 Resetting the service indicator

1 On completion of the service, reset the service interval indicator as follows.

2 With the ignition switched off, press and hold the trip meter button.

3 Turn on the ignition switch, and the display begins a countdown. When the countdown reaches 0, release the trip meter button, and the spanner service symbol in the display will disappear.

4 Turn off the ignition switch.

5 Turn on the ignition switch and check the correct mileage to the next service interval is displayed on the indicator.

Note: *If you need to disconnect the battery after carrying out this procedure, lock the vehicle and wait at least 5 minutes. Otherwise the display reset may not register.*

Every 20 000 miles (30 000 km) or two years

9 Pollen filter renewal

1 Release the carpet trim panel from under the facia on the passenger's side.

2 Remove the three securing screws, and withdraw the lid from the pollen filter housing on the heater assembly. If no screws are visible, slide the lid sideways to release the internal retaining lugs.

3 Withdraw the pollen filter.

4 Clean the filter housing and the lid, then fit the new filter using a reversal of the removal procedure.

10 Auxiliary drivebelt check and renewal

Note: *Peugeot/Citroën specify the use of a special electronic tool (SEEM C.TRONIC type 105 belt tensioning measuring tool) to correctly set the auxiliary drivebelt tension on manually-adjusted drivebelts. This is an* involved process that varies significantly according to engine type, model year, and belt type and condition. The following procedure is an alternative method assuming that the electronic equipment is not being used. If any problems arise (such as screeching noises when driving) the tension should be checked by a dealer using the special electronic tool at the earliest opportunity.

1 Depending on specification, either one or two auxiliary drivebelts are fitted. Where two belts are fitted, it will obviously be necessary to remove the outer belt in order to renew the inner belt.

10.8a Slacken the alternator upper mounting bolt . . .

10.8b . . . the lower mounting bolt and the adjuster strap (arrowed) – models with a manual adjuster on the alternator lower mounting

Correct tensioning of the drivebelt will ensure it has a long life. A belt which is too slack will slip and squeal. Beware of overtightening, as this can cause wear in the alternator bearings.

Check

2 Chock the rear wheels then jack up the front of the vehicle and support it on axle stands (see *Jacking and vehicle support*). Remove the right-hand front roadwheel.

3 From underneath the front of the car, undo the screws, prise out the retaining clips, and remove the wheel arch liner from the wing valance to gain access to the crankshaft sprocket/pulley bolt. Where necessary, unclip the coolant hoses from the wing to improve access further.

4 Using a suitable socket and extension bar fitted to the crankshaft sprocket/pulley bolt, rotate the crankshaft so that the entire length of the drivebelt(s) can be examined. Examine the drivebelt(s) for cracks, splitting, fraying or damage. Check also for signs of glazing (shiny patches) and for separation of the belt plies. Renew the belt if worn or damaged.

5 If the condition of the belt is satisfactory, on models where the belt is adjusted manually, check the drivebelt tension as described below, bearing in mind the Note at the start of this Section. On models with an automatic spring-loaded tensioner, there is no need to check the drivebelt tension.

Manual adjuster on alternator lower mounting

Removal

6 If not already done, proceed as described in paragraphs 2 and 3.

7 Disconnect the battery negative terminal (refer to *Disconnecting the battery* in the Reference Chapter).

8 Slacken the alternator upper and lower mounting bolts and, where applicable, the adjuster strap mounting bolt (see illustrations).

9 Turn the adjuster bolt as necessary to relieve the tension in the drivebelt, then slip the drivebelt from the pulleys (see illustrations). **Note:** *If the belt is going to be re-used, mark the direction of rotation on the belt prior to removal. This will ensure it is refitted the correct way around.*

Refitting

10 If the belt is being renewed, ensure that the correct type is used and if the original belt is being refitted, use the mark made on removal to ensure it is fitted the correct way around. Fit the belt around the pulleys, and take up the slack in the belt by means of the adjuster bolt.

11 Tension the drivebelt as described in the following paragraphs.

Tensioning

12 If not already done, proceed as described in paragraphs 2 and 3.

13 The belt should be tensioned so that, under firm thumb pressure, there is about 5.0 mm of free movement at the mid-point between the pulleys on the longest belt run (see the note at the start of this Section).

14 To adjust, with the mounting bolts just holding the alternator, but still allowing slight movement, turn the adjuster bolt until the correct tension is achieved.

15 Rotate the crankshaft a couple of times, recheck the tension, then tighten both the alternator mountings. Where applicable, also tighten the bolt securing the adjuster strap to its mounting bracket.

16 Reconnect the battery negative terminal.

17 Clip the coolant hoses into position (where necessary), then refit the wheel arch liner. Refit the roadwheel, and lower the vehicle to the ground.

Manually-adjusted sliding tensioning pulley

Removal

18 If not already done, proceed as described in paragraphs 2 and 3.

19 Disconnect the battery negative terminal (refer to *Disconnecting the battery* in the Reference Chapter).

20 Slacken the two bolts securing the tensioning pulley assembly to the engine (see illustration).

21 Rotate the adjuster bolt to move the tensioning pulley away from the drivebelt until there is sufficient slack for the drivebelt to be removed from the pulleys. **Note:** *If the belt is going to be re-used, mark the direction of rotation on the belt prior to removal. This will ensure it is refitted the correct way around.*

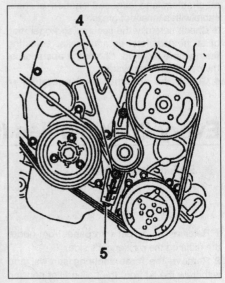

10.20 Tensioning pulley securing screws (4) and adjuster bolt (5) – models with a manually-adjusted sliding tensioning pulley

10.9a Turn the adjuster bolt to relieve the tension in the drivebelt . . .

10.9b . . . then slip the drivebelt from the pulleys – models with a manual adjuster on the alternator lower mounting

Every 20 000 miles - petrol models 1A•11

Refitting

22 If the belt is being renewed, ensure that the correct type is used and if the original belt is being refitted, use the mark made on removal to ensure it is fitted the correct way around. Fit the belt around the pulleys, ensuring that the ribs on the belt are correctly engaged with the grooves in the pulleys, and that the drivebelt is correctly routed. Take all the slack out of the belt by turning the tensioner pulley adjuster bolt. Tension the belt as follows.

Tensioning

23 If not already done, proceed as described in paragraphs 2 and 3.
24 Correct tensioning of the drivebelt will ensure that it has a long life – see Haynes Hint above.
25 The belt should be tensioned so that, under firm thumb pressure, there is approximately 5.0 mm of free movement at the mid-point between the pulleys on the longest belt run (see Note at the start of this Section).
26 To adjust the tension, with the two tensioner pulley assembly retaining bolts slackened, rotate the adjuster bolt until the correct tension is achieved. Once the belt is correctly tensioned, rotate the crankshaft a couple of times and recheck the tension.
27 When the belt is correctly tensioned, securely tighten the tensioner pulley assembly retaining bolts, then reconnect the battery negative terminal.
28 Clip the coolant hoses into position, then refit the wheel arch liner. Refit the roadwheel, and lower the vehicle to the ground.

Manually-adjusted fixed tensioning pulley

Removal

29 If not already done, proceed as described in paragraphs 2 and 3.
30 Disconnect the battery negative terminal (refer to *Disconnecting the battery* in the Reference Chapter).
31 Slacken the tensioning pulley nut and rotate the centre bolt to move the pulley away from the drivebelt until there is sufficient slack for the belt to be removed from the pulleys **(see illustration)**. **Note:** *If the belt is going to be re-used, mark the direction of rotation on the belt prior to removal. This will ensure it is refitted the correct way around.*

Refitting

32 If the belt is being renewed, ensure that the correct type is used and if the original belt is being refitted, use the mark made on removal to ensure it is fitted the correct way around. Fit the belt around the pulleys, ensuring that the ribs on the belt are correctly engaged with the grooves in the pulleys, and that the drivebelt is correctly routed. Tension the belt as follows.

Tensioning

33 If not already done, proceed as described in paragraphs 2 and 3.

34 Correct tensioning of the drivebelt will ensure that it has a long life – see Haynes Hint above.
35 The belt should be tensioned so that, under firm thumb pressure, there is approximately 5.0 mm of free movement at the mid-point between the pulleys on the longest belt run (see Note at the start of this Section).
36 To adjust the tension, slacken the tensioning pulley nut and rotate the centre bolt until the correct tension is achieved. Once the belt is correctly tensioned, hold the centre bolt stationary and securely tighten the pulley nut. Rotate the crankshaft a couple of times and recheck the tension.
37 Clip the coolant hoses into position, then refit the wheel arch liner. Refit the roadwheel, and lower the vehicle to the ground.

Automatic spring-loaded tensioning pulley

Removal

38 If not already done, proceed as described in paragraphs 2 and 3.
39 Disconnect the battery negative terminal (refer to *Disconnecting the battery* in the Reference Chapter).
40 Where necessary, remove the retaining screws from the power steering pump pulley shield, and remove the shield to gain access to the top of the drivebelt.
41 Move the tensioning pulley away from the drivebelt, using a spanner on the tensioning pulley retaining nut. Rotate the tensioning pulley anti-clockwise away from the belt. **Note:** *The tensioning pulley has a left-hand thread so it will not slacken when releasing the tension on the belt.*

42 Once the tension is released, retain the pulley in the released position by inserting a 4.0 mm Allen key in the hole provided in the base of the assembly. Disengage the drivebelt from all the pulleys, noting its correct routing, and remove the drivebelt from the engine. **Note:** *If the belt is going to be re-used, mark the direction of rotation on the belt prior to removal. This will ensure it is refitted the correct way around.*

Refitting and tensioning

43 If the belt is being renewed, ensure that the correct type is used and if the original belt is being refitted, use the mark made on removal to ensure it is fitted the correct way around. Fit the belt around the pulleys, ensuring that the ribs on the belt are correctly engaged with the grooves in the pulleys, and that the drivebelt is correctly routed.
44 Take the load off the tensioning pulley and remove the Allen key. Release the pulley and allow the tensioner to automatically tension the belt.
45 Refit the power steering pump pulley shield (where removed), and securely tighten its retaining screws.
46 Reconnect the battery negative terminal.
47 Clip the coolant hoses into position, then refit the wheel arch liner. Refit the roadwheel, and lower the vehicle to the ground.

11 Front brake pad check

1 Firmly apply the handbrake, then jack up the front of the car and support it securely on

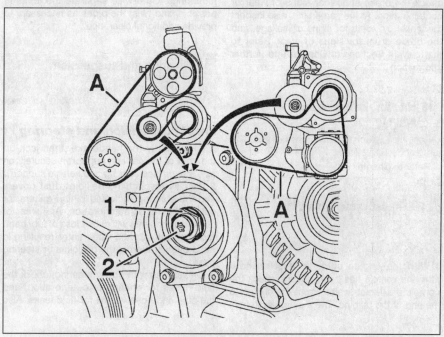
10.31 Slacken the pulley nut (1) and rotate the centre bolt (2) to adjust the drivebelt tension. Inset shows belt tension checking point (A) – models with a manually-adjusted fixed tensioning pulley

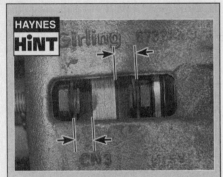

For a quick check, the thickness of friction material on each brake pad can be measured through the aperture in the caliper body.

axle stands (see *Jacking and vehicle support*). Remove the front roadwheels.

2 If any pad's friction material is worn to the specified thickness or less, *all four pads must be renewed as a set.*

3 For a comprehensive check, the brake pads should be removed and cleaned **(see Haynes Hint)**. The operation of the caliper can then be checked, and the brake disc itself can be fully examined on both sides. Refer to Chapter 9 for details.

12 Rear brake shoe check

1 Remove the rear brake drums, and check the brake shoes for signs of wear or contamination. At the same time, also inspect the wheel cylinders for signs of leakage, and the brake drum for signs of wear. Refer to the relevant Sections of Chapter 9 for further information.

13 Handbrake check and adjustment

Refer to Chapter 9.

14 Exhaust system check

1 With the engine cold (at least an hour after the vehicle has been driven), check the complete exhaust system from the engine to the end of the tailpipe. The exhaust system is

15.4 Check for wear in the hub bearings by grasping the wheel and trying to rock it

most easily checked with the vehicle raised on a hoist, or suitably-supported on axle stands, so that the exhaust components are readily visible and accessible (see *Jacking and vehicle support*).

2 Check the exhaust pipes and connections for evidence of leaks, severe corrosion and damage. Make sure that all brackets and mountings are in good condition, and that all relevant nuts and bolts are tight. Leakage at any of the joints or in other parts of the system will usually show up as a black sooty stain in the vicinity of the leak.

3 Rattles and other noises can often be traced to the exhaust system, especially the brackets and mountings. Try to move the pipes and silencers. If the components are able to come into contact with the body or suspension parts, secure the system with new mountings. Otherwise separate the joints (if possible) and twist the pipes as necessary to provide additional clearance.

15 Steering and suspension check

Front suspension and steering

1 Firmly apply the handbrake, then jack up the front of the car and support it securely on axle stands (see *Jacking and vehicle support*).

2 Visually inspect the balljoint dust covers and the steering rack-and-pinion gaiters for splits, chafing or deterioration. Any wear of these components will cause loss of lubricant, together with dirt and water entry, resulting in rapid deterioration of the balljoints or steering gear.

3 On vehicles with power steering, check the fluid hoses for chafing or deterioration, and the pipe and hose unions for fluid leaks. Also

check for signs of fluid leakage under pressure from the steering gear rubber gaiters, which would indicate failed fluid seals within the steering gear.

4 Grasp the roadwheel at the 12 o'clock and 6 o'clock positions, and try to rock it **(see illustration)**. Very slight free play may be felt, but if the movement is appreciable, further investigation is necessary to determine the source. Continue rocking the wheel while an assistant depresses the footbrake. If the movement is now eliminated or significantly reduced, it is likely that the hub bearings are at fault. If the free play is still evident with the footbrake depressed, then there is wear in the suspension joints or mountings.

5 Now grasp the wheel at the 9 o'clock and 3 o'clock positions, and try to rock it as before. Any movement felt now may again be caused by wear in the hub bearings or the steering track rod balljoints. If the inner or outer balljoint is worn, the visual movement will be obvious.

6 Using a large screwdriver or flat bar, check for wear in the suspension mounting bushes by levering between the relevant suspension component and its attachment point. Some movement is to be expected as the mountings are made of rubber, but excessive wear should be obvious. Also check the condition of any visible rubber bushes, looking for splits, cracks or contamination of the rubber.

7 With the car standing on its wheels, have an assistant turn the steering wheel back-and-forth about an eighth of a turn each way. There should be very little, if any, lost movement between the steering wheel and roadwheels. If this is not the case, closely observe the joints and mountings previously described, but in addition, check the steering column universal joints for wear, and the rack-and-pinion steering gear itself.

Strut/shock absorbers

8 Check for any signs of fluid leakage around the suspension strut/shock absorber body, or from the rubber gaiter around the piston rod. Should any fluid be noticed, the suspension strut/shock absorber is defective internally, and should be renewed.

Note: *Suspension struts/shock absorbers should always be renewed in pairs on the same axle.*

9 The efficiency of the suspension strut/shock absorber may be checked by bouncing the vehicle at each corner. Generally speaking, the body will return to its normal position and stop after being depressed. If it rises and returns on a rebound, the suspension strut/shock absorber is probably suspect. Examine also the suspension strut/shock absorber upper and lower mountings for any signs of wear.

Every 40 000 miles (60 000 km)

16 Timing belt renewal

Refer to Chapter 2A.

Every 40 000 miles (60 000 km) or two years

17 Brake fluid renewal

Warning: Brake hydraulic fluid can harm your eyes and damage painted surfaces, so use extreme caution when handling and pouring it. Do not use fluid that has been standing open for some time, as it absorbs moisture from the air. Excess moisture can cause a dangerous loss of braking effectiveness.

1 The procedure is similar to that for the bleeding of the hydraulic system as described in Chapter 9, except that the brake fluid reservoir should be emptied by syphoning,

using a clean poultry baster or similar before starting, and allowance should be made for the old fluid to be expelled when bleeding a section of the circuit.

2 Working as described in Chapter 9, open the first bleed screw in the sequence, and pump the brake pedal gently until nearly all the old fluid has been emptied from the master cylinder reservoir.

> **HAYNES HINT** *Old hydraulic fluid is invariably much darker in colour than the new, making it easy to distinguish the two.*

3 Top-up to the MAX level with new fluid, and continue pumping until only the new fluid

remains in the reservoir, and new fluid can be seen emerging from the bleed screw. Tighten the screw, and top the reservoir level up to the MAX level line.

4 Work through all the remaining bleed screws in the sequence until new fluid can be seen at all of them. Be careful to keep the master cylinder reservoir topped-up to above the MIN level at all times, or air may enter the system and increase the length of the task.

5 When the operation is complete, check that all bleed screws are securely tightened, and that their dust caps are refitted. Wash off all traces of spilt fluid, and recheck the master cylinder reservoir fluid level.

6 Check the operation of the brakes before taking the car on the road.

Every 40 000 miles (60 000 km) or four years

18 Spark plug renewal

1 The correct functioning of the spark plugs is vital for the correct running and efficiency of the engine. It is essential that the plugs fitted are appropriate for the engine (a suitable type is specified at the beginning of this Chapter). If this type is used and the engine is in good condition, the spark plugs should not need attention between scheduled renewal intervals. Spark plug cleaning is rarely necessary, and should not be attempted unless specialised equipment is available, as damage can easily be caused to the firing ends.

2 On later 1.4 litre models and all 1.6 litre models, to gain access to the spark plugs, remove the ignition HT coil as described in Chapter 5B.

3 On early 1.4 litre models, if the marks on the original-equipment spark plug (HT) leads cannot be seen, mark the leads 1 to 4, to correspond to the cylinder the lead serves (No 1 cylinder is at the transmission end of the engine). Pull the leads from the plugs by gripping the end fitting, not the

lead, otherwise the lead connection may be fractured.

4 It is advisable to remove the dirt from the spark plug recesses using a clean brush, vacuum cleaner or compressed air before removing the plugs, to prevent dirt dropping into the cylinders.

5 Unscrew the plugs using a spark plug spanner, suitable box spanner or a deep socket and extension bar **(see illustration)**. Keep the socket aligned with the spark plug – if it is forcibly moved to one side, the ceramic insulator may be broken off. As each plug is removed, examine it as follows.

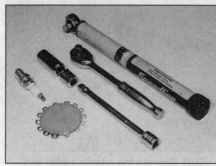

18.5 Tools required for spark plug removal, gap adjustment and refitting

6 Examination of the spark plugs will give a good indication of the condition of the engine. If the insulator nose of the spark plug is clean and white, with no deposits, this is indicative of a weak mixture or too hot a plug (a hot plug transfers heat away from the electrode slowly, a cold plug transfers heat away quickly).

7 If the tip and insulator nose are covered with hard black-looking deposits, then this is indicative that the mixture is too rich. Should the plug be black and oily, then it is likely that the engine is fairly worn, as well as the mixture being too rich.

8 If the insulator nose is covered with light tan to greyish-brown deposits, then the mixture is correct and it is likely that the engine is in good condition.

9 The spark plug electrode gap is of considerable importance as, if it is too large or too small, the size of the spark and its efficiency will be seriously impaired. Where given, the gap should be set as specified. **Note:** *Spark plugs with multiple earth electrodes are becoming an increasingly common fitment, especially to vehicles equipped with catalytic converters. Unless there is clear information to the contrary, no attempt should be made to adjust the plug gap on a spark plug with more than one earth electrode.*

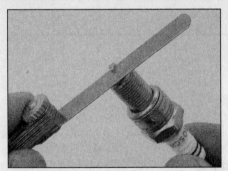

18.10 Measuring the spark plug gap with a feeler blade

10 To set the gap, measure it with a feeler blade, and then bend open, or closed, the outer plug electrode until the correct gap is achieved **(see illustration)**. The centre electrode should never be bent, as this may crack the insulator and cause plug failure, if nothing worse. If using feeler blades, the gap is correct when the appropriate-size blade is a firm sliding fit.

11 Special spark plug electrode gap adjusting tools are available from most motor accessory shops, or from spark plug manufacturers.

12 Before fitting the spark plugs, check that the threaded connector sleeves are tight, and that the plug exterior and threads are clean **(see Haynes Hint)**.

13 Remove the rubber hose (if used), and tighten the plug to the specified torque using

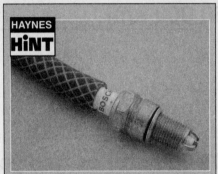

It is very often difficult to insert spark plugs into their holes without cross-threading them. To avoid this possibility, fit a short length of 5/16 inch internal diameter rubber hose over the end of the spark plug. The flexible hose acts as a universal joint to help align the plug with the plug hole. Should the plug begin to cross-thread, the hose will slip on the spark plug, preventing thread damage to the cylinder head.

the spark plug socket and a torque wrench. Refit the remaining spark plugs in the same manner.

14 On later models, refit the ignition HT coil as described in Chapter 5B.

15 On early models, connect the HT leads in the correct order, and refit any components removed for access.

19 Air cleaner filter element renewal

1 Remove the air cleaner assembly from the car as described in Chapter 4A.

2 With the air cleaner assembly on the bench, undo the screws securing the air cleaner lid to the base. Lift off the lid and remove the air filter element, noting which way up it is fitted **(see illustrations)**.

3 Wipe clean the inside of the air cleaner lid and base then fit the new element, ensuring it is correctly located.

4 Locate the lid correctly on the base and securely tighten the retaining screws.

5 Refit the air cleaner assembly to the car as described in Chapter 4A.

20 Fuel filter renewal

⚠️ **Warning: Before carrying out the following operation, refer to the precautions given in 'Safety first!' at the beginning of this manual, and follow them implicitly. Petrol is a highly-dangerous and volatile liquid, and the precautions necessary when handling it cannot be overstressed.**

1 The fuel filter is situated underneath the rear of the vehicle, on the side of the fuel tank. To gain access to the filter, chock the front wheels then jack up the rear of the car and support it on axle stands (see *Jacking and vehicle support*).

2 Place a container beneath the filter to catch any spilt fuel.

3 Position a large rag around the fuel pipe union, to catch any fuel spray which may be expelled as the fuel pressure is released, then depress the retaining clips and slowly disconnect the fuel pipe. Disconnect the other pipe from the opposite end of the filter and allow the filter contents to drain into the container **(see illustration)**.

4 Release the tab of the retaining strap and slide the fuel filter out of its holder, noting which way around it is fitted **(see illustration)**. Dispose of

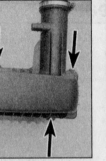

19.2a Undo the screws (arrowed) securing the air cleaner lid to the base . . .

19.2b . . . lift off the air cleaner lid . . .

19.2c . . . and remove the air filter element

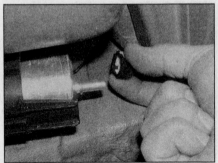

20.3 Depress the retaining clips and disconnect the fuel pipes from the fuel filter

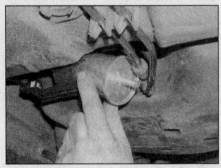

20.4 Release the tab of the retaining strap and slide the fuel filter out of its holder

the old filter safely; it will be highly inflammable, and may explode if thrown on a fire.

5 Slide the new filter into position, ensuring it is fitted the correct way around; the filter will either have an arrow on its body (indicating the correct direction of fuel flow) or be stamped OUT on one end (indicating the fuel outlet end of the filter).

6 Ensure the filter is clipped securely in its holder then reconnect both fuel pipes. Ensure the pipes 'click' into position on the filter and are securely retained by their quick-release fittings.

7 Start the engine and check the fuel filter for signs leaks.

21 Manual transmission oil level check

Note: *A suitable square-section wrench may be required to undo the transmission filler/ level plug on some models. These wrenches can be obtained from most motor factors or your Peugeot/Citroën dealer.*

1 Park the car on a level surface. The oil level must be checked before the car is driven, or at least 5 minutes after the engine has been switched off. If the oil is checked immediately after driving the car, some of the oil will remain distributed around the transmission, resulting in an inaccurate level reading.

2 Prise out the clips and remove the access cover from the left-hand wheel arch liner.

3 Wipe clean the area around the filler/level plug, which is on the left-hand end of the transmission **(see illustrations)**. Unscrew the plug and clean it; discard the sealing washer.

4 The oil level should reach the lower edge of the filler/level hole. A certain amount of oil will have gathered behind the filler/level plug, and will trickle out when it is removed; this does **not** necessarily indicate that the level is correct. To ensure that a true level is established, wait until the initial trickle has stopped, then add oil as necessary until a trickle of new oil can be seen emerging. The level will be correct when the flow ceases; use only good-quality oil of the specified type (refer to *Lubricants and fluids*).

5 Filling the transmission with oil is an extremely awkward operation; above all, allow plenty of time for the oil level to settle properly before checking it. If a large amount is added to the transmission, and a large amount flows out on checking the level, refit the filler/level plug and take the vehicle on a short journey so that the new oil is distributed fully around the transmission components, then recheck the level when it has settled again.

6 If the transmission has been overfilled so that oil flows out as soon as the filler/level plug is removed, check that the car is completely level (front-to-rear and side-to-side), and allow the surplus to drain off into a container.

7 When the level is correct, fit a new sealing washer to the filler/level plug. Refit the plug, tightening it to the specified torque setting.

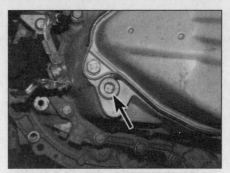

21.3a Oil filler/level plug (arrowed) – 1.4 litre models

Wash off any spilt oil then refit the access cover securing it in position with the clips.

22 Emissions control systems check

1 Details of the emissions control system components are given in Chapter 4D.

2 Checking consists simply of a visual check for obvious signs of damaged or leaking hoses and joints.

3 Detailed checking of the evaporative and/ or exhaust emissions systems (as applicable) should be entrusted to a Peugeot/Citroën dealer.

23 Coolant renewal

⚠ *Warning: Wait until the engine is cold before starting this procedure. Do not allow antifreeze to come in contact with your skin, or with the painted surfaces of the vehicle. Rinse off spills immediately with plenty of water. Never leave antifreeze lying around in an open container, or in a puddle in the driveway or on the garage floor. Children and pets are attracted by its sweet smell, but antifreeze can be fatal if ingested.*

Cooling system draining

1 With the engine completely cold, remove

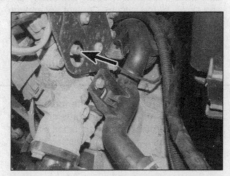

23.3b . . . thermostat housing bleed screw (arrowed) . . .

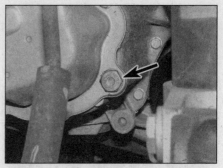

21.3b Oil filler/level plug (arrowed) – 1.6 litre models

the expansion tank filler cap. Turn the cap anti-clockwise until it reaches the first stop. Wait until any pressure remaining in the system is released, then push the cap down, turn it anti-clockwise to the second stop, and lift it off.

2 Position a suitable container beneath the lower left-hand side of the radiator. On early models, loosen the drain plug (there is no need to remove it completely) and allow the coolant to drain into the container. On later models a drain plug is not provided, so it will be necessary to disconnect the radiator bottom hose to allow the coolant to drain.

3 To assist draining, open the cooling system bleed screws. These are located in the heater matrix outlet hose union (to improve access, it may be located in an extension hose), on the engine compartment bulkhead, and on the thermostat housing. On some models, there may also be a bleed screw in the top left-hand end of the radiator **(see illustrations)**.

23.3a Heater matrix bleed screw (arrowed) . . .

23.3c . . . and radiator bleed screw (arrowed)

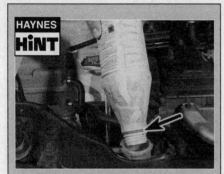

Cut the bottom off an old antifreeze container to make a 'header tank' for use when refilling the cooling system. The seal at the point arrowed must be as airtight as possible.

4 When the flow of coolant stops, reposition the container below the cylinder block drain plug located at the front left-hand side of the cylinder block.

5 Remove the drain plug, and allow the coolant to drain into the container.

6 If the coolant has been drained for a reason other than renewal, then provided it is clean and less than four years old, it can be re-used, though this is not recommended.

7 Refit the radiator and cylinder block drain plugs on completion of draining. Also refit the radiator bottom hose (later models) if the system is not to be flushed.

Cooling system flushing

8 If coolant renewal has been neglected, or if the antifreeze mixture has become diluted, then in time, the cooling system may gradually lose efficiency, as the coolant passages become restricted due to rust, scale deposits, and other sediment. The cooling system efficiency can be restored by flushing the system clean.

9 The radiator should be flushed separately from the engine, to avoid excess contamination.

Radiator flushing

10 To flush the radiator, first tighten the radiator drain plug, and the radiator bleed screw, where applicable.

11 Disconnect the top and bottom hoses and any other relevant hoses from the radiator, with reference to Chapter 3.

12 Insert a garden hose into the radiator top inlet. Direct a flow of clean water through the radiator, and continue flushing until clean water emerges from the radiator bottom outlet.

13 If after a reasonable period, the water still does not run clear, the radiator can be flushed with a good proprietary cleaning agent. It is important that their manufacturer's instructions are followed carefully. If the contamination is particularly bad, insert the hose in the radiator bottom outlet, and reverse-flush the radiator.

Engine flushing

14 To flush the engine, first refit the cylinder block drain plug, and tighten the cooling system bleed screws.

15 Remove the thermostat (see Chapter 3), then temporarily refit the thermostat cover.

16 With the top and bottom hoses disconnected from the radiator, insert a garden hose into the radiator top hose. Direct a clean flow of water through the engine, and continue flushing until clean water emerges from the radiator bottom hose.

17 When flushing is complete, refit the thermostat and reconnect the hoses with reference to Chapter 3.

Cooling system filling

18 Before attempting to fill the cooling system, make sure that all hoses and clips are in good condition, and that the clips are tight. Note that an antifreeze mixture must be used all year round, to prevent corrosion of the engine components (see following sub-Section). Also check that the radiator and cylinder block drain plugs are in place and tight.

19 Remove the expansion tank filler cap.

20 Open all the cooling system bleed screws (see paragraph 3).

21 Some of the cooling system hoses are positioned at a higher level than the top of the radiator expansion tank. It is therefore necessary to use a 'header tank' when refilling the cooling system, to reduce the possibility of air being trapped in the system. Although Peugeot/Citroën dealers use a special header tank, the same effect can be achieved by using a suitable bottle, with a seal between the bottle and the expansion tank **(see Haynes Hint)**.

22 Fit the 'header tank' to the expansion tank and slowly fill the system. Coolant will emerge from each of the bleed screws in turn, starting with the lowest screw. As soon as coolant free from air bubbles emerges from the lowest screw, tighten that screw, and watch the next bleed screw in the system. Repeat the procedure until the coolant is emerging from the highest bleed screw in the cooling system and all bleed screws are securely tightened.

23 Continue to fill the cooling system until bubbles stop appearing in the expansion tank. Help to bleed the air from the system by repeatedly squeezing the radiator bottom hose.

24 When no more bubbles appear, ensure the header tank is full (at least 1.0 litre of coolant) then start the engine. Run the engine at a fast idle speed (do not exceed 2000 rpm) until the cooling fan cuts in and out TWICE, then when the fan has stopped for the second time, switch the engine off.

Caution: The coolant will be hot. Take great care not to scald yourself.

25 Allow the engine to cool, then remove the 'header tank'.

26 When the engine has cooled, check the coolant level with reference to *Weekly checks*. Top-up the level if necessary, and refit the expansion tank cap.

Antifreeze mixture

27 The antifreeze should always be renewed at the specified intervals. This is necessary not only to maintain the antifreeze properties, but also to prevent corrosion which would otherwise occur as the corrosion inhibitors become progressively less effective.

28 Always use an ethylene-glycol based antifreeze of the specified type (see *Lubricants and fluids*). The quantity of antifreeze and level of protection are indicated in the Specifications.

29 Before adding antifreeze, the cooling system should be completely drained, preferably flushed, and all hoses checked for condition and security.

30 After filling with antifreeze, a label should be attached to the expansion tank, stating the type and concentration of antifreeze used, and the date installed. Any subsequent topping-up should be made with the same type and concentration of antifreeze.

31 Do not use engine antifreeze in the windscreen/tailgate washer system, as it will damage the vehicle paintwork. A screenwash additive should be added to the washer system in the quantities stated on the bottle.

Every ten years

24 Airbags and seat belt pretensioners renewal

1 Peugeot/Citroën recommend that the airbags and seat belt pretensioners are renewed regardless of their condition every ten years. Refer to Chapter 12 for airbag renewal, and Chapter 11 for seat belt pretensioner renewal.

Chapter 1 Part B:
Routine maintenance and servicing – diesel models

Contents

Degrees of difficulty

Easy, suitable for novice with little experience	**Fairly easy,** suitable for beginner with some experience	**Fairly difficult,** suitable for competent DIY mechanic	**Difficult,** suitable for experienced DIY mechanic	**Very difficult,** suitable for expert DIY or professional 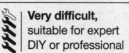

Lubricants and fluids. . . . . Refer to *Weekly checks*

Capacities (approximate)

Engine oil (including filter)

1.6 litre engines	3.75 litres

1.8 and 1.9 litre XUD series engines:

With steel sump	4.2 litres
With aluminium sump.	4.0 litres

1.9 litre DW series engines:

With steel sump	4.7 litres
With aluminium sump.	4.5 litres

2.0 litre engines:

With steel sump	4.5 litres
With aluminium sump.	4.2 litres
Difference between MAX and MIN dipstick marks.	1.5 litres

Cooling system

1.6 litre engines	11.0 litres
1.8 and 1.9 litre XUD series engines	8.0 litres

1.9 litre DW series engines:

Pre-September 2002 models.	10.5 litres
September 2002 models onward.	9.0 litres
2.0 litre engines	9.0 litres

Transmission.	2.0 litres
Power-assisted steering	1.0 litre
Fuel tank	60.0 litres

Cooling system

50% antifreeze	Protection down to –35°C

Note: *Refer to antifreeze manufacturer for latest recommendations.*

Brakes

Brake pad friction material minimum thickness.	2.0 mm
Brake shoe friction material minimum thickness	1.5 mm

Tyre pressures . . . . See end of *Weekly checks*

Torque wrench settings

	Nm	lbf ft
Roadwheel bolts.	90	66
Transmission filler/level plugs.	25	18

Note: *This maintenance schedule is a guide recommended by Haynes, for servicing your own vehicle. For the manufacturer's maintenance schedule, check with your local dealer.*

The maintenance intervals in this manual are provided with the assumption that you will be carrying out the work yourself. These are the minimum maintenance intervals recommended by ourselves for vehicles driven daily, based on the schedule produced by the manufacturer. If you wish to keep your vehicle in peak condition at all times, you may wish to perform some of these procedures more often. We encourage frequent maintenance, because it enhances the efficiency, performance and resale value of your vehicle.

If the vehicle is driven in dusty areas, used to tow a trailer, or driven frequently at slow speeds (idling in traffic) or on short journeys, more frequent maintenance intervals are recommended.

When the vehicle is new, it should be serviced by a dealer service department (or other workshop recognised by the vehicle manufacturer as providing the same standard of service) in order to preserve the warranty. The vehicle manufacturer may reject warranty claims if you are unable to prove that servicing has been carried out as and when specified, using only original equipment parts or parts certified to be of equivalent quality.

Every 250 miles or weekly
☐ Refer to *Weekly checks*

Every 6000 miles (10 000 km) or 12 months – whichever comes first
☐ Renew the engine oil and filter (Section 3).

Note: *Citroën/Peugeot recommend that the engine oil and filter are changed every 12 000 miles (20 000 km). However, oil and filter changes are good for the engine and we recommend that the oil and filter are renewed more frequently, especially if the vehicle is used on a lot of short journeys.*

Every 12 000 miles (20 000 km) or two years – whichever comes first
☐ Drain any water from the fuel filter (Section 4).
☐ Check all underbonnet components for fluid leaks (Section 5).
☐ Check the condition of the driveshaft rubber gaiters (Section 6).
☐ Lubricate all hinges and locks (Section 7).
☐ Carry out road test (Section 8).
☐ Reset the service interval indicator (Section 9).
☐ Check the pollen filter (Section 10).
☐ Check the condition of the auxiliary drivebelt (Section 13).
☐ Check the condition of the front brake pads (Section 14).
☐ Check the condition of the rear brake shoes (Section 15).
☐ Check the operation of the handbrake (Section 16).
☐ Check the condition of the exhaust system (Section 17).
☐ Check the steering and suspension components (Section 18).

Every 36 000 miles (60 000 km) or six years – whichever comes first
☐ Renew the fuel filter (Section 19).
☐ Renew the air cleaner filter element (Section 20).
☐ Check the manual transmission oil level (Section 21).
☐ Check the exhaust emissions (Section 22).
☐ Renew the brake fluid (Section 24).
☐ Renew the coolant (Section 25)*.

*Note: *This work is not included in the Citroën/Peugeot schedule, and should not be required if the recommended Citroën/Peugeot anti-freeze/inhibitor is used.*

Every 75 000 miles (120 000 km) or ten years – whichever comes first
☐ Renew the timing belt (Section 23).

Note: *Although the normal interval for timing belt renewal is 150 000 miles (240 000 km), it is strongly recommended that the interval is reduced to 75 000 miles (120 000 km), especially on vehicles which are subjected to intensive use, ie, mainly short journeys or a lot of stop-start driving. The actual belt renewal interval is therefore very much up to the individual owner, but bear in mind that severe engine damage will result if the belt breaks.*

Every fifteen years
☐ Renew the airbags and seat belt pretensioners (Section 26).

Note: *This maintenance schedule is a guide recommended by Haynes, for servicing your own vehicle. For the manufacturer's maintenance schedule, check with your local dealer.*

The maintenance intervals in this manual are provided with the assumption that you, not the dealer, will be carrying out the work. These are the minimum maintenance intervals recommended by us for vehicles driven daily. If you wish to keep your vehicle in peak condition at all times, you may wish to perform some of these procedures more often. We encourage frequent maintenance, because it enhances the efficiency, performance and resale value of your vehicle.

If the vehicle is driven in dusty areas, used to tow a trailer, or driven frequently at slow speeds (idling in traffic) or on short journeys, more frequent maintenance intervals are recommended.

When the vehicle is new, it should be serviced by a dealer service department (or other workshop recognised by the vehicle manufacturer as providing the same standard of service) in order to preserve the warranty. The vehicle manufacturer may reject warranty claims if you are unable to prove that servicing has been carried out as and when specified, using only original equipment parts or parts certified to be of equivalent quality.

Every 250 miles (400 km) or weekly
☐ Refer to *Weekly checks*

Every 5000 miles (7500 km) or 12 months – whichever comes first
☐ Renew the engine oil and filter (Section 3)*.
☐ Drain any water from the fuel filter (Section 4).
☐ Check all underbonnet components for fluid leaks (Section 5).
☐ Check the condition of the driveshaft rubber gaiters (Section 6).
☐ Lubricate all hinges and locks (Section 7).
☐ Carry out a road test (Section 8).
☐ Reset the service interval indicator (Section 9).

***Note:** On 1.9 litre (DW series) engines, Peugeot/Citroën recommend the engine oil and filter are changed every 10 000 miles or two years. However, oil and filter changes are good for the engine and we recommend that the oil and filter are renewed at least once a year, especially if the vehicle is used on a lot of short journeys.*

Every 10 000 miles (15 000 km) or two years – whichever comes first
☐ Check the pollen filter (Section 10).
☐ Check the idle speed and anti-stall speed (Section 11).
☐ Check the condition of the auxiliary drivebelt (Section 12).
☐ Check the condition of the front brake pads (Section 14).
☐ Check the condition of the rear brake shoes (Section 15).
☐ Check the operation of the handbrake (Section 16).
☐ Check the condition of the exhaust system (Section 17).
☐ Check the steering and suspension components (Section 18).

Every 30 000 miles (45 000 km) or four years – whichever comes first
☐ Renew the fuel filter (Section 19).
☐ Renew the air cleaner filter element (Section 20).
☐ Check the manual transmission oil level (Section 21).
☐ Check the exhaust emissions (Section 22).

Every 40 000 miles (60 000 km)
☐ Renew the timing belt (Section 23).
Note: *Although the normal interval for timing belt renewal is 80 000 miles (120 000 km), it is strongly recommended that the interval is reduced to 40 000 miles (60 000 km), especially on vehicles which are subjected to intensive use, ie, mainly short journeys or a lot of stop-start driving. The actual belt renewal interval is therefore very much up to the individual owner, but bear in mind that severe engine damage will result if the belt breaks.*

Every 40 000 miles (60 000 km) or two years – whichever comes first
☐ Renew the brake fluid (Section 24).

Every 40 000 miles (60 000 km) or four years – whichever comes first
☐ Renew the coolant (Section 25).

Every ten years
☐ Renew the airbags and seat belt pretensioners (Section 26).

Note: *This maintenance schedule is a guide recommended by Haynes, for servicing your own vehicle. For the manufacturer's maintenance schedule, check with your local dealer.*

The maintenance intervals in this manual are provided with the assumption that you, not the dealer, will be carrying out the work. These are the minimum maintenance intervals recommended by us for vehicles driven daily. If you wish to keep your vehicle in peak condition at all times, you may wish to perform some of these procedures more often. We encourage frequent maintenance, because it enhances the efficiency, performance and resale value of your vehicle.

If the vehicle is driven in dusty areas, used to tow a trailer, or driven frequently at slow speeds (idling in traffic) or on short journeys, more frequent maintenance intervals are recommended.

When the vehicle is new, it should be serviced by a dealer service department (or other workshop recognised by the vehicle manufacturer as providing the same standard of service) in order to preserve the warranty. The vehicle manufacturer may reject warranty claims if you are unable to prove that servicing has been carried out as and when specified, using only original equipment parts or parts certified to be of equivalent quality.

Every 250 miles (400 km) or weekly
☐ Refer to *Weekly checks*

Every 6000 miles (10 000 km) or 12 months – whichever comes first
☐ Renew the engine oil and filter (Section 3)*.
☐ Drain any water from the fuel filter (Section 4).
☐ Check all underbonnet components for fluid leaks (Section 5).
☐ Check the condition of the driveshaft rubber gaiters (Section 6).
☐ Lubricate all hinges and locks (Section 7).
☐ Carry out a road test (Section 8).
☐ Reset the service interval indicator (Section 9).

***Note:** Peugeot/Citroën recommend the engine oil and filter are changed every 12 000 miles or two years. However, oil and filter changes are good for the engine and we recommend that the oil and filter are renewed at least once a year, especially if the vehicle is used on a lot of short journeys.*

Every 12 000 miles (20 000 km) or two years – whichever comes first
☐ Check the pollen filter (Section 10).
☐ Check the condition of the auxiliary drivebelt (Section 13).
☐ Check the condition of the front brake pads (Section 14).
☐ Check the condition of the rear brake shoes (Section 15).
☐ Check the operation of the handbrake (Section 16).
☐ Check the condition of the exhaust system (Section 17).
☐ Check the steering and suspension components (Section 18).

Every 36 000 miles (60 000 km) or two years – whichever comes first
☐ Renew the brake fluid (Section 24).

Every 36 000 miles (60 000 km) or 4 years – whichever comes first
☐ Renew the fuel filter (Section 19).
☐ Renew the air cleaner filter element (Section 20).
☐ Check the manual transmission oil level (Section 21).
☐ Check the exhaust emissions (Section 22).
☐ Renew the coolant (Section 25).

Every 48 000 miles (80 000 km)
☐ Renew the timing belt (Section 23).

Note: *Although the normal interval for timing belt renewal is 96 000 miles (160 000 km), it is strongly recommended that the interval is reduced to 48 000 miles (80 000 km), especially on vehicles which are subjected to intensive use, ie, mainly short journeys or a lot of stop-start driving. The actual belt renewal interval is therefore very much up to the individual owner, but bear in mind that severe engine damage will result if the belt breaks.*

Every ten years
☐ Renew the airbags and seat belt pretensioners (Section 26).

Underbonnet view of a 1.6 litre model

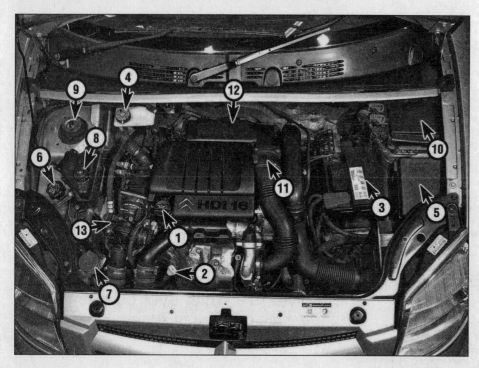

1 Engine oil filler cap
2 Engine oil dipstick
3 Battery
4 Brake/clutch fluid reservoir
5 Fuse/relay box
6 Coolant system expansion tank
7 Windscreen/tailgate washer fluid reservoir
8 Power steering fluid reservoir
9 Suspension strut upper mounting
10 Engine management ECU
11 Airflow meter
12 Air cleaner housing
13 Throttle housing

Underbonnet view of a pre-September 2002 1.9 litre model (DW series)

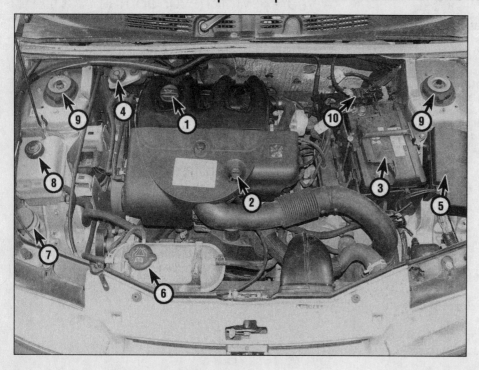

1 Engine oil filler cap
2 Engine oil dipstick
3 Battery
4 Master cylinder brake fluid reservoir
5 Fuse/relay box
6 Cooling system expansion tank
7 Windscreen/tailgate washer fluid reservoir
8 Power steering fluid reservoir
9 Suspension strut upper mounting
10 Engine management ECU

Underbonnet view of a post-September 2002 1.9 litre model (DW series)

1 Engine oil filler cap
2 Engine oil dipstick
3 Battery
4 Master cylinder brake fluid reservoir
5 Fuse/relay box
6 Cooling system expansion tank
7 Windscreen/tailgate washer fluid reservoir
8 Power steering fluid reservoir
9 Suspension strut upper mounting
10 Engine management ECU
11 Airflow meter
12 Air cleaner housing

Underbonnet view of a 2.0 litre model

1 Engine oil filler cap
2 Engine oil dipstick
3 Battery
4 Master cylinder brake fluid reservoir
5 Fuse/relay box
6 Cooling system expansion tank
7 Windscreen/tailgate washer fluid reservoir
8 Power steering fluid reservoir
9 Suspension strut upper mounting
10 Engine management ECU
11 Airflow meter
12 Air cleaner housing
13 Accelerator pedal position sensor

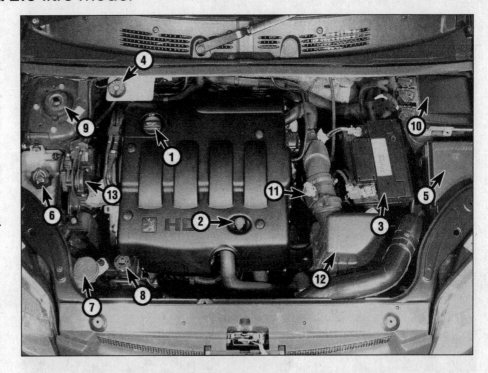

Front underbody view

1 Sump drain plug
2 Oil filter
3 Engine/transmission rear mounting
4 Alternator
5 Radiator bottom hose
6 Clutch cable
7 Front suspension subframe
8 Front brake caliper
9 Front suspension lower arm
10 Track rod balljoint
11 Front anti-roll bar
12 Steering gear assembly

Rear underbody view

1 Spare wheel
2 Rear silencer
3 Fuel tank
4 Handbrake cable
5 Rear suspension torsion bar
6 Rear suspension tubular crossmember
7 Rear shock absorber
8 Rear suspension trailing arm

1 General information

This Chapter is designed to help the home mechanic maintain his/her vehicle for safety, economy, long life and peak performance.

The Chapter contains a master maintenance schedule, followed by Sections dealing specifically with each task in the schedule. Visual checks, adjustments, component renewal and other helpful items are included. Refer to the accompanying illustrations of the engine compartment and the underside of the vehicle for the locations of the various components.

Servicing your vehicle in accordance with the mileage/time maintenance schedule and the following Sections will provide a planned maintenance programme, which should result in a long and reliable service life. This is a comprehensive plan, so maintaining some items but not others at the specified service intervals will not produce the same results.

As you service your vehicle, you will discover that many of the procedures can – and should – be grouped together, because of the particular procedure being performed, or because of the proximity of two otherwise-unrelated components to one another. For example, if the vehicle is raised for any reason, the exhaust can be inspected at the same time as the suspension and steering components.

The first step in this maintenance programme is to prepare yourself before the actual work begins. Read through all the Sections relevant to the work to be carried out, then make a list and gather all the parts and tools required. If a problem is encountered, seek advice from a parts specialist, or a dealer service department.

2 Routine maintenance

1 If, from the time the vehicle is new, the routine maintenance schedule is followed closely, and frequent checks are made of fluid levels and high-wear items, as suggested throughout this manual, the engine will be kept in relatively good running condition, and the need for additional work will be minimised.

2 It is possible that there will be times when the engine is running poorly due to the lack of regular maintenance. This is even more likely if a used vehicle, which has not received regular and frequent maintenance checks, is purchased. In such cases, additional work may need to be carried out, outside of the regular maintenance intervals.

3 If engine wear is suspected, a compression test or leakdown test (refer to the relevant Part of Chapter 2) will provide valuable information regarding the overall performance of the main internal components. Such a test can

be used as a basis to decide on the extent of the work to be carried out. If, for example, a compression or leakdown test indicates serious internal engine wear, conventional maintenance as described in this Chapter will not greatly improve the performance of the engine, and may prove a waste of time and money, unless extensive overhaul work is carried out first.

4 The following series of operations are those most often required to improve the performance of a generally poor-running engine:

Primary operations

  a) *Clean, inspect and test the battery (See 'Weekly checks').*
  b) *Check all the engine-related fluids (See 'Weekly checks').*
  c) *Check the condition and tension of the auxiliary drivebelt (Sections 12 and 13).*
  d) *Check the condition of the air cleaner filter element, and renew if necessary (Section 20).*
  e) *Check the fuel filter (Section 19).*
  f) *Check the condition of all hoses, and check for fluid leaks (Section 5).*
  g) *Check the idle speed and anti-stall speed – 1.8 and 1.9 litre engines (Section 11).*

5 If the above operations do not prove fully effective, carry out the following secondary operations:

Secondary operations

All items listed under *Primary operations*, **plus the following:**
  a) *Check the charging system (Chapter 5A).*
  b) *Check the preheating system (Chapter 5C).*
  c) *Check the fuel system (Chapter 4B or 4C).*

3 Engine oil and filter renewal

1.6 and 2.0 litre engines – every 6000 miles (10 000 km)

1.8 and 1.9 litre engines – every 5000 miles (7500 km)

Note: *A suitable square-section wrench may be required on some models to undo the sump drain plug. These wrenches can be*

obtained from most motor factors, or from your Peugeot/Citroën dealer.

1 Frequent oil and filter changes are among the most important preventative maintenance procedures for the DIY owner. As engine oil ages, it becomes diluted and contaminated, which leads to premature engine wear.

2 Before starting this procedure, gather together all the necessary tools and materials. Also make sure that you have plenty of clean rags and newspapers handy, to mop-up any spills. Ideally, the engine oil should be warm, as it will drain better, and more built-up sludge will be removed with it. Take care, however, not to touch the exhaust or any other hot parts of the engine when working under the vehicle. To avoid any possibility of scalding, and to protect yourself from possible skin irritants and other harmful contaminants in used engine oils, it is advisable to wear gloves when carrying out this work. Access to the underside of the vehicle will be greatly improved if it can be raised on a lift, driven onto ramps, or jacked up and supported on axle stands (see *Jacking and vehicle support*). Whichever method is chosen, make sure that the vehicle remains level, or if it is at an angle, that the drain plug is at the lowest point. Where fitted, undo the retaining screws and remove the engine undertray.

3 Slacken the drain plug about half a turn; on some models, a square-section wrench may be needed to slacken the plug **(see illustration)**. Position the draining container under the drain plug, then remove the plug completely. If possible, try to keep the plug pressed into the sump while unscrewing it by hand the last couple of turns **(see Haynes Hint)**. Recover the sealing ring from the drain plug.

4 Allow some time for the old oil to drain, noting that it may be necessary to reposition the container as the oil flow slows to a trickle.

5 After all the oil has drained, wipe off the drain plug with a clean rag, and fit a new sealing washer. Clean the area around the drain plug opening, and refit the plug. Tighten the plug securely.

6 Move the container into position under the

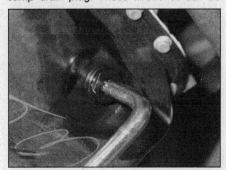

3.3 Slackening the sump drain plug with a square-section wrench

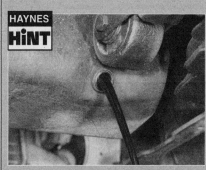

As the drain plug releases from the threads, move it away sharply so the stream of oil issuing from the sump runs into the container, not up your sleeve

3.7 Using an oil filter removal tool to slacken the oil filter

4.3 Opening the fuel filter drain plug – XUD series engines

oil filter, which is located on the front side of the cylinder block, below the inlet manifold.

7 Using an oil filter removal tool if necessary, slacken the filter initially, then unscrew it by hand the rest of the way **(see illustration)**. Empty the oil in the old filter into the container.

8 Use a clean rag to remove all oil, dirt and sludge from the filter sealing area on the engine. Check the old filter to make sure that the rubber sealing ring hasn't stuck to the engine. If it has, carefully remove it.

9 Apply a light coating of clean engine oil to the sealing ring on the new filter, then screw it into position on the engine. Tighten the filter firmly by hand only – **do not** use any tools.

10 Remove the old oil and all tools from under the car, then lower the car to the ground (if applicable).

11 Remove the dipstick, then unscrew the oil filler cap from the cylinder head cover or

oil filler/breather neck (as applicable). Fill the engine, using the correct grade and type of oil (see *Weekly checks*). An oil can spout or funnel may help to reduce spillage. Pour in half the specified quantity of oil first, then wait a few minutes for the oil to fall to the sump. Continue adding oil a small quantity at a time until the level is up to the lower mark on the dipstick. Adding approximately 1.5 litres will bring the level up to the upper mark on the dipstick. Refit the filler cap.

12 Start the engine and run it for a few minutes; check for leaks around the oil filter seal and the sump drain plug. Note that there may be a brief delay before the oil pressure warning light goes out when the engine is first started, as the oil circulates through the engine oil galleries and the new oil filter (where fitted) before the pressure builds-up.

13 Switch off the engine, and wait a few

minutes for the oil to settle in the sump once more. With the new oil circulated and the filter completely full, recheck the level on the dipstick, and add more oil as necessary.

14 Dispose of the used engine oil and filter safely, with reference to *General repair procedures* at the rear of this manual. Do not discard the old filter with domestic household waste. The facility for waste oil disposal provided by many local council refuse tips generally has a filter receptacle alongside.

4 Fuel filter water draining

**1.6 litre engines –
every 12 000 miles (20 000 km)**

**1.8 and 1.9 litre engines –
every 5000 miles (7500 km)**

**2.0 litre engines –
every 6000 miles (10 000 km)**

> **HAYNES HiNT** *This is a somewhat messy operation. Wear disposable plastic gloves and spread out a good quantity of rags or newspapers to catch any spillage. Be particularly careful not to spill fuel onto cooling system hoses, wiring harnesses, engine mountings or accessory drivebelts; protect them with a plastic sheet. Catch the fuel in a clean container in order to be able to observe any water or foreign bodies drained from the filter.*

1.8 and 1.9 litre XUD series engines

1 A water drain plug and tube are provided at the base of the fuel filter housing.

2 Place a suitable container beneath the drain tube, and cover the clutch bellhousing.

3 Open the drain plug by turning it anti-clockwise, and allow fuel and water to drain until fuel, free from water, emerges from the end of the tube **(see illustration)**. Close the drain plug, and tighten it securely.

4 Dispose of the drained fuel safely.

5 Start the engine. If difficulty is experienced, prime the fuel system (see Chapter 4B).

1.9 litre DW series engines

6 Release the fasteners from the right-hand side and top of the engine cover then lift off the cover, taking care not to lose its mounting rubbers **(see illustrations)**.

7 Wipe clean the exterior of the fuel filter housing then position a suitable container beneath the drain plug at the base of the housing **(see illustration)**. If necessary attach a short length of hose to the housing drain outlet to allow the flow of fuel to be directed into the container (on some models a hose may be fitted in production).

4.6a On 1.9 litre DW series engines, remove the fasteners from the right-hand side . . .

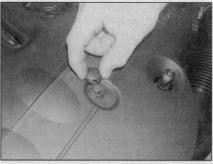

4.6b . . . and top of the engine cover . . .

4.6c . . . then remove the cover from the engine

4.7 Fuel filter drain plug location – 1.9 litre DW series engines

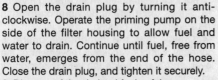

4.11a Release the fixings by turning them through 90° . . .

4.11b . . . and remove the engine cover

4.14 Fuel filter drain plug location – 2.0 litre engines

8 Open the drain plug by turning it anti-clockwise. Operate the priming pump on the side of the filter housing to allow fuel and water to drain. Continue until fuel, free from water, emerges from the end of the hose. Close the drain plug, and tighten it securely.

9 Dispose of the drained fuel safely.

10 Refit the engine cover and start the engine. If difficulty is experienced, prime the fuel system (see Chapter 4C).

1.6 and 2.0 litre engines

Caution: It is vital to observe the intervals specified for draining the water from the fuel filter. The high pressure injection system is particularly susceptible to the presence of water in the fuel, which can cause seizure of the injectors and/or injection pump. The result is the destruction of the engine, either as a result of the 'blowlamp' effect of an injector stuck open, or by breakage of the timing belt consequent upon the seizure of the pump.

Note: *Always renew the drain plug and its O-ring after each draining. On completion, prime the fuel system (see Chapter 4C) and make sure that there are no signs of leakage at the drain plug after restarting the engine.*

11 Release the fixings by turning them through 90°, and remove the engine cover (see illustrations).

12 Cover the clutch bellhousing with rags to protect it from any fuel spillage.

13 On 1.6 litre models only, remove the air inlet ducts from the left-hand side of the engine compartment as described in Chapter 4C, Section 3, for access to the fuel filter.

14 Clean the outside of the filter housing, then place a suitable container below the drain plug at the base of the housing (see illustration). If necessary attach a short length of hose to the housing drain outlet to allow the flow of fuel to be directed into the container (on some models a hose may be fitted in production).

15 Undo the drain plug and allow the contents of the filter housing to drain into the container. Note that it may be necessary to release one of the fuel hose unions on the filter housing cover to allow the draining to take place. Discard the drain plug and its O-ring.

16 Once the housing is empty, fit a new drain plug and O-ring. Tighten the drain plug and,

if necessary, reconnect the hose union on the housing cover, making sure it is correctly engaged.

17 Move the container away and if necessary remove the hose. Wipe up any spillage and recover the rags.

18 Dispose of the drained fuel safely.

19 Prime the fuel system as described in Chapter 4C, then refit the engine cover and air inlet ducts (1.6 litre models).

5 Hose and fluid leak check

1.6 litre engines – every 12 000 miles (20 000 km)

1.8 and 1.9 litre engines – every 5000 miles (7500 km)

2.0 litre engines – every 6000 miles (10 000 km)

1 On 1.9 litre DW series engines, release the fasteners from the right-hand side and top of the engine cover then lift off the cover, taking care not to lose its mounting rubbers (see illustrations 4.6a to 4.6c). On 1.6 and 2.0 litre engines, release the fixings by turning them through 90°, and remove the engine cover (see illustrations 4.11a and 4.11b).

2 Visually inspect the engine joint faces, gaskets and seals for any signs of water or oil leaks. Pay particular attention to the areas around the camshaft cover, cylinder head, oil filter and sump joint faces. Bear in mind that, over a period of time, some very slight seepage from these areas is to be expected – what you are really looking for is any indication of a serious leak. Should a leak be found, renew the gasket or oil seal by referring to the appropriate Chapters in this manual.

3 Also check the security and condition of all the engine-related pipes and hoses. Ensure that all cable ties or securing clips are in place, and in good condition. Clips which are broken or missing can lead to chafing of the hoses, pipes or wiring, which could cause more serious problems in the future.

4 Carefully check the radiator hoses and heater hoses along their entire length. Renew any hose which is cracked, swollen

or deteriorated. Cracks will show up better if the hose is squeezed. Pay close attention to the hose clips that secure the hoses to the cooling system components. Hose clips can pinch and puncture hoses, resulting in cooling system leaks. If the original Peugeot/Citroën crimped-type hose clips are used, it may be a good idea to use worm-drive clips.

5 Inspect all the cooling system components (hoses, joint faces, etc) for leaks (see Haynes Hint).

6 Where any problems are found on system components, renew the component or gasket with reference to Chapter 3.

7 With the vehicle raised, inspect the fuel tank and filler neck for punctures, cracks and other damage. The connection between the filler neck and tank is especially critical. Sometimes a rubber filler neck or connecting hose will leak due to loose retaining clamps or deteriorated rubber.

8 Carefully check all rubber hoses and metal fuel lines leading away from the fuel tank. Check for loose connections, deteriorated hoses, crimped lines, and other damage. Pay particular attention to the vent pipes and hoses, which often loop up around the filler neck and can become blocked or crimped. Follow the lines to the front of the vehicle, carefully inspecting them all the way. Renew damaged sections as necessary.

9 From within the engine compartment, check the security of all fuel hose attachments and pipe unions, and inspect the fuel hoses

HAYNES HiNT

A leak in the cooling system will usually show up as white- or rust-coloured deposits on the area adjoining the leak.

and vacuum hoses for kinks, chafing and deterioration.

10 Where applicable, check the condition of the power steering fluid hoses and pipes.

11 On completion, refit the engine covers (where applicable).

6 Driveshaft gaiter check

1.6 litre engines –
every 12 000 miles (20 000 km)

1.8 and 1.9 litre engines –
every 5000 miles (7500 km)

2.0 litre engines –
every 6000 miles (10 000 km)

1 With the vehicle raised and securely supported on axle stands (see *Jacking and vehicle support*), turn the steering onto full lock, then slowly rotate the roadwheel. Inspect the condition of the outer constant velocity (CV) joint rubber gaiters, squeezing the gaiters to open out the folds **(see illustration)**. Check for signs of cracking, splits or deterioration of the rubber, which may allow the grease to escape, and lead to water and grit entry into the joint. Also check the security and condition of the retaining clips. Repeat these checks on the inner CV joints. If any damage or deterioration is found, the gaiters should be renewed (see Chapter 8).

2 At the same time, check the general condition of the CV joints themselves by first holding the driveshaft and attempting to rotate the wheel. Repeat this check by holding the inner joint and attempting to rotate the driveshaft. Any appreciable movement indicates wear in the joints, wear in the driveshaft splines, or a loose driveshaft retaining nut.

7 Hinge and lock lubrication
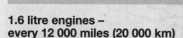

1.6 litre engines –
every 12 000 miles (20 000 km)

1.8 and 1.9 litre engines –
every 5000 miles (7500 km)

2.0 litre engines –
every 6000 miles (10 000 km)

1 Work around the vehicle, and lubricate the hinges of the bonnet, doors and tailgate with a general-purpose light oil.

2 Lightly lubricate the bonnet release mechanism and exposed section of inner cable with a smear of grease.

3 Check carefully the security and operation of all hinges, latches and locks, adjusting

6.1 Check the condition of the driveshaft gaiters (arrowed)

them where required. Check the operation of the central locking system (if fitted).

4 Check the condition and operation of the tailgate struts, renewing them if either is leaking or no longer able to support the tailgate securely when raised.

8 Road test

1.6 litre engines –
every 12 000 miles (20 000 km)

1.8 and 1.9 litre engines –
every 5000 miles (7500 km)

2.0 litre engines –
every 6000 miles (10 000 km)

Instruments and electrical equipment

1 Check the operation of all instruments and electrical equipment.

2 Make sure that all instruments read correctly, and switch on all electrical equipment in turn to check that it works properly.

Steering and suspension

3 Check for any abnormalities in the steering, suspension, handling or road 'feel'.

4 Drive the vehicle, and check that there are no unusual vibrations or noises.

5 Check that the steering feels positive, with no excessive 'sloppiness', or roughness, and check for any suspension noises when cornering, or when driving over bumps.

Drivetrain

6 Check the performance of the engine, clutch, transmission and driveshafts.

7 Listen for any unusual noises from the engine, clutch and transmission.

8 Make sure that the engine runs smoothly when idling, and that there is no hesitation when accelerating.

9 Check that the clutch action is smooth and progressive, that the drive is taken up smoothly, and that the pedal travel is not excessive. Also listen for any noises when the clutch pedal is depressed.

10 Check that all gears can be engaged smoothly, without noise, and that the gear lever action is smooth and not abnormally vague or 'notchy'.

11 Listen for a metallic clicking sound from the front of the vehicle, as the vehicle is driven slowly in a circle with the steering on full lock. Carry out this check in both directions. If a clicking noise is heard, this indicates wear in a driveshaft joint, in which case, the complete driveshaft must be renewed (see Chapter 8).

Braking system

12 Make sure that the vehicle does not pull to one side when braking, and that the wheels do not lock prematurely when braking hard.

13 Check that there is no vibration through the steering when braking.

14 Check that the handbrake operates correctly, without excessive movement of the lever, and that it holds the vehicle stationary on a slope.

15 Test the operation of the brake servo unit as follows. With the engine off, depress the footbrake four or five times to exhaust the vacuum. Start the engine, holding the brake pedal depressed. As the engine starts, there should be a noticeable 'give' in the brake pedal as vacuum builds-up. Allow the engine to run for at least two minutes, and then switch it off. If the brake pedal is depressed now, it should be possible to detect a hiss from the servo as the pedal is depressed. After about four or five applications, no further hissing should be heard, and the pedal should feel considerably firmer.

9 Resetting the service indicator

1.6 litre engines –
every 12 000 miles (20 000 km)

1.8 and 1.9 litre engines –
every 5000 miles (7500 km)

2.0 litre engines –
every 6000 miles (10 000 km)

1 On completion of the service, reset the service interval indicator as follows.

2 With the ignition switched off, press and hold the trip meter button.

3 Turn on the ignition switch, and the display begins a countdown. When the countdown reaches 0, release the trip meter button, and the spanner service symbol in the display will disappear.

4 Turn off the ignition switch.

5 Turn on the ignition switch and check the correct mileage to the next service interval is displayed on the indicator.

Note: *If you need to disconnect the battery after carrying out this procedure, lock the vehicle and wait at least 5 minutes. Otherwise the display reset may not register.*

10 Pollen filter renewal

1.6 and 2.0 litre engines – every 12 000 miles (20 000 km)

1.8 and 1.9 litre engines – every 10 000 miles (15 000 km)

1 Release the carpet trim panel from under the facia on the passenger's side.
2 Remove the three securing screws, and withdraw the lid from the pollen filter housing on the heater assembly. If no screws are visible, slide the lid sideways to release the internal retaining lugs.
3 Withdraw the pollen filter.
4 Clean the filter housing and the lid, then fit the new filter using a reversal of the removal procedure.

11 Idle speed and anti-stall speed check and adjustment – 1.8 and 1.9 litre engines

1.8 and 1.9 litre engines – every 10 000 miles (15 000 km)

Refer to Chapter 4B, Section 9.

12 Auxiliary drivebelt check and renewal – 1.8 and 1.9 litre engines

1.8 and 1.9 litre engines – every 10 000 miles (15 000 km)

Note: *Peugeot/Citroën specify the use of a special electronic tool (SEEM C.TRONIC type 105 belt tensioning measuring tool) to correctly set the auxiliary drivebelt tension on manually-adjusted drivebelts. This is an involved process that varies significantly according to engine type, model year, and belt type and condition. The following procedure is an alternative method assuming that the electronic equipment is not being used. If any problems arise (such as screeching noises when driving) the tension should be checked by a Peugeot/Citroën dealer using the special electronic tool at the earliest opportunity.*

Check

1 Chock the rear wheels then jack up the front of the vehicle and support it on axle stands (see *Jacking and vehicle support*). Remove the right-hand front roadwheel.
2 From underneath the front of the car, undo the screws, prise out the retaining clips, and remove the wheel arch liner to gain access to the crankshaft sprocket/pulley bolt. Where necessary, unclip the coolant hoses from the wing to improve access further.
3 Using a suitable socket and extension bar fitted to the crankshaft sprocket/pulley bolt,

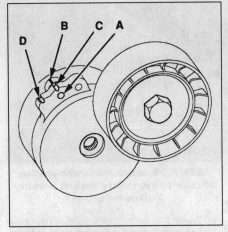

12.4 Auxiliary drivebelt automatic tensioner details

A *Tensioner arm locking pin hole*
B *Backplate indicator mark and locking pin locating hole*
C *Tensioner arm right-hand (zero) wear mark*
D *Tensioner arm left-hand (maximum) wear mark*

rotate the crankshaft so that the entire length of the drivebelt(s) can be examined. Examine the drivebelt(s) for cracks, splitting, fraying or damage. Check also for signs of glazing (shiny patches) and for separation of the belt plies. Renew the belt if worn or damaged.
4 On 1.9 litre DW series engines with power steering (but without air conditioning) which are equipped with an automatic belt tensioner, check the position of the wear indicators on the tensioner pulley arm and backplate **(see illustration)**. The indicator mark on the backplate must be positioned between the two marks on the tensioner arm. If not, the belt is stretched and should be renewed.
5 If the condition of the belt is satisfactory, on models where the belt is adjusted manually, check the drivebelt tension as described below, bearing in mind the Note at the start of this Section. On models with an automatic spring-loaded tensioner, there is no need to check the drivebelt tension.

XUD series engines with manual adjuster on alternator upper mounting

Removal

6 If not already done, proceed as described in paragraphs 1 and 2.
7 Disconnect the battery negative terminal (refer to *Disconnecting the battery* in the Reference Chapter).
8 Slacken both the alternator upper and lower mounting nuts/bolts (as applicable) and the adjuster strap bolt.
9 Back off the adjuster bolt to relieve the tension in the drivebelt, then slip the drivebelt from the pulleys **(see illustration)**. **Note:** *If the belt is going to be re-used, mark the direction of rotation on the belt prior to removal. This will ensure it is refitted the correct way around.*

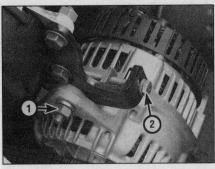

12.9 Alternator upper mounting nut (1) and adjuster bolt (2) – XUD series engines

Refitting

10 If the belt is being renewed, ensure that the correct type is used and if the original belt is being refitted, use the mark made on removal to ensure it is fitted the correct way around. Fit the belt around the pulleys, and take up the slack in the belt by tightening the adjuster bolt.
11 Tension the drivebelt as described in the following paragraphs.

Tensioning

> **HAYNES HINT**   *Correct tensioning of the drivebelt will ensure that it has a long life. A belt which is too slack will slip and squeal. Beware, however, of over-tightening, as this can cause wear in the alternator bearings.*

12 If not already done, proceed as described in paragraphs 1 and 2.
13 The belt should be tensioned so that, under firm thumb pressure, there is about 5.0 mm of free movement at the mid-point between the pulleys on the longest belt run (see the note at the start of this Section).
14 To adjust, with the mounting nut/bolts just holding the alternator firm, turn the adjuster bolt until the correct tension is achieved.
15 Rotate the crankshaft a couple of times, recheck the tension, then securely tighten both the alternator mounting nuts/bolts. Where applicable, also tighten the bolt securing the adjuster strap to its mounting bracket.
16 Reconnect the battery negative terminal.
17 Clip the coolant hoses into position (where necessary), then refit the wheel arch liner. Refit the roadwheel, and lower the vehicle to the ground.

XUD series engines with manually-adjusted tensioning pulley

Removal

18 If not already done, proceed as described in paragraphs 1 and 2.
19 Disconnect the battery negative terminal (refer to *Disconnecting the battery* in the Reference Chapter).

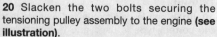

12.20 Slacken the two tensioner roller retaining screws (arrowed) . . .

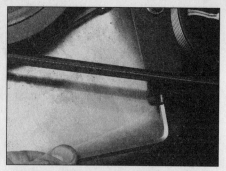

12.21 . . . then turn the tensioner roller adjuster bolt to release the belt tension – XUD series engines

20 Slacken the two bolts securing the tensioning pulley assembly to the engine **(see illustration)**.

21 Rotate the adjuster bolt to move the tensioning pulley away from the drivebelt until there is sufficient slack for the drivebelt to be removed from the pulleys **(see illustration)**. *Note: If the belt is going to be re-used, mark the direction of rotation on the belt prior to removal. This will ensure it is refitted the correct way around.*

Refitting

22 If the belt is being renewed, ensure that the correct type is used and if the original belt is being refitted, use the mark made on removal to ensure it is fitted the correct way around. Fit the drivebelt around the pulleys ensuring that the ribs on the belt are correctly engaged with the pulley grooves, and that the drivebelt is correctly routed.

23 Take all the slack out of the belt by turning the tensioner pulley adjuster bolt, then tension the belt as follows.

Tensioning

24 If not already done, proceed as described in paragraphs 1 and 2.

25 Correct tensioning of the drivebelt will ensure that it has a long life – see Haynes Hint above.

26 The belt should be tensioned so that, under firm thumb pressure, there is approximately 5.0 mm of free movement at the mid-point between the pulleys on the longest belt run.

27 To adjust the tension, with the two tensioner pulley assembly retaining screws slackened, rotate the adjuster bolt until the correct tension is achieved. Once the belt is correctly tensioned, rotate the crankshaft a couple of times and recheck the tension.

28 When the belt is correctly tensioned, securely tighten the tensioner pulley assembly retaining screws, then reconnect the battery negative terminal.

29 Clip the coolant hoses into position, then refit the plastic cover to the wing valance. Refit the roadwheel, and lower the vehicle to the ground.

XUD series engines with automatic spring-loaded tensioning pulley

Removal

30 If not already done, proceed as described in paragraphs 1 and 2.

31 Disconnect the battery negative terminal (refer to *Disconnecting the battery* in the Reference Chapter).

32 Where necessary, remove the retaining screws from the power steering pump pulley shield, and remove the shield to gain access to the top of the drivebelt.

33 Working under the wheel arch, slacken the retaining bolt located in the centre of the eccentric tensioning pulley.

34 Insert a cranked 7.0 mm square section bar (a quarter inch square section drive socket bar for example) into the square hole on the front face of the eccentric tensioning pulley.

35 Using the bar, turn the eccentric tensioning pulley until the hole in the arm of the automatic tensioner pulley is aligned with the hole in the mounting bracket behind. When the holes are aligned, slide a suitable setting tool (a bolt or cranked length of bar of approximately 8.0 mm diameter) through the hole in the arm and into the mounting bracket.

36 With the automatic tensioner locked, turn the eccentric tensioning pulley until the drivebelt tension is released sufficiently to enable the belt to be removed. *Note: If the belt is going to be re-used, mark the direction of rotation on the belt prior to removal. This will ensure it is refitted the correct way around.*

Refitting and tensioning

37 If the belt is being renewed, ensure that the correct type is used and if the original belt is being refitted, use the mark made on removal to ensure it is fitted the correct way around. Fit the drivebelt around the pulleys ensuring that the ribs on the belt are correctly engaged with the pulley grooves, and that the drivebelt is correctly routed.

38 Turn the eccentric tensioning pulley to apply tension to the drivebelt, until the load is released from the setting bolt. Without altering the position of the eccentric tensioning pulley, tighten its retaining bolt securely.

39 Remove the setting bolt from the automatic tensioner arm, then rotate the crankshaft four complete revolutions in the normal direction of rotation.

40 Check that the holes in the automatic adjuster arm and the mounting bracket are still aligned by re-inserting the setting bolt. If the bolt will not slide in easily, repeat the tensioning procedure from paragraph 38 onward.

41 On completion, reconnect the battery negative terminal, and all other disturbed components.

DW series engines without power steering

Removal

42 If not already done, proceed as described in paragraphs 2 and 3.

43 Disconnect the battery negative terminal (refer to *Disconnecting the battery* in the Reference Chapter).

44 Slacken the two bolts securing the tensioner pulley assembly to the engine **(see illustration)**.

45 Rotate the adjuster bolt to move the tensioner pulley away from the drivebelt until there is sufficient slack for the drivebelt to be removed from the pulleys. *Note: If the belt is going to be re-used, mark the direction of rotation on the belt prior to removal. This will ensure it is refitted the correct way around.*

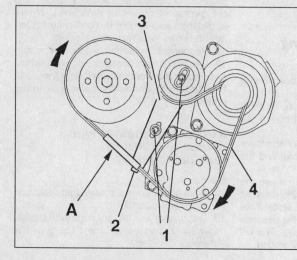

12.44 Auxiliary drivebelt and tensioner details – DW series engines without power steering

1 *Retaining bolts*
2 *Adjuster bolt*
3 *Tensioner pulley assembly*
4 *Drivebelt*
A *Tension checking point*

Refitting

46 If the belt is being renewed, ensure that the correct type is used and if the original belt is being refitted, use the mark made on removal to ensure it is fitted the correct way around.

47 Fit the drivebelt around the pulleys ensuring that the ribs on the belt are correctly engaged with the pulley grooves, and that the drivebelt is correctly routed.

48 Take all the slack out of the belt by turning the tensioner pulley adjuster bolt, then tension the belt as follows.

Tensioning

Correct tensioning of the drivebelt will ensure that it has a long life. A belt which is too slack will slip and squeal. Beware, however, of over-tightening, as this can cause wear in the alternator bearings.

49 If not already done, proceed as described in paragraphs 2 and 3.

50 The belt should be tensioned so that, under firm thumb pressure, there is approximately 5.0 mm of free movement at the mid-point between the pulleys on the longest belt run.

51 To adjust the tension, with the two tensioner pulley assembly retaining bolts slackened, rotate the adjuster bolt until the correct tension is achieved. Once the belt is correctly tensioned, rotate the crankshaft a couple of times and recheck the tension.

52 When the belt is correctly tensioned, securely tighten the tensioner pulley assembly retaining bolts, then reconnect the battery negative terminal.

53 Clip the coolant hoses into position (where applicable), then refit the plastic cover to the wing valance. Refit the roadwheel, and lower the vehicle to the ground.

DW series engines with power steering (without air conditioning) with a manual tensioner

Removal

54 If not already done, proceed as described in paragraphs 2 and 3.

55 Disconnect the battery negative terminal (refer to *Disconnecting the battery* in the Reference Chapter).

56 Release the fasteners from the right-hand side and top of the engine cover then lift off the cover, taking care not to lose its mounting rubbers **(see illustrations 4.6a to 4.6c)**.

57 Slacken the tensioner pulley backplate bolt and back off the pulley adjuster nut, located behind the power steering pump, to move the pulley away from the drivebelt **(see illustration)**. Once there is sufficient slack in the drivebelt, slip the belt off the pulleys and remove it from the engine. **Note:** *If the belt is going to be re-used, mark the direction of rotation on the belt prior to removal. This will ensure it is refitted the correct way around.*

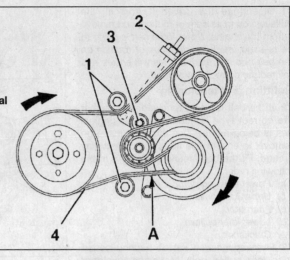
12.57 Auxiliary drivebelt and tensioner details – DW series engines with power steering and manual tensioner assembly

1 Idler pulleys
2 Adjuster nut
3 Tensioner pulley backplate bolt
4 Drivebelt
A Tension checking point

Refitting

58 If the belt is being renewed, ensure that the correct type is used and if the original belt is being refitted, use the mark made on removal to ensure it is fitted the correct way around. Fit the belt around the pulleys in the following order:
a) Power steering pump.
b) Tensioner pulley.
c) Alternator.
d) Lower idler pulley.
e) Crankshaft.
f) Upper idler pulley.

59 Ensure that the ribs on the belt are correctly engaged with the pulley grooves, then take up the slack in the belt by tightening the adjuster bolt. Tension the drivebelt as described in the following paragraphs.

Tensioning

60 If not already done, proceed as described in paragraphs 2 and 3.

61 Correct tensioning of the drivebelt will ensure that it has a long life – see Haynes Hint above.

62 The belt should be tensioned so that, under firm thumb pressure, there is approximately 5.0 mm of free movement at the mid-point between the alternator and idler pulleys on the lower belt run.

63 To adjust the tension, with the tensioner pulley backplate bolt slackened, rotate the adjuster nut until the correct tension is achieved. Once the belt is correctly tensioned, rotate the crankshaft a couple of times and recheck the tension.

64 When the belt is correctly tensioned, securely tighten the tensioner pulley backplate bolt, then lightly tighten the adjuster nut.

65 Clip the coolant hoses into position (where applicable), then refit the plastic cover to the wing valance. Refit the roadwheel, and lower the vehicle to the ground.

66 Ensure that the mounting rubbers are all correctly fitted then install the engine cover, securing it in position with the fasteners.

67 On completion, reconnect the battery negative terminal.

DW series engines with power steering (without air conditioning) with an automatic tensioner

Note: *A 4.0 mm diameter bolt or pin will be required to lock the spring-loaded tensioner pulley in position (see Tool Tip).*

Removal

68 If not already done, proceed as described in paragraphs 2 and 3.

69 Disconnect the battery negative terminal (refer to *Disconnecting the battery* in the Reference Chapter).

70 Using a spanner/socket fitted to the spring-loaded tensioner pulley centre bolt, move the tensioner pulley away from the belt until it is possible to slip the drivebelt off one of the pulleys. Once the drivebelt has been displaced, align the tensioner arm right-hand (zero) wear mark **(see illustration 12.4)** with the backplate indicator mark and lock the tensioner in position by inserting the 4.0 mm diameter bolt/pin **(see illustrations 13.8a and 13.8b)**. Ensure the bolt/pin is correctly located in the backplate, then release the tensioner.

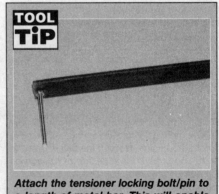
Attach the tensioner locking bolt/pin to a length of metal bar. This will enable you to manoeuvre the bolt/pin easily down between the engine and body and into position.

71 Disengage the drivebelt from all the pulleys, noting its correct routing, and remove it from the engine. **Note:** *If the belt is going to be re-used, mark the direction of rotation on the belt prior to removal. This will ensure it is refitted the correct way around.*

Refitting and tensioning

72 If the belt is being renewed, ensure that the correct type is used and if the original belt is being refitted, use the mark made on removal to ensure it is fitted the correct way around. Fit the belt around the pulleys in the following order:
a) *Power steering pump.*
b) *Upper idler pulley.*
c) *Alternator.*
d) *Lower idler pulley.*
e) *Crankshaft.*

73 Fit the spanner/socket to the spring-loaded tensioner pulley bolt. Move the tensioner pulley away from the belt until it is possible to withdraw the locking bolt/pin, then slip the belt over the pulley. Ensure the belt ribs are correctly seated in all the pulley grooves, then slowly release the spring-loaded tensioner to tension the drivebelt.

74 Clip the coolant hoses into position (where applicable), then refit the plastic cover to the wing valance. Refit the roadwheel, and lower the vehicle to the ground.

75 On completion, reconnect the battery negative terminal.

DW series engines with air conditioning

Note: *A 6.0 mm diameter bolt or pin will be required to lock the spring-loaded tensioner pulley in position.*

76 If not already done, proceed as described in paragraphs 2 and 3.

77 Disconnect the battery negative terminal (refer to *Disconnecting the battery* in the Reference Chapter).

78 Slacken the manual tensioner pulley bolt.

79 Pivot the manual tensioner pulley in a clockwise direction, using a square-section key fitted to the hole in the pulley hub, to move the spring-loaded tensioner pulley. Position the tensioner pulley so that the hole in its arm aligns with the corresponding hole in the bracket, then lock the pulley in position by inserting the 6.0 mm diameter bolt/pin **(see illustration)**. Ensure that the spring-loaded tensioner pulley is locked securely in position, then release the manual tensioner pulley.

80 Disengage the drivebelt from all the pulleys, noting its correct routing, and remove it from the engine. **Note:** *If the belt is going to be re-used, mark the direction of rotation on the belt prior to removal. This will ensure it is refitted the correct way around.*

Refitting and tensioning

81 Ensure that the spring loaded tensioner pulley is locked in position (see paragraph 79).
Note: *The pulley arm has a square-section*

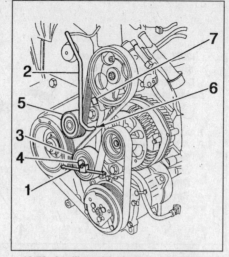

12.79 Auxiliary drivebelt and tensioner details – DW series engines with air conditioning

1 *Peugeot/Citroën tool for moving the manual tensioner pulley*
2 *Peugeot/Citroën locking pin for spring-loaded tensioner*
3 *Drivebelt*
4 *Manual tensioner pulley*
5 *Spring-loaded tensioner pulley*
6 *Spring-loaded tensioner pulley arm locking hole*
7 *Spring-loaded tensioner pulley arm square-section hole (only accessible with drivebelt removed)*

cut-out to allow the pulley to be moved using a ratchet/bar, but this hole is only accessible with the drivebelt removed.

82 If the belt is being renewed, ensure that the correct type is used and if the original belt is being refitted, use the mark made on removal to ensure it is fitted the correct way around. Fit the belt around the pulleys in the following order:
a) *Power steering pump.*
b) *Manual tensioner pulley.*
c) *Alternator.*
d) *Air conditioning compressor.*
e) *Crankshaft.*
f) *Spring-loaded tensioner pulley.*

83 Ensure the belt ribs are correctly seated in all the pulley grooves, then rotate the manual tensioner pulley in a clockwise direction to remove all slack from the belt.

84 To correctly set the drivebelt tension, position the manual tensioner pulley so that all spring pressure is removed from the locking bolt/pin fitted to the spring-loaded tensioner arm. Once the manual tensioner pulley is correctly positioned, securely tighten its retaining bolt.

85 Remove the locking bolt/pin then rotate the crankshaft through four complete revolutions. Check that the locking bolt/pin can still be easily inserted. If not, slacken the manual tensioner pulley bolt and repeat the adjustment procedure.

86 Once the belt is correctly tensioned, remove the locking bolt/pin, clip the coolant hoses into position (where applicable), then refit the plastic cover to the wing valance. Refit the roadwheel, and lower the vehicle to the ground.

87 On completion, reconnect the battery negative terminal.

13 Auxiliary drivebelt check and renewal – 1.6 and 2.0 litre engines

1.6 and 2.0 litre engines – every 12 000 miles (20 000 km)

Check

1 Chock the rear wheels then jack up the front of the vehicle and support it on axle stands (see *Jacking and vehicle support*). Remove the right-hand front roadwheel.

2 From underneath the front of the car, undo the screws, prise out the retaining clips, and remove the wheel arch liner to gain access to the crankshaft sprocket/pulley bolt. Where necessary, unclip the coolant hoses from the wing to improve access further.

3 Using a suitable socket and extension bar fitted to the crankshaft sprocket/pulley bolt, rotate the crankshaft so that the entire length of the drivebelt can be examined. Examine the drivebelt for cracks, splitting, fraying or damage. Check also for signs of glazing (shiny patches) and for separation of the belt plies. Renew the belt if worn or damaged.

4 Check the position of the wear indicators on the tensioner pulley arm and backplate **(see illustration 12.4)**. The indicator mark on the backplate must be positioned between the two marks on the tensioner arm. If not, the belt is stretched and should be renewed.

5 If the condition of the belt is satisfactory, refit the wheel arch liner and roadwheel, then lower the vehicle to the ground.

Removal

Note: *A 4.0 mm diameter bolt or pin will be required to lock the spring-loaded tensioner pulley in position (see Tool Tip in Section 12).*

6 If not already done, proceed as described in paragraphs 1 and 2.

7 Disconnect the battery negative terminal (refer to *Disconnecting the battery* in the Reference Chapter).

8 Using a spanner/socket fitted to the spring-loaded tensioner pulley centre bolt, move the tensioner pulley away from the belt (clockwise on 1.6 litre models, anti-clockwise on 2.0 litre models) until it is possible to slip the drivebelt off one of the pulleys. Once the drivebelt has been displaced, align the tensioner arm (zero) wear mark **(see illustration 12.4)** with the backplate indicator mark and lock the tensioner in position by inserting the 4.0 mm diameter bolt/pin **(see**

illustrations). Ensure the bolt/pin is correctly located in the backplate, then release the tensioner.

9 Disengage the drivebelt from all the pulleys, noting its correct routing, and remove it from the engine. **Note:** *If the belt is going to be re-used, mark the direction of rotation on the belt prior to removal. This will ensure it is refitted the correct way around.*

Refitting

Except new belt on 2.0 litre models

10 If the original belt is being refitted, use the mark made on removal to ensure it is fitted the correct way around. Fit the belt around the pulleys in the following order:
  a) *Power steering pump.*
  b) *Manual tensioning pulley (2.0 litre models) or upper idler pulley (1.6 litre models).*
  c) *Alternator*
  d) *Air conditioning compressor or lower idler pulley (as applicable)*
  e) *Crankshaft pulley*

11 Fit the spanner/socket to the spring-loaded tensioner pulley bolt. Move the tensioner pulley away from the belt until it is possible to withdraw the locking bolt/pin, then slip the belt over the pulley. Ensure the belt ribs are correctly seated in all the pulley grooves, then slowly release the spring-loaded tensioner to tension the drivebelt.

12 Clip the coolant hoses into position (where applicable), then refit the wheel arch liner. Refit the roadwheel, and lower the vehicle to the ground.

13 On completion, reconnect the battery negative terminal.

New belt on 2.0 litre models only

14 Ensure that the spring loaded tensioner pulley is locked in position with its right-hand (zero) wear mark correctly aligned with the backplate indicator (see paragraph 8).

15 Slacken the manual tensioner pulley bolt, then fit the new drivebelt around the pulleys in the following order:
  a) *Power steering pump.*
  b) *Manual tensioner pulley.*
  c) *Alternator.*
  d) *Air conditioning compressor/lower idler pulley (as applicable).*
  e) *Crankshaft.*
  f) *Spring-loaded tensioner pulley.*

16 Ensure the belt ribs are correctly seated in all the pulley grooves, then rotate the manual tensioner pulley in a clockwise direction to remove all slack from the belt. Rotate the pulley using a square-section key fitted to the hole in the pulley hub.

17 To correctly set the drivebelt tension, position the manual tensioner pulley so that all spring pressure is removed from the locking bolt/pin fitted to the spring-loaded tensioner pulley backplate **(see illustration).** Once the manual tensioner pulley is correctly

positioned, securely tighten its retaining bolt.

18 Remove the locking bolt/pin then rotate the crankshaft through four complete revolutions. Check that the holes in the tensioner pulley and backplate are still aligned, and that it is now possible to insert a setting tool of 2.0 mm diameter through both holes. If not, slacken the manual tensioner pulley bolt and repeat the adjustment procedure.

19 Once the belt is correctly tensioned, remove the setting tool, clip the coolant hoses into position (where applicable), then refit the wheel arch liner. Refit the roadwheel, and lower the vehicle to the ground.

20 On completion, reconnect the battery negative terminal.

14 Front brake pad check

1.6 and 2.0 litre engines – every 12 000 miles (20 000 km)

1.8 and 1.9 litre engines – every 10 000 miles (15 000 km)

1 Firmly apply the handbrake, then jack up the front of the car and support it securely on axle stands (see *Jacking and vehicle support*). Remove the front roadwheels.

2 If any pad's friction material is worn to the specified thickness or less, *all four pads must be renewed as a set.*

3 For a comprehensive check, the brake

13.8a Using a spanner/socket on the tensioner pulley bolt, align the arm zero wear mark with the backplate indicator . . .

13.8b . . . and lock it in position by inserting the bolt/pin through the arm and backplate holes – 2.0 litre engines

13.8c On 1.6 litre engines, use a spanner/ socket to turn the tensioner pulley bolt clockwise in order to align the arm zero wear mark with the backplate indicator . . .

13.8d . . . then lock it in position by inserting the bolt/pin through the arm into the backplate hole

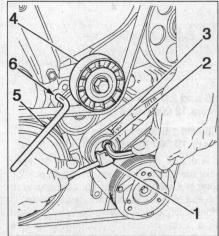

13.17 Auxiliary drivebelt adjustment details – 2.0 litre engines

1 *Peugeot/Citroën tool for moving the manual tensioner pulley*
2 *Manual tensioner pulley retaining bolt*
3 *Manual tensioner pulley*
4 *Spring loaded tensioner pulley*
5 *Peugeot/Citroën locking pin for spring-loaded tensioner*
6 *Spring-loaded tensioner pulley arm locking hole*

pads should be removed and cleaned (see Haynes Hint). The operation of the caliper can then also be checked, and the condition of the brake disc itself can be fully examined on both sides. Refer to Chapter 9 for further information.

15 Rear brake shoe check

**1.6 and 2.0 litre engines –
every 12 000 miles (20 000 km)**

**1.8 and 1.9 litre engines –
every 10 000 miles (15 000 km)**

1 Remove the rear brake drums, and check the brake shoes for wear or contamination. At the same time, also inspect the wheel cylinders for signs of leakage, and the brake drum for signs of wear. Refer to the relevant Sections of Chapter 9 for further information.

16 Handbrake check and adjustment

**1.6 and 2.0 litre engines –
every 12 000 miles (20 000 km)**

**1.8 and 1.9 litre engines –
every 10 000 miles (15 000 km)**

Refer to Chapter 9.

17 Exhaust system check

**1.6 and 2.0 litre engines –
every 12 000 miles (20 000 km)**

**1.8 and 1.9 litre engines –
every 10 000 miles (15 000 km)**

1 With the engine cold (at least an hour after the vehicle has been driven), check the complete exhaust system from the engine to the end of the tailpipe. The exhaust system is most easily checked with the vehicle raised on a hoist, or suitably-supported on axle stands, so that the exhaust components are readily visible and accessible (see *Jacking and vehicle support*).
2 Check the exhaust pipes and connections for evidence of leaks, severe corrosion and damage. Make sure that all brackets and mountings are in good condition, and that all relevant nuts and bolts are tight. Leakage at any of the joints or in other parts of the system will usually show up as a black sooty stain in the vicinity of the leak.

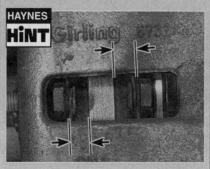

For a quick check, the thickness of friction material remaining on each brake pad can be measured through the aperture in the caliper body.

3 Rattles and other noises can often be traced to the exhaust system, especially the brackets and mountings. Try to move the pipes and silencers. If the components are able to come into contact with the body or suspension parts, secure the system with new mountings. Otherwise separate the joints (if possible) and twist the pipes as necessary to provide additional clearance.

18 Steering and suspension check

**1.6 and 2.0 litre engines –
every 12 000 miles (20 000 km)**

**1.8 and 1.9 litre engines –
every 10 000 miles (15 000 km)**

Front suspension and steering

1 Raise the front of the vehicle, and securely support it on axle stands (see *Jacking and vehicle support*).
2 Inspect the balljoint dust covers and the steering rack-and-pinion gaiters for splits, chafing or damage. Any wear of these parts will cause loss of lubricant, together with dirt and water entry, resulting in rapid deterioration of the balljoints or steering gear.

18.4 Check for wear in the hub bearings by grasping the wheel and trying to rock it

3 On models with power steering, check the fluid hoses for chafing or damage, and the pipe and hose unions for leaks. Also check for signs of leakage under pressure from the steering gear rubber gaiters, which would indicate failed fluid seals within the steering gear.
4 Grasp the roadwheel at the 12 o'clock and 6 o'clock positions, and try to rock it (see illustration). Very slight free play may be felt, but if the movement is appreciable, further investigation is necessary to determine the source. Continue rocking the wheel while an assistant depresses the footbrake. If the movement is now eliminated or significantly reduced, it is likely that the hub bearings are at fault. If the free play is still evident with the footbrake depressed, then there is wear in the suspension joints or mountings.
5 Now grasp the wheel at the 9 o'clock and 3 o'clock positions, and try to rock it as before. Any movement felt now may again be caused by wear in the hub bearings or the steering track rod balljoints. If the inner or outer balljoint is worn, the movement will be obvious.
6 Using a large screwdriver or flat bar, check for wear in the suspension mounting bushes by levering between the relevant suspension component and its attachment point. Some movement is to be expected as the mountings are made of rubber, but excessive wear should be obvious. Also check the condition of any visible rubber bushes, looking for splits, cracks or contamination of the r ubber.
7 With the car standing on its wheels, have an assistant turn the steering wheel back-and-forth about an eighth of a turn each way. There should be very little, if any, lost movement between the steering wheel and roadwheels. If this is not the case, closely observe the joints and mountings previously described, but in addition, check the steering column universal joints for wear, and the steering gear itself.

Strut/shock absorbers

8 Check for any signs of fluid leakage around the suspension strut/shock absorber body, or from the rubber gaiter around the piston rod. Should any fluid be noticed, the suspension strut/shock absorber is defective internally, and should be renewed.
Note: *Suspension struts/shock absorbers should always be renewed in pairs on the same axle.*
9 The efficiency of the suspension strut/shock absorber may be checked by bouncing the vehicle at each corner. Generally speaking, the body will return to its normal position and stop after being depressed. If it rises and returns on a rebound, the suspension strut/shock absorber is probably suspect. Examine also the suspension strut/shock absorber upper and lower mountings for any signs of wear.

19 Fuel filter renewal

1.6 and 2.0 litre engines – every 36 000 miles (60 000 km)

1.8 and 1.9 litre engines – every 30 000 miles (45 000 km)

Caution: Take care not to allow dirt into the fuel filter housing during this procedure or to spill fuel onto the clutch assembly

1.8 and 1.9 litre XUD series engines

1 The fuel filter is located in a plastic housing at the front of the engine.

2 Where applicable, cover the clutch bellhousing with a piece of plastic sheeting, to protect the clutch from fuel spillage.

3 Remove all traces of dirt from the exterior of the filter housing then drain the fuel filter as described in Section 4.

4 Undo the four retaining bolts and lift off the filter housing cover **(see illustration)**.

5 Lift the filter from the housing **(see illustration)**. Ensure that the rubber sealing ring comes away with the filter, and does not stick to the housing/lid.

6 Remove all traces of dirt or debris from inside the filter housing then, making sure its sealing ring is in position, fit the new fuel filter.

7 Coat the threads of the filter cover securing bolts with thread-locking compound, then refit the cover and secure with the bolts.

8 Prime the fuel system as described in Chapter 4B.

1.9 litre DW series engines

9 Release the fasteners from the right-hand side and top of the engine cover then lift off the cover, taking care not to lose its mounting rubbers **(see illustrations 4.6a to 4.6c)**.

10 Remove all traces of dirt from the exterior of the filter housing then drain the fuel filter as described in Section 4.

11 Release the retaining clip and detach the fuel outlet pipe from the filter housing cover **(see illustration)**.

12 Unclip the filter housing cover retaining clip then position the cover clear of the housing **(see illustration)**. Discard the cover sealing ring – a new ring must be used on refitting.

13 Lift the fuel filter and sealing ring out of the housing **(see illustration)**.

14 Remove all traces of dirt or debris from inside the filter housing.

15 Ensure that the housing and cover are spotlessly clean then fit the new fuel filter.

16 Ensure that the new small sealing ring is correctly fitted to the top of the filter, then fit the new large sealing ring to the cover **(see illustrations)**.

17 Locate the cover correctly on the filter housing and refit the retaining clip. Ensure that the clip is correctly engaged with the housing and cover and secure it firmly in position.

18 Reconnect the fuel outlet pipe to the cover.

19 Check that the filter housing drain plug is securely closed, then prime the fuel system as described in Chapter 4C.

20 Once the engine is idling smoothly, ensure that the mounting rubbers are all correctly fitted then install the engine cover, securing it in position with the fasteners.

2.0 litre engines

Note: Check with your dealer for the availability of fuel filter/housing before removal. On some models the fuel filter/housing may come as a complete assembly.

Caution: The need for scrupulous cleanliness when working on the fuel system of HDi engines cannot be over-emphasised. It is

19.4 Lift off the fuel filter cover . . .

19.5 . . . then lift the filter from the housing – XUD series engines

19.11 Release the retaining clip and detach the fuel outlet pipe from the filter housing cover – 1.9 litre DW series engines

19.12 Release the clip and lift off the filter housing cover – 1.9 litre DW series engines

19.13 Lift the fuel filter and sealing ring out of the housing – 1.9 litre DW series engines

19.16a Ensure that the new small sealing ring (arrowed) is correctly fitted to the fuel filter . . .

19.16b . . . and the new large sealing ring (arrowed) is correctly fitted to the housing cover – 1.9 litre DW series engines

19.24 Disconnect the fuel supply and return hose quick-release fittings (arrowed) from the filter housing cover – early 2.0 litre engines

19.26a Lift off the filter housing cover . . .

19.26b . . . remove the metal sealing ring . . .

19.26c . . . and the O-ring seal . . .

19.26d . . . then lift out the filter element – early 2.0 litre engines

particularly important to keep foreign matter – dust, water or any other contaminant – out of the fuel lines. Bear in mind also, the following specific points:

• When renewing the fuel filter element, the filter housing must be cleaned in a solvent bath using injector test fluid, paraffin or similar. DO NOT use compressed air or ordinary rags to dry it off; special Resistel cleaning cloths, available from Peugeot/ Citroën dealers, are the only items approved for this purpose.

• Before undertaking any work on the high pressure side of the system, remove any loose debris with a vacuum cleaner, then clean around the components to be removed with a paint brush and an approved solvent (Sodimac No 35, Mecanet or equivalent).

• DO NOT clean the engine using a steam cleaner or a high pressure water jet; use one of the solvents mentioned above.

• After disconnection of any fuel union, cover the open ends immediately to keep dirt out. Special plugs for this purpose can be obtained from your dealer.

21 Two different filter assemblies may be encountered and cab be identified by the design of the filter housing cover. On early engines the housing cover has a hexagonal moulding to enable it to be unscrewed using a suitable socket. On later engines the filter housing cover is secured by a ribbed locking ring which can be unscrewed using a strap wrench. Identify the type of filter fitted and proceed as described under the relevant sub-heading.

Early models

22 Release the fixings by turning them through 90°, and remove the engine cover (see illustrations 4.11a and 4.11b).
23 Remove all traces of dirt from the exterior of the filter housing then drain the fuel filter as described in Section 4.
24 At the connections on the filter housing cover, disconnect the fuel supply and return hose quick-release fittings using a small screwdriver to release the locking clip (see illustration). Suitably plug or cover the open hose unions to prevent dirt entry.

25 Using a suitable socket engaged with the hexagonal moulding on the filter housing cover, turn the cover approximately a quarter turn anti-clockwise to release the locking lugs.
26 Lift off the housing cover, and collect the metal sealing ring and the O-ring seal, then lift out the filter element (see illustrations).
27 Undo the two bolts and remove the filter housing from its mounting bracket. Thoroughly clean the filter housing and cover, bearing in mind the information on cleanliness given above. When the cleaning operations are complete, refit the housing to its mounting bracket and secure with the two retaining bolts.
28 Fit the new fuel filter element to the housing.
29 Lubricate the new O-ring with clean diesel fuel and locate the seal in position, followed by the metal sealing ring.
30 Refit the housing cover and turn it

19.35 Disconnect the wiring connector from the top of the filter housing cover – later 2.0 litre engines

clockwise until the arrow on the housing cover is in line with the filter drain outlet.
31 Reconnect the fuel supply and return hoses, then prime the fuel system as described in Chapter 4C.
32 On completion, refit the engine cover.

Later models

33 Release the fixings by turning them through 90°, and remove the engine cover (see illustrations 4.11a and 4.11b).
34 Remove all traces of dirt from the exterior of the filter housing then drain the fuel filter as described in Section 4.
35 Where applicable, disconnect the wiring connector from the top of the filter housing cover (see illustration).
36 Disconnect the fuel lines from the top of the fuel filter housing by releasing the quick-release fittings using a small screwdriver (see illustration). Move them to one side,

19.36 Disconnect the fuel supply and return hose quick-release fittings – later 2.0 litre engines

19.37 Using a strap wrench or similar, unscrew the locking ring from the filter housing – later 2.0 litre engines

19.46 Removing the front inlet duct . . .

19.47 . . . and air filter housing air duct

19.48 Removing the air cleaner assembly from the rear of the engine

19.49 Free the manual priming pump from its clips

covering the ends of the fuel lines to prevent dirt entry.

37 Using a strap wrench or similar tool, unscrew the locking ring from the filter housing. Lift off the housing cover then remove the filter element and the O-ring seal **(see illustration)**. **Note:** *Although in theory the locking ring on the filter housing unscrews, in practice we have found it impossible to unscrew the locking ring without damaging the housing, necessitating the renewal of the complete filter housing.*

38 Undo the two bolts and remove the filter housing from its mounting bracket. Thoroughly clean the filter housing and cover, bearing in mind the information on cleanliness given above. When the cleaning operations are complete, refit the housing to its mounting bracket and secure with the two retaining bolts.

39 Fit the new fuel filter element to the housing.

40 Lubricate the new O-ring with clean diesel fuel and locate the seal in position on the housing.

41 Refit the housing cover and position it so the fuel inlet and outlet unions are parallel with the engine.

42 Screw the locking ring onto the housing and tighten it until the notches on the ring and housing are aligned.

43 Reconnect the fuel supply and return

hoses and, where applicable, the wiring connector. Prime the fuel system as described in Chapter 4C.

44 On completion, refit the engine cover.

1.6 litre engines

Note: *The fuel filter is only available as a complete assembly. First, note the list of* **Cautions** *given earlier in this Section under 2.0 litre engines.*

45 Disconnect the battery negative lead (see Chapter 5A), then remove the plastic cover from the top of the engine.

46 Remove the air inlet duct from the front of the engine compartment and twist to remove it from the intermediate duct **(see illustration)**.

47 Disconnect the inlet air duct from the

left-hand end of the air filter housing **(see illustration)**.

48 Loosen the clip and disconnect the turbocharger air duct from the air mass meter on the front of the air cleaner assembly, then remove the assembly from the rear of the engine **(see illustration)**.

49 Without disconnecting the fuel lines, remove the manual priming pump from its mounting clips and position to one side **(see illustration)**.

50 If necessary, remove the air duct from the turbocharger, at the same time releasing the breather tube from the oil trap housing **(see illustration)**.

51 Note their fitted positions and disconnect the pipes and wiring plug from the fuel filter assembly **(see illustration)**. Plug the openings to prevent contamination.

19.50 Removing the air duct from the turbocharger and air mass meter

19.51 Disconnect the pipes and wiring from the fuel filter

19.52 Release the retaining clip and remove the fuel filter

19.53a Release the clip (arrowed) . . .

19.53b . . . and slide the heater from the filter body

52 Release the retaining clip and lift the filter from place **(see illustration)**.
53 Release the clip and detach the fuel heater from the side of the filter assembly **(see illustrations)**.
54 Clip the fuel heater into place on the new filter.
55 Fit the new filter into place, remove the plugs and reconnect the pipes, and the wiring plug.
56 Refit the air pipes and reconnect the battery negative lead (see Chapter 5A).
57 Prime the fuel system as described in Chapter 4C.
58 On completion, refit the engine top cover.

20 Air cleaner filter element renewal

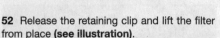

1.6 and 2.0 litre engines – every 36 000 miles (60 000 km)

1.8 and 1.9 litre engines – every 30 000 miles (45 000 km)

1.8 and 1.9 litre XUD series engines

1 Slacken the retaining clip and disconnect the intake duct from the top of the filter housing. Slacken the retaining clips, and

remove the duct linking the intake to the rear of the filter housing.
2 Release the retaining clips, then lift off the filter housing lid **(see illustrations)**.
3 Remove the filter element from the housing **(see illustration)**.
4 Wipe clean the inside of the filter housing and fit the new filter element, making sure that it is correctly seated.
5 Refit the lid, and secure it in position with the retaining clips.
6 Reconnect the intake ducts, securing them in position with the retaining clips.

1.9 litre DW series engines

WJZ engine models

7 Proceed as described above for XUD series engines.

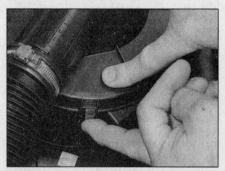

20.2a Release the clips securing the filter housing lid . . .

20.2b . . . then lift off the lid . . .

WJY engine models – pre-September 2002

8 Access to the filter element is obtained from under the front of the vehicle. If necessary, to improve access, firmly apply the handbrake then jack up the front of the vehicle and support it on axle stands (see *Jacking and vehicle support*).
9 Release the retaining clips, and remove the cover from the base of the air filter housing **(see illustration)**.
10 Withdraw the filter element from the housing **(see illustration)**.
11 Wipe clean the inside of the filter housing, then fit the new filter.
12 Refit the cover to the base of the housing, and secure it in position with the retaining clips. Where necessary, lower the vehicle to the ground.

20.3 . . . and withdraw the filter element – XUD series engines

20.9 Release the retaining clips, and remove the cover from the base of the air cleaner filter housing – early DW series engines

20.10 Withdraw the filter element from the housing – early DW series engines

20.13 Disconnect the wiring connector from the airflow meter – later DW series engines

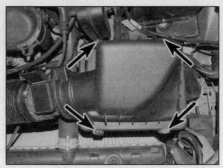

20.14 Undo the screws securing the lid to the air filter housing – later DW series engines

20.15 Lift up the lid and withdraw the filter element – later DW series engines

20.19 Disconnect the wiring connector from the airflow meter – 2.0 litre engines

20.20 Slacken the retaining clip and disconnect the air inlet duct from the airflow meter – 2.0 litre engines

20.21a Undo the two screws securing the lid to the air cleaner housing . . .

WJY engine models – post-September 2002

13 Disconnect the wiring connector from the airflow meter, mounted on the side of the air cleaner lid **(see illustration)**.
14 Undo the screws securing the lid to the air filter housing **(see illustration)**.
15 Lift up the lid and withdraw the filter element from the housing **(see illustration)**.
16 Wipe clean the inside of the filter housing, then fit the new filter element making sure that it is correctly seated.
17 Refit the lid to the filter housing and secure with the retaining screws.
18 Reconnect the airflow meter wiring connector.

2.0 litre engines

19 Disconnect the wiring connector from the airflow meter, located on the air cleaner lid **(see illustration)**.
20 Slacken the retaining clip and disconnect the air inlet duct from the airflow meter **(see illustration)**.
21 Undo the two screws securing the lid to the air cleaner housing. Lift up the right-hand side of the lid and disengage the two left-hand retaining lugs from the air cleaner housing **(see illustrations)**.
22 Withdraw the filter element from the housing **(see illustration)**.
23 Wipe clean the inside of the filter housing, then fit the new filter element making sure that it is correctly seated.

24 Refit the lid to the filter housing and secure with the retaining screws.
25 Reconnect the air inlet duct to the airflow meter, then reconnect the wiring connector.

1.6 litre engines

26 Remove the engine top cover.
27 Disconnect the wiring plug from the airflow meter attached to the air cleaner cover **(see illustration)**.
28 For improved access, loosen the clip and disconnect the air duct from the left-hand side of the turbocharger, at the same time releasing the breather tube from the oil trap housing **(see illustration)**. This work will allow better access to the filter element, making it easier to clean the lower section of the air cleaner.

20.21b . . . lift up the lid and disengage the two retaining lugs from the air cleaner housing – 2.0 litre engines

20.22 Withdraw the filter element from the housing – 2.0 litre engines

20.27 Disconnect the wiring plug from the airflow meter

20.28 Removing the turbocharger to air cleaner air duct

20.30a Undo the screws . . .

20.30b . . . and lift the cover from the air cleaner housing

20.31 Removing the air filter element

29 Without disconnecting the fuel lines, remove the manual priming pump from its mounting clips and position to one side.
30 Undo the screws and lift the air filter cover together with the airflow meter and air duct from the engine **(see illustrations)**.
31 Withdraw the filter element from the air cleaner housing **(see illustration)**.
32 Wipe clean the inside of the housing and cover, then fit the new filter element making sure that it is correctly seated.
33 Refit the air filter cover together with the airflow meter and air duct, and tighten the screws.
34 Refit the manual priming pump and air duct, and reconnect the airflow meter wiring.
35 Refit the engine top cover.

21 Manual transmission oil level check

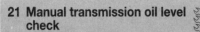

1.6 and 2.0 litre engines – every 36 000 miles (60 000 km)

1.8 and 1.9 litre engines – every 30 000 miles (45 000 km)

Note: *A suitable square-section wrench may be required to undo the transmission filler/level plug on some models. These wrenches can be obtained from most motor factors or your Peugeot/Citroën dealer.*

1 Park the car on a level surface. The oil level must be checked before the car is driven, or at least 5 minutes after the engine has been switched off. If the oil is checked immediately after driving the car, some of the oil will remain distributed around the transmission, resulting in an inaccurate level reading.
2 Prise out the clips and remove the access cover from the left-hand wheel arch liner.
3 Wipe clean the area around the filler/level plug, which is on the left-hand end of the transmission **(see illustration)**. Unscrew the plug and clean it; discard the sealing washer.
4 The oil level should reach the lower edge of the filler/level hole. A certain amount of oil will have gathered behind the filler/level plug, and will trickle out when it is removed; this does not necessarily indicate that the level is correct.

To ensure that a true level is established, wait until the initial trickle has stopped, then add oil as necessary until a trickle of new oil can be seen emerging **(see illustration)**. The level will be correct when the flow ceases; use only good-quality oil of the specified type (refer to *Lubricants and fluids*).
5 Filling the transmission with oil is an extremely awkward operation; above all, allow plenty of time for the oil level to settle properly before checking it. If a large amount is added to the transmission, and a large amount flows out on checking the level, refit the filler/level plug and take the vehicle on a short journey so that the new oil is distributed fully around the transmission components, then recheck the level when it has settled again.
6 If the transmission has been overfilled so that oil flows out as soon as the filler/level plug is removed, check that the car is completely level (front-to-rear and side-to-side), and allow the surplus to drain off into a suitable container.
7 When the level is correct, fit a new sealing washer to the filler/level plug. Refit the plug, tightening it to the specified torque wrench setting. Wash off any spilt oil then refit the access cover securing it in position with the retaining clips.

22 Emissions control systems check

1.6 and 2.0 litre engines – every 36 000 miles (60 000 km)

1.8 and 1.9 litre engines – every 36 000 miles (45 000 km)

1 Details of the emissions control system components are given in Chapter 4D.
2 Checking consists simply of a visual check for obvious signs of damaged or leaking hoses and joints.
3 Detailed checking and testing of the evaporative and/or exhaust emissions systems (as applicable) should be entrusted to a Peugeot/Citroën dealer.

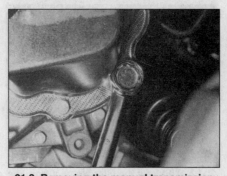

21.3 Removing the manual transmission filler/level plug

21.4 Oil level is correct when the oil stops flowing out of the filler/level hole

23 Timing belt renewal

**1.6 litre engines –
every 75 000 miles (120 000 km)**

**1.8 and 1.9 litre engines –
every 40 000 miles (60 000 km)**

**2.0 litre engines –
every 48 000 miles (80 000 km)**

Refer to the relevant Part of Chapter 2.

24 Brake fluid renewal

**1.6 and 2.0 litre engines –
every 36 000 miles (60 000 km)**

**1.8 and 1.9 litre engines –
every 40 000 miles (60 000 km)**

 Warning: Brake hydraulic fluid can harm your eyes and damage painted surfaces, so use extreme caution when handling and pouring it. Do not use fluid that has been standing open for some time, as it absorbs moisture from the air. Excess moisture can cause a dangerous loss of braking effectiveness.

1 The procedure is similar to that for the bleeding of the hydraulic system as described in Chapter 9, except that the brake fluid reservoir should be emptied by syphoning, using a clean poultry baster or similar before starting, and allowance should be made for the old fluid to be expelled when bleeding a section of the circuit.

2 Working as described in Chapter 9, open the first bleed screw in the sequence, and pump the brake pedal gently until nearly all the old fluid has been emptied from the master cylinder reservoir.

 HAYNES HiNT *Old hydraulic fluid is invariably much darker in colour than the new, making it easy to distinguish the two.*

3 Top-up to the MAX level with new fluid, and continue pumping until only the new fluid remains in the reservoir, and new fluid can be seen emerging from the bleed screw. Tighten the screw, and top the reservoir level up to the MAX level line.

4 Work through all the remaining bleed screws in the sequence until new fluid can be seen at all of them. Be careful to keep the master cylinder reservoir topped-up to above the MIN level at all times, or air may enter the system and greatly increase the length of the task.

5 When the operation is complete, check that all bleed screws are securely tightened, and that their dust caps are refitted. Wash off all traces of spilt fluid, and recheck the master cylinder reservoir fluid level.

6 Check the operation of the brakes before taking the car on the road.

25 Coolant renewal

**1.6 and 2.0 litre engines –
every 36 000 miles (60 000 km)**

**1.8 and 1.9 litre engines –
every 40 000 miles (60 000 km)**

Cooling system draining

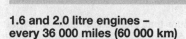 *Warning: Wait until the engine is cold before starting this procedure. Do not allow antifreeze to come in contact with your skin, or with the painted surfaces of the vehicle. Rinse off spills immediately with plenty of water. Never leave antifreeze lying around in an open container, or in a puddle in the driveway or on the garage floor. Children and pets are attracted by its sweet smell, but antifreeze can be fatal if ingested.*

1 On 1.9 litre DW series engines, release the fasteners from the right-hand side and top of the engine cover then lift off the cover, taking care not to lose its mounting rubbers **(see illustrations 4.6a to 4.6c)**. On 2.0 litre engines, release the fixings by turning them through 90°, and remove the engine cover **(see illustrations 4.11a and 4.11b)**.

2 With the engine completely cold, remove the expansion tank filler cap. Turn the cap anti-clockwise until it reaches the first stop. Wait until any pressure remaining in the system is released, then push the cap down, turn it anti-clockwise to the second stop, and lift it off.

3 Position a suitable container beneath the lower left-hand side of the radiator. On early models, loosen the drain plug (there is no need to remove it completely) and allow the coolant to drain into the container. On later models a drain plug is not provided, so it will be necessary to disconnect the radiator bottom hose to allow the coolant to drain.

4 To assist draining, open the cooling system bleed screws. These are located in the heater matrix outlet hose union (to improve access, it may be located in an extension hose), on the engine compartment bulkhead and, on 2.0 litre engines, on the top of the thermostat housing **(see illustrations)**.

5 When the flow of coolant stops, reposition the container below the cylinder block drain plug. The drain plug is located at the rear of the cylinder block.

6 Remove the drain plug, and allow the coolant to drain into the container.

7 If the coolant has been drained for a reason other than renewal, then provided it is clean and less than two years old, it can be re-used, though this is not recommended.

8 Refit the radiator and cylinder block drain plugs on completion of draining. Also refit the radiator bottom hose (later models) if the system is not to be flushed.

25.4a Heater hose bleed screw (arrowed)

25.4b Thermostat housing bleed screw (arrowed)

Cooling system flushing

9 If coolant renewal has been neglected, or if the antifreeze mixture has become diluted, then in time, the cooling system may gradually lose efficiency, as the coolant passages become restricted due to rust, scale deposits, and other sediment. The cooling system efficiency can be restored by flushing the system clean.

10 The radiator should be flushed independently of the engine, to avoid unnecessary contamination.

Radiator flushing

11 To flush the radiator, first tighten the radiator drain plug, and the radiator bleed screw, where applicable.

12 Disconnect the top and bottom hoses and any other relevant hoses from the radiator, with reference to Chapter 3.

13 Insert a garden hose into the radiator top inlet. Direct a flow of clean water through the radiator, and keep flushing until clean water emerges from the radiator bottom outlet.

14 If after a reasonable period, the water still does not run clear, the radiator can be flushed with a good proprietary cleaning agent. It is important that their manufacturer's instructions are followed carefully. If the contamination is particularly bad, insert the hose in the radiator bottom outlet, and reverse-flush the radiator.

Engine flushing

15 To flush the engine, first refit the cylinder block drain plug, and tighten the cooling system bleed screws.

16 Remove the thermostat as described in Chapter 3, then temporarily refit the thermostat cover.

17 With the top and bottom hoses disconnected from the radiator, insert a garden hose into the radiator top hose. Direct a clean flow of water through the engine, and continue flushing until clean water emerges from the radiator bottom hose.

18 On completion of flushing, refit the thermostat and reconnect the hoses with reference to Chapter 3.

Cooling system filling

19 Before attempting to fill the cooling system, make sure that all hoses and clips are in good condition, and that the clips are tight. An antifreeze mixture must be used all year round, to prevent corrosion of the engine components (see following sub-Section). Also check that the radiator and cylinder block

drain plugs are in place and tight.

20 Remove the expansion tank filler cap.

21 Open all the cooling system bleed screws (see paragraph 4).

22 Some of the cooling system hoses are positioned at a higher level than the top of the radiator expansion tank. It is therefore necessary to use a 'header tank' when refilling the cooling system, to reduce the possibility of air being trapped in the system. Although Peugeot/Citroën dealers use a special header tank, the same effect can be achieved by using a suitable bottle, with a seal between the bottle and the expansion tank **(see Haynes Hint)**.

23 Fit the 'header tank' to the expansion tank and slowly fill the system. Coolant will emerge from each of the bleed screws in turn, starting with the lowest screw. As soon as coolant free from air bubbles emerges from the lowest screw, tighten that screw and, where applicable, watch the next bleed screw in the system. Repeat the procedure until the coolant is emerging from the highest bleed screw in the cooling system and all bleed screws are securely tightened.

24 Continue to fill the cooling system until bubbles stop appearing in the expansion tank. Help to bleed the air from the system by repeatedly squeezing the radiator bottom hose.

25 Ensure that the 'header tank' is full (at least 0.5 litres of coolant). Start the engine, and run it at a fast idle speed (do not exceed 2000 rpm) until the cooling fan cuts in, and then cuts out. Stop the engine. **Note:** *Take great care not to scald yourself with the hot coolant during this operation.*

26 Allow the engine to cool, then remove the 'header tank'.

27 When the engine has cooled, check the coolant level as described in *Weekly checks*. Top-up the level if necessary, and refit the expansion tank cap. Refit the engine cover (where applicable).

Antifreeze mixture

28 The antifreeze should always be renewed at the specified intervals. This is necessary not only to maintain the antifreeze properties, but also to prevent corrosion which would otherwise occur as the corrosion inhibitors become progressively less effective.

29 Always use an ethylene-glycol based antifreeze of the specified type (see *Lubricants and fluids*). The quantity of antifreeze and

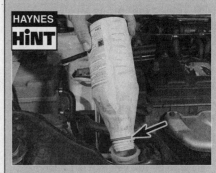

Cut the bottom off an old antifreeze container to make a 'header tank' for use when refilling the cooling system. The seal at the point arrowed should be as airtight as possible – use an O-ring if available, or seal the joint by some other means.

level of protection are indicated in the Specifications.

30 Before adding antifreeze, the cooling system should be completely drained, preferably flushed, and all hoses checked for condition and security.

31 After filling with antifreeze, a label should be attached to the expansion tank, stating the type and concentration of antifreeze used, and the date installed. Any subsequent topping-up should be made with the same type and concentration of antifreeze.

32 Do not use engine antifreeze in the windscreen/tailgate washer system, as it will cause damage to the vehicle paintwork. A screenwash additive should be added to the washer system in the quantities stated on the bottle.

26 Airbags and seat belt pretensioners renewal

1.6 litre engines – every 15 years

1.8, 1.9 and 2.0 litre engines – every 10 years

1 Peugeot/Citroën recommend that the airbags and seat belt pretensioners are renewed regardless of their condition every ten/fifteen years. Refer to Chapter 12 for airbag renewal, and Chapter 11 for seat belt pretensioner renewal.

Chapter 2 Part A:
Petrol engine in-car repair procedures

Contents

Degrees of difficulty

Easy, suitable for novice with little experience	Fairly easy, suitable for beginner with some experience	Fairly difficult, suitable for competent DIY mechanic	Difficult, suitable for experienced DIY mechanic	Very difficult, suitable for expert DIY or professional

Specifications

Engine (general)

Designation:
  1.4 litre (1360 cc) engine TU3JP
  1.6 litre (1587 cc) engine TU5JP4
Engine codes*:
  1.4 litre engine:
    Up to 2001 . . . . KFX
    2001 onwards. . . . . KFW
  1.6 litre engine . . . . NFU
Bore:
  1.4 litre engine . . . . 75.00 mm
  1.6 litre engine . . . . 78.50 mm
Stroke:
  1.4 litre engine . . . . 77.00 mm
  1.6 litre engine . . . . 82.00 mm
Direction of crankshaft rotation . . . . Clockwise (viewed from right-hand side of vehicle)
No 1 cylinder location. . . . . At transmission end of the block
Compression ratio:
  1.4 litre engine . . . . 10.5 : 1
  1.6 litre engine . . . . 11.0 : 1
Maximum power output:
  1.4 litre engine . . . . 55 kW @ 5400 rpm
  1.6 litre engine . . . . 80 kW @ 5800 rpm
Maximum torque output:
  1.4 litre engine . . . . 120 Nm @ 3400 rpm
  1.6 litre engine . . . . 147 Nm @ 4000 rpm

The engine code is situated on front, left-hand end of the cylinder block.

Camshaft(s)
Drive . . . .   Toothed belt

Valve clearances (engine cold)
1.4 litre engine:
   Inlet . . . .   0.20 mm
   Exhaust. . . . .   0.40 mm
1.6 litre engine . . . .   Hydraulic adjusters

Lubrication system
Oil pump type. . . . .   Gear type, chain-driven off the crankshaft
Minimum oil pressure at 80°C . . . .   4 bars @ 4000 rpm
Oil pressure warning switch operating pressure . . . .   0.8 bars

Torque wrench settings

	Nm	lbf ft
Big-end bearing cap nuts*	40	30
Camshaft bearing housing to cylinder head (1.6 litre engine)	10	7
Camshaft sprocket retaining bolt(s):		
1.4 litre engine:		
M11 bolt with plain washer.	80	59
M10 bolt with captive washer.	45	33
1.6 litre engine	45	33
Camshaft thrust fork retaining bolt (1.4 litre engine)	16	12
Crankshaft oil seal housing bolts	8	6
Crankshaft pulley retaining bolts	25	18
Crankshaft sprocket retaining bolt*:		
Stage 1.	40	30
Stage 2.	Angle-tighten a further 45°	
Cylinder head bolts:		
1.4 litre engine:		
Stage 1	20	15
Stage 2	Angle-tighten a further 240°	
1.6 litre engine:		
Stage 1	20	15
Stage 2	Angle-tighten a further 260°	
Cylinder head cover screws/nuts.	8	6
Engine-to-transmission bolts:		
1.4 litre engine	40	30
1.6 litre engine	50	37
Engine/transmission left-hand mounting:		
Centre nut.	65	48
Mounting bracket-to-transmission nuts:		
1.4 litre engine	25	18
1.6 litre engine	60	44
Mounting bracket-to-body bolts	22	16
Mounting rubber nuts/bolts	25	18
Engine/transmission rear mounting:		
Connecting link-to-mounting rubber nut/bolt.	54	40
Connecting link-to-subframe nut/bolt	65	48
Engine/transmission right-hand mounting:		
1.4 litre engine:		
Rubber mounting to body.	40	30
Upper bracket-to-cylinder block bracket nuts	45	33
Upper bracket-to-rubber mounting nut	45	33
Support bracket (later models):		
Bracket-to-mounting upper bracket bolt	45	33
Bracket-to-cylinder head bolt.	25	18
Lower bracket-to-engine nut/bolt.	25	18
1.6 litre engine:		
Rubber mounting to body.	40	30
Upper bracket-to-engine bracket bolts	60	44
Upper bracket-to-rubber mounting nut	45	33
Engine bracket-to-cylinder head bolts	45	33
Flywheel bolts*	70	52
Main bearing cap bolts (1.6 litre engine):		
Stage 1	20	15
Stage 2	Angle-tighten a further 49°	

Torque wrench settings (continued)

	Nm	lbf ft
Main bearing ladder casting (1.4 litre engine):		
M11 bolts:		
Stage 1	20	15
Stage 2	Angle-tighten a further 44°	
M6 bolts	8	6
Oil filter plastic housing (later models)	25	18
Oil filter housing to engine block (1.6 litre engine)	10	7
Oil pressure switch	30	22
Oil pump retaining bolts	9	7
Piston oil jet spray tube bolts	10	7
Roadwheel bolts	90	66
Sump drain plug	30	22
Sump retaining nuts and bolts	8	6
Timing belt cover bolts	8	6
Timing belt tensioner/idler pulley nut:		
1.4 litre engine	20	15
1.6 litre engine	22	16

New nuts/bolts must be used

1 General information

How to use this Chapter

This Part of Chapter 2 describes those repair procedures that can reasonably be carried out on the engine while it remains in the car. If the engine has been removed from the car and is being dismantled, as described in Part E, any preliminary dismantling procedures can be ignored.

Note that, while it may be possible physically to overhaul items such as the piston/connecting rod assemblies while the engine is in the car, such tasks are not normally carried out as separate operations. Usually, several additional procedures (not to mention the cleaning of components and of oilways) have to be carried out. For this reason, all such tasks are classed as major overhaul procedures, and are described in Part E of this Chapter.

Part E describes the removal of the engine/transmission from the vehicle, and the full overhaul procedures that can then be carried out.

Engine description

The TU series engine is a well-proven unit which has been fitted to many previous Peugeot and Citroën vehicles. The engine is of the in-line four-cylinder, single overhead camshaft (SOHC) 8-valve type on 1.4 litre models, or double overhead camshaft (DOHC) 16-valve type on 1.6 litre models, mounted transversely at the front of the car with the transmission attached to its left-hand end.

The crankshaft runs in five main bearings. Thrustwashers are fitted to No 2 main bearing (upper half) to control crankshaft endfloat.

The connecting rods rotate on horizontally-split bearing shells at their big-ends. The pistons are attached to the connecting rods by gudgeon pins, which are an interference fit in the connecting rod small-end eyes. The aluminium-alloy pistons are fitted with three piston rings – two compression rings and an oil control ring.

On 1.4 litre engines, the cylinder block is made of aluminium, and wet liners are fitted to the cylinder bores. Sealing O-rings are fitted at the base of each liner, to prevent the escape of coolant into the sump.

On 1.6 litre engines, the cylinder block is made from cast-iron, and the cylinder bores are an integral part of the cylinder block. On this type of engine, the cylinder bores are sometimes referred to as having dry liners.

The inlet and exhaust valves are each closed by coil springs, and operate in guides pressed into the cylinder head; the valve seat inserts are also pressed into the cylinder head, and can be renewed separately if worn.

On 1.4 litre engines, the camshaft is driven by a toothed timing belt, and operates the eight valves via rocker arms. Valve clearances are adjusted by a screw-and-locknut arrangement. The camshaft rotates directly in the cylinder head. The timing belt also drives the coolant pump.

On 1.6 litre engines, the camshafts are driven by a timing belt, and operate the 16 valves via followers incorporating hydraulic compensator units (clearance adjusters). The camshafts rotate directly in the cylinder head and are retained by a one-piece bearing housing. The belt also drives the coolant pump.

Lubrication is by means of an oil pump, which is driven (via a chain and sprocket) off the right-hand end of the crankshaft. It draws oil through a strainer located in the sump, and then forces it through an externally-mounted filter into galleries in the cylinder block/crankcase. From there, the oil is distributed to the crankshaft (main bearings) and camshaft. The big-end bearings are supplied with oil via internal drillings in the crankshaft, while the camshaft bearings also receive a pressurised supply. On 1.6 litre engines, piston cooling oil spray jets are fitted to spray oil on the underside of each piston. The camshaft lobes and valves are lubricated by splash, as are all other engine components.

Operations with engine in car

The following work can be carried out with the engine in the car:

a) Compression pressure – testing.
b) Cylinder head cover – removal and refitting.
c) Timing belt covers – removal and refitting.
d) Timing belt – removal, refitting and adjustment.
e) Timing belt tensioner and sprockets – removal and refitting.
f) Camshaft oil seal(s) – renewal.
g) Camshaft(s) and rocker arms/followers – removal, inspection and refitting.
h) Cylinder head – removal and refitting.
i) Cylinder head and pistons – decarbonising.
j) Sump – removal and refitting.
k) Oil pump – removal, overhaul and refitting.
l) Crankshaft oil seals – renewal.
m) Engine/transmission mountings – inspection and renewal.
n) Flywheel – removal, inspection and refitting.

2 Compression test – description and interpretation

1 When engine performance is down, or if misfiring occurs which cannot be attributed to the ignition or fuel systems, a compression test can provide diagnostic clues as to the engine's condition. If the test is performed regularly, it can give warning of trouble before any other symptoms become apparent.

2 The engine must be fully warmed-up to normal operating temperature and the battery must be fully charged. The aid of an assistant will also be required.

3 Referring to Chapter 5B, on early 1.4 litre models, disconnect the LT wiring connector from the ignition HT coil(s). On later 1.4 litre, and all 1.6 litre models, remove the ignition HT coil assembly from the top of the spark plugs. On all models, remove the spark plugs as described in Chapter 1A.

4 Fit a compression tester to the No 1 cylinder spark plug hole – the type of tester which screws into the plug thread is to be preferred.

5 Have the assistant hold the throttle wide open, and crank the engine on the starter motor; after one or two revolutions, the compression pressure should build-up to a maximum figure, and then stabilise. Record the highest reading obtained.

6 Repeat the test on the remaining cylinders, recording the pressure in each.

7 All cylinders should produce very similar pressures; a difference of more than 2 bars between any two cylinders indicates a fault. Note that the compression should build-up quickly in a healthy engine; low compression on the first stroke, followed by gradually-increasing pressure on successive strokes, indicates worn piston rings. A low compression reading on the first stroke, which does not build-up during successive strokes, indicates leaking valves or a blown head gasket (a cracked head could also be the cause). Deposits on the undersides of the valve heads can also cause low compression.

8 Although the manufacturer does not specify exact compression pressures, as a guide, any cylinder pressure of below 10 bars can be considered as less than healthy. Refer to a Peugeot/Citroën dealer or other specialist if in doubt as to whether a particular pressure reading is acceptable.

9 If the pressure in any cylinder is low, carry out the following test to isolate the cause. Introduce a teaspoonful of clean oil into that cylinder through its spark plug hole, and repeat the test.

10 If the addition of oil temporarily improves the compression pressure, this indicates that bore or piston wear is responsible for the pressure loss. No improvement suggests that leaking or burnt valves, or a blown head gasket, may be to blame.

11 A low reading from two adjacent cylinders is almost certainly due to the head gasket having blown between them; the presence of coolant in the engine oil will confirm this.

12 If one cylinder is about 20 percent lower than the others and the engine has a slightly rough idle, a worn camshaft lobe could be the cause.

13 If the compression reading is unusually high, the combustion chambers are probably coated with carbon deposits. If this is the case, the cylinder head should be removed and decarbonised.

14 On completion of the test, refit the spark plugs, ignition HT coil and/or wiring connectors (see Chapters 1A and 5B).

---

3 Engine assembly/valve timing holes – general information and usage

Note: *Do not attempt to rotate the engine whilst the crankshaft/camshaft are locked in position. If the engine is to be left in this state for a long period of time, it is a good idea to place warning notices inside the vehicle, and in the engine compartment. This will reduce the possibility of the engine being accidentally cranked on the starter motor, which is likely to cause damage with the locking pins in place.*

1 On all models, timing holes are drilled in the camshaft sprocket(s) and in the rear of the flywheel. The holes are used to ensure that the crankshaft and camshaft(s) are correctly positioned when assembling the engine (to prevent the possibility of the valves contacting the pistons when refitting the cylinder head), or refitting the timing belt. When the timing holes are aligned with access holes in the cylinder head and the front of the cylinder block, suitable diameter bolts/pins can be inserted to lock both the camshaft and crankshaft in position, preventing them from rotating. Proceed as follows.

2 Remove the timing belt upper cover as described in Section 5.

3 On later engines with a plastic oil filter housing, access to the flywheel timing hole is improved if the oil filter is removed (see Chapter 1A).

1.4 litre engines

4 The crankshaft must now be turned until the timing hole in the camshaft sprocket is aligned with the corresponding hole in the cylinder head. The holes are aligned when the camshaft sprocket hole is in the 2 o'clock position, when viewed from the right-hand end of the engine. The crankshaft can be turned by using a spanner on the crankshaft sprocket bolt, noting that it should always be rotated in a clockwise direction (viewed from the right-hand end of the engine).

5 With the camshaft sprocket hole correctly positioned, insert a 6 mm diameter stud or pin, 90 mm long, (ideally welded to a length of weld rod bent to the appropriate shape), through the hole in the front left-hand flange of the cylinder block, and locate it in the timing hole in the rear of the flywheel **(see illustration)**. A purpose-made tool is available from dealers. Note that it may be necessary to rotate the crankshaft slightly to get the holes to align.

6 With the flywheel correctly positioned, insert a 10 mm diameter bolt or pin through the timing hole in the camshaft sprocket, and locate it in the hole in the cylinder head **(see illustration)**.

7 The crankshaft and camshaft are now locked in position, preventing unnecessary rotation.

1.6 litre engines

8 Turn the crankshaft until the holes in the camshaft sprockets align with the corresponding holes in the cylinder head. The crankshaft can be turned by using a spanner

3.5 Insert a 6 mm diameter bolt/pin (arrowed) into the hole in the cylinder block flange and into the flywheel hole

3.6 Lock the camshaft sprocket in position with a 10 mm diameter bolt/pin (arrowed) – 1.4 litre engines

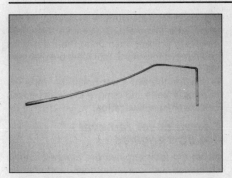

3.9a Weld a 90 mm length of 6 mm rod/ stud to a length of weld rod . . .

3.9b . . . and insert it into the hole in the cylinder block flange (arrowed)

3.10 Use 10 mm diameter bolts/pins (arrowed) to lock the camshaft sprockets in position – 1.6 litre engines

on the crankshaft sprocket bolt, noting that it should always be rotated in a clockwise direction (viewed from the right-hand end of the engine).

9 With the camshaft sprocket holes correctly positioned, insert a 6 mm diameter stud or pin, 80 mm long, welded to a length of weld rod bent to the appropriate shape, through the hole in the front left-hand flange of the cylinder block, and locate it in the timing hole in the rear of the flywheel **(see illustrations)**. A purpose-made tool is available from dealers. Note that it may be necessary to rotate the crankshaft slightly to get the holes to align.

10 With the crankshaft correctly positioned, insert 10 mm diameter bolts or pins through the timing holes in the camshaft sprockets, and locate them in the holes in the cylinder head **(see illustration)**.

11 The crankshaft and camshafts are now locked in position, preventing unnecessary rotation.

---

4 Cylinder head cover – removal and refitting

1.4 litre engines

Removal

1 Disconnect the battery negative terminal (refer to *Disconnecting the battery* in the Reference Chapter).

2 Depress the clip and disconnect the breather hose from the cylinder head cover **(see illustration)**.

3 On later models, remove the ignition HT coil assembly from the top of the spark plugs as described in Chapter 5B.

4 Undo the two retaining nuts and sealing washers (where fitted) then lift off the cylinder head cover, complete with its rubber seal. Examine the seal for signs of damage and deterioration, and if necessary, renew it.

5 Remove the spacer from each cover stud then lift off the oil baffle plate **(see illustrations)**.

Refitting

6 Carefully clean the cylinder head and cover mating surfaces, and remove all traces of oil.

7 Fit the rubber seal over the edge of the cylinder head cover, ensuring that it is correctly located along its entire length **(see illustration)**.

8 Refit the oil baffle plate then fit the spacers to the cover studs.

9 Carefully refit the cylinder head cover to the engine, taking great care not to displace the rubber seal.

10 Fit the sealing washers (where fitted) and cover retaining nuts, tightening them to the specified torque.

11 Where applicable, refit the ignition HT coil (see Chapter 5B) then reconnect the breather hose to the cylinder head cover. On completion reconnect the battery.

1.6 litre engines

Removal

12 Disconnect the battery negative terminal (refer to *Disconnecting the battery* in the Reference Chapter), and remove the ignition coil as described in Chapter 5B.

13 Working in a spiral pattern, progressively and evenly slacken the cylinder head cover bolts, and remove the covers. Recover the gaskets.

Refitting

14 Carefully clean the cylinder head and cover mating surfaces, and remove all traces of oil.

15 Check the condition of the cover's composite gasket, and re-use it if undamaged. If it is damaged, a repair may be effected using silicone sealing compound.

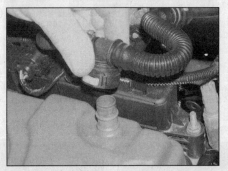

4.2 Disconnect the breather hose from the cylinder head cover

4.5a Remove the spacers (arrowed) from the studs . . .

4.5b . . . then lift off the baffle plate

4.7 Ensure the rubber seal is correctly located on the cylinder head cover

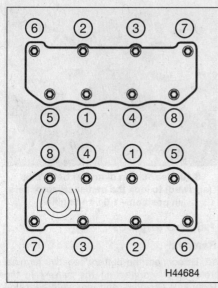

4.16 Cylinder head cover bolts tightening sequence

16 Refit the cover(s) and tighten the bolts in sequence **(see illustration)**.
17 Refit the ignition coil (Chapter 5B).
18 Reconnect the battery.

5 Timing belt covers – removal and refitting

Upper cover removal

1.4 litre engines

1 Slacken and remove the two retaining bolts (one at the front and one at the rear), and remove the upper timing cover from the cylinder head **(see illustrations)**.

1.6 litre engines

2 Position a trolley jack under the engine, with a block of wood between the jack head and the sump to prevent damage. Raise the jack to take the weight of the engine.
3 Undo the two bolts and move the accelerator pedal position sensor and mounting bracket clear of the right-hand engine mounting **(see illustration)**.
4 Release the purge valve vapour hose from the clip on the right-hand engine mounting and move the hose aside slightly.
5 Undo the three bolts securing the right-hand engine mounting upper bracket to the bracket on the engine, and the centre nut securing

the bracket to the rubber mounting on the body **(see illustration)**. Remove the upper mounting bracket, then undo the three bolts and remove the engine mounting bracket from the engine.
6 Slacken the two lower bolts, the undo the five upper bolts and remove the upper timing belt cover **(see illustration)**.

Centre cover removal – 1.4 litre engines

Note: On later engines the centre cover is combined with the lower cover and is not a separate component.
7 Remove the upper cover as described in paragraph 1, then free the wiring from its retaining clips on the centre cover.
8 Slacken and remove the three retaining bolts (one at the rear of the cover, beneath the engine mounting plate, and two directly above the crankshaft pulley), and manoeuvre the centre cover out from the engine compartment **(see illustration)**.

Lower cover removal

9 Remove the auxiliary drivebelt as described in Chapter 1A.
10 Remove the upper and, where applicable, the centre covers as described previously.

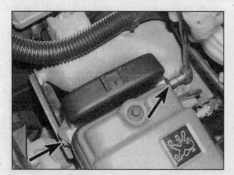

5.1a Unscrew the retaining bolts (arrowed) . . .

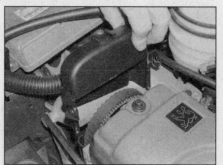

5.1b . . . and remove the timing belt upper cover

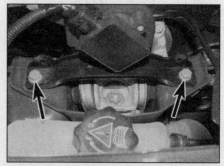

5.3 Accelerator pedal position sensor mounting bracket retaining bolts (arrowed)

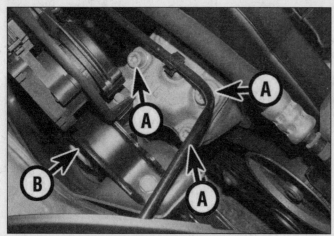

5.5 Undo the three bolts (A) and the centre nut (B) then remove the engine mounting upper bracket

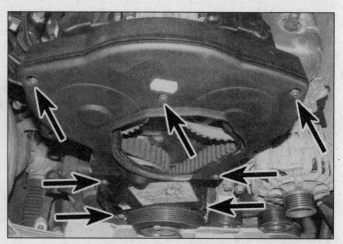

5.6 Timing belt upper cover retaining bolts (arrowed)

5.8 Undo the three bolts (locations arrowed) and remove the centre cover

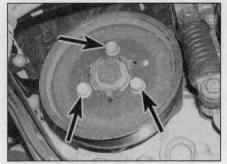

5.11a Undo the retaining bolts (arrowed) . . .

5.11b . . . and remove the crankshaft pulley

11 Undo the three crankshaft pulley retaining bolts and remove the pulley, noting which way round it is fitted **(see illustrations)**.

12 Slacken and remove the retaining bolts then remove the lower cover from the engine **(see illustration)**.

Inner cover removal – 1.6 litre engines

13 Remove the camshaft sprockets and tensioner pulley as described in Section 7.

14 Undo the bolts and remove the inner cover **(see illustration)**.

Refitting

Upper cover

15 Refitting is the reverse of removal. On 1.6 litre engines, tighten the engine mounting retaining bolts to the specified torque.

Centre cover – 1.4 litre engines

16 Manoeuvre the centre cover back into position, ensuring it is correctly located with the lower cover, and tighten its retaining bolts.

17 Clip the wiring loom into its retaining clips on the front of the centre cover, then refit the upper cover as described in paragraph 15.

Lower cover

18 Locate the lower cover over the timing belt sprocket, and tighten its retaining bolts.

19 Fit the pulley to the end of the crankshaft, ensuring it is fitted the correct way round, and tighten its bolts to the specified torque.

20 Refit centre (where applicable) and upper covers as described above.

21 Refit and tension the auxiliary drivebelt as described in Chapter 1A.

Inner cover – 1.6 litre engines

22 Refitting is a reversal of removal. Ensure that the cupped lower edge of the cover engages correctly with the lip at the top of the crankshaft oil seal housing as the cover is refitted.

---

6 Timing belt – general information, removal and refitting

Note: *On early 1.4 litre engines, the manufacturer's specify the use of a special electronic tool (SEEM C.TRONIC type 105 belt tensioning measuring tool, and valve rocker contact plate (–).0132 AE) to correctly set the timing belt tension. If access to this equipment cannot be obtained, an approximate setting can be achieved using the method described below. If the method described is used, the tension must be checked using the special electronic tool at the earliest possible*

opportunity. Do not drive the vehicle over large distances, or use high engine speeds, until the belt tension is known to be correct.

General information

1 The timing belt drives the camshaft(s) and coolant pump from a toothed sprocket on the front of the crankshaft. If the belt breaks or slips in service, the pistons are likely to hit the valve heads, resulting in extensive (and expensive) damage.

2 The timing belt should be renewed at the specified intervals (see Chapter 1A), or earlier if it is contaminated with oil, or if it is at all noisy in operation (a 'scraping' noise due to uneven wear).

3 If the timing belt is being removed, it is a wise precaution to check the condition of the coolant pump at the same time (check for signs of coolant leakage). This may avoid the need to remove the timing belt again at a later stage, should the coolant pump fail.

4 On later 1.4 litre engines an automatic timing belt tensioner is used to maintain the correct tension on the timing belt after the initial setting procedure has been carried out. The automatic type tensioner can be identified by the index arm and tension position marks on the side of the tensioner body **(see illustration 6.33)**. If this type of tensioner is

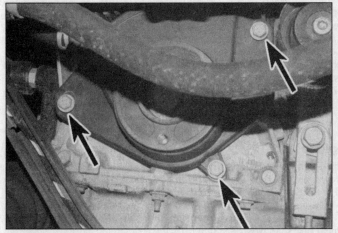

5.12 Undo the bolts (arrowed) and remove the timing belt lower cover

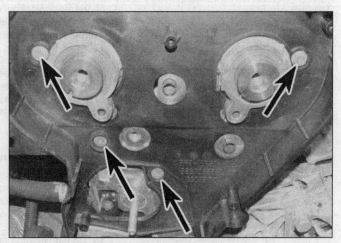

5.14 Undo the bolts (arrowed) and remove the inner cover

6.8 Slacken the nut then pivot the tensioner pulley clockwise to relieve the timing belt tension – 1.4 litre engines

fitted, follow the procedures for 'later 1.4 litre engines' when refitting the timing belt.

Removal

5 Disconnect the battery negative terminal (refer to *Disconnecting the battery* in the Reference Chapter).

6 Align the engine assembly/valve timing holes as described in Section 3, and lock both the camshaft sprocket and the flywheel in position.
Caution: Do not attempt to rotate the engine whilst the locking tools are in position.

7 Remove the remaining timing belt cover(s) as described in Section 5.

1.4 litre engines

8 Loosen the timing belt tensioner pulley retaining nut **(see illustration)**. Pivot the pulley approximately 60° in a clockwise direction, using a key fitted to the hole in the pulley hub, then retighten the retaining nut. On early engines, an 8 mm square section key will be required **(see Tool Tip)**, and on later engines with an automatic tensioner, an Allen key will be needed.

9 If the timing belt is to be re-used, use white paint or similar to mark the direction of rotation on the belt (if markings do not already exist). Slip the belt off the sprockets.

1.6 litre engines

10 Slacken the timing belt tensioner pulley retaining nut and, using a hexagonal key, rotate the pulley clockwise until the index

6.16 Pivot the tensioner pulley anti-clockwise to remove all freeplay from the timing belt then tighten the pulley nut

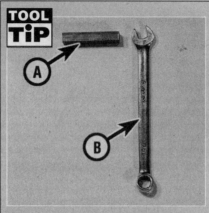

If you're having difficulty finding a square-section tool that will fit the tensioner pulley, obtain a length of standard 8 mm door handle rod from a DIY shop and cut it to length (A). Insert the rod into the pulley hub and rotate the pulley with an 8 mm spanner (B).

arm is in the minimum tension position **(see illustration)**. Temporarily tighten the tensioner pulley nut in this position.

11 If the timing belt is to be re-used, use white paint or similar to mark the direction of rotation on the belt (if markings do not already exist). Slip the belt off the sprockets.

All engines

12 Check the timing belt carefully for any signs of uneven wear, splitting, or oil contamination. Pay particular attention to the roots of the teeth. Renew the belt if there is the slightest doubt about its condition. If the engine is undergoing an overhaul, and has covered more than 40 000 miles (60 000 km) with the existing belt fitted, renew the belt as a matter of course, regardless of its apparent condition. The cost of a new belt is nothing when compared to the cost of repairs, should the belt break in service. If signs of oil contamination are found, trace the source of the oil leak, and rectify it. Wash down the engine timing belt area and all related components, to remove all traces of oil.

13 Prior to refitting, thoroughly clean the timing belt sprockets. Check that the tensioner and pulleys rotate freely, without any sign of roughness. If necessary, renew the pulleys as described in Section 7. Make sure that the locking tools are still in place, as described in Section 3.

Refitting –
early 1.4 litre engines

14 Manoeuvre the timing belt into position, ensuring that the arrows on the belt are pointing in the direction of rotation (clockwise, when viewed from the right-hand end of the engine).

15 Do not twist the timing belt sharply while refitting it. Fit the belt over the crankshaft and camshaft sprockets. Make sure that the 'front

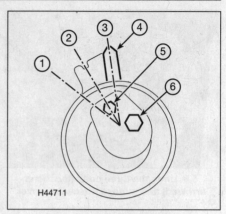

6.10 Timing belt tensioner – 1.6 litre engines

1 Minimum tension position
2 Normal tension position
3 Maximum tension position
4 Index arm
5 Hole for hexagonal key
6 Tensioner pulley bolt

run' of the belt is taut – ie, ensure that any slack is on the tensioner pulley side of the belt. Fit the belt over the coolant pump sprocket and tensioner pulley. Ensure that the belt teeth are seated centrally in the sprockets.

16 Loosen the tensioner pulley retaining nut. Pivot the pulley anti-clockwise to remove all free play from the timing belt, then retighten the nut **(see illustration)**. Tension the timing belt as described under the relevant sub-heading.

Tensioning without the special electronic measuring tool

Note: *If this method is used, ensure that the belt tension is checked using the electronic measuring tool at the earliest possible opportunity.*

17 If the special tool is not available, an approximate setting may be achieved as follows. Slacken the tensioner pulley retaining nut and pivot the pulley anti-clockwise until it is just possible to twist the timing belt through 90° by finger and thumb, midway between the crankshaft and camshaft sprockets. The deflection of the belt at the mid-point between the sprockets should be approximately 6.0 mm. Hold the tensioner pulley in this position and tighten the retaining nut.

18 Remove the locking tools from the camshaft sprocket and flywheel.

19 Using a suitable socket and extension bar on the crankshaft sprocket bolt, rotate the crankshaft through four complete rotations in a clockwise direction (viewed from the right-hand end of the engine).
Caution: Do not at any time rotate the crankshaft anti-clockwise.

20 Slacken the tensioner pulley nut, retension the belt as described in paragraph 17, then tighten the tensioner pulley nut to the specified torque.

21 Rotate the crankshaft through a further

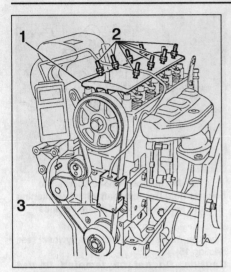

6.26 Fit the rocker arm plate (1) to the cylinder head and use the contact bolts (2) to lift the rocker arms clear of the camshaft (see text). Note the correct location for the measuring tool (3)

two turns clockwise, and check that both the camshaft sprocket and flywheel timing holes are still correctly aligned.

22 If all is well, refit the timing belt covers as described in Section 5, and reconnect the battery negative terminal.

Tensioning using the special electronic measuring tool

23 Fit the special belt tensioning measuring equipment to the front run of the timing belt, approximately midway between the camshaft and crankshaft sprockets. Position the tensioner pulley so that the belt is tensioned to a setting of 44 SEEM units, then retighten its retaining nut.

24 Remove the locking tools from the camshaft sprocket and flywheel, and remove the measuring tool from the belt.

25 Using a suitable socket and extension bar on the crankshaft sprocket bolt, rotate the crankshaft through four complete rotations in a clockwise direction (viewed from the right-hand end of the engine). *Do not* at any time rotate the crankshaft anti-clockwise. Refit the locking tool to the flywheel and check that the camshaft sprocket timing hole is aligned.

26 To ensure an accurate reading, it is necessary to remove the valve spring load from the camshaft by fitting the valve rocker contact plate (–).0132 AE. Remove the cylinder head cover (see Section 4), then slacken the eight rocker arm contact bolts in the valve rocker contact plate. Fit the contact plate to the cylinder head cover studs, observing the correct fitted direction, and secure it with the cover nuts **(see illustration)**. Tighten each rocker arm contact bolt until the rockers are just free of the camshaft lobes. Do not over-tighten the contact bolts otherwise the valves will contact the pistons.

27 Refit the measuring tool to the belt,

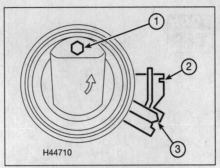

6.33 Timing belt tensioner – later 1.4 litre engines

1 Hole for hexagonal key
2 Normal tension position
3 Maximum tension position

slacken the tensioner pulley retaining nut, and gradually release the tensioner pulley until a setting of between 29 and 33 SEEM units is indicated on the measuring tool. Retighten the tensioner pulley retaining nut to the specified torque.

28 Remove the measuring tool from the belt then unscrew the nuts and remove the rocker arm contact plate from the cylinder head.

29 Remove the flywheel locking tool, then rotate the crankshaft through another four complete rotations in a clockwise direction. Refit the flywheel locking tool and check that the camshaft timing hole is correctly aligned with the cylinder head hole.

30 If all is well, refit the timing belt covers and cylinder head cover as described in Sections 4 and 5. **Note:** *If the rocker arm adjusting screws were moved, adjust the valve clearances before refitting the cylinder head cover.*

Refitting – later 1.4 litre engines

31 Manoeuvre the timing belt into position, ensuring that the arrows on the belt are pointing in the direction of rotation (clockwise, when viewed from the right-hand end of the engine).

32 Do not twist the timing belt sharply while refitting it. Fit the belt over the crankshaft and camshaft sprockets. Make sure that the 'front

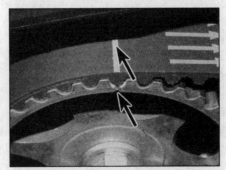

6.40 Note the timing belt marks which correspond to the camshaft sprockets and crankshaft sprocket – 1.6 litre engines

run' of the belt is taut – ie, ensure that any slack is on the tensioner pulley side of the belt. Fit the belt over the coolant pump sprocket and tensioner pulley. Ensure that the belt teeth are seated centrally in the sprockets.

33 Remove the crankshaft and camshaft locking tools, then slacken the tensioner pulley nut and, using a hexagonal key, rotate the pulley anti-clockwise until the index arm is in the maximum tension position **(see illustration)**. Tighten the pulley retaining nut.

34 Using a socket on the crankshaft pulley bolt, rotate the crankshaft clockwise 10 complete revolutions, and refit the crankshaft locking tool as described in Section 3.

35 Check the timing is correct by inserting the camshaft sprocket locking tool (Section 3). If the tool cannot be inserted, slacken the tensioner, remove the belt, refit the locking tools, and start again from paragraph 31.

36 Remove the crankshaft and camshaft locking tools.

37 Hold the hexagonal key in the tensioner pulley to maintain the tension, then slacken the pulley nut, and rotate the tensioner to bring the index arm to the normal tension position **(see illustration 6.33)**. Tighten the pulley nut to the specified torque.

38 Rotate the crankshaft two complete revolutions, and check that the crankshaft and camshaft locking tools can still be inserted.

39 The remainder of refitting is a reversal of removal.

Refitting – 1.6 litre engines

40 Manoeuvre the timing belt into position, ensuring that the arrows on the belt are pointing in the direction of rotation (clockwise, when viewed from the right-hand end of the engine). Note that there are three marks on a new belt which correspond to marks on the crankshaft and camshaft sprockets **(see illustration)**.

41 Do not twist the timing belt sharply while refitting it. Fit the belt over the crankshaft and camshaft sprockets aligning the marks on the belt with those on the crankshaft and camshaft sprockets. Make sure that the 'front run' of the belt is taut – ie, ensure that any slack is on the tensioner pulley side of the belt. Fit the belt over the coolant pump sprocket, idler pulley and tensioner pulley. Ensure that the belt teeth are seated centrally in the sprockets.

42 Insert the hexagonal key on the tensioner pulley, slacken the pulley nut and rotate the key to bring the index arm to the maximum tension position **(see illustration 6.10)**. Tighten the tensioner roller nut securely.

43 Remove the camshaft and crankshaft locking tools, and rotate the crankshaft 4 complete revolutions clockwise, and refit the crankshaft locking tool.

44 Insert the hexagon key in the tensioner, slacken the nut and rotate the tensioner using the key, until the index arm is in the normal tension position **(see illustration 6.10)**. Tighten the tensioner nut to the specified torque.

45 Remove the crankshaft locking tool, and rotate the crankshaft two complete revolutions clockwise. Check the position of the tensioner index arm – it should be no more than 2.0 mm away from the normal tension position. If it is, repeat the belt fitting procedure from paragraph 40.

46 Refit the timing belt covers as described in Section 5, then on completion, reconnect the battery.

7 Timing belt tensioner and sprockets – removal, inspection and refitting

Removal

Camshaft sprocket – 1.4 litre engines

1 Remove the timing belt as described in Section 6.

2 Withdraw the crankshaft and camshaft locking tools, and using a spanner or socket on the crankshaft pulley bolt, rotate the crankshaft backwards (anti-clockwise) 90°. This is to prevent any accidental contact between the pistons and valves.

3 Slacken the camshaft sprocket retaining bolt and remove it, along with its washer. To prevent the camshaft rotating as the bolt is slackened, a sprocket-holding tool will be required. In the absence of the manufacturer's special tool, an acceptable substitute can be fabricated as follows. Use two lengths of steel strip (one long, the other short), and three nuts and bolts; one nut and bolt forms the pivot of a forked tool, with the remaining two nuts and bolts at the tips of the 'forks' to engage with the sprocket spokes **(see Tool Tip)**.
Caution: Do not attempt to use the sprocket locking pin to prevent the sprocket from rotating whilst the bolt is slackened.

4 With the retaining bolt removed, slide the sprocket off the end of the camshaft. If the sprocket locating pin is a loose fit, remove it for safe-keeping. Examine the camshaft oil seal for signs of oil leakage and, if necessary, renew it as described in Section 8.

TOOL TiP

Using a home-made tool to hold the camshaft sprocket stationary whilst the bolt is tightened (shown with the cylinder head removed).

Camshaft sprockets – 1.6 litre engines

5 Remove the cylinder head covers as described in Section 4.

6 Remove the timing belt as described in Section 6.

7 Withdraw the crankshaft and camshaft locking tools, and using a spanner or socket on the crankshaft pulley bolt, rotate the crankshaft backwards (anti-clockwise) 90°. This is to prevent any accidental contact between the pistons and valves.

8 Using an open-ended spanner on the square section to counter-hold the camshaft, undo the sprocket retaining bolt **(see illustration)**.
Caution: Do not attempt to use the sprocket locking pin to prevent the sprocket from rotating whilst the bolt is slackened.

9 With the retaining bolt removed, slide the sprocket off the end of the camshaft. Note that the key is integral with the sprocket. Examine the camshaft oil seals for signs of oil leakage and, if necessary, renew as described in Section 8.

Crankshaft sprocket

10 Remove the timing belt as described in Section 6.

11 Slacken the crankshaft sprocket bolt. To prevent crankshaft rotation as the bolt is slackened, select top gear, and have an assistant apply the brakes firmly. If the engine has been removed from the vehicle,

7.8 Use an open-ended spanner to counter-hold the camshaft whilst slackening the sprocket bolt – 1.6 litre engines

it will be necessary to lock the flywheel (see Section 15).
Caution: Do not be tempted to use the flywheel locking pin to prevent the crankshaft from rotating; temporarily remove the locking pin prior to slackening the pulley bolt, then refit it once the bolt has been slackened.

12 Unscrew the retaining bolt and washer, then slide the sprocket off the end of the crankshaft **(see illustrations)**.

13 If the Woodruff key is a loose fit in the crankshaft, remove it and store it with the sprocket for safe-keeping. If necessary, also slide the flanged spacer (where fitted) off the end of the crankshaft **(see illustration)**. Examine the crankshaft oil seal for signs oil leakage and, if necessary, renew as described in Section 14.

Tensioner pulley

14 Remove the lower timing belt cover (see Section 5).

15 Lock the camshaft and crankshaft at TDC on No 1 cylinder as described in Section 3.

16 Slacken and remove the timing belt tensioner pulley retaining nut, and slide the pulley off its mounting stud. Examine the mounting stud for signs of damage and, if necessary, renew it.

Idler pulley

17 Remove the lower timing belt cover (see Section 5).

18 Lock the camshaft and crankshaft at TDC on No 1 cylinder as described in Section 3.

7.12a Remove the retaining bolt and washer . . .

7.12b . . . then slide off the crankshaft sprocket

7.13 Remove the Woodruff key and flanged spacer (where fitted) from the crankshaft

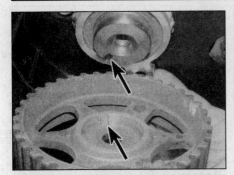

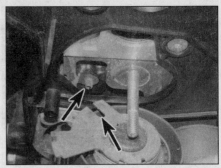

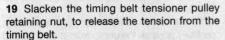

7.24a The locating pin must engage with the slot (arrowed)

7.24b On 1.6 litre engines, the inlet sprocket is marked A (arrowed) and the exhaust E

7.37 The cut-out aligns the locating pin (arrowed)

19 Slacken the timing belt tensioner pulley retaining nut, to release the tension from the timing belt.

20 Slacken and remove the timing belt idler pulley retaining nut, and slide the pulley off its mounting stud. Examine the mounting stud for signs of damage and, if necessary, renew it.

Inspection

21 Clean the sprockets thoroughly, and renew any that show signs of wear, damage or cracks.

22 Clean the tensioner/idler pulleys, but do not use any strong solvent which may enter the pulley bearings. Check that the pulleys rotate freely about their hubs, with no sign of stiffness or of free play. Renew them if there is any doubt about their condition, or if there are any obvious signs of wear or damage.

23 Inspect the timing belt (see Section 6). Renew the belt if there is any doubt about its condition.

Refitting

Camshaft sprocket

24 Refit the locating pin (where removed) then locate the sprocket on the end of the camshaft. Ensure that the locating pin is correctly engaged with the sprocket and the cut-out in the camshaft end. Note that on 1.6 litre engines, the exhaust sprocket is marked E and the inlet sprocket is marked A **(see illustrations)**.

25 Refit the sprocket retaining bolt and washer. Tighten the bolt to the specified torque, whilst retaining the sprocket/camshaft with the method used on removal.

26 Realign the timing hole in the camshaft sprocket (see Section 3) with the corresponding hole in the cylinder head, and refit the locking pin.

27 Rotate the crankshaft 90° in the normal direction of rotation (clockwise), until the crankshaft locking pin can be inserted.

28 Refit the timing belt as described in Section 6. On 1.6 litre engines, refit the cylinder head covers as described in Section 4.

Crankshaft sprocket

29 Locate the Woodruff key in the crankshaft

end, then slide on the flanged spacer (where fitted) aligning its slot with the Woodruff key.

30 Align the crankshaft sprocket slot with the Woodruff key, and slide it onto the end of the crankshaft.

31 Temporarily remove the locking pin from the rear of the flywheel, then refit the crankshaft sprocket retaining bolt and washer. Tighten the bolt to the specified torque, whilst preventing crankshaft rotation using the method employed on removal. Refit the locking pin to the rear of the flywheel.

32 Refit the timing belt as described in Section 6.

Idler pulley

33 Refit the idler pulley to its mounting stud, refit the retaining nut and tighten it to the specified torque.

34 Ensure that the 'front run' of the timing belt is taut – ie, ensure that any slack is on the pulley side of the belt. Check that the belt is centrally located on all its sprockets. Rotate the tensioner pulley anti-clockwise to remove all free play from the timing belt, then tighten the pulley retaining nut securely.

35 Tension the timing belt as described in Section 6.

36 Once the belt is correctly tensioned, refit the timing belt covers as described in Section 5.

Tensioner pulley

37 Refit the tensioner pulley to its mounting stud, ensuring the cut-out aligns with the

8.3 Carefully prise the camshaft oil seal out with a flat-bladed screwdriver

pin **(see illustration)**, and fit the retaining nut.

38 Ensure that the 'front run' of the belt is taut – ie, ensure that any slack is on the pulley side of the belt. Check that the belt is centrally located on all its sprockets. Rotate the pulley anti-clockwise to remove all free play from the timing belt, then tighten the pulley retaining nut securely.

39 Tension the timing belt as described in Section 6.

40 Once the belt is correctly tensioned, refit the timing belt covers as described in Section 5.

8 Camshaft oil seal(s) – renewal

Note: *If the camshaft oil seal has been leaking, check the timing belt for signs of oil contamination; the belt must be renewed if signs of oil contamination are found. Ensure that all traces of oil are removed from the sprockets and surrounding area before the new belt is fitted.*

1 Remove the camshaft sprocket as described in Section 7.

2 Noted the fitted depth of the oil seal in relation to the cylinder head face as a guide for refitting.

3 Punch or drill two small holes opposite each other in the oil seal. Screw a self-tapping screw into each, and pull on the screws with pliers to extract the seal. Alternatively, carefully prise the seal out using a flat-bladed screwdriver **(see illustration)**.

4 Clean the seal housing, and polish off any burrs or raised edges, which may have caused the seal to fail in the first place.

5 Lubricate the lips of the new seal with clean engine oil, and drive it into position until it is at the fitted depth as noted during removal. Use a suitable tubular drift, such as a socket, which bears only on the hard outer edge of the seal. Take care not to damage the seal lips during fitting. Note that the seal lips should face inwards.

6 Refit the camshaft sprocket as described in Section 7.

9.5 Check the valve clearances using feeler gauges

9 Valve clearances – checking and adjustment

Note 1: *The valve clearances must be checked and adjusted only when the engine is cold.*
Note 2: *This procedure applies only to 1.4 litre engines – the valve clearances on 1.6 litre engines are maintained by hydraulic compensator units built into the cam followers.*
1 The importance of having the valve clearances correctly adjusted cannot be overstressed, as they vitally affect the performance of the engine. If the clearances are too big, the engine will be noisy (characteristic rattling or tapping noises) and engine efficiency will be reduced, as the valves open too late and close too early. A more serious problem arises if the clearances are too small, however. If this is the case, the valves may not close fully when the engine is hot, resulting in serious damage to the engine (eg, burnt valve seats and/or cylinder head warping/cracking). The clearances are checked and adjusted as follows.
2 Remove the cylinder head cover as described in Section 4.
3 The engine can now be turned using a suitable socket and extension bar fitted to the crankshaft sprocket bolt.
4 It is important that the clearance of each valve is checked and adjusted only when the valve is fully closed, with the rocker arm resting on the heel of the cam (directly opposite the peak). This can be ensured by carrying out the adjustments in the following sequence, noting

that No 1 cylinder is at the transmission end of the engine. The correct valve clearances are given in the Specifications at the start of this Chapter. The valve locations can be determined from the position of the manifolds.

Valve fully open	Adjust valves
No 1 exhaust	No 3 inlet and No 4 exhaust
No 3 exhaust	No 4 inlet and No 2 exhaust
No 4 exhaust	No 2 inlet and No 1 exhaust
No 2 exhaust	No 1 inlet and No 3 exhaust

5 With the relevant valve fully open, check the clearances of the two valves specified. The clearances are checked by inserting a feeler blade of the correct thickness between the valve stem and the rocker arm adjusting screw. The feeler blade should be a light, sliding fit. If adjustment is necessary, slacken the adjusting screw locknut, and turn the screw as necessary **(see illustration)**. Once the correct clearance is obtained, hold the adjusting screw and tighten the locknut securely. Once the locknut has been tightened, recheck the valve clearance, and adjust again if necessary.
6 Rotate the crankshaft until the next valve in the sequence is fully open, and check the clearances of the next two specified valves.
7 Repeat the procedure until all eight valve clearances have been checked (and if necessary, adjusted), then refit the cylinder head cover as described in Section 4.

10 Camshaft(s) and rocker arms/followers – removal, inspection and refitting

General information

1 On 1.6 litre engines, the valves are operated by followers incorporating hydraulic compensator units, between the camshafts and the top of the valves. On 1.4 litre engines, the valves are operated by rocker arms between the camshaft and the top of the valves. The rocker arm assembly is secured to the top of the cylinder head by the cylinder head bolts. Although in theory it is possible to undo the head bolts and remove the rocker arm assembly without removing the head, in practice, this is not recommended. Once the bolts have been removed, the head gasket

will be disturbed, and the gasket will almost certainly leak or blow after refitting. For this reason, removal of the rocker arm assembly cannot be done without removing the cylinder head and renewing the head gasket.
2 On 1.6 litre engines, the camshafts can be removed upwards from the cylinder head. On 1.4 litre engines, the camshaft is slid out of the right-hand end of the cylinder head, and it therefore cannot be removed without first removing the cylinder head, due to a lack of clearance.

Removal

Rocker arms – 1.4 litre engines

3 Remove the cylinder head as described in Section 11.
4 To dismantle the rocker arm assembly, carefully prise off the circlip from the right-hand end of the rocker shaft; retain the rocker pedestal, to prevent it being sprung off the end of the shaft. Slide the various components off the end of the shaft, keeping all components in their correct fitted order **(see illustration)**. Make a note of each component's correct fitted position and orientation as it is removed, to ensure it is fitted correctly on reassembly.
Note: *Avoid touching the rocker arm roller bearing surfaces with your fingers.*
5 To separate the left-hand pedestal and shaft, first unscrew the cylinder head cover retaining stud from the top of the pedestal; this can be achieved using a stud extractor, or two nuts locked together **(see illustration)**. With the stud removed, unscrew the grub screw from the top of the pedestal, and withdraw the rocker shaft.

Camshaft – 1.4 litre engines

6 Remove the cylinder head as described in Section 11.
7 With the head on a bench, remove the locking tool, then remove the camshaft sprocket as described in Section 7.
8 On early models, remove the ignition coil module from the left-hand end of the cylinder head (see Chapter 5B) then undo the bolts and remove the coil mounting bracket. On later models, unbolt the coolant housing from the left-hand end of the cylinder head.
9 Undo the retaining bolt and slide out the camshaft thrust fork **(see illustration)**.

10.4 Remove the circlip and slide the components from the rocker shaft – 1.4 litre engines

10.5 Lock two nuts together to enable the stud to be unscrewed from the left-hand end pedestal – 1.4 litre engines

10.9 Undo the bolt and slide out the camshaft thrust fork (arrowed) – 1.4 litre engines

10 Note the fitted depth of the camshaft oil seal in relation to the cylinder head face as a guide for refitting. Using a large flat-bladed screwdriver, carefully prise the oil seal out of the right-hand end of the cylinder head, then slide out the camshaft (see illustrations).

Camshafts/followers – 1.6 litre engines

11 Remove the camshaft sprockets as described in Section 7, then remove the timing belt inner cover as described in Section 5.

12 Starting from the outside, working in a spiral pattern, progressively and evenly slacken the camshaft bearing housing retaining bolts, and lift the housing from the cylinder head (see illustration).

13 Identify each camshaft for position – the inlet camshaft is at the rear and the exhaust camshaft is at the front of the cylinder head. Also note the TDC position of each camshaft for correct refitting.

14 Remove the camshafts by pressing on the transmission ends to release the opposite ends from their bearings. Withdrawn the camshafts from the cylinder head and slide the oil seals from the ends.

15 Obtain 16 small, clean plastic containers, and number them inlet 1 to 8 and exhaust 1 to 8; alternatively, divide a larger container into 16 compartments and number each compartment accordingly. Using a rubber sucker, withdraw each follower in turn, and place it in its respective container. Don't interchange the followers, the wear rate will be much increased.

Inspection

Rocker arm assembly

16 Examine the rocker arm roller surfaces which contact the camshaft lobes for wear ridges and scoring. Renew any rocker arms on which the rollers show signs of damage. If a rocker arm roller surface is badly scored, also examine the corresponding lobe on the camshaft for wear, as both will likely be worn. Renew worn components as necessary. The rocker arm assembly can be dismantled as described in paragraphs 4 and 5.

17 Inspect the ends of the (valve clearance)

10.12 Evenly and progressively slacken the camshaft housing retaining bolts – 1.6 litre engines

10.10a Prise out the oil seal . . .

adjusting screws for signs of wear or damage, and renew as required.

18 If the rocker arm assembly has been dismantled, examine the rocker arm and shaft bearing surfaces for wear ridges and scoring. If there are obvious signs of wear, the relevant rocker arm(s) and/or the shaft must be renewed.

Camshaft(s)

19 Examine the camshaft bearing surfaces and cam lobes for signs of wear ridges and scoring. Renew the camshaft if any of these conditions are apparent. Examine the condition of the bearing surfaces, both on the camshaft journals and in the cylinder head/bearing housing. If the head bearing surfaces are worn excessively, the cylinder head will need to be renewed.

20 On 1.4 litre engines, examine the thrust fork for signs of wear or scoring, and renew as necessary.

21 On 1.6 litre engines, examine the hydraulic follower surfaces which contact the camshaft lobes for wear ridges and scoring. Renew any follower where these conditions are apparent. If a follower bearing surface is badly scored, also examine the corresponding lobe on the camshaft for wear, as it is likely that both will be worn. Renew any components as necessary.

Refitting

Rocker arms – 1.4 litre engines

22 If the rocker arm assembly was dismantled, refit the rocker shaft to the left-hand pedestal, aligning its locating hole with the pedestal threaded hole. Refit the grub screw, and tighten it securely. With the grub screw in position, refit the cylinder head cover mounting stud to the pedestal, and tighten it securely. Apply a smear of clean engine oil to the shaft, then slide on all removed components, ensuring each is correctly fitted in its original position. **Note:** *Avoid touching the rocker arm roller bearing surfaces with your fingers*. Once all components are in position on the shaft, compress the right-hand pedestal and refit the circlip. Ensure that the circlip is correctly located in its groove on the shaft.

23 Refit the cylinder head and rocker arm assembly as described in Section 11.

10.10b . . . then slide out the camshaft from the cylinder head – 1.4 litre engines

Camshaft – 1.4 litre engines

24 Ensure that the cylinder head and camshaft bearing surfaces are clean, then liberally oil the camshaft bearings and lobes. Slide the camshaft back into position in the cylinder head.

25 Locate the thrust fork with the left-hand end of the camshaft. Refit the fork retaining bolt, tightening it to the specified torque setting.

26 On early models, refit the mounting bracket, then refit the ignition coil module with reference to Chapter 5B. On later models, ensure that the coolant housing and cylinder head mating surfaces are clean and dry, then apply a smear of sealant to the housing mating surface. Refit the housing to the cylinder head, and securely tighten its retaining bolts.

27 Lubricate the lips of the new seal with clean engine oil, then drive it into position until it is at the fitted depth noted during removal. Use a suitable tubular drift, such as a socket, which bears only on the hard outer edge of the seal. Take care not to damage the seal lips during fitting. Note that the seal lips should face inwards.

28 Refit the camshaft sprocket as described in Section 7.

29 Refit the cylinder head as described in Section 11.

Camshafts/followers – 1.6 litre engines

30 Before commencing refitting, remove all traces of oil from the bearing housing retaining bolts holes in the cylinder head, using a clean rag. Also ensure that both the cylinder head and bearing housing mating faces are clean and free from oil.

31 Liberally oil the cylinder head hydraulic follower bores and the followers. Carefully refit the followers to the cylinder head, ensuring that each follower is refitted to its original bore. Some care will be required to enter the followers squarely into their bores. Check that each follower rotates freely.

32 Liberally oil the camshaft bearings in the cylinder head and the camshaft lobes, then refit the camshafts to the cylinder head in the previously noted positions. The locating notch in the right-hand end of the camshafts should

10.32 Position the inlet camshaft locking notch at the 7 o'clock position and the exhaust camshaft at 8 o'clock (arrowed) – 1.6 litre engines

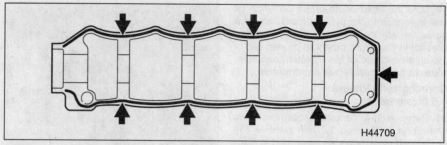

10.33 Apply a bead of silicone sealant to the cylinder head mating surface (arrowed) – 1.6 litre engines

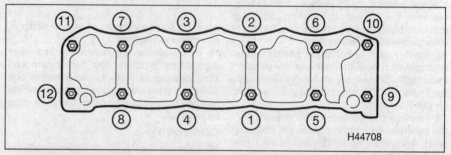

10.34 Camshaft bearing housing bolts tightening sequence – 1.6 litre engines

be positioned at the 7 o'clock position on the inlet camshaft, and the 8 o'clock position on the exhaust camshaft (see illustration).

33 Apply a bead of silicone-based jointing compound around the perimeter of the mating faces and around the retaining bolt hole locations (see illustration).

34 Refit the bearing housing, and tighten the bolts progressively, in sequence, to the specified torque (see illustration).

35 Fit new oil seals with reference to Section 8.

36 Refit the timing belt inner cover as described in Section 5.

37 Refit the camshaft sprockets as described in Section 7.

11 Cylinder head – removal and refitting

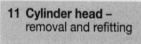

Note: Ensure the engine is cold before removing the cylinder head.

Removal

1 Disconnect the battery negative terminal (refer to Disconnecting the battery in the Reference Chapter).

2 Drain the cooling system as described in Chapter 1A.

3 Remove the ignition coil assembly (see Chapter 5B) then remove the spark plugs (see Chapter 1A).

4 Remove the cylinder head cover(s) as described in Section 4.

5 Remove the timing belt upper and lower covers as described in Section 5.

6 Align the engine assembly/valve timing holes as described in Section 3, and lock both the camshaft sprocket(s) and flywheel in position.

Caution: Do not attempt to rotate the engine whilst the tools are in position.

1.4 litre engines

7 Note that the following text assumes that the cylinder head will be removed with both inlet and exhaust manifolds attached; this is easier, but makes it a bulky and heavy assembly to handle. If it is wished to remove

11.14 Slacken and remove the cylinder head bolts – 1.4 litre engines

the manifolds first, proceed as described in Chapter 4A.

8 Carry out the following operations as described in Chapter 4A:

a) Remove the air cleaner assembly and air intake ducting.

b) Disconnect the exhaust system front pipe from the manifold and from the bracket on the transmission. Disconnect or release the oxygen sensor wiring.

c) Disconnect the fuel feed hose (and, where applicable, the return hose) from the fuel rail (plug all openings, to prevent loss of fuel and entry of dirt into the fuel system).

d) Note their fitted positions, then disconnect the relevant electrical connectors and vacuum/breather hoses from the inlet manifold and throttle housing.

e) Where necessary unbolt the support bracket from the inlet manifold.

f) Disconnect the accelerator cable (where fitted).

g) On models with air injection, disconnect the hose from the injection valve which is fitted to the exhaust manifold.

9 Note their fitted positions, then slacken the retaining clips, and disconnect the coolant hoses from the cylinder head. Likewise, note the routing, then disconnect all electrical connectors from the cylinder head.

10 Slacken and remove the bolt securing the engine oil dipstick tube to the cylinder head.

11 On later models with power steering, referring to Chapter 10, unbolt the power steering pump from its mounting bracket. Undo the power steering pipe retaining clip screws then position the pump clear of the engine. Support the weight of the pump by

tying it to the vehicle body to prevent any excess strain being placed on the hydraulic pipes/hoses. **Note:** *There is no need to disconnect the pipe/hose from the pump.*

12 Loosen the timing belt tensioner pulley retaining nut. Pivot the pulley approximately 60° in a clockwise direction, using a key fitted to the hole in the pulley hub, then retighten the retaining nut. On early engines, an 8 mm square section key will be required, and on later engines with an automatic tensioner, an Allen key will be needed.

13 Disengage the timing belt from the camshaft sprocket, and position the belt clear of the sprocket. Ensure that the belt is not bent or twisted sharply.

14 Working in the reverse of the tightening sequence (see illustration 11.39a), progressively slacken the cylinder head bolts by half a turn at a time, until all bolts can be unscrewed by hand (see illustration).

15 With all the cylinder head bolts removed, lift the rocker arm assembly off the cylinder

11.15 Lift off the rocker arm assembly – 1.4 litre engines

11.16 Use two stout screwdrivers to rock the cylinder head free from the block –

1.4 litre engines

11.17 Clamp the cylinder liners in position

before rotating the crankshaft (clamps arrowed) – 1.4 litre engines

head **(see illustration)**. Note: *Avoid touching the rocker arm roller bearing surfaces with your fingers.* Note the locating pins which are fitted to the base of each rocker arm pedestal. If any pin is a loose fit in the head or pedestal, remove it for safe-keeping.

16 The joint between the cylinder head and gasket, and the cylinder block/crankcase must now be broken without disturbing the wet liners. To break the joint, obtain two stout screwdrivers which fit into the cylinder head bolt holes. Gently 'rock' the cylinder head free towards the front of the car **(see illustration)**. Do not try to swivel the head on the cylinder block/crankcase; it is located by dowels, as well as by the tops of the liners. **Note:** *If care is not taken and the liners are moved, there is also a possibility of the bottom seals being disturbed, causing leakage after refitting the head.* When the joint is broken, lift the cylinder head away; seek assistance if possible, as it is a heavy assembly, especially if it is being removed complete with the manifolds.

17 Remove the gasket from the top of the block, noting the two locating dowels. If the locating dowels are a loose fit, remove them and store them with the head for safe-keeping. Do not discard the gasket – it will be needed for identification purposes (see paragraphs 29 and 30). Operations that require the rotation of the crankshaft (eg, cleaning the piston crowns), should only be carried out once the cylinder liners are firmly clamped in position **(see illustration)**. In the absence of the manufacturer's special liner clamps, the liners can be clamped in position using large flat washers positioned underneath suitable-length bolts. Alternatively, the original head bolts could be temporarily refitted, with suitable spacers fitted to their shanks.

18 If the cylinder head is to be dismantled for overhaul, remove the camshaft as described in Section 10, then refer to Part D of this Chapter.

1.6 litre engines

19 Note their fitted positions, then slacken the retaining clips, and disconnect the coolant hoses from the cylinder head. Likewise, note the routing, then disconnect all electrical connectors from the cylinder head.

20 Remove the inlet and exhaust manifolds as described in Chapter 4A.

21 Remove the timing belt inner cover as described in Section 5.

22 Working in the *reverse* of the tightening sequence **(see illustration 11.39b)**, progressively slacken the cylinder head bolts by half a turn at a time, until all bolts can be unscrewed by hand.

23 Lift the cylinder head away; seek assistance if possible, as it is a heavy assembly.

24 Remove the gasket from the top of the block, noting the two locating dowels. If the locating dowels are a loose fit, remove them and store them with the head for safe-keeping. Do not discard the gasket – it will be needed for identification purposes (see paragraphs 29 and 30).

25 If the cylinder head is to be dismantled for overhaul, remove the camshafts as described in Section 10, then refer to Part D of this Chapter.

Preparation for refitting

26 The mating faces of the cylinder head and cylinder block/crankcase must be perfectly clean before refitting the head. Use a hard plastic or wood scraper to remove all traces of gasket and carbon; also clean the piston crowns. **Note:** *On 1.4 litre engines, clamp the liners in position before turning the crankshaft (see paragraph 17).* Take particular care during the cleaning operations, as aluminium alloy is easily damaged. Also, make sure that the carbon is not allowed to enter the oil and water passages – this is particularly important for the lubrication system, as carbon could block the oil supply to the engine's components. Using adhesive tape and paper, seal the water, oil and bolt holes in the cylinder block/crankcase. To prevent carbon entering the gap between the pistons and bores, smear a little grease in the gap. After cleaning each piston, use a small brush to remove all traces of grease and carbon from the gap, then wipe away the remainder with a clean rag. Clean all the pistons in the same way.

27 Check the mating surfaces of the cylinder block/crankcase and the cylinder head for nicks, deep scratches and other damage. If slight, they may be removed carefully with a file, but if excessive, machining may be the only alternative to renewal.

28 If warpage of the cylinder head gasket surface is suspected, use a straight-edge to

check it for distortion. Refer to Part D of this Chapter if necessary.

29 When purchasing a new cylinder head gasket, it is essential that a gasket of the correct thickness is obtained. On some models only one thickness of gasket is available, so this is not a problem. On other models, there are two different thicknesses available – the standard gasket, and a slightly thicker 'repair' gasket (+ 0.2 mm). The gaskets can be identified as described in the following paragraph, using the cut-outs on the left-hand end of the gasket.

30 With the gasket fitted the correct way up on the cylinder block, there will be a single or double cut-out at the rear of the left-hand side of the gasket identifying the engine type (eg, TU3JP engine). In the centre of the gasket there will likely be another series of between 0 and 4 cut-outs, identifying the manufacturer of the gasket and whether or not it contains asbestos (these cut-outs are of little importance). The important cut-out location is at the front of the gasket; on the standard gasket there will be no cut-out in this position, whereas on the thicker 'repair' gasket there will be a single cut-out **(see illustration)**. Identify

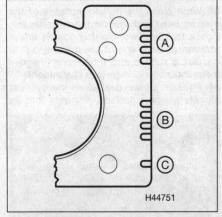

H44751

11.30 Cylinder head gasket identification markings

A *Engine type identification cut-out locations*
B *Gasket manufacturer identification cut-out locations*
C *Gasket thickness identification cut-out locations*

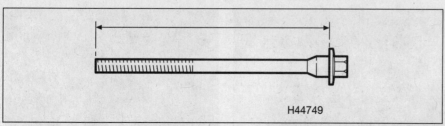

11.31 Measure the bolt length from the underside of the bolt head to the end of the bolt

the gasket type, and ensure that the new gasket obtained is of the correct thickness. If there is any doubt as to which gasket is fitted, take the old gasket along to your dealer, and have him confirm the gasket type.

31 Check the condition of the cylinder head bolts, and particularly their threads, whenever they are removed. Wash the bolts in suitable solvent, and wipe them dry. Check each for any sign of visible wear or damage, renewing any bolt if necessary. Measure the length of each bolt, from the underside of its head to the bolt end, to check for stretching **(see illustration)**. The bolts for 1.4 litre engines are 175.5 mm in length when new; if any bolt has stretched to more than 176.5 mm, renew all the cylinder head bolts as a set. On 1.6 litre engines, the maximum length for the bolts is 122.6 mm. Although the manufacturer's do not actually specify that the bolts must be renewed, it is strongly recommended that the bolts should be renewed as a complete set, regardless of their apparent condition, whenever they are disturbed.

32 On 1.4 litre engines, prior to refitting the cylinder head, check the cylinder liner protrusion as described Chapter 2D, Section 11.

Refitting

1.4 litre engines

33 Wipe clean the mating surfaces of the cylinder head and cylinder block/crankcase. Check that the two locating dowels are in position at each end of the cylinder block/crankcase surface and, if necessary, remove the cylinder liner clamps **(see illustration)**.

34 Position a new gasket on the cylinder block/crankcase surface, ensuring that its identification cut-outs are at the left-hand end of the gasket, and the side marked TOP is uppermost.

35 Check that the flywheel and camshaft sprocket are still correctly locked in position with their respective tools then, with the aid of an assistant, carefully refit the cylinder head assembly to the block, aligning it with the locating dowels.

36 Ensure that the locating pins are in position in the base of each rocker pedestal, then refit the rocker arm assembly to the cylinder head.

37 Lubricate the threads and underside of the heads of the cylinder head bolts lightly with clean engine oil.

38 Carefully enter each bolt into its relevant hole (*do not drop them in*) and screw in, by hand only, until finger-tight.

39 Working progressively and in sequence, tighten the cylinder head bolts to their Stage 1 torque setting, using a torque wrench and suitable socket **(see illustrations)**.

40 Once all the bolts have been tightened to their Stage 1 setting, working again in the given sequence, angle-tighten the bolts through the specified Stage 2 angle, using a socket and extension bar. It is recommended that an angle-measuring gauge is used during this stage of the tightening, to ensure accuracy. If a gauge is not available, use white paint to make alignment marks between the bolt head and cylinder head prior to tightening; the marks can then be used to check that the bolt has been rotated through the correct angle during tightening.

41 Refit the timing belt as described in Section 6.

42 Reconnect all coolant hoses and wiring connectors to the cylinder head, inlet manifold and throttle housing.

43 Refit the bolt securing the engine oil dipstick tube to the cylinder head.

44 Working as described in the Chapter 4A, carry out the following tasks:

   a) *Refit all disturbed fuel hoses and control cable(s) to the inlet manifold and fuel system components.*

   b) *Reconnect and adjust the accelerator cable (where fitted).*

   c) *Reconnect the exhaust system front pipe to the manifold and transmission bracket and reconnect the oxygen sensor wiring connector.*

   d) *Refit the air cleaner assembly and intake ducts.*

45 Check and, if necessary, adjust the valve clearances as described in Section 9.

46 Refit the cylinder head cover as described in Section 4.

47 Refit the spark plugs and install the ignition HT coil (see Chapters 1A and 5B).

48 Refit the power steering pump as described in Chapter 10.

49 On completion, reconnect the battery, and refill the cooling system as described in Chapter 1A.

1.6 litre engines

50 Remove the flywheel locking tool and, using a spanner or socket on the crankshaft pulley bolt, rotate the crankshaft backwards (anti-clockwise) 90°. This is to prevent any accidental contact between the pistons and valves as the cylinder head is refitted.

51 Check that the camshafts are correctly positioned in the cylinder head. The locating notch in the right-hand end of the camshafts should be at the 7 o'clock position on the inlet camshaft, and the 8 o'clock position on the exhaust camshaft **(see illustration 10.32)**. If necessary, reposition the camshafts using an open-ended spanner on the square section between the lobes.

52 Wipe clean the mating surfaces of the cylinder head and cylinder block/crankcase. Check that the two locating dowels are in position at each end of the cylinder block/crankcase surface.

53 Position a new gasket on the cylinder block/crankcase surface, ensuring that its identification cut-outs are at the left-hand end

11.33 Ensure the locating dowels (arrowed) are in position then fit the new head gasket

11.39a Cylinder head bolt tightening sequence – 1.4 litre engines

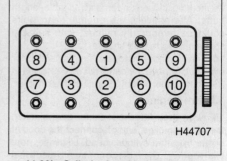

11.39b Cylinder head bolt tightening sequence – 1.6 litre engines

of the gasket, and the side marked TOP is uppermost.

54 Lubricate the threads and underside of the heads of the cylinder head bolts lightly with clean engine oil, then refit and tighten the bolts as described in paragraphs 38 to 40.

55 Refit the timing belt inner cover as described in Section 5, then refit the camshaft sprockets as described in Section 7.

56 Refit the timing belt as described in Section 6.

57 Working as described in the Chapter 4A, carry out the following tasks:
a) *Refit the inlet and exhaust manifolds.*
b) *Refit all disturbed fuel hoses and control cable(s) to the inlet manifold and fuel system components.*
c) *Refit the air cleaner assembly and intake ducts.*

58 Reconnect all coolant hoses and wiring connectors to the cylinder head, inlet manifold and throttle housing.

59 Refit the cylinder head covers as described in Section 4.

60 Refit the spark plugs and install the ignition HT coil (see Chapters 1A and 5B).

61 On completion, reconnect the battery, and refill the cooling system as described in Chapter 1A.

12 Sump – removal and refitting

Removal

1 Firmly apply the handbrake, then jack up the front of the vehicle and support it on axle stands (see *Jacking and vehicle support*). Where fitted, undo the screws and remove the engine undershield.

2 Drain the engine oil, then clean and refit the engine oil drain plug, tightening it to the specified torque. If the engine is nearing its service interval when the oil and filter are due for renewal, it is recommended that the filter is also removed, and a new one fitted. After reassembly, the engine can then be refilled with fresh oil. Refer to Chapter 1A for further information.

3 Remove the exhaust system front pipe as described in Chapter 4A.

4 Progressively slacken and remove all the sump nuts and bolts/nuts and position the wiring harness guide clear of the sump **(see illustrations)**.

5 Break the joint by striking the sump with the palm of your hand, then lower and withdraw the sump from under the car. On 1.4 litre engines, it may be necessary to use a putty knife or similar carefully inserted between the sump and block. Ease the knife along the joint until the sump is released. On 1.6 litre engines, recover the gasket.

6 While the sump is removed, take the opportunity to check the oil pump pick-up/

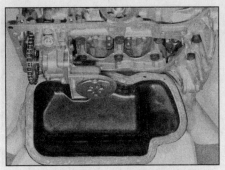

12.4a Undo the nuts and bolts, then remove the sump from the engine – 1.4 litre engines

strainer for signs of clogging or splitting. If necessary, remove the pump as described in Section 13, and clean or renew the strainer.

Refitting

7 Clean all traces of sealant from the mating surfaces of the cylinder block/crankcase and sump, then use a clean rag to wipe out the sump and the engine's interior.

8 Ensure that the sump and cylinder block/crankcase mating surfaces are clean and dry then, on 1.4 litre engines, apply a coating of suitable sealant to the sump mating surface. On 1.6 litre engines, if the gasket is undamaged, refit it to the sump, otherwise fit a new gasket.

9 Offer up the sump and locate it on its studs. Locate the wiring harness guide back in position then refit the sump retaining nuts and bolts. Tighten the nuts and bolts evenly and progressively to the specified torque.

10 Refit the exhaust front pipe as described in Chapter 4A, and refit the engine undershield (where applicable).

11 Replenish the engine oil (see Chapter 1A).

13 Oil pump – removal, inspection and refitting

Removal

1 Remove the sump (see Section 12).

2 Slacken and remove the three bolts securing the oil pump in position **(see illustration)**. Disengage the pump sprocket from the chain, and remove the oil pump. If the pump locating dowel is a loose fit, remove and store it with the bolts for safe-keeping.

Inspection

3 Examine the oil pump sprocket for signs of damage and wear, such as chipped or missing teeth. If the sprocket is worn, the pump assembly must be renewed, as the sprocket is not available separately. It is also recommended that the chain and drive sprocket, fitted to the crankshaft, are renewed at the same time. On 1.4 litre engines, renewal of the chain and drive sprocket is an involved

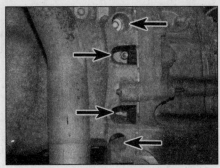

12.4b Access to the sump end bolts/nuts is through holes in the casing (arrowed) – 1.6 litre engines

operation requiring the removal of the main bearing ladder, and therefore cannot be carried out with the engine still fitted to the vehicle. On 1.6 litre engines, the oil pump drive sprocket and chain can be removed with the engine *in situ*, once the crankshaft sprocket has been removed and the crankshaft oil seal housing has been unbolted.

4 Slacken and remove the bolts securing the strainer cover to the pump body, then lift off the strainer cover. Remove the relief valve piston and spring (and guide pin – 1.6 litre engines only), noting which way round they are fitted.

5 Examine the pump rotors and body for signs of wear ridges and scoring. If worn, the complete pump assembly must be renewed.

6 Examine the relief valve piston for signs of wear or damage, and renew if necessary. The condition of the relief valve spring can only be measured by comparing it with a new one; if there is any doubt about its condition, it should also be renewed. Both the piston and spring are available individually.

7 Thoroughly clean the oil pump strainer with a suitable solvent, and check it for signs of clogging or splitting. If the strainer is damaged, the strainer and cover assembly must be renewed.

8 Locate the relief valve spring, piston and (where fitted) the guide pin in the strainer cover, then refit the cover to the pump body. Align the relief valve piston with its bore in the pump. Refit the cover retaining bolts, tightening them securely.

13.2 Unscrew the three bolts securing the oil pump is position

14.2 Use a screwdriver to lever out the crankshaft right-hand oil seal

15.2 Use a tool to lock the flywheel ring gear and prevent rotation

Refitting

9 Ensure that the locating dowel is in position, then engage the pump sprocket with its drive chain. Locate the pump on its dowel, and refit the pump retaining bolts, tightening them to the specified torque setting.
10 Refit the sump as described in Section 12.

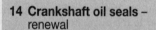

14 Crankshaft oil seals – renewal

Right-hand oil seal

1 Remove the crankshaft sprocket and flanged spacer (where fitted) as described in Section 7.
2 Make a note of the correct fitted depth of the seal in its housing then carefully punch or drill two small holes opposite each other in the seal. Screw a self-tapping screw into each, and pull on the screws with pliers to extract the seal. Alternatively, the seal can be levered out of position using a suitable flat-bladed screwdriver, taking great care not to damage the crankshaft/oil pump drive gear shoulder or seal housing **(see illustration)**.
3 Clean the seal housing, and polish off any burrs or raised edges, which may have caused the seal to fail in the first place.
4 Lubricate the lips of the new seal with clean engine oil, and carefully locate the seal on the end of crankshaft. Note that its sealing lip must face inwards. Take care not to damage the seal lips during fitting.
5 Using a suitable tubular drift (such as a socket) which bears only on the hard outer edge of the seal, tap the seal into position, to the same depth in the housing as the original was prior to removal. The inner face of the seal must be flush with the inner wall of the crankcase.
6 Wash off any traces of oil, then refit the crankshaft sprocket as described in Section 7.

Left-hand oil seal

7 Remove the flywheel (see Section 15).
8 Make a note of the correct fitted depth of the seal in its housing. Punch or drill two small holes opposite each other in the seal. Screw a

self-tapping screw into each, and pull on the screws with pliers to extract the seal.
9 Clean the seal housing, and polish off any burrs or raised edges, which may have caused the seal to fail in the first place.
10 Lubricate the lips of the new seal with clean engine oil, and carefully locate the seal on the end of the crankshaft.
11 Using a suitable tubular drift, which bears only on the hard outer edge of the seal, drive the seal into position, to the same depth in the housing as the original was prior to removal.
12 Wash off any traces of oil, then refit the flywheel as described in Section 15.

15 Flywheel – removal, inspection and refitting

Removal

1 Remove the transmission as described in Chapter 7, then remove the clutch assembly as described in Chapter 6.
2 Prevent the flywheel from turning by locking the ring gear teeth **(see illustration)**. Alternatively, bolt a strap between the flywheel and the cylinder block/crankcase.
Caution: Do not attempt to lock the flywheel in position using the locking pin described in Section 3.
3 Slacken and remove the flywheel retaining bolts.
4 Remove the flywheel. Do not drop it, as it is very heavy. If the locating dowel is a loose fit in the crankshaft end, remove and store it with the flywheel for safe-keeping.

Inspection

5 If the flywheel's clutch mating surface is deeply scored, cracked or otherwise damaged, the flywheel must be renewed. However, it may be possible to have it surface-ground; seek the advice of a dealer or engine reconditioning specialist.
6 If the ring gear is badly worn or has missing teeth, it must be renewed. This job is best left to a dealer or engine reconditioning specialist. The temperature to which the new ring gear must be heated for installation is critical and, if not done accurately, the hardness of the teeth will be destroyed.

Refitting

7 Clean the mating surfaces of the flywheel and crankshaft.
8 If the new flywheel retaining bolts are not supplied with their threads already precoated, apply a suitable thread-locking compound to the threads of each bolt.
9 Ensure that the locating dowel is in position. Offer up the flywheel, locating it on the dowel, and fit the retaining bolts.
10 Lock the flywheel using the method employed on dismantling, and tighten the retaining bolts evenly and progressively to the specified torque.
11 Refit the clutch as described in Chapter 6. Remove the locking tool, and refit the transmission as described in Chapter 7.

16 Engine/transmission mountings – inspection and renewal

Inspection

1 If improved access is required, raise the front of the car and support it on axle stands (see *Jacking and vehicle support*).
2 Check the mounting rubber to see if it is cracked, hardened or separated from the metal at any point; renew the mounting if any such damage or deterioration is evident.
3 Check that all the mounting's fasteners are securely tightened; use a torque wrench to check if possible **(see illustrations)**.
4 Using a large screwdriver or a crowbar, check for wear in the mounting by carefully levering against it to check for free play. Where this is not possible, enlist the aid of an assistant to move the engine/transmission back-and-forth, or from side-to-side, while you watch the mounting. While some free play is to be expected even from new components, excessive wear should be obvious. If excessive free play is found, check first that the fasteners are secure, then renew any worn components as described below.

Renewal

Right-hand mounting – 1.4 litre engines

Note: *The construction of the right-hand mounting differs slightly between early and later models, however the removal and refitting procedures are similar for both types.*
5 Place a jack beneath the engine, with a block of wood on the jack head. Raise the jack until it is supporting the weight of the engine.
6 Release the wiring harness and/or vacuum hoses from the clips on the right-hand engine mounting upper bracket.
7 Slacken and remove the three nuts securing the upper bracket to the bracket on the cylinder block.
8 On later models, undo the bolt securing the

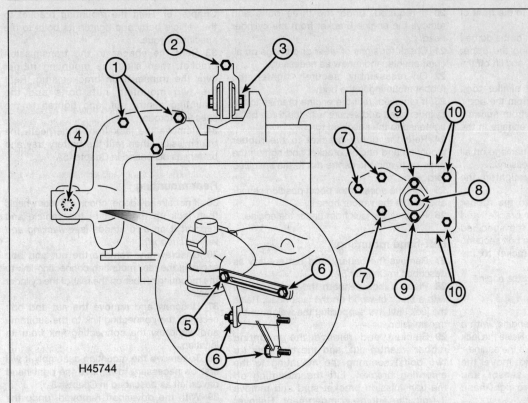

1 Right-hand mounting upper bracket-to-cylinder block bracket nuts
2 Rear mounting connecting link-to-subframe nut/bolt
3 Rear mounting connecting link-to-mounting rubber nut/bolt
4 Right-hand mounting upper bracket-to-rubber mounting nut
5 Cylinder head support bracket-to-upper bracket bolt
6 Cylinder head support bracket-to-engine nut/bolts
7 Left-hand mounting transmission bracket nuts
8 Left-hand mounting rubber centre nut
9 Left-hand mounting-to-body bracket nuts/bolts
10 Left-hand mounting body bracket bolts

H45744

16.3a Engine/transmission mounting components and attachments – later 1.4 litre engines

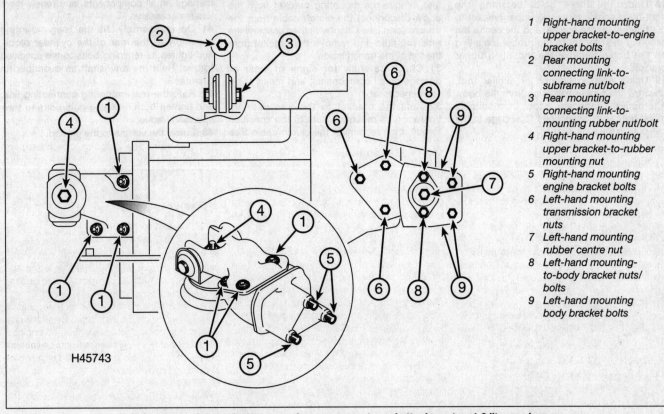

1 Right-hand mounting upper bracket-to-engine bracket bolts
2 Rear mounting connecting link-to-subframe nut/bolt
3 Rear mounting connecting link-to-mounting rubber nut/bolt
4 Right-hand mounting upper bracket-to-rubber mounting nut
5 Right-hand mounting engine bracket bolts
6 Left-hand mounting transmission bracket nuts
7 Left-hand mounting rubber centre nut
8 Left-hand mounting-to-body bracket nuts/bolts
9 Left-hand mounting body bracket bolts

H45743

16.3b Engine/transmission mounting components and attachments – 1.6 litre engines

cylinder head support bracket to the front of the mounting upper bracket.

9 Either unscrew the single nut, or the domed buffer and spacer nut, securing the upper bracket to the rubber mounting, and lift off the bracket.

10 Using a strap wrench or similar tool, unscrew the rubber mounting from the body. Alternatively, fabricate a tool from suitable metal tube with projections to engage in the cut-outs in the mounting.

11 Check for signs of wear or damage on all components, and renew as necessary.

12 On reassembly, securely tighten the rubber mounting in the body.

13 Refit the upper bracket to the rubber mounting and cylinder block bracket and tighten the retaining nuts to the specified torque. On later models, refit the bolt securing the cylinder head support bracket to the mounting upper bracket.

14 Remove the jack from under the engine.

Right-hand mounting – 1.6 litre engines

15 Place a jack beneath the engine, with a block of wood on the jack head. Raise the jack until it is supporting the weight of the engine.

16 Undo the two bolts and move the accelerator pedal position sensor and mounting bracket clear of the right-hand engine mounting.

17 Release the purge valve vapour hose from the clip on the right-hand mounting and move the hose aside slightly.

18 Undo the three bolts securing the right-hand engine mounting upper bracket to the bracket on the engine, and the centre nut securing the bracket to the rubber mounting on the body. Remove the mounting upper bracket.

19 Using a strap wrench or similar tool, unscrew the rubber mounting from the body. Alternatively, fabricate a tool from suitable metal tube with projections to engage in the cut-outs in the mounting.

20 If required, undo the three bolts and remove the engine bracket from the cylinder head.

21 Check for signs of wear or damage on all components, and renew as necessary.

22 On reassembly, securely tighten the rubber mounting in the body.

23 If removed, refit the engine bracket to the cylinder head and secure with the three bolts, tightened to the specified torque.

24 Refit the upper bracket to the rubber mounting and engine bracket and tighten the three bolts and the centre nut to the specified torque.

25 Refit the accelerator pedal position sensor and secure the vapour hose.

26 Remove the jack from under the engine.

Left-hand mounting

27 Remove the battery, and battery tray as described in Chapter 5A.

28 Place a jack beneath the transmission, with a block of wood on the jack head. Raise the jack until it is supporting the weight of the transmission.

29 Slacken and remove the mounting rubber's centre nut, and the two nuts (or two bolts) securing the mounting to the mounting bracket. Lift the mounting off the transmission bracket stud and remove it from the engine compartment. Recover the spacer from the transmission bracket stud.

30 If necessary, undo the retaining bolts and remove the mounting bracket from the body. Disconnect the clutch cable from the transmission (see Chapter 6) then unscrew the retaining nuts and remove the bracket from the top of the transmission.

31 Check carefully for signs of wear or damage on all components, and renew them where necessary.

32 Refit the bracket to the transmission, tightening its mounting nuts to the specified torque, then reconnect the clutch cable (see

Chapter 6). Refit the mounting bracket to the vehicle body and tighten its bolts to the specified torque.

33 Refit the spacer to the transmission bracket, then slide the mounting rubber over the transmission bracket stud. Refit the two mounting nuts/bolts and the mounting centre nut, and tighten to the specified torque.

34 Remove the jack from underneath the transmission, then refit the battery tray and battery as described in Chapter 5A.

Rear mounting

35 If not already done, chock the rear wheels then jack up the front of the vehicle and support it on axle stands (see *Jacking and vehicle support*).

36 Unscrew and remove the nut and bolt securing the rear mounting connecting link to the mounting rubber on the rear of the cylinder block.

37 Unscrew and remove the nut and bolt securing the connecting link to the subframe and withdraw the connecting link from its location.

38 To remove the mounting assembly it will first be necessary to remove the right-hand driveshaft as described in Chapter 8.

39 With the driveshaft removed, undo the retaining bolts and remove the mounting from the rear of the cylinder block.

40 Check carefully for signs of wear or damage on all components, and renew them where necessary.

41 On reassembly, fit the rear mounting assembly to the rear of the cylinder block, and tighten its retaining bolts to the specified torque. Refit the driveshaft as described in Chapter 8.

42 Refit the rear mounting connecting link, and tighten both retaining nuts/bolts to their specified torque.

43 Lower the vehicle to the ground.

Chapter 2 Part B:
1.6 litre diesel engine in-car repair procedures

Contents

Degrees of difficulty

Easy, suitable for novice with little experience	**Fairly easy,** suitable for beginner with some experience	**Fairly difficult,** suitable for competent DIY mechanic	**Difficult,** suitable for experienced DIY mechanic	**Very difficult,** suitable for expert DIY or professional

Specifications

General

Designation:	
Without intercooler	DV6TED4
With intercooler	DV6ATED4 and DV6BTED4
Engine codes:*	
DV6TED4	9HY
DV6ATED4	9HX
DV6BTED4	9HW
Capacity	1560 cc
Bore	75.0 mm
Stroke	88.3 mm
Direction of crankshaft rotation	Clockwise (viewed from the right-hand side of vehicle)
No 1 cylinder location	At the transmission end of block
Maximum power output:	
DV6TED4 (9HY)	110 bhp (80 kW) @ 4000 rpm
DV6ATED4 (9HX).	90 bhp (66 kW) @ 4000 rpm
DV6BTED4 (9HW).	90 bhp (66 kW) @ 4000 rpm
Maximum torque output:	
DV6TED4 (9HY)	240 Nm @ 1750 rpm
DV6ATED4 (9HX)	215 Nm @ 1750 rpm
DV6BTED4 (9HW)	215 Nm @ 1750 rpm
Compression ratio	18.0 : 1

* The engine code is stamped on a plate attached to the front of the cylinder block, next to the oil filter

Compression pressures (engine hot, at cranking speed)
Normal . . . .   20 ± 5 bar
Minimum . . . .   15 bar
Maximum difference between any two cylinders . . . .   5 bar

Camshaft
Drive:
  Inlet camshaft . . . .   Toothed belt from crankshaft
  Exhaust camshaft . . . .   Chain-drive from inlet camshaft
Number of teeth   19
Length:
  Inlet camshaft . . . .   401.0 ± 0.15 mm
  Exhaust camshaft . . . .   389.0 ± 0.5 mm
Endfloat . . . .   0.195 to 0.300 mm

Lubrication system
Oil pump type . . . .   Gear-type, driven directly by the right-hand end of the crankshaft, by two flats machined along the crankshaft journal.

Minimum oil pressure at 80°C:
  1000 rpm . . . .   1.3 bar
  4000 rpm . . . .   3.5 bar

Torque wrench settings

	Nm	lbf ft
Ancillary drivebelt tensioner roller	20	15
Big-end bolts:*		
Stage 1	5	4
Stage 2	10	7
Stage 3	Angle-tighten a further 130°	
Camshaft bearing caps	10	7
Camshaft cover/bearing ladder:		
Studs	10	7
Bolts	10	7
Camshaft position sensor bolt	5	4
Camshaft sprocket:		
Stage 1	20	15
Stage 2	Angle-tighten a further 50°	
Coolant outlet housing bolts	7	5
Crankshaft position/speed sensor bolt	5	4
Crankshaft pulley/sprocket bolt:*		
Stage 1	35	26
Stage 2	Angle-tighten a further 190 °	
Cylinder head bolts:		
Stage 1	20	15
Stage 2	40	30
Stage 3	Angle-tighten a further 260°	
Cylinder head cover/manifold	13	10
EGR valve	10	7
Engine-to-transmission fixing bolts	40	30
Flywheel bolt:*		
Dual mass flywheel:		
Stage 1	25	18
Stage 2	Fully slacken	
Stage 3	8	6
Stage 4	30	22
Stage 5	Angle-tighten a further 90°	
Normal flywheel:		
Stage 1	25	18
Stage 2	Fully slacken	
Stage 3	8	6
Stage 4	17	13
Stage 5	Angle-tighten a further 75°	
Fuel pump sprocket	50	37
Left-hand engine/transmission mounting:		
Mounting bracket to body	21	15
Mounting bracket to transmission	57	42
Rubber mounting to body bracket	19	14
Rubber mounting nut to centre pin	50	37

Torque wrench settings (continued)

	Nm	lbf ft
Main bearing ladder outer seam bolts:		
Stage 1	6	4
Stage 2	8	6
Main bearing ladder to cylinder block:		
Stage 1	10	7
Stage 2	Slacken 180°	
Stage 3	30	22
Stage 4	Angle-tighten a further 140°	
Piston oil jet spray tube bolt	20	15
Oil filter cover	25	18
Oil pick-up pipe	10	7
Oil pressure switch	32	24
Oil pump to cylinder block:		
Stage 1	5	4
Stage 2	9	7
Engine/transmission rear mounting:		
Connecting link-to-subframe nut/bolt	64	47
Mounting/driveshaft intermediate bearing housing to cylinder block	54	40
Mounting centre bolt	60	44
Right-hand engine mounting:		
Top bracket to body bracket	20	15
Mounting centre bolt to rubber mounting	45	33
Support pin to centre bolt	21	15
Rubber mounting to body bracket	45	33
Mounting bracket to engine:		
Upper	61	45
Lower	55	41
Sump drain plug	25	18
Sump bolts/nuts	12	9
Timing belt idler pulley	37	27
Timing belt tensioner pulley	23	17
Timing chain tensioner	10	7
Vacuum pump:		
Stage 1	3	2
Stage 2	5	4
Stage 3	20	15

* Do not re-use

1 General information

How to use this Chapter

This Part of Chapter 2 describes the repair procedures that can reasonably be carried out on the engine whilst it remains in the vehicle. If the engine has been removed from the vehicle and is being dismantled as described in Part F, any preliminary dismantling procedures can be ignored.

Note that, while it may be possible physically to overhaul items such as the piston/connecting rod assemblies while the engine is in the car, such tasks are not usually carried out as separate operations. Usually, several additional procedures are required (not to mention the cleaning of components and oilways); for this reason, all such tasks are classed as major overhaul procedures, and are described in Part F of this Chapter.

Part F describes the removal of the engine/transmission from the car, and the full overhaul procedures that can then be carried out.

DV series engines

The 1.6 litre DV series engine is the result of development collaboration between Citroën, Peugeot and Ford. The engine is of double overhead camshaft (DOHC) 16-valve design. The direct injection, turbocharged, four-cylinder engine is mounted transversely, with the transmission mounted on the left-hand side.

A toothed timing belt drives the inlet camshaft, high-pressure fuel pump and coolant pump. The inlet camshaft drives the exhaust camshaft via a chain. The camshafts operate the inlet and exhaust valves via rocker arms which are supported at their pivot ends by hydraulic self-adjusting tappets. The camshafts are supported by bearings machined directly in the cylinder head and camshaft bearing housing.

The high-pressure fuel pump supplies fuel to the fuel rail, and subsequently to the electronically-controlled injectors which inject the fuel direct into the combustion chambers. This design differs from the previous type where an injection pump supplies the fuel at high-pressure to each injector. The earlier, conventional type injection pump required fine calibration and timing, and these functions are now completed by the high-pressure pump, electronic injectors and engine management ECU.

The crankshaft runs in five main bearings of the usual shell type. Endfloat is controlled by thrustwashers either side of No 2 main bearing.

The pistons are selected to be of matching weight, and incorporate fully-floating gudgeon pins retained by circlips.

Repair operations precaution

The engine is a complex unit with numerous accessories and ancillary components. The design of the engine compartment is such that every conceivable space has been utilised, and access to virtually all of the engine components is extremely limited. In many cases, ancillary components will have to be removed, or moved to one side, and wiring, pipes and hoses will have to be disconnected or removed from various cable clips and support brackets.

When working on this engine, read through the entire procedure first, look at the car and engine at the same time, and establish whether you have the necessary tools, equipment, skill and patience to proceed. Allow considerable time for any operation, and be prepared for the unexpected.

Because of the limited access, many of the engine photographs appearing in this Chapter were, by necessity, taken with the engine removed from the vehicle.

 Warning: It is essential to observe strict precautions when working on the fuel system components of the engine, particularly the high-pressure side of the system. Before carrying out any engine operations that entail working on, or near, any part of the fuel system, refer to the special information given in Chapter 4C.

Operations with engine in vehicle

a) *Compression pressure – testing.*
b) *Cylinder head cover – removal and refitting.*
c) *Crankshaft pulley – removal and refitting.*
d) *Timing belt covers – removal and refitting.*
e) *Timing belt – removal, refitting and adjustment.*
f) *Timing belt tensioner and sprockets – removal and refitting.*
g) *Camshaft oil seal – renewal.*
h) *Camshaft, rocker arms and hydraulic tappets – removal, inspection and refitting.*
i) *Sump – removal and refitting.*
j) *Oil pump – removal and refitting.*
k) *Crankshaft oil seals – renewal.*
l) *Engine/transmission mountings – inspection and renewal.*
m) *Flywheel – removal, inspection and refitting.*

2 Compression and leakdown tests – description and interpretation

Compression test

Note: *A compression tester specifically designed for diesel engines must be used for this test.*

1 When engine performance is down, or if misfiring occurs which cannot be attributed to the fuel system, a compression test can provide diagnostic clues as to the engine's condition. If the test is performed regularly, it can give warning of trouble before any other symptoms become apparent.

2 A compression tester specifically intended for diesel engines must be used, because of the higher pressures involved. The tester is connected to an adapter which screws into the glow plug hole. On this engine, an adapter suitable for use in the glow plug holes will be required, so as not to disturb the fuel system components. It is unlikely to be worthwhile buying such a tester for occasional use, but it

may be possible to borrow or hire one – if not, have the test performed by a garage.

3 Unless specific instructions to the contrary are supplied with the tester, observe the following points:

a) *The battery must be in a good state of charge, the air filter must be clean, and the engine should be at normal operating temperature.*
b) *All the glow plugs should be removed as described in Chapter 5C before starting the test.*
c) *The wiring connectors on the engine management system ECU (located in the plastic box behind the battery) must be disconnected.*

4 The compression pressures measured are not so important as the balance between cylinders. Values are given in the Specifications.

5 The cause of poor compression is less easy to establish on a diesel engine than on a petrol one. The effect of introducing oil into the cylinders ('wet' testing) is not conclusive, because there is a risk that the oil will sit in the swirl chamber or in the recess on the piston crown instead of passing to the rings. However, the following can be used as a rough guide to diagnosis.

6 All cylinders should produce very similar pressures; any difference greater than that specified indicates the existence of a fault. Note that the compression should build-up quickly in a healthy engine; low compression on the first stroke, followed by gradually-increasing pressure on successive strokes, indicates worn piston rings. A low compression reading on the first stroke, which does not build-up during successive strokes, indicates leaking valves or a blown head gasket (a cracked head could also be the cause). Deposits on the undersides of the valve heads can also cause low compression.

7 A low reading from two adjacent cylinders is almost certainly due to the head gasket having blown between them; the presence of coolant in the engine oil will confirm this.

8 If the compression reading is unusually high, the cylinder head surfaces, valves and pistons are probably coated with carbon deposits. If this is the case, the cylinder head should be removed and decarbonised (see Part F).

Leakdown test

9 A leakdown test measures the rate at which compressed air fed into the cylinder is lost. It is an alternative to a compression test, and in many ways it is better, since the escaping air provides easy identification of where pressure loss is occurring (piston rings, valves or head gasket).

10 The equipment needed for leakdown testing is unlikely to be available to the home mechanic. If poor compression is suspected, have the test performed by a suitably-equipped garage.

3 Engine assembly/valve timing holes – general information and usage

Note: *Do not attempt to rotate the engine whilst the crankshaft and camshaft are locked in position. If the engine is to be left in this state for a long period of time, it is a good idea to place suitable warning notices inside the vehicle, and in the engine compartment. This will reduce the possibility of the engine being accidentally cranked on the starter motor, which is likely to cause damage with the locking pins in place.*

1 Timing holes or slots are located only in the crankshaft pulley flange and camshaft sprocket hub. The holes/slots are used to position the pistons halfway up the cylinder bores. This will ensure that the valve timing is maintained during operations that require removal and refitting of the timing belt. When the holes/slots are aligned with their corresponding holes in the cylinder block and cylinder head, suitable diameter bolts/pins can be inserted to lock the crankshaft and camshaft in position, preventing rotation.

2 Note that the HDi type fuel system used on these engines does not have a conventional diesel injection pump, but instead uses a high-pressure fuel pump. Although it may be argued that timing of the fuel pump is irrelevant because it merely pressurises the fuel in the fuel rail, Citroën/Peugeot include this procedure for engines fitted with a Bosch high-pressure fuel pump, using the same timing rod/pin used for crankshaft sprocket timing. **Note:** *On the Bosch pump, the drive sprocket is keyed to the shaft.* In addition, note that the hole in the fuel pump sprocket only aligns correctly with the hole in the mounting bracket every 12 revolutions of the crankshaft (or every 6 revolutions of the camshaft sprocket).

3 To align the engine assembly/valve timing holes, proceed as follows.

4 Apply the handbrake then jack up the front of the vehicle and support it on axle stands (see *Jacking and vehicle support*). Remove the right-hand front roadwheel.

5 To gain access to the crankshaft pulley, to enable the engine to be turned, the front right-hand wheel arch plastic liner must be removed. The liner is secured by several plastic expanding rivets/nut/screws. To remove the rivets, push in the centre pins a little, then prise the clips from place. Remove the liner from under the front wing. The crankshaft can then be turned using a suitable socket and extension bar fitted to the pulley bolt.

6 Remove the upper and lower timing belt covers as described in Section 6.

7 Temporarily refit the crankshaft pulley bolt, remove the crankshaft locking tool, then turn the crankshaft until the timing hole in the camshaft sprocket hub is aligned with the corresponding hole in the cylinder head. Note that the crankshaft must always be turned in a clockwise direction (viewed from the right-hand side of vehicle). Use a small mirror so that the position of the sprocket hub timing slot can be observed. When the slot is aligned with the corresponding hole in the cylinder head, the camshaft is positioned correctly.

8 Remove the crankshaft drivebelt pulley as described in Section 5.

9 Insert a 5 mm diameter bolt, rod or drill through the hole in crankshaft sprocket flange and into the corresponding hole in the oil pump **(see illustration)**, if necessary, carefully turn the crankshaft either way until the rod enters the timing hole in the block.

10 Insert an 8 mm bolt, rod or drill through the hole in the camshaft sprocket hub and into engagement with the cylinder head. Note that a modified 3-segment camshaft sprocket is fitted to later models **(see illustrations)**.

11 If using this procedure during refitting of the timing belt, insert a 5 mm diameter bolt, rod or drill through the hole in the fuel pump sprocket and into the corresponding hole in the cylinder head **(see illustration)**. **Note:** *On some engines, a hole is provided at the 5 o'clock position for locking purposes only, however, the timing hole is at the 12 o'clock position.* Note the comment in paragraph 2 – if the fuel pump sprocket holes are not aligned during removal of the timing belt, it is of no consequence, however, it is important to align the holes during the refitting procedure. If timing alignment alone is being *checked* there is no need to check alignment of the pump sprocket.

12 The crankshaft and camshaft are now locked in position, preventing unnecessary rotation.

---

4 Cylinder head cover/ manifold – removal and refitting

Removal

1 Pull the plastic cover upwards from the top of the engine.

2 Disconnect the mass airflow meter wiring plug **(see illustration)**.

3 Remove the inlet and outlet air ducting from the air filter housing **(see illustrations)**.

4 Unscrew the air filter housing cover bolts,

3.9 Insert a 5.0 mm drill bit/bolt through the round hole in the sprocket flange, into the hole in the oil pump housing (lower timing belt cover removed for clarity)

3.10a Insert an 8.0 mm drill bit/bolt through the hole in the camshaft sprocket into the corresponding hole in the cylinder head

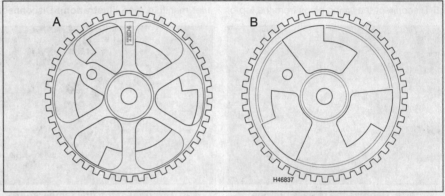

3.10b Early (A) and late (B) camshaft sprocket

3.11 Insert a 5.0 mm drill bit/bolt through the round hole in the fuel pump sprocket into the cylinder head

4.2 Release the clip (arrowed) and disconnect the mass airflow meter wiring plug

4.3a Undo the screw (arrowed) and remove the inlet ducting

4.3b Disconnect the hose to the turbocharger . . .

4.3c . . . release the clips (arrowed) and disconnect the breather hose . . .

4.4a ... then undo the cover screws (arrowed) ...

4.4b ... and remove the ducting/cover assembly

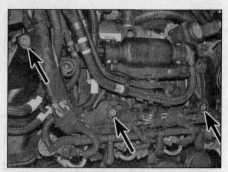

4.5 Undo the Allen screws (arrowed) and position the wiring harness/guide to one side

then remove the cover and filter element – refer to Chapter 4C **(see illustrations)**. Pull the air filter housing from its mountings.
5 Disconnect the wiring plugs from the top of each injector, undo the guide bolts, then make sure all wiring harnesses are freed from any retaining brackets on the cylinder head cover/inlet manifold **(see illustration)**. Disconnect any vacuum pipes as necessary, having first noted their fitted positions.
6 Remove the EGR cooler as described in Chapter 4C.
7 Depress the release buttons and disconnect the fuel feed and return hoses at the right-hand end of the cylinder head, then disconnect the fuel temperature sensor wiring plug, and move the pipe/priming bulb assembly to the rear **(see illustrations)**.
8 Release the clamps, undo the bolts and remove the inlet ducting between the turbocharger and the inlet manifold. Make a note of their fitted positions, then disconnect the various wiring plugs as the assembly is withdrawn **(see illustrations)**.
9 Undo the retaining bolts and remove the oil separator from the top of the cylinder head **(see illustration)**. Recover the rubber seal.
10 Prise out the retaining clips and

4.7a Depress the release buttons (arrowed) and disconnect the fuel feed and return hoses

4.7b Disconnect the fuel temperature sensor wiring plug (arrowed) ...

4.7c ... then unclip the fuel priming bulb/pipes (arrowed)

4.8a Slacken the left-hand turbocharger outlet hose bolt, undo the right-hand bolt (arrowed) ...

4.8b ... then slacken the hose clamps (arrowed), disconnect the wiring plugs ...

4.8c ... undo the bolt on the end (arrowed) ...

4.8d ... and the 2 at the front (arrowed), then remove the assembly

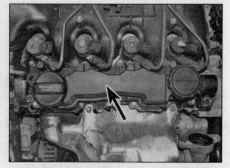

4.9 Undo the bolts and remove the oil separator (arrowed)

4.10a Prise out the clip and pull the return hose from the top of each injector

4.10b Use a second spanner to hold the injector port whilst slackening the fuel pipe unions

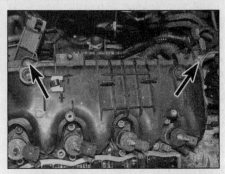

4.11 Undo the 2 remaining bolts (arrowed) and pull the cover/manifold upwards

disconnect the fuel return pipes from the injectors, then undo the unions and remove the high-pressure fuel pipes from the injectors and the common fuel rail at the rear of the cylinder head – counterhold the unions with a second spanner **(see illustrations)**. Plug the openings to prevent dirt ingress.

11 Undo the 2 bolts securing the cylinder head cover/inlet manifold. Lift the assembly away **(see illustration)**. Recover the manifold rubber seals.

Refitting

12 Refitting is a reversal of removal, bearing in mind the following points:
  a) *Examine the seals for signs of damage and deterioration, and renew if necessary. Smear a little clean engine oil on the manifold seals.*
  b) *Renew the fuel injector high-pressure pipes – see Chapter 4C.*

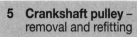

5	Crankshaft pulley – removal and refitting

Removal

1 Remove the auxiliary drivebelt as described in Chapter 1B.
2 To lock the crankshaft, working underneath the engine, insert Citroën/Peugeot tool No 0194-C into the hole in the right-hand face of the engine block casting over the lower section of the flywheel. Rotate the crankshaft until the tool engages in the corresponding hole in the flywheel. In the absence of the Citroën/Peugeot tool, insert a 12 mm rod or drill into the hole **(see illustration)**. **Note:** *The hole in the casting and the hole in the flywheel are provided purely to lock the crankshaft whilst the pulley bolt is undone, it does not position the crankshaft at TDC.*
3 Using a suitable socket and extension bar, unscrew the retaining bolt, remove the washer, then slide the pulley off the end of the crankshaft **(see illustration)**. If the pulley is tight fit, it can be drawn off the crankshaft using a suitable puller. If a puller is being used, refit the pulley retaining bolt without the washer to avoid damaging the crankshaft as the puller is tightened.

5.2 The locking pin/bolt (arrowed) must locate in the hole in the flywheel (arrowed) to prevent rotation

Caution: Do not touch the outer magnetic sensor ring of the sprocket with your fingers, or allow metallic particles to come into contact with it.

Refitting

4 Refit the pulley to the end of the crankshaft.
5 Thoroughly clean the threads of the pulley retaining bolt, then apply a coat of locking compound to the bolt threads. Citroën/Peugeot recommend the use of Loctite (available from your Citroën/Peugeot dealer); in the absence of this, any good-quality locking compound may be used.
6 Refit the crankshaft pulley retaining bolt and washer. Tighten the bolt to the specified torque, then through the specified angle, preventing the crankshaft from turning using the method employed on removal.

6.2a Unclip the fuel pipes (arrowed) . . .

5.3 Undo the crankshaft pulley retaining bolt (arrowed)

7 Refit and tension the auxiliary drivebelt as described in Chapter 1B.

6	Timing belt covers – removal and refitting

⚠ *Warning: Refer to the precautionary information contained in Section 1 before proceeding.*

Removal

Upper cover

1 Remove the plastic cover from the top of the engine.
2 Release the wiring harness and fuel pipes from the upper cover **(see illustrations)**.

6.2b . . . and the wiring harness (arrowed) from the timing belt upper cover

3 Undo the five screws and remove the timing belt upper cover **(see illustration)**.

Lower cover

4 Remove the upper cover as described previously.

5 Remove the crankshaft pulley as described in Section 5.

6 Remove the auxiliary drivebelt tensioner locking tool (where applicable), then undo the five bolts and remove the lower cover **(see illustration)**.

Refitting

7 Refitting of all the covers is a reversal of the relevant removal procedure, ensuring that each cover section is correctly located, and that the cover retaining bolts are securely tightened. Ensure that all disturbed hoses are reconnected and retained by their relevant clips.

---

7 Timing belt – removal, inspection, refitting and tensioning

General

1 The timing belt drives the inlet camshaft, high-pressure fuel pump, and coolant pump from a toothed sprocket on the end of the crankshaft. If the belt breaks or slips in service, the pistons are likely to hit the valve heads, resulting in expensive damage.

2 The timing belt should be renewed at the specified intervals, or earlier if it is contaminated with oil, or at all noisy in operation (a 'scraping' noise due to uneven wear).

3 If the timing belt is being removed, it is a wise precaution to check the condition of the coolant pump at the same time (check for signs of coolant leakage). This may avoid the need to remove the timing belt again at a later stage should the coolant pump fail.

Removal

4 Apply the handbrake then jack up the front of the vehicle and support it on axle stands (see *Jacking and vehicle support*). Remove the front right-hand roadwheel, wheel arch liner (to expose the crankshaft pulley), and the engine

6.3 Upper timing belt cover screws (arrowed)

undershield. The wheel arch liner is secured by several plastic expanding rivets/nuts/plastic clips. Push the centre pins in a little then prise the rivets from place. The engine undershield is retained by several screws.

5 Remove the auxiliary drivebelt as described in Chapter 1B.

6 Remove the upper and lower timing belt covers, as described in Section 6.

7 Refer to Chapter 4C and disconnect the front exhaust pipe at the flexible section.

8 Position a trolley jack under the engine, and using a block of wood on the jack head, take the weight of the engine.

9 Undo the bolts/nut and remove the right-hand engine mounting and support bracket – see Section 17.

10 Undo the screw and remove the crankshaft position sensor adjacent to the crankshaft sprocket flange, and move it to one side **(see illustration)**.

11 Undo the retaining screw and remove the timing belt protection bracket, again adjacent to the crankshaft sprocket flange **(see illustration)**.

12 Lock the crankshaft and camshaft in the correct position as described in Section 3. If necessary, temporarily refit the crankshaft pulley bolt to enable the crankshaft to be rotated. At this stage, it is of no consequence that the fuel pump sprocket aligns correctly with the hole in the pump mounting bracket.

13 Insert a hexagon key into the belt tensioner pulley centre, slacken the pulley bolt, and allow the tensioner to rotate, relieving the belt tension **(see illustration)**. With the belt slack, temporarily tighten the pulley bolt.

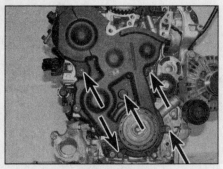

6.6 Lower timing belt cover screws (arrowed)

14 Note its routing, then remove the timing belt from the sprockets.

Inspection

15 Renew the belt as a matter of course, regardless of its apparent condition. The cost of a new belt is nothing compared with the cost of repairs should the belt break in service. If signs of oil contamination are found, trace the source of the oil leak and rectify it. Wash down the engine timing belt area and all related components, to remove all traces of oil. Check that the tensioner and idler pulleys rotate freely without any sign of roughness, and also check that the coolant pump pulley rotates freely. If necessary, renew these items.

Refitting and tensioning

16 Commence refitting by ensuring that the crankshaft and camshaft timing pins are still in position correctly. Also, where a Bosch high-pressure fuel pump is fitted, locate and lock the fuel pump sprocket in its correct position as described in Section 3.

17 Locate the timing belt on the crankshaft sprocket, then keeping it taut, locate it around the idler pulley, camshaft sprocket, high-pressure pump sprocket, coolant pump sprocket, and the tensioner pulley **(see illustration)**. If the timing belt has directional arrows on it, make sure that they point in the direction of normal engine rotation.

18 Refit the timing belt protection bracket and tighten the retaining bolt securely.

19 Slacken the tensioner pulley bolt, and using a hexagonal key, rotate the tensioner anti-clockwise, which moves the index arm

7.10 Undo the bolt (arrowed) and remove the crankshaft position sensor

7.11 Remove the timing belt protection bracket

7.13 Slacken the bolt and allow the tensioner to rotate, relieving the tension on the belt

7.17 Timing belt routing

7.19 The index arm must align with the lug (arrowed)

clockwise, until the index arm is aligned as shown **(see illustration)**.

20 Remove the camshaft and crankshaft and fuel pump timing pins and, using a socket on the crankshaft pulley bolt, crankshaft clockwise 10 complete revolutions. Align the camshaft and crankshaft timing holes and check that the timing pins can be inserted, then remove them. There is no requirement to check the fuel pump sprocket alignment, as it will only be aligned after 12 complete revolutions.

A sprocket holding tool can be made from two lengths of steel strip bolted together to form a forked end. Drill holes and insert bolts in the ends of the fork to engage with the sprocket spokes.

21 Check that the tensioner index arm is still aligned between the edges of the area shown **(see illustration 7.19)**. If it is not, remove and belt and begin the refitting process again, starting at Paragraph 19.

22 The remainder of refitting is a reversal of removal. Tighten all fasteners to the specified torque where given.

8 Timing belt sprockets and tensioner – removal and refitting

Camshaft sprocket

Removal

1 Remove the timing belt as described in Section 7.

2 Remove the locking tool from the camshaft sprocket/hub. Slacken the sprocket hub retaining bolt. To prevent the camshaft rotating as the bolt is slackened, a sprocket holding tool will be required. In the absence of the special Citroën/Peugeot tool, an acceptable substitute can be fabricated at home **(see Tool Tip 1)**. *Do not* attempt to use the engine assembly/valve timing locking tool to prevent the sprocket from rotating whilst the bolt is slackened.

3 Remove the sprocket hub retaining bolt,

and slide the sprocket and hub off the end of the camshaft.

4 Clean the camshaft sprocket thoroughly, and renew it if there are any signs of wear, damage or cracks.

Refitting

5 Refit the camshaft sprocket to the camshaft **(see illustration)**.

6 Refit the sprocket hub retaining bolt. Tighten the bolt to the specified torque, preventing the camshaft from turning as during removal.

7 Align the engine assembly/valve timing slot in the camshaft sprocket hub with the hole in the cylinder head and refit the timing pin to lock the camshaft in position.

8 Fit the timing belt around the pump sprocket and camshaft sprocket, and tension the timing belt as described in Section 7.

Crankshaft sprocket

Removal

9 Remove the timing belt as described in Section 7.

10 Check that the engine assembly/valve timing holes are still aligned as described in Section 3, and the camshaft sprocket and flywheel are locked in position.

11 Slide the sprocket off the end of the crankshaft and collect the Woodruff key **(see illustrations)**.

8.5 Ensure the lug on the sprocket hub engages with the slot on the end of the camshaft (arrowed)

8.11a Slide the sprocket from the crankshaft . . .

8.11b . . . and recover the Woodruff key

8.17 Insert a suitable drill bit through the sprocket into the hole in the backplate

12 Examine the crankshaft oil seal for signs of oil leakage and, if necessary, renew it as described in Section 14.

13 Clean the crankshaft sprocket thoroughly, and renew it if there are any signs of wear, damage or cracks. Recover the crankshaft locating key.

Refitting

14 Refit the key to the end of the crankshaft, then refit the crankshaft sprocket (with the flange facing the crankshaft pulley).

15 Fit the timing belt around the crankshaft sprocket, and tension the timing belt as described in Section 7.

Fuel pump sprocket

Removal

16 Remove the timing belt as described in Section 7.

17 Using a suitable socket, undo the pump sprocket retaining nut. The sprocket can be held stationary by inserting a suitably sized locking pin, drill or rod through the hole in the sprocket, and into the corresponding hole in the backplate **(see illustration)**, or by using a suitable forked tool engaged with the holes in the sprocket **(see Tool Tip 1 on previous page)**. **Note:** *On some engines, a hole is provided at the 5 o'clock position for locking purposes only, however, the timing position hole is at the 12 o'clock position.*

18 The pump sprocket is a taper fit on the pump shaft and it will be necessary to make up another tool to release it from the taper **(see Tool Tip 2)**.

19 On late models where the sprocket is keyed to the shaft, unscrew the retaining nut and remove the sprocket, then recover the Woodruff key. On early models where the sprocket is **not** keyed to the shaft, partially unscrew the sprocket retaining nut, then fit the home-made tool, and secure it to the sprocket with two suitable bolts. Prevent the sprocket from rotating as before, and unscrew the sprocket retaining nut. The nut will bear against the tool as it is undone, forcing the sprocket off the shaft taper. Once the taper is released, remove the tool, unscrew the nut fully, and remove the sprocket from the pump shaft.

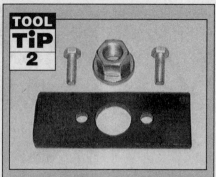

Make a sprocket releasing tool from a short strip of steel. Drill two holes in the strip to correspond with the two holes in the sprocket. Drill a third hole just large enough to accept the flats of the sprocket retaining nut.

20 Clean the sprocket thoroughly, and renew it if there are any signs of wear, damage or cracks.

Refitting

21 Refit the Woodruff key (late models only) then refit the pump sprocket and retaining nut, and tighten the nut to the specified torque. Prevent the sprocket rotating as the nut is tightened using the sprocket holding tool.

22 Fit the timing belt around the pump sprocket, and tension the timing belt as described in Section 7.

Coolant pump sprocket

23 The coolant pump sprocket is integral with the pump, and cannot be removed. Coolant pump removal is described in Chapter 3.

Tensioner pulley

Removal

24 Remove the timing belt as described in Section 7.

25 Remove the tensioner pulley retaining bolt, and slide the pulley off its mounting stud.

26 Clean the tensioner pulley, but do not use any strong solvent which may enter the pulley bearings. Check that the pulley rotates freely, with no sign of stiffness or free play. Renew the pulley if there is any doubt about its condition, or if there are any obvious signs of wear or damage.

27 Examine the pulley mounting stud for signs of damage and if necessary, renew it.

Refitting

28 Refit the tensioner pulley to its mounting stud, and fit the retaining bolt.

29 Refit the timing belt as described in Section 7.

Idler pulley

Removal

30 Remove the timing belt as described in Section 7.

31 Undo the retaining bolt/nut and withdraw the idler pulley from the engine **(see illustration)**.

8.31 Timing belt idler pulley retaining nut (arrowed)

32 Clean the idler pulley, but do not use any strong solvent which may enter the bearings. Check that the pulley rotates freely, with no sign of stiffness or free play. Renew the idler pulley if there is any doubt about its condition, or if there are any obvious signs of wear or damage.

Refitting

33 Locate the idler pulley on the engine, and fit the retaining bolt/nut. Tighten the bolt/nut to the specified torque.

34 Refit the timing belt (see Section 7).

9 Camshafts, rocker arms and hydraulic tappets – removal, inspection and refitting

Removal

1 Remove the cylinder head cover/manifold as described in Section 4.

2 Remove the injectors as described in Chapter 4C.

3 Remove the camshaft sprocket as described in Section 8.

4 Refit the right-hand engine mounting, but only tighten the bolts moderately; this will keep the engine supported during the camshaft removal.

5 Undo the bolts and remove the vacuum pump. Recover the pump O-ring seals **(see illustration)**.

6 Remove the fuel filter (see Chapter 1B), then undo the bolts and remove the fuel filter mounting bracket.

9.5 Vacuum pump bolts (arrowed)

7 Release the wiring harness clips, then undo the 3 bolts and remove the timing belt inner, upper cover **(see illustration)**.

8 Disconnect the wiring plug, unscrew the retaining bolt, and remove the camshaft position sensor from the camshaft cover/bearing ladder.

9 Undo the 5 bolts and remove the upper rear section of the turbocharger heat shield, then working gradually and evenly, slacken and remove the bolts securing the camshaft cover/bearing ladder to the cylinder head in sequence **(see illustrations)**. Lift the cover/ladder from position complete with the camshafts.

10 Undo the retaining bolts and remove the bearing caps. Note their fitted positions, as they must be refitted into their original positions **(see illustration)**. Note that the bearing caps are marked A for inlet, and E for exhaust, and 1 to 4 from the flywheel end of the cylinder head.

11 Undo the bolts securing the chain tensioner assembly to the camshaft cover/bearing ladder, then lift the camshafts, chain and tensioner from place **(see illustrations)**. Discard the camshaft oil seal.

12 Obtain 16 small, clean plastic containers, and number them 1 to 8 inlet and 1 to 8 exhaust; alternatively, divide a larger container into 16 compartments.

13 Lift out each rocker arm. Place the rocker arms in their respective positions in the box or containers.

14 A compartmentalised container filled with engine oil is now required to retain the hydraulic tappets while they are removed from the cylinder head. Withdraw each hydraulic follower and place it in the container, keeping them each identified for correct refitting. The tappets must be totally submerged in the oil to prevent air entering them.

Inspection

15 Inspect the cam lobes and the camshaft bearing journals for scoring or other visible evidence of wear. Once the surface hardening of the cam lobes has been eroded, wear will occur at an accelerated rate. **Note:** *If these symptoms are visible on the tips of the camshaft lobes, check the corresponding rocker arm, as it will probably be worn as well.*

16 Examine the condition of the bearing surfaces in the cylinder head and camshaft bearing housing. If wear is evident, the cylinder head and bearing housing will both have to be renewed, as they are a matched assembly.

17 Inspect the rocker arms and tappets for scuffing, cracking or other damage and renew any components as necessary. Also check the condition of the tappet bores in the cylinder head. As with the camshafts, any wear in this area will necessitate cylinder head renewal.

Refitting

18 Thoroughly clean the sealant from the mating surfaces of the cylinder head and camshaft bearing housing. Use a suitable liquid gasket dissolving agent (available from Citroën/Peugeot dealers) together with a soft putty knife; do not use a metal scraper or the faces will be damaged. As there is no conventional gasket used, the cleanliness of the mating faces is of the utmost importance. Prise out the oil injector oil seals from the camshaft bearing housing.

19 Clean off any oil, dirt or grease from both components and dry with a clean lint-free cloth. Ensure that all the oilways are completely clean.

20 Liberally lubricate the hydraulic tappet bores in the cylinder head with clean engine oil.

9.7 Timing belt inner, upper cover bolts (arrowed)

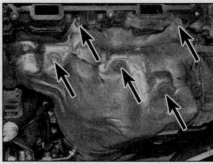
9.9a Undo the bolts (arrowed) and remove the rear section of the heat shield

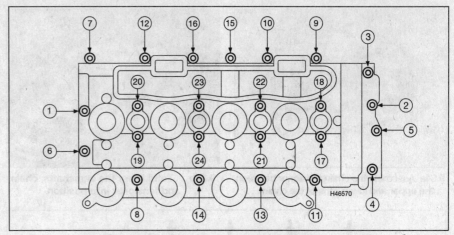
9.9b Camshaft cover/bearing ladder bolt slackening sequence

9.10 The camshaft bearing caps are numbered 1 to 4 from the flywheel end – A for inlet, and E for exhaust (arrowed)

9.11a Undo the tensioner bolts (arrowed) . . .

9.11b . . . then lift the camshafts, chain and tensioner from place

9.21 Refit the hydraulic tappets . . .

9.22 . . . and rocker arms to their original locations

9.23 Align the marks on the sprockets with the centre of the black-coloured chain links (arrowed). There must be 12 link pins between the sprocket marks

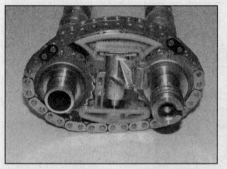

9.24a Assemble the chain tensioner between the upper and lower runs of the chain . . .

9.24b . . . and lower the camshafts, chain and tensioner into position

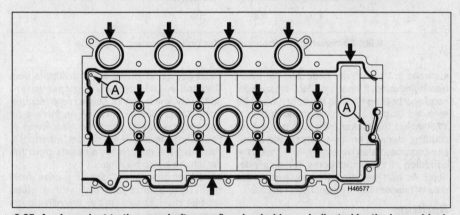

9.25 Apply sealant to the camshaft cover/bearing ladder as indicated by the heavy black lines. Ensure sealant does not enter the tensioner oil holes – marked A

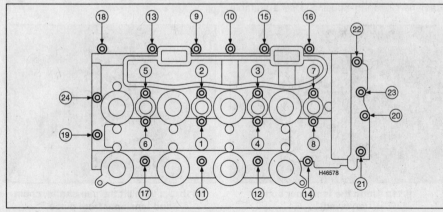

9.26 Camshaft cover/bearing ladder bolt tightening sequence

21 Insert the hydraulic tappets into their original bores in the cylinder head unless they have been renewed (see illustration).

22 Lubricate the rocker arms and place them over their respective tappets and valve stems (see illustration).

23 Engage the timing chain around the camshaft sprockets, aligning the black-coloured links with the marked teeth on the camshaft sprockets (see illustration). If the black colouring has been lost, there must be 12 chain link pins between the marks on the sprockets.

24 Fit the chain tensioner between the upper and lower runs of the chain, then lubricate the bearing surfaces with clean engine oil, and fit the camshafts into position on the underside of the camshaft cover/bearing ladder. Refit the bearing caps to their original positions and tighten the retaining bolts to the specified torque (see illustrations). Tighten the tensioner retaining bolts to the specified torque.

25 Apply a thin bead of sealant to the mating surface of the camshaft cover/bearing ladder as shown. Citroën/Peugeot recommend the use of Autojoint Noir (see illustration). Do not allow the sealant to obstruct the oil channels for the hydraulic chain tensioner.

26 Check that the black-coloured links on the chain are still aligned with the marks on the camshaft sprockets, then refit the camshaft cover/bearing ladder, and gradually and evenly tighten the retaining bolts until the cover/ladder is in contact with the cylinder head, then tighten the bolts to the specified torque in sequence (see illustration). Note: Ensure the cover/ladder is correctly located by checking the bores of the vacuum pump and camshaft oil seal at each end of the cover/ladder.

27 Fit a new camshaft oil seal as described in Section 14.

28 Refit the camshaft sprocket, and tighten the retaining bolt finger-tight.

29 Using a spanner on the camshaft sprocket bolt, rotate the camshafts approximately 40 complete revolutions clockwise. Check the black-coloured links on the chain still align with the marks on the camshaft sprockets.

30 If the marks still align, refit the camshaft sprocket as described in Section 8.

31 Refit and adjust the camshaft position sensor as described in Chapter 4C.
32 Press the new oil seals into the bearing housing, using a tube/socket of approximately 20 mm outside diameter, ensuring the inner lip of the seal fits around the injector guide tube **(see illustrations)**. Refit the injectors as described in Chapter 4C.
33 Refit the cylinder head cover/manifold as described in Section 4.

10 Cylinder head –
removal and refitting

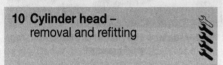

9.32a Fit the new seal around a 20 mm outside diameter socket . . .

9.32b . . . and push it into place

Removal

1 Apply the handbrake then jack up the front of the vehicle and support it on axle stands (see *Jacking and vehicle support*). Remove the front right-hand roadwheel, the engine undershield, and the front wheel arch liner. The undershield is secured by several screws, and the wheel arch liner is secured by several plastic expanding rivets/nuts/plastic clips. Push the centre pins in a little, then prise the rivet from place.
2 Disconnect the battery negative lead as described in Chapter 5A.
3 Drain the cooling system as described in Chapter 1B.
4 Remove the camshafts, rocker arms and hydraulic tappets as described in Section 9.
5 Remove the turbocharger as described in Chapter 4C.

6 Remove the glow plugs as described in Chapter 5C.
7 Where applicable, undo the 3 mounting bolts and move the power steering pump to one side (there's no need to disconnect the hoses).
8 Undo the upper mounting bolts, and pivot the alternator away from the engine, undo the oil dipstick guide tube bolt, then undo the bolts securing the alternator/power steering pump mounting bracket to the cylinder head/block **(see illustration)**.
9 Undo the coolant outlet housing (left-hand end of the cylinder head) retaining bolts, slacken the two bolts securing the housing support bracket to the top of the transmission bellhousing, and move the outlet housing away from the cylinder head a little **(see illustration)**. There is no need to disconnect the hoses.
10 Disconnect the high-pressure fuel pipe from the common rail to the pump, and

disconnect the fuel supply and return hoses. Remove the bracket at the rear of the pump, then undo the bolt/nut and remove the pump and mounting bracket as an assembly **(see illustrations)**. Note that a new high-pressure pipe must be fitted – see Chapter 4C.
11 Working in the **reverse** of the sequence shown **(see illustration 10.32)** undo the cylinder head bolts.
12 Release the cylinder head from the cylinder block and location dowels by rocking it. The Citroën/Peugeot tool for doing this consists simply of two metal rods with 90-degree angled ends **(see illustration)**. Do not prise between the mating faces of the cylinder head and block, as this may damage the gasket faces.
13 Lift the cylinder head from the block, and recover the gasket.
14 If necessary, remove the exhaust manifold with reference to Chapter 4C.

10.8 The engine oil level dipstick is secured to the alternator bracket by a Torx bolt (arrowed)

10.9 Undo the bolts (arrowed) and pull the coolant outlet housing from the left-hand end of the cylinder head

10.10a Remove the high-pressure pipe (arrowed) . . .

10.10b . . . and the bracket (arrowed)

10.10c Pump mounting bracket upper nut and lower mounting bolt (arrowed)

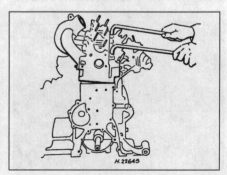

10.12 Free the cylinder head using angled rods

10.17a Pull the non-return valve from the cylinder head . . .

10.17b . . . and push a new one into place

10.21 Measure the piston protrusion using a DTI gauge

Preparation for refitting

15 The mating faces of the cylinder head and cylinder block must be perfectly clean before refitting the head. Citroën/Peugeot recommend the use of a scouring agent for this purpose, but acceptable results can be achieved by using a hard plastic or wood scraper to remove all traces of gasket and carbon. The same method can be used to clean the piston crowns. Take particular care to avoid scoring or gouging the cylinder head/cylinder block mating surfaces during the cleaning operations, as aluminium alloy is easily damaged. Make sure that the carbon is not allowed to enter the oil and water passages – this is particularly important for the lubrication system, as carbon could block the oil supply to the engine's components. Using adhesive tape and paper, seal the water, oil and bolt holes in the cylinder block. To prevent carbon entering the gap between the pistons and bores, smear a little grease in the gap. After cleaning each piston, use a small brush to remove all traces of grease and carbon from the gap, then wipe away the remainder with a clean rag.

16 Check the mating surfaces of the cylinder block and the cylinder head for nicks, deep scratches and other damage. If slight, they may be removed carefully with a file, but if excessive, machining may be the only alternative to renewal. If warpage of the cylinder head gasket surface is suspected, use a straight-edge to check it for distortion. Refer to Part F of this Chapter if necessary.

17 Thoroughly clean the threads of the cylinder head bolt holes in the cylinder block. Ensure that the bolts run freely in their threads, and that all traces of oil and water are removed from each bolt hole. If required, pull the oil feed non-return valve from the cylinder head, and check the ball moves freely. Push a new valve into place if necessary **(see illustrations)**.

Gasket selection

18 Remove the crankshaft timing pin, then turn the crankshaft until pistons 1 and 4 are at TDC (Top Dead Centre). Position a dial test indicator (dial gauge) on the cylinder block adjacent to the rear of No 1 piston, and zero it on the block face. Transfer the probe to the crown of No 1 piston (10.0 mm in from the rear edge), then slowly turn the crankshaft back-and-forth past TDC, noting the highest reading on the indicator. Record this reading as protrusion A.

19 Repeat the check described in paragraph 18, this time 10.0 mm in from the front edge of the No 1 piston crown. Record this reading as protrusion B.

20 Add protrusion A to protrusion B, then divide the result by 2 to obtain an average reading for piston No 1.

21 Repeat the procedure described in paragraphs 18 to 20 on piston 4, then turn the crankshaft through 180° and carry out the procedure on the piston Nos 2 and 3 **(see illustration)**. Check that there is a maximum difference of 0.07 mm protrusion between any two pistons.

22 If a dial test indicator is not available, piston protrusion may be measured using a straight-edge and feeler blades or Vernier calipers. However, this is much less accurate, and cannot therefore be recommended.

23 Note the greatest piston protrusion measurement, and use this to determine the correct cylinder head gasket from the following table. The series of notches/holes on the side of the gasket are used for thickness identification **(see illustration)**.

Piston protrusion	Gasket identification
0.6115 to 0.720 mm	2 notches
0.721 to 0.770 mm	3 notches
0.771 to 0.820 mm	1 notches
0.821 to 0.870 mm	4 notches
0.871 to 0.977 mm	5 notches

Head bolt examination

24 Carefully examine the cylinder head bolts for signs of damage to the threads or head, and for any sign of corrosion. If the bolts are in a satisfactory condition, measure the length of each bolt from the underside of the head to the end of the shank. The bolts may be re-used providing that the measured length does not exceed 149.0 mm **(see illustration)**. **Note:** *Considering the stress to which the cylinder head bolts are subjected, it is highly recommended that they are all renewed, regardless of their apparent condition.*

Refitting

25 Turn the crankshaft and position Nos 1 and 4 pistons at TDC, then turn the crankshaft a quarter turn (90°) anti-clockwise.

26 Thoroughly clean the surfaces of the cylinder head and block.

27 Make sure that the locating dowels are in place, then fit the correct gasket the right way round on the cylinder block **(see illustration)**.

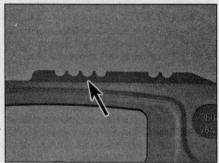

10.23 Cylinder head gasket thickness identification notches (arrowed)

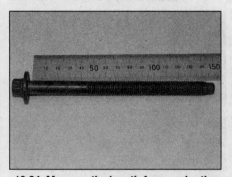

10.24 Measure the length from under the bolt head to its end

10.27 Ensure the gasket locates over the dowels (arrowed)

28 If necessary, refit the exhaust manifold to the cylinder head as described in Chapter 4C.
29 Carefully lower the cylinder head onto the gasket and block, making sure that it locates correctly onto the dowels.
30 Apply a smear of grease to the threads, and to the underside of the heads, of the cylinder head bolts. Citroën/Peugeot recommend the use of Molykote G Rapid Plus (available from your Citroën/Peugeot dealer); in the absence of the specified grease, any good-quality high melting-point grease may be used.
31 Carefully insert the cylinder head bolts into their holes (*do not drop them in*) and initially finger-tighten them.
32 Working progressively and in sequence, tighten the cylinder head bolts to their Stage 1 torque setting, using a torque wrench and suitable socket **(see illustration)**.
33 Once all the bolts have been tightened to their Stage 1 torque setting, working again in the specified sequence, tighten each bolt to the specified Stage 2 setting. Finally, angle-tighten the bolts through the specified Stage 3 angle. It is recommended that an angle-measuring gauge is used during this stage of tightening, to ensure accuracy. **Note:** *Retightening of the cylinder head bolts after running the engine is not required.*
34 Refit the hydraulic tappets, rocker arms, and camshaft housing (complete with camshafts) as described in Section 9.
35 Refit the timing belt as described in Section 7.
36 The remainder of refitting is a reversal of removal, noting the following points.
  a) *Use a new seal when refitting the coolant outlet housing.*
  b) *When refitting a cylinder head, it is good practice to renew the thermostat.*
  c) *Refit the camshaft position sensor and set the air gap with reference to Chapter 4C.*
  d) *Tighten all fasteners to the specified torque where given.*
  e) *Refill the cooling system as described in Chapter 1B.*
  f) *The engine may run erratically for the first few miles, until the engine management ECU relearns its stored values.*

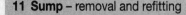

11 Sump – removal and refitting

Removal

1 Drain the engine oil, then clean and refit the engine oil drain plug, tightening it securely. If the engine is nearing the service interval when the oil and filter are due for renewal, it is recommended that the filter is also removed, and a new one fitted. After reassembly, the engine can then be refilled with fresh oil. Refer to Chapter 1B for further information.
2 Apply the handbrake then jack up the front of the vehicle and support it on axle stands

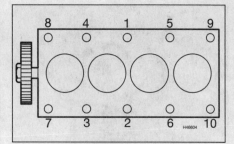

10.32 Cylinder head bolt tightening sequence

(see *Jacking and vehicle support*). Undo the screws and remove the engine undershield.
3 Remove the exhaust front pipe as described in Chapter 4C.
4 Where necessary, disconnect the wiring connector from the oil temperature sender unit, which is screwed into the sump. Also where necessary, unscrew the bolts securing the air conditioning compressor to the sump.
5 Progressively slacken and remove all the sump retaining bolts/nuts. Since the sump bolts vary in length, remove each bolt in turn, and store it in its correct fitted order by pushing it through a clearly-marked cardboard template. This will avoid the possibility of installing the bolts in the wrong locations on refitting.
6 Try to break the joint by striking the sump with the palm of your hand, then lower and withdraw the sump from under the car. If the sump is stuck (which is quite likely) use a putty knife or similar, carefully inserted between the sump and block. Ease the knife along the joint until the sump is released. While the sump is removed, take the opportunity to check the oil pump pick-up/strainer for signs of clogging or splitting. If necessary, remove the pump as described in Section 12, and clean or renew the strainer.

Refitting

7 Clean all traces of sealant from the mating surfaces of the cylinder block/crankcase and sump, then use a clean rag to wipe out the sump and the engine's interior.
8 On engines where the sump was fitted without a gasket, ensure that the sump mating surfaces are clean and dry, then apply a thin coating of suitable sealant to the sump or crankcase mating surface **(see illustration)**.
9 Offer up the sump to the cylinder block/crankcase. Refit its retaining bolts/nuts, ensuring

11.9 Refit the sump and tighten the bolts

11.8 Apply a bead of sealant to the sump or crankcase mating surface. Ensure the sealant is applied on the inside of the retaining bolt holes

that each bolt is screwed into its original location. Tighten the bolts evenly and progressively to the specified torque setting **(see illustration)**.
10 Where necessary, align the air conditioning compressor with its mountings on the sump, and insert the retaining bolts. Securely tighten the compressor retaining bolts, then refit the drivebelt as described in Chapter 1B.
11 Refit the exhaust front pipe as described in Chapter 4C.
12 Reconnect the wiring connector to the oil temperature sensor (where fitted).
13 Refit the undershield and lower the vehicle to the ground, then refill the engine with oil as described in Chapter 1B.

12 Oil pump – removal, inspection and refitting

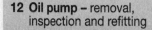

Removal

1 Remove the crankshaft sprocket as described in Section 8. Recover the locating key from the crankshaft.
2 Temporarily refit the right-hand engine mounting and support bracket, and remove the trolley jack, then remove the sump as described in Section 11.
3 Disconnect the wiring plug, undo the bolts and remove the crankshaft position sensor, located on the right-hand end of the cylinder block.
4 Undo the three Allen screws and remove the oil pump pick-up tube from the pump/block **(see illustration)**. Discard the oil seal, a new one must be fitted.

12.4 Oil pick-up tube Allen screws (arrowed)

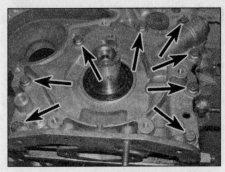

12.5 Oil pump retaining bolts (arrowed)

12.6 Undo the Torx bolts and remove the pump cover

12.7a Remove the circlip . . .

12.7b . . . cap . . .

12.7c . . . spring . . .

12.7d . . . and piston

5 Undo the 8 bolts, and remove the oil pump (see illustration).

Inspection

6 Undo and remove the Torx bolts securing the cover to the oil pump (see illustration). Examine the pump rotors and body for signs of wear and damage. If worn, the complete pump must be renewed.

7 Remove the circlip, and extract the cap, valve piston and spring, noting which way around they are fitted (see illustrations). The condition of the relief valve spring can only be measured by comparing it with a new one; if there is any doubt about its condition, it should also be renewed.

8 Refit the relief valve piston and spring, then secure them in place with the circlip.

9 Refit the cover to the oil pump, and tighten the Torx bolts securely.

Refitting

10 Remove all traces of sealant, and thoroughly clean the mating surfaces of the oil pump and cylinder block.

11 Apply a 4 mm wide bead of silicone sealant to the mating face of the cylinder block (see illustration). Ensure that no sealant enters any of the holes in the block.

12 With a new oil seal fitted, refit the oil pump over the end of the crankshaft, aligning the flats in the pump drivegear with the flats machined in the crankshaft (see illustrations). Note that new oil pumps are supplied with the oil seal already fitted, and a seal protector sleeve. The sleeve fits over the end of the crankshaft to protect the seal as the pump is fitted.

13 Install the oil pump bolts and tighten them to the specified torque.

14 Refit the oil pick-up tube to the pump/ cylinder block using a new O-ring seal. Ensure the oil dipstick guide tube is correctly refitted.

15 Refit the Woodruff key to the crankshaft, and slide the crankshaft sprocket into place.

16 The remainder of refitting is a reversal of removal.

12.11 Apply a bead of sealant to the cylinder block mating surface

12.12a Fit a new seal . . .

12.12b . . . align the pump gear flats (arrowed) . . .

12.12c . . . with those of the crankshaft (arrowed)

13 Oil cooler – removal and refitting

Removal

1 Apply the handbrake then jack up the front of the vehicle and support it on axle stands (see *Jacking and vehicle support*). Undo the screws and remove the engine undershield.
2 The oil cooler is fitted to the front of the oil filter housing. Drain the coolant as described in Chapter 1B.
3 Drain the engine oil as described in Chapter 1B, or be prepared for fluid spillage.
4 Undo the 5 bolts/stud and remove the oil cooler. Recover the O-ring seals **(see illustrations)**.

Refitting

5 Fit new O-ring seals into the recesses in the oil filter housing, and refit the cooler. Tighten the bolts securely.
6 Refill or top-up the cooling system and engine oil level as described in Chapter 1B or *Weekly checks* (as applicable). Start the engine, and check the oil cooler for signs of leakage.

14 Oil seals – renewal
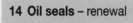

Crankshaft

Right-hand oil seal

1 Remove the crankshaft sprocket and Woodruff key as described in Section 8.
2 Measure and note the fitted depth of the oil seal.
3 Pull the oil seal from the housing using a screwdriver. Alternatively, drill a small hole in the oil seal, and use a self-tapping screw and a pair of pliers to remove it **(see illustration)**.
4 Clean the oil seal housing and the crankshaft sealing surface.
5 The seal has a Teflon lip and must not be oiled or marked. The new seal should be supplied with a protector sleeve, which fits over the end of the crankshaft to prevent any

13.4a Undo the oil cooler bolts/stud (arrowed)

damage to the seal lip. With the sleeve in place, press the seal (open end first) into the pump to the previously-noted depth, using a suitable tube or socket **(see illustrations)**.
6 Where applicable, remove the plastic sleeve from the end of the crankshaft.
7 Refit the timing belt crankshaft sprocket as described in Section 8.

Left-hand oil seal

8 Remove the flywheel, as described in Section 16.
9 Measure and note the fitted depth of the oil seal.
10 Pull the oil seal from the housing using a screwdriver. Alternatively, drill a small hole in the oil seal, and use a self-tapping screw and a pair of pliers to remove it **(see illustration 14.3)**.
11 Clean the oil seal housing and the crankshaft sealing surface.
12 The seal has a Teflon lip and must not be oiled or marked. The new seal should be

14.3 Take great care not to mark the crankshaft whilst levering out the oil seal

13.4b Renew the O-ring seals (arrowed)

supplied with a protector sleeve, which fits over the end of the crankshaft to prevent any damage to the seal lip **(see illustration)**. With the sleeve in place, press the seal (open end first) into the housing to the previously-noted depth, using a suitable tube or socket.
13 Where applicable, remove the plastic sleeve from the end of the crankshaft.
14 Refit the flywheel, as described in Section 16.

Camshaft

15 Remove the camshaft sprocket as described in Section 8. In principle there is no need to remove the timing belt completely, but remember that if the belt has been contaminated with oil, it must be renewed.
16 Pull the oil seal from the housing using a hooked instrument. Alternatively, drill a small hole in the oil seal and use a self-tapping screw and a pair of pliers to remove it **(see illustration)**.

14.5a Slide the seal and protective sleeve over the end of the crankshaft . . .

14.5b . . . and press the seal into place

14.12 Slide the seal and protective sleeve over the left-hand end of the crankshaft

14.16 Drill a hole, insert a self-tapping screw, and pull the seal from place using pliers

14.18 Fit the protective sleeve and seal over the end of the camshaft

17 Clean the oil seal housing and the camshaft sealing surface.

18 The seal has a Teflon lip and must not be oiled or marked. The new seal should be supplied with a protector sleeve which fits over the end of the camshaft to prevent any damage to the seal lip **(see illustration)**. With the sleeve in place, press the seal (open end first) into the housing, using a suitable tube or socket which bears only of the outer edge of the seal.

19 Refit the camshaft sprocket as described in Section 8.

20 Where necessary, fit a new timing belt with reference to Section 7.

15 Oil pressure switch and level sensor – removal and refitting

Removal

Oil pressure switch

1 The oil pressure switch is located at the front of the cylinder block, adjacent to the oil dipstick guide tube. Note that on some models, access to the switch may be improved if the vehicle is jacked up and supported on axle stands, then undo the screws and remove the engine undershield so that the switch can be reached from underneath (see *Jacking and vehicle support*).

2 Remove the protective sleeve from the wiring plug (where applicable), then disconnect the wiring from the switch.

3 Unscrew the switch from the cylinder block, and recover the sealing washer **(see illustration)**.

15.3 The oil pressure switch is located on the front face of the cylinder block (arrowed)

Be prepared for oil spillage, and if the switch is to be left removed from the engine for any length of time, plug the hole in the cylinder block.

Oil level sensor

4 The oil level sensor is located at the rear of the cylinder block. Jack up the front of the vehicle and support it securely on axle stands (see *Jacking and vehicle support*). Undo the screws and remove the engine undershield.

5 Reach up between the driveshaft and the cylinder block and disconnect the sensor wiring plug **(see illustration)**.

6 Using an open-ended spanner, unscrew the sensor and withdraw it from position.

Refitting

Oil pressure switch

7 Examine the sealing washer for any signs of damage or deterioration, and if necessary renew.

8 Refit the switch, complete with washer, and tighten it to the specified torque.

9 Refit the engine undershield, and lower the vehicle to the ground.

Oil level sensor

10 Smear a little silicone sealant on the threads and refit the sensor to the cylinder block, tightening it securely.

11 Reconnect the sensor wiring plug.

12 Refit the engine undershield, and lower the vehicle to the ground.

16 Flywheel – removal, inspection and refitting

Removal

1 Remove the transmission as described in Chapter 7A, then remove the clutch assembly as described in Chapter 6.

2 Prevent the flywheel from turning by locking the ring gear teeth **(see illustration 5.2)**. Alternatively, bolt a strap between the flywheel and the cylinder block/crankcase. *Do not* attempt to lock the flywheel in position using the crankshaft pulley locking tool described in Section 3. Insert a 12 mm diameter rod or drill bit through the hole in the flywheel cover casting, and into a slot in the flywheel.

3 Make alignment marks between the

15.5 The oil level sensor is located on the rear face of the cylinder block (arrowed)

flywheel and crankshaft to aid refitting. Slacken and remove the flywheel retaining bolts, and remove the flywheel from the end of the crankshaft. Be careful not to drop it; it is heavy. If the flywheel locating dowel (where fitted) is a loose fit in the crankshaft end, remove it and store it with the flywheel for safe-keeping. Discard the flywheel bolts; new ones must be used on refitting.

Inspection

4 Examine the flywheel for scoring of the clutch face, and for wear or chipping of the ring gear teeth. If the clutch face is scored, the flywheel may be surface-ground, but renewal is preferable. Seek the advice of a Citroën/Peugeot dealer or engine reconditioning specialist to see if machining is possible. If the ring gear is worn or damaged, the flywheel must be renewed, as it is not possible to renew the ring gear separately.

Refitting

5 Clean the mating surfaces of the flywheel and crankshaft. Remove any remaining locking compound from the threads of the crankshaft holes, using the correct size of tap, if available.

6 If the new flywheel retaining bolts are not supplied with their threads already pre-coated, apply a suitable thread-locking compound to the threads of each bolt.

> **HAYNES HiNT**
>
> *If a suitable tap is not available, cut two slots along the threads of one of the old flywheel bolts, and use the bolt to remove the locking compound from the threads.*

Except engines with dual mass flywheel

7 Ensure that the locating dowel is in position. Offer up the flywheel, locating it on the dowel (where fitted), and fit the new retaining bolts. Where no locating dowel is fitted, align the previously-made marks to ensure the flywheel is refitted in its original position.

8 Lock the flywheel using the method employed on dismantling, and tighten the retaining bolts to the specified torque **(see illustration)**.

16.8 Flywheel retaining Torx bolts

17.7a Unscrew the mounting nut . . .

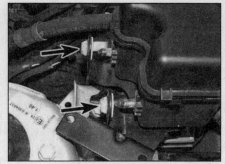

17.7b . . . then release the power steering fluid reservoir location pins from the support bracket . . .

17.7c . . . unbolt the reservoir support bracket . . .

Engines with dual mass flywheel

9 The dual mass flywheel is designed to reduce harshness and vibration in the action of the engine, clutch and transmission. With this type of flywheel, two flywheel centralising tools are needed (available from Citroën/Peugeot dealers). These are screwed into two opposite flywheel bolt holes in the crankshaft. As the tools are screwed down, their conical shape centralises the flywheel with regard to the crankshaft.

10 With the flywheel centralised, fit the new bolts into the remaining flywheel holes, then lock the flywheel using the same method employed on dismantling, and tighten the bolts to the specified torque.

11 Remove the two centralising tools, fit the new bolts and tighten them to the specified torque.

All models

12 Refit the clutch as described in Chapter 6. Remove the flywheel locking tool, and refit the transmission as described in Chapter 7A.

17 Engine/transmission mountings – inspection and renewal

Inspection

1 Apply the handbrake then jack up the front of the car and support it on axle stands (see *Jacking and vehicle support*). Undo the screws and remove the engine undershield.

2 Check the mounting rubbers to see if they are cracked, hardened or separated from the metal at any point; renew the mounting if any such damage or deterioration is evident.

3 Check that all the mountings' fasteners are securely tightened; use a torque wrench to check if possible.

4 Using a large screwdriver or a crowbar, check for wear in each mounting by carefully levering against it to check for free play. Where this is not possible, enlist the aid of an assistant to move the engine/transmission back-and-forth, or from side-to-side, while you watch the mounting. While some free play is to be expected even from new components, excessive wear should be obvious. If excessive free play is found, check first that the fasteners are correctly secured, then renew any worn components as described below.

Renewal

Right-hand mounting

5 Release all the relevant hoses and wiring from their retaining clips. Place the hoses/wiring clear of the mounting so that the removal procedure is not hindered. Undo the screws and remove the engine undershield.

6 Place a jack beneath the engine, with a block of wood on the jack head. Raise the jack until it is supporting the weight of the engine.

7 Unscrew the mounting nut and withdraw the power steering fluid reservoir from the mounting top bracket then place to one side without disconnecting the hoses. Unbolt and remove the reservoir support bracket and mounting top bracket (see illustrations).

8 Undo the three bolts securing the upper mounting bracket to the lower bracket on the engine (see illustration).

9 Unscrew the support pin from the mounting centre bolt.

10 Unscrew the centre bolt from the rubber mounting and remove the upper mounting bracket and buffers.

11 Unscrew the rubber mounting from the body bracket. The top rim of the mounting is slotted and a suitable tool will be required to engage the slots in order to unscrew the mounting.

12 If necessary, unbolt the lower mounting bracket from the engine (see illustration).

13 Check all components carefully for signs of wear or damage, and renew as necessary.

14 Where removed, refit the lower mounting bracket to the engine and tighten to the specified torque.

15 Refit the rubber mounting and tighten securely.

16 Refit the upper mounting bracket and buffers, insert the centre bolt and tighten to the specified torque.

17 Refit the support pin and tighten to the specified torque.

18 Refit the upper mounting bracket to the lower bracket, insert the bolts and tighten to the specified torque.

19 Refit the top bracket and tighten the bolts to the specified torque.

20 Refit the power steering fluid reservoir and tighten the nut securely.

17.7d . . . and mounting top bracket

17.8 Right-hand engine mounting upper bracket and support pin

17.12 Bolts securing the right-hand engine mounting lower bracket to the engine

17.24 Left-hand engine/transmission mounting

17.31 Rear engine mounting torque link

21 Refit the engine undershield, then remove the jack from underneath the engine.

Left-hand mounting

22 Remove the engine management ECU and module box as described in Chapter 4C.

23 Place a jack beneath the gearbox, with a block of wood on the jack head. Raise the jack until it is supporting the weight of the gearbox/engine.

24 Unscrew the nut from the centre pin, then unscrew the mounting nuts and remove the mounting upwards from the body and centre pin **(see illustration)**.

25 If necessary, unbolt the centre pin and bracket from the gearbox, noting the location of the spacer sleeve.

26 Check all components carefully for signs of wear or damage, and renew as necessary.

27 Where removed, refit the centre pin and bracket and tighten the bolts to the specified torque.

28 Refit the mounting and tighten the nuts to the specified torque, then refit the centre pin nut and tighten to the specified torque.

29 Remove the jack from underneath the transmission.

30 Refit the module box and ECU as described in Chapter 4C.

Rear engine mounting torque link

31 Unscrew and remove the centre bolt securing the movement limiter link to the driveshaft intermediate bearing housing **(see illustration)**.

32 Remove the bolt securing the link to the subframe. Withdraw the link.

33 To remove the intermediate bearing housing assembly it will first be necessary to remove the right-hand driveshaft as described in Chapter 8.

34 With the driveshaft removed, undo the retaining bolts and remove the bearing housing from the rear of the cylinder block.

35 Check carefully for signs of wear or damage on all components, and renew them where necessary. The rubber bush fitted to the bearing housing is available as a separate item (at the time of writing), and can be pressed out of, and back into place.

36 On reassembly, fit the bearing housing assembly to the rear of the cylinder block, and tighten its retaining bolts to the specified torque. Refit the driveshaft as described in Chapter 8.

37 Refit the movement limiter link, and tighten both its bolts to their specified torque settings. Refit the engine undershield.

38 Lower the vehicle to the ground.

Chapter 2 Part C:
1.8 and 1.9 litre diesel engine (XUD series) in-car repair procedures

Contents

Degrees of difficulty

Easy, suitable for novice with little experience	Fairly easy, suitable for beginner with some experience	Fairly difficult, suitable for competent DIY mechanic	Difficult, suitable for experienced DIY mechanic	Very difficult, suitable for expert DIY or professional

Specifications

Engine (general)

Designation:
1.8 litre (1769 cc) engine	XUD7
1.9 litre (1905 cc) engines.	XUD9

Engine codes*:
1.8 litre engine	A9A (XUD7L)
1.9 litre engine	D9B (XUD9A) or DJY (XUD9Y)

Bore:
1.8 litre engines	80.00 mm
1.9 litre engines	83.00 mm
Stroke	88.00 mm
Direction of crankshaft rotation	Clockwise (viewed from the right-hand side of vehicle)
No 1 cylinder location.	At the transmission end of block
Compression ratio	23 : 1

** The engine code is stamped on a plate attached to the front of the cylinder block.
The code given in brackets is the factory identification number.*

Compression pressures (engine hot, at cranking speed)

Normal	25 to 30 bars (363 to 435 psi)
Minimum	18 bars (261 psi)
Maximum difference between any two cylinders.	5 bars (73 psi)

Camshaft

Drive	Toothed belt
No of bearings	3
Endfloat	0.07 to 0.16 mm

Valve clearances (engine cold)

Inlet	0.15 ± 0.05 mm
Exhaust	0.30 ± 0.05 mm

Lubrication system

Oil pump type	Gear-type, chain-driven off the crankshaft right-hand end
Minimum oil pressure at 90°C	3.5 bars at 4000 rpm
Oil pressure warning switch operating pressure	0.8 bars

Torque wrench settings

	Nm	lbf ft
Big-end bearing cap nuts:*		
Stage 1	20	15
Stage 2	Angle-tighten a further 70°	
Camshaft bearing cap nuts	20	15
Camshaft sprocket bolt	45	33
Crankshaft oil seal housing bolts	16	12
Crankshaft pulley bolt:		
Stage 1	40	30
Stage 2	Angle-tighten a further 60°	
Cylinder head bolts (Torx type, see text, Section 13):		
Stage 1	20	15
Stage 2	60	44
Stage 3	Angle-tighten a further 180°	
Cylinder head cover bolts	20	15
Engine-to-transmission fixing bolts	50	37
Engine/transmission left-hand mounting:		
Centre nut	65	48
Mounting bracket to body bolts	25	18
Mounting rubber nuts/bolts	25	18
Mounting stud-to-bracket	50	37
Engine/transmission rear mounting:		
Connecting link-to-mounting rubber nut/bolt	50	37
Connecting link-to-subframe nut/bolt	50	37
Mounting assembly-to-block bolts	45	33
Engine/transmission right-hand mounting:		
Engine (tensioner assembly) bracket bolts	18	13
Mounting bracket retaining nuts	45	33
Rubber mounting to body	40	30
Flywheel bolts*	50	37
Injection pump sprocket nut	50	37
Injection pump sprocket puller retaining screws	10	7
Main bearing cap bolts	70	52
Oil pump mounting bolts	13	10
Sump bolts	19	14
Timing belt cover bolts	8	6
Timing belt tensioner adjustment bolt	18	13
Timing belt tensioner pivot nut	18	13

New nuts/bolts must be used

1 General information

How to use this Chapter

This Part of Chapter 2 describes those repair procedures that can reasonably be carried out on the engine while it remains in the car. If the engine has been removed from the car and is being dismantled, as described in Part F, any preliminary dismantling procedures can be ignored.

Note that, while it may be possible physically to overhaul items such as the piston/connecting rod assemblies while the engine is in the car, such tasks are not normally carried out as separate operations. Usually, several additional procedures (not to mention the cleaning of components and of oilways) have to be carried out. For this reason, all such tasks are classed as major overhaul procedures, and are described in Part F of this Chapter.

Part F describes the removal of the engine/transmission from the vehicle, and the full overhaul procedures that can then be carried out.

Engine description

The XUD engine is a well-proven unit which has appeared in many Peugeot and Citroën vehicles. The engine is of four-cylinder overhead camshaft design, mounted transversely, with the transmission mounted on the left-hand side.

A toothed timing belt drives the camshaft, fuel injection pump and coolant pump. Followers are fitted between the camshaft and valves. Valve clearance adjustment is by means of shims. The camshaft is supported by three bearings machined directly in the cylinder head.

The crankshaft runs in five main bearings of the usual shell type. Endfloat is controlled by thrustwashers either side of No 2 main bearing.

The pistons are selected to be of matching weight, and incorporate fully-floating gudgeon pins retained by circlips.

The oil pump is chain-driven from the front of the crankshaft. An oil cooler is fitted to all engines.

Throughout the manual, it is often necessary to identify the engines not only by their cubic capacity, but also by their engine code. The engine code, consists of three letters (eg, D9B). The code is stamped on a plate attached to the front of the cylinder block.

Operations with engine in car

The following work can be carried out with the engine in the car:
a) Compression pressure – testing.
b) Cylinder head cover – removal and refitting.
c) Crankshaft pulley – removal and refitting.
d) Timing belt covers – removal and refitting.
e) Timing belt – removal, refitting and adjustment.
f) Timing belt tensioner and sprockets – removal and refitting.
g) Camshaft oil seal – renewal.
h) Camshaft and followers – removal, inspection and refitting.
i) Valve clearances – checking and adjustment.
j) Cylinder head – removal and refitting.
k) Cylinder head and pistons – decarbonising.
l) Sump – removal and refitting.
m) Oil pump – removal and refitting.
n) Crankshaft oil seals – renewal.
o) Engine/transmission mountings – inspection and renewal.
p) Flywheel – removal, inspection and refitting.

2 Compression and leakdown tests – description and interpretation

Compression test

Note: *A compression tester specifically designed for diesel engines must be used for this test.*

1 When engine performance is down, or if misfiring occurs which cannot be attributed to the fuel system, a compression test can provide diagnostic clues as to the engine's condition. If the test is performed regularly, it can give warning of trouble before any other symptoms become apparent.

2 A compression tester specifically intended for diesel engines must be used, because of the higher pressures involved. The tester is connected to an adapter which screws into the glow plug or injector hole. On these models, an adapter suitable for use in the injector holes will be required, due to the limited access to the glow plug holes **(see illustration)**. It is

2.2 Performing a compression test

unlikely to be worthwhile buying such a tester for occasional use, but it may be possible to borrow or hire one – if not, have the test performed by a garage.

3 Unless specific instructions to the contrary are supplied with the tester, observe the following points:
a) *The battery must be in a good state of charge, the air filter must be clean, and the engine should be at normal operating temperature.*
b) *All the injectors or glow plugs should be removed before starting the test. If removing the injectors, also remove the flame shield washers, otherwise they may be blown out.*
c) *The anti-theft system electronic engine immobiliser unit wiring connector at the rear of the injection pump must be disconnected.*

4 There is no need to hold the accelerator pedal down during the test, because the diesel engine air inlet is not throttled.

5 The actual compression pressures measured are not so important as the balance between cylinders. Values are given in the Specifications.

6 The cause of poor compression is less easy to establish on a diesel engine than on a petrol one. The effect of introducing oil into the cylinders ('wet' testing) is not conclusive, because there is a risk that the oil will sit in the swirl chamber or in the recess on the piston crown instead of passing to the rings. However, the following can be used as a rough guide to diagnosis.

7 All cylinders should produce very similar pressures; any difference greater than that specified indicates the existence of a fault. Note that the compression should build-up quickly in a healthy engine; low compression on the first stroke, followed by gradually-increasing pressure on successive strokes, indicates worn piston rings. A low compression reading on the first stroke, which does not build-up during successive strokes, indicates leaking valves or a blown head gasket (a cracked head could also be the cause). Deposits on the undersides of the valve heads can also cause low compression.

8 A low reading from two adjacent cylinders is almost certainly due to the head gasket having blown between them; the presence of coolant in the engine oil will confirm this.

9 If the compression reading is unusually high, the cylinder head surfaces, valves and pistons are probably coated with carbon deposits. If this is the case, the cylinder head should be removed and decarbonised (see Part F).

Leakdown test

10 A leakdown test measures the rate at which compressed air fed into the cylinder is lost. It is an alternative to a compression test, and in many ways it is better, since the escaping air provides easy identification of where pressure loss is occurring (piston rings, valves or head gasket).

11 The equipment needed for leakdown testing is unlikely to be available to the home mechanic. If poor compression is suspected, have the test performed by a suitably-equipped garage.

3 Engine assembly/valve timing holes – general information and usage

Note: *Do not attempt to rotate the engine whilst the crankshaft/camshaft/injection pump are locked in position. If the engine is to be left in this state for a long period of time, it is a good idea to place suitable warning notices inside the vehicle, and in the engine compartment. This will reduce the possibility of the engine being accidentally cranked on the starter motor, which is likely to cause damage with the locking pins in place.*

1 On all engines, timing holes are drilled in the camshaft sprocket, injection pump sprocket and flywheel. The holes are used to align the crankshaft, camshaft and injection pump, and to prevent the possibility of the valves contacting the pistons when refitting the cylinder head, or when refitting the timing belt. When the holes are aligned with their corresponding holes in the cylinder head and cylinder block (as appropriate), suitable diameter bolts/pins can be inserted to lock both the camshaft, injection pump and crankshaft in position, preventing them from rotating unnecessarily. Proceed as follows. **Note:** *With the timing holes aligned, No 4 cylinder is at TDC on its compression stroke.*

2 Remove the upper timing belt covers as described in Section 6.

3 Firmly apply the handbrake, then jack up the front of the car and support it securely on axle stands (see *Jacking and vehicle support*). Remove the right-hand front roadwheel.

4 The crankshaft must now be turned until the three bolt holes in the camshaft and injection pump sprockets (one hole in the camshaft sprocket, two holes in the injection pump sprocket) are aligned with the corresponding holes in the engine front plate. To gain access to the right-hand end of the engine, the wheel arch plastic liner must be removed. The liner is secured by various screws and clips under the wheel arch. Release all the fasteners, and remove liner from under the front wing. Where necessary, unclip the coolant hoses from under the wing to improve access further. The crankshaft can then be turned using a suitable socket and extension bar fitted to the pulley bolt. Note that the crankshaft must always be turned in a clockwise direction (viewed from the right-hand side of vehicle).

5 Insert an 8 mm diameter rod or drill through the hole in the left-hand flange of the cylinder block by the starter motor; if necessary, carefully turn the crankshaft either way until

3.5a Suitable tools available for locking the engine in the TDC position

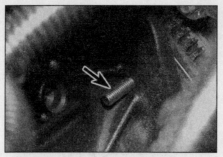

3.5b Rod (arrowed) inserted through cylinder block into timing hole in the flywheel

3.6a Bolt (arrowed) inserted through timing hole in the camshaft sprocket

the rod enters the timing hole in the flywheel (see illustrations).

6 Insert three 8 mm bolts through the holes in the camshaft and fuel injection pump sprockets, and screw them into the engine finger-tight (see illustrations).

7 The crankshaft, camshaft and injection pump are now locked in position, preventing unnecessary rotation.

4 Cylinder head cover – removal and refitting

Removal

1 On the 1.9 litre (D9B) engine, remove the air distribution housing as described in Chapter 4B.

2 Disconnect the breather hose from the front of the camshaft cover and, where necessary,

remove the inlet duct from the inlet manifold.

3 Unscrew the securing bolt and remove the fuel hose bracket from the right-hand end of the cylinder head cover (see illustration).

4 Note the locations of any brackets secured by the three cylinder head cover bolts, then unscrew the bolts. Recover the metal and fibre washers under each bolt (see illustration).

5 Carefully move any hoses clear of the cylinder head cover.

6 Lift off the cover, and recover the rubber seal (see illustration). Examine the seal for signs of damage and deterioration, and if necessary, renew it.

Refitting

7 Refitting is a reversal of removal, bearing in mind the following points:
   a) Refit any brackets in their original positions noted before removal.
   b) Where applicable, refit the air distribution housing, as described in Chapter 4B.

5 Crankshaft pulley – removal and refitting

Removal

1 Remove the auxiliary drivebelt as described in Chapter 1B.

2 To prevent crankshaft turning whilst the pulley retaining bolt is being slackened, select top gear and have an assistant apply the brakes firmly. Alternatively, the flywheel ring gear can be locked using a suitable tool made from steel angle (see illustration). Remove the cover plate from the base of the transmission bellhousing and bolt the tool to the bellhousing flange so it engages with the ring gear teeth. Do not attempt to lock the pulley by inserting a bolt/drill through the timing hole. If the timing hole bolt/drill is in position, temporarily remove it prior to slackening the pulley bolt, then refit it once the bolt has been slackened.

3 Unscrew the retaining bolt and washer, then slide the pulley off the end of the crankshaft. If the pulley locating roll pin or Woodruff key (as applicable) is a loose fit, remove it and store it with the pulley for safe-keeping. If the pulley is tight fit, it can be drawn off the crankshaft using a suitable puller.

Refitting

4 Ensure that the Woodruff key is correctly located in its crankshaft groove, or that the roll pin is in position (as applicable). Refit the

3.6b Bolts (arrowed) inserted through timing holes in the injection pump sprocket

4.3 Removing the fuel hose bracket from the cylinder head cover

4.4 Remove the retaining bolts and washers . . .

4.6 . . . and lift off the cylinder head cover

5.2 Use a fabricated tool similar to this to lock the flywheel ring gear and prevent crankshaft rotation

pulley to the end of the crankshaft, aligning its locating groove or hole with the Woodruff key or pin.

5 Thoroughly clean the threads of the pulley retaining bolt, then apply a coat of locking compound to the bolt threads. Peugeot/ Citroën recommend the use of Loctite (available from your dealer); in the absence of this, any good-quality locking compound may be used.

6 Refit the crankshaft pulley retaining bolt and washer. Tighten the bolt to the specified torque, then through the specified angle, preventing the crankshaft from turning using the method employed on removal.

7 Refit and tension the auxiliary drivebelt as described in Chapter 1B.

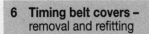

6 Timing belt covers – removal and refitting

Removal

Upper covers

1 If procedures are to be carried out which involve removal of the timing belt, remove the right-hand engine mounting-to-body bracket as described in Section 9. This will greatly improve access.

2 Undo the two bolts securing the camshaft sprocket cover and the nut and bolt securing the injection pump sprocket cover.

3 Release the covers from their locations and lift them off the engine.

Lower cover

4 Remove the crankshaft pulley as described in Section 5.

5 Remove both upper covers as described previously.

6 Undo the two remaining securing nuts, and remove the lower cover.

Refitting

7 Refitting is a reversal of the relevant removal procedure, ensuring that each cover section is correctly located, and that the cover retaining nuts and/or bolts are tightened securely.

7 Timing belt – removal, inspection, refitting and tensioning

General

1 The timing belt drives the camshaft, injection pump, and coolant pump from a toothed sprocket on the front of the crankshaft. The belt also drives the brake vacuum pump indirectly via the flywheel end of the camshaft. If the belt breaks or slips in service, the pistons are likely to hit the valve heads, resulting in expensive damage.

2 The timing belt should be renewed at

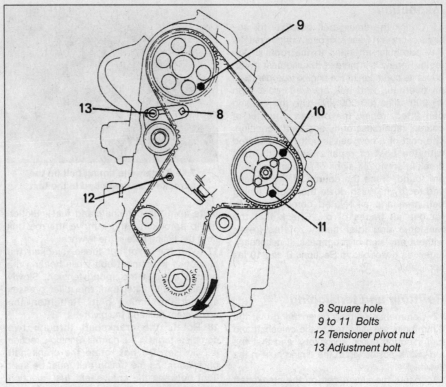

8 Square hole
9 to 11 Bolts
12 Tensioner pivot nut
13 Adjustment bolt

7.9 Removing the timing belt

the specified intervals, or earlier if it is contaminated with oil, or at all noisy in operation (a 'scraping' noise due to uneven wear).

3 If the timing belt is being removed, it is a wise precaution to check the condition of the coolant pump at the same time (check for signs of coolant leakage). This may avoid the need to remove the timing belt again at a later stage, should the coolant pump fail.

Removal

4 Disconnect the battery negative terminal (refer to *Disconnecting the battery* in the Reference Chapter).

5 Remove the crankshaft pulley as described in Section 5.

6 Remove the timing belt covers as described in Section 6.

7 Temporarily refit the crankshaft pulley to

enable the engine to be turned, then align the engine assembly/valve timing holes as described in Section 3, and lock the camshaft sprocket, injection pump sprocket and flywheel in position. *Do not* attempt to rotate the engine whilst the pins are in position.

8 Remove the right-hand engine mounting-to-body bracket as described in Section 9.

9 Loosen the timing belt tensioner pivot nut and adjustment bolt, then turn the tensioner bracket anti-clockwise to release the tension. Retighten the adjustment bolt to hold the tensioner in the released position. If available, use a 10 mm square drive extension in the hole provided, to turn the tensioner bracket against the spring tension **(see illustration)**.

10 Mark the timing belt with an arrow to indicate its running direction, if it is to be re-used. Remove the belt from the sprockets **(see illustrations)**.

7.10a Mark the timing belt with an arrow to indicate its running direction

7.10b Removing the timing belt

Inspection

11 Check the timing belt carefully for any signs of uneven wear, split or oil contamination. Pay particular attention to the roots of the teeth. Renew it if there is the slightest doubt about its condition. If the engine is undergoing an overhaul, and has covered more than 40 000 miles (60 000 km) with the existing belt fitted, renew the belt as a matter of course, regardless of its apparent condition. The cost of a new belt is nothing compared with the cost of repairs, should the belt break in service. If signs of oil contamination are found, trace the source of the oil leak and rectify it. Wash down the engine timing belt area and all related components, to remove all traces of oil. Check that the tensioner and idler pulley rotates freely, without any sign of roughness. If necessary, renew as described in Sections 9 and 10 (as applicable).

Refitting and tensioning

12 Commence refitting by ensuring that the 8 mm bolts are still fitted to the camshaft and fuel injection pump sprockets, and that the rod/drill is positioned in the timing hole in the flywheel.

13 Locate the timing belt on the crankshaft sprocket, making sure that, where applicable, the direction of rotation arrow is facing the correct way.

14 Engage the timing belt with the crankshaft sprocket, hold it in position, then feed the belt over the remaining sprockets in the following order:
   a) Idler roller.
   b) Fuel injection pump.
   c) Camshaft.
   d) Tensioner roller.
   e) Coolant pump.

15 Be careful not to kink or twist the belt. To ensure correct engagement, locate only a half-width on the injection pump sprocket before feeding the timing belt onto the camshaft sprocket, keeping the belt taut and fully engaged with the crankshaft sprocket. Locate the timing belt fully onto the sprockets (see illustration).

16 Unscrew and remove the 8 mm locking

7.15 Locate the timing belt on the sprockets as described in the text

bolts from the camshaft and fuel injection pump sprockets, and remove the rod/drill from the timing hole in the flywheel.

17 With the pivot nut loose, slacken the tensioner adjustment bolt while holding the bracket against the spring tension. Slowly release the bracket until the roller presses against the timing belt. Retighten the adjustment bolt and the pivot nut.

18 Rotate the crankshaft through two complete turns in the normal running direction (clockwise). **Do not** rotate the crankshaft backwards, as the timing belt must be kept tight between the crankshaft, fuel injection pump and camshaft sprockets.

19 Loosen the tensioner adjustment bolt and the pivot nut to allow the tensioner spring to push the roller against the timing belt, then tighten both the adjustment bolt and pivot nut to the specified torque.

20 Check that the timing holes are all correctly positioned by reinserting the sprocket locking bolts and the rod/drill in the flywheel timing hole, as described in Section 3. If the timing holes are not correctly positioned, the timing belt has been incorrectly fitted (possibly one tooth out on one of the sprockets) – in this case, repeat the refitting procedure from the beginning.

21 Refit the upper timing belt covers as described in Section 6.

22 Refit the right-hand engine mounting-to-body bracket, with reference to Section 9.

23 Refit the crankshaft pulley as described in Section 5.

8 Timing belt sprockets – removal and refitting

Camshaft sprocket

Removal

1 Remove the upper timing belt covers as described in Section 6.

2 The camshaft sprocket bolt must now be loosened. The camshaft must be prevented from turning as the sprocket bolt is unscrewed, and this can be done in one of two ways, as follows (see illustrations). Do not remove the camshaft sprocket bolt at this stage.
   a) Make up a tool similar to that shown, and use it to hold the sprocket stationary by means of the holes in the sprocket.
   b) Remove the cylinder head cover as described in Section 4. Prevent the camshaft from turning by holding it with a suitable spanner on the lug between Nos 3 and 4 camshaft lobes.

3 Align the engine assembly/valve timing holes as described in Section 3, and lock the camshaft sprocket, injection pump sprocket and flywheel in position. Do not attempt to rotate the engine whilst the pins are in position.

4 Loosen the timing belt tensioner pivot nut and adjustment bolt, then turn the tensioner bracket anti-clockwise to release the tension, and retighten the adjustment bolt to hold the tensioner in the released position. If available, use a 10 mm square drive extension in the hole provided, to turn the tensioner bracket against the spring tension. Slip the timing belt off the sprocket.

5 Remove the previously slackened camshaft sprocket retaining bolt and washer.

6 Remove the locking bolt securing the camshaft sprocket in the TDC position.

7 Slide the sprocket off the end of the camshaft (see illustration). If the locating peg is a loose fit in the rear of the sprocket, remove it for safe-keeping. Examine the camshaft oil seal for signs of oil leakage and, if necessary, renew it as described in Section 16.

8.2a Using a home-made tool to prevent the camshaft sprocket from turning

8.2b Holding the camshaft using a spanner on the lug between Nos 3 and 4 lobes

8.7 Withdrawing the camshaft sprocket

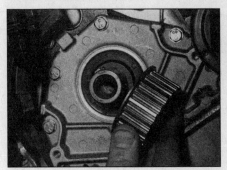

8.16 Withdrawing the crankshaft sprocket

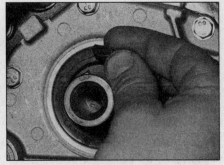

8.17 Removing the Woodruff key from the end of the crankshaft

Refitting

8 Where applicable, refit the Woodruff key to the end of the camshaft, then refit the camshaft sprocket. Note that the sprocket will only fit one way round (with the protruding centre boss against the camshaft), as the end of the camshaft is tapered.

9 Refit the sprocket retaining bolt and washer. Tighten the bolt to the specified torque, preventing the camshaft from turning as during removal.

10 Where applicable, refit the cylinder head cover as described in Section 4.

11 Align the holes in the camshaft sprocket and the engine front plate, and refit the 8 mm bolt to lock the camshaft in position.

12 Fit the timing belt around the fuel injection pump sprocket (where applicable) and the camshaft sprocket, and tension the timing belt as described in Section 7.

13 Refit the upper timing belt covers as described in Section 6.

Crankshaft sprocket

Removal

14 Remove the crankshaft pulley as described in Section 5.

15 Proceed as described in paragraphs 1, 3 and 4.

16 Disengage the timing belt from the crankshaft sprocket, and slide the sprocket off the end of the crankshaft **(see illustration)**.

17 Remove the Woodruff key from the crankshaft, and store it with the sprocket for safe-keeping **(see illustration)**.

18 Examine the crankshaft oil seal for signs

of oil leakage and, if necessary, renew it as described in Section 16.

Refitting

19 Refit the Woodruff key to the end of the crankshaft, then refit the crankshaft sprocket (with the flange nearest the cylinder block).

20 Fit the timing belt around the crankshaft sprocket, and tension the timing belt as described in Section 7. Refit the timing belt covers as described in Section 6.

21 Refit the crankshaft pulley as described in Section 5.

Fuel injection pump sprocket

Removal

22 Proceed as described in paragraphs 1, 3 and 4.

23 Make alignment marks on the fuel injection pump sprocket and the timing belt, to ensure that the sprocket and timing belt are correctly aligned on refitting.

24 Remove the 8 mm bolts securing the fuel injection pump sprocket in the TDC position.

25 On certain models, the sprocket may be fitted with a built-in puller, which consists of a plate bolted to the sprocket. The plate contains a captive nut (the sprocket securing nut), which is screwed onto the fuel injection pump shaft. On models not fitted with the built-in puller, a suitable puller can be made up using a short length of bar, and two M7 bolts screwed into the holes provided in the sprocket.

26 The fuel injection pump shaft must be prevented from turning as the sprocket nut is unscrewed, and this can be achieved using a tool similar to that shown **(see illustration)**.

8.26 Using a home-made tool to prevent the injection pump sprocket from turning

8.28 Home-made puller fitted to the fuel injection pump sprocket

Use the tool to hold the sprocket stationary by means of the holes in the sprocket.

27 On models with a built-in puller, unscrew the sprocket securing nut until the sprocket is freed from the taper on the pump shaft, then withdraw the sprocket. Recover the Woodruff key from the end of the pump shaft if it is loose. If desired, the puller assembly can be removed from the sprocket by removing the two securing screws and washers.

28 On models not fitted with a built-in puller, partially unscrew the sprocket securing nut, then fit the improvised puller, and tighten the two bolts (forcing the bar against the sprocket nut), until the sprocket is freed from the taper on the pump shaft **(see illustration)**. Withdraw the sprocket, and recover the Woodruff key from the end of the pump shaft if it is loose. Remove the puller from the sprocket.

Refitting

29 Where applicable, refit the Woodruff key to the pump shaft, ensuring that it is correctly located in its groove.

30 Where applicable, if the built-in puller assembly has been removed from the sprocket, refit it, and tighten the two securing screws to the specified torque, ensuring that the washers are in place.

31 Refit the sprocket, then tighten the securing nut to the specified torque, preventing the pump shaft from turning as during removal.

32 Make sure that the 8 mm bolts are fitted to the camshaft and fuel injection pump sprockets, and that the rod/drill is positioned in the flywheel timing hole.

33 Fit the timing belt around the fuel injection pump sprocket, ensuring that the marks made on the belt and sprocket before removal are aligned.

34 Tension the timing belt (see Section 7).

35 Refit the upper timing belt covers as described in Section 6.

Coolant pump sprocket

36 The coolant pump sprocket is integral with the pump, and cannot be removed.

9 Right-hand mounting bracket and timing belt tensioner – removal and refitting

General

1 The timing belt tensioner is operated by a spring and plunger housed in the right-hand engine mounting bracket, which is bolted to the end face of the engine. The engine mounting is attached to the mounting on the body via the engine mounting-to-body bracket.

Right-hand engine mounting-to-body bracket

Removal

2 Before removing the bracket, the engine must be supported, preferably using a suitable

9.4 Removing the engine mounting-to-body bracket

hoist and lifting tackle attached to the lifting bracket at the right-hand end of the engine. Alternatively, the engine can be supported using a trolley jack and interposed block of wood beneath the sump, in which case, be prepared for the engine to tilt backwards when the bracket is removed.

3 Release the retaining clips and brackets, and position the diesel priming pump and all the relevant hoses and cables clear of the engine mounting assembly and suspension top mounting.

4 Unscrew the three nuts securing the mounting bracket to the engine bracket, and the single nut securing the bracket to the rubber mounting on the body, then lift off the bracket **(see illustration)**.

Refitting

5 Refitting is a reversal of removal. Tighten the nuts and bolts to the specified torque.

Timing belt tensioner and right-hand engine mounting bracket

Note: *A suitable tool will be required to retain the timing belt tensioner plunger during this operation.*

Removal

6 Remove the engine mounting-to-body bracket as described previously in this Section, and remove the auxiliary drivebelt as described in Chapter 1B.

7 If not already done, support the engine with a trolley jack and interposed block of wood beneath the sump.

8 Where applicable, disconnect the hoist and lifting tackle supporting the engine from the right-hand lifting bracket (this is necessary because the lifting bracket is attached to the engine mounting bracket, and must be removed).

9 Unscrew the two retaining bolts and remove the engine lifting bracket.

10 Align the engine assembly/valve timing holes as described in Section 3, and lock the camshaft sprocket, injection pump sprocket and flywheel in position. *Do not* rotate the engine whilst the pins are in position.

11 Loosen the timing belt tensioner pivot nut and adjustment bolt, then turn the tensioner bracket anti-clockwise until the adjustment bolt is in the middle of the slot, and retighten the adjustment bolt. Use a 10 mm square drive extension in the hole provided, to turn the tensioner bracket against the spring tension.

12 Mark the timing belt with an arrow to indicate its running direction, if it is to be re-used. Remove the belt from the sprockets.

13 A tool must now be obtained in order to hold the tensioner plunger in the engine mounting bracket.

14 The Peugeot/Citroën tool is designed to slide in the two lower bolt holes of the mounting bracket. It should be easy to fabricate a similar tool out of sheet metal, using 10 mm bolts and nuts instead of metal rods **(see Tool Tip)**.

15 Unscrew the two lower engine mounting bracket bolts, then fit the special tool **(see illustrations)**. Grease the inner surface of the tool, to prevent any damage to the end of the tensioner plunger. Unscrew the pivot nut and adjustment bolt, and withdraw the tensioner assembly.

16 Remove the two remaining engine mounting bracket bolts, and withdraw the bracket.

17 Compress the tensioner plunger into the

engine mounting bracket, remove the special tool, then withdraw the plunger and spring.

Refitting

18 Refitting is a reversal of removal, bearing in mind the following points:
- a) *Tighten all fixings to the specified torque.*
- b) *Refit and tension the timing belt as described in Section 7.*
- c) *Refit and tighten the auxiliary drivebelt as described in Chapter 1B.*

10 Timing belt idler roller – removal and refitting

Removal

1 Remove the auxiliary drivebelt as described in Chapter 1B.

2 Align the engine assembly/valve timing holes as described in Section 3, and lock the camshaft sprocket, injection pump sprocket and flywheel in position. *Do not* rotate the engine whilst the pins are in position.

3 Loosen the timing belt tensioner pivot nut and adjustment bolt, then turn the tensioner bracket anti-clockwise to release the tension, and retighten the adjustment bolt to hold the tensioner in the released position. If available, use a 10 mm square drive extension in the hole provided, to turn the tensioner bracket against the spring tension.

4 Unscrew the two bolts and the stud securing the idler roller assembly to the cylinder block, noting that the upper bolt also secures the engine mounting bracket.

5 Slightly loosen the remaining four engine mounting bolts, noting that the uppermost bolt is on the inside face of the engine front plate, and also secures the engine lifting bracket. Slide out the idler roller assembly.

Refitting

6 Refitting is a reversal of removal, bearing in mind the following points:
- a) *Tighten all fixings to the specified torque.*
- b) *Tension the timing belt as described in Section 7.*
- c) *Refit and tension the auxiliary drivebelt as described in Chapter 1B.*

TOOL TiP

Fabricated tool for holding tensioner plunger in the engine mounting bracket.

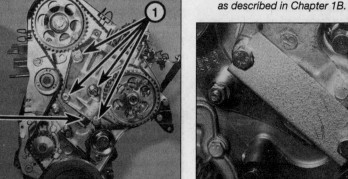

9.15a View of timing belt end of engine

1 *Engine mounting bracket retaining bolts*
2 *Timing belt tensioner plunger*

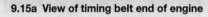

9.15b Tool in place to hold tensioner plunger in engine mounting bracket – timing belt removed for clarity

11.4 Camshaft bearing cap identification mark (arrowed)

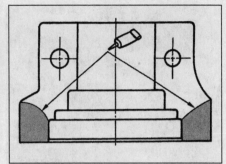

11.17 Apply sealing compound to the end camshaft bearing caps on the areas shown

11.19 Checking the camshaft endfloat using a feeler blade

11 Camshaft and followers – removal, inspection and refitting

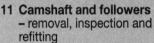

Removal

1 Remove the cylinder head cover as described in Section 4.

2 Remove the camshaft sprocket as described in Section 8.

3 Remove the braking system vacuum pump as described in Chapter 9.

4 The camshaft bearing caps should be numbered from the flywheel end of the engine (see illustration). If the caps are not already numbered, identify them, numbering them from the flywheel end of the engine, and making the marks on the manifold side.

5 Progressively unscrew the nuts, then remove the bearing caps.

6 Lift the camshaft from the cylinder head. Remove the oil seal from the timing belt end of the camshaft. Discard the seal, a new one should be used on refitting.

7 Obtain eight small, clean plastic containers, and number them 1 to 8; alternatively, divide a larger container into eight compartments. Using a rubber sucker, withdraw each follower in turn, and place it in its respective container. Do not interchange the cam followers, or the rate of wear will be much-increased. If necessary, also remove the shim from the top of the valve stem, and store it with its respective follower. Note that the shim may stick to the inside of the follower as it is withdrawn. If this happens, take care not to allow it to drop out as the follower is removed.

Inspection

8 Examine the camshaft bearing surfaces and cam lobes for signs of wear ridges and scoring. Renew the camshaft if any of these conditions are apparent. Examine the condition of the bearing surfaces, both on the camshaft journals and in the cylinder head/bearing caps. If the head bearing surfaces are worn excessively, the cylinder head will need to be renewed.

9 Examine the cam follower bearing surfaces which contact the camshaft lobes for wear ridges and scoring. Renew any follower on which these conditions are apparent. If a follower bearing surface is badly scored, also examine the corresponding lobe on the camshaft for wear, as it is likely that both will be worn. Renew worn components as necessary.

Refitting

10 To prevent any possibility of the valves contacting the pistons as the camshaft is refitted, remove the locking rod/drill from the flywheel and turn the crankshaft a quarter turn in the *opposite* direction to normal rotation, to position all the pistons at mid-stroke. Release the timing belt from the injection pump sprocket while turning the crankshaft.

11 Where removed, refit each shim to the top of its original valve stem. *Do not* interchange the shims, as this will upset the valve clearances (see Section 12).

12 Liberally oil the cylinder head cam follower bores and the followers. Carefully refit the followers to the cylinder head, ensuring that each follower is refitted to its original bore. Some care will be required to enter the followers squarely into their bores.

13 Lubricate the cam lobes and bearing journals with clean engine oil of the specified grade.

14 Position the camshaft in the cylinder head, passing it through the engine front plate.

15 Temporarily locate the sprocket on the end of the camshaft, and turn the shaft so that the sprocket timing hole is aligned with the corresponding cut-out in the cylinder head. Remove the sprocket.

16 Fit the centre bearing cap the correct way round as previously noted, then screw on the nuts and tighten them two or three turns.

17 Apply sealing compound to the end bearing caps on the areas shown (see illustration). Fit them in the correct positions, and tighten the nuts two or three turns.

18 Tighten all the nuts progressively to the specified torque, making sure that the camshaft remains correctly positioned.

19 Check that the camshaft endfloat is as given in the Specifications, using a feeler blade. If not, the camshaft and/or the cylinder head must be renewed. To check the endfloat, push the camshaft fully towards one end of the cylinder head, and insert a feeler blade between the thrust faces of one of the camshaft lobes and a bearing cap (see illustration).

20 If the original camshaft is being refitted, and it is known that the valve clearances are correct, proceed to the next paragraph. Otherwise, check and adjust the valve clearances as described in Section 12.

21 Smear the lips of the new oil seal with clean engine oil and fit it onto the camshaft end, making sure its sealing lip is facing inwards. Press the oil seal in until it is flush with the end face of the camshaft bearing cap.

22 Refit the braking system vacuum pump as described in Chapter 9.

23 Again, temporarily locate the sprocket on the end of the camshaft, and make sure that the sprocket timing hole is aligned with the corresponding cut-out in the cylinder head.

24 Turn the crankshaft a quarter turn in the normal direction of rotation so that pistons 1 and 4 are again at TDC.

25 Refit the rod/drill to the flywheel timing hole.

26 Refit the camshaft sprocket as described in Section 8.

27 Refit the cylinder head cover as described in Section 4.

12 Valve clearances – checking and adjustment

Checking

1 The importance of having the valve clearances correctly adjusted cannot be overstressed, as they vitally affect the performance of the engine. Checking should not be regarded as a routine operation, however. It should only be necessary when the valve gear has become noisy, after engine overhaul, or when trying to trace the cause of power loss. The clearances are checked as follows. The engine must be cold for the check to be accurate.

2 Firmly apply the handbrake, then jack up the front of the car and support it securely on axle stands (see *Jacking and vehicle support*). Remove the right-hand front roadwheel.

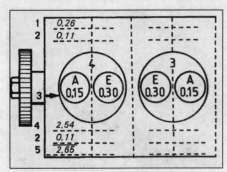

12.6 Example of valve shim thickness calculation

A Inlet
E Exhaust
1 Measured clearance
2 Difference between 1 and 3
3 Specified clearance
4 Thickness of shim fitted
5 Thickness of shim required

3 From underneath the front of the car, remove the wheel arch plastic liner, which is secured by various screws and clips under the wheel arch. Release all the fasteners, and remove liner from under the front wing. Where necessary, unclip the coolant hoses from under the wing to improve access to the crankshaft pulley.
4 The engine can now be turned over using a suitable socket and extension bar fitted to the crankshaft pulley bolt.

 HAYNES HiNT *The engine will be easier to turn if the fuel injectors or glow plugs are removed.*

5 Remove the cylinder head cover as described in Section 4.
6 On a piece of paper, draw the outline of the engine with the cylinders numbered from the flywheel end. Show the position of each valve, together with the specified valve clearance. Above each valve, draw lines for noting (1) the actual clearance and (2) the amount of adjustment required **(see illustration)**.
7 Turn the crankshaft until the inlet valve of

13.4 Disconnecting the vacuum hose from the braking system vacuum pump

12.8 Measuring a valve clearance using a feeler blade

No 1 cylinder (nearest the transmission) is fully closed, with the tip of the cam facing directly away from the follower.
8 Using feeler blades, measure the clearance between the base of the cam and the follower **(see illustration)**. Record the clearance on line (1).
9 Repeat the measurement for the other seven valves, turning the crankshaft as necessary so that the cam lobe in question is always facing directly away from the relevant follower.
10 Calculate the difference between each measured clearance and the desired value, and record it on line (2). Since the clearance is different for inlet and exhaust valves – make sure that you are aware which valve you are dealing with. The valve sequence from either end of the engine is:

In – Ex – Ex – In – In – Ex – Ex – In

11 If all the clearances are within tolerance, refit the cylinder head cover with reference to Section 4, and where applicable, lower the vehicle to the ground. If any clearance measured is outside the specified tolerance, adjustment must be carried out as described in the following paragraphs.

Adjustment

12 Remove the camshaft as described in Section 11.
13 Withdraw the first follower and its shim. Clean the shim, and measure its thickness with a micrometer. The shims carry

13.5 Disconnecting a fuel injector leak-off hose

thickness markings, but wear may have reduced the original thickness, so be sure to check.
14 Refer to the clearance recorded for the valve concerned. If the clearance was more than that specified, the shim thickness must be increased by the difference recorded (2). If the clearance was less than that specified, the thickness of the shim must be decreased by the difference recorded (2).
15 Draw three more lines beneath each valve on the calculation paper, as shown in illustration 12.6. On line (4) note the measured thickness of the shim, then add or deduct the difference from line (2) to give the final shim thickness required on line (5).
16 Repeat the procedure given in paragraphs 13 to 15 on the remaining valves, keeping each follower identified for position.
17 Obtain the shims required to bring each valve clearance within tolerance. Note that the shims can be swapped around, but not the followers.
18 When reassembling, oil the shim and fit it into the valve retainer, with the size marking face downwards. Oil the follower, and lower it onto the shim. Do not raise the follower after fitting, as the shim may become dislodged.
19 When all the followers are in position, complete with their shims, refit the camshaft as described in Section 11. Recheck the valve clearances before refitting the camshaft cover, to make sure they are correct.

13 Cylinder head – removal and refitting

Note: *This is an involved procedure, and it is suggested that the Section is read thoroughly before starting work. To aid refitting, make notes on the locations of all relevant brackets and the routing of hoses and cables before removal.*

Removal

1 Disconnect the battery negative terminal (refer to *Disconnecting the battery* in the Reference Chapter).
2 Drain the cooling system as described in Chapter 1B.
3 Remove the inlet and exhaust manifolds as described in Chapter 4B.
4 Slacken the retaining clip and disconnect the vacuum hose from the braking system vacuum pump **(see illustration)**.
5 Disconnect and remove the fuel injector leak-off hoses **(see illustration)**.
6 Disconnect the fuel pipes from the fuel injectors and the fuel injection pump, and remove the pipes as described in Chapter 4B.
7 Unscrew the securing nut and disconnect the feed wire from the relevant glow plug. Recover the washers.
8 Disconnect the coolant hose from the

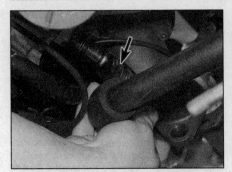

13.8 Disconnecting the coolant hose (arrowed) from the rear of the cylinder head

13.9 Disconnecting the coolant hose (arrowed) from the front of the head

13.10 Unclip the fuel return hose from its brackets

rear, left-hand end of the cylinder head **(see illustration)**.

9 Disconnect the small coolant hose from the front timing belt end of the cylinder head **(see illustration)**.

10 Unclip the fuel return hose from the brackets on the cylinder head, and move it to one side **(see illustration)**.

11 Disconnect the accelerator cable from the fuel injection pump (refer to Chapter 4B if necessary), and move the cable clear of the cylinder head.

12 Remove the fuel filter/thermostat housing as described in Chapter 3.

13 Unscrew the nut or stud securing the coolant hose bracket and the engine lifting bracket to the transmission end of the cylinder head.

14 Remove the camshaft sprocket as described in Section 8.

15 Remove the timing belt tensioner and the right-hand engine mounting bracket as described in Section 9.

16 Remove the timing belt idler roller as described in Section 10.

17 Remove the bolt securing the engine front plate to the fuel injection pump mounting bracket.

18 Remove the nut and bolt securing the engine front plate and the alternator mounting bracket to the fuel injection pump mounting bracket, then remove the engine front plate.

19 Progressively unscrew the cylinder head bolts, in the reverse order to that shown in illustration 13.37.

20 Lift out the bolts and recover the spacers **(see illustration)**.

21 Release the cylinder head from the cylinder block and location dowel by rocking it. The Peugeot/Citroën tool for doing this consists simply of two metal rods with 90-degree angled ends **(see illustration)**. Do not prise between the mating faces of the cylinder head and block, as this may damage the gasket faces.

22 Lift the cylinder head from the block, and recover the gasket **(see illustration)**.

Preparation for refitting

23 The mating faces of the cylinder head and cylinder block/crankcase must be perfectly clean before refitting the head. The manufacturer's recommend the use of a scouring agent for this purpose, but acceptable results can be achieved by using a hard plastic or wood scraper to remove all traces of gasket and carbon. The same method can be used to clean the piston crowns. Take particular care to avoid scoring or gouging the cylinder head/cylinder block mating surfaces during the cleaning operations, as aluminium alloy is easily damaged. Make sure that the carbon is not allowed to enter the oil and water passages – this is particularly important for the lubrication system, as carbon could block the

oil supply to the engine's components. Using adhesive tape and paper, seal the water, oil and bolt holes in the cylinder block/crankcase. To prevent carbon entering the gap between the pistons and bores, smear a little grease in the gap. After cleaning each piston, use a small brush to remove all traces of grease and carbon from the gap, then wipe away the remainder with a clean rag.

24 Check the mating surfaces of the cylinder block/crankcase and the cylinder head for nicks, deep scratches and other damage. If slight, they may be removed carefully with a file, but if excessive, machining may be the only alternative to renewal. If warpage of the cylinder head gasket surface is suspected, use a straight-edge to check it for distortion. Refer to Part E of this Chapter if necessary.

25 Thoroughly clean the threads of the cylinder head bolt holes in the cylinder block. Ensure that the bolts run freely in their threads, and that all traces of oil and water are removed from each bolt hole.

Gasket selection

26 Check that the timing belt is clear of the fuel injection pump sprocket, then turn the crankshaft until pistons 1 and 4 are at TDC. Position a dial test indicator (dial gauge) on the cylinder block, and zero it on the block face. Transfer the probe to the centre of No 1 piston, then slowly turn the crankshaft back and forth past TDC, noting the highest reading on the indicator. Record this reading.

27 Repeat this measurement procedure on No 4 piston, then turn the crankshaft half a

13.20 Removing a cylinder head bolt and spacer

13.21 Freeing the cylinder head using angled rods

H.22645

13.22 Removing the cylinder head

13.27 Measuring piston protrusion

turn (180°) and repeat the procedure on Nos 2 and 3 pistons **(see illustration)**.

28 If a dial test indicator is not available, piston protrusion may be measured using a straight-edge and feeler blades or vernier calipers. However, this is much less accurate, and cannot therefore be recommended.

29 Note down the greatest piston protrusion measurement, and use this to determine the correct cylinder head gasket from the following table. The notches or holes at the corner of the gasket are used for thickness identification. The notches or holes near the centre-line of the gasket identify the engine capacity and type, and have no significance for the gasket thickness **(see illustration)**.

Piston protrusion	Gasket identification
0.56 to 0.67 mm	1 notch
0.68 to 0.71 mm	2 notches
0.72 to 0.75 mm	3 notches
0.76 to 0.79 mm	4 notches
0.80 to 0.83 mm	5 notches

Cylinder head bolt examination

30 A number of different cylinder head bolt types have been used on the XUD engines during the course of production, of both hexagon head and Torx head arrangement. If working on an engine fitted with the earlier hexagon head type bolts, these **must** be renewed once disturbed, and the latest Torx head type used. The Torx head type bolts are supplied in two versions, one version with a guiding end-piece at the base of the thread, and one version without an end-piece. It

is permissible to re-use the Torx type bolts providing that their length does not exceed the figures shown below. Note that, if a bolt is modified to locate the gasket (see paragraph 33), a new bolt will be required when finally refitting the cylinder head.

31 Measure the length of each bolt from the base of the head to the end of the shank (or guiding end-piece) **(see illustration)**. Compare the results with the values given in the following table, to determine whether the bolts and spacers should be renewed. **Note:** *Considering the stress which the cylinder head bolts are under, it is highly recommended that they are renewed, regardless of their apparent condition.*

Bolt length	Action required
Bolts without guiding end-piece:	
Below 121.5 mm	*Re-use bolts/spacers*
Above 121.5 mm	*Renew bolts/spacers*
Bolts with guiding end-piece:	
Below 125.5 mm	*Re-use bolts/spacers*
Above 125.5 mm	*Renew bolts/spacers*

Refitting

32 Turn the crankshaft clockwise (viewed from the timing belt end) until Nos 1 and 4 pistons pass bottom dead centre (BDC) and begin to rise, then position them halfway up their bores. Nos 2 and 3 pistons will also be at their mid-way positions, but descending their bores.

33 Fit the correct gasket the right way round on the cylinder block, with the identification notches or holes at the flywheel/driveplate end of the engine. Make sure that the locating dowel is in place at the timing belt end of the block. Note that, as there is only one locating dowel, it is possible for the gasket to move as the cylinder head is fitted, particularly when the cylinder head is fitted with the engine in the car (due to the inclination of the engine). In the worst instance, this can allow the pistons and/or the valves to hit the gasket, causing engine damage. To avoid this problem, saw the head off a cylinder head bolt, and file (or cut) a slot in the end of the bolt, to enable it to be turned with a screwdriver. Screw the bolt into one of the bolt holes at the flywheel end of the cylinder block, then fit the gasket over the bolt and location dowel. This will ensure that

the gasket is held in position as the cylinder head is fitted.

34 Lower the cylinder head onto the block.

35 Apply a smear of grease to the threads, and to the underside of the heads, of the cylinder head bolts. Peugeot/Citroën recommend the use of Molykote G Rapid Plus (available from your dealer); in the absence of the specified grease, any good-quality high-melting-point grease may be used.

36 Carefully enter each bolt and spacer (convex sides uppermost, where applicable) into its relevant hole (*do not drop it in*) and screw it in finger-tight. Where applicable, after fitting three or four bolts to locate the cylinder head, unscrew the modified bolt fitted in paragraph 33, and fit a new bolt in its place.

37 Working progressively and in sequence, tighten the cylinder head bolts to their Stage 1 torque setting, using a torque wrench and suitable socket **(see illustration)**.

38 Once all the bolts have been tightened to their Stage 1 torque setting, working again in the specified sequence, tighten each bolt to the specified Stage 2 setting. Finally, angle-tighten the bolts through the specified Stage 3 angle. It is recommended that an angle-measuring gauge is used during this stage of tightening, to ensure accuracy.

39 The remainder of the refitting procedure is a reversal of removal, noting the following points:

a) *Ensure that all wiring is correctly routed, and that all connectors are securely reconnected to the correct components.*

b) *Ensure that the coolant hoses are correctly reconnected, and that their retaining clips are securely tightened.*

c) *Ensure that all vacuum/breather hoses are correctly reconnected.*

d) *Refit the cylinder head cover as described in Section 4.*

e) *Reconnect the exhaust system to the manifold, refit the air cleaner housing and ducts, and adjust the accelerator cable, as described in Chapter 4B. If the manifolds were removed, refit these as described in Chapter 4B.*

f) *Refill the cooling system as described in Chapter 1B.*

g) *Reconnect the battery and bleed the fuel system as described in Chapter 4B.*

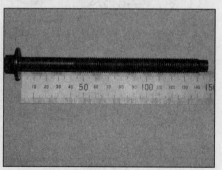

13.29 Cylinder head gasket thickness identification notches (A). Also note engine capacity and type identification notches (B)

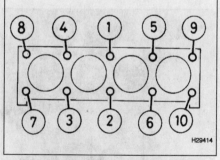

13.31 Measure the length of the cylinder head bolts, to determine whether renewal is required

13.37 Cylinder head bolt tightening sequence

H29414

14 Sump – removal and refitting

Removal

1 Disconnect the battery negative terminal (refer to *Disconnecting the battery* in the Reference Chapter).
2 Drain the engine oil, then clean and refit the engine oil drain plug, tightening it securely. If the engine is nearing its service interval when the oil and filter are due for renewal, it is recommended that the filter is also removed, and a new one fitted. After reassembly, the engine can then be refilled with fresh oil. Refer to Chapter 1B for further information.
3 Firmly apply the handbrake, then jack up the front of the car and support it securely on axle stands (see *Jacking and vehicle support*).
4 On models with air conditioning, where the compressor is mounted onto the side of the sump, remove the drivebelt as described in Chapter 1B. Unbolt the compressor, and position it clear of the sump. Support the weight of the compressor by tying it to the vehicle, to prevent any excess strain being placed on the compressor lines. *Do not* disconnect the refrigerant lines from the compressor (refer to the warnings given in Chapter 3).
5 Where necessary, disconnect the wiring connector from the oil level sender unit, which is screwed into the sump.
6 Progressively slacken and remove all the sump retaining bolts. Since the sump bolts vary in length, remove each bolt in turn, and store it in its correct fitted order by pushing it through a clearly-marked cardboard template. This will avoid the possibility of installing the bolts in the wrong locations on refitting.
7 Try to break the joint by striking the sump with the palm of your hand, then lower and withdraw the sump from under the car. If the sump is stuck (which is quite likely) use a putty knife or similar, carefully inserted between the sump and block. Ease the knife along the joint until the sump is released. Remove the gasket (where fitted), and discard it; a new one must be used on refitting. While the sump is removed, take the opportunity to check the oil pump pick-up/strainer for signs of clogging or splitting. If necessary, remove the pump as described in Section 15, and clean or renew the strainer.
8 On some engines, a large spacer plate is fitted between the sump and the base of the cylinder block/crankcase. If this plate is fitted, undo the two retaining screws from diagonally-opposite corners of the plate. Remove the plate from the base of the engine, noting which way round it is fitted.

Refitting

9 Clean all traces of sealant/gasket from the mating surfaces of the cylinder block/crankcase and sump, then use a clean rag to wipe out the sump and the engine's interior.
10 Where a spacer plate is fitted, remove all traces of sealant/gasket from the spacer plate, then apply a thin coating of suitable sealant to the plate upper mating surface. Offer up the plate to the base of the cylinder block/crankcase, and securely tighten its retaining screws.

11 On engines where the sump was fitted without a gasket, ensure that the sump mating surfaces are clean and dry, then apply a thin coating of suitable sealant to the sump mating surface.
12 On engines where the sump was fitted with a gasket, ensure that all traces of the old gasket have been removed, and that the sump mating surfaces are clean and dry. Position the new gasket on the top of the sump, using a dab of grease to hold it in position.
13 Offer up the sump to the cylinder block/crankcase. Refit its retaining bolts, ensuring that each is screwed into its original location. Tighten the bolts evenly and progressively to the specified torque setting.
14 Where necessary, align the air conditioning compressor with its mountings on the sump, and insert the retaining bolts. Securely tighten the compressor retaining bolts, then refit the drivebelt as described in Chapter 1B.
15 Reconnect the wiring connector to the oil level sensor (where fitted).
16 Lower the vehicle to the ground, then refill the engine with oil as described in Chapter 1B.

15 Oil pump and drive chain – removal, inspection and refitting

Removal

1 Remove the sump as described in Section 14.
2 Where necessary, undo the two retaining screws, and slide the sprocket cover off the front of the oil pump.
3 Slacken and remove the three bolts securing the oil pump to the base of the cylinder block/crankcase. Disengage the pump sprocket from the chain, and remove the oil pump **(see illustration)**. Where necessary, also remove the spacer plate which is fitted behind the oil pump.

Inspection

4 Examine the oil pump sprocket for signs of damage and wear, such as chipped or missing teeth. If the sprocket is worn, the pump assembly must be renewed, since the sprocket is not available separately. It is also recommended that the chain and drive sprocket, fitted to the crankshaft, be renewed at the same time. To renew the chain and drive sprocket, first remove the crankshaft timing belt sprocket as described in Section 9. Unbolt the oil seal carrier from the cylinder block. The sprocket, spacer (where fitted) and chain can then be slid off the end of the crankshaft. See Part E of this Chapter for further information.
5 Slacken and remove the bolts (along with the baffle plate, where fitted) securing the strainer cover to the pump body. Lift off the strainer cover, and take off the relief valve piston and spring, noting which way round they are fitted **(see illustrations)**.

15.3 Removing the oil pump

15.5a Remove the oil pump cover retaining bolts . . .

15.5b . . . then lift off the cover and remove the spring . . .

15.5c . . . and relief valve piston, noting which way round it is fitted

6 Examine the pump rotors and body for signs of wear ridges or scoring. If worn, the complete pump assembly must be renewed.

7 Examine the relief valve piston for signs of wear or damage, and renew if necessary. The condition of the relief valve spring can only be measured by comparing it with a new one; if there is any doubt about its condition, it should also be renewed. Both the piston and spring are available individually.

8 Thoroughly clean the oil pump strainer with a suitable solvent, and check it for signs of clogging or splitting. If the strainer is damaged, the strainer and cover assembly must be renewed.

9 Locate the relief valve spring and piston in the strainer cover. Refit the cover to the pump body, aligning the relief valve piston with its bore in the pump. Refit the baffle plate (where fitted) and the cover retaining bolts, and tighten them securely.

10 Prime the pump by filling it with clean engine oil before refitting.

Refitting

11 Offer up the spacer plate (where fitted), then locate the pump sprocket with its drive chain. Seat the pump on the base of the cylinder block/crankcase. Refit the pump retaining bolts, and tighten them to the specified torque setting.

12 Where necessary, slide the sprocket cover into position on the pump. Refit its retaining bolts, tightening them securely.

13 Refit the sump as described in Section 14.

16 Oil seals – renewal

Crankshaft

Right-hand oil seal

1 Remove the timing belt crankshaft sprocket as described in Section 8.

2 Note the fitted depth of the oil seal.

3 Pull the oil seal from the housing using a hooked instrument. Alternatively, drill a small hole in the oil seal, and use a self-tapping

screw and a pair of pliers to remove it (**see illustration**).

4 Clean the oil seal housing and the crankshaft sealing surface.

5 Dip the new oil seal in clean engine oil, and press it into the housing (open end first) to the previously-noted depth, using a suitable tube or socket. A piece of thin plastic or tape wound around the front of the crankshaft is useful to prevent damage to the oil seal as it is fitted.

6 Where applicable, remove the plastic or tape from the end of the crankshaft.

7 Refit the timing belt crankshaft sprocket as described in Section 8.

Left-hand oil seal

8 Remove the flywheel as described in Section 18.

9 Proceed as described in paragraphs 2 to 6, noting that when fitted, the outer lip of the oil seal must point outwards; if it is pointing inwards, use a piece of bent wire to pull it out. Take care not to damage the oil seal.

10 Refit the flywheel as described in Section 18.

Camshaft

Right-hand oil seal

11 Remove the camshaft sprocket as described in Section 8. In principle there is no need to remove the timing belt completely, but remember that if the belt has been contaminated with oil, it must be renewed.

12 Pull the oil seal from the housing using a hooked instrument (**see illustration**). Alternatively, drill a small hole in the oil seal and use a self-tapping screw and a pair of pliers to remove it.

13 Clean the oil seal housing and the camshaft sealing surface.

14 Smear the new oil seal with clean engine oil, then fit it over the end of the camshaft, open end first. A piece of thin plastic or tape wound round the front of the camshaft should prevent damage to the oil seal as it is fitted.

15 Press the seal into the housing until it is flush with the end face of the cylinder head. Use an M10 bolt (screwed into the end of the camshaft), washers and a suitable tube or socket to press the seal into position.

16 Refit the camshaft sprocket as described in Section 8.

17 Where applicable, fit a new timing belt as described in Section 7.

Left-hand oil seal

18 No oil seal is fitted to the left-hand end of the camshaft. The sealing is provided by an O-ring fitted to the vacuum pump flange. The O-ring can be renewed after unbolting the pump from the cylinder head (see Chapter 9). Note the smaller O-ring which seals the oil feed gallery to the pump – this may also cause leakage from the pump/cylinder head mating faces if it deteriorates or fails (**see illustration**).

17 Oil level and pressure sensors – general

Refer to Chapter 5A for details.

18 Flywheel – removal, inspection and refitting

Removal

1 Remove the transmission as described in Chapter 7, then remove the clutch assembly as described in Chapter 6.

2 Prevent the flywheel from turning by locking the ring gear teeth (**see illustration 5.2**). Alternatively, bolt a strap between the flywheel and the cylinder block/crankcase. *Do not* attempt to lock the flywheel in position using the crankshaft pulley locking tool described in Section 3.

3 Slacken and remove the flywheel retaining bolts, and remove the flywheel from the end of the crankshaft. Be careful not to drop it; it is heavy. If the flywheel locating dowel is a loose fit in the crankshaft end, remove it and store it with the flywheel for safe-keeping. Discard the flywheel bolts; new ones must be used on refitting.

Inspection

4 Examine the flywheel for scoring of the

16.3 Self-tapping screw and pliers used to remove the crankshaft right-hand oil seal

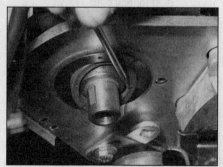

16.12 Removing the camshaft right-hand oil seal

16.18 Camshaft left-hand oil seal (1) and oil feed gallery O-ring (2) on rear of the brake vacuum pump

clutch face, and for wear or chipping of the ring gear teeth. If the clutch face is scored, the flywheel may be surface-ground, but renewal is preferable. Seek the advice of a Peugeot/Citroën dealer or engine reconditioning specialist to see if machining is possible. If the ring gear is worn or damaged, the flywheel must be renewed, as it is not possible to renew the ring gear separately.

Refitting

5 Clean the mating surfaces of the flywheel and crankshaft. Remove any remaining locking compound from the threads of the crankshaft holes, using the correct size of tap, if available.

 HAYNES HINT *If a suitable tap is not available, cut two slots along the threads of one of the old flywheel bolts, and use the bolt to remove the locking compound from the threads.*

6 If the new flywheel retaining bolts are not supplied with their threads already precoated, apply a suitable thread-locking compound to the threads of each bolt.
7 Ensure that the locating dowel is in position. Offer up the flywheel, locating it on the dowel, and fit the new retaining bolts.
8 Lock the flywheel using the method employed on dismantling, and tighten the retaining bolts to the specified torque.
9 Refit the clutch as described in Chapter 6. Remove the flywheel locking tool, and refit the transmission as described in Chapter 7.

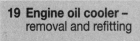 **19 Engine oil cooler –** removal and refitting

Removal

1 Firmly apply the handbrake, then jack up the front of the car and support it securely on axle stands (see *Jacking and vehicle support*).
2 Drain the cooling system as described in Chapter 1B. Alternatively, clamp the oil cooler coolant hoses directly above the cooler, and be prepared for some coolant loss as the hoses are disconnected.
3 Position a suitable container beneath the oil filter. Unscrew the filter using an oil filter removal tool if necessary, and drain the oil into the container. If the oil filter is damaged or distorted during removal, it must be renewed. Given the low cost of a new oil filter relative to the cost of repairing the damage which could result if a re-used filter springs a leak, it is probably a good idea to renew the filter in any case.
4 Release the hose clips, and disconnect the coolant hoses from the oil cooler.
5 Unscrew the oil cooler/oil filter mounting bolt from the cylinder block, and withdraw the

19.5 Oil cooler/oil filter mounting bolt (A) and locating notch (B)

cooler. Note the locating notch in the cooler flange, which fits over the lug on the cylinder block **(see illustration)**. Discard the oil cooler sealing ring; a new one must be used on refitting.

Refitting

6 Fit a new sealing ring to the recess in the rear of the cooler, then offer the cooler to the cylinder block.
7 Ensure that the locating notch in the cooler flange is correctly engaged with the lug on the cylinder block, then refit the mounting bolt and tighten it securely.
8 Fit the oil filter, then lower the vehicle to the ground. Top-up the engine oil level as described in *Weekly checks*.
9 Refill or top-up the cooling system as described in Chapter 1B or *Weekly checks*. Start the engine, and check the oil cooler for signs of leakage.

20 Engine/transmission mountings – inspection and renewal

Inspection

1 If improved access is required, firmly apply the handbrake, then jack up the front of the car and support it securely on axle stands (see *Jacking and vehicle support*).
2 Check the mounting rubbers to see if they are cracked, hardened or separated from the metal at any point; renew the mounting if any such damage or deterioration is evident.
3 Check that all the mountings' fasteners are securely tightened; use a torque wrench to check if possible.
4 Using a large screwdriver or a crowbar, check for wear in each mounting by carefully levering against it to check for free play. Where this is not possible, enlist the aid of an assistant to move the engine/transmission back-and-forth, or from side-to-side, while you watch the mounting. While some free play is to be expected even from new components, excessive wear should be obvious. If excessive free play is found, check first that the fasteners are correctly secured, then renew any worn components as described below.

Renewal

Right-hand mounting

5 Place a jack beneath the engine, with a block of wood on the jack head. Raise the jack until it is supporting the weight of the engine.
6 Release the retaining clips and brackets, and position the diesel priming pump and all the relevant hoses and cables clear of the engine mounting assembly and suspension top mounting.
7 Slacken and remove the three nuts securing the mounting bracket to the engine bracket.
8 Unscrew the single nut securing the mounting bracket to the rubber mounting, and lift off the bracket.
9 Using a strap wrench or similar tool, unscrew the rubber mounting from the body. Alternatively, fabricate a tool from suitable metal tube with projections to engage in the cut-outs in the mounting.
10 Check for signs of wear or damage on all components, and renew as necessary.
11 On reassembly, securely tighten the rubber mounting in the body.
12 Refit the mounting bracket to the rubber mounting and engine bracket and tighten the retaining nuts to the specified torque.
13 Reposition the diesel priming pump and the hoses and cables move clear for access.
14 Remove the jack from under the engine.

Left-hand mounting

15 Remove the battery, battery tray, and mounting plate as described in Chapter 5A.
16 Place a jack beneath the transmission, with a block of wood on the jack head. Raise the jack until it is supporting the weight of the transmission.
17 Slacken and remove the centre nut and washer from the left-hand mounting, then undo the nuts securing the mounting in position and remove it from the engine compartment.
18 If necessary, slide the spacer (where fitted) off the mounting stud, then unscrew the stud from the top of the transmission housing, and remove it along with its washer. If the mounting stud is tight, a universal stud extractor can be used to unscrew it.
19 Check all components carefully for signs of wear or damage, and renew as necessary.
20 Clean the threads of the mounting stud, and apply a coat of thread-locking compound to its threads. Refit the stud and washer to the top of the transmission, and tighten it securely.
21 Slide the spacer (where fitted) onto the mounting stud, then refit the rubber mounting. Tighten both the mounting-to-body bolts and the mounting centre nut to their specified torque settings, and remove the jack from underneath the transmission.
22 Refit the battery mounting plate, battery tray and battery as described in Chapter 5A.

Rear mounting

23 Refer to Chapter 2A, Section 16.

Chapter 2 Part D:
1.9 and 2.0 litre diesel engine (DW series) in-car repair procedures

Contents

Degrees of difficulty

Easy, suitable for novice with little experience	**Fairly easy,** suitable for beginner with some experience	**Fairly difficult,** suitable for competent DIY mechanic	**Difficult,** suitable for experienced DIY mechanic	**Very difficult,** suitable for expert DIY or professional

Specifications

Engine (general)

Designation:
  1.9 litre (1868 cc) engines. DW8
  2.0 litre (1997 cc) engines. DW10
Engine codes*:
  1.9 litre engines:
    Engines with mechanical injection pump . . . .   WJZ (DW8)
    Engines with electronically controlled injection pump . . . .   WJY (DW8B)
  2.0 litre engines . . . .   RHY (DW10TD)
Bore:
  1.9 litre engines . . . .   82.2 mm
  2.0 litre engines . . . .   85.0 mm
Stroke . . . .   88.00 mm
Direction of crankshaft rotation . . . .   Clockwise (viewed from right-hand side of vehicle)
No 1 cylinder location. . . . .   At transmission end of block
Compression ratio:
  1.9 litre engines . . . .   23 : 1
  2.0 litre engines . . . .   17.6 : 1

* The engine code is stamped on front of the cylinder block, just to the left of the oil filter/cooler.
The code given in brackets is the factory identification number.

Compression pressures (engine hot, at cranking speed)
Normal .... 25 to 30 bars (363 to 435 psi)
Maximum difference between any two cylinders.................. 5 bars (73 psi)

Camshaft
Drive .... Toothed belt
No of bearings:
   1.9 litre engines 3
   2.0 litre engines 5
Endfloat:
   1.9 litre engines .... 0.02 to 0.07 mm
   2.0 litre engines .... 0.07 to 0.38 mm

Valve clearances (engine cold)
1.9 litre engines:
   Inlet .... 0.15 ± 0.07 mm
   Exhaust... 0.30 ± 0.07 mm
2.0 litre engines .... Automatically adjusted by hydraulic tappets

Lubrication system
Oil pump type... Gear-type, chain-driven off the crankshaft right-hand end
Minimum oil pressure at 80°C:
   1.9 litre engines .... 4.5 bar at 4000 rpm
   2.0 litre engines .... 4 bar at 4000 rpm

Torque wrench settings

	Nm	lbf ft
Big-end bearing cap nuts:*		
Stage 1	20	15
Stage 2	Angle-tighten a further 70°	
Camshaft:		
Bearing cap nuts – 1.9 litre engines	20	15
Bearing cap casting bolts – 2.0 litre engines	10	7
Camshaft sprocket:		
Hub-to-camshaft bolt	43	32
Sprocket-to-hub bolts:		
1.9 litre engines	23	17
2.0 litre engines	20	15
Crankshaft right-hand (timing belt end) oil seal housing bolts	14	10
Crankshaft pulley bolt:		
1.9 litre engines:		
To RPO 10063 (bolted to sprocket)	10	7
From RPO 10064 (not bolted to sprocket):		
Stage 1	70	52
Stage 2	Angle-tighten a further 60°	
2.0 litre engines (see text – Section 5):		
Early type pulley without green paint mark:		
Stage 1	50	37
Stage 2	Angle-tighten a further 62°	
Later type pulley with green paint mark:		
Stage 1	70	52
Stage 2	Angle-tighten a further 60°	
Crankshaft sprocket bolt – 1.9 litre engines (to RPO 10063):		
Stage 1	40	30
Stage 2	Angle-tighten a further 55°	
Cylinder head bolts:		
1.9 litre engines:		
Stage 1	20	15
Stage 2	60	44
Stage 3	Angle-tighten a further 180°	
2.0 litre engines:		
Stage 1	20	15
Stage 2	60	44
Stage 3	Angle-tighten a further 220°	
Cylinder head cover bolts:		
1.9 litre engines:		
Upper cover bolts	10	7
Lower cover bolts	5	4

	Nm	lbf ft
2.0 litre engines	10	7
Engine-to-transmission fixing bolts	50	37
Engine/transmission left-hand mounting:		
Centre nut	65	48
Mounting bracket-to-body bolts	25	18
Mounting rubber nuts/bolts	25	18
Mounting stud to bracket	50	37
Mounting bracket to transmission	60	44

Torque wrench settings (continued)

	Nm	lbf ft
Engine/transmission rear mounting:		
Connecting link-to-mounting rubber nut/bolt	50	37
Connecting link-to-subframe nut/bolt	50	37
Mounting assembly-to-block bolts	45	33
Engine/transmission right-hand mounting:		
1.9 litre engines:		
Engine bracket to cylinder block/head	45	33
Movement restrictors	45	33
Rubber mounting to body	45	33
Upper bracket to engine bracket	45	33
Upper bracket to rubber mounting	45	33
2.0 litre engines:		
Domed buffer nut	20	15
Engine bracket bolts:		
M8 bolts	20	15
M10 bolts	45	33
Rubber mounting to body	45	33
Stiffener bracket bolts	22	16
Upper bracket to engine bracket	61	45
Upper bracket to rubber mounting	45	33
Flywheel bolts*	48	35
Fuel filter/thermostat housing bolts – 1.9 litre engines	15	11
Fuel filter plastic housing bolt – 1.9 litre engines	18	13
Injection pump sprocket:		
Sprocket-to-hub bolts – 1.9 litre engines	23	17
Sprocket nut – 2.0 litre engines	50	37
Main bearing cap bolts:		
1.9 litre engines	70	52
2.0 litre engines:		
Stage 1	25	18
Stage 2	Angle-tighten a further 60°	
Oil cooler centre bolt	50	37
Oil pump mounting bolts	16	12
Piston oil jet spray tube bolt	10	7
Roadwheel bolts	85	63
Sump bolts	16	12
Sump drain plug	34	25
Thermostat housing fixings – 2.0 litre engines:		
Housing studs	25	18
Retaining nuts and bolts	20	15
Timing belt cover bolts	8	6
Timing belt tensioner pulley bolt	23	17
Timing belt idler pulley bolt	43	32

* New nuts/bolts must be used.

1 General information

How to use this Chapter

This Part of Chapter 2 describes those repair procedures that can reasonably be carried out on the engine while it remains in the car. If the engine has been removed from the car and is being dismantled, as described in Part F, any preliminary dismantling procedures can be ignored.

Note that, while it may be possible physically to overhaul items such as the piston/connecting rod assemblies while the engine is in the car, such tasks are not normally carried out as separate operations. Usually, several additional procedures (not to mention the cleaning of components and of oilways) have to be carried out. For this reason, all such tasks are classed as major overhaul procedures, and are described in Part F of this Chapter.

Part F describes the removal of the engine/transmission from the vehicle, and the full overhaul procedures that can then be carried out.

Engine description

The DW series engine is a relatively new power unit based on the well-proven XUD series engine which has appeared in many Peugeot and Citroën vehicles. The engine is of four-cylinder single overhead camshaft design, mounted transversely, with the transmission mounted on the left-hand side.

The crankshaft runs in five main bearings of the usual shell type. Endfloat is controlled by thrustwashers either side of No 2 main bearing.

The connecting rods rotate on horizontally-split bearing shells at their big-ends. The pistons are attached to the connecting rods by gudgeon pins, which are secured in position with circlips. The aluminium-alloy pistons are fitted with three piston rings – two compression rings and an oil control ring.

The cylinder block is made from cast-iron, and the cylinder bores are an integral part of the cylinder block. On this type of engine, the cylinder bores are sometimes referred to as having dry liners.

The camshaft is driven by a toothed timing belt which also operates the coolant pump. On 1.9 litre engines, the camshaft operates the eight valves via bucket-type followers; valve clearances are adjusted by shims fitted between the valve stem and follower. On 2.0 litre engines, the camshaft operates the valves via followers and hydraulic tappets which automatically adjust the valve clearances. On all engines the camshaft runs in bearing caps which are bolted to the top of the cylinder head. The inlet and exhaust valves are each closed by coil springs, and operate in guides pressed into the cylinder head.

Lubrication is by means of an oil pump, which is driven (via a chain and sprocket) off the right-hand end of the crankshaft. It draws oil through a strainer located in the sump, and then forces it through an externally-mounted filter into galleries in the cylinder block/crankcase. From there, the oil is distributed to the crankshaft (main bearings) and camshaft. The big-end bearings are supplied with oil via internal drillings in the crankshaft, while the camshaft bearings also receive a pressurised supply. The camshaft lobes and valves are lubricated by splash, as are all other engine components. An oil cooler is mounted between the oil filter and cylinder block to keep the oil temperature stable under arduous operating temperatures.

Repair operations – precaution

The 2.0 litre engine is a complex unit with numerous accessories and ancillary components. The design of the engine compartment is such that every conceivable space has been utilised, and access to virtually all of the engine components is extremely limited. In many cases, ancillary components will have to be removed, or moved to one side, and wiring, pipes and hoses will have to be disconnected or removed from various cable clips and support brackets.

When working on this engine, read through the entire procedure first, look at the vehicle and engine at the same time, and establish whether you have the necessary tools, equipment, skill and patience to proceed. Allow considerable time for any operation, and be prepared for the unexpected. Any major work on this engine is not for the faint-hearted!

Because of the limited access, many of the engine photographs appearing in this Chapter were, by necessity, taken with the engine removed from the vehicle.

 Warning: It is essential to observe strict precautions when working on the fuel system components of the 2.0 litre engine, particularly the high pressure side of the system. Before carrying out any engine operations that entail working on, or near, any part of the fuel system, refer to the precautionary information given in Chapter 4C, Section 1.

Operations with engine in car

The following work can be carried out with the engine in the car:
a) Compression and leakdown tests.
b) Cylinder head cover – removal and refitting.
c) Timing belt covers – removal and refitting.
d) Timing belt – removal, refitting and adjustment.
e) Timing belt sprockets and tensioner/idler pulleys – removal and refitting.
f) Camshaft oil seal – renewal.
g) Camshaft and followers – removal, inspection and refitting.
h) Cylinder head (1.9 litre engines) – removal and refitting*.
i) Cylinder head and pistons – decarbonising.
j) Sump – removal and refitting.
k) Oil pump – removal, overhaul and refitting.
l) Crankshaft oil seals – renewal.
m) Engine/transmission mountings – inspection and renewal.
n) Flywheel – removal, inspection and refitting.

* **Note:** On 2.0 litre engines, access between the cylinder head and engine compartment bulkhead, and to the rear underside of the engine is so restricted that it is impossible to remove the cylinder head with the engine in the car unless considerable additional dismantling is carried out first (eg, removal of the front suspension subframe and related components). Cylinder head removal and refitting procedures are therefore contained in Part F, assuming that the engine/transmission has been removed from the vehicle.

2 Compression and leakdown tests – description and interpretation

Compression test

Note: A compression tester specifically designed for diesel engines must be used for this test, because of the high pressures involved.

1 When engine performance is down, or if misfiring occurs which cannot be attributed to the fuel system, a compression test can provide diagnostic clues as to the engine's condition. If the test is performed regularly, it can give warning of trouble before any other symptoms become apparent.

2 A compression tester specifically intended for diesel engines must be used, because of the higher pressures involved. The tester is connected to an adapter which screws into the glow plug or injector hole. On these engines, an adapter suitable for use in the glow plug holes will be required, so as not to disturb the fuel system components. It is unlikely to be worthwhile buying such a tester for occasional use, but it may be possible to borrow or hire one – if not, have the test performed by a garage.

3 Unless specific instructions to the contrary are supplied with the tester, observe the following points:
a) The battery must be in a good state of charge, the air filter must be clean, and the engine should be at normal operating temperature.
b) All the glow plugs should be removed as described in Chapter 5C before starting the test.
c) On 1.9 litre WJZ engines, the anti-theft system electronic engine immobiliser unit wiring connector at the rear of the injection pump must be disconnected.
d) On 1.9 litre WJY engines and all 2.0 litre engines, the wiring connector on the engine management system ECU must be disconnected. Refer to Chapter 4C for further information.

4 Crank the engine on the starter motor; after one or two revolutions, the compression pressure should build-up to a maximum figure, and then stabilise. Record the highest reading obtained.

5 Repeat the test on the remaining cylinders, recording the pressure in each.

6 All cylinders should produce very similar pressures; a difference of more than 5 bars between any two cylinders indicates a fault. Note that the compression should build-up quickly in a healthy engine; low compression on the first stroke, followed by gradually-increasing pressure on successive strokes, indicates worn piston rings. A low compression reading on the first stroke, which does not build-up during successive strokes, indicates leaking valves or a blown head gasket (a cracked head could also be the cause). Deposits on the undersides of the valve heads can also cause low compression.

7 As a guide, any cylinder pressure of below 20 bars can be considered as less than healthy. Refer to a Peugeot/Citroën dealer or other specialist if in doubt as to whether a particular pressure reading is acceptable.

8 The cause of poor compression is less easy to establish on a diesel engine than on a petrol one. The effect of introducing oil into the cylinders ('wet' testing) is not conclusive, because there is a risk that the oil will sit in the swirl chamber or in the recess on the piston crown instead of passing to the rings. A low reading from two adjacent cylinders is almost certainly due to the head gasket having blown between them; the presence of coolant in the engine oil will confirm this.

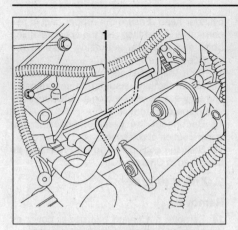

3.4 Insert the bolt/drill (special tool shown – 1) in through the hole in the cylinder block flange (shown with the starter motor moved forwards for clarity) and locate it in the rear of the flywheel

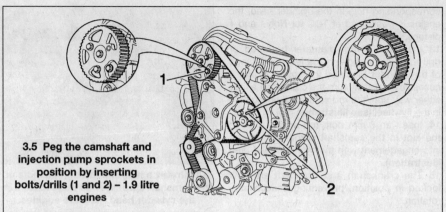

3.5 Peg the camshaft and injection pump sprockets in position by inserting bolts/drills (1 and 2) – 1.9 litre engines

Leakdown test

9 A leakdown test measures the rate at which compressed air fed into the cylinder is lost. It is an alternative to a compression test, and in many ways it is better, since the escaping air provides easy identification of where pressure loss is occurring (piston rings, valves or head gasket).

10 The equipment needed for leakdown testing is unlikely to be available to the home mechanic. If poor compression is suspected, have the test performed by a suitably-equipped garage.

3 Engine assembly/valve timing holes – general information and usage

Note: *Do not attempt to rotate the engine whilst the crankshaft/camshaft/injection pump (as applicable) are locked in position. If the engine is to be left in this state for a long period of time, it is a good idea to place suitable warning notices inside the vehicle, and in the engine compartment. This will reduce the possibility of the engine being accidentally cranked on the starter motor, which is likely to cause damage with the locking pins in place.*

1.9 litre engines

1 Timing holes are drilled in the camshaft sprocket hub, injection pump sprocket hub and flywheel. The holes are used to align the crankshaft, camshaft and injection pump, and to prevent the possibility of the valves contacting the pistons when refitting the cylinder head, and to ensure the valve timing/injection pump timing is correct when refitting the timing belt. When the holes are aligned with their corresponding holes in the cylinder head and cylinder block (as appropriate), suitable diameter bolts/pins can be inserted to lock the camshaft, injection pump and crankshaft in position, preventing them from rotating unnecessarily. Proceed as follows.

2 Remove the timing belt upper and intermediate covers as described in Section 6 to gain access to the sprockets.

3 Using a suitable socket and extension bar, turn the crankshaft by means of the pulley bolt, until the holes in the camshaft and injection pump sprocket hubs are aligned with the corresponding holes in the cylinder head/pump. Note that the crankshaft must always be turned in a clockwise direction (viewed from the right-hand side of vehicle).

4 With the camshaft sprocket hole correctly positioned, insert an 8 mm diameter bolt or drill through the hole in the front, left-hand flange of the cylinder block, located behind the starter motor, and locate it in the timing hole in the rear of the flywheel (**see illustration**). Note that it may be necessary to rotate the crankshaft slightly, to get the holes to align.

5 With the flywheel correctly positioned, lock the camshaft sprocket in position by inserting an 8 mm diameter bolt or a drill through the timing hole in the sprocket hub, and locating it in the hole in the cylinder head (**see illustration**).

6 Lock the injection pump sprocket in position by inserting a 6 mm diameter bolt or a drill through the timing hole in the sprocket hub and locating it in the hole in the pump.

7 The crankshaft, camshaft and injection pump are now locked in position, preventing unnecessary rotation.

2.0 litre engines

8 Timing holes or slots are located in the flywheel and in the camshaft sprocket or sprocket hub. The holes/slots are used to align the crankshaft and camshaft at the TDC position for Nos 1 and 4 pistons. This will ensure that the valve timing is maintained during operations that require removal and refitting of the timing belt and, on later engines, the crankshaft pulley. When the holes/slots are aligned with their corre-sponding holes in the cylinder block and cylinder head, suitable diameter bolts/pins can be inserted to lock the crankshaft and camshaft in position, preventing rotation.

9 The HDi type fuel system used on these engines does not have a conventional diesel injection pump, but instead uses a high-pressure fuel pump that does not have to be timed. The alignment of the fuel pump sprocket (and hence the fuel pump itself) with respect to crankshaft and camshaft position is therefore irrelevant.

10 To align the engine assembly/valve timing holes, proceed as follows.

11 Remove the upper timing belt cover as described in Section 6.

12 Using a suitable socket and extension bar, turn the crankshaft by means of the pulley bolt, until the timing slot in the camshaft sprocket hub is aligned with the corresponding hole in the cylinder head. Note that the crankshaft must always be turned in a clockwise direction (viewed from the right-hand side of vehicle). Use a small mirror so that the position of the sprocket hub timing slot can be observed (**see illustrations**). When the slot is aligned with the

3.12a Use a mirror to observe the camshaft sprocket hub timing slot – 2.0 litre engines

3.12b Camshaft sprocket hub timing slot (A) aligned with the cylinder head timing hole (B) – 2.0 litre engines

corresponding hole in the cylinder head, the engine is positioned at TDC for Nos 1 and 4 pistons.

13 Insert an 8 mm diameter bolt, rod or drill through the hole in the left-hand flange of the cylinder block by the starter motor; if necessary, carefully turn the crankshaft a little either way until the rod enters the timing hole in the flywheel **(see illustration 3.4)**.

14 Insert an 8 mm bolt, rod or drill through the slot in the camshaft sprocket hub and into engagement with the cylinder head **(see illustration)**.

15 The crankshaft and camshaft are now locked in position, preventing unnecessary rotation.

4 Cylinder head cover – removal and refitting

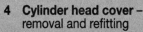

1.9 litre engines

Removal

1 Release the fasteners from the right-hand side and top of the engine cover then lift off the cover, taking care not to lose its mounting rubbers **(see illustrations)**. Disconnect the battery negative terminal (refer to *Disconnecting the battery* in the Reference Chapter).

2 Remove the upper section of the inlet manifold as described in Chapter 4C.

3 Unscrew the bolts securing the EGR pipe to the top of the exhaust manifold and the cylinder head cover. Free the pipe from the manifold and position it clear of the cylinder

4.1a Remove the fasteners from the right-hand side . . .

4.1c . . . then remove the cover from the engine – 1.9 litre engines

3.14 Insert a bolt/drill through the hole in the camshaft sprocket hub and locate it in the cylinder head – 2.0 litre engines

head cover. Recover the gasket and discard it; a new one should be used on refitting.

4 Slacken the retaining clips and disconnect the breather hoses from the upper section of the cylinder head cover.

5 Unscrew the eight retaining bolts then lift off the upper section of the cylinder head cover, complete with its rubber seal.

6 Unscrew the three retaining bolts and washers then remove the lower section of the cylinder head cover, complete with its rubber seal.

7 Inspect the cover seals for signs of damage or deterioration and, if necessary, renew.

Refitting

8 Carefully clean the cylinder head and cover mating surfaces, and remove all traces of oil.

9 Fit the rubber seals to both the cylinder head cover sections, ensuring they are correctly located along their entire length.

10 Fit the lower section of the cover the

4.1b . . . and top of the engine cover . . .

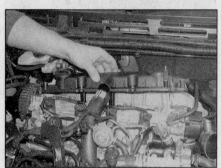

4.19 Removing the cylinder head cover – 2.0 litre engines

cylinder head. Ensure the rubber seal is still correctly located then refit the cover retaining bolts and washers, tightening them to the specified torque.

11 Refit the upper section of the cover to the lower section, ensuring its seal remains correctly seated, and tighten its retaining bolts to the specified torque.

12 Reconnect the breather hoses to the upper section of the cover.

13 Refit the EGR pipe and inlet manifold as described in Chapter 4C.

2.0 litre engines

Removal

14 Remove the timing belt upper cover as described in Section 6.

15 Slacken or release the clips securing the crankcase ventilation hoses to the centre and left-hand end of the cylinder head cover and disconnect the hoses.

16 Undo the bolts as necessary and move the engine cover and cable guide support bracket clear of the right-hand end of the cylinder head cover.

17 Disconnect the camshaft position sensor wiring connector.

18 Release the wiring harness from the clip on the cylinder head cover and move the harness to one side.

19 Undo the bolts securing the cylinder head cover to the camshaft carrier and collect the washers. Carefully lift off the cover taking care not to damage the camshaft position sensor as the cover is removed **(see illustration)**. Recover the seal from the cover.

Refitting

20 Refitting is a reversal of removal, bearing in mind the following points:
  a) *Examine the cover seal for signs of damage and deterioration, and renew if necessary.*
  b) *Tighten the cylinder head cover bolts to the specified torque.*
  c) *On early engines with a two-piece camshaft sprocket (see Section 9), adjust the camshaft position sensor air gap as described in Chapter 4C before refitting the upper timing belt cover.*

5 Crankshaft pulley – removal and refitting

Removal – 1.9 litre engines

Note: *As from RPO 10064 the camshaft sprocket is fixed, and the crankshaft sprocket is 'floating' as for the 2.0 litre engine. Refer to the 2.0 litre procedure described later in this Section.*

1 Remove the auxiliary drivebelt as described in Chapter 1B.

2 Undo the four crankshaft pulley retaining bolts and remove the pulley, noting which way round it is fitted.

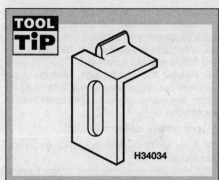

TOOL TiP

H34034

A flywheel ring gear locking tool can be made from a short strip of steel bent to form a right-angle. Cut a slot in the upper part and bend this part up to engage with the ring gear teeth. File the edges to form a tooth profile. Drill a hole in the lower part to enable the tool to be bolted to the bellhousing flange.

Refitting – 1.9 litre engines

3 Fit the pulley to the end of the crankshaft, ensuring it is fitted the correct way round. Apply locking compound (Peugeot/Citroën recommend the use of Loctite Frenetanch) to the retaining bolt threads, then refit and tighten the bolts to the specified torque.

4 Refit and tension the auxiliary drivebelt as described in Chapter 1B.

Removal – 2.0 litre engines

5 Remove the auxiliary drivebelt as described in Chapter 1B.

6 It is now necessary to determine the type of pulley fitted, as there are two different removal and refitting procedures accordingly.

7 From under the wheel arch, observe the flat front face of the pulley. If there is a green paint mark on the pulley face it is of the later type. If no paint mark is present, the pulley is an early type. Proceed as described in the appropriate following sub-sections, according to pulley type.

Pulley without green paint mark

8 To prevent crankshaft rotation whilst the pulley retaining bolt is being slackened, the flywheel ring gear must be locked using a suitable tool made from steel angle (see **Tool Tip**). Release the power steering fluid pipes from the clamps on the cover plate at the base of the transmission bellhousing. Remove the cover plate from the bellhousing and bolt the tool to the lower bolt hole in the bellhousing flange so it engages with the ring gear teeth.

9 Using a suitable socket and extension bar, unscrew the retaining bolt, remove the washer, then slide the pulley off the end of the crankshaft (see **illustration**). If the pulley is a tight fit, it can be drawn off the crankshaft using a suitable puller. If a puller is being used, refit the pulley retaining bolt without the washer, to avoid damaging the crankshaft as the puller is tightened.

5.9 Unscrew the bolt and washer and remove the crankshaft pulley – 2.0 litre engines

Pulley with green paint mark

10 Align the engine assembly/valve timing holes as described in Section 3, and lock the crankshaft and the camshaft sprocket in position. The crankshaft timing belt sprocket used with the later type pulley incorporates a wider keyway for the locating Woodruff key. When the pulley retaining bolt is slackened, the sprocket is free to turn on the crankshaft within the limits afforded by the wider keyway. This provides a certain degree of lateral movement of the sprocket for accurate adjustment of the timing belt tension. It is therefore essential that the flywheel and camshaft are locked in the engine assembly/valve timing position when the pulley bolt is slackened, otherwise the sprockets will turn slightly and the valve timing will be lost.

11 To prevent crankshaft rotation whilst the pulley retaining bolt is being slackened, make up and fit a flywheel ring gear locking tool as described in paragraph 8. *Do not* attempt to use only the engine assembly/valve timing locking tools to prevent rotation whilst the bolt is slackened.

12 Using a suitable socket and extension bar, unscrew the retaining bolt, remove the washer, then slide the pulley off the end of the crankshaft. If the pulley is a tight fit, it can be drawn off the crankshaft using a suitable puller. If a puller is being used, refit the pulley retaining bolt without the washer, to avoid damaging the crankshaft as the puller is tightened.

Refitting – 2.0 litre engines

13 If working on the later type pulley, ensure that the engine assembly/valve timing holes are still aligned as described in Section 3, and the crankshaft and camshaft sprocket are locked in position.

14 Locate the pulley in position on the end of the crankshaft.

15 Thoroughly clean the threads of the pulley retaining bolt, then apply a coat of locking compound to the bolt threads (Peugeot/Citroën recommend the use of Loctite Frenetanch).

16 Refit the crankshaft pulley retaining bolt and washer. Tighten the bolt to the specified torque, then through the specified angle, preventing the crankshaft from turning using the tool employed for removal. Note that

different torque and angle settings are given in the Specifications, according to pulley type.

17 Remove the flywheel ring gear locking tool and, where applicable, the crankshaft and camshaft sprocket locking tools.

18 Refit the cover plate to the transmission bellhousing and secure the power steering fluid pipes in position.

19 If working on the later type pulley, refit the upper timing belt cover as described in Section 6.

20 Refit and tension the auxiliary drivebelt as described in Chapter 1B.

6 Timing belt covers – removal and refitting

1.9 litre engines

Upper cover removal

1 Disconnect the battery negative terminal (refer to *Disconnecting the battery* in the Reference Chapter).

2 Release the clip in the centre of the engine cover and undo the retaining screw on the right-hand side. Lift off the engine cover (see **illustrations 4.1a to 4.1c**).

3 Firmly apply the handbrake, then jack up the front of the vehicle and support it securely on axle stands (see *Jacking and vehicle support*). Remove the right-hand front roadwheel.

4 To gain access to the right-hand end of the engine, the wheel arch plastic liner must be removed. The liner is secured by various screws and clips under the wheel arch. Release all the fasteners, and remove liner from under the front wing. Where necessary, unclip the coolant hoses from under the wing to improve access further.

5 At the connections adjacent to the fuel pump, disconnect the fuel supply and return hose quick-release fittings using a small screwdriver to release the locking clip. Cover the open unions to prevent dirt entry, using small plastic bags, or fingers cut from clean rubber gloves.

6 Release the two hoses from the retaining clips on the upper timing belt cover and move them to one side (see **illustration**).

6.6 Unclip the fuel pipes from the top of the timing belt covers – 1.9 litre engines

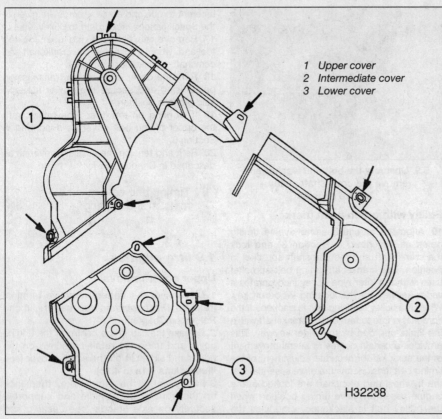

1 Upper cover
2 Intermediate cover
3 Lower cover

H32238

6.12 Timing belt cover retaining bolt locations (arrowed) – 1.9 litre engines

7 Connect an engine hoist or suitable lifting gear to the two lifting brackets on the cylinder head. Raise the hoist to just take the weight of the engine.
8 For additional stability, place a jack beneath the right-hand side of the engine, with a block of wood on the jack head. Raise the jack until it is just contacting the sump.
9 Slacken and remove the three bolts securing the right-hand engine/transmission mounting upper bracket to the lower (engine) bracket. Unscrew the single nut securing the upper bracket to the rubber mounting. Remove the upper bracket from the rubber mounting and lower (engine) bracket.
10 Undo the two nuts and remove the through-bolts securing the rear engine/

transmission mounting connecting link to the mounting bracket on the subframe and on the rear of the cylinder block. Release and remove the connecting link from the mounting brackets.
11 With the two engine mountings removed, alternatively raise and lower the lifting gear and the jack under the engine, as necessary, for access to the timing belt cover retaining bolts.
12 Undo the bolt securing the upper cover to the cylinder head cover (see illustration).
13 Undo the two bolts at the joint between the upper cover and lower cover; one in the centre just below the engine mounting bracket, and one on the outer edge. Note that the bolt on the outer edge also retains the

coolant pump. To avoid coolant leakage, after the cover is removed, refit the bolt fitted with a 5.0 mm spacer, and tighten it securely.
14 Undo the remaining bolt directly above the injection pump sprocket.
15 Release the locating lugs, ease the upper section out from behind the intermediate cover and manipulate the upper cover from its location.

Intermediate cover removal
16 Remove the upper cover as described previously.
17 Undo the remaining bolt at the base of the cover just below the engine mounting bracket.
18 Release the locating lugs and manipulate the intermediate cover from its location.

Lower cover removal
19 Remove the upper and intermediate covers as described previously.
20 Remove the crankshaft pulley as described in Section 5.
21 Undo the two remaining bolts on the edge of the cover, one on either side of the crankshaft pulley location.
22 Lift the cover off the front of the engine.

Refitting
23 Refitting of all the covers is a reversal of the relevant removal procedure, ensuring that each cover section is correctly located, and that the cover retaining bolts are securely tightened. Ensure that all disturbed hoses are reconnected and retained by their relevant clips, and that all nuts/bolts are tightened to their specified torque wrench settings (where given). On completion, prime and bleed the fuel system as described in Chapter 4C.

2.0 litre engines

⚠ Warning: Refer to the precautionary information contained in Section 1 before proceeding.

Upper cover removal
24 Disconnect the battery negative terminal (refer to Disconnecting the battery in the Reference Chapter).
25 Turn the four plastic fasteners through 90° and lift off the engine cover (see illustrations).
26 Firmly apply the handbrake, then jack up the front of the vehicle and support it securely on axle stands (see Jacking and vehicle support). Remove the right-hand front roadwheel.
27 To gain access to the right-hand end of the engine, the wheel arch plastic liner must be removed. The liner is secured by various screws and clips under the wheel arch. Release all the fasteners, and remove liner from under the front wing. Where necessary, unclip the coolant hoses from under the wing to improve access further.
28 At the connections adjacent to the fuel pump, disconnect the fuel supply and return hose quick-release fittings using a small

6.25a Rotate each fastener 90° to release it . . .

6.25b . . . then lift off the engine cover – 2.0 litre engines

6.28 Disconnect the fuel supply and return hose quick-release fittings – 2.0 litre engines

6.29 Release the two hoses from the retaining clips on the upper timing belt cover – 2.0 litre engines

6.31 Undo the two bolts (arrowed) and lift off the stiffener bracket and pedal position sensor – later 2.0 litre engines

screwdriver to release the locking clip **(see illustration)**. Cover the open unions to prevent dirt entry, using small plastic bags, or fingers cut from clean rubber gloves.

29 Release the two hoses from the retaining clips on the upper timing belt cover and move them to one side **(see illustration)**.

30 On early engines, undo the EGR solenoid valve mounting bracket bolt and move the valve to one side.

31 Undo the two bolts securing the right-hand mounting stiffener bracket to the body and lift off the bracket, complete with the accelerator pedal position sensor on later engines **(see illustration)**.

32 Connect an engine hoist or suitable lifting gear to the two lifting brackets on the cylinder head. Raise the hoist to just take the weight of the engine. For additional stability, place a jack beneath the right-hand side of the engine, with a block of wood on the jack head. Raise the jack until it is just contacting the sump.

33 Slacken and remove the three bolts securing the right-hand engine/transmission mounting upper bracket to the lower (engine) bracket.

34 Unscrew the domed buffer nut, then unscrew the single nut securing the upper bracket to the rubber mounting. Remove the upper bracket from the rubber mounting and lower (engine) bracket.

35 Undo the two nuts and remove the through-bolts securing the rear engine/transmission mounting connecting link to the mounting bracket on the subframe and on the rear of the cylinder block. Release and remove the connecting link from the mounting brackets.

36 With the two engine mountings removed, alternatively raise and lower the lifting gear and the jack under the engine, as necessary, for access to the timing belt cover retaining bolts.

37 Undo the bolt securing the upper cover to the cylinder head cover **(see illustration)**.

38 Undo the upper bolt on the edge of the cover nearest to the engine compartment bulkhead.

39 Undo the lower bolt on the bulkhead side of the cover, at the join between the upper and lower covers. Note that this bolt also retains the coolant pump. To avoid coolant leakage,

after the upper cover is removed, refit the bolt fitted with a 17.0 mm spacer, and tighten it securely.

40 Undo the remaining bolt in the centre of the cover, just above the engine mounting bracket.

41 Disengage the upper cover from the intermediate cover and manipulate the upper cover from its location.

Intermediate cover removal

42 Remove the upper cover as described previously.

43 Undo the upper bolt on the top edge of the intermediate cover.

44 Undo the two remaining bolts at the join between the intermediate cover and lower cover, then manipulate the intermediate cover from its location.

Lower cover removal

45 Remove the crankshaft pulley as described in Section 5.

46 Remove the upper and intermediate covers as described previously.

47 Undo the two remaining bolts on the edge of the cover, one on either side of the crankshaft pulley location.

48 Lift the cover off the front of the engine and manipulate it from its location.

Refitting

49 Refitting of all the covers is a reversal of the relevant removal procedure, ensuring that each cover section is correctly located, and that the cover retaining bolts are securely tightened. Ensure that all disturbed hoses are reconnected and retained by their relevant clips, and that all nuts/bolts are tightened to their specified torque wrench settings (where given). On completion, prime and bleed the fuel system as described in Chapter 4C.

7 Timing belt (1.9 litre engines) – general information, removal and refitting

Note 1: *The manufacturer's specify the use of a special electronic tool (SEEM C.TRONIC type 105 belt tensioning measuring tool, to correctly set the timing belt tension. The following procedure assumes that this equipment (or*

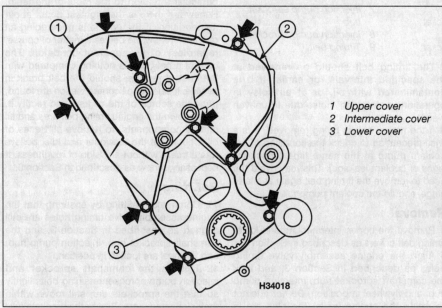

1 Upper cover
2 Intermediate cover
3 Lower cover

6.37 Timing belt cover retaining bolt locations (arrowed) – 2.0 litre engines

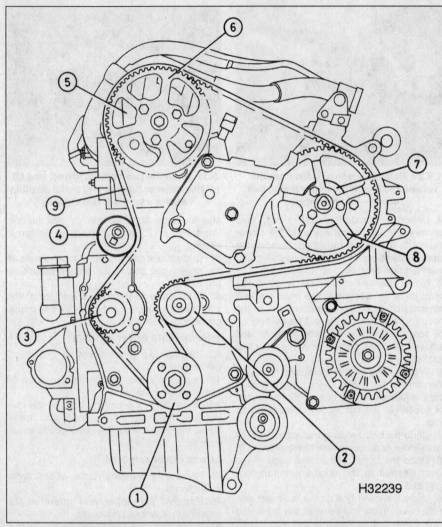

7.6 Timing belt, sprocket and tensioner details – 1.9 litre engines

1 *Crankshaft sprocket*	4 *Tensioner pulley*	7 *Injection pump sprocket*
2 *Idler pulley*	5 *Camshaft sprocket*	*hub*
3 *Coolant pump*	*hub*	8 *Injection pump sprocket*
sprocket	6 *Camshaft sprocket*	9 *Timing belt*

suitable alternative equipment calibrated to display belt tension in SEEM units) is available. Accurate tensioning of the timing belt is essential, and if the electronic equipment is not available, it is recommended that the work is entrusted to a Peugeot/Citroën dealer or suitably-equipped garage.

Note 2: *As from RPO 10064 the camshaft sprocket is fixed, and the crankshaft sprocket is 'floating' as for the 2.0 litre engine. Refer to Section 8.*

General information

1 The timing belt drives the camshaft, injection pump and coolant pump from a toothed sprocket on the right-hand end of the crankshaft. The belt also drives the brake vacuum pump indirectly via the flywheel end of the camshaft. If the belt breaks or slips in service, the pistons are likely to hit the valve heads, resulting in expensive damage.

2 The timing belt should be renewed at the specified intervals, or earlier if it is contaminated with oil, or at all noisy in operation (a 'scraping' noise due to uneven wear).

3 If the timing belt is being removed, it is a wise precaution to check the condition of the coolant pump at the same time (check for signs of coolant leakage). This may avoid the need to remove the timing belt again at a later stage, should the coolant pump fail.

Removal

4 Remove the upper, intermediate and lower timing belt covers as described in Section 6.
5 Align the engine assembly/valve timing holes as described in Section 3, and lock the camshaft sprocket hub, injection pump hub, and flywheel in position. *Do not* attempt to rotate the engine whilst the pins are in position.

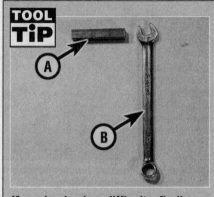

If you're having difficulty finding a square-section tool that will fit the tensioner pulley, obtain a length of standard 8 mm door handle rod from a DIY shop and cut it to length (A). Insert the rod into the pulley hub and rotate the pulley with an 8 mm spanner (B).

6 Slacken the three bolts securing the camshaft sprocket to the sprocket hub **(see illustration)**.
7 Similarly slacken the three bolts securing the injection pump sprocket to the pump hub.
8 Loosen the timing belt tensioner pulley retaining bolt. Pivot the pulley in a clockwise direction, using a square-section key fitted to the hole in the pulley hub, then retighten the retaining bolt **(see Tool Tip)**.
9 If the timing belt is to be re-used, use white paint or chalk to mark the direction of rotation on the belt (if markings do not already exist), then slip the belt off the sprockets. Note that the crankshaft must not be rotated whilst the belt is removed.
10 Check the timing belt carefully for any signs of uneven wear, split or oil contamination. Pay particular attention to the roots of the teeth. Renew it if there is the slightest doubt about its condition. If the engine is undergoing an overhaul, renew the belt as a matter of course, regardless of its apparent condition. The cost of a new belt is nothing compared with the cost of repairs, should the belt break in service. If signs of oil contamination are found, trace the source of the oil leak and rectify it. Wash down the engine timing belt area and all related components, to remove all traces of oil. Check that the tensioner and idler pulleys rotate freely, without any sign of roughness. If necessary, renew as described in Section 9.

Refitting

11 Commence refitting by ensuring that the engine assembly/valve timing holes are still aligned as described in Section 3, and the camshaft sprocket hub, injection pump hub, and flywheel are locked in position.
12 Tighten the camshaft sprocket and injection pump sprocket retaining bolts lightly so that the sprockets can still move within their elongated slots. Turn both sprockets fully clockwise to the ends of the slots.

13 Manoeuvre the timing belt into position, ensuring that the arrows on the belt are pointing in the direction of rotation (clockwise, when viewed from the right-hand end of the engine).

14 Locate the belt on the crankshaft sprocket, taking care not to twist it sharply while refitting it, and route the belt round the idler pulley.

15 Ensure the 'front run' of the belt is taut then align the belt with the injection pump sprocket. Rotate the sprocket anti-clockwise on its hub until the belt and sprocket teeth are correctly aligned then engage the belt on the sprocket. **Note:** *Do not rotate the sprocket anti-clockwise any more than is necessary and never rotate it through more than one sprocket tooth of movement.*

16 Once the belt is correctly seated on the injection pump sprocket, ensure the belt 'front' and 'top' runs are taut then align the belt with the camshaft sprocket. Rotate the camshaft sprocket anti-clockwise on its hub until the belt and sprocket teeth are correctly aligned then engage the belt on the sprocket. **Note:** *Do not rotate the sprocket anti-clockwise any more than is necessary and never rotate it through more than one sprocket tooth of movement.*

17 Ensure that any slack is on the tensioner pulley side of the belt then locate the belt over the coolant pump sprocket and behind the tensioner pulley.

18 Ensure that the belt teeth are seated centrally in the sprockets then loosen the tensioner pulley retaining bolt. Pivot the pulley anti-clockwise to remove all free play from the timing belt, then retighten the bolt.

19 Remove one of the sprocket bolts from both the injection pump and camshaft sprockets and check that the sprockets are not at the end of their retaining bolt slots **(see illustration)**. If they are, the sprocket was rotated through more than one tooth of

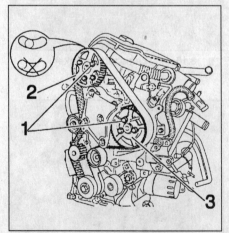

7.19 Remove one of the bolts (1) from both the camshaft (2) and injection pump (3) sprockets and check that each sprocket is not at the end of its bolt slots (see inset) – 1.9 litre engines

movement whilst installing the belt; remove the timing belt and repeat the refitting procedure. If the sprockets are correctly positioned, tension the timing belt as follows.

20 Fit the sensor head of the electronic belt tension measuring equipment to the 'top run' of the timing belt, approximately midway between the camshaft and injection pump sprockets.

21 Pivot the tensioner pulley anti-clockwise until an initial setting of 106 ± 2 SEEM units is displayed on the tension measuring equipment. Hold the tensioner pulley in that position and retighten the retaining bolt.

22 Check that the sprockets have not been turned so far that the retaining bolts are at the end of their slots. If this is the case, repeat the refitting operation. If all is satisfactory, tighten the camshaft and injection pump sprocket retaining bolts to the specified torque.

23 Remove the belt tension measuring equipment and the crankshaft, camshaft sprocket hub and injection pump hub locking tools.

24 Rotate the crankshaft through eight complete rotations in a clockwise direction (viewed from the right-hand end of the engine). Realign the engine assembly/valve timing holes and refit the crankshaft, camshaft and injection pump locking tools.

25 Slacken the camshaft and injection pump sprocket retaining bolts, retighten them finger-tight, then slacken them all by one sixth of a turn.

26 Slacken the tensioner pulley retaining bolt once more. Refit the belt tension measuring equipment to the top run of the belt, and turn the tensioner pulley to give a final setting of 42 ± 2 SEEM units on the tensioning gauge. Hold the tensioner pulley in this position and tighten the retaining bolt to the specified torque.

27 Retighten all sprocket retaining bolts to the specified torque.

28 Release the sensor head of the belt tension measuring equipment, then refit it again and check that a reading of between 38 and 46 SEEM units is indicated. Remove the tension measuring equipment.

29 Remove the locking tools, then rotate the crankshaft once again through two complete rotations in a clockwise direction. Realign the engine assembly/valve timing holes and refit the crankshaft locking tool.

30 Check that it is possible to insert the camshaft sprocket hub and injection pump hub locking tools. If the tools cannot be inserted, check that the offset between the timing holes in the sprocket hubs and the corresponding holes in the cylinder head and injection pump is not greater than 1.0 mm. If it is, repeat the complete timing belt refitting and tensioning procedure.

31 Refit the lower, intermediate and upper timing belt covers as described in Section 6.

32 Refit the crankshaft pulley as described in Section 5.

8 Timing belt (2.0 litre engines) – general information, removal and refitting

Note: *The manufacturer's specify the use of a special electronic tool (SEEM C.TRONIC type 105 belt tensioning measuring tool, to correctly set the timing belt tension. The following procedure assumes that this equipment (or suitable alternative equipment calibrated to display belt tension in SEEM units) is available. Accurate tensioning of the timing belt is essential, and if the electronic equipment is not available, it is recommended that the work is entrusted to a Peugeot/Citroën dealer or suitably-equipped garage.*

General information

1 The timing belt drives the camshaft, high-pressure fuel pump and coolant pump from a toothed sprocket on the end of the crankshaft. The belt also drives the brake servo vacuum pump indirectly via the flywheel end of the camshaft. If the belt breaks or slips in service, the pistons are likely to hit the valve heads, resulting in expensive damage.

2 The timing belt should be renewed at the specified intervals, or earlier if it is contaminated with oil, or at all noisy in operation (a 'scraping' noise due to uneven wear).

3 If the timing belt is being removed, it is a wise precaution to check the condition of the coolant pump at the same time (check for signs of coolant leakage). This may avoid the need to remove the timing belt again at a later stage, should the coolant pump fail.

4 Two types of timing belt sprocket arrangements may be encountered. On early engines, the camshaft sprocket is of the 'floating' type, secured to the sprocket hub with three bolts. The bolt holes are elongated and allow for a certain degree of lateral movement of the sprocket for accurate tensioning of the timing belt when refitting. On later engines, the camshaft sprocket is fixed, but the crankshaft sprocket becomes the 'floating' component. Lateral movement of the crankshaft sprocket is achieved by using a wider keyway for the locating Woodruff key. Timing belt removal procedures are the same for both types, but different procedures must be used when refitting.

Removal

5 Remove the crankshaft pulley as described in Section 5. Refit and tighten the pulley retaining bolt to allow the engine to be turned in subsequent operations.

6 Remove the upper, intermediate and lower timing belt covers as described in Section 6.

7 It is now necessary to identify the type of timing belt sprocket arrangement fitted by observing the design of the camshaft sprocket. On early engines the sprocket and hub is a two-piece assembly. The sprocket is secured

8.9 On early engines, slacken the bolts (arrowed) and rotate the camshaft sprocket fully clockwise on its hub – 2.0 litre engines

to the sprocket hub by three retaining bolts, with the hub being secured to the camshaft by a single centre bolt. On later engines the sprocket and hub are a single fixed assembly secured to the camshaft by a centre retaining bolt only. When refitting, proceed as described in the appropriate sub-Sections according to sprocket type.

8 If not already done, align the engine assembly/valve timing holes as described in Section 3, and lock the crankshaft and the camshaft sprocket in position. *Do not* attempt to rotate the engine whilst the locking pins are in position.

9 On early engines, slacken the three bolts securing the camshaft sprocket to the sprocket hub **(see illustration)**.

10 Slacken the timing belt tensioner pulley retaining bolt and insert a short length of 8.0 mm square bar into the square hole on the front face of the tensioner pulley **(see Tool Tip in Section 7)**. Alternatively, although clearance is restricted, the square end of a 1/4 inch drive socket bar can also be used. Using the bar and a spanner, turn the pulley in a clockwise direction, to relieve the tension from the timing belt. Retighten the tensioner pulley retaining bolt to secure it in the slackened position.

11 If the timing belt is to be re-used, use white paint or chalk to mark the direction of rotation on the belt (if markings do not already exist), then slip the belt off the sprockets. Note that the crankshaft must not be rotated whilst the belt is removed.

12 Check the timing belt carefully for any signs of uneven wear, splits or oil contamination. Pay particular attention to the roots of the teeth. Renew it if there is the slightest doubt about its condition. If the engine is undergoing an overhaul, renew the belt as a matter of course, regardless of its apparent condition. The cost of a new belt is nothing compared with the cost of repairs, should the belt break in service. If signs of oil contamination are found, trace the source of the oil leak and rectify it. Wash down the engine timing belt area and all related components, to remove all traces of oil. Check that the tensioner and idler pulleys rotate freely, without any sign of roughness. If necessary, renew them as described in Section 9.

Refitting

Two-piece camshaft sprocket

13 Commence refitting by ensuring that the engine assembly/valve timing holes are still aligned as described in Section 3, and the crankshaft, and camshaft sprocket hub are locked in position.

14 Tighten the camshaft sprocket retaining bolts lightly so that the sprocket can still move within the elongated slots. Turn the sprocket fully clockwise to the ends of the slots.

15 Locate the timing belt on the crankshaft sprocket making sure that the direction of rotation arrow is facing the correct way.

16 Hold the belt on the crankshaft sprocket and, while keeping the 'lower run' of the belt taut (between the crankshaft and idler pulley), feed the belt over the remaining sprockets and pulleys in the following order **(see illustrations)**:

   a) *Idler pulley.*
   b) *High-pressure fuel pump.*
   c) *Camshaft.*
   e) *Coolant pump.*
   d) *Tensioner pulley.*

17 Fit the sensor head of the electronic belt tension measuring equipment to the 'top run' of the timing belt, approximately midway between the camshaft and fuel pump sprockets.

18 Slacken the tensioner pulley retaining bolt and, using the square bar and spanner, pivot the tensioner pulley anti-clockwise until an initial setting of 98 ± 2 SEEM units is displayed on the tension measuring equipment **(see**

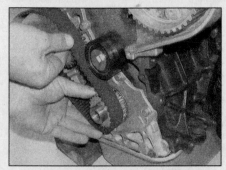

8.16a Retain the timing belt on the crankshaft sprocket and feed it around the idler pulley . . .

8.16b . . . high pressure fuel pump sprocket . . .

8.16c . . . camshaft sprocket . . .

8.16d . . . coolant pump and tensioner pulley – 2.0 litre engines

8.18a Pivot the tensioner pulley anti-clockwise, then tighten the retaining bolt . . .

8.18b . . . when the specified tension value is shown on the measuring equipment – 2.0 litre engines

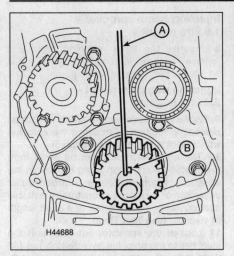

8.31 Insert a 2 mm rod (A) on the left-hand side of the Woodruff key (B) – 2.0 litre engines

illustrations). Hold the tensioner pulley in that position and retighten the retaining bolt.

19 Check that the camshaft sprocket retaining bolts are not at the ends of their slots (if necessary, remove one of the sprocket bolts to check this). If they are, repeat the refitting operation. If all is satisfactory, refit the removed bolt and tighten all three sprocket retaining bolts to the specified torque.

20 Remove the belt tension measuring equipment and the crankshaft, and camshaft sprocket hub locking tools.

21 Rotate the crankshaft through eight complete rotations in a clockwise direction (viewed from the right-hand end of the engine). Realign the engine assembly/valve timing holes and refit the crankshaft locking tool only.

22 Slacken the camshaft sprocket retaining bolts and refit the camshaft sprocket hub locking tool.

23 Slacken the tensioner pulley retaining bolt once more.

24 Refit the belt tension measuring equipment to the top run of the belt, and turn the tensioner pulley to give a final setting of 54 ± 2 SEEM units on the tensioning gauge. Hold the tensioner pulley in this position and tighten the retaining bolt to the specified torque.

25 Retighten the camshaft sprocket retaining bolts to the specified torque.

26 Release the sensor head of the belt tension measuring equipment, then refit it again and check that a reading of 54 ± 3 SEEM units is indicated. Remove the tension measuring equipment.

27 Remove the locking tools, then rotate the crankshaft once again through two complete rotations in a clockwise direction. Realign the engine assembly/valve timing holes and refit the crankshaft locking tool.

28 Check that it is possible to insert the camshaft sprocket hub locking tool. If the tool cannot be inserted, check that the offset

between the timing slot in the sprocket hub and the corresponding hole in the cylinder head is not greater than 1.0 mm. If it is, repeat the complete timing belt refitting and tensioning procedure.

29 Refit the lower, intermediate and upper timing belt covers as described in Section 6. Refit the crankshaft pulley as described in Section 5 after refitting the lower cover.

Fixed camshaft sprocket

30 Ensure that the engine assembly/valve timing holes are still aligned as described in Section 3, and the crankshaft and camshaft sprocket are locked in position.

31 Turn the crankshaft sprocket anti-clockwise to the limit of the movement afforded by the keyway. Lock the sprocket in this position by inserting a 2.0 mm diameter rod down the left-hand side of the Woodruff key **(see illustration)**.

32 Locate the timing belt on the camshaft sprocket, making sure that the direction of rotation arrow is facing the correct way.

33 Retain the timing belt on the camshaft sprocket using a cable tie to ensure that it does not jump a tooth. Keeping the 'top run' of the belt taut (between the camshaft and fuel pump sprockets), feed the belt over the remaining sprockets and pulleys in the following order:

  a) *High-pressure fuel pump.*
  b) *Idler pulley.*
  c) *Crankshaft.*
  d) *Coolant pump.*
  e) *Tensioner pulley.*

34 Cut off the cable tie securing the timing belt to the camshaft sprocket and remove the rod from the crankshaft sprocket keyway.

35 Fit the sensor head of the electronic belt tension measuring equipment to the 'top run' of the timing belt, approximately midway between the camshaft and fuel pump sprockets.

36 Slacken the tensioner pulley retaining bolt and, using the square bar and spanner, pivot the tensioner pulley anti-clockwise until an initial setting of 98 ± 2 SEEM units is displayed on the tension measuring equipment. Hold the tensioner pulley in that position and retighten the retaining bolt.

37 If not already in place, refit the crankshaft pulley retaining bolt and washer and tighten the bolt to 70 Nm (52 lbf ft). Prevent the crankshaft from turning using the flywheel ring gear locking tool described for pulley removal in Section 5. *Do not* attempt to use only the engine assembly/valve timing locking tools to prevent rotation whilst the bolt is tightened.

38 Remove the belt tension measuring equipment, the flywheel ring gear locking tool and the engine assembly/valve timing locking tools.

39 Rotate the crankshaft through eight complete rotations in a clockwise direction (viewed from the right-hand end of the engine). Realign the engine assembly/valve timing holes and refit the crankshaft and camshaft sprocket locking tools.

40 Refit the flywheel ring gear locking tool

and slacken the crankshaft pulley retaining bolt.

41 Slacken the tensioner pulley retaining bolt once more. Refit the belt tension measuring equipment to the top run of the belt, and turn the tensioner pulley to give a final setting of 54 ± 2 SEEM units on the tensioning gauge. Hold the tensioner pulley in this position and tighten the retaining bolt to the specified torque.

42 Release the sensor head of the belt tension measuring equipment, then refit it again and check that a reading of 54 ± 3 SEEM units is indicated. If not, repeat the complete tensioning procedure. If the reading is correct, remove the tension measuring equipment.

43 Remove all the locking tools, then rotate the crankshaft once again through two complete rotations in a clockwise direction. Realign the engine assembly/valve timing holes and refit the crankshaft and camshaft sprocket locking tools. If it is not possible to fit both locking tools, repeat the complete tensioning procedure.

44 If all is satisfactory, locate the lower timing belt cover in position, refit the retaining bolts and tighten them securely.

45 With the engine assembly/valve timing holes aligned and the crankshaft and camshaft sprocket locking tools in place, refit the flywheel ring gear locking tool and unscrew the crankshaft pulley retaining bolt.

46 Locate the crankshaft pulley in position on the end of the crankshaft.

47 Thoroughly clean the threads of the pulley retaining bolt, then apply a coat of locking compound to the bolt threads (Peugeot/Citroën recommend the use of Loctite Frenetanch).

48 Refit the crankshaft pulley retaining bolt and washer. Tighten the bolt to the specified torque, then through the specified angle.

49 Remove the flywheel ring gear locking tool and the crankshaft and camshaft sprocket locking tools.

50 Refit the intermediate and upper timing belt covers as described in Section 6, then refit and tension the auxiliary drivebelt as described in Chapter 1B.

---

9   Timing belt sprockets and idler/tensioner pulleys – removal, inspection and refitting

Note: *As from RPO 10064 the camshaft sprocket is fixed, and the crankshaft sprocket is 'floating' as for the 2.0 litre engine. Refer to the 2.0 litre procedure described later in this Section.*

Removal

1 Disconnect the battery negative terminal (refer to *Disconnecting the battery* in the Reference Chapter).

2 Position the engine assembly/valve timing holes as described in Section 3, and lock the sprocket hub(s) and flywheel in position.

Caution: Do not attempt to rotate the engine whilst the pins are in position.

A sprocket holding tool can be made from two lengths of steel strip bolted together to form a forked end. Bend the end of the strip through 90° to form the fork 'prongs'.

Make a sprocket releasing tool from a short strip of steel. Drill two holes in the strip to correspond with the two holes in the sprocket. Drill a third hole just large enough to accept the flats of the sprocket retaining nut.

3 Remove the timing belt as described in Section 7 or 8, as applicable, then proceed as described under the relevant sub-heading.

Camshaft sprocket

4 As a precaution, remove the flywheel locking pin then rotate the crankshaft **backwards** (anti-clockwise) through 90°; this will position

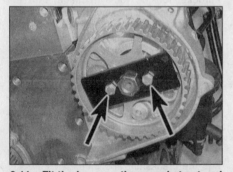

9.11a Fit the bar over the sprocket nut and screw in the two bolts (arrowed) – 2.0 litre engines

the pistons midway up the bores and remove the risk of the valves contacting the pistons during the following operation.
5 Slacken the sprocket hub retaining bolt, and the three sprocket-to-hub retaining bolts (where applicable). To prevent the camshaft rotating as the bolt is slackened, a sprocket-holding tool will be required. In the absence of the special Peugeot/Citroën tool, an acceptable substitute can be fabricated at home **(see Tool Tip 1)**. *Do not* attempt to use the engine assembly/valve timing locking tool to prevent the sprocket from rotating whilst the bolt is slackened.
6 Unscrew the sprocket hub retaining bolt and slide the sprocket and hub off the end of the camshaft. If the Woodruff key is a loose fit, remove it for safe-keeping. Examine the camshaft oil seal for signs of oil leakage and, if necessary, renew it as described in Section 10.
7 If necessary on engines with a two-piece sprocket, the sprocket can be separated from the hub after removing the three retaining bolts.

Injection pump sprocket – 1.9 litre engines

8 Unscrew the three retaining bolts and remove the sprocket from its hub; The hub is an integral part of the injection pump.

Injection pump sprocket – 2.0 litre engines

9 Slacken the sprocket retaining nut whilst preventing rotation by retaining the sprocket with a holding tool (see paragraph 5).
10 The sprocket must then be freed from the injection pump shaft using a puller. In the absence of correct Peugeot/Citroën puller assembly or a pattern substitute, a suitable alternative can be made out of a short length of steel bar **(see Tool Tip 2)**.
11 Loosen the sprocket nut then bolt the steel bar to the sprocket by screwing two M7 bolts in the threaded holes provided. Evenly tighten the bolts, so the bar is forced into contact with nut, then unscrew the sprocket nut to draw the sprocket off the pump shaft. Once the sprocket has been released, unscrew the bolts and remove the bar then unscrew the nut and remove the sprocket **(see illustrations)**.

Crankshaft sprocket – 1.9 litre engines

12 As a precaution, remove the flywheel locking pin then rotate the crankshaft **backwards** (anti-clockwise) through 90°; this will position the pistons midway up the bores and remove the risk of the valves contacting the pistons during the following operation.
13 Slacken the crankshaft sprocket bolt. To prevent crankshaft rotation, select top gear, and have an assistant apply the brakes firmly. Alternatively, the flywheel ring gear can be locked using a suitable tool made from steel angle **(see Tool Tip in Section 5)**.
14 Unscrew the retaining bolt and washer, then slide the sprocket off the end of the crankshaft. If the Woodruff key is a loose fit in the crankshaft, remove it and store it

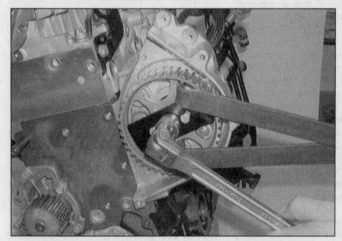

9.11b With the puller in position, retain the sprocket then unscrew the sprocket nut to release the sprocket from the pump shaft – 2.0 litre engines

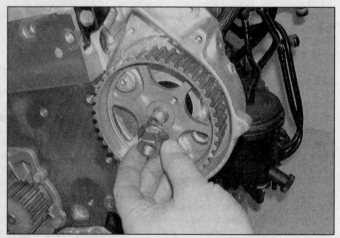

9.11c Once the sprocket is free, remove the puller then unscrew the nut and lift off the sprocket – 2.0 litre engines

9.15a Slide the sprocket off the crankshaft . . .

9.15b . . . then remove the Woodruff key – 2.0 litre engines

9.18 Unscrew the mounting bolt and remove the idler pulley from the block

with the sprocket for safe-keeping. Examine the crankshaft oil seal for signs oil leakage and, if necessary, renew as described in Section 17.

Crankshaft sprocket – 2.0 litre engines

15 Slide the sprocket and off the end of the crankshaft. If the Woodruff key is a loose fit in the crankshaft, remove it and store it with the sprocket for safe-keeping (see illustrations). Examine the crankshaft oil seal for signs oil leakage and, if necessary, renew as described in Section 17.

Coolant pump sprocket

16 The coolant pump sprocket is integral with the pump, and cannot be removed. Coolant pump removal is described in Chapter 3.

Tensioner pulley

17 Unscrew the bolt and remove the pulley from its mounting pin. Examine the mounting stud for signs of damage and, if necessary, renew it.

Idler pulley

18 Unscrew the mounting bolt and remove the idler pulley from the cylinder block (see illustration).

Inspection

19 Clean the sprockets thoroughly, and renew any that show signs of wear, damage or cracks.
20 Clean the tensioner and idler pulleys, but do not use any strong solvent which may enter the pulley bearing. Check that each pulley rotates freely about its hub, with no sign of stiffness or of free play. Renew the pulley if there is any doubt about its condition, or if there are any obvious signs of wear or damage.
21 Inspect the timing belt (see Sections 7 or 8). Renew the belt is there is any doubt about its condition.

Refitting

Camshaft sprocket

22 On engines with a two-piece sprocket, refit the sprocket to the hub (if removed) and

secure with the three retaining bolts, tightened finger tight only at this stage.
23 Refit the Woodruff key to the end of the camshaft, then refit the camshaft sprocket and hub.
24 Refit the sprocket hub retaining bolt and washer. Tighten the bolt to the specified torque, preventing the camshaft from turning as during removal.
25 Align the hub timing hole with the cylinder head and insert the locking tool. Rotate the crankshaft 90° clockwise and lock the flywheel in position with the locking tool.
26 Refit the timing belt (see Section 7 or 8).

Injection pump sprocket – 1.9 litre engines

27 Seat the sprocket on the hub and lightly tighten its bolts.
28 Refit the timing belt (see Section 7).

Injection pump sprocket – 2.0 litre engines

29 Ensure the pump shaft and sprocket taper surfaces are clean and dry then fit the sprocket to the pump. Refit the sprocket nut and tighten it to the specified torque, using the holding tool to prevent rotation.
30 Refit the timing belt (see Section 8).

Crankshaft sprocket – 1.9 litre engines

31 Where removed, locate the Woodruff key in the crankshaft end.
32 Align the crankshaft pulley slot with the Woodruff key, and slide it onto the end of the crankshaft.
33 Remove all traces of locking compound from the threads of the pulley bolt and crankshaft. Apply a drop of locking compound (Peugeot/Citroën recommend the use of Loctite Frenetanch) to the threads of the bolt then refit the bolt and washer to the crankshaft
34 Tighten the bolt to the specified torque Stage 1 torque setting, whilst preventing crankshaft rotation using the method employed on removal.
35 Angle-tighten the pulley bolt through the specified Stage 2 angle, using a socket and extension bar. It is recommended that an

angle-measuring gauge is used during this stage of the tightening, to ensure accuracy.
36 Rotate the crankshaft 90° clockwise and lock the flywheel in position with the locking tool.
37 Refit the timing belt (see Section 7).

Crankshaft sprocket – 2.0 litre engines

38 Where removed, locate the Woodruff key in the crankshaft end.
39 Align the crankshaft pulley slot with the Woodruff key, and slide it onto the end of the crankshaft.
40 Refit the timing belt (see Section 8).

Tensioner pulley

41 Refit the tensioner pulley to its mounting pin, and fit the retaining bolt.
42 Refit the timing belt (see Section 7 or 8).

Idler pulley

43 Refit the idler pulley to the cylinder block and tighten its retaining bolt to the specified torque.
44 Refit the timing belt (see Section 7 or 8).

10 Camshaft oil seal – renewal

Note: *If the camshaft oil seal has been leaking, check the timing belt for signs of oil contamination; the belt must be renewed if signs of oil contamination are found. Ensure that all traces of oil are removed from the sprockets and surrounding area before the new belt is fitted.*

1 Remove the camshaft sprocket as described in Section 9.
2 Punch or drill two small holes opposite each other in the oil seal. Screw a self-tapping screw into each, and pull on the screws with pliers to extract the seal.
3 Clean the seal housing, and polish off any burrs or raised edges, which may have caused the seal to fail in the first place.
4 Lubricate the lips of the new seal with clean engine oil, and drive/press it into position until it seats on its locating shoulder. Use a suitable tubular drift, such as a socket, which bears only on the hard outer edge of the seal (see

10.4 Using a socket, a length of stud and a nut to press the camshaft oil seal into position

11.4 The camshaft bearing caps should be numbered (arrowed) for identification – 1.9 litre engines

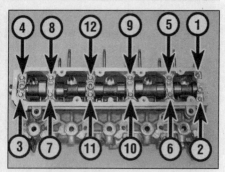

11.9 Camshaft bearing cap casting bolt slackening sequence – 2.0 litre engines

illustration). Take care not to damage the seal lips during fitting. Note that the seal lips should face inwards.
5 Refit the camshaft sprocket as described in Section 9.

11 Camshaft and followers
– removal, inspection and refitting

Note: *On 1.9 litre engines, valve clearance adjustment requires the removal of the camshaft. If the original camshaft is being refitted, it is worthwhile recording the valve clearances before it is removed, so any adjustments can be made before refitting it (see Section 12).*

Removal

1 Remove the cylinder head cover as described in Section 4.
2 Remove the braking system vacuum pump as described in Chapter 9.

3 Remove the camshaft sprocket as described in Section 9. Proceed as described under the relevant sub-heading.

1.9 litre engines

4 The camshaft bearing caps should be numbered 1 to 3, number 1 being at the transmission end of the engine **(see illustration)**. If not, make identification marks on the caps, using white paint or a suitable marker pen. Also mark each cap in some way to indicate its correct fitted orientation. This will avoid the possibility of installing the caps the wrong way around on refitting.
5 Evenly and progressively slacken the camshaft bearing cap retaining nuts by one turn at a time. This will relieve the valve spring pressure on the bearing caps gradually and evenly. Once the pressure has been relieved, the nuts can be fully unscrewed and removed.
Caution: If the bearing cap nuts are carelessly slackened, the bearing caps may break. If any bearing cap breaks then the

complete cylinder head assembly must be renewed; the bearing caps are matched to the head and are not available separately.
6 Note the correct fitted orientation of the bearing caps, then remove them from the cylinder head.
7 Lift the camshaft away from the cylinder head, and slide the oil seal off the camshaft end.
8 Obtain eight small, clean plastic containers, and number them 1 to 8; alternatively, divide a larger container into eight compartments. Using a rubber sucker, withdraw each follower in turn, and place it in its respective container. Do not interchange the cam followers, or the rate of wear will be much-increased. If necessary, also remove the shim from the top of the valve stem, and store it with its respective follower. **Note:** *The shim may stick to the inside of the follower as it is withdrawn. If this happens, take care not to allow it to drop out as the follower is removed.*

2.0 litre engines

9 Working in sequence, evenly and progressively slacken the camshaft bearing cap casting retaining bolts by one turn at a time **(see illustration)**. This will relieve the valve spring pressure on the bearing caps gradually and evenly. Once the pressure has been relieved, the bolts can be fully unscrewed and removed.
Caution: If the bearing cap casting bolt are carelessly slackened, the casting may break. If the casting breaks then the complete cylinder head assembly must be renewed; the casting is matched to the head and is not available separately.
10 Remove the camshaft bearing cap casting from the cylinder head **(see illustration)**. If the casting locating dowels are a loose fit in the head, remove them and store them with the casting for safe-keeping.
11 Lift the camshaft away from the cylinder head, and slide the oil seal off the camshaft end **(see illustration)**.
12 Obtain eight, oil tight, clean plastic containers, and number them 1 to 8. Each container must be deep enough to allow the tappets to be almost totally submerged in oil. Lift each follower and hydraulic tappet out of position and place it in its respective container **(see illustrations)**. Add clean engine oil to each container so that the tappet

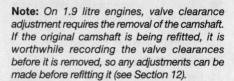

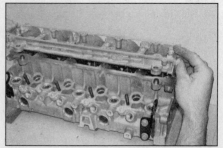

11.10 Remove the bearing cap casting . . .

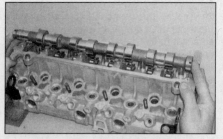

11.11 . . . then lift the camshaft out of position (shown with cylinder head removed) – 2.0 litre engines

11.12a Lift the camshaft followers . . .

11.12b . . . and hydraulic tappets out from the cylinder head – 2.0 litre engines

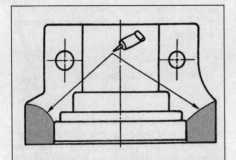

11.22 Apply sealant to the areas shown on the camshaft end bearing caps – 1.9 litre engines

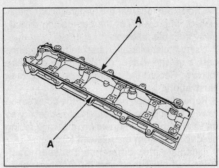

11.31 Apply a thin bead of sealant (A) to the mating surface of the camshaft bearing cap casting as shown – 2.0 litre engines

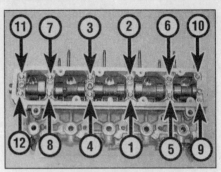

11.33 Camshaft bearing cap bolt tightening sequence – 2.0 litre engines

is submerged. Do not interchange the cam followers or tappets, or the rate of wear will be much-increased.

Inspection

13 Examine the camshaft bearing surfaces and cam lobes for signs of wear ridges and scoring. Renew the camshaft if any of these conditions are apparent. Examine the condition of the bearing surfaces, both on the camshaft journals and in the cylinder head/bearing caps. If the head bearing surfaces are worn excessively, the cylinder head will need to be renewed.

14 Examine the cam follower bearing surfaces which contact the camshaft lobes for wear ridges and scoring. Renew any follower on which these conditions are apparent. If a follower bearing surface is badly scored, also examine the corresponding lobe on the camshaft for wear, as it is likely that both will be worn. Renew worn components as necessary.

15 On 2.0 litre engines, if the hydraulic tappets are thought to be faulty they should be renewed.

Refitting

1.9 litre engines

16 If the original camshaft is being refitted, and it is known that the valve clearances are correct, proceed to the next paragraph, otherwise, adjust the valves as described in Section 12 using the clearances noted before camshaft removal. If a new camshaft is used, fit it as described in paragraphs 17 to 23, and then adjust the valve clearances (Section 12).

Caution: Ensure the crankshaft is correctly positioned with the pistons midway up the bores before rotating the camshaft.

17 Fit each shim to the top of its valve stem.

Caution: Do not interchange the shims, as this will upset the valve clearances (see Section 12).

18 Liberally oil the cylinder head cam follower bores and the followers. Carefully refit the followers to the cylinder head, ensuring that each follower is refitted to its original bore. Some care will be required to enter the followers squarely into their bores.

19 Lubricate the cam lobes and bearing journals with clean engine oil of the specified

grade. Then refit the camshaft back into position on the cylinder head.

20 Temporarily refit the sprocket to the end of the camshaft and position it so that the hub timing hole is aligned with the corresponding cut-out in the cylinder head. Ensure the crankshaft is still positioned 90° BTDC so the pistons are midway up the bores.

21 Fit the centre bearing cap the correct way round as previously noted, then screw on the nuts and tighten them two or three turns.

22 Apply sealing compound to the end bearing caps on the areas shown **(see illustration)**. Fit them in the correct positions, and tighten the nuts two or three turns.

23 Tighten all the nuts evenly and progressively to the specified torque, making sure that the camshaft remains correctly positioned.

Caution: If the bearing cap nuts are carelessly tightened, the bearing caps may break. If any bearing cap breaks then the complete cylinder head assembly must be renewed; the bearing caps are matched to the head and are not available separately.

24 Smear the lips of the new oil seal with clean engine oil and fit it onto the camshaft end, making sure its sealing lip is facing inwards. Press the oil seal in until it is flush with the end face of the camshaft bearing cap.

25 Refit the camshaft sprocket as described in Section 9.

26 Refit the braking system vacuum pump as described in Chapter 9.

27 Refit the cylinder head cover as described in Section 4.

2.0 litre engines

28 Liberally oil the cylinder head tappet bores and the followers. Ensure the followers and hydraulic tappets are correctly clipped together then carefully refit them to the cylinder head, ensuring that each assembly is refitted in its original location.

29 Lubricate the cam bearing journals and followers with clean engine oil of the specified grade.

30 Ensure the crankshaft is still positioned 90° BTDC so the pistons are midway up the bores.

31 Ensure the mating surfaces of the camshaft bearing cap casting and cylinder head are clean and dry. Apply a thin bead of sealant (Peugeot/Citroën recommend the use

of Autojoint NOIR) to the mating surface of casting as shown **(see illustration)**.

32 Locate the camshaft correctly in the bearing cap casting then, ensuring the locating dowels are in position, refit the camshaft and bearing cap casting assembly to the head.

33 Install the bearing cap casting bolts, tightening all bolts by hand. Working in sequence, evenly and progressively tighten the bolts to draw the casting squarely down onto the cylinder head **(see illustration)**. Once the casting is in contact with the head, go around in the specified sequence and tighten the bolts to the specified torque.

Caution: If the bearing cap casting bolt are carelessly tightened, the casting may break. If the casting breaks then the complete cylinder head assembly must be renewed; the casting is matched to the head and is not available separately.

34 Smear the lips of the new oil seal with clean engine oil and fit it onto the camshaft end, making sure its sealing lip is facing inwards. Press the oil seal in until it is flush with the end face of the camshaft bearing cap.

35 Refit the camshaft sprocket and hub as described in Section 9.

36 Refit the braking system vacuum pump as described in Chapter 9.

37 Refit the cylinder head cover as described in Section 4.

---

12 Valve clearances –
checking and adjustment

1.9 litre engines

Checking

1 The importance of having the valve clearances correctly adjusted cannot be overstressed, as they vitally affect the performance of the engine. Checking should not be regarded as a routine operation, however. It should only be necessary when the valve gear has become noisy, after engine overhaul, or when trying to trace the cause of power loss. The clearances are checked as follows. The engine must be cold for the check to be accurate.

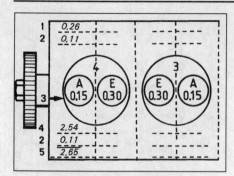

1	0.26	
2	0.11	
3	A 0.15	E 0.30	E 0.30	A 0.15
4	2.54	
2	0.11	
5	2.65	

12.5 Example of valve shim thickness calculation – 1.9 litre engines

A Inlet valve
B Exhaust valve
1 Measured clearance
2 Difference from specified clearance (3)
3 Specified clearance
4 Thickness of shim fitted
5 Correct thickness of shim required

2 Firmly apply the handbrake, then jack up the front of the car and support it securely on axle stands (see *Jacking and vehicle support*). To gain access to the right-hand end of the engine, the wheel arch plastic liner must be removed. The liner is secured by various screws and clips under the wheel arch. Release all the fasteners, and remove liner from under the front wing. Where necessary, unclip the coolant hoses from under the wing to improve access further.

3 The engine can now be turned over using a suitable socket and extension bar fitted to the crankshaft pulley bolt. Note that the crankshaft must always be turned in a clockwise direction (viewed from the right-hand side of the vehicle).

4 Remove the cylinder head cover as described in Section 4.

5 On a piece of paper, draw the outline of the engine with the cylinders numbered from the flywheel end. Show the position of each valve, together with the specified valve clearance. Above each valve, draw lines for recording (1) the actual clearance and (2) the amount of adjustment required **(see illustration)**.

6 Turn the crankshaft until the inlet valve of

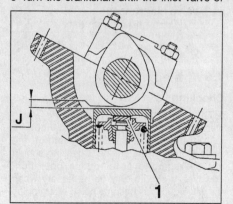

12.7 Valve clearance measurement (J). Clearance is altered by changing the shim (1) – 1.9 litre engines

No 1 cylinder (nearest the transmission) is fully closed, with the tip of the cam facing directly away from the follower.

7 Using feeler blades, measure the clearance between the base of the cam and the follower. Record the clearance on line (1) **(see illustration)**.

8 Repeat the measurement for the other seven valves, turning the crankshaft as necessary so that the cam lobe in question is always facing directly away from the relevant follower.

9 Calculate the difference between each measured clearance and the desired value, and record it on line (2). Since the clearance is different for inlet and exhaust valves – make sure that you are aware which valve you are dealing with. The valve sequence from either end of the engine is:

In – Ex – Ex – In – In – Ex – Ex – In

10 If all the clearances are within tolerance, refit the cylinder head cover with reference to Section 4. Refit the wheel arch liner then lower the vehicle to the ground. If any clearance measured is outside the specified tolerance, adjustment must be carried out as described in the following paragraphs.

Adjustment

11 Remove the camshaft as described in Section 11.

12 Withdraw the first follower and its shim. Clean the shim, and measure its thickness with a micrometer. The shims carry thickness markings, but wear may have reduced the original thickness, so be sure to check.

13 Refer to the clearance recorded for the valve concerned. If the clearance was more than that specified, the shim thickness must be increased by the difference recorded (2). If the clearance was less than that specified, the thickness of the shim must be decreased by the difference recorded (2).

14 Draw three more lines beneath each valve on the calculation paper as shown in illustration 12.5. On line (4) note the measured thickness of the shim, then add or deduct the difference from line (2) to give the final shim thickness required on line (5).

15 Repeat the procedure given in paragraphs 13 to 15 on the remaining valves, keeping each follower identified for position.

16 Obtain the shims required to bring each valve clearance within tolerance. Note that the shims can be swapped around, but not the followers.

17 When reassembling, oil the shim and fit it into the valve retainer, with the size marking face downwards. Oil the follower, and lower it onto the shim. Do not raise the follower after fitting, as the shim may become dislodged.

18 When all the followers are in position, complete with their shims, refit the camshaft as described in Section 11. Recheck the valve clearances before refitting the cylinder head cover, to make sure they are correct.

2.0 litre engines

19 The 2.0 litre engine is equipped with hydraulic tappets which automatically adjust the valve clearances. Therefore there is no need to check or adjust the valve clearances at any time.

13 Cylinder head (1.9 litre engines) – removal and refitting

Note 1: *This is an involved procedure, and it is suggested that the Section is read thoroughly before starting work. To aid refitting, make notes on the locations of all relevant brackets and the routing of hoses and cables before removal.*

Note 2: *On 2.0 litre engines, due to the limited access, it is impossible to remove the cylinder head with the engine in the car unless considerable additional dismantling is carried out first (eg, removal of the front suspension subframe and related components). Cylinder head removal and refitting procedures are therefore contained in Part E, assuming that the engine/transmission has been removed from the vehicle.*

Removal

1 Disconnect the battery negative terminal (refer to *Disconnecting the battery* in the Reference Chapter).

2 Drain the cooling system as described in Chapter 1B.

3 Remove the braking system vacuum pump as described in Chapter 9.

4 Remove the timing belt as described in Section 7.

5 Once the timing belt has been removed, unscrew the single bolt securing the right-hand engine/transmission mounting bracket to the cylinder head. Leave all the bolts securing the bracket to the cylinder block then refit the upper bracket, securing the engine bracket to the mounting, and securely tighten its nuts and bolts. This will ensure the engine/transmission unit is securely supported through out the following procedure.

6 If the cylinder head is to be overhauled, remove the camshaft sprocket and camshaft (see Sections 9 and 11).

7 Referring to Chapter 4C, carry out the following operations:

   a) Remove the air cleaner housing.
   b) Remove the inlet and exhaust manifolds.
   c) Disconnect and remove the fuel return hose from the end injector.
   d) Unscrew the union nuts and disconnect the fuel pipes from the fuel injectors and the fuel injection pump. Remove the pipes.
   e) If the cylinder head is being overhauled, remove the injectors.

8 Remove the cylinder head cover as described in Section 4.

9 Remove the fuel filter as described in Chapter 1B.

10 Unscrew the retaining bolt and remove the filter plastic housing, complete with its sealing ring **(see illustration)**. Discard the sealing ring; a new one must be used on refitting.

11 Slacken and remove the three bolts, noting the correct fitted location of the sealing washer,

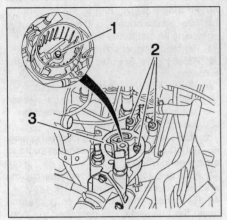

13.10 Unscrew the bolt (1) and remove the fuel filter housing then undo the three bolts (2) and free the filter/thermostat housing (3) from the cylinder head – 1.9 litre engines

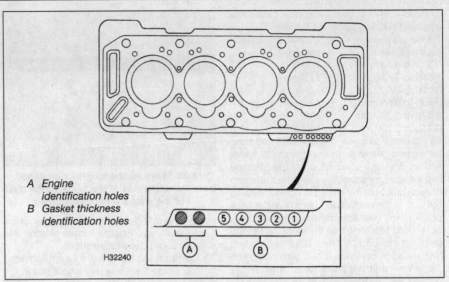

A Engine identification holes
B Gasket thickness identification holes

H32240

13.22 Cylinder head gasket identification holes – 1.9 litre engines

securing the fuel filter/thermostat housing to the front of the cylinder head. Disconnect the coolant hose connecting the housing to the coolant pipe then free the housing from the cylinder head. Recover the housing gasket and discard it; a new one must be used on refitting.

12 Unscrew the securing nut and disconnect the feed wire from the relevant glow plug. Recover the washers.

13 Unscrew the bolt securing the coolant pipe to the left-hand end of the cylinder head.

14 Check that the wiring and hoses is released from all the relevant clips or guides on the cylinder head and positioned clear.

15 Working in the *reverse* of the sequence shown in illustration 13.32, progressively slacken the ten cylinder head bolts by half a turn at a time, until all bolts can be unscrewed by hand.

16 With all the cylinder head bolts removed, release the cylinder head from the cylinder block and locating dowel by rocking it. The Peugeot/Citroën tool for doing this consists simply of two metal rods with 90-degree angled ends. Do not prise between the mating faces of the cylinder head and block, as this may damage the gasket faces. Lift the cylinder head away; seek assistance if possible.

17 Remove the gasket from the top of the block, noting the locating dowel. If the locating dowel is a loose fit, remove it and store it with the head for safe-keeping. Do not discard the gasket – it will be needed for identification purposes (see paragraphs 22 to 25).

18 If the cylinder head is to be dismantled for overhaul, remove the camshaft and followers as described in Section 11, then refer to Part E of this Chapter.

Preparation for refitting

19 The mating faces of the cylinder head and cylinder block must be perfectly clean before refitting the head. Use a hard plastic or wood scraper to remove all traces of gasket and carbon; also clean the piston crowns. Take particular care during the cleaning operations,

as aluminium alloy is easily damaged. Also, make sure that the carbon is not allowed to enter the oil and water passages – this is particularly important for the lubrication system, as carbon could block the oil supply to the engine's components. Using adhesive tape and paper, seal the water, oil and bolt holes in the cylinder block/crankcase. To prevent carbon entering the gap between the pistons and bores, smear a little grease in the gap. After cleaning each piston, use a small brush to remove all traces of grease and carbon from the gap, then wipe away the remainder with a clean rag. Clean all the pistons in the same way.

20 Check the mating surfaces of the cylinder block and the cylinder head for nicks, deep scratches and other damage. If slight, they may be removed carefully with a file, but if excessive, machining may be the only alternative to renewal.

21 If warpage of the cylinder head gasket surface is suspected, use a straight-edge to check it for distortion. Refer to Part E of this Chapter if necessary.

22 When purchasing a new cylinder head gasket, it is essential that a gasket of the correct thickness is obtained. There are six different thicknesses of gasket available to

13.23 Measuring piston protrusion – 1.9 litre engines

enable the cylinder head-to-piston clearance to be accurately set. The gasket thickness can be determined by looking at the tab situated in front of No 1 cylinder **(see illustration)**. There will be between 3 and 7 holes in the tab; the first two holes (in location A) identify the engine type (DW8), these are present on all gaskets and are of no real significance. It is the last group of between 1 and 5 holes (in location B) which identify the gasket thickness as follows.

Number of holes (hole locations)	Gasket thickness (when compressed)
1 (1)	1.26 mm
2 (1 and 2)	1.30 mm
3 (1, 2 and 3)	1.34 mm
4 (1, 2, 3 and 4)	1.38 mm
5 (1, 2, 3, 4 and 5)	1.42 mm
2 (1 and 5)	1.46 mm

The correct thickness of gasket required is selected by measuring the piston protrusions as follows.

23 Ensure the flywheel is correctly locked in position so pistons 1 and 4 are exactly at TDC. Mount a dial test indicator securely on the block so that its pointer can be easily pivoted between the piston crown and block mating surfaces. Zero the dial test indicator on the gasket surface of the cylinder block then carefully move the indicator over No 1 piston and measure its protrusion **(see illustration)**. Take measurements at the front and rear of the piston, and take the average of the two measurements to be the piston protrusion. Repeat this procedure on No 4 piston.

24 Remove the locking tool then rotate the crankshaft half-a-turn (180°) clockwise to bring pistons 2 and 3 to TDC. Ensure the crankshaft is accurately positioned then measure the protrusions of pistons No 2 and 3. Once all four pistons have been measured, rotate the crankshaft through a further half-a-turn (180°) clockwise to bring pistons 1 and 4 back to TDC then lock the flywheel in position again.

25 Using the largest protrusion measurement

of the four pistons, select the correct thickness of gasket required using the following:

Piston protrusion measurement	Gasket thickness required
0.510 to 0.549 mm	1.26 mm
0.550 to 0.589 mm	1.30 mm
0.590 to 0.629 mm	1.34 mm
0.630 to 0.669 mm	1.38 mm
0.670 to 0.709 mm	1.42 mm
0.710 to 0.750 mm	1.46 mm

26 Carefully examine the cylinder head bolts for signs of damage to the threads or head, and for any sign of corrosion. If the bolts are in a satisfactory condition, measure the length of each bolt from the underside of the head, to the end of the unthreaded portion at the base of the shank (see illustration). The bolts may be re-used providing that the measured length does not exceed 125.5 mm. Note that, if a bolt is modified to locate the gasket (see paragraph 28), a new bolt will be required when finally refitting the cylinder head. Note: *Considering the stress to which the cylinder head bolts are subjected, it is highly recommended that they are all renewed, regardless of their apparent condition.*

Refitting

27 Turn the crankshaft clockwise (viewed from the timing belt end) until Nos 1 and 4 pistons pass bottom dead centre (BDC) and begin to rise, then position them halfway up their bores. Nos 2 and 3 pistons will also be at their midway positions, but descending their bores.
28 Wipe clean the mating surfaces of the cylinder head and cylinder block. Fit the correct gasket the right way round on the cylinder block, with the identification holes toward the front facing side of the engine, and adjacent to cylinder No 1 (flywheel end). Make sure that the locating dowel is in place at the timing belt end of the block. Note that, as there is only one locating dowel, it is possible for the gasket to move as the cylinder head is fitted, particularly when the cylinder head is fitted with the engine in the car (due to the inclination of the engine). In the worst instance, this can allow the pistons and/or the valves to hit the gasket, causing engine damage. To avoid this problem, saw the head off an old cylinder head bolt, and file (or cut) a slot in the end of the bolt, to enable it to be turned with a screwdriver. Screw the bolt into one of the bolt holes at the flywheel end of the cylinder block, then fit the gasket over the bolt and location dowel. This will ensure that the gasket is held in position as the cylinder head is fitted.
29 With the aid of an assistant, carefully refit the cylinder head assembly to the block, aligning it with the locating dowel.
30 Lubricate the threads and underside of the heads of the cylinder head bolts with a smear of grease (Peugeot/Citroën recommend the use of Molykote G Rapid Plus grease).
31 Carefully enter each bolt into its relevant hole (*do not drop them in*) and screw in, by hand only, until finger-tight.
32 Working progressively and in sequence,

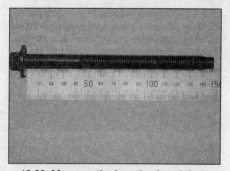

13.26 Measure the length of each bolt from the underside of the head, to the base of the shank – 1.9 litre engines

tighten the cylinder head bolts to their Stage 1 torque setting, using a torque wrench and suitable socket (see illustration).
33 Once all the bolts have been tightened to their Stage 1 setting, working again in the given sequence, tighten the cylinder head bolts to the specified Stage 2 torque setting.
34 Finally angle-tighten the bolts through the specified Stage 3 angle, using a socket and extension bar. It is recommended that an angle-measuring gauge is used during this stage of the tightening, to ensure accuracy. If a gauge is not available, use white paint to make alignment marks between the bolt head and cylinder head prior to tightening; the marks can then be used to check that the bolt has been rotated through the correct angle during tightening.
35 Where necessary, refit the camshaft and/or camshaft sprocket (see Sections 9 and 11). If the cylinder head has been overhauled, check the valve clearances before proceeding.
36 Ensure the engine/transmission unit is securely supported then remove the mounting bracket from the right-hand engine/trans-mission mounting. Refit the bolt securing the bracket to the cylinder head and tighten it to the specified torque.
37 Refit the timing belt as described in Section 7.
38 Refit the coolant pipe bolt and securely reconnect the glow plug wiring.
39 Ensure the mating surfaces are clean and dry then refit the fuel filter/thermostat housing to the cylinder head, using a new gasket. Fit the housing retaining bolts, ensuring the sealing washer is fitted to the bolt located inside the filter housing, and tighten them to the specified torque. Reconnect the coolant hose securely to the housing.

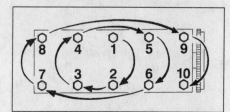

13.32 Cylinder head bolt tightening sequence – 1.9 litre engines

40 Fit a new sealing ring to the base of the fuel filter plastic housing and refit the housing, tightening its bolt to the specified torque.
41 Refit the cylinder cover (see Section 4).
42 Referring to Chapter 4C, carry out the following:
   a) *Refit the injectors (where removed).*
   b) *Refit the fuel pipes connecting the injection pump to the injectors and reconnect the leak off hoses to the injectors.*
   c) *Refit the manifolds and air cleaner housing.*
43 Refit the braking system vacuum pump as described in Chapter 9.
44 Fit a new fuel filter and refill the cooling system as described in Chapter 1B.
45 Reconnect the battery, then prime and bleed the fuel system as described in Chapter 4C.

14 Sump – removal and refitting

Removal

1 Firmly apply the handbrake, then jack up the front of the car and support it securely on axle stands (see *Jacking and vehicle support*). Disconnect the battery negative terminal (refer to *Disconnecting the battery* in the Reference Chapter).
2 Where necessary, remove the retaining bolts, screws and clips and remove the undercover from beneath the engine/ transmission unit.
3 Drain the engine oil, then clean and refit the engine oil drain plug, tightening it to the specified torque. If the engine is nearing its service interval when the oil and filter are due for renewal, it is recommended that the filter is also removed, and a new one fitted. After reassembly, the engine can then be refilled with fresh oil. Refer to Chapter 1B for further information.
4 On models with air conditioning, remove the auxiliary drivebelt as described in Chapter 1B. Unscrew the compressor mounting bolts and nuts. Free the compressor from the sump and support its weight by tying it to the vehicle, to prevent any excess strain being placed on the compressor lines. Take care not to lose the spacers from the compressor rear mountings (where fitted).
Caution: Do not disconnect the refrigerant lines from the compressor (refer to the warnings given in Chapter 3). Ensure the compressor is securely supported to prevent the refrigerant lines being damaged.
5 Progressively slacken and remove all the sump retaining bolts. On some models, it may be necessary to unbolt the flywheel cover plate from the transmission to gain access to the left-hand sump fasteners.
6 Progressively slacken and remove all the sump retaining bolts/nuts. Since the sump bolts vary in length, remove each bolt in turn, and store it in its correct fitted order by pushing it through a clearly-marked cardboard template. This will avoid the possibility of installing the bolts in the wrong locations on refitting.

7 Try to break the joint by striking the sump with the palm of your hand, then lower and withdraw the sump from under the car. If the sump is stuck (which is quite likely) use a putty knife, or similar, carefully inserted between the sump and block. Ease the knife along the joint until the sump is released. While the sump is removed, take the opportunity to check the oil pump pick-up/strainer for signs of clogging or splitting. If necessary, remove the pump as described in Section 15, and clean or renew the strainer. Note that on later 2.0 litre engine, the oil dipstick tube extends to the bottom of the sump in order to allow the oil to sucked out of the tube using special equipment.

Refitting

8 Clean all traces of sealant from the mating surfaces of the cylinder block/crankcase and sump, then use a clean rag to wipe out the sump and the engine's interior.
9 Apply a thin coating of suitable sealant to the sump mating surface.
10 On models with air conditioning ensure the sump locating dowel(s) is/are correctly fitted (as applicable).
11 Offer up the sump to the cylinder block/crankcase and refit its retaining bolts. Tighten all bolts by hand then evenly and progressively tighten them to the specified torque setting.
12 Where necessary, ensure the spacers (where fitted) are correctly located to the rear mountings then align the air conditioning compressor with the sump. Refit the mounting bolts and nuts; tighten compressor front (drivebelt pulley end) mounting bolts to the

specified torque first, then tighten the rear mounting bolts to the specified torque (see Chapter 3). Refit the auxiliary drivebelt as described in Chapter 1B.
13 Refit the undercover (where fitted) then lower the vehicle to the ground and refill the engine with oil (see Chapter 1B).

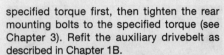

15 Oil pump – removal, inspection and refitting

Removal

1 Remove the sump (see Section 14).
2 Unscrew the bolt securing the dipstick guide tube to the oil pump and remove the guide tube from the cylinder block (see illustrations).
3 On 1.9 litre engines slacken and remove the three bolts securing the oil pump in position, noting the correct fitted location of the longer bolt. Disengage the pump sprocket from the chain, and remove the oil pump and spacer plate from the engine.
4 On 2.0 litre engines slacken and remove the three bolts securing the oil pump in position, noting the correct fitted location of the each bolt (they are all different sizes) and the sealing washer (see illustration). Disengage the pump sprocket from the chain, and remove the oil pump from the engine.

Inspection

5 Examine the oil pump sprocket for signs

of damage and wear, such as chipped or missing teeth. If the sprocket is worn, the pump assembly must be renewed, as the sprocket is not available separately. It is also recommended that the chain and drive sprocket, fitted to the crankshaft, is renewed at the same time. The oil pump drive sprocket and chain can be removed with the engine in situ, once the crankshaft sprocket has been removed and the crankshaft oil seal housing has been unbolted. See Part E for further information.
6 Slacken and remove the bolts securing the strainer cover to the pump body, then lift off the strainer cover. Remove the relief valve piston and spring (and guide pin – 2.0 litre engines only), noting which way round they are fitted (see illustrations).
7 Examine the pump rotors and body for signs of wear ridges and scoring. If worn, the complete pump assembly must be renewed.
8 Examine the relief valve piston for signs of wear or damage, and renew if necessary. The condition of the relief valve spring can only be measured by comparing it with a new one; if there is any doubt about its condition, it should also be renewed. Both the piston and spring are available individually.
9 Thoroughly clean the oil pump strainer with a suitable solvent, and check it for signs of clogging or splitting. If the strainer is damaged, the strainer and cover assembly must be renewed.
10 Locate the relief valve spring, piston and (where fitted) the guide pin in the strainer cover, then refit the cover to the pump body.

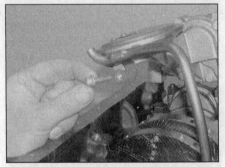

15.2a Unscrew the bolt securing the dipstick guide tube to the oil pump . . .

15.2b . . . then remove the guide tube from the block (shown with engine removed)

15.4 Note the correct fitted location of each oil pump retaining bolt (arrowed) as it is removed – 2.0 litre engines

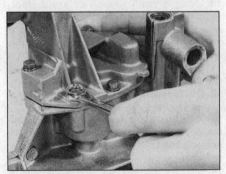

15.6a Unscrew the retaining bolts . . .

15.6b . . . then lift off the cover and remove the spring . . .

15.6c . . . and relief valve piston, noting which way around it is fitted

Align the relief valve piston with its bore in the pump. Refit the cover retaining bolts, tightening them securely.

Refitting

11 On 1.9 litre engines, fit the spacer plate then offer up the pump, engaging the pump sprocket with its drive chain. Refit the pump retaining bolts, ensuring the longer bolt is fitted to the rear hole, and tighten them to the specified torque setting.

12 On 2.0 litre engines, engage the pump sprocket with the drive chain then install the retaining bolts. Fit the sealing washer to the rear bolt then install the pump retaining bolts, ensuring they are fitted in their original locations. Tighten the bolts to the specified torque.

13 On all engines, refit the dipstick guide tube to the cylinder block and securely tighten its retaining bolt.

14 Refit the sump as described in Section 14.

16 Engine oil cooler –
removal and refitting

Refer to Chapter 2B, Section 19.

17 Crankshaft oil seals –
renewal

Right-hand oil seal

1 Remove the crankshaft sprocket as described in Section 9.

2 Make a note of the correct fitted depth of the seal in its housing then carefully punch or drill two small holes opposite each other in the seal. Screw a self-tapping screw into each, and pull on the screws with pliers to extract the seal **(see illustration)**. Alternatively, the seal can be levered out of position using a suitable flat-bladed screwdriver, taking great care not to damage the oil pump drive gear shoulder or seal housing.

3 Clean the seal housing, and polish off any burrs or raised edges, which may have caused the seal to fail in the first place.

4 Lubricate the lips of the new seal with clean engine oil, and carefully locate the seal on the end of crankshaft. Note that its sealing lip must face inwards. Take care not to damage the seal lips during fitting.

5 Using a suitable tubular drift (such as a socket) which bears only on the hard outer edge of the seal, tap the seal into position to the same depth in the housing as the original was prior to removal. The inner face of the seal must be flush with the inner wall of the crankcase.

6 Wash off any traces of oil, then refit the crankshaft sprocket as described in Section 9.

17.2 Using a self-tapping screw and pliers to remove the crankshaft right-hand oil seal

Left-hand oil seal

7 Remove the flywheel as described in Section 19.

8 Make a note of the correct fitted depth of the seal in its housing. Punch or drill two small holes opposite each other in the seal. Screw a self-tapping screw into each, and pull on the screws with pliers to extract the seal.

9 Clean the seal housing, and polish off any burrs or raised edges, which may have caused the seal to fail in the first place.

10 Lubricate the lips of the new seal with clean engine oil, and carefully locate the seal on the end of the crankshaft.

11 Using a suitable tubular drift, which bears only on the hard outer edge of the seal, drive the seal into position, to the same depth in the housing as the original was prior to removal.

12 Wash off any traces of oil, then refit the flywheel as described in Section 19.

18 Oil level and pressure
sensors – general

Refer to Chapter 5A.

19 Flywheel – removal,
inspection and refitting

Refer to Chapter 2B, Section 18.

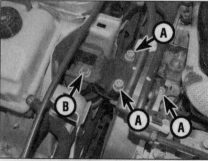

20.8 Unscrew the bolts (A) and nut (B) and remove the bracket from the top of the right-hand mounting – 1.9 litre engines

20 Engine/transmission
mountings – inspection and renewal

Inspection

1 If improved access is required, raise the front of the car and support it on axle stands (see *Jacking and vehicle support*).

2 Check the mounting rubber to see if it is cracked, hardened or separated from the metal at any point; renew the mounting if any such damage or deterioration is evident.

3 Check that all the mounting's fasteners are securely tightened; use a torque wrench to check if possible.

4 Using a large screwdriver or a crowbar, check for wear in the mounting by carefully levering against it to check for free play. Where this is not possible, enlist the aid of an assistant to move the engine/transmission back-and-forth, or from side-to-side, while you watch the mounting. While some free play is to be expected even from new components, excessive wear should be obvious. If excessive free play is found, check first that the fasteners are secure, then renew any worn components as described below.

Renewal

**Right-hand mounting –
1.9 litre engines**

5 Disconnect the battery negative terminal (refer to *Disconnecting the battery* in the Reference Chapter).

6 Remove the fasteners from the right-hand side and top of the engine cover then lift off the cover, taking care not to lose its mounting rubbers **(see illustrations 4.1a to 4.1c)**.

7 Place a jack beneath the engine, with a block of wood on the jack head. Raise the jack until it is supporting the weight of the engine.

8 Slacken and remove the three bolts securing the right-hand engine/transmission mounting upper bracket to the lower (engine) bracket. Unscrew the single nut securing the upper bracket to the rubber mounting **(see illustration)**.

9 Remove the upper bracket from the rubber mounting and lower (engine) bracket, then lift off the rubber buffer plate (where fitted).

10 Using a strap wrench or similar tool, unscrew the rubber mounting from the body. Alternatively, fabricate a tool from suitable metal tube with projections to engage in the cut-outs in the mounting.

11 Check for signs of wear or damage on all components, and renew as necessary.

12 On reassembly, screw the mounting rubber into the body, tightening it securely.

13 Refit the rubber buffer plate, then install the upper mounting bracket, tightening its retaining bolts and nut to their specified torque settings.

14 Remove the jack from under the engine then reconnect the battery negative lead and refit the engine cover.

20.21 Unscrew the domed buffer nut from the top of the mounting to gain access to the mounting nut – 2.0 litre engines

Right-hand mounting – 2.0 litre engines

15 Disconnect the battery negative terminal (refer to *Disconnecting the battery* in the Reference Chapter).

16 Turn the four plastic fasteners through 90° and lift off the engine cover **(see illustrations 6.25a and 6.25b)**.

17 Remove the engine undercover, then place a jack beneath the engine, with a block of wood on the jack head. Raise the jack until it is supporting the weight of the engine.

18 On early engines, undo the EGR solenoid valve mounting bracket bolt and move the valve to one side.

19 Undo the two bolts securing the right-hand mounting stiffener bracket to the body and lift off the bracket, complete with the accelerator pedal position sensor on later engines **(see illustration 6.31)**.

20 Slacken and remove the three bolts securing the right-hand engine/transmission mounting upper bracket to the lower (engine) bracket.

21 Unscrew the domed buffer nut, then unscrew the single nut securing the upper bracket to the rubber mounting **(see illustration)**.

22 Remove the upper bracket from the rubber mounting and lower (engine) bracket, then lift off the rubber buffer plate.

23 Using a strap wrench or similar tool, unscrew the rubber mounting from the body.

Alternatively, fabricate a tool from suitable metal tube with projections to engage in the cut-outs in the mounting.

24 Check for signs of wear or damage on all components, and renew as necessary.

25 On reassembly, screw the mounting rubber into the body, tightening it securely.

26 Refit the rubber buffer plate, then install the upper mounting bracket, tightening its retaining bolts and nut to their specified torque settings.

27 Refit the stiffener bracket and secure with the two retaining bolts, tightened to the specified torque. On early engines, refit the EGR solenoid valve mounting bracket to the stiffener bracket, insert the retaining bolt and tighten the bolt securely.

28 Remove the jack from under the engine then refit the undercover. Reconnect the battery negative lead then refit the engine cover.

Left-hand mounting

29 Refer to Chapter 2B, Section 20.

Rear mounting

30 Refer to Chapter 2A, Section 16.

Notes

Chapter 2 Part E:
Petrol engine removal and overhaul procedures

Contents

Degrees of difficulty

Easy, suitable for novice with little experience 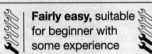	Fairly easy, suitable for beginner with some experience	Fairly difficult, suitable for competent DIY mechanic	Difficult, suitable for experienced DIY mechanic	Very difficult, suitable for expert DIY or professional

Specifications

Cylinder head

Maximum gasket face distortion	0.05 mm
New cylinder head height:	
1.4 litre engines	111.20 mm
1.6 litre engines	N/A
Minimum cylinder head height after machining:	
1.4 litre engines	111.00 mm
1.6 litre engines	N/A

Valves

	Inlet	Exhaust
Valve head diameter:		
1.4 litre engines	36.7 mm	29.4 mm
1.6 litre engines	N/A	N/A
Valve stem diameter:		
1.4 litre engines	6.965 to 6.980 mm	6.945 to 6.960 mm
1.6 litre engines	N/A	N/A

Cylinder block

Cylinder bore diameter:	
1.4 litre engines	75.00 mm (nominal)
1.6 litre engines	78.50 mm (nominal)
Liner protrusion – 1.4 litre engines:	
Standard	0.03 to 0.10 mm
Maximum difference between any two liners	0.05 mm

Pistons

Piston diameter:
1.4 litre engines	74.950 mm (nominal)
1.6 litre engines	78.455 mm (nominal)

Check with your Peugeot/Citroën dealer or engine specialist regarding piston oversizes

Crankshaft

Endfloat	0.07 to 0.27 mm
Main bearing journal diameter	49.965 to 49.981 mm
Big-end bearing journal diameter	44.975 to 44.991 mm

Piston rings

End gaps:
Top compression ring	0.20 to 0.45 mm
Second compression ring	0.30 to 0.50 mm
Oil control ring	0.30 to 0.50 mm

Torque wrench settings

Refer to Chapter 2A Specifications

1 General information

Included in this Part of Chapter 2 are details of removing the engine/transmission from the car and general overhaul procedures for the cylinder head, cylinder block/crankcase and all other engine internal components.

The information given ranges from advice concerning preparation for an overhaul and the purchase of new parts, to detailed step-by-step procedures covering removal, inspection, renovation and refitting of engine internal components.

After Section 5, all instructions are based on the assumption that the engine has been removed from the car. For information concerning in-car engine repair, as well as the removal and refitting of those external components necessary for full overhaul, refer to Part A of this Chapter, and to Section 5. Ignore any preliminary dismantling operations described in Part A that are no longer relevant once the engine has been removed from the car.

Apart from torque wrench settings, which are given at the beginning of Part A, all specifications relating to engine overhaul are at the beginning of this Part of Chapter 2.

2 Engine overhaul –
general information

It is not always easy to determine when, or if, an engine should be completely overhauled, as a number of factors must be considered.

High mileage is not necessarily an indication that an overhaul is needed, while low mileage does not preclude the need for an overhaul. Frequency of servicing is probably the most important consideration. An engine which has had regular and frequent oil and filter changes, as well as other required maintenance, should give many thousands of miles of reliable service. Conversely, a neglected engine may require an overhaul very early in its life.

Excessive oil consumption is an indication that piston rings, valve seals and/or valve guides are in need of attention. Make sure that oil leaks are not responsible before deciding that the rings and/or guides are worn. Perform a compression test, as described in Part A of this Chapter, to determine the likely cause of the problem.

Check the oil pressure with a gauge fitted in place of the oil pressure switch, and compare it with that specified. If it is extremely low, the main and big-end bearings, and/or the oil pump, are probably worn out.

Loss of power, rough running, knocking or metallic engine noises, excessive valve gear noise, and high fuel consumption may also point to the need for an overhaul, especially if they are all present at the same time. If a complete service does not remedy the situation, major mechanical work is the only solution.

A full engine overhaul involves restoring all internal parts to the specification of a new engine. During a complete overhaul, the pistons and the piston rings are renewed, and the cylinder bores are reconditioned. New main and big-end bearings are generally fitted; if necessary, the crankshaft may be reground, to compensate for wear in the journals. The valves are also serviced as well, since they are usually in less-than-perfect condition at this point. Always pay careful attention to the condition of the oil pump when overhauling the engine, and renew it if there is any doubt as to its serviceability. The end result should be an as-new engine that will give many trouble-free miles.

Critical cooling system components such as the hoses, thermostat and water pump should be renewed when an engine is overhauled. The radiator should be checked carefully, to ensure that it is not clogged or leaking. Also, it is a good idea to renew the oil pump whenever the engine is overhauled.

Before beginning the engine overhaul, read through the entire procedure, to familiarise yourself with the scope and requirements of the job. Check on the availability of parts and make sure that any necessary special tools and equipment are obtained in advance. Most work can be done with typical hand tools, although a number of precision measuring tools are required for inspecting parts to determine if they must be renewed.

The services provided by an engineering machine shop or engine reconditioning specialist will almost certainly be required, particularly if major repairs such as crankshaft regrinding or cylinder reboring are necessary. Apart from carrying out machining operations, these establishments will normally handle the inspection of parts, offer advice concerning reconditioning or renewal and supply new components such as pistons, piston rings and bearing shells. It is recommended that the establishment used is a member of the Federation of Engine Re-Manufacturers, or a similar society.

Always wait until the engine has been completely dismantled, and until all components (especially the cylinder block/crankcase and the crankshaft) have been inspected, before deciding what service and repair operations must be performed by an engineering works. The condition of these components will be the major factor to consider when determining whether to overhaul the original engine, or to buy a reconditioned unit. Do not, therefore, purchase parts or have overhaul work done on other components until they have been thoroughly inspected. As a general rule, time is the primary cost of an overhaul, so it does not pay to fit worn or sub-standard parts.

As a final note, to ensure maximum life and minimum trouble from a reconditioned engine, everything must be assembled with care, in a spotlessly-clean environment.

3 Engine/transmission removal
– methods and precautions

If you have decided that the engine must be removed for overhaul or major repair work, several preliminary steps should be taken.

Locating a suitable place to work is extremely important. Adequate work space, along with storage space for the car, will be needed. If a workshop or garage is not available, at the very least, a flat, level, clean work surface is required.

Cleaning the engine compartment and engine/transmission before beginning the removal procedure will help keep tools clean and organised.

An engine hoist will also be necessary. Make sure the equipment is rated in excess of the combined weight of the engine and transmission. Safety is of primary importance, considering the potential hazards involved in removing the engine/transmission from the car.

The help of an assistant is essential. Apart from the safety aspects involved, there are many instances when one person cannot simultaneously perform all of the operations required during engine/transmission removal.

Plan the operation ahead of time. Before starting work, arrange for the hire of or obtain all of the tools and equipment you will need. Some of the equipment necessary to perform engine/transmission removal and installation safely (in addition to an engine hoist) is as follows: a heavy duty trolley jack, complete sets of spanners and sockets as described in the rear of this manual, wooden blocks, and plenty of rags and cleaning solvent for mopping-up spilled oil, coolant and fuel. If the hoist must be hired, make sure that you arrange for it in advance, and perform all of the operations possible without it beforehand. This will save you money and time.

Plan for the car to be out of use for quite a while. An engineering machine shop or engine reconditioning specialist will be required to perform some of the work which cannot be accomplished without special equipment. These places often have a busy schedule, so it would be a good idea to consult them before removing the engine, in order to accurately estimate the amount of time required to rebuild or repair components that may need work.

During the engine/transmission removal procedure, it is advisable to make notes of the locations of all brackets, cable ties, earthing points, etc, as well as how the wiring harnesses, hoses and electrical connections are attached and routed around the engine and engine compartment. An effective way of doing this is to take a series of photographs of the various components before they are disconnected or removed; the resulting photographs will prove invaluable when the engine/transmission is refitted.

Always be extremely careful when removing and refitting the engine/transmission. Serious injury can result from careless actions. Plan ahead and take your time, and a job of this nature, although major, can be accomplished successfully.

The engine and transmission assembly is removed and refitted as follows:

a) *Upwards from the engine compartment on pre-September 2002 models.*
b) *Downwards from the engine compartment on September 2002 models onward.*

4 Engine/transmission –
removal and refitting

Note: *Such is the complexity of the power unit arrangement on these vehicles, and the variations that may be encountered according to model and optional equipment fitted, that the following should be regarded as a guide to the work involved, rather than a step-by-step procedure. Where differences are encountered, or additional component disconnection or removal is necessary, make notes of the work involved as an aid to refitting.*

Removal

Note: *The engine can be removed from the car only as a complete unit with the transmission; the two are then separated for overhaul.*

1 Remove the battery, battery tray and mounting plate as described in see Chapter 5A.

2 Apply the handbrake, then jack up the front of the vehicle and support it on axle stands (see *Jacking and vehicle support*). Remove both front roadwheels.

3 Where fitted, remove the plastic cover from the top of the engine.

4 To improve access, remove the bonnet as described in Chapter 11.

5 Remove the air cleaner housing and intake ducting as described in Chapter 4A.

6 Drain the cooling system with reference to Chapter 1A.

7 Drain the transmission oil as described in Chapter 7. Refit the drain and filler plugs, and tighten them to their specified torque settings.

8 If the engine is to be dismantled, drain the engine oil and remove the oil filter as described in Chapter 1A. Clean and refit the drain plug, tightening it securely.

9 Remove both the front wheel arch liners. The liners are secured by various screws and clips under the wheel arch. Release all the fasteners, and remove liners from under the front wings.

10 Refer to Chapter 1A and remove the auxiliary drivebelt.

11 Refer to Chapter 8 and remove both front driveshafts.

12 Disconnect the radiator top and bottom hoses, the heater hoses at the engine compartment bulkhead, and the expansion tank hose. On September 2002 models onward, remove the radiator as described in Chapter 3.

13 On models with air conditioning, refer to Chapter 3 and unbolt the compressor from the engine. **Do not** disconnect the refrigerant lines. Support or tie the compressor to one side.

14 On models with power steering, remove the power steering pump as described in Chapter 10.

15 Remove the exhaust system with reference to Chapter 4A.

16 Note their fitted positions and harness routing, then disconnect all relevant wiring plugs from the transmission. If necessary label the connectors as they are unplugged.

17 Disconnect the engine wiring harness connectors at the fusebox, fuel injection relay and front body panel (as applicable). Release the wiring harness from the retaining clips and ties so the harness is free to be removed with the engine.

18 Disconnect the engine earth leads at the fusebox; under the left-hand wheel arch and on the left-hand chassis member.

19 Disconnect the brake servo unit vacuum pipe from the inlet manifold.

20 Disconnect the accelerator cable with reference to Chapter 4A.

21 Where fitted, on later engines, undo the two bolts securing the right-hand engine mounting stiffener bracket to the body and lift off the bracket, complete with the accelerator pedal position sensor.

22 Disconnect the fuel feed and return hoses and plug the hoses and unions to prevent dirt ingress. Release the fuel hoses from the retaining clips on the engine and move them aside.

23 Disconnect the clutch cable from the release lever and transmission bracket as described in Chapter 6.

24 Disconnect the gearchange selector mechanism from the transmission as described in Chapter 7.

25 Using a hoist attached to the lifting eyes on the cylinder head, take the weight of the engine and transmission.

26 Remove the right-hand, left-hand and rear engine mountings and support brackets as described in Chapter 2A.

27 Make a final check to ensure all wiring, hoses and brackets that would prevent the removal of the assembly have been disconnected.

28 On pre-September 2002 models, lift the engine/transmission assembly from the engine compartment, ensuring that nothing is trapped or damaged. Enlist the help of an assistant during this procedure as it will be necessary to tilt the assembly slightly to clear the body panels. Once the unit is high enough, lift it out over the front of the body and lower it to the ground.

29 On September 2002 models onward, carefully lower the engine/transmission from the engine compartment taking care not to damage the surrounding components. Ideally lower the unit onto a low trolley so that it may be withdrawn from under the car. Disconnect the hoist from the engine/transmission assembly.

Separation

30 With the engine/transmission assembly removed, support the assembly on suitable blocks of wood on a workbench (or failing that, on a clean area of the workshop floor).
31 Undo the retaining bolts, and remove the flywheel lower cover plate (where fitted) from the transmission.
32 Slacken and remove the retaining bolts, and remove the starter motor from the transmission.
33 Disconnect any remaining wiring connectors at the transmission, then move the main engine wiring harness to one side.
34 Ensure that both engine and transmission are adequately supported, then slacken and remove the remaining bolts securing the transmission housing to the engine. Note the correct fitted positions of each bolt (and the relevant brackets) as they are removed, to use as a reference on refitting.
35 Carefully withdraw the transmission from the engine, ensuring that the weight of the transmission is not allowed to hang on the input shaft while it is engaged with the clutch friction disc.
36 If they are loose, remove the locating dowels from the engine or transmission, and keep them in a safe place.

Refitting

37 If the engine and transmission have not been separated, perform the operations described below from paragraph 44 onwards.
38 Apply a smear of high melting-point grease (Peugeot/Citroën recommend the use of Molykote BR2 plus) to the splines of the transmission input shaft. Do not apply too much, otherwise there is a possibility of the grease contaminating the clutch friction disc.
39 Ensure that the locating dowels are correctly positioned in the engine or transmission.
40 Carefully offer the transmission to the engine, until the locating dowels are engaged. Ensure that the weight of the transmission is not allowed to hang on the input shaft as it is engaged with the clutch friction disc.
41 Refit the transmission housing-to-engine bolts, ensuring that all the necessary brackets are correctly positioned, and tighten them to the specified torque.
42 Refit the starter motor, and securely tighten its retaining bolts.
43 Refit the lower flywheel cover plate (where fitted) to the transmission, and securely tighten the bolts.
44 Position the engine/transmission assembly

ready for installation, then reconnect the hoist and lifting tackle. With the aid of an assistant, locate the assembly into the engine compartment, using the same procedure as for removal.
45 Refit the right-hand, left-hand and rear engine mountings and support brackets as described in Chapter 2A.
46 Remove the hoist from the engine.
47 The remainder of the refitting procedure is a direct reversal of the removal sequence, with reference to the relevant chapters and noting the following points:
a) Ensure that the wiring loom is correctly routed and retained by all the relevant retaining clips; all connectors should be correctly and securely reconnected.
b) Ensure that all coolant hoses are correctly reconnected, and securely retained by their retaining clips.
c) Refill the engine and transmission with the correct quantity and type of lubricant, as described in Chapters 1A and 7.
d) Refill the cooling system as described in Chapter 1A.
e) Pressurise/prime the fuel system as described in Chapter 4A.
f) Bleed the power steering system as described in Chapter 10.
g) Initialise the engine management ECU as follows. Start the engine and run to normal temperature. Carry out a road test during which the following procedure should be made. Engage third gear and stabilise the engine at 1000 rpm. Now accelerate fully to 3500 rpm.

---

5 Engine overhaul – dismantling sequence

1 It is much easier to dismantle and work on the engine if it is mounted on a portable engine stand. These stands can often be hired from a tool hire shop. Before the engine is mounted on a stand, the flywheel should be removed, so that the stand bolts can be tightened into the end of the cylinder block/crankcase.
2 If a stand is not available, it is possible to dismantle the engine with it blocked up on a sturdy workbench, or on the floor. Be extra careful not to tip or drop the engine when working without a stand.
3 If you are going to obtain a reconditioned engine, all the external components must be removed first, to be transferred to the new engine (just as they will if you are doing a complete engine overhaul yourself). These components include the following:
a) Ancillary unit mounting brackets (oil filter, starter, alternator, power steering pump, etc)
b) Thermostat and housing (Chapter 3).
c) Dipstick tube/sensor.
d) All electrical switches and sensors.

e) Inlet and exhaust manifolds – where applicable (Chapter 4A).
f) Ignition coils and spark plugs – as applicable (Chapter 5B and 1A).
g) Flywheel (Part A of this Chapter).

Note: When removing the external components from the engine, pay close attention to details that may be helpful or important during refitting. Note the fitted position of gaskets, seals, spacers, pins, washers, bolts, and other small items.
4 If you are obtaining a 'short' engine (which consists of the engine cylinder block/crankcase, crankshaft, pistons and connecting rods all assembled), then the cylinder head, sump, oil pump, and timing belt will have to be removed also.
5 If you are planning a complete overhaul, the engine can be dismantled, and the internal components removed, in the order given below, referring to Part A of this Chapter unless otherwise stated.
a) Inlet and exhaust manifolds – where applicable (Chapter 4A).
b) Timing belts, sprockets and tensioner(s).
c) Cylinder head.
d) Flywheel.
e) Sump.
f) Oil pump.
g) Piston/connecting rod assemblies (Section 9).
h) Crankshaft (Section 10).
6 Before beginning the dismantling and overhaul procedures, make sure that you have all of the correct tools necessary. Refer to *Tools and working facilities* for further information.

---

6 Cylinder head – dismantling

Note: New and reconditioned cylinder heads are available from the manufacturer, and from engine overhaul specialists. Be aware that some specialist tools are required for the dismantling and inspection procedures, and new components may not be readily available. It may therefore be more practical and economical for the home mechanic to purchase a reconditioned head, rather than dismantle, inspect and recondition the original head.
1 Remove the cylinder head as described in Part A of this Chapter.
2 If not already done, remove the inlet and exhaust manifolds with reference to Chapter 4A. Remove any remaining brackets or housings as required.
3 Remove the camshaft(s), hydraulic tappets and rockers (as applicable) as described in Part A of this Chapter.
4 If not already done, remove the spark plugs as described in Chapter 1A.
5 Using a valve spring compressor, compress

6.5 Compress the valve spring using a spring compressor until the collets can be removed

6.7 Use a pair of pliers to remove the valve stem oil seal

6.8 Place each valve and its associated components in a labelled bag

each valve spring in turn until the split collets can be removed **(see illustration)**. Release the compressor, and lift off the spring retainer and spring.

6 If, when the valve spring compressor is screwed down, the spring retainer refuses to free and expose the split collets, gently tap the top of the tool, directly over the retainer, with a light hammer. This will free the retainer.

7 Withdraw the valve from the combustion chamber then, using a pair of pliers, carefully extract the valve stem oil seal from the top of the guide **(see illustration)**. Lift out the spring seat, where fitted.

8 It is essential that each valve is stored together with its collets, retainer, spring, and spring seat. The valves should also be kept in their correct sequence, unless they are so badly worn that they are to be renewed. If they are going to be kept and used again, place each valve assembly in a labelled polythene bag or similar small container **(see illustration)**. Note that No 1 valve is nearest to the transmission (flywheel) end of the engine.

---

7 Cylinder head and valves – cleaning and inspection

1 Thorough cleaning of the cylinder head and valve components, followed by a detailed inspection, will enable you to decide how much valve service work must be carried out during the engine overhaul. **Note:** *If the engine has been severely overheated, it is best to assume that the cylinder head is warped – check carefully for signs of this.*

Cleaning

2 Scrape away all traces of old gasket material from the cylinder head.

3 Scrape away the carbon from the combustion chambers and ports, then wash the cylinder head thoroughly with paraffin or a suitable solvent.

4 Scrape off any heavy carbon deposits that may have formed on the valves, then use a power-operated wire brush to remove deposits from the valve heads and stems.

Inspection

Note: *Be sure to perform all the following inspection procedures before concluding that the services of a machine shop or engine overhaul specialist are required. Make a list of all items that require attention.*

Cylinder head

5 Inspect the head very carefully for cracks, evidence of coolant leakage, and other damage. If cracks are found, a new cylinder head should be obtained. Use a straight-edge and feeler blade to check that the cylinder head gasket surface is not distorted **(see illustration)**. If it is, it may be possible to have it machined, provided that the cylinder head height is not significantly reduced.

6 Examine the valve seats in each of the combustion chambers. If they are severely pitted, cracked, or burned, they will need to be renewed or recut by an engine overhaul specialist. If they are only slightly pitted, this can be removed by grinding-in the valve heads and seats with fine valve-grinding compound, as described below.

7 Check the valve guides for wear by inserting the relevant valve, and checking for side-to-side motion of the valve. A very small amount of movement is acceptable. If the movement seems excessive, remove the valve. Measure the valve stem diameter (see below), and renew the valve if it is worn. If the valve stem is not worn, the wear must be in the valve guide, and the guide must be renewed. The renewal of valve guides is best carried out by an engine overhaul specialist,

who will have the necessary tools available. Where no valve stem diameter is specified, seek the advice of a Peugeot/Citroën dealer or engine overhaul specialist on the best course of action.

8 If renewing the valve guides, the valve seats should be recut or reground only *after* the guides have been fitted.

Valves

9 Examine the head of each valve for pitting, burning, cracks, and general wear. Check the valve stem for scoring and wear ridges. Rotate the valve, and check for any obvious indication that it is bent. Look for pits or excessive wear on the tip of each valve stem. Renew any valve that shows any such signs of wear or damage.

10 If the valve appears satisfactory at this stage, measure the valve stem diameter at several points using a micrometer **(see illustration)**. Any significant difference in the readings obtained indicates wear of the valve stem. Should any of these conditions be apparent, the valve must be renewed.

11 If the valves are in satisfactory condition, they should be ground (lapped) into their respective seats, to ensure a smooth, gas-tight seal. If the seat is only lightly pitted, or if it has been recut, fine grinding compound only should be used to produce the required finish. Coarse valve-grinding compound should not be used, unless a seat is badly burned or deeply pitted. If this is the case, the cylinder head and valves should be inspected by an expert, to decide whether seat recutting, or

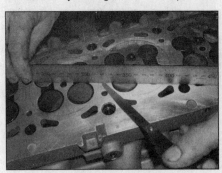

7.5 Check the cylinder head gasket surface for distortion

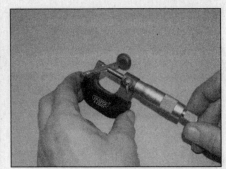

7.10 Measure the valve stem diameter with a micrometer

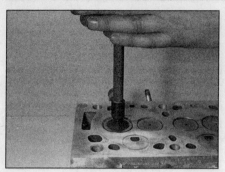

7.13 Grinding-in a valve

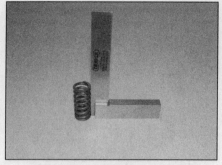

7.17 Check each valve spring for squareness

8.1 Press the new oil seal firmly onto the guide using a suitable socket

even the renewal of the valve or seat insert (where possible) is required.

12 Valve grinding is carried out as follows. Place the cylinder head upside-down on a bench.

13 Smear a trace of (the appropriate grade of) valve-grinding compound on the seat face, and press a suction grinding tool onto the valve head **(see illustration)**. With a semi-rotary action, grind the valve head to its seat, lifting the valve occasionally to redistribute the grinding compound. A light spring placed under the valve head will greatly ease this operation.

14 If coarse grinding compound is being used, work only until a dull, matt even surface is produced on both the valve seat and the valve, then wipe off the used compound, and repeat the process with fine compound. When

a smooth unbroken ring of light grey matt finish is produced on both the valve and seat, the grinding operation is complete. *Do not* grind-in the valves any further than absolutely necessary, or the seat will be prematurely sunk into the cylinder head.

15 When all the valves have been ground-in, carefully wash off *all* traces of grinding compound using paraffin or a suitable solvent, before reassembling the cylinder head.

Valve components

16 Examine the valve springs for signs of damage and discoloration. No minimum free length is specified by Peugeot/Citroën, so the only way of judging valve spring wear is by comparison with a new component.

17 Stand each spring on a flat surface, and check it for squareness **(see illustration)**. If any of the springs are damaged, distorted

or have lost their tension, obtain a complete new set of springs. It is normal to renew the valve springs as a matter of course if a major overhaul is being carried out.

18 Renew the valve stem oil seals regardless of their apparent condition.

8 Cylinder head – reassembly

1 Working on the first valve assembly, refit the spring seat then dip the new valve stem oil seal in fresh engine oil. Locate the seal on the valve guide and press the seal firmly onto the guide using a suitable socket **(see illustration)**.

2 Lubricate the stem of the first valve, and insert it in the guide **(see illustration)**.

3 Locate the valve spring on top of its seat, then refit the spring retainer **(see illustrations)**.

4 Compress the valve spring, and locate the split collets in the recess in the valve stem **(see illustration)**. Release the compressor, then repeat the procedure on the remaining valves. Ensure that each valve is inserted into its original location. If new valves are being fitted, insert them into the locations to which they have been ground.

8.2 Lubricate the valve stem and insert it in the guide

8.3a Fit the valve spring . . .

 HAYNES HiNT *Haynes hint: Use a little dab of grease to hold the collets in position on the valve stem while the spring compressor is released.*

5 With all the valves installed, support the cylinder head and, using a hammer and interposed block of wood, tap the end of each valve stem to settle the components.

6 Refit the camshafts, hydraulic tappets and rocker arms (as applicable) as described in Part A of this Chapter.

7 Refit any remaining components using the reverse of the removal sequence and with new seals or gaskets as necessary.

8 The cylinder head can then be refitted as described in Part A of this Chapter.

8.3b . . . then place the spring retainer over the spring

8.4 Compress the valve spring, and locate the collets in the recess in the valve stem

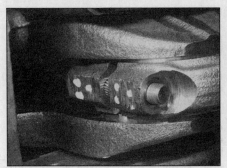

9.3 Connecting rod and big-end bearing cap identification marks (No 3 shown)

9 Piston/connecting rod assembly – removal

1 Remove the cylinder head, sump and oil pump as described in Part A.
2 If there is a pronounced wear ridge at the top of any bore, it may be necessary to remove it with a scraper or ridge reamer, to avoid piston damage during removal. Such a ridge indicates excessive wear of the cylinder bore.
3 Using quick-drying paint, mark each connecting rod and big-end bearing cap with its respective cylinder number on the flat machined surface provided; if the engine has been dismantled before, note carefully any identifying marks made previously **(see illustration)**. Note that No 1 cylinder is at the transmission (flywheel) end of the engine.
4 Turn the crankshaft to bring pistons 1 and 4 to BDC (bottom dead centre).
5 Unscrew the nuts or bolts, as applicable, from No 1 piston big-end bearing cap. Take off the cap, and recover the bottom half bearing shell **(see illustration)**. If the bearing shells are to be re-used, tape the cap and the shell together.
6 To prevent the possibility of damage to the crankshaft bearing journals, tape over the connecting rod stud threads, where fitted **(see illustration)**.
7 Using a hammer handle, push the piston up through the bore, and remove it from the top of the cylinder block. Recover the bearing

9.6 To protect the crankshaft journals, tape over the connecting rod stud threads

9.5 Remove the big-end bearing shell and cap

shell, and tape it to the connecting rod for safe-keeping.
8 Loosely refit the big-end cap to the connecting rod, and secure with the nuts/bolts – this will help to keep the components in their correct order.
9 Remove No 4 piston assembly in the same way.
10 Turn the crankshaft through 180° to bring pistons 2 and 3 to BDC (bottom dead centre), and remove them in the same way.

10 Crankshaft – removal

1 Remove the crankshaft sprocket and the oil pump as described in Part A of this Chapter.
2 Remove the pistons and connecting rods, as described in Section 9. If no work is to be done on the pistons and connecting rods, there is no need to remove the cylinder head, or to push the pistons out of the cylinder bores. The pistons should just be pushed far enough up the bores so that they are positioned clear of the crankshaft journals.
3 Check the crankshaft endfloat as described in Section 13, then proceed as follows.

1.4 litre engines

4 Work around the outside of the cylinder block, and unscrew all the small (M6) bolts securing the main bearing ladder to the base of the cylinder block. Note the correct fitted depth of both the left- and right-hand crankshaft oil seals in the cylinder block/main bearing ladder.

11.1 Cylinder block core plugs (arrowed)

5 Working in a diagonal sequence, evenly and progressively slacken the ten large (M11) main bearing ladder retaining bolts by a turn at a time. Once all the bolts are loose, remove them from the ladder.
6 With all the retaining bolts removed, carefully lift the main bearing ladder casting away from the base of the cylinder block. Recover the lower main bearing shells, and tape them to their respective locations in the casting. If the two locating dowels are a loose fit, remove them and store them with the casting for safe-keeping.
7 Lift out the crankshaft, and discard both the oil seals. Remove the oil pump drive chain from the end of the crankshaft. Where necessary, slide off the drive sprocket, and recover the Woodruff key.
8 Recover the upper main bearing shells, and store them along with the relevant lower bearing shell. Also recover the two thrustwashers (one fitted either side of No 2 main bearing) from the cylinder block.

1.6 litre engines

9 Unbolt and remove the crankshaft left- and right-hand oil seal housings from each end of the cylinder block, noting the correct fitted locations of the locating dowels. If the locating dowels are a loose fit, remove them and store them with the housings for safe-keeping.
10 Remove the oil pump drive chain, and slide the drive sprocket off the end of the crankshaft. Remove the Woodruff key, and store it with the sprocket for safe-keeping.
11 The main bearing caps should be numbered 1 to 5 from the transmission (flywheel) end of the engine. If not, mark them accordingly using a centre-punch or paint.
12 Unscrew and remove the main bearing cap retaining bolts, and withdraw the caps. Recover the lower main bearing shells, and tape them to their respective caps for safe-keeping.
13 Carefully lift out the crankshaft, taking care not to displace the upper main bearing shell.
14 Recover the upper bearing shells from the cylinder block, and tape them to their respective caps for safe-keeping. Remove the thrustwasher halves from the side of No 2 main bearing, and store them with the bearing cap.

11 Cylinder block/crankcase – cleaning and inspection

Cleaning

1 Remove all external components and electrical switches/sensors from the block. For complete cleaning, the core plugs should ideally be removed **(see illustration)**. Drill a small hole in the plugs, then insert a self-tapping screw into the hole. Pull out the plugs by pulling on the screw with a pair of grips, or by using a slide hammer.

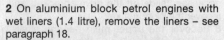

11.3 Piston oil jet spray tube (arrowed) in the cylinder block

11.9 Use a suitable tap to clean the cylinder block threaded holes

2 On aluminium block petrol engines with wet liners (1.4 litre), remove the liners – see paragraph 18.

3 Where applicable, undo the retaining bolts and remove the piston oil jet spray tubes (there is one for each piston) from inside the cylinder block **(see illustration)**.

4 Scrape all traces of gasket from the cylinder block/crankcase, and from the main bearing ladder/caps (as applicable), taking care not to damage the gasket/sealing surfaces.

5 Remove all oil gallery plugs (where fitted). The plugs are usually very tight – they may have to be drilled out, and the holes retapped. Use new plugs when the engine is reassembled.

6 If any of the castings are extremely dirty, all should be steam-cleaned.

7 After the castings are returned, clean all oil holes and oil galleries one more time. Flush all internal passages with warm water until the water runs clear. Dry thoroughly, and apply a light film of oil to all mating surfaces, to prevent rusting. On cast-iron block engines, also oil the cylinder bores. If you have access to compressed air, use it to speed up the drying process, and to blow out all the oil holes and galleries.

 Warning: Wear eye protection when using compressed air.

8 If the castings are not very dirty, you can do an adequate cleaning job with hot, soapy water and a stiff brush. Take plenty of time, and do a thorough job. Regardless of the cleaning method used, be sure to clean all oil holes and galleries very thoroughly, and to dry all components well. On cast-iron block engines, protect the cylinder bores as described above, to prevent rusting.

9 All threaded holes must be clean, to ensure accurate torque readings during reassembly. To clean the threads, run the correct-size tap into each of the holes to remove rust, corrosion, thread sealant or sludge, and to restore damaged threads **(see illustration)**. If possible, use compressed air to clear the holes of debris produced by this operation.

10 Apply suitable sealant to the new oil gallery plugs, and insert them into the holes in the block. Tighten them securely. Also

apply suitable sealant to new core plugs, and drive them into the block using a tube or socket.

11 Where applicable, clean the threads of the piston oil jet retaining bolts, and apply a drop of thread-locking compound (Peugeot/Citroën recommend Loctite Frenetanch) to each bolt threads. Refit the piston oil jet spray tubes to the cylinder block, and tighten the retaining bolts to the specified torque setting.

12 If the engine is not going to be reassembled right away, cover it with a large plastic bag to keep it clean; protect all mating surfaces and the cylinder bores as described above, to prevent rusting.

Inspection

Cast-iron cylinder block

13 Visually check the castings for cracks and corrosion. Look for stripped threads in the threaded holes. If there has been any history of internal water leakage, it may be worthwhile having an engine overhaul specialist check the cylinder block/crankcase with special equipment. If defects are found, have them repaired if possible, or renew the assembly.

14 Check each cylinder bore for scuffing and scoring. Check for signs of a wear ridge at the top of the cylinder, indicating that the bore is excessively worn.

15 Accurate measuring of the cylinder bores requires specialised equipment and experience. We recommend having the

bores measured by an engine reconditioning specialist who will also be able to supply appropriate pistons (where possible) should a rebore be necessary.

16 If the cylinder bores and pistons are in reasonably good condition, and not worn beyond the specified limits, and if the piston-to-bore clearances can be maintained, then it will only be necessary to renew the piston rings. If this is the case, the cylinder bores must be honed to allow the new piston rings to bed in correctly and provide the best possible seal. An engine reconditioning specialist will carry out this work at moderate cost.

17 At the time of writing, it was not clear whether oversize pistons were available for all models. Consult your Peugeot/Citroën dealer or engine specialist for the latest information on piston availability. If oversize pistons are available (either from Peugeot/Citroën, or from another source), then it may be possible to have the cylinder bores rebored and fit the oversize pistons. If oversize pistons are not available, and the bores are worn, renewal of the block seems to be the only option.

Aluminium cylinder block

18 Remove the liner clamps (where used), then use a hardwood drift to tap out each liner from the inside of the cylinder block. When all the liners are released, tip the cylinder block/crankcase on its side and remove each liner from the top of the block. As each liner is removed, stick masking tape on its left-hand (transmission side) face, and write the cylinder number on the tape. No 1 cylinder is at the transmission (flywheel) end of the engine. Remove the sealing ring from the base of each liner, and discard **(see illustrations)**.

19 Check each cylinder liner for scuffing and scoring. Check for signs of a wear ridge at the top of the liner, indicating that the bore is excessively worn.

20 Take the liners to an engine reconditioning specialist and have their bores measured to determine if renewal is necessary. If it is, the specialist will be able to advise you regarding piston/liner availability.

21 Prior to installing the liners, check the liner protrusion as follows. Thoroughly clean the mating surfaces of the liner and cylinder

11.18a On aluminium block engines, remove each liner . . .

11.18b . . . and recover the bottom O-ring seal (arrowed)

block. Insert the liners into the block ensuring each one is correctly seated; if the original liners are being refitted, ensure the liners are fitted in their original locations. With all four liners correctly installed, use a dial gauge (or a straight-edge and feeler blade) to check that the protrusion of each liner above the upper surface of the cylinder block is within the limits given in the Specifications. The maximum difference between any two liners must not be exceeded. **Note:** *If new liners are being fitted, it is permissible to interchange them to bring the difference in protrusion within limits. Remember to keep each piston with its respective liner.* If liner protrusion is not within the specified limits, seek the advice of an engine reconditioning specialist before proceeding with the engine rebuild.

22 Once the protrusions have been checked, remove the liners from the block and fit a new sealing ring carefully to the base of each liner. Lubricate the base of each liner with a smear of oil to aid installation.

23 Insert each liner into the cylinder block, taking care not to damage the O-ring, and press it home as far as possible by hand. Using a hammer and a block of wood, tap each liner lightly but fully onto its locating shoulder. If the original liners are being refitted, use the marks made on removal to ensure that each is refitted the correct way round, and is inserted into its original bore.

24 Wipe clean, then lightly oil all exposed liner surfaces, to prevent rusting. Where necessary, clamp the liners back in position.

12 Piston/connecting rod assembly – inspection

1 Before the inspection process can begin, the piston/connecting rod assemblies must be cleaned, and the original piston rings removed from the pistons.

2 Carefully expand the old rings over the top of the pistons. The use of two or three old feeler blades will be helpful in preventing the rings dropping into empty grooves **(see illustration)**. Be careful not to scratch the piston with the ends of the ring. The rings are brittle, and will snap if they are spread too far. They are also very sharp – protect your hands and fingers. Note that the third ring incorporates an expander. Always remove the rings from the top of the piston. Keep each set of rings with its piston if the old rings are to be re-used.

3 Scrape away all traces of carbon from the top of the piston. A hand-held wire brush (or a piece of fine emery cloth) can be used, once the majority of the deposits have been scraped away.

4 Remove the carbon from the ring grooves in the piston, using an old ring. Break the ring

in half to do this (be careful not to cut your fingers – piston rings are sharp). Be careful to remove only the carbon deposits – do not remove any metal, and do not nick or scratch the sides of the ring grooves.

5 Once the deposits have been removed, clean the piston/connecting rod assembly with paraffin or a suitable solvent, and dry thoroughly. Make sure that the oil return holes in the ring grooves are clear.

6 If the pistons and cylinder bores are not damaged or worn excessively, and if the cylinder block does not need to be rebored (where possible), the original pistons can be refitted. Normal piston wear shows up as even vertical wear on the piston thrust surfaces, and slight looseness of the top ring in its groove. New piston rings should always be used when the engine is reassembled.

7 Carefully inspect each piston for cracks around the skirt, around the gudgeon pin holes, and at the piston ring 'lands' (between the ring grooves).

8 Look for scoring and scuffing on the piston skirt, holes in the piston crown, and burned areas at the edge of the crown. If the skirt is scored or scuffed, the engine may have been suffering from overheating, and/or abnormal combustion which caused excessively high operating temperatures. The cooling and lubrication systems should be checked thoroughly. Scorch marks on the sides of the pistons show that blow-by has occurred. A hole in the piston crown, or burned areas at the edge of the piston crown, indicates that abnormal combustion (pre-ignition, knocking, or detonation) has been occurring. If any of the above problems exist, the causes must be investigated and corrected, or the damage will occur again. The causes are likely to be attributable to a faulty injector or engine management system fault.

9 Corrosion of the piston, in the form of pitting, indicates that coolant has been leaking into the combustion chamber and/or the crankcase. Again, the cause must be corrected, or the problem may persist in the rebuilt engine.

10 On aluminium block engines with wet liners, it is not possible to renew the pistons separately; pistons are only supplied with piston rings and a liner, as a part of a matched assembly (see Section 11). On iron-block engines, pistons can be purchased from a Peugeot/Citroën dealer or engine reconditioning specialist.

11 Examine each connecting rod carefully for signs of damage, such as cracks around the big-end and small-end bearings. Check that the rod is not bent or distorted. Damage is highly unlikely, unless the engine has been seized or badly overheated. Detailed checking of the connecting rod assembly can only be carried out by an engine specialist with the necessary equipment.

12 The connecting rod big-end cap nuts must be renewed whenever they are

12.2 Remove the piston rings with the aid of a feeler gauge

disturbed. Although Peugeot/Citroën do not specify that the bolts must also renewed, it is recommended that the nuts and bolts are replaced as a complete set.

13 The gudgeon pins are an interference fit in the connecting rod small-end bearing. Therefore, piston and/or connecting rod renewal should be entrusted to an engine reconditioning specialist, who will have the necessary tooling to remove and install the gudgeon pins.

13 Crankshaft – inspection

Checking endfloat

1 If the crankshaft endfloat is to be checked, this must be done when the crankshaft is still installed in the cylinder block/crankcase, but is free to move (see Section 10).

2 Check the endfloat using a dial gauge in contact with the end of the crankshaft. Push the crankshaft fully one way, and then zero the gauge. Push the crankshaft fully the other way, and check the endfloat. The result can be compared with the specified amount, and will give an indication as to whether new thrustwashers are required **(see illustration)**.

3 If a dial gauge is not available, feeler blades can be used. First push the crankshaft fully towards the flywheel end of the engine, then use feeler blades to measure the gap between

13.2 The crankshaft endfloat can be checked with a dial gauge . . .

13.3 . . . or with feeler gauges

the web of No 2 crankpin and the thrustwasher **(see illustration)**.

Inspection

4 Clean the crankshaft using paraffin or a suitable solvent, and dry it, preferably with compressed air if available. Be sure to clean the oil holes with a pipe cleaner or similar probe, to ensure that they are not obstructed.

 Warning: Wear eye protection when using compressed air.

5 Check the main and big-end bearing journals for uneven wear, scoring, pitting and cracking.
6 Big-end bearing wear is accompanied by distinct metallic knocking when the engine is running (particularly noticeable when the engine is pulling from low speed) and some loss of oil pressure.
7 Main bearing wear is accompanied by severe engine vibration and rumble – getting progressively worse as engine speed increases – and again by loss of oil pressure.
8 Check the bearing journal for roughness by running a finger lightly over the bearing surface. Any roughness (which will be accompanied

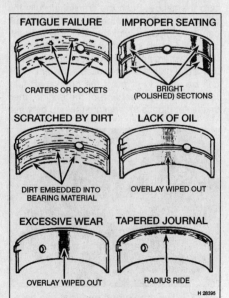

14.2 Typical bearing failures

by obvious bearing wear) indicates that the crankshaft requires regrinding (where possible) or renewal.
9 Check the oil seal contact surfaces at each end of the crankshaft for wear and damage. If the seal has worn a deep groove in the surface of the crankshaft, consult an engine overhaul specialist; repair may be possible, but otherwise a new crankshaft will be required.
10 Take the crankshaft to an engine reconditioning specialist to have it measured for journal wear. If excessive wear is evident, they will be able to advise you with regard to regrinding the crankshaft and supplying new bearing shells.
11 If the crankshaft has been reground, check for burrs around the crankshaft oil holes (the holes are usually chamfered, so burrs should not be a problem unless regrinding has been carried out carelessly). Remove any burrs with a fine file or scraper, and thoroughly clean the oil holes as described previously.
12 At the time of writing, it was not clear whether Peugeot/Citroën produce oversize bearing shells for all of these engines. On some engines, if the crankshaft journals have not already been reground, it may be possible to have the crankshaft reconditioned, and to fit oversize shells. If no oversize shells are available and the crankshaft has worn beyond the specified limits, it will have to be renewed. Consult your dealer or engine specialist for further information on parts availability.

14 Main and big-end bearings – inspection

1 Even though the main and big-end bearings should be renewed during the engine overhaul, the old bearings should be retained for close examination, as they may reveal valuable information about the condition of the engine. The bearing shells are graded by thickness, the grade of each shell being indicated by the colour code marked on it.
2 Bearing failure can occur due to lack of lubrication, the presence of dirt or other foreign particles, overloading the engine, or corrosion **(see illustration)**. Regardless of the cause of bearing failure, the cause must be corrected (where applicable) before the engine is reassembled, to prevent it from happening again.
3 When examining the bearing shells, remove them from the cylinder block/crankcase, the connecting rods and the connecting rod big-end bearing caps. Lay them out on a clean surface in the same general position as their location in the engine. This will enable you to match any bearing problems with the corresponding crankshaft journal. *Do not* touch any shell's bearing surface with your fingers while checking it, or the delicate surface may be scratched.
4 Dirt and other foreign matter gets into the

engine in a variety of ways. It may be left in the engine during assembly, or it may pass through filters or the crankcase ventilation system. It may get into the oil, and from there into the bearings. Metal chips from machining operations and normal engine wear are often present. Abrasives are sometimes left in engine components after reconditioning, especially when parts are not thoroughly cleaned using the proper cleaning methods. Whatever the source, these foreign objects often end up embedded in the soft bearing material, and are easily recognised. Large particles will not embed in the bearing, and will score or gouge the bearing and journal. The best prevention for this cause of bearing failure is to clean all parts thoroughly, and keep everything spotlessly-clean during engine assembly. Frequent and regular engine oil and filter changes are also recommended.
5 Lack of lubrication (or lubrication breakdown) has a number of interrelated causes. Excessive heat (which thins the oil), overloading (which squeezes the oil from the bearing face) and oil leakage (from excessive bearing clearances, worn oil pump or high engine speeds) all contribute to lubrication breakdown. Blocked oil passages, which usually are the result of misaligned oil holes in a bearing shell, will also oil-starve a bearing, and destroy it. When lack of lubrication is the cause of bearing failure, the bearing material is wiped or extruded from the steel backing of the bearing. Temperatures may increase to the point where the steel backing turns blue from overheating.
6 Driving habits can have a definite effect on bearing life. Full-throttle, low-speed operation (labouring the engine) puts very high loads on bearings, tending to squeeze out the oil film. These loads cause the bearings to flex, which produces fine cracks in the bearing face (fatigue failure). Eventually, the bearing material will loosen in pieces, and tear away from the steel backing.
7 Short-distance driving leads to corrosion of bearings, because insufficient engine heat is produced to drive off the condensed water and corrosive gases. These products collect in the engine oil, forming acid and sludge. As the oil is carried to the engine bearings, the acid attacks and corrodes the bearing material.
8 Incorrect bearing installation during engine assembly will lead to bearing failure as well. Tight-fitting bearings leave insufficient bearing running clearance, and will result in oil starvation. Dirt or foreign particles trapped behind a bearing shell result in high spots on the bearing, which lead to failure.
9 *Do not* touch any shell's bearing surface with your fingers during reassembly; there is a risk of scratching the delicate surface, or of depositing particles of dirt on it.
10 As mentioned at the beginning of this Section, the bearing shells should be renewed as a matter of course during engine overhaul; to do otherwise is false economy.

15 Engine overhaul – reassembly sequence

1 Before reassembly begins, ensure that all new parts have been obtained, and that all necessary tools are available. Read through the entire procedure to familiarise yourself with the work involved, and to ensure that all items necessary for reassembly of the engine are at hand. In addition to all normal tools and materials, thread-locking compound will be needed. A tube of suitable liquid sealant will also be required for the joint faces that are fitted without gaskets. It is recommended that Peugeot/Citroën's own product(s) are used, which are specially formulated for this purpose; the relevant product names are quoted in the text of each Section where they are required.

2 In order to save time and avoid problems, engine reassembly can be carried out in the following order, referring to Part A of this Chapter unless otherwise stated:
a) *Crankshaft (See Section 17).*
b) *Piston/connecting rod assemblies (See Section 18).*
c) *Oil pump.*
d) *Sump.*
e) *Flywheel.*
f) *Cylinder head.*
g) *Timing belt tensioner pulley(s) and sprockets, and timing belt.*
h) *Engine external components.*

3 At this stage, all engine components should be absolutely clean and dry, with all faults repaired. The components should be laid out (or in individual containers) on a completely clean work surface.

16 Piston rings – refitting

1 Before fitting new piston rings, the ring end gaps must be checked as follows.

2 Lay out the piston/connecting rod assemblies and the new piston ring sets, so that the ring sets will be matched with the same piston and cylinder during the end gap measurement and subsequent engine reassembly.

3 Insert the top ring into the first cylinder, and push it down the bore using the top of the piston. This will ensure that the ring remains square with the cylinder walls. Position the ring near the bottom of the cylinder bore, at the lower limit of ring travel. Note that the top and second compression rings are different. The second ring can be identified by its taper; it also has a step on its lower surface.

4 Measure the end gap using feeler blades.

5 Repeat the procedure with the ring at the top of the cylinder bore, at the upper limit of its travel **(see illustration)**, and compare the measurements with the figures given in the Specifications. If the end gaps are incorrect,

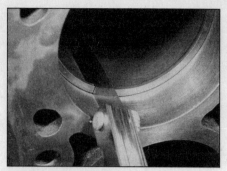

16.5 Measure the piston rings end gaps with a feeler gauge

check that you have the correct rings for your engine and for the cylinder bore size.

6 Repeat the checking procedure for each ring in the first cylinder, and then for the rings in the remaining cylinders. Remember to keep rings, pistons and cylinders matched up.

7 Once the ring end gaps have been checked, the rings can be fitted to the pistons.

8 Fit the oil control ring expander (where fitted) then install the ring.

9 The second and top rings are different and can be identified from their cross-sections; the top ring is symmetrical whilst the second ring is tapered. Fit the second ring, ensuring its identification (TOP) marking is facing upwards, then install the top ring **(see illustration)**. Arrange the oil control, second and top ring end gaps so they are equally spaced 120° apart. **Note:** *Always follow any instructions supplied with the new piston ring sets – different manufacturers may specify different procedures. Do not mix up the top and second compression rings, as they have different cross-sections.*

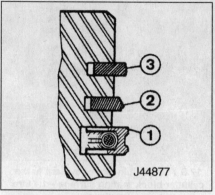

16.9 Typical piston ring fitting diagram
1 *Oil control ring*
2 *Second compression ring*
3 *Top compression ring*

Crankshaft refitting

Note: *New main bearing cap/lower crankcase bolts must be used when refitting the crankshaft.*

2 Where applicable, ensure that the oil spray jets are fitted to the bearing locations in the cylinder block.

1.4 litre engines

3 Using a little grease, stick the upper thrustwashers to each side of the No 2 main bearing upper location; ensure that the oilway grooves on each thrustwasher face outwards (away from the block).

4 Clean the backs of the bearing shells, and the bearing locations in both the cylinder block/crankcase and the main bearing ladder/bearing caps.

5 Press the bearing shells into their locations, ensuring that the tab on each shell engages in the notch in the cylinder block/crankcase or main bearing ladder/bearing cap. Take care not to touch any shell's bearing surface with your fingers. Note that the grooved bearing shells, both upper and lower, are fitted to Nos 2 and 4 main bearings **(see illustration)**.

6 Liberally lubricate each bearing shell in the cylinder block/crankcase with clean engine oil.

7 Refit the Woodruff key, then slide on the oil pump drive sprocket, and locate the drive chain on the sprocket **(see illustration)**.

17 Crankshaft – refitting

Selection of bearing shells

1 Have the crankshaft inspected and measured by an engine reconditioning specialist. They will be able to carry out any regrinding/repairs, and supply suitable main and big-end bearing shells.

17.5 Fit the grooved bearing shells to No 2 and 4 main bearings – 1.4 litre engines

17.7 Fit the oil pump drive chain and sprocket – 1.4 litre engines

17.8 Apply a thin film of sealant to the cylinder block mating surface – 1.4 litre engines

17.10 Tighten the ten main bearing bolts to the specified torque – 1.4 litre engines

Lower the crankshaft into position so that Nos 2 and 3 cylinder crankpins are at TDC; Nos 1 and 4 cylinder crankpins will be at BDC, ready for fitting No 1 piston. Check the crankshaft endfloat as described in Section 13.

8 Thoroughly degrease the mating surfaces of the cylinder block/crankcase and the main bearing ladder. Apply a thin bead of suitable sealant to the cylinder block mating surface of the main bearing ladder casting, then spread to an even film **(see illustration)**.

9 Ensure the locating dowels are in position then lubricate the lower bearing shells with clean engine oil. Refit the main bearing ladder to the cylinder block, ensuring that the lower bearings remain correctly fitted.

10 Install the main bearing ladder retaining bolts, and tighten them all by hand only. Working in a spiral pattern from the centre bolts outwards, evenly and progressively tighten the bolts to the specified Stage 1 torque wrench setting **(see illustration)**. Once all the bolts have been tightened to the Stage 1 setting, working in the same sequence, angle-tighten the bolts through the specified Stage 2 angle using a socket and extension bar. It is recommended that an angle-measuring gauge is used during this stage of the tightening, to ensure accuracy. If a gauge is not available, use a dab of white paint to make alignment marks between the bolt head and casting prior to tightening; the marks can then be used to check that the bolt has been rotated sufficiently during tightening.

11 Refit all the smaller bolts securing the main bearing ladder to the base of the cylinder block, and tighten them to the specified torque. Check that the crankshaft rotates freely.

12 Refit the piston/connecting rod assemblies to the crankshaft as described in Section 18.

13 Ensuring that the drive chain is correctly located on the sprocket, refit the oil pump and sump as described in Part A of this Chapter.

14 Fit two new crankshaft oil seals as described in Part A of this Chapter.

15 Refit the flywheel as described in Part A of this Chapter.

16 Refit the cylinder head (where removed) as described in Part A. Also refit the crankshaft sprocket and timing belt (see Part A).

1.6 litre engines

17 Using a little grease, stick the upper thrustwashers to each side of the No 2 main bearing upper location. Ensure that the oilway grooves on each thrustwasher face outwards (away from the cylinder block) **(see illustration)**.

18 Place the bearing shells in their locations as described in paragraphs 4 and 5 **(see illustration)**. If new shells are being fitted, ensure that all traces of protective grease are cleaned off using paraffin. Wipe dry the shells and connecting rods with a lint-free cloth. Liberally lubricate each bearing shell in the cylinder block/crankcase and cap with clean engine oil.

19 Lower the crankshaft into position so that

Nos 2 and 3 cylinder crankpins are at TDC; Nos 1 and 4 cylinder crankpins will be at BDC, ready for fitting No 1 piston. Check the crankshaft endfloat as described in Section 13.

20 Lubricate the lower bearing shells in the main bearing caps with clean engine oil. Make sure that the locating lugs on the shells engage with the corresponding recesses in the caps.

21 Fit the main bearing caps to their correct locations, ensuring that they are fitted the correct way round (the bearing shell lug recesses in the block and caps must be on the same side).

22 Lightly lubricate the threads and the underside of the heads of the main bearing cap bolts with engine oil then refit the bolts. Working in a spiral sequence from the centre bolts outwards, tighten the main bearing cap bolts evenly and progressively to the specified Stage 1 torque wrench setting. Once all the bolts have been tightened to the Stage 1 setting, working in the same sequence, angle-tighten the bolts through the specified Stage 2 angle, using a socket and extension bar. It is recommended that an angle-measuring gauge is used during this stage of the tightening, to ensure accuracy. If a gauge is not available, use a dab of white paint to make alignment marks between the bolt head and casting prior to tightening; the marks can then be used to check that the bolt has been rotated sufficiently during tightening.

23 Check that the crankshaft rotates freely.

24 Refit the piston/connecting rod assemblies to the crankshaft as described in Section 18.

25 Refit the Woodruff key to the crankshaft groove, and slide on the oil pump drive sprocket. Locate the drive chain on the sprocket.

26 Ensure that the mating surfaces of right-hand (timing belt end) oil seal housing and cylinder block are clean and dry. Note the correct fitted depth of the oil seal then, using a large flat-bladed screwdriver, lever the seal out of the housing.

27 Apply a smear of suitable sealant to the oil seal housing mating surface, and make sure that the locating dowels are in position. Slide the housing over the end of the crankshaft, and into position on the cylinder block. Tighten the housing retaining bolts securely.

28 Repeat the operations in paragraphs 26 and 27, and fit the left-hand (flywheel end) oil seal housing.

29 Fit new crankshaft oil seals as described in Part A of this Chapter.

30 Ensuring that the chain is correctly located on the drive sprocket, refit the oil pump and sump as described in Part A of this Chapter.

31 Refit the flywheel as described in Part A of this Chapter.

32 Refit the cylinder head (where removed) and install the crankshaft sprocket and timing belt as described in the relevant Sections of Part A.

17.17 Fit the thrustwashers to either side of the No 2 main bearing, with the oilway grooves facing outwards – 1.6 litre engines

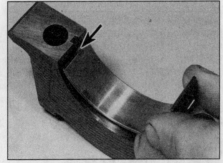

17.18 Ensure the tab (arrowed) is located in the cut-out when fitting the bearing shells – 1.6 litre engines

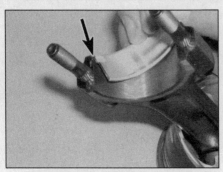

18.3 Ensure the bearing shell tab (arrowed) locates correctly in the cut-out

18 Piston/connecting rod assembly – refitting

Note: *New big-end cap nuts/bolts must be used on refitting.*

1 Note that the following procedure assumes that the cylinder liners (aluminium block engines) are in position in the cylinder block/crankcase as described in Section 11, and that the crankshaft and main bearing ladder/caps are in place.
2 Clean the backs of the bearing shells, and the bearing locations in both the connecting rod and bearing cap.

18.8 Fit the big-end bearing cap, ensuring it is fitted the right way around, and screw on the new nuts

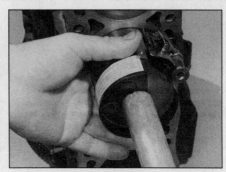

18.7 Tap the piston into the bore using a hammer handle

3 Press the bearing shells into their locations, ensuring that the tab on each shell engages in the notch in the connecting rod and cap. Take care not to touch any shell's bearing surface with your fingers **(see illustration)**.
4 Lubricate the cylinder bores, the pistons, and piston rings, then lay out each piston/connecting rod assembly in its respective position.
5 Start with assembly No 1. Make sure that the piston rings are still spaced as described in Section 16, then clamp them in position with a piston ring compressor.
6 Insert the piston/connecting rod assembly into the top of cylinder/liner No 1, ensuring that the arrow on the piston crown is pointing towards the timing belt end of the engine.
7 Once the piston is correctly positioned, using a block of wood or hammer handle against the piston crown, tap the assembly into the cylinder/liner until the piston crown is flush with the top of the cylinder/liner **(see illustration)**.
8 Ensure that the bearing shell is still correctly installed. Liberally lubricate the crankpin and both bearing shells. Taking care not to mark the cylinder/liner bores, pull the piston/connecting rod assembly down the bore and onto the crankpin. Refit the big-end bearing cap and fit the new nuts, tightening them finger-tight at first **(see illustration)**. Note that the faces with the identification marks must

match (which means that the bearing shell locating tabs abut each other).
9 Tighten the bearing cap retaining nuts evenly and progressively to the specified torque setting.
10 Once the bearing cap retaining nuts have been correctly tightened, rotate the crankshaft. Check that it turns freely; some stiffness is to be expected if new components have been fitted, but there should be no signs of binding or tight spots.
11 Refit the cylinder head and oil pump as described in Part A of this Chapter.

19 Engine – initial start-up after overhaul

1 With the engine refitted in the vehicle, double-check the engine oil and coolant levels. Make a final check that everything has been reconnected, and that there are no tools or rags left in the engine compartment.
2 Switch on the ignition and immediately turn the engine on the starter until the oil pressure warning light goes out.
3 Pressurise the fuel system as described in Chapter 4A, then start the engine, noting that this may take a little longer than usual, due to the fuel system components having been disturbed.
4 While the engine is idling, check for fuel, water and oil leaks. Don't be alarmed if there are some odd smells and smoke from parts getting hot and burning off oil deposits.
5 Assuming all is well, keep the engine idling until hot water is felt circulating through the top hose, then switch off the engine.
6 Allow the engine to cool then recheck the oil and coolant levels as described in *Weekly checks*, and top-up as necessary.
7 If new pistons, rings or crankshaft bearings have been fitted, the engine must be treated as new, and run-in for the first 500 miles (800 km). Do not operate the engine at full-throttle, or allow it to labour at low engine speeds in any gear. It is recommended that the oil and filter be changed at the end of this period.

Chapter 2 Part F:
Diesel engine removal and overhaul procedures

Contents

Degrees of difficulty

Easy, suitable for novice with little experience | **Fairly easy,** suitable for beginner with some experience | **Fairly difficult,** suitable for competent DIY mechanic | **Difficult,** suitable for experienced DIY mechanic | **Very difficult,** suitable for expert DIY or professional

Specifications

Cylinder head
Maximum gasket face distortion:
Except DV engines	0.03 mm
DV engines	0.05 mm

Cylinder head height:
DV series engines	124 ± 0.05 mm
XUD series engines	157.4 to 157.7 mm

DW series engines:
1.9 litre engines (from centre of camshaft to head mating surface)	139.95 to 140.25 mm
2.0 litre engines	133.0 mm
Swirl chamber protrusion – 1.8 and 1.9 litre engines only	0 to 0.03 mm

Valves

Valve head diameter:	Inlet	Exhaust
1.6 litre engines	25.6 ± 0.1 mm	23.4 ± 0.1 mm
1.8 and 1.9 litre engines	38.6 mm	33.0 mm
2.0 litre engines	35.6 mm	33.8 mm
Valve stem diameter:	Inlet	Exhaust
1.6 litre engines	5.485 +0.0, -0.015 mm	5.475 +0.0, -0.015 mm
1.8 and 1.9 litre engines	7.96 to 7.99 mm	7.95 to 7.98 mm
2.0 litre engines	5.978 ± 0.007 mm	5.968 ± 0.007 mm
Overall length:	Inlet	Exhaust
1.6 litre engines	96.43 ± 0.25 mm	96.65 ± 0.2 mm
1.8 and 1.9 litre engines	112.10 to 112.70 mm	111.55 to 112.15 mm
2.0 litre engines:		
Standard	107.18 mm	107.18 mm
Minimum	106.78 mm	106.78 mm

Cylinder block
Cylinder bore diameter:
1.6 litre engine (reboring not possible)	75.00 mm
1.8 litre engines	80.00 mm (nominal)

1.9 litre:
XUD series engines	83.00 mm (nominal)
DW series engines	82.20 mm (nominal)
2.0 litre engines	85.00 mm (nominal)

Pistons

Piston diameter:	
1.6 litre engines	74.945 ± 0.075 mm
1.8 litre engines	79.92 mm (nominal)
1.9 litre:	
XUD series engines	82.92 mm (nominal)
DW series engines	82.12 mm (nominal)
2.0 litre engines	84.21 mm (nominal)

Check with your Peugeot/Citroën dealer or engine specialist regarding piston oversizes

Crankshaft

Endfloat:		
Except DV engines	0.07 to 0.32 mm	
DV engines	2.4 ± 0.05 mm	
Main bearing journal diameter:	**Standard**	**Undersize**
All engines	59.977 to 60.000 mm	59.677 to 59.700 mm
Big-end bearing journal diameter:	**Standard**	**Undersize**
All engines	49.984 to 50.000 mm	49.681 to 49.700 mm
Maximum bearing journal out-of-round	0.007 mm	
Main bearing running clearance*	0.025 to 0.050 mm	
Big-end bearing running clearance*	0.025 to 0.050 mm	

* These are suggested figures, typical for this type of engine – no exact values are stated by the manufacturer.

Piston rings

End gaps:*	
Top and second compression rings	0.20 to 0.40 mm
Oil control ring	0.25 to 0.50 mm

*These are suggested figures, typical for this type of engine – no exact values are stated by the manufacturer.

Torque wrench settings

1.6 litre (DV series) engines
Refer to Chapter 2B Specifications

1.8 and 1.9 litre (XUD series) engines
Refer to Chapter 2C Specifications.

1.9 and 2.0 litre (DW series) engines
Refer to Chapter 2D Specifications.

1 General information

Included in this Part of Chapter 2 are details of removing the engine/transmission from the car and general overhaul procedures for the cylinder head, cylinder block/crankcase and all other engine internal components.

The information given ranges from advice concerning preparation for an overhaul and the purchase of new parts, to detailed step-by-step procedures covering removal, inspection, renovation and refitting of engine internal components.

After Section 5, all instructions are based on the assumption that the engine has been removed from the car. For information concerning in-car engine repair, as well as the removal and refitting of those external components necessary for full overhaul, refer to Part B, C or D of this Chapter, and to Section 6. Ignore any preliminary dismantling operations described in Part B, C or D that are no longer relevant once the engine has been removed from the car.

Apart from torque wrench settings, which are given at the beginning of Part B, C or D, all specifications relating to engine overhaul are at the beginning of this Part of Chapter 2.

2 Engine overhaul – general information

It is not always easy to determine when, or if, an engine should be completely overhauled, as a number of factors must be considered.

High mileage is not necessarily an indication that an overhaul is needed, while low mileage does not preclude the need for an overhaul. Frequency of servicing is probably the most important consideration. An engine which has had regular and frequent oil and filter changes, as well as other required maintenance, should give many thousands of miles of reliable service. Conversely, a neglected engine may require an overhaul very early in its life.

Excessive oil consumption is an indication that piston rings, valve seals and/or valve guides are in need of attention. Make sure that oil leaks are not responsible before deciding that the rings and/or guides are worn. Perform a compression or leakdown test, as described in Part B, C or D of this Chapter, to determine the likely cause of the problem.

Check the oil pressure with a gauge fitted in place of the oil pressure switch, and compare it with that specified. If it is extremely low, the main and big-end bearings, and/or the oil pump, are probably worn out.

Loss of power, rough running, knocking or metallic engine noises, excessive valve gear noise, and high fuel consumption may also point to the need for an overhaul, especially if they are all present at the same time. If a complete service does not remedy the situation, major mechanical work is the only solution.

A full engine overhaul involves restoring all internal parts to the specification of a new engine. During a complete overhaul, the pistons and the piston rings are renewed, and the cylinder bores are reconditioned. New main and big-end bearings are generally fitted; if necessary, the crankshaft may be reground, to compensate for wear in the journals. The valves are also serviced as well, since they are usually in less-than-perfect condition at this point. Always pay careful attention to the condition of the oil pump when overhauling the engine, and renew it if there is any doubt as to its serviceability. The end result should be an as-new engine that will give many trouble-free miles.

Critical cooling system components such as the hoses, thermostat and water pump should be renewed when an engine is overhauled. The radiator should be checked carefully, to ensure that it is not clogged or leaking. Also, it is a good idea to renew the oil pump whenever the engine is overhauled.

Before beginning the engine overhaul, read through the entire procedure, to familiarise yourself with the scope and requirements of the job. Check on the availability of parts and make sure that any necessary special tools and equipment are obtained in advance. Most work can be done with typical hand tools, although a number of precision measuring tools are required for inspecting parts to determine if they must be renewed.

The services provided by an engineering machine shop or engine reconditioning specialist will almost certainly be required, particularly if major repairs such as crankshaft regrinding or cylinder reboring are necessary. Apart from carrying out machining operations, these establishments will normally handle the inspection of parts, offer advice concerning reconditioning or renewal and supply new components such as pistons, piston rings and bearing shells. It is recommended that the establishment used is a member of the Federation of Engine Re-Manufacturers, or a similar society.

Always wait until the engine has been completely dismantled, and until all components (especially the cylinder block/crankcase and the crankshaft) have been inspected, before deciding what service and repair operations must be performed by an engineering works. The condition of these components will be the major factor to consider when determining whether to overhaul the original engine, or to buy a reconditioned unit. Do not, therefore, purchase parts or have overhaul work done on other components until they have been thoroughly inspected. As a general rule, time is the primary cost of an overhaul, so it does not pay to fit worn or sub-standard parts.

As a final note, to ensure maximum life and minimum trouble from a reconditioned engine, everything must be assembled with care, in a spotlessly-clean environment.

3 Engine/transmission removal – methods and precautions

If you have decided that the engine must be removed for overhaul or major repair work, several preliminary steps should be taken.

Locating a suitable place to work is extremely important. Adequate work space, along with storage space for the car, will be needed. If a workshop or garage is not available, at the very least, a flat, level, clean work surface is required.

Cleaning the engine compartment and engine/transmission before beginning the removal procedure will help keep tools clean and organised.

An engine hoist will also be necessary.

Make sure the equipment is rated in excess of the combined weight of the engine and transmission. Safety is of primary importance, considering the potential hazards involved in removing the engine/transmission from the car.

The help of an assistant is essential. Apart from the safety aspects involved, there are many instances when one person cannot simultaneously perform all of the operations required during engine/transmission removal.

Plan the operation ahead of time. Before starting work, arrange for the hire of or obtain all of the tools and equipment you will need. Some of the equipment necessary to perform engine/transmission removal and installation safely (in addition to an engine hoist) is as follows: a heavy duty trolley jack, complete sets of spanners and sockets as described in the rear of this manual, wooden blocks, and plenty of rags and cleaning solvent for mopping-up spilled oil, coolant and fuel. If the hoist must be hired, make sure that you arrange for it in advance, and perform all of the operations possible without it beforehand. This will save you money and time.

Plan for the car to be out of use for quite a while. An engineering machine shop or engine reconditioning specialist will be required to perform some of the work which cannot be accomplished without special equipment. These places often have a busy schedule, so it would be a good idea to consult them before removing the engine, in order to accurately estimate the amount of time required to rebuild or repair components that may need work.

During the engine/transmission removal procedure, it is advisable to make notes of the locations of all brackets, cable ties, earthing points, etc, as well as how the wiring harnesses, hoses and electrical connections are attached and routed around the engine and engine compartment. An effective way of doing this is to take a series of photographs of the various components before they are disconnected or removed; the resulting photographs will prove invaluable when the engine/transmission is refitted.

Always be extremely careful when removing and refitting the engine/transmission. Serious injury can result from careless actions. Plan ahead and take your time, and a job of this nature, although major, can be accomplished successfully.

The engine and transmission assembly is removed downwards from the engine compartment on all models described in this Chapter.

4 Engine/transmission – removal and refitting

Note: *Such is the complexity of the power unit arrangement on these vehicles, and the variations that may be encountered according to model and optional equipment fitted, that the following should be regarded as a guide to*

the work involved, rather than a step-by-step procedure. Where differences are encountered, or additional component disconnection or removal is necessary, make notes of the work involved as an aid to refitting.

⚠️ **Warning: It is essential to observe strict precautions when working on the fuel system components of the 1.6 or 2.0 litre engine.** **Before carrying out any of the following operations, refer to the special information given in Chapter 4C, Section 1.**

Removal

Note: *The engine can be removed from the car only as a complete unit with the transmission; the two are then separated for overhaul.*

1 Remove the battery, battery tray and mounting plate as described in see Chapter 5A.

2 Apply the handbrake, then jack up the front of the vehicle and support it on axle stands (see *Jacking and vehicle support*). Remove both front roadwheels.

3 On 1.9 litre (DW series) engines, release the fasteners from the right-hand side and top of the engine cover then lift off the cover, taking care not to lose its mounting rubbers. On 1.6 and 2.0 litre engines, turn the four plastic fasteners through 90° and lift off the engine cover

4 To improve access, remove the bonnet as described in Chapter 11.

5 Remove the air cleaner housing and intake ducting as described in Chapter 4B or 4C.

6 Drain the cooling system with reference to Chapter 1B.

7 Drain the transmission oil as described in Chapter 7. Refit the drain and filler plugs, and tighten them to their specified torque settings.

8 If the engine is to be dismantled, drain the engine oil and remove the oil filter as described in Chapter 1B. Clean and refit the drain plug, tightening it securely.

9 Remove both the front wheel arch liners. The liners are secured by various screws and clips under the wheel arch. Release all the fasteners, and remove liners from under the front wings.

10 Refer to Chapter 1B and remove the auxiliary drivebelt.

11 Refer to Chapter 8 and remove both front driveshafts.

12 Disconnect the radiator top and bottom hoses, the heater hoses at the engine compartment bulkhead, and the expansion tank hose. Remove the radiator as described in Chapter 3.

13 On models with air conditioning, refer to Chapter 3 and unbolt the compressor from the engine. **Do not** disconnect the refrigerant lines. Support or tie the compressor to one side.

14 On models with power steering, remove the power steering pump as described in Chapter 10. Release the power steering pipe from the retaining clips on the underside of the transmission.

15 On 1.8 and 1.9 litre (XUD series) engines, carry out the following operations with reference to Chapter 4B:

a) *Disconnect the fuel supply hose from the thermostat/fuel filter housing and the return hose from the fuel injection pump.*

b) *Release the fuel hoses and priming pump from their retaining clips and move them clear of the engine.*

c) *Disconnect the accelerator cable from the fuel injection pump.*

d) *Disconnect the exhaust front pipe/ catalytic converter from the exhaust manifold.*

16 On 1.6, 1.9 (DW series) and 2.0 litre engines, carry out the following operations with reference to Chapter 4C:

a) *At the connections above the fuel pump, disconnect the fuel supply and return hose quick-release fittings using a small screwdriver to release the locking clip. Suitably plug or cover the open unions to prevent dirt entry.*

b) *Release the fuel hoses from their retaining clips and move them clear of the engine.*

c) *Disconnect the accelerator cable from the fuel injection pump or accelerator pedal position sensor (as applicable).*

d) *Disconnect the wiring connectors at the engine management ECU.*

e) *Disconnect the catalytic converter from the exhaust manifold/turbocharger.*

17 Disconnect the vacuum hoses and wiring connector at the EGR solenoid valve.

18 Unbolt the preheating system control unit located at the front of the engine compartment.

19 Open the engine compartment fuse/relay box and disconnect the engine related wiring connectors.

20 Trace the wiring harness back from the engine to the main harness connectors at the fuse/relay box, and/or at the bulkhead connection or front body panel connection. Release the locking rings by twisting them anti-clockwise and disconnect the connectors. Also trace the wiring connectors back to the transmission and disconnect all engine related wiring and earth leads in this area. Check that all the relevant connectors have been disconnected, and that the harness is released from all the clips or ties, so that it is free to be removed with the engine/ transmission.

21 Disconnect the engine earth leads at the fusebox, under the left hand wheel arch and on the left-hand chassis member.

22 Disconnect the brake servo unit vacuum pipe from the vacuum pump, or at the quick-release connector on the pipe.

23 Disconnect the clutch cable from the release lever and transmission bracket as described in Chapter 6.

24 Disconnect the gearchange selector mechanism from the transmission as described in Chapter 7.

25 Remove the front subframe as described in Chapter 10.

26 Using a hoist attached to the lifting eyes on the cylinder head, take the weight of the engine and transmission.

27 Remove the right-hand and left-hand engine mountings and support brackets as described in Chapter 2B, 2C or 2D.

28 Make a final check to ensure all wiring, hoses and brackets that would prevent the removal of the assembly have been disconnected.

29 Carefully lower the engine/transmission from the engine compartment taking care not to damage the surrounding components. Ideally lower the unit onto a low trolley so that it may be withdrawn from under the car. Disconnect the hoist from the engine/ transmission assembly.

Separation

30 With the engine/transmission assembly removed, support the assembly on suitable blocks of wood on a workbench (or failing that, on a clean area of the workshop floor).

31 Undo the retaining bolts, and remove the flywheel lower cover plate from the transmission.

32 Slacken and remove the retaining bolts, and remove the starter motor from the transmission.

33 Disconnect any remaining wiring connectors at the transmission, then move the main engine wiring harness to one side.

34 Ensure that both engine and transmission are adequately supported, then slacken and remove the remaining bolts securing the transmission housing to the engine. Note the correct fitted positions of each bolt (and the relevant brackets) as they are removed, to use as a reference on refitting.

35 Carefully withdraw the transmission from the engine, ensuring that the weight of the transmission is not allowed to hang on the input shaft while it is engaged with the clutch friction disc.

36 If they are loose, remove the locating dowels from the engine or transmission, and keep them in a safe place.

Refitting

37 If the engine and transmission have not been separated, perform the operations described below from paragraph 44 onwards.

38 Apply a smear of high melting-point grease (Peugeot/Citroën recommend the use of Molykote BR2 plus) to the splines of the transmission input shaft. Do not apply too much, otherwise there is a possibility of the grease contaminating the clutch friction disc.

39 Ensure that the locating dowels are correctly positioned in the engine or transmission.

40 Carefully offer the transmission to the engine, until the locating dowels are engaged. Ensure that the weight of the transmission is not allowed to hang on the input shaft as it is engaged with the clutch friction disc.

41 Refit the transmission housing-to-engine

bolts, ensuring that all the necessary brackets are correctly positioned, and tighten them to the specified torque.

42 Refit the starter motor, and securely tighten its retaining bolts.

43 Refit the lower flywheel cover plate to the transmission, and securely tighten the bolts.

44 Position the engine/transmission assembly ready for installation, then reconnect the hoist and lifting tackle. With the aid of an assistant, locate the assembly into the engine compartment, using the same procedure as for removal.

45 Refit the right-hand and left-hand engine mountings and support brackets as described in Chapter 2B, 2C or 2D.

46 Remove the hoist from the engine.

47 Refit the front subframe as described in Chapter 10.

48 The remainder of the refitting procedure is a direct reversal of the removal sequence, with reference to the relevant chapters and noting the following points:

a) *Ensure that the wiring loom is correctly routed and retained by all the relevant retaining clips; all connectors should be correctly and securely reconnected.*

b) *Ensure that all coolant hoses are correctly reconnected, and securely retained by their retaining clips.*

c) *Refill the engine and transmission with the correct quantity and type of lubricant, as described in Chapters 1B and 7.*

d) *Refill the cooling system as described in Chapter 1B.*

e) *Prime the fuel system as described in Chapter 4B.*

f) *Bleed the power steering system as described in Chapter 10.*

5 Cylinder head (2.0 litre engines) – removal and refitting

Note: *Due to the limited access at the rear of the engine, it is impossible to remove the cylinder head with the engine in the car unless considerable additional dismantling is carried out first (eg, removal of the front suspension subframe and related components). The following information describes the cylinder head removal and refitting procedure with the engine/transmission removed from the car.*

Removal

1 Remove the engine/transmission assembly as described in Section 4.

2 Remove the timing belt as described in Chapter 2D.

3 Carry out the following operations as described in Chapter 4C:

a) *Remove the exhaust manifold and turbocharger.*

b) *Remove the inlet manifold.*

c) *Remove the fuel system accumulator rail.*

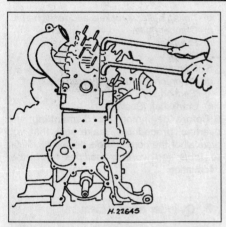

5.14 Free the cylinder head using angled rods

4 Undo the three bolts and remove the right-hand engine mounting upper bracket from the engine bracket. Undo the bolts securing the engine bracket to the cylinder head and block and remove the bracket.

5 Remove the braking system vacuum pump as described in Chapter 9.

6 Disconnect the wiring connectors and coolant hoses at the thermostat housing on the left-hand end of the cylinder head.

7 Undo the bolts and release the wiring harness guide from the thermostat housing.

8 Undo the retaining nuts and bolts and remove the fuel injector wiring harness guide left-hand support bracket.

9 Undo the mounting bolt and release the dipstick tube from the cylinder head.

10 Move all the adjacent components clear, then undo the three bolts and two nuts securing the thermostat housing to the cylinder head. Lift off the hose and cable support bracket, then withdraw the thermostat housing. Recover the housing gasket.

11 Remove the cylinder head cover as described in Chapter 2D.

12 Progressively slacken the cylinder head bolts, in the **reverse** order to that in illustration 5.29.

13 When all the bolts are loose, unscrew them fully and remove them from the cylinder head.

14 Release the cylinder head from the cylinder block and location dowels by rocking it. The Peugeot/Citroën tool for doing this consists simply of two metal rods with 90-degree angled ends **(see illustration)**. Do not prise between the mating faces of the cylinder head and block, as this may damage the gasket faces.

15 Lift the cylinder head from the block, and recover the gasket.

Preparation for refitting

16 The mating faces of the cylinder head and cylinder block must be perfectly clean before refitting the head. Peugeot/Citroën recommend the use of a scouring agent for this purpose, but acceptable results can be achieved by using a hard plastic or wood scraper to remove all traces of gasket and carbon. The same method can be used to clean the piston crowns. Take particular care to avoid scoring or gouging the cylinder head/cylinder block mating surfaces during the cleaning operations, as aluminium alloy is easily damaged. Make sure that the carbon is not allowed to enter the oil and water passages – this is particularly important for the lubrication system, as carbon could block the oil supply to the engine's components. Using adhesive tape and paper, seal the water, oil and bolt holes in the cylinder block. To prevent carbon entering the gap between the pistons and bores, smear a little grease in the gap. After cleaning each piston, use a small brush to remove all traces of grease and carbon from the gap, then wipe away the remainder with a clean rag.

17 Check the mating surfaces of the cylinder block and the cylinder head for nicks, deep scratches and other damage. If slight, they may be removed carefully with a file, but if excessive, machining may be the only alternative to renewal. If warpage of the cylinder head gasket surface is suspected, use a straight-edge to check it for distortion. Refer to Section 8 if necessary.

18 Thoroughly clean the threads of the cylinder head bolt holes in the cylinder block. Ensure that the bolts run freely in their threads, and that all traces of oil and water are removed from each bolt hole.

Gasket selection

19 Turn the crankshaft until pistons 1 and 4 are at TDC. Position a dial test indicator (dial gauge) on the cylinder block, and zero it on the block face. Transfer the probe to the edge of No 1 piston, then slowly turn the crankshaft back-and-forth past TDC, noting the highest reading on the indicator. Record this reading.

20 Repeat this measurement procedure on No 4 piston, then turn the crankshaft half a turn (180°) and repeat the procedure on Nos 2 and 3 pistons **(see illustration)**.

21 If a dial test indicator is not available, piston protrusion may be measured using a straight-edge and feeler blades or vernier calipers. However, this is much less accurate, and cannot therefore be recommended.

22 Note down the greatest piston protrusion measurement, and use this to determine the correct cylinder head gasket from the following table. The series of up to five notches on the side of the gasket are used for thickness identification **(see illustration)**.

Piston protrusion	Gasket identification
0.470 to 0.605 mm	1 notch
0.605 to 0.655 mm	2 notches
0.655 to 0.705 mm	3 notches
0.705 to 0.755 mm	4 notches
0.755 to 0.830 mm	5 notches

Cylinder head bolt examination

23 Carefully examine the cylinder head bolts for signs of damage to the threads or head, and for any sign of corrosion. If the bolts are in a satisfactory condition, measure the length of each bolt from the underside of the head, to the end of the shank. The bolts may be re-used providing that the measured length does not exceed 133.3 mm. **Note:** *Considering the stress to which the cylinder head bolts are subjected, it is highly recommended that they are all renewed, regardless of their apparent condition.*

Refitting

24 Turn the crankshaft clockwise (viewed from the timing belt end) until Nos 1 and 4 pistons pass bottom dead centre (BDC) and begin to rise, then position them halfway up their bores. Nos 2 and 3 pistons will also be at their midway positions, but descending their bores.

25 Make sure that the locating dowels are in place, then fit the correct gasket the right way round on the cylinder block, with the identification notches toward the fuel pump side of the engine.

26 Lower the cylinder head onto the block.

27 Apply a smear of grease to the threads, and to the underside of the heads, of the cylinder head bolts. Peugeot/Citroën recommend the use of Molykote G Rapid Plus.

28 Carefully enter each bolt into its relevant hole (*do not drop it in*) and screw it in finger-tight.

29 Working progressively and in sequence, tighten the cylinder head bolts to their

5.20 Measure the piston protrusion using a DTI gauge

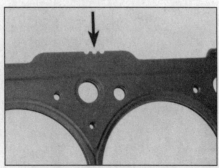

5.22 Cylinder head gasket thickness identification notches (arrowed)

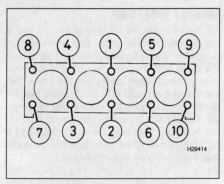

5.29 Cylinder head bolt tightening sequence

Stage 1 torque setting, using a torque wrench and suitable socket (see illustration).

30 Once all the bolts have been tightened to their Stage 1 torque setting, working again in the specified sequence, tighten each bolt to the specified Stage 2 setting. Finally, angle-tighten the bolts through the specified Stage 3 angle. It is recommended that an angle-measuring gauge is used during this stage of tightening, to ensure accuracy.

31 Refit the cylinder head cover as described in Chapter 2D.

32 Ensure that the mating face of the cylinder head and thermostat housing are clean then refit the housing using a new gasket. Refit the hose and cable support bracket and the thermostat housing retaining nuts and bolts. Tighten the nuts and bolts securely.

33 Refit and tighten the dipstick tube retaining bolt.

34 Refit the wiring harness guide support brackets.

35 Reconnect the coolant hoses to the thermostat housing.

36 Refit the timing belt as described in Chapter 2D.

37 Refit the accumulator rail, inlet manifold, and the exhaust manifold and turbocharger, in strict accordance with the procedures described in Chapter 4C.

38 Refit the braking system vacuum pump as described in Chapter 9.

39 Refit the right-hand engine mounting components with reference to Chapter 2D.

40 Refit the engine/transmission assembly as described in Section 4.

6 Engine overhaul – dismantling sequence

1 It is much easier to dismantle and work on the engine if it is mounted on a portable engine stand. These stands can often be hired from a tool hire shop. Before the engine is mounted on a stand, the flywheel should be removed, so that the stand bolts can be tightened into the end of the cylinder block/crankcase.

2 If a stand is not available, it is possible to dismantle the engine with it blocked up on a sturdy workbench, or on the floor. Be extra careful not to tip or drop the engine when working without a stand.

3 If you are going to obtain a reconditioned engine, all the external components must be removed first, to be transferred to the new engine (just as they will if you are doing a complete engine overhaul yourself). These components include the following:

a) *Ancillary unit mounting brackets (oil filter, starter, alternator, power steering pump, etc).*
b) *Fuel filter/thermostat housing (Chapter 3).*
c) *Dipstick tube/sensor.*
d) *All electrical switches and sensors.*
e) *Inlet and exhaust manifolds – where applicable (Chapter 4B or 4C).*
f) *Flywheel (Part B, C or D of this Chapter).*

Note: *When removing the external components from the engine, pay close attention to details that may be helpful or important during refitting. Note the fitted position of gaskets, seals, spacers, pins, washers, bolts, and other small items.*

4 If you are obtaining a 'short' engine (which consists of the engine cylinder block/ crankcase, crankshaft, pistons and connecting rods all assembled), then the cylinder head, sump, oil pump, and timing belt will have to be removed also.

5 If you are planning a complete overhaul, the engine can be dismantled, and the internal components removed, in the order given below, referring to Part B, C or D of this Chapter unless otherwise stated.

a) *Inlet and exhaust manifolds – where applicable (Chapter 4B or 4C).*
b) *Timing belts, sprockets and tensioner(s).*
c) *Cylinder head.*
d) *Flywheel.*
e) *Sump.*
f) *Oil pump.*
g) *Piston/connecting rod assemblies (Section 10).*
h) *Crankshaft (Section 11).*

6 Before beginning the dismantling and overhaul procedures, make sure that you have all of the correct tools necessary. Refer to *Tools and working facilities* for further information.

7 Cylinder head – dismantling

Note: *New and reconditioned cylinder heads are available from the manufacturer, and from engine overhaul specialists. Some specialist tools are required for dismantling and inspection, and new components may not be readily available. It may therefore be more practical and economical for the home mechanic to purchase a reconditioned head, rather than dismantle, inspect and recondition the original head.*

1 Remove the cylinder head as described in Part B, C or D of this Chapter, or in Section 5 of this Part (as applicable).

2 If not already done, remove the inlet and exhaust manifolds with reference to the relevant Part of Chapter 4.

3 Remove the camshaft(s), followers and shims, or hydraulic tappets (as applicable) as described in Part B, C or D of this Chapter.

4 Remove the glow plugs as described in Chapter 5C and the injectors as described in Chapter 4B or 4C.

5 Using a valve spring compressor, compress each valve spring in turn until the split collets can be removed. Release the compressor, and lift off the spring retainer and spring. Using a pair of pliers, carefully extract the valve stem oil seal from the top of the guide, then lift out the spring seat (see illustrations).

6 If, when the valve spring compressor is screwed down, the spring retainer refuses to free and expose the split collets, gently tap the top of the tool, directly over the retainer, with a light hammer. This will free the retainer.

7.5a Compress the valve spring using a spring compressor . . .

7.5b . . . then extract the collets and release the spring compressor

7.5c Remove the spring retainer . . .

7.5d . . . followed by the valve spring

7.5e Remove the valve stem oil seal using
a pair of pliers . . .

7.5f . . . then lift out the spring seat

7 Withdraw the valve through the combustion chamber.

8 It is essential that each valve is stored together with its collets, retainer, spring, and spring seat. The valves should also be kept in their correct sequence, unless they are so badly worn that they are to be renewed. If they are going to be kept and used again, place each valve assembly in a labelled polythene bag or similar small container **(see illustration)**. Note that No 1 valve is nearest to the transmission (flywheel) end of the engine.

8 Cylinder head and valves – cleaning and inspection

1 Thorough cleaning of the cylinder head and valve components, followed by a detailed inspection, will enable you to decide how much valve service work must be carried out during the engine overhaul.

Note: *If the engine has been severely overheated, it is best to assume that the cylinder head is warped – check carefully for signs of this.*

Cleaning

2 Scrape away all traces of old gasket material from the cylinder head.

3 Scrape away the carbon from the combustion chambers and ports, then wash the cylinder head thoroughly with paraffin or a suitable solvent.

4 Scrape off any heavy carbon deposits that may have formed on the valves, then

use a power-operated wire brush to remove deposits from the valve heads and stems.

Inspection

Note: *Be sure to perform all the following inspection procedures before concluding that the services of a machine shop or engine overhaul specialist are required. Make a list of all items that require attention.*

Cylinder head

5 Inspect the head very carefully for cracks, evidence of coolant leakage, and other damage. If cracks are found, a new cylinder head should be obtained.

6 Use a straight-edge and feeler blade to check that the cylinder head gasket surface is not distorted **(see illustration)**. If it is, it may be possible to have it machined, provided that the cylinder head is not reduced to less than the specified height.

Note: *It may be necessary to recut the valve seats if the cylinder head is machined. This is necessary in order to maintain the correct dimensions between the valve heads, valve guides and cylinder head gasket face.*

7 Examine the valve seats in each of the combustion chambers. If they are severely pitted, cracked, or burned, they will need to be renewed or recut by an engine overhaul specialist. If they are only slightly pitted, this can be removed by grinding-in the valve heads and seats with fine valve-grinding compound, as described below.

8 Check the valve guides for wear by inserting the relevant valve, and checking for side-to-side motion of the valve. A very

small amount of movement is acceptable. If the movement seems excessive, remove the valve. Measure the valve stem diameter (see below), and renew the valve if it is worn. If the valve stem is not worn, the wear must be in the valve guide, and the guide must be renewed. The renewal of valve guides is best carried out by a Peugeot/Citroën dealer or engine overhaul specialist, who will have the necessary tools available.

9 If renewing the valve guides, the valve seats should be recut or reground only *after* the guides have been fitted.

10 On 1.8 and 1.9 litre engines, inspect the swirl chambers for burning or damage such as cracking. Small cracks in the chambers are acceptable; renewal of the chambers will only be required if chamber tracts are badly burned and disfigured, or if they are no longer a tight fit in the cylinder head. If there is any doubt as to the swirl chamber condition, seek the advice of a Peugeot/Citroën dealer or a suitable repairer who specialises in diesel engines. Swirl chamber renewal should be entrusted to a specialist. Using a dial test indicator, check that the swirl chamber protrusion is within the limits given in the Specifications **(see illustration)**. Zero the dial test indicator on the gasket surface of the cylinder head, then measure the protrusion of the swirl chamber. If the protrusion is not within the specified limits, the advice of a Peugeot/Citroën dealer or suitable repairer who specialises in diesel engines should be sought.

Valves

11 Examine the head of each valve for pitting, burning, cracks, and general wear. Check the

7.8 Place each valve and its associated
components in a labelled polythene bag

8.6 Checking the cylinder head gasket
surface for distortion

8.10 Checking a swirl chamber protrusion
– 1.8 and 1.9 litre engines

8.12 Measuring a valve stem diameter

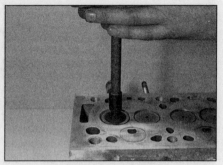

8.15 Grinding-in a valve

valve stem for scoring and wear ridges. Rotate the valve, and check for any obvious indication that it is bent. Look for pits or excessive wear on the tip of each valve stem. Renew any valve that shows any such signs of wear or damage.

12 If the valve appears satisfactory at this stage, measure the valve stem diameter at several points using a micrometer **(see illustration)**. Any significant difference in the readings obtained indicates wear of the valve stem. Should any of these conditions be apparent, the valve(s) must be renewed.

13 If the valves are in satisfactory condition, they should be ground (lapped) into their respective seats, to ensure a smooth, gas-tight seal. If the seat is only lightly pitted, or if it has been recut, fine grinding compound *only* should be used to produce the required finish. Coarse valve-grinding compound should *not* be used, unless a seat is badly burned or deeply pitted. If this is the case, the cylinder head and valves should be inspected by an expert, to decide whether seat recutting, or even the renewal of the valve or seat insert (where possible) is required.

14 Valve grinding is carried out as follows. Place the head upside-down on a bench.

15 Smear a trace of (the appropriate grade of) valve-grinding compound on the seat face, and press a suction grinding tool onto the valve head **(see illustration)**. With a semi-rotary action, grind the valve head to its seat, lifting the valve occasionally to redistribute the grinding compound. A light spring placed under the valve head will greatly ease this operation.

16 If coarse grinding compound is being used, work only until a dull, matt even surface is produced on both the valve seat and the valve, then wipe off the used compound, and

repeat the process with fine compound. When a smooth unbroken ring of light grey matt finish is produced on both the valve and seat, the grinding operation is complete. *Do not* grind-in the valves any further than absolutely necessary, or the seat will be prematurely sunk into the cylinder head.

17 When all the valves have been ground-in, carefully wash off *all* traces of grinding compound using paraffin or a suitable solvent, before reassembling the cylinder head.

Valve components

18 Examine the valve springs for signs of damage and discoloration. No minimum free length is specified by Peugeot/Citroën, so the only way of judging valve spring wear is by comparison with a new component.

19 Stand each spring on a flat surface, and check it for squareness. If any of the springs are damaged, distorted or have lost their tension, obtain a complete new set of springs. It is normal to fit new springs as a matter of course if a major overhaul is being carried out.

20 Renew the valve stem oil seals regardless of their apparent condition.

9 Cylinder head – reassembly

1 Lubricate the stems of the valves, and insert the valves into their original locations **(see illustration)**. If new valves are being fitted, insert them into the locations to which they have been ground.

2 Refit the spring seat then, working on the first valve, dip the new valve stem seal in fresh

engine oil. Carefully locate it over the valve and onto the guide. Take care not to damage the seal as it is passed over the valve stem. Use a suitable socket or tube to press the seal firmly onto the guide **(see illustration)**.

3 Locate the valve spring on top of its seat, then refit the spring retainer.

4 Compress the valve spring, and locate the split collets in the recess in the valve stem. Release the compressor, then repeat the procedure on the remaining valves.

 Use a little dab of grease to hold the collets in position on the valve stem while the spring compressor is released.

5 With all the valves installed, place the cylinder head flat on the bench and, using a hammer and interposed block of wood, tap the end of each valve stem to settle the components.

6 Refit the camshaft(s), followers and shims, or hydraulic tappets (as applicable) as described in Part B or C of this Chapter.

7 The cylinder head can then be refitted as described in Part B or C of this Chapter, or in Section 5 of this Part (as applicable).

10 Piston/connecting rod assembly – removal

1 Remove the cylinder head, sump and oil pump as described in Part B, C or D of this Chapter, or in Section 5 of this Part (as applicable). **Note:** *On the 1.6 litre engine the main bearing ladder must be removed as described in Section 11 before removal of the piston/connecting rod assemblies.*

2 If there is a pronounced wear ridge at the top of any bore, it may be necessary to remove it with a scraper or ridge reamer, to avoid piston damage during removal. Such a ridge indicates excess bore wear.

3 Using a hammer and centre-punch, paint or similar, mark each connecting rod and big-end bearing cap with its respective cylinder number on the flat machined surface provided; if the engine has been dismantled before, note carefully any identifying marks made previously **(see illustration)**. Note that

9.1 Lubricate the valve stems prior to refitting

9.2 Fitting a valve stem oil seal using a socket

10.3 Connecting rod and big-end bearing cap identification marks (No 3 shown)

No 1 cylinder is at the transmission (flywheel) end of the engine.

4 Turn the crankshaft to bring pistons 1 and 4 to BDC (bottom dead centre).

5 Unscrew the nuts from No 1 piston big-end bearing cap. Take off the cap, and recover the bottom half bearing shell **(see illustration)**. If the bearing shells are to be re-used, tape the cap and the shell together.

6 To prevent the possibility of damage to the crankshaft bearing journals, tape over the connecting rod stud threads **(see illustration)**.

7 Using a hammer handle, push the piston up through the bore, and remove it from the top of the cylinder block. Recover the bearing shell, and tape it to the connecting rod for safe-keeping.

8 Loosely refit the big-end cap to the connecting rod, and secure with the nuts – this will help to keep the components in their correct order.

9 Remove No 4 assembly in the same way.

10 Turn the crankshaft through 180° to bring pistons 2 and 3 to BDC (bottom dead centre), and remove them in the same way.

11 Crankshaft – removal

1 Remove the crankshaft sprocket and the oil pump as described in Part B or C of this Chapter (as applicable).

1.6 litre engine

2 Working around the inner periphery of the crankcase, unscrew the small bolts securing the crankshaft bearing cap housing to the base of the cylinder block. Note the correct fitted depth of the left-hand crankshaft oil seal in the cylinder block/bearing cap housing.

10.5 Removing a big-end bearing cap and shell

10.6 To protect the crankshaft journals, tape over the connecting rod stud threads

3 Working in the reverse of the tightening sequence, evenly and progressively slacken the ten large bearing cap housing retaining bolts by a turn at a time. Once all the bolts are loose, remove them from the housing. **Note:** *Prise up the flywheel end of the housing to expose the two end main bearing bolts* **(see illustration)**.

4 With all the retaining bolts removed, tap around the outer periphery of the bearing cap housing using a soft-faced mallet to break the seal between the housing and cylinder block. Once the seal is released and the housing is clear of the locating dowels, lift it up and off the crankshaft and cylinder block **(see illustration)**. Recover the lower main bearing shells, and tape them to their respective locations in the housing. If the two locating dowels are a loose fit, remove them and store them with the housing for safe-keeping.

5 Remove the pistons and connecting rods with reference to Section 10. If no work is to be done on the pistons and connecting rods, there is no need to remove the cylinder head, or to push the pistons out of the cylinder bores. The pistons should just be pushed far enough up the bores so that they are positioned clear of the crankshaft journals.

6 Check the crankshaft endfloat as described in Section 14, then proceed as follows.

7 Lift out the crankshaft, and collect the left-hand oil seal.

8 Recover the upper main bearing shells, and store them along with the relevant lower bearing shell. Also recover the two thrustwashers one fitted either side of No 2 main bearing) from the cylinder block.

1.9 and 2.0 litre engines

9 Remove the pistons and connecting rods, as described in Section 10. If no work is to be done on the pistons and connecting rods, there is no need to remove the cylinder head, or to push the pistons out of the cylinder bores. The pistons should just be pushed far enough up the bores so that they are positioned clear of the crankshaft journals.

10 Check the crankshaft endfloat as described in Section 14, then proceed as follows.

11 Slacken and remove the retaining bolts, and remove the oil seal carrier from the timing belt end of the cylinder block, along

11.3 On 1.6 litre diesel engines, prise up the two caps to expose the main bearing bolts at the flywheel end

11. 4 Remove the crankshaft bearing cap housing

11.11 Removing the oil seal carrier from the block

11.12a Remove the oil pump drive chain . . .

11.12b . . . then slide off the drive sprocket . . .

11.12c . . . and remove the Woodruff key from the crankshaft

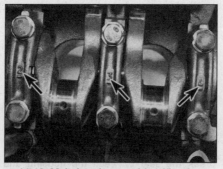

11.13 Main bearing cap identification markings (arrowed)

11.14 Removing No 2 main bearing cap. Note the thrustwasher (arrowed)

with its gasket (where fitted) **(see illustration)**.

12 Remove the oil pump drive chain, and slide the drive sprocket and spacer (where fitted) off the end of the crankshaft. Remove the Woodruff key, and store it with the sprocket for safe-keeping **(see illustrations)**.

13 The main bearing caps should be numbered 1 to 5, starting from the transmission (flywheel) end of the engine **(see illustration)**. If not, mark them accordingly using a centre-punch. Also note the correct fitted depth of the crankshaft oil seal in the bearing cap.

14 Slacken and remove the main bearing cap

retaining bolts, and lift off each bearing cap. Recover the lower bearing shells, and tape them to their respective caps for safe-keeping. Also recover the lower thrustwasher halves from the side of No 2 main bearing cap **(see illustration)**. Remove the sealing strips from the sides of No 1 main bearing cap, and discard them.

15 Lift out the crankshaft **(see illustration)**, and discard the oil seal.

16 Recover the upper bearing shells from the cylinder block **(see illustration)**, and tape them to their respective caps for safe-keeping. Remove the upper thrustwasher halves from

the side of No 2 main bearing, and store them with the lower halves.

12 Cylinder block/crankcase – cleaning and inspection

Cleaning

1 Remove all external components and electrical switches/sensors from the block. For complete cleaning, the core plugs

11.15 Lifting out the crankshaft

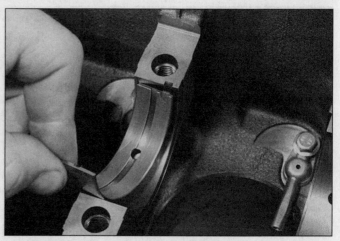

11.16 Remove the upper main bearing shells from the cylinder block/crankcase, and store them with their lower shells

12.1 Cylinder block core plugs (arrowed)

12.9 Cleaning a cylinder block threaded hole using a suitable tap

should ideally be removed (see illustration). Drill a small hole in the plugs, then insert a self-tapping screw into the hole.

2 Pull out the plugs by pulling on the screw with a pair of grips, or by using a slide hammer.

3 Where fitted, undo the retaining bolts and remove the piston oil jet spray tubes from inside the cylinder block.

4 Scrape all traces of gasket from the cylinder block/crankcase, taking care not to damage the gasket/sealing surfaces.

5 Remove all oil gallery plugs (where fitted). The plugs are usually very tight – they may have to be drilled out, and the holes retapped. Use new plugs when the engine is reassembled.

6 If any of the castings are extremely dirty, all should be steam-cleaned.

7 After the castings are returned, clean all oil holes and oil galleries one more time. Flush all internal passages with warm water until the water runs clear. Dry thoroughly, and apply a light film of oil to the cylinder bores and all mating surfaces, to prevent rusting. If you have access to compressed air, use it to speed up the drying process, and to blow out all the oil holes and galleries.

 Warning: Wear eye protection when using compressed air.

8 If the castings are not very dirty, you can do an adequate cleaning job with hot, soapy water and a stiff brush. Take plenty of time, and do a thorough job. Regardless of the cleaning method used, be sure to clean all oil holes and galleries very thoroughly, and to dry all components well. Protect the cylinder bores as described above, to prevent rusting.

9 All threaded holes must be clean, to ensure accurate torque readings during reassembly. To clean the threads, run the correct-size tap into each of the holes to remove rust, corrosion, thread sealant or sludge, and to restore damaged threads (see illustration). If possible, use compressed air to clear the holes of debris produced by this operation.

 Warning: Wear eye protection when using compressed air.

10 Apply suitable sealant to the new oil gallery plugs, and insert them into the holes in the block. Tighten them securely. Also apply suitable sealant to new core plugs, and drive them into the block using a tube or socket.

11 On engines with piston oil jet spray tubes, clean the threads of each oil jet retaining bolt, and apply a drop of thread-locking compound to the bolt threads. Refit the piston oil jet spray tubes to the cylinder block, and tighten the retaining bolts to the specified torque setting.

12 If the engine is not going to be reassembled right away, cover it with a large plastic bag to keep it clean; protect all mating surfaces and the cylinder bores as described above, to prevent rusting.

Inspection

13 Visually check the castings for cracks and corrosion. Look for stripped threads in the threaded holes. If there has been any history of internal water leakage, it may be worthwhile having an engine overhaul specialist check the cylinder block/crankcase with special equipment. If defects are found, have them repaired if possible, or renew the assembly.

14 Check each cylinder bore for scuffing and scoring. Check for signs of a wear ridge at the top of the cylinder, indicating that the bore is excessively worn.

15 Accurate measuring of the cylinder bores requires specialised equipment and experience. We recommend having the bores measured by an engine reconditioning specialist who will also be able to supply appropriate pistons (where possible) should a rebore be necessary.

16 If the cylinder bores and pistons are in reasonably good condition, and not worn beyond the specified limits, and if the piston-to-bore clearances can be maintained, then it will only be necessary to renew the piston rings. If this is the case, the cylinder bores must be honed to allow the new piston rings to

bed in correctly and provide the best possible seal. An engine reconditioning specialist will carry out this work at moderate cost.

17 At the time of writing, it was not clear whether oversize pistons were available for all models. Consult your Peugeot/Citroën dealer or engine specialist for the latest information on piston availability. If oversize pistons are available (either from Peugeot/Citroën, or from another source), then it may be possible to have the cylinder bores rebored and fit the oversize pistons. If oversize pistons are not available, and the bores are worn, renewal of the block seems to be the only option.

13 Piston/connecting rod assembly – inspection

1 Before the inspection process can begin, the piston/connecting rod assemblies must be cleaned, and the original piston rings removed from the pistons.

2 Carefully expand the old rings over the top of the pistons. The use of two or three old feeler blades will be helpful in preventing the rings dropping into empty grooves (see illustration). Be careful not to scratch the piston with the ends of the ring. The rings are brittle, and will snap if they are spread too far. They are also very sharp – protect your hands and fingers.

13.2 Removing a piston ring with the aid of a feeler blade

13.13a Prise out the circlip . . .

13.13b . . . withdraw the gudgeon pin . . .

13.13c . . . and separate the piston from the connecting rod

Note that the third ring incorporates an expander. Always remove the rings from the top of the piston. Keep each set of rings with its piston if the old rings are to be re-used.

3 Scrape away all traces of carbon from the top of the piston. A hand-held wire brush (or a piece of fine emery cloth) can be used, once the majority of the deposits have been scraped away.

4 Remove the carbon from the ring grooves in the piston, using an old ring. Break the ring in half to do this (be careful not to cut your fingers – piston rings are sharp).
Caution: Be careful to remove only the carbon deposits – do not remove any metal, and do not nick or scratch the sides of the ring grooves.

5 Once the deposits have been removed, clean the piston/connecting rod assembly with paraffin or a suitable solvent, and dry thoroughly. Make sure that the oil return holes in the ring grooves are clear.

6 If the pistons and cylinder bores are not damaged or worn excessively, and if the cylinder block does not need to be rebored, the original pistons can be refitted. Normal piston wear shows up as even vertical wear on the piston thrust surfaces, and slight looseness of the top ring in its groove. New piston rings should always be used when the engine is reassembled.

7 Carefully inspect each piston for cracks around the skirt, around the gudgeon pin holes, and at the piston ring 'lands' (between the ring grooves).

8 Look for scoring and scuffing on the piston skirt, holes in the piston crown, and burned areas at the edge of the crown. If the skirt is scored or scuffed, the engine may have been suffering from overheating, and/or abnormal combustion which caused excessively high operating temperatures. The cooling and lubrication systems should be checked thoroughly. Scorch marks on the sides of the pistons show that blow-by has occurred. A hole in the piston crown, or burned areas at the edge of the piston crown, indicates that abnormal combustion has been occurring. If any of the above problems exist, the causes must be investigated and corrected, or the damage will occur again. The causes may include incorrect injection pump timing, or a faulty injector (as applicable).

9 Corrosion of the piston, in the form of pitting, indicates that coolant has been leaking into the combustion chamber and/or the crankcase. Again, the cause must be

corrected, or the problem may persist in the rebuilt engine.

10 Examine each connecting rod carefully for signs of damage, such as cracks around the big-end and small-end bearings. Check that the rod is not bent or distorted. Damage is highly unlikely, unless the engine has been seized or badly overheated. Detailed checking of the connecting rod assembly can only be carried out by an engine specialist with the necessary equipment.

11 The connecting rod big-end cap nuts must be renewed whenever they are disturbed. Although Peugeot/Citroën do not specify that the bolts must also be renewed, it is recommended that the nuts and bolts are renewed as a complete set.

12 The gudgeon pins are of the floating type, secured in position by two circlips. The pistons and connecting rods can be separated as follows.

13 Using a small flat-bladed screwdriver, prise out the circlips, and push out the gudgeon pin (see illustrations). Hand pressure should be sufficient to remove the pin. Identify the piston and rod to ensure correct reassembly. Discard the circlips – new ones must be used on refitting.

14 Examine the gudgeon pin and connecting rod small-end bearing for signs of wear or damage. Wear can be cured by renewing both the pin and bush. Bush renewal, however, is a specialist job – press facilities are required, and the new bush must be reamed accurately.

15 The connecting rods themselves should not be in need of renewal, unless seizure or some other major mechanical failure has occurred. Check the alignment of the connecting rods visually, and if the rods are not straight, take them to an engine overhaul specialist for a more detailed check.

16 Examine all components, and obtain any new parts from your Peugeot/Citroën dealer or engine reconditioning specialist. If new pistons are purchased, they will be supplied complete with gudgeon pins and circlips. Circlips can also be purchased individually.

17 Position the piston so that the cut-out or arrow on the piston crown, or the valve recesses on the piston crown, are positioned as shown in relation to the connecting rod big-end bearing shell cut-outs (see illustrations). Apply a smear of clean engine

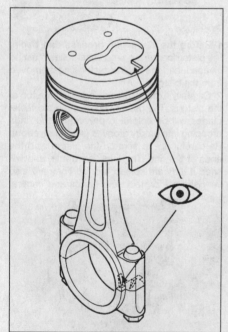

13.17a On 1.8 and 1.9 litre engines, ensure that the piston cut-out is positioned as shown, in relation to the connecting rod bearing shell cut-out

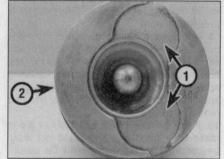

13.17b On 2.0-litre engines, the valve recesses (1) on the piston crown must be on the opposite side to the connecting rod bearing shell cut-out (2 – not visible)

14.2 Checking crankshaft endfloat using a dial gauge

14.3 Checking crankshaft endfloat using feeler blades

oil to the gudgeon pin. Slide it into the piston and through the connecting rod small-end. Check that the piston pivots freely on the rod, then secure the gudgeon pin in position with two new circlips. Ensure that each circlip is correctly located in its groove in the piston.

14 Crankshaft – inspection

Checking endfloat

1 If the crankshaft endfloat is to be checked, this must be done when the crankshaft is still installed in the cylinder block/crankcase, but is free to move (see Section 11).
2 Check the endfloat using a dial gauge in contact with the end of the crankshaft. Push the crankshaft fully one way, and then zero the gauge. Push the crankshaft fully the other way, and check the endfloat. The result can be compared with the specified amount, and will give an indication as to whether new thrustwashers are required (see illustration).
3 If a dial gauge is not available, feeler blades can be used. First push the crankshaft fully towards the flywheel end of the engine, then use feeler blades to measure the gap between the web of No 2 crankpin and the thrustwasher (see illustration).

Inspection

4 Clean the crankshaft using paraffin or a suitable solvent, and dry it, preferably with compressed air if available. Be sure to clean the oil holes with a pipe cleaner or similar probe, to ensure that they are not obstructed.

 Warning: Wear eye protection when using compressed air.

5 Check the main and big-end bearing journals for uneven wear, scoring, pitting and cracking.
6 Big-end bearing wear is accompanied by distinct metallic knocking when the engine

is running (particularly noticeable when the engine is pulling from low speed) and some loss of oil pressure.
7 Main bearing wear is accompanied by severe engine vibration and rumble – getting progressively worse as engine speed increases – and again by loss of oil pressure.
8 Check the bearing journal for roughness by running a finger lightly over the bearing surface. Any roughness (which will be accompanied by obvious bearing wear) indicates that the crankshaft requires regrinding (where possible) or renewal.
9 Check the oil seal contact surfaces at each end of the crankshaft for wear and damage. If the seal has worn a deep groove in the surface of the crankshaft, consult an engine overhaul specialist; repair may be possible, but otherwise a new crankshaft will be required.
10 Take the crankshaft to an engine reconditioning specialist to have it measured

for journal wear. If excessive wear is evident, they will be able to advise you with regard to regrinding the crankshaft and supplying new bearing shells.
11 If the crankshaft has been reground, check for burrs around the crankshaft oil holes (the holes are usually chamfered, so burrs should not be a problem unless regrinding has been carried out carelessly). Remove any burrs with a fine file or scraper, and thoroughly clean the oil holes as described previously.
12 At the time of writing, it was not clear whether Peugeot/Citroën produce oversize bearing shells for all of these engines. On some engines, if the crankshaft journals have not already been reground, it may be possible to have the crankshaft reconditioned, and to fit oversize shells. If no oversize shells are available and the crankshaft has worn beyond the specified limits, it will have to be renewed. Consult your dealer or engine specialist for further information on parts availability.

15 Main and big-end bearings – inspection

1 Even though the main and big-end bearings should be renewed during the engine overhaul, the old bearings should be retained for close examination, as they may reveal valuable information about the condition of the engine. The bearing shells are graded by thickness, the grade of each shell being indicated by the colour code marked on it.
2 Bearing failure can occur due to lack of lubrication, the presence of dirt or other foreign particles, overloading the engine, or corrosion (see illustration). Regardless of the cause of bearing failure, the cause must be corrected (where applicable) before the engine is reassembled, to prevent it from happening again.
3 When examining the bearing shells, remove them from the cylinder block/crankcase, the

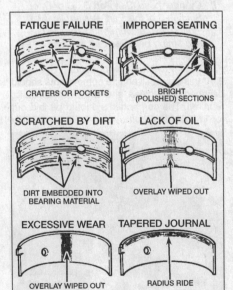

FATIGUE FAILURE	IMPROPER SEATING
CRATERS OR POCKETS	BRIGHT (POLISHED) SECTIONS
SCRATCHED BY DIRT	LACK OF OIL
DIRT EMBEDDED INTO BEARING MATERIAL	OVERLAY WIPED OUT
EXCESSIVE WEAR	TAPERED JOURNAL
OVERLAY WIPED OUT	RADIUS RIDE

H 28395

15.2 Typical bearing failures

main bearing ladder/caps (as appropriate), the connecting rods and the connecting rod big-end bearing caps. Lay them out on a clean surface in the same general position as their location in the engine. This will enable you to match any bearing problems with the corresponding crankshaft journal.

Caution: Do not touch any shell's bearing surface with your fingers while checking it, or the delicate surface may be scratched.

4 Dirt and other foreign matter gets into the engine in a variety of ways. It may be left in the engine during assembly, or it may pass through filters or the crankcase ventilation system. It may get into the oil, and from there into the bearings. Metal chips from machining operations and normal engine wear are often present. Abrasives are sometimes left in engine components after reconditioning, especially when parts are not thoroughly cleaned using the proper cleaning methods. Whatever the source, these foreign objects often end up embedded in the soft bearing material, and are easily recognised. Large particles will not embed in the bearing, and will score or gouge the bearing and journal. The best prevention for this cause of bearing failure is to clean all parts thoroughly, and keep everything spotlessly-clean during engine assembly. Frequent and regular engine oil and filter changes are also recommended.

5 Lack of lubrication (or lubrication breakdown) has a number of interrelated causes. Excessive heat (which thins the oil), overloading (which squeezes the oil from the bearing face) and oil leakage (from excessive bearing clearances, worn oil pump or high engine speeds) all contribute to lubrication breakdown. Blocked oil passages, which usually are the result of misaligned oil holes in a bearing shell, will also oil-starve a bearing, and destroy it. When lack of lubrication is the cause of bearing failure, the bearing material is wiped or extruded from the steel backing of the bearing. Temperatures may increase to the point where the steel backing turns blue from overheating.

6 Driving habits can have a definite effect on bearing life. Full-throttle, low-speed operation (labouring the engine) puts very high loads on bearings, tending to squeeze out the oil film. These loads cause the bearings to flex, which produces fine cracks in the bearing face (fatigue failure). Eventually, the bearing material will loosen in pieces, and tear away from the steel backing.

7 Short-distance driving leads to corrosion of bearings, because insufficient engine heat is produced to drive off the condensed water and corrosive gases. These products collect in the engine oil, forming acid and sludge. As the oil is carried to the engine bearings, the acid attacks and corrodes the bearing material.

8 Incorrect bearing installation during engine assembly will lead to bearing failure as well. Tight-fitting bearings leave insufficient bearing running clearance, and will result in oil starvation. Dirt or foreign particles trapped

behind a bearing shell result in high spots on the bearing, which lead to failure.

Caution: Do not touch any shell's bearing surface with your fingers during reassembly; there is a risk of scratching the delicate surface, or of depositing particles of dirt on it.

9 As mentioned at the beginning of this Section, the bearing shells should be renewed as a matter of course during engine overhaul; to do otherwise is false economy.

16 Engine overhaul – eassembly sequence

1 Before reassembly begins, ensure that all new parts have been obtained, and that all necessary tools are available. Read through the entire procedure to familiarise yourself with the work involved, and to ensure that all items necessary for reassembly of the engine are at hand. In addition to all normal tools and materials, thread-locking compound will be needed. A suitable tube of liquid sealant will also be required for the joint faces that are fitted without gaskets. It is recommended that Peugeot/Citroën's own product(s) are used, which are specially formulated for this purpose; the relevant product names are quoted in the text of each Section where they are required.

2 In order to save time and avoid problems, engine reassembly can be carried out in the following order:
   a) *Crankshaft (See Section 18).*
   b) *Piston/connecting rod assemblies (See Section 19).*
   c) *Oil pump (See Part B, C or D – as applicable).*
   d) *Sump (See Part B, C or D – as applicable).*
   e) *Flywheel (See Part B, C or D – as applicable).*
   f) *Cylinder head (See Part B , C or D, or Section 5 of this Part – as applicable).*
   g) *Timing belt tensioner and sprockets, and timing belt (See Part B, C or D – as applicable).*
   h) *Engine external components.*

3 At this stage, all engine components should be absolutely clean and dry, with all faults repaired. The components should be laid out (or in individual containers) on a completely

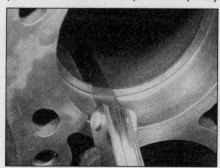

17.5 Measuring a piston ring end gap

17 Piston rings – refitting

1 Before fitting new piston rings, the ring end gaps must be checked as follows.

2 Lay out the piston/connecting rod assemblies and the new piston ring sets, so that the ring sets will be matched with the same piston and cylinder during the end gap measurement and subsequent engine reassembly.

3 Insert the top ring into the first cylinder, and push it down the bore using the top of the piston. This will ensure that the ring remains square with the cylinder walls. Position the ring near the bottom of the cylinder bore, at the lower limit of ring travel. Note that the top and second compression rings are different. The second ring is easily identified by the step on its lower surface, and by the fact that its outer face is tapered.

4 Measure the end gap using feeler blades.

5 Repeat the procedure with the ring at the top of the cylinder bore, at the upper limit of its travel **(see illustration)**, and compare the measurements with the figures given in the Specifications. If the end gaps are incorrect, check that you have the correct rings for your engine and for the cylinder bore size.

6 Repeat the checking procedure for each ring in the first cylinder, and then for the rings in the remaining cylinders. Remember to keep rings, pistons and cylinders matched up.

7 Once the ring end gaps have been checked and if necessary corrected, the rings can be fitted to the pistons.

8 Fit the piston rings using the same technique as for removal. Fit the bottom (oil control) ring first, and work up. When fitting the oil control ring, first insert the expander (where fitted), then fit the ring with its gap positioned 180° from the expander gap. Ensure that the second compression ring is fitted the correct way up, with its identification mark (either a dot of paint or the word TOP stamped on the ring surface) at the top, and the stepped surface at the bottom **(see illustration)**. Arrange the gaps of

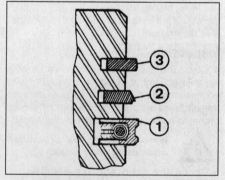

17.8 Piston ring fitting diagram (typical)
1 *Oil control ring*
2 *Second compression ring*
3 *Top compression ring*

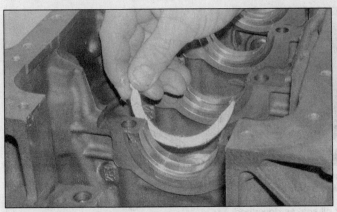

18.3 Fit the upper thrustwashers to the No 2 main bearing location with the oilway grooves facing outwards

18.4a Fit the bearing shells, ensuring that the tab engages in the notch in the cylinder block/crankcase . . .

the top and second compression rings 120° either side of the oil control ring gap.

Note: *Always follow any instructions supplied with the new piston ring sets – different manufacturers may specify different procedures. Do not mix up the top and second compression rings, as they have different cross-sections.*

18 Crankshaft – refitting

Selection of bearing shells

1 Have the crankshaft inspected and measured by an engine reconditioning specialist. They will be able to carry out any regrinding/repairs, and supply suitable main and big-end bearing shells.

Crankshaft refitting

1.9 and 2.0 litre engines

2 Where applicable, ensure that the oil spray jets are fitted to the bearing locations in the cylinder block.
3 Using a little grease, stick the upper thrustwashers to each side of the No 2 main bearing upper location. Ensure that the oilway grooves on each thrustwasher face outwards (away from the cylinder block) **(see illustration).**

4 Clean the backs of the bearing shells, and the bearing locations in both the cylinder block/crankcase and the main bearing caps. Press the bearing shells into their locations, ensuring that the tab on each shell engages in the notch in the cylinder block/crankcase or main bearing cap. Take care not to touch any shell's bearing surface with your fingers. Note that the upper bearing shells all have a grooved bearing surface, whereas the lower shells have a plain bearing surface **(see illustrations).** If new shells are being fitted, ensure that all traces of protective grease are cleaned off using paraffin. Wipe dry the shells and connecting rods with a lint-free cloth. Liberally lubricate each bearing shell in the cylinder block/crankcase and cap with clean engine oil.
5 Lower the crankshaft into position so that Nos 2 and 3 cylinder crankpins are at TDC; Nos 1 and 4 cylinder crankpins will be at BDC, ready for fitting No 1 piston. Check the crankshaft endfloat as described in Section 14.
6 Lubricate the lower bearing shells in the main bearing caps with clean engine oil. Make sure that the locating lugs on the shells engage with the corresponding recesses in the caps.
7 Fit main bearing caps Nos 2 to 5 to their correct locations, ensuring that they are fitted the correct way round (the bearing shell tab recesses in the block and caps must be on

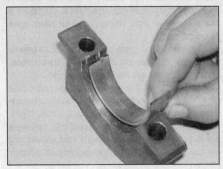

18.4b . . . and bearing cap

the same side). Insert the bolts, tightening them only loosely at this stage.
8 Apply a small amount of sealant to the No 1 main bearing cap mating face on the cylinder block, around the sealing strip holes **(see illustration).**
9 Locate the tab of each sealing strip over the pins on the base of No 1 bearing cap, and press the strips into the bearing cap grooves. It is now necessary to obtain two thin metal strips, of 0.25 mm thickness or less, in order to prevent the strips moving when the cap is being fitted. Peugeot/Citroën garages use the tool shown, which acts as a clamp. Metal strips (such as old feeler blades) can be used, provided all burrs which may damage the sealing strips are first removed **(see illustrations).**

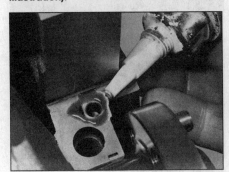

18.8 Applying sealant to the cylinder block No 1 main bearing cap mating face

18.9a Fitting a sealing strip to No 1 main bearing cap

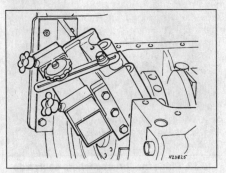

18.9b Using the Peugeot special tool to fit No 1 main bearing cap

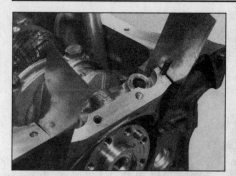

18.10a Fitting No 1 main bearing cap, using metal strips to retain the side seals

18.10b Removing a metal strip from No 1 main bearing cap using a pair of pliers

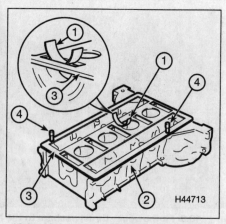

18.21 Main bearing shell fitment (1.6 litre engine)

1 Bearing shell
2 Main bearing ladder
3 Citroen tool No 0194-QZ
4 Aligning pins

10 Oil both sides of the metal strips, and hold them on the sealing strips. Fit the No 1 main bearing cap, insert the bolts loosely, then carefully pull out the metal strips in a horizontal direction, using a pair of pliers (see illustrations).

11 Tighten all the main bearing cap bolts evenly to the specified torque and, on 2.0 litre engines, additionally through the specified angle.

12 Check that the sealing strips protrude slightly from above the cylinder block/crankcase mating surface by approximately 1.0 mm. If not, remove the bearing cap again and refit; the seals are supplied the correct length and should not be cut. Also check that the crankshaft rotates freely.

13 Fit a new crankshaft oil seal as described in Chapter 2B or 2C (as applicable).

14 Refit the piston/connecting rod assemblies to the crankshaft as described in Section 19.

15 Refit the Woodruff key, then slide on the oil pump drive sprocket and spacer (where fitted), and locate the drive chain on the sprocket.

16 Ensure that the mating surfaces of the oil seal carrier and cylinder block are clean and dry. Note the correct fitted depth of the oil seal then, using a large flat-bladed screwdriver, lever the old seal out of the housing.

17 Apply a smear of suitable sealant to the oil seal carrier mating surface. Ensure that the locating dowels are in position, then slide the carrier over the end of the crankshaft and into position on the cylinder block. Tighten the carrier retaining bolts to the specified torque.

18 Fit a new crankshaft oil seal as described in Chapter 2B or 2C (as applicable).

19 Ensuring that the drive chain is correctly located on the sprocket, refit the oil pump and sump as described in Chapter 2B or 2C (as applicable).

20 Where removed, refit the cylinder head as described in Part B or C of this Chapter, or in Section 5 of this Part (as applicable).

1.6 litre engine

21 Place the bearing shells in their locations. If new shells are being fitted, ensure that all traces of protective grease are cleaned off using paraffin. Wipe dry the shells with a lint-free cloth. The upper bearing shells all have a grooved surface, whereas the lower shells have a plain surface. On these engines, it's essential that the lower bearing shells are centrally located in the bearing cap housing/ladder. To ensure this use a Citroën/Peugeot tool positioned over the housing/ladder, and insert the bearing shells through the slots in the tool (see illustration).

22 Liberally lubricate each bearing shell in the cylinder block with clean engine oil then lower the crankshaft into position.

23 Insert the thrustwashers to either side of No 2 main bearing upper location and push them around the bearing journal until their edges are horizontal (see illustration). Ensure that the oil way grooves on each thrustwasher face outwards (away from the bearing journal).

24 Thoroughly degrease the mating surfaces of the cylinder block and the crankshaft

bearing cap housing. Apply a thin bead of RTV sealant to the bearing cap housing mating surface (see illustration). Citroën/Peugeot recommend the use of Loctite Autojoint Noir for this purpose.

25 Lubricate the lower bearing shells with clean engine oil, then refit the bearing cap housing, ensuring that the shells are not displaced, and that the locating dowels engage correctly.

26 Install the ten large diameter, and sixteen smaller diameter crankshaft bearing cap housing retaining bolts, and screw them in until they are just making contact with the housing.

27 Working in the sequence shown, tighten the bolts to the torque settings given in the Specifications (see illustration).

28 With the bearing cap housing in place, check that the crankshaft rotates freely.

29 Refit the piston/connecting rod assemblies to the crankshaft as described in Section 19.

30 Refit the oil pump and sump.

31 Fit a new crankshaft left-hand oil seal, then refit the flywheel.

32 Where removed, refit the cylinder head, crankshaft sprocket and timing belt.

18.23 Place the thrustwashers each side of the No 2 bearing upper location

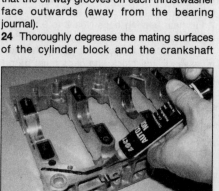

18.24 Apply a thin bead of RTV sealant to the bearing cap housing mating surface

18.27 Main bearing cap housing/ladder retaining bolt tightening sequence – 1.6 litre engines

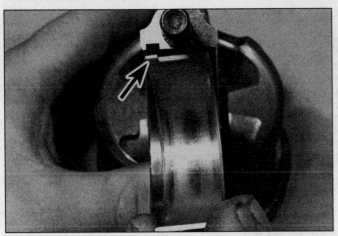

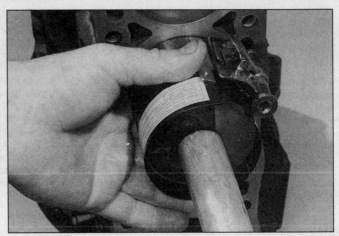

19.3 Fitting a bearing shell to a connecting rod – ensure the tab (arrowed) engages with the recess in the connecting rod

19.6 Tap the piston into the bore using a hammer handle

19 Piston/connecting rod assembly – refitting

Note: *New big-end bearing cap nuts must be used on refitting.*

1 Note that the following procedure assumes that the crankshaft and main bearing caps/ladder are in place (see Section 18).

2 Clean the backs of the bearing shells, and the bearing locations in both the connecting rod and bearing cap.

1.9 and 2.0 litre engines

3 Press the bearing shells into their locations, ensuring that the tab on each shell engages in the notch in the connecting rod and cap **(see illustration)**. Take care not to touch any shell's bearing surface with your fingers. If new shells are being fitted, ensure that all traces of the protective grease are cleaned off using paraffin. Wipe dry the shells and connecting rods with a lint-free cloth.

All engines

4 Lubricate the cylinder bores, the pistons, and piston rings, then lay out each piston/connecting rod assembly in its respective position.

5 Start with assembly No 1. Make sure that the piston rings are still spaced as described in Section 17, then clamp them in position with a piston ring compressor. Insert the piston/connecting rod assembly into the top of cylinder No 1, ensuring the piston is correctly positioned as follows.

  a) On 1.8 and 1.9 litre engines, ensure that the cloverleaf-shaped cut-out on the piston crown is towards the front (oil filter side) of the cylinder block.
  b) On 2.0 litre engines, ensure that the valve recesses on the piston crown are towards the rear of the cylinder block.
  c) On 1.6 litre engines, ensure that the 'DIST' mark or arrow on the piston crown

is towards the timing belt end of the engine.

6 Using a block of wood or hammer handle against the piston crown, tap the assembly into the cylinder/liner until the piston crown is flush with the top of the cylinder **(see illustration)**.

1.9 and 2.0 litre engines

7 Ensure that the bearing shell is still correctly installed. Liberally lubricate the crankpin and both bearing shells. Taking care not to mark the cylinder bores, pull the piston/connecting rod assembly down the bore and onto the crankpin. Refit the big-end bearing cap, tightening the nuts finger-tight at first. Note that the faces with the identification marks must match (which means that the bearing shell locating tabs abut each other).

8 Tighten the bearing cap retaining nuts

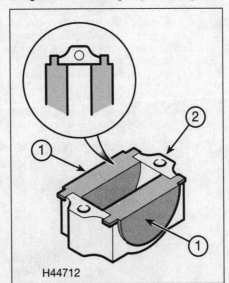

19.10 Big-end bearing shell positioning (1.6 litre engine)

1 Citroen tool No 0194-P
2 Bearing shell in the cap

evenly and progressively to the Stage 1 torque setting. Once both nuts have been tightened to the Stage 1 setting, angle-tighten them through the specified Stage 2 angle, using a socket and extension bar. It is recommended that an angle-measuring gauge is used during this stage of the tightening, to ensure accuracy.

1.6 litre engine

9 On these engines, the connecting rod is made in one piece, then the big-end bearing cap is 'cracked' off. This ensures that the cap fits onto the connecting rod only in one position, and with maximum rigidity. Consequently, there are no locating notches for the bearing shells to fit into.

10 To ensure that the big-end bearing shells are centrally located in the connecting rod and cap, two special tools are available from Citroën/Peugeot. These half-moon shaped tools are pressed in from either side of the rod/cap and locate the shell exactly in the centre **(see illustration)**. Fit the shells into the connecting rods and big-end caps and lubricate them with plenty of clean engine oil.

11 Pull the connecting rods and pistons down the bores and onto the crankshaft journals. Fit the big-end caps – they will only fit properly one way round (see paragraph 10), and insert the new bolts.

12 Tighten the bolts to the specified torque settings.

All engines

13 Once the bearing cap retaining nuts have been correctly tightened, rotate the crankshaft. Check that it turns freely; some stiffness is to be expected if new components have been fitted, but there should be no signs of binding or tight spots.

14 Refit the other three piston/connecting rod assemblies in the same way.

15 Refit the cylinder head and oil pump as described in Part B, C or D of this Chapter and/or in Section 5 of this Part (as applicable).

20 Engine – initial start-up after overhaul

1 With the engine refitted in the vehicle, double-check the engine oil and coolant levels (see *Weekly checks*). Make a final check that everything has been reconnected, and that there are no tools or rags left in the engine compartment.

Early models

2 Switch on the ignition and immediately turn the engine on the starter (do not allow the glow plugs to heat up) until the oil pressure warning light goes out.
3 Prime the fuel system as described in the relevant Part of Chapter 4.

Later models

4 On later models, the oil pressure warning light is linked to the STOP warning light, and is not illuminated when the ignition is initially switched on. Therefore it is not possible to check the oil pressure warning light when turning the engine on the starter motor.
5 Prime the fuel system (refer to relevant Part of Chapter 4). Although the system is self-priming, it will help if the ignition is switched on and off several times before attempting to start the engine in order to purge air from the system.
6 Fully depress the accelerator pedal, turn the ignition key to position M, and wait for the preheating warning light to go out.

All models

7 Start the engine, noting that this may take a little longer than usual, due to the fuel system components having been disturbed.
8 While the engine is idling, check for fuel, water and oil leaks. Don't be alarmed if there are some odd smells and smoke from parts getting hot and burning off oil deposits.
9 Assuming all is well, keep the engine idling until hot water is felt circulating through the top hose, then switch off the engine.
10 Allow the engine to cool then recheck the oil and coolant levels as described in *Weekly checks*, and top-up as necessary.
11 If they were tightened as described, there is no need to retighten the cylinder head bolts once the engine has first run after reassembly.
12 If new pistons, rings or crankshaft bearings have been fitted, the engine must be treated as new, and run-in for the first 500 miles (800 km). *Do not* operate the engine at full-throttle, or allow it to labour at low engine speeds in any gear. It is recommended that the oil and filter be changed at the end of this period.

Chapter 3
Cooling, heating and air conditioning systems

Contents

Degrees of difficulty

Easy, suitable for novice with little experience	Fairly easy, suitable for beginner with some experience	Fairly difficult, suitable for competent DIY mechanic	Difficult, suitable for experienced DIY mechanic	Very difficult, suitable for expert DIY or professional

Specifications

General
Maximum system pressure . . . . 1.4 bars

Thermostat
Opening temperatures:
  Starts to open:
    Petrol engine models . . . . 89°C
    Diesel engine models . . . . 83°C
  Fully-open. . . . . 99°C

Torque wrench settings

	Nm	lbf ft
Coolant pump housing bolts (aluminium block petrol engines):		
Smaller bolts.	30	22
Larger bolts.	65	48
Coolant pump securing bolts (cast-iron iron block engines)	15	11

1 General information and precautions

General information

The cooling system is of pressurised type, comprising a coolant pump driven by the timing belt, an aluminium crossflow radiator, expansion tank, electric cooling fan(s), a thermostat, heater matrix, and all associated hoses and switches.

The system functions as follows. Cold coolant in the bottom of the radiator passes through the bottom hose to the coolant pump, where it is pumped around the cylinder block and head passages, and through the oil cooler(s) (where fitted). After cooling the cylinder bores, combustion surfaces and valve seats, the coolant reaches the underside of the thermostat, which is initially closed. The coolant passes through the heater, and is returned via the cylinder block to the coolant pump.

When the engine is cold, the coolant circulates only through the cylinder block, cylinder head, and heater. When the coolant reaches a predetermined temperature, the thermostat opens, and the coolant passes through the top hose to the radiator. As the coolant circulates through the radiator, it is cooled by the inrush of air when the car is in forward motion. The airflow is supplemented by the action of the electric cooling fan(s) when necessary. Upon reaching the bottom of the radiator, the coolant has now cooled, and the cycle is repeated.

When the engine is at normal operating temperature, the coolant expands, and some of it is displaced into the expansion tank. Coolant collects in the tank, and is returned to the radiator when the system cools.

The electric cooling fan(s) mounted in front of the radiator are controlled by a thermostatic switch/sensor. At a predetermined coolant temperature, the switch/sensor actuates the fan.

Precautions

 Warning: Do not attempt to remove the expansion tank filler cap, or to disturb any part of the cooling system, while the engine is hot, as there is a high risk of scalding. If the expansion tank filler cap must be removed before the engine and radiator have fully cooled (even though this is not recommended), the pressure in the cooling system must first be relieved. Cover the cap with a thick layer of cloth to avoid scalding, and slowly unscrew the filler cap until a hissing sound is heard. When the hissing has stopped, indicating that the pressure has reduced, slowly unscrew the filler cap until it can be removed; if more hissing sounds are heard, wait until they have stopped before unscrewing the cap. At all times, keep well away from the filler cap opening, and protect your hands.

 Warning: Do not allow antifreeze to come into contact with your skin, or with the painted surfaces of the vehicle. Rinse off spills immediately, with plenty of water. Never leave antifreeze lying around in an open container, or in a puddle in the driveway or on the garage floor. Children and pets are attracted by its sweet smell, but antifreeze can be fatal if ingested.

 Warning: If the engine is hot, the electric cooling fan may start rotating even if the engine is not running. Be careful to keep your hands, hair and any loose clothing well clear when working in the engine compartment.

 Warning: Refer to Section 11 for precautions to be observed when working on models equipped with air conditioning.

---

2 Cooling system hoses – disconnection and renewal

Note: *Refer to the warnings given in Section 1 of this Chapter before proceeding. Hoses should only be disconnected once the engine has cooled sufficiently to avoid scalding.*

1 If the checks described in Chapter 1A or 1B reveal a faulty hose, it must be renewed as follows.

2 First drain the cooling system (Chapter 1A or 1B). If the coolant is not due for renewal, it may be re-used, providing it is collected in a clean container.

3 To disconnect a hose, proceed as follows, according to the type of hose connection.

2.5 Disconnecting the radiator top hose

Conventional connections – general instructions

4 On conventional connections, the clips used to secure the hoses in position may be either standard worm-drive clips or disposable crimped types. The crimped type of clip is not designed to be re-used and worm drive clips should be used on reassembly.

5 To disconnect a hose, use a screwdriver to slacken or release the clips, then move them along the hose, clear of the relevant inlet/outlet. Carefully work the hose free **(see illustration)**. The hoses can be removed with relative ease when new – on an older car, they may have stuck.

6 If a hose proves to be difficult to remove, try to release it by rotating its ends before attempting to free it. Gently prise the end of the hose with a blunt instrument (such as a flat-bladed screwdriver), but do not apply too much force, and take care not to damage the pipe stubs or hoses. Note in particular that the radiator inlet stub is fragile; do not use excessive force when attempting to remove the hose. If all else fails, cut the hose with a sharp knife, then slit it so that it can be peeled off in two pieces. Although this may prove expensive if the hose is otherwise undamaged, it is preferable to buying a new radiator. Check first, however, that a new hose is readily available.

7 When fitting a hose, first slide the clips onto

---

the hose, then work the hose into position. If crimped-type clips were originally fitted, use standard worm-drive clips when refitting the hose.

8 Work the hose into position, checking that it is correctly routed, then slide each clip back along the hose until it passes over the flared end of the relevant inlet/outlet, before tightening the clip securely.

> **HAYNES HiNT** *If the hose is stiff, use a little soapy water as a lubricant, or soften the hose by soaking it in hot water. Do not use oil or grease, which may attack the rubber.*

9 Refill the cooling system (see Chapter 1A or 1B).

10 Check thoroughly for leaks as soon as possible after disturbing any part of the cooling system.

Bayonet-type connections

Note: *A new O-ring should be used when reconnecting the hose.*

Removal

11 On certain models, the radiator bottom and/or top hose(s) may be connected to the radiator using a plastic bayonet-type connection. To disconnect this type of connector, proceed as follows.

12 Turn the locking ring (2) anti-clockwise until it contacts the stop (1) **(see illustration)**.

13 Press the connector away from the hose, to ensure that the two retaining lugs (3) are free **(see illustration)**.

14 Pull the hose, complete with the connector, from the radiator.

15 Recover the O-ring from the connector, and discard it; a new one must be used on refitting.

Refitting

16 Wipe the connector and the stub on the radiator thoroughly with a clean, lint-free cloth.

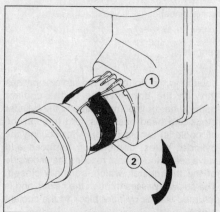

2.12 To release the bayonet-type radiator hose connection, turn the locking ring (2) until it contacts the stop (1)

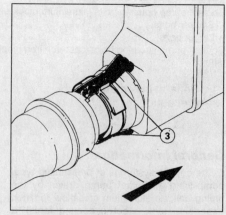

2.13 Press the connector away from the hose, to ensure that the two retaining lugs (3) are free

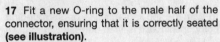

2.17 On refitting, fit a new O-ring (arrowed) to the hose union

2.19 Offer the hose to the stub on the radiator, cut-out (arrowed) at the bottom

2.25 Where spring clip hose connections are used, remove the spring clip then disconnect the hose

17 Fit a new O-ring to the male half of the connector, ensuring that it is correctly seated (see illustration).
18 Turn the locking ring clockwise until it clicks.
19 Offer the hose to the stub on the radiator, with the locating cut-out in the male part of the connector located at the bottom (see illustration).
20 Push the connector into the stub until both the retaining lugs click into position. Make sure that the O-ring is not trapped.
21 Pull the connector rearwards (away from the stub) to adjust the position of the retaining lugs if necessary.
22 Refill the cooling system (see Chapter 1A or 1B).
23 Check thoroughly for leaks as soon as possible after disturbing any part of the cooling system.

Spring clip type connections

Note: A new sealing ring should be used when reconnecting the hose.

Removal

24 Some cooling system hoses may be secured in position using a wire spring clip. To disconnect this type of connector, proceed as follows.
25 Using a small screwdriver, extract the retaining spring clip and disconnect the hose connection (see illustration). Once the hose has been disconnected, refit the spring clip to the hose union.

26 Inspect the hose unit sealing ring for signs of damage or deterioration and renew if necessary.

Refitting

27 Ensure that the sealing ring is in position and the spring clip is correctly located in the groove in the union (see illustration).
28 Lubricate the sealing ring with a smear of soapy water, to ease installation, then push the hose into position until it is heard to click into position.
29 Ensure that the hose is securely retained by the spring clip then refill the cooling system (see Chapter 1A or 1B).
30 Check thoroughly for leaks as soon as possible after disturbing any part of the cooling system.

3 Radiator – removal, inspection and refitting

Note: If leakage is the reason for removing the radiator, bear in mind that minor leaks can often be cured using a radiator sealant with the radiator in situ.

Removal – pre-September 2002 models

Petrol models

1 Disconnect the battery negative terminal (refer to Disconnecting the battery in the Reference Chapter).

2 Drain the cooling system as described in Chapter 1A.
3 Remove the air cleaner assembly and air intake ducts as necessary for access to the radiator, as described in Chapter 4A.
4 Disconnect the coolant hoses from the radiator with reference to Section 2.
5 On models without air conditioning, where applicable, disconnect the wiring connector from the cooling fan switch or temperature sensor located on the left-hand side of the radiator.
6 Working at the top of the radiator, lift the ends of the radiator retaining clips (one each side) and move the top of the radiator toward the engine (see illustration). Lift the radiator upward to disengage the lower locating lugs and remove the radiator from the engine compartment. Take care not to damage the radiator fins on surrounding components as it is lifted out.

Diesel models

7 Disconnect the battery negative terminal (refer to Disconnecting the battery in the Reference Chapter).
8 Drain the cooling system as described in Chapter 1B.
9 Remove the air cleaner assembly and air intake ducts as necessary for access to the radiator, as described in Chapter 4B or 4C.
10 Slacken the clips and disconnect the upper hoses at the coolant expansion tank (see illustration).
11 Where applicable, disconnect the wiring

2.27 Ensure that the sealing ring and spring clip (arrowed) are correctly fitted to the hose union before reconnecting

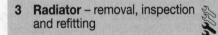

3.6 Lift the ends of the radiator retaining clips (arrowed) and move the top of the radiator toward the engine

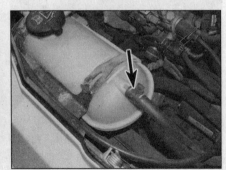

3.10 Disconnect the upper hoses (left-hand hose arrowed) at the coolant expansion tank on diesel models

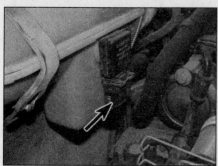

3.11 Disconnect the wiring connector (arrowed) from the coolant level sensor on the expansion tank

3.21a Undo the nut (arrowed) securing the radiator support frame to the front body panel . . .

3.21b . . . then withdraw the metal spacer from the rubber mounting bush

connector from the coolant level sensor on the rear of the expansion tank **(see illustration)**.

12 Release the retaining straps and lift the expansion tank off its mounting bracket. Slacken the clip and disconnect the hose from the underside of the expansion tank, then remove the tank.

13 Remove the radiator grille as described in Chapter 11, then undo the two bolts and remove the expansion tank support bracket from the front body panel.

14 Where applicable, disconnect the wiring connector from the cooling fan switch or temperature sensor located on the left-hand side of the radiator.

15 Disconnect all the coolant hoses from the radiator with reference to Section 2.

16 Working at the top of the radiator, lift the ends of the radiator retaining clips (one each side) and move the top of the radiator toward the engine **(see illustration 3.6)**. Lift the radiator upward to disengage the lower locating lugs and remove the radiator from the engine compartment. Take care not to damage the radiator fins on surrounding components as it is lifted out.

Removal – post-September 2002 models to RPO 9456

17 Disconnect the battery negative terminal (refer to *Disconnecting the battery* in the Reference Chapter).

18 Drain the cooling system as described in Chapter 1A or 1B.

19 Remove the air cleaner assembly and air intake ducts as necessary for access to the radiator, as described in Chapter 4A, 4B or 4C.

20 On models without air conditioning, where applicable, disconnect the wiring connector from the cooling fan switch or temperature sensor located on the left-hand side of the radiator.

21 Working at the top of the radiator, undo the nut (one each side) securing the radiator support frame to the front body panel. Withdraw the metal spacer from the rubber mounting bush **(see illustrations)**.

22 Move the top of the radiator support frame towards the engine and undo the bolt securing each radiator upper mounting bracket to the frame **(see illustration)**.

23 Withdraw the brackets from their locations in the support frame, and lift them off the plastic studs on the radiator **(see illustration)**.

24 Slide out the retaining clips and disconnect the expansion tank hoses from the radiator. Release the hose(s) from the clips on the radiator and move them to one side.

25 Disconnect the remaining coolant hoses from the radiator with reference to Section 2.

26 Lift the radiator upward to disengage the lower locating lugs and remove the radiator from the engine compartment. Take care not

to damage the radiator fins on surrounding components as it is lifted out.

Removal – post-September 2002 models from RPO 9457

Note: *The air conditioning system must be evacuated during this work.*

27 Disconnect the battery negative terminal (refer to *Disconnecting the battery* in the Reference Chapter).

28 Drain the cooling system as described in Chapter 1A or 1B.

29 Refer to Chapter 11 and remove the front bumper and front bumper crossmember.

30 Refer to Chapter 12 and remove the headlights.

31 Unbolt and remove the front crossmember panel for access to the radiator and air conditioning condenser.

32 Have the air conditioning system evacuated and sealed by a suitably qualified engineer.

33 Unclip the two air deflectors from the electric cooling fan shroud.

34 Unscrew the three bolts and remove the fan and the electric cooling fan motor from the shroud. As the unit is removed, disconnect it from the wiring socket on the shroud.

35 Disconnect the cooling motor wiring and feed through the shroud.

36 Unscrew the securing bolt and disconnect the air conditioning refrigerant pipe from the

3.22 Undo the bolt securing each radiator upper mounting bracket to the support frame

3.23 Withdraw the brackets from their locations in the support frame, and lift them off the plastic studs on the radiator

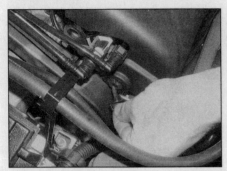

4.2a On 1.9 litre diesel engines, remove the fasteners from the right-hand side . . .

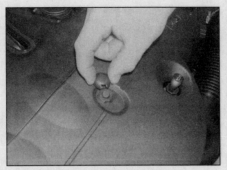

4.2b . . . and top of the engine cover . . .

4.2c . . . then remove the cover from the engine

4.2d On 2.0 litre diesel engines, rotate each fastener through 90° to release it . . .

4.2e . . . then lift off the engine cover

Refitting

47 Refitting is a reversal of removal, bearing in mind the following points:

a) *Ensure that the lower lugs on the radiator are correctly engaged with the mounting rubbers in the body panel.*

b) *Reconnect the hoses with reference to Section 2, using new O-rings where applicable.*

c) *On completion, refill the cooling system as described in Chapter 1A or 1B.*

d) *On models from RPO 9457, have the air conditioning system recharged by a suitably qualified engineer.*

4 Thermostat –
removal, testing and refitting

condenser. Immediately fit sealing plugs to the pipe and condenser.

37 Unscrew the shroud upper mounting bolts then lift the shroud and unclip the wiring socket from the motor mounting location.

38 Twist the radiator upper mountings from the location pins on the top of the radiator.

39 Unscrew the bolts and remove the wiring socket unit from the rear of the shroud, at the same time releasing the wiring from the clips. Position the unit to one side. Also unclip the wiring from the bottom of the shroud.

40 Disconnect the remaining coolant hoses from the radiator with reference to Section 2.

41 Carefully lift the condenser and radiator from their locations in the bottom mounting rubbers.

Inspection

42 If the radiator has been removed due

to suspected blockage, reverse-flush it as described in Chapter 1A or 1B. Clean dirt and debris from the radiator fins, using an air line (in which case, wear eye protection) or a soft brush.

Caution: Be careful, as the fins are sharp, and easily damaged.

43 If necessary, a radiator specialist can perform a 'flow test' on the radiator, to establish whether an internal blockage exists.

44 A leaking radiator must be referred to a specialist for permanent repair. Do not attempt to weld or solder a leaking radiator, as damage to the plastic components may result.

45 If the radiator is to be sent for repair or renewed, remove all hoses and the cooling fan switch (where fitted).

46 Inspect the condition of the radiator mounting rubbers, and renew them if necessary.

Removal

1 Disconnect the battery negative terminal (refer to *Disconnecting the battery* in the Reference Chapter).

2 On 1.9 litre DW series diesel engines, release the clip in the centre of the engine cover and undo the retaining screw on the right-hand side. Lift off the engine cover. On 1.6 and 2.0 litre diesel engines, turn the four plastic fasteners through 90° and lift off the engine cover **(see illustrations)**.

3 Drain the cooling system as described in Chapter 1A or 1B.

4 Remove the air cleaner assembly and air intake ducts as described in Chapter 4A, 4B or 4C.

Early models

5 Unscrew the retaining bolts, and carefully withdraw the thermostat housing cover to expose the thermostat **(see illustration)**. Take care not to strain the coolant hose(s) connected to the cover. Note that the design of the thermostat housing varies between engine types, but the thermostat removal procedure for each type is similar.

6 Lift the thermostat from the housing, noting which way round the thermostat is fitted, and recover the sealing ring(s) **(see illustration)**.

Later models

7 The thermostat is an integral part of the

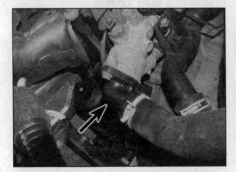

4.5 Thermostat housing cover location (arrowed) – 1.4 litre petrol model

4.6 Removing the sealing ring from the thermostat flange

4.7a Depress the release button (arrowed) and disconnect the hoses

4.7b Undo the bolts (arrowed) and detach the coolant outlet housing

6.5 Engine management system coolant temperature sensor (arrowed) on later 1.4 litre petrol models

coolant outlet housing on the left-hand end of the cylinder head. Disconnect the coolant hoses from the outlet housing, and the wiring plug from the coolant temperature sensor. Note that some of the hoses are disconnected after pressing down on the white-coloured release button. Undo the retaining bolts and remove the housing **(see illustrations)**.

Testing

8 A rough test of the thermostat may be made by suspending it with a piece of string in a container full of water. Heat the water to bring it to the boil – the thermostat must open by the time the water boils. If not, renew it.

9 If a thermometer is available, the precise opening temperature of the thermostat may be determined; compare with the figures given in the Specifications. The opening temperature is also marked on the thermostat.

10 A thermostat which fails to close as the water cools must also be renewed.

Refitting

11 Refitting is a reversal of removal, bearing in mind the following points:

a) *Examine the sealing ring(s) for damage or deterioration, and if necessary, renew.*

b) *Ensure that the thermostat is fitted the correct way round as noted during removal.*

c) *On completion, refill the cooling system as described in Chapter 1A or 1B.*

5 Electric cooling fan(s) – removal and refitting

Removal

1 Remove the radiator as described in Section 3.

2 Unscrew the locking ring and disconnect the round wiring connector from the lower left-hand corner of the fan shroud. Where individual connectors are used, trace the wiring back from the fan and disconnect the relevant connectors.

3 On early models, lift the ends of the fan shroud retaining clips (one each side) and move the top of the shroud toward the engine. On all models, lift the assembly upward to

disengage the lower locating lugs and remove it from the engine compartment.

4 To remove the fan motor(s) from the shroud, undo the three nuts and bolts securing the relevant motor to the shroud. Withdraw the motor and fan assembly and disconnect the wiring connector. The fan can be removed from the motor spindle after extracting the retaining clip, or undoing the retaining bolt, as applicable.

5 To gain access to the motor relays, unclip and lift off the cover over the relay box located in the centre of the fan shroud. Note that on some models the relay box cover may be secured by a screw.

6 Lift the relay mounting plate from the shroud, disconnect the wiring connector and remove the relevant relay.

Refitting

7 Refitting is a reversal of removal. Refit the radiator as described in Section 3.

6 Cooling system electrical switches and sensors – removal and refitting

Petrol models

Cooling fan switch – early models

1 On models without air conditioning, the cooling fan switch has a blue wiring connector and is located in the left-hand side of the radiator.

2 On models with air conditioning, the cooling fans are controlled by the air conditioning system control unit in conjunction with a temperature sensor located in the top of the thermostat housing. The sensor can be identified by its brown wiring connector.

Temperature warning light switch/ temperature gauge sensor

3 The coolant temperature warning light switch/temperature gauge sensor has a blue wiring connector and is located in the thermostat housing or at the left-hand end of the cylinder head.

Engine management system coolant temperature sensor

4 The engine management system coolant temperature sensor has a green wiring connector and is located in the thermostat housing.

5 On later engines (approximately 2001 onward) the coolant temperature sensor has a blue or green wiring connector and is located above the thermostat in the coolant outlet housing at the left-hand end of the cylinder head **(see illustration)**. The temperature signal from this sensor is used by the engine management ECU for fuel injection/ignition regulation and to control the operation of the cooling fan, air conditioning system and temperature warning light/gauge.

1.8 and 1.9 litre diesel models

Cooling fan switch

6 On models without air conditioning, the cooling fan switch has a blue wiring connector and is located in the left-hand side of the radiator.

7 On models with air conditioning, the cooling fans are controlled by the air conditioning system control unit in conjunction with a temperature sensor located in the thermostat housing. The sensor can be identified by its brown wiring connector.

Temperature warning light switch/ temperature gauge sensor

8 The coolant temperature warning light switch/temperature gauge sensor has a blue wiring connector and is located in the thermostat housing.

Preheating/EGR system coolant temperature switch/sensor

9 The coolant temperature switch or sensor used for control of the preheating and EGR systems has a green wiring connector and is located in the thermostat housing.

1.6 and 2.0 litre diesel models

Engine management system coolant temperature sensor

10 On 1.6 and 2.0 litre diesel engines the coolant temperature sensor has a green wiring connector and is mounted in the thermostat/coolant outlet housing at the left-hand end of the cylinder head. The temperature signal from

6.15 On later models, prise out the sensor retaining circlip then remove the sensor and sealing ring from the housing

7.4a Withdraw the coolant pump . . .

7.4b . . . and recover the O-ring – 1.4 litre petrol engine shown

this sensor is used by the engine management ECU for diesel injection regulation and to control the operation of the exhaust gas recirculation, cooling fans, pre/post-heating control unit, air conditioning system and temperature warning light/gauge.

Removal

Warning: The engine should be cold before removing a cooling system switch or sensor.

11 Disconnect the battery negative terminal (refer to *Disconnecting the battery* in the Reference Chapter).

12 Partially drain the cooling system to just below the level of the switch/sensor (as described in Chapter 1A or 1B). Alternatively, have ready a suitable bung to plug the switch aperture in the housing when the switch is removed. If this method is used, take care not to use anything which will allow foreign matter to enter the cooling system.

13 Where necessary, refer to Chapter 4A, 4B or 4C and remove the air cleaner assembly and air intake ducts for access to the switches/sensors located in the thermostat housing or cylinder head.

14 Unplug the wiring connector from the relevant switch/sensor.

15 On later engines fitted with a plastic thermostat/coolant outlet housing, prise out the sensor retaining circlip then remove the sensor and sealing ring from the housing **(see illustration)**. If the system has not been drained, plug the sensor aperture to prevent further coolant loss.

16 On all other engines, carefully unscrew the switch/sensor from its mounting and recover the sealing ring (where applicable). If the system has not been drained, plug the switch/sensor aperture to prevent further coolant loss.

Refitting

17 On models fitted with a plastic thermostat/coolant outlet housing, fit a new sealing ring to the sensor. Push the sensor firmly into the housing and secure it in position with the circlip, ensuring it is correctly located in the housing groove. Reconnect the sensor wiring connector.

18 On all other engines, if the switch/sensor

was originally fitted using sealing compound, clean the switch/sensor threads thoroughly, and coat them with fresh sealing compound. If the switch was originally fitted using a sealing ring, use a new sealing ring on refitting.

19 Fit the switch/sensor to its location, tighten it securely and reconnect the wiring connector.

20 On all engines, refill and bleed the cooling system as described in Chapter 1A or 1B. Follow the bleeding instructions carefully, to ensure that all air is expelled from the cooling system.

21 On completion, refit any components removed for access, then start the engine and run it until it reaches normal operating temperature. Continue to run the engine, and check that the component(s) controlled by the switch/sensor operate correctly.

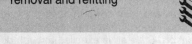

7 Coolant pump – removal and refitting

Aluminium cylinder block

Note: *A new impeller assembly O-ring and, where applicable, a new impeller housing O-ring, will be required on refitting.*

Removal

1 The coolant pump is driven by the timing belt, and is located in a housing at the timing belt end of the engine.

2 Drain the cooling system as described in the relevant Part of Chapter 1.

3 Remove the timing belt as described in the relevant Part of Chapter 2.

4 Remove the securing bolts, and withdraw the pump impeller assembly from the pump housing (access is most easily obtained from under the wheel arch). Recover the O-ring **(see illustrations)**.

5 If desired, the pump impeller housing can be removed from the rear of the coolant pump housing. Access is most easily obtained from underneath the vehicle (it may be necessary to remove the exhaust heat shield). Disconnect the coolant hoses from the impeller housing (be prepared for coolant spillage), then remove the securing bolts and withdraw the impeller housing. Again, recover the O-ring.

Refitting

6 Ensure that all mating faces are clean.

7 Where applicable, refit the impeller housing to the rear of the coolant pump housing, using a new O-ring. Reconnect the coolant hoses securely.

8 Refit the impeller assembly to the pump housing, using a new O-ring.

9 Refit the timing belt as described in the relevant Part of Chapter 2.

10 Refill the cooling system as described in the relevant Part of Chapter 1.

Cast-iron cylinder block

Note: *A new pump O-ring must be used on refitting.*

11 The pump is driven by the timing belt, and is located directly in the cylinder block.

12 Proceed as described previously for engines with an aluminium cylinder block, but note that there is no separate impeller housing.

8 Thermostat/fuel filter housing (1.8 and 1.9 litre diesel models) – removal and refitting

Note: *A new gasket must be used when refitting the main housing.*

Removal

1 Disconnect the battery negative terminal (refer to *Disconnecting the battery* in the Reference Chapter).

2 Drain the cooling system as described in Chapter 1B.

3 Place a plastic sheet over the transmission bellhousing and the starter motor, to prevent any fuel spilled during the following procedure from causing damage.

4 Remove the fuel filter as described in Chapter 1B.

5 Disconnect the wiring plugs from the coolant sensors mounted in the top of the housing.

6 Disconnect the coolant hoses from the plastic thermostat housing.

7 Disconnect the coolant hose from the stub at the rear of the housing.

8.8a Unscrew the securing bolt (arrowed) . . .

8.8b . . . withdraw the plastic housing . . .

8.8c . . . and recover the O-ring

8 Unscrew the bolt securing the plastic fuel filter housing to the main housing, then withdraw the plastic housing and move it clear of the main housing. Recover the O-ring from the base of the plastic housing (see illustrations).
9 Unscrew the three securing bolts, and withdraw the main housing from the cylinder head (see illustrations). Recover the gasket.
10 Disconnect the coolant hose from the base of the housing, and remove the housing.

Refitting

11 Refitting is a reversal of removal, bearing in mind the following points:
 a) *Examine the condition of the O-ring on the base of the plastic housing, and renew if necessary.*
 b) *Use a new gasket when refitting the main housing.*
 c) *Ensure that all hoses, pipes and wires are correctly reconnected.*
 d) *Refill the cooling system as described in Chapter 1B.*
 e) *On completion, prime and bleed the fuel system as described in Chapter 4B or 4C.*

9 Heating and ventilation system – general information

The heating/ventilation system consists of a four-speed blower motor (housed behind the facia), face level vents in the centre and at each end of the facia, and air ducts to the front footwells.
The control unit is located in the facia, and the controls operate flap valves to deflect and mix the air flowing through the various parts of the heating/ventilation system. The flap valves are contained in the air distribution housing, which acts as a central distribution unit, passing air to the various ducts and vents.
Cold air enters the system through the grille at the rear of the engine compartment. If required, the airflow is boosted by the blower, and then flows through the various ducts, according to the settings of the controls. Stale air is expelled through ducts at the rear of the vehicle. If warm air is required, the cold air is passed over the heater matrix, which is heated by the engine coolant.
On models fitted with air conditioning,

a recirculation switch enables the outside air supply to be closed off, while the air inside the vehicle is recirculated. This can be useful to prevent unpleasant odours entering from outside the vehicle, but should only be used briefly, as the recirculated air inside the vehicle will soon become stale.

10 Heater/ventilation components – removal and refitting

Heater/ventilation control unit

Removal

1 Disconnect the battery negative terminal (refer to *Disconnecting the battery* in the Reference Chapter).
2 Remove the relevant panels in the centre of the facia, for access to the control unit, as described in Chapter 11.
3 Undo the two upper retaining screws at each corner of the control unit.
4 Using a small screwdriver, release the retaining lug at the lower centre of the control

8.9a Unscrew the three securing bolts (arrowed) . . .

8.9b . . . and withdraw the main thermostat housing

unit and withdraw the unit from the facia **(see illustration)**.

5 Pivot the control unit upwards, as far as clearance will allow, then release the securing clips and disconnect the control cables from the unit. Note the locations of the cables to ensure correct refitting **(see illustration)**.

6 Disconnect the wiring plug from the rear of the control unit, then withdraw the unit.

Refitting

7 Refitting is a reversal of removal, but ensure that the control cables are securely reconnected to their original locations.

Heater/ventilation control cables

Removal

8 Disconnect the cables from the heater/ventilation control unit, as described previously in this Section during the control unit removal procedure.

9 Working through the facia aperture or under the facia (it may be necessary to remove certain facia panels for access – see Chapter 11 – depending on which cable is to be removed), release the clips and disconnect the cable from the heater assembly. Note the routing of the cable to ensure correct refitting.

Refitting

10 Refitting is a reversal of removal, ensuring that the cables are correctly routed, and securely reconnected.

10.4 Release the lug at the lower centre of the heater/ventilation control unit and withdraw the unit from the facia

Heater matrix

Note 1: *New heater hose connector O-rings must be used on refitting.*

Note 2: *The design, layout and construction of the heater assembly varies considerably according to model type, engine type and year of manufacture. The following procedures describe a typical installation.*

Removal

11 Drain the cooling system (see Chapter 1A or 1B).

12 Remove the complete facia assembly as described in Chapter 11.

13 Working in the engine compartment, disconnect the heater hoses from the matrix pipes. Where the hoses are connected

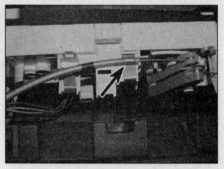

10.5 Pivot the control unit upwards, then release the clips (arrowed) and disconnect the control cables

individually, release the retaining clips and disconnect the hoses from the heater matrix pipe unions on the engine compartment bulkhead. Where the hoses are connected to a block connector, prise the metal retaining clip from the top of the connector, then release the plastic retaining clip by pushing it towards the left-hand hose connection. Pull the connector assembly from the heater matrix. Recover the O-ring seals from the connector, and discard them; new ones should be used on refitting **(see illustrations)**.

14 Undo the two screws securing the cover plate over the matrix pipes bulkhead seal. Lift off the cover plate, noting the orientation of the D-shaped cut-out.

15 Withdraw the rubber bulkhead seal from the matrix pipes.

16 Working inside the car, disconnect and withdraw the ventilation ducts on the driver's and passenger's side.

17 Unscrew the bolt securing the bottom of the heater to the bracket on the floor **(see illustration)**.

18 Check that all cables, wiring and related components are disconnected or moved clear to allow the heater assembly to be withdrawn into the vehicle interior.

19 Again working in the engine compartment, unscrew the two nuts securing the heater assembly to the bulkhead.

20 With the aid of an assistant working in the engine compartment, ease the matrix pipes from the bulkhead, and carefully pull the heater assembly into the vehicle interior.

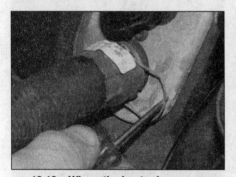

10.13a Where the heater hoses are connected individually, prise out the retaining clip and disconnect the hoses from the matrix pipe unions

10.13b Where the hoses are connected to a block connector, remove the metal clip from the heater matrix connector . . .

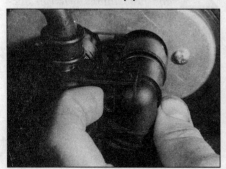

10.13c . . . then release the plastic retaining clip . . .

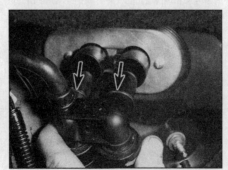

10.13d . . . and pull the connector away from the bulkhead – recover the O-rings (arrowed)

10.17 Unscrew the bolt securing the bottom of the heater to the bracket on the floor

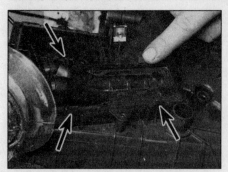

10.21 Release the four securing clips (arrowed) then withdraw the matrix from the heater casing

10.26 Unscrew the screws securing the motor assembly to the heater unit and lower the motor from its location

21 With the heater assembly removed, release the four securing clips, then withdraw the matrix from the heater casing **(see illustration)**.

Refitting

22 Refitting is a reversal of removal bearing in mind the following points.
  a) *Before refitting the heater assembly, lubricate the heater pipe grommet, then refit it to the matrix pipes.*
  b) *Offer the heater assembly into position, pushing the heater pipe grommet through the bulkhead as the assembly is refitted (again, an assistant working in the engine compartment will ease the task).*
  c) *When reconnecting the heater hoses to the pipes, fit new O-rings to the matrix pipes, then reconnect the hose connector to the pipes.*

Heater blower motor

Removal

23 The blower motor assembly is located on the passenger side of the vehicle.
24 Disconnect the battery negative terminal (refer to *Disconnecting the battery* in the Reference Chapter).
25 Referring to Chapter 11, remove the facia panels as necessary for access under the facia on the passenger's side.
26 Unscrew the screws securing the motor assembly to the heater unit and lower the motor from its location **(see illustration)**.
27 Cut the cable tie securing the wiring to the motor cover then pull the rubber wiring grommet away, and disconnect the wiring connector.

Refitting

28 Refitting is a reversal of removal.

11 Air conditioning system – general information and precautions

General information

An air conditioning system is available on certain models. It enables the temperature of incoming air to be lowered, and also dehumidifies the air, which makes for rapid demisting and increased comfort.

The cooling side of the system works in the same way as a domestic refrigerator. Refrigerant gas is drawn into a belt-driven compressor, and passes into a condenser mounted on the front of the radiator, where it loses heat and becomes liquid. The liquid passes through an expansion valve to an evaporator, where it changes from liquid under high pressure to gas under low pressure. This change is accompanied by a drop in temperature, which cools the evaporator. The refrigerant returns to the compressor, and the cycle begins again.

Air blown through the evaporator passes to the air distribution unit, where it is mixed with hot air blown through the heater matrix to achieve the desired temperature in the passenger compartment.

The heating side of the system works in the same way as on models without air conditioning (see Section 9).

The operation of the system is controlled by an electronic control unit, which controls the electric cooling fan(s), the compressor and the facia-mounted warning light. Any problems with the system should be referred to a Peugeot/Citroën dealer.

Precautions

When an air conditioning system is fitted, it is necessary to observe special precautions whenever dealing with any part of the system, or its associated components. If for any reason the system must be disconnected, entrust this task to your Peugeot/Citroën dealer or a refrigeration engineer.

⚠ *Warning: The refrigeration circuit contains a liquid refrigerant, and it is therefore dangerous to disconnect any part of the system without specialised knowledge and equipment.*

The refrigerant is potentially dangerous, and should only be handled by qualified persons. If it is splashed onto the skin, it can cause frostbite. It is not itself poisonous, but in the presence of a naked flame (including a cigarette) it forms a poisonous gas. Uncontrolled discharging of the refrigerant is dangerous, and potentially damaging to the environment.

12 Air conditioning system components – removal and refitting

Note: *Do not operate the air conditioning system if it is known to be short of refrigerant, as this may damage the compressor.*
1 The only operation which can be carried out easily without discharging the refrigerant is the renewal of the auxiliary (compressor) drivebelt. This is described in the relevant Part of Chapter 1. All other operations must be referred to a Peugeot/Citroën dealer or an air conditioning specialist.
2 If necessary, the compressor can be unbolted and moved aside, without disconnecting its flexible hoses, after removing the drivebelt.

⚠ *Warning: Do not attempt to open the refrigerant circuit. Refer to the precautions given in Section 11.*

Chapter 4 Part A:
Fuel and exhaust systems – petrol models

Contents

Degrees of difficulty

Easy, suitable for novice with little experience	**Fairly easy,** suitable for beginner with some experience	**Fairly difficult,** suitable for competent DIY mechanic	**Difficult,** suitable for experienced DIY mechanic	**Very difficult,** suitable for expert DIY or professional

Specifications

System type

1.4 litre models:
  Engine code KFX:
    Pre-1999 models . . . . Magneti Marelli 1AP
    1999 models onward:
      To emission standard L3 . . . . Sagem Lucas SL96
      To emission standard L4 . . . . Bosch Motronic MP7.3
  Engine code KFW . . . . Sagem S2000
1.6 litre models . . . . Bosch Motronic ME7.4.4

Fuel system data

Fuel pump type . . . . Electric, immersed in tank
Specified idle speed . . . . 850 ± 50 rpm (not adjustable – controlled by ECU)
Idle mixture CO content . . . . Less than 1.0 % (not adjustable– controlled by ECU)

Recommended fuel

Minimum octane rating . . . . 95 RON unleaded

Torque wrench settings

	Nm	lbf ft
Exhaust manifold-to-cylinder head nuts	20	15
Inlet manifold nuts:		
M6	10	7
M8	20	15

1 General information and precautions

The fuel supply system consists of a fuel tank (which is mounted under the rear of the car, with an electric fuel pump immersed in it), a fuel filter, fuel feed lines and, on early models, fuel return lines.

The fuel pump supplies fuel to the fuel rail, which acts as a reservoir for the four fuel injectors which inject fuel into the inlet tracts. The fuel filter incorporated in the feed line from the pump to the fuel rail ensures that the fuel supplied to the injectors is clean.

Refer to Section 6 for further information on the operation of each engine management system, and to Section 16 for information on the exhaust system.

 Warning: Many of the procedures in this Chapter require the removal of fuel lines and connections, which may result in some fuel spillage. Before carrying out any operation on the fuel system, refer to the precautions given in 'Safety first!' at the beginning of this manual, and follow them implicitly. Petrol is a highly dangerous

and volatile liquid, and the precautions necessary when handling it cannot be overstressed.

Note: *Residual pressure will remain in the fuel lines long after the vehicle was last used. When disconnecting any fuel line, first depressurise the fuel system as described in Section 7.*

2   Air cleaner assembly and intake ducts – removal and refitting

Note: *Where crimped-type hose clips or ties are fitted, cut and discard them and use standard worm-drive hose clips, or new cable ties on refitting.*

Removal

Pre-September 2002 1.4 litre models

1 Slacken the retaining clip securing the air cleaner lid to the throttle housing **(see illustration)**.
2 Disconnect the breather hose at the front of the air cleaner lid by slackening the retaining clip (where fitted) or depressing the sides of the quick-release fitting.
3 Undo the bolt securing the air intake duct to the support bracket on the engine, and the two screws securing the intake duct to the front body panel **(see illustration)**.
4 Detach the air cleaner lid from the throttle housing, while at the same time lifting the air

2.1 Slacken the retaining clip (arrowed) securing the air cleaner lid to the throttle housing – early 1.4 litre models

cleaner housing upwards to release the lower mounting. Slide the unit sideways slightly and withdraw it, together with the intake duct, from the engine compartment. Recover the throttle housing sealing ring from the air cleaner lid.
5 If required, the intake duct components can be separated after cutting off the retaining cable ties.

1.6 litre models and post-September 2002 1.4 litre models

6 Slacken the clip securing the air cleaner lid to the throttle housing **(see illustration)**.
7 Depress the sides of the quick-release fitting and detach the engine breather hose from the air cleaner lid **(see illustration)**.
8 Undo the nut securing the air intake duct

2.3 Undo the bolt (arrowed) securing the air intake duct to the support bracket – early 1.4 litre models

to the front body panel **(see illustration)**. Lift the duct off the mounting stud and slide it sideways slightly to disengage the additional retaining tab.
9 Release the plastic retainer securing the air cleaner housing to the support bracket by turning it through 90° **(see illustration)**.
10 Detach the air cleaner lid from the throttle housing, while at the same time lifting the air cleaner housing upwards to release the lower mounting. Slide the unit sideways slightly and withdraw it, together with the intake duct, from the engine compartment **(see illustrations)**. Recover the throttle housing sealing ring from the air cleaner lid.
11 If required, the intake duct can be removed from the air cleaner housing by pulling it outwards from the base of the housing.

2.6 Slacken the clip securing the air cleaner lid to the throttle housing – later models

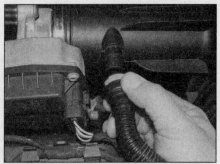

2.7 Depress the quick-release fitting and detach the breather hose from the air cleaner lid

2.8 Undo the nut (arrowed) securing the air intake duct to the front body panel – later models

2.9 Turn the plastic retainer through 90° to release it – later models

2.10a Detach the air cleaner lid from the throttle housing . . .

2.10b . . . then lift the air cleaner assembly upwards to release the lower mounting – later models

3.1 Remove the spring clip from the accelerator outer cable

Refitting

12 Refitting is a reversal of the removal procedure, ensuring that all hoses are properly reconnected, and that all ducts are correctly seated and securely held by their retaining clips or cable ties.

---

3 Accelerator cable – removal, refitting and adjustment

Note: *All 2005-on models (from RPO 10281) are fitted with an electronic accelerator pedal/position sensor without a cable.*

Removal

1 Working in the engine compartment, free the accelerator inner cable from the throttle housing cam, or accelerator pedal position sensor, then pull the outer cable out from its mounting bracket rubber grommet. Recover the spring clip from the outer cable **(see illustration)**.
2 Working back along the length of the cable, free it from any retaining clips or ties, noting its correct routing.
3 Working inside the car, remove the fusebox cover and the under cover from beneath the facia on the driver's side.
4 Reach up under the facia, depress the ends of the cable end fitting and detach the inner cable from the top of the accelerator pedal. Where fitted, pull out the clip securing the bulkhead grommet.
5 Tie a length of string to the end of the cable.
6 Return to the engine compartment, release the cable grommet from the bulkhead and withdraw the cable. When the end of the cable appears, untie the string and leave it in position – it can then be used to draw the cable back into position on refitting.

Refitting

7 Tie the string to the end of the cable, then use the string to draw the cable into position through the bulkhead. Once the cable end is visible, untie the string, then attach the inner cable to the pedal. Where applicable, refit the bulkhead grommet clip.
8 From within the engine compartment, ensure the outer cable is correctly seated in the bulkhead grommet, then work along the cable, securing it in position with the retaining clips and ties, and ensuring that the cable is correctly routed.
9 Pass the outer cable through its mounting bracket grommet, and reconnect the inner cable to the throttle cam or accelerator pedal position sensor. Adjust the cable as described below.

Adjustment

10 Remove the spring clip from the accelerator outer cable **(see illustration 3.1)**. Ensuring that the throttle cam or position sensor is fully against its stop, gently pull the cable out of its grommet until all free play is removed from the inner cable.
11 With the cable held in this position, refit the spring clip to the last exposed outer cable groove in front of the rubber grommet. When the clip is refitted and the outer cable is released, there should be only a small amount of free play in the inner cable.
12 Have an assistant depress the accelerator pedal, and check that the throttle cam or position sensor opens fully and returns smoothly to its stop.

---

4 Accelerator pedal – removal and refitting

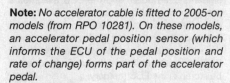

Note: *No accelerator cable is fitted to 2005-on models (from RPO 10281). On these models, an accelerator pedal position sensor (which informs the ECU of the pedal position and rate of change) forms part of the accelerator pedal.*

Removal

1 Disconnect the accelerator cable (where fitted) from the pedal as described in Section 3, or disconnect the wiring plug from the accelerator pedal position sensor.

Right-hand drive models

2 Unscrew the nut from the end of the pedal pivot shaft, whilst retaining the pivot shaft with an open-ended spanner on the flats provided.
3 Withdraw the pedal and pivot shaft assembly from the support bracket.
4 Examine the pivot shaft for signs of wear or damage and, if necessary, renew it. The pivot shaft is a screw fit in the pedal.

Left-hand drive models

5 Unscrew the two nuts and lift off the pedal pivot housing cover and upper bearing.
6 Withdraw the pedal from the lower bearing.
7 Examine the pivot bushes and shaft for signs of wear and renew as necessary.

Refitting

8 Refitting is a reversal of the removal procedure, applying a little multi-purpose grease to the pedal pivot point. On completion, adjust the accelerator cable as described in Section 3 (where applicable).

---

5 Unleaded petrol – general information and usage

Note: *The information given in this Chapter is correct at the time of writing. If updated information is thought to be required, check with a Peugeot/Citroën dealer. If travelling abroad, consult one of the motoring organisations (or a similar authority) for advice on the fuel available.*

1 All petrol engine models covered by this manual are designed to run on unleaded fuel with a minimum octane rating of 95 (RON). All engines have a catalytic converter, and so must be run on unleaded fuel **only**. Under no circumstances should leaded fuel, or lead replacement petrol (LRP) be used, as this will damage the converter.
2 Super unleaded petrol (98 octane) can also be used in all models if wished, though there is no advantage in doing so.

---

6 Engine management system – general information

Note: *The fuel injection ECU is of the 'self-learning' type, meaning that as it operates, it also monitors and stores the settings which give optimum engine performance under all operating conditions. When the battery is disconnected, these settings are lost and the ECU reverts to the base settings programmed into its memory at the factory. On restarting, this may lead to the engine running/idling roughly for a short while, until the ECU has relearned the optimum settings. This process is best accomplished by taking the vehicle on a road test (for approximately 15 minutes), covering all engine speeds and loads, concentrating mainly in the 2500 to 3500 rpm region.*

On all models, the fuel injection and ignition functions are combined into a single engine management system. The systems fitted are manufactured by Bosch, Magneti Marelli and Sagem, and are very similar to each other in most respects, the only significant differences being in the software contained in the system ECU, and specific component location according to engine type. Each system incorporates a closed-loop catalytic converter and an evaporative emission control system, and complies with the latest emission control standards. Refer to Chapter 5B for information on the ignition side of each system; the fuel side of the system operates as follows.

The fuel pump supplies fuel from the tank to the fuel rail, via a renewable cartridge filter mounted on the side of the fuel tank. The pump itself is mounted inside the tank, with the pump motor permanently immersed in fuel, to keep it cool. The fuel rail is mounted directly above the fuel injectors and acts as a fuel reservoir.

Fuel rail supply pressure is controlled by the pressure regulator, mounted at the end of the fuel rail, on the fuel tank, or integrated into the fuel pump assembly. The regulator contains a spring-loaded valve, which lifts to allow excess fuel to return to the tank when the optimum operating pressure of the fuel system is exceeded (eg, during low speed, light load cruising).

The fuel injectors are electromagnetic pintle valves, which spray atomised fuel into the combustion chambers under the control of the engine management system ECU. There are four injectors, one per cylinder, mounted in the inlet manifold close to the cylinder head. Each injector is mounted at an angle that allows it to spray fuel directly onto the back of the inlet valve(s). The ECU controls the volume of fuel injected by varying the length of time for which each injector is held open.

The electrical control system consists of the ECU, along with the following sensors:

a) *Throttle potentiometer – informs the ECU of the throttle valve position, and the rate of throttle opening/closing.*

b) *Coolant temperature sensor – informs the ECU of engine temperature.*

c) *Inlet air temperature sensor – informs the ECU of the temperature of the air passing through the throttle housing.*

d) *Lambda (oxygen) sensors – inform the ECU of the oxygen content of the exhaust gases (explained in greater detail in Part D of this Chapter).*

e) *Manifold pressure sensor – informs the ECU of the load on the engine (expressed in terms of inlet manifold vacuum).*

f) *Crankshaft position sensor – informs the ECU of engine speed and crankshaft angular position.*

g) *Vehicle speed sensor – informs the ECU of the vehicle speed.*

h) *Knock sensor – informs the ECU of pre-ignition (detonation) within the cylinders.*

i) *Camshaft sensor (Motronic MP7.3) – informs the ECU of which cylinder is on the firing stroke.*

j) *Accelerator pedal position sensor (Sagem S2000 and Motronic ME7.4.4) – informs the ECU of the pedal position and rate of change.*

k) *Accelerometer sensor (Motronic MP7.3) – informs the ECU of the quality of the road surface on which the vehicle is being driven. This ensures the ECU does not diagnose variations in engine speed due to an uneven road surface as an ignition misfire.*

Signals from each of the sensors are compared by the ECU and, based on this information, the ECU selects the response appropriate to those values, and controls the fuel injectors (varying the pulse width – the length of time the injectors are held open – to provide a richer or weaker air/fuel mixture, as appropriate). The air/fuel mixture is constantly varied by the ECU, to provide the best settings for cranking, starting (with either a hot or cold engine) and engine warm-up, idle, cruising and acceleration.

The ECU also has full control over the engine idle speed, via a stepper motor fitted to the throttle housing. The stepper motor either controls the amount of air passing through a bypass drilling at the side of the throttle or controls the position of the throttle valve itself, depending on model. On Sagem S2000 and Motronic ME7.4.4 systems, a sensor informs the ECU of the position, and rate of change, of the accelerator pedal. The ECU then controls the throttle valve by means of a throttle positioning motor integral with the throttle body. The ECU also carries out 'fine tuning' of the idle speed by varying the ignition timing to increase or reduce the torque of the engine as it is idling. This helps to stabilise the idle speed when electrical or mechanical loads (such as headlights, air conditioning, etc) are switched on and off.

The throttle housing may also fitted with an electric heating element. The heater is supplied with current by the ECU, warming the throttle housing on cold starts to help prevent icing of the throttle valve.

The exhaust and evaporative loss emission control systems are described in more detail in Chapter 4D.

If there is any abnormality in any of the readings obtained from the coolant temperature sensor, the inlet air temperature sensor or the lambda sensor, the ECU enters its 'back-up' mode. If this happens, the erroneous sensor signal is overridden, and the ECU assumes a pre-programmed 'back-up' value, which will allow the engine to continue running, albeit at reduced efficiency. If the ECU enters this mode, the warning lamp on the instrument panel will be illuminated, and the relevant fault code will be stored in the ECU memory.

If the warning light illuminates, the vehicle should be taken to a Peugeot/Citroën dealer or engine diagnostic specialist at the earliest opportunity. Once there, a complete test of the engine management system can be carried out, using a special electronic diagnostic test unit, which is plugged into the system's diagnostic connector located adjacent to the passenger's compartment fusebox.

7 Fuel system – depressurisation and pressurising

Note: *Refer to the warning note in Section 1 before proceeding.*

Depressurisation

 Warning: The following procedure will merely relieve the pressure in the fuel system – remember that fuel will still be present in the system components and take precautions accordingly before disconnecting any of them.

1 The fuel system referred to in this Section is defined as the tank-mounted fuel pump, the fuel filter, the fuel injectors, the fuel rail and the pipes of the fuel lines between these components. All

7.3 Fuel rail pressure relief valve (arrowed) – 1.6 litre model shown

these contain fuel which will be under pressure while the engine is running, and/or while the ignition is switched on. The pressure will remain for some time after the ignition has been switched off, and must be relieved in a controlled fashion when any of these components are disturbed for servicing work.

2 Disconnect the battery negative terminal (refer to *Disconnecting the battery* in the Reference Chapter).

3 Some models are equipped with a pressure relief valve on the fuel rail **(see illustration)**. On these models, unscrew the cap from the valve and position a container beneath the valve. Hold a wad of rag over the valve and relieve the pressure in the system by depressing the valve core with a suitable screwdriver. Be prepared for the squirt of fuel as the valve core is depressed and catch it with the rag. Hold the valve core down until no more fuel is expelled from the valve. Once the pressure is relieved, securely refit the valve cap.

4 Where no valve is fitted to the fuel rail, it will be necessary to release the pressure as a fuel pipe is disconnected. Place a container beneath the union and position a large rag around the union to catch any fuel spray which may be expelled. Slowly release and disconnect the fuel pipe and catch any spilt fuel in the container. Plug the pipe/union to minimise fuel loss and prevent the entry of dirt into the fuel system.

Pressurising

5 After any work is carried out on the fuel system, the system should be pressurised as follows.

6 Depress the accelerator pedal fully then switch on the ignition. Hold the pedal depressed for approximately 1 second then release it. The ECU should then operate the fuel pump for between 20 and 30 seconds to refill the fuel system. Once the fuel pump stops the ignition can be switched off.

8 Fuel pump – removal and refitting

Removal

1 Remove the fuel tank as described in Section 10.

2 Depress the retaining tabs on the quick-release fitting(s) and disconnect the fuel pipe(s) from the top of the pump. Plug the pipe end(s) to prevent the entry of dirt.

3 Check to see if alignment marks are present on the tank, pump cover and the locking ring. If no marks are visible, make your own marks using quick-drying paint such as correction fluid.

4 Unscrew the locking ring and remove it from the tank. This is best accomplished by using a screwdriver on the raised ribs of the locking ring. Carefully tap the screwdriver to turn the ring anti-clockwise until it can be unscrewed by hand. Alternatively, a Peugeot/Citroën special tool is available which fits over the collar and allows it to be released using a ratchet and extension.

5 Carefully lift the fuel pump assembly out of the fuel tank, taking great care not to damage the fuel gauge sender unit float arm. Recover the rubber sealing ring and discard it – a new one must be used on refitting.

6 Note that the fuel pump is only available as a complete assembly – no components are available separately.

Refitting

7 Fit the new sealing ring to the top of the fuel tank.

8 Carefully manoeuvre the pump assembly into the fuel tank, taking care not to damage the float arm.

9 Position the pump so that the marks on the pump and tank, or made prior to removal are aligned. On some pump types, a notch in the pump body engages with a cut-out in the tank to ensure correct alignment.

10 Refit the locking ring and tighten it securely until its alignment mark aligns with the mark on the pump.

11 Reconnect the fuel pipe(s) to the pump, then refit the fuel tank as described in Section 10.

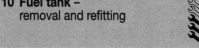

9 Fuel gauge sender unit – removal and refitting

The fuel gauge sender unit is an integral part of the fuel pump assembly and is not available separately. Refer to Section 8 for removal and refitting details.

10 Fuel tank – removal and refitting

Note: *Refer to the warning note in Section 1 before proceeding.*

Removal

1 Before removing the fuel tank, all fuel must be drained from the tank. Since a fuel tank drain plug is not provided, it is therefore preferable to carry out the removal operation when the tank is nearly empty. Before proceeding, disconnect the battery negative terminal (refer to *Disconnecting the battery* in the Reference Chapter), and syphon or hand-pump the remaining fuel from the tank.

2 Chock the front wheels then jack up the rear of the car and securely support it on axle stands (see *Jacking and vehicle support*).

3 Remove the exhaust system heat shield from the base of the fuel tank as described in Section 16.

4 Working at the right-hand side of the fuel tank, release the retaining clips then disconnect the filler neck vent pipe and main filler neck hose from the fuel tank. Similarly, disconnect the breather and vent hoses at their connections on the right-hand side of the tank.

5 Disconnect the accessible fuel feed and, where applicable, return hoses at the quick-release fittings on the fuel filter and on the hoses themselves. Bear in mind the information given in Section 7 on depressurising the fuel system when disconnecting the fuel pipes. Plug the pipe ends to minimise fuel loss and prevent the entry of dirt.

6 Disconnect the fuel pump wiring at the connector adjacent to the fuel filter.

7 Release the two handbrake cables from their guides on the underside of the fuel tank.

8 Place a trolley jack with an interposed block of wood beneath the tank, then raise the jack until it is supporting the weight of the tank.

9 Slacken and remove the two retaining bolts, then remove the support brace from the underside of the tank.

10 Undo and remove the two additional retaining bolts, one on each side of the tank.

11 Slowly lower the fuel tank from its location, until there is sufficient clearance available to disconnect the remaining fuel and vent pipes from the tank.

12 Position the right-hand handbrake cable over the top of the tank, lower the jack slightly and withdraw the tank from the right-hand side of the vehicle.

13 If the tank is contaminated with sediment or water, remove the fuel pump as described in Section 8, and swill the tank out with clean fuel. The tank is injection-moulded from a synthetic material – if seriously damaged, it should be renewed. However, in certain cases, it may be possible to have small leaks or minor damage repaired. Seek the advice of a specialist before attempting to repair the fuel tank.

Refitting

14 Refitting is the reverse of the removal procedure, noting the following points:

a) *When manoeuvering the tank back into position, take care to ensure that none of the hoses become trapped between the tank and vehicle body.*

b) *Ensure all pipes and hoses are correctly routed, and securely held in position with their retaining clips.*

c) *On completion, refill the tank with a small amount of fuel, and check for signs of leakage prior to taking the vehicle out on the road.*

11 Engine management system – testing and adjustment

Testing

1 If a fault appears in the engine management system, first ensure that all the system wiring connectors are securely connected and free of corrosion. Ensure that the fault is not due to poor maintenance; ie, check that the air cleaner filter element is clean, the spark plugs are in good condition and correctly gapped, the cylinder compression pressures are correct and that the engine breather hoses are clear and undamaged, referring to Chapters 1A, 2A and 5B for further information.

2 If these checks fail to reveal the cause of the problem, the vehicle should be taken to a suitably-equipped Peugeot/Citroën dealer or engine management diagnostic specialist for testing. A diagnostic socket is located adjacent to the passenger's compartment fusebox, to which a fault code reader or other suitable test equipment can be connected **(see illustration)**. By using the code reader or test equipment, the engine management ECU (and the various other vehicle system ECUs) can be interrogated, and any stored fault codes can be retrieved. This will allow the fault to be quickly and simply traced, alleviating the need to test all the system components individually, which is a time-consuming operation that carries a risk of damaging the ECU.

Adjustment

3 Whilst it is possible to check the exhaust CO level and the idle speed, if these are found to be in need of adjustment, the car *must* be taken to a suitably-equipped dealer or specialist or further testing. Neither the mixture adjustment (exhaust gas CO level) nor the idle speed are adjustable, and should either be incorrect, a fault must be present in the engine management system.

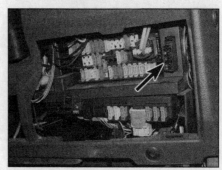

11.2 The diagnostic socket (arrowed) is located adjacent to the passenger's compartment fusebox

12 Throttle housing – removal and refitting

Removal

1 Remove the air cleaner assembly as described in Section 2.

2 Free the accelerator inner cable from the throttle cam (where applicable).

3 Note their fitted positions, then depress the retaining clip and disconnect the wiring connectors from the throttle housing **(see illustration)**.

4 Slacken and remove the retaining screws and remove the throttle housing from the inlet manifold **(see illustrations)**. Recover the sealing ring from manifold and discard it; a new one must be used on refitting.

Refitting

5 Refitting is a reversal of the removal procedure, noting the following points:

   a)   Fit a new sealing ring to the manifold, then refit the throttle housing and securely tighten its retaining screws (see illustration).

   b)   Ensure all wiring is correctly routed, and that the connectors are securely reconnected.

   c)   On completion, adjust the accelerator cable (where applicable) as described in Section 3.

13 Engine management system components – removal and refitting

Fuel rail and injectors

Note: *Refer to the warning note in Section 1 before proceeding.*

Note: *If a faulty injector is suspected, before condemning the injector, it is worth trying the effect of one of the proprietary injector-cleaning treatments which are available from car accessory shops.*

1.4 litre models

1 Disconnect the battery negative terminal

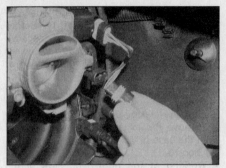

12.3 Disconnect the wiring connectors from all the throttle housing components – 1.4 litre model shown

12.4b . . . then remove the throttle housing from the manifold and recover the sealing ring – 1.4 litre model shown

(refer to *Disconnecting the battery* in the Reference Chapter).

2 Remove the air cleaner assembly as described in Section 2.

3 On later models with the ignition HT coil module mounted above the fuel rail, remove the coil module as described in Chapter 5B.

4 Free the accelerator inner cable (where applicable) from the throttle housing cam, then pull the outer cable out from its mounting bracket rubber grommet, complete with its spring clip.

5 Undo the screws and remove the accelerator cable bracket from the manifold/cylinder head **(see illustration)**.

6 On early models, disconnect the vacuum pipe from the fuel pressure regulator.

7 Bearing in mind the information given in

12.4a Undo the three retaining screws (arrowed) . . .

12.5 On refitting ensure the new sealing ring is correctly fitted to the manifold-- 1.4 litre model shown

Section 7, disconnect the fuel feed and, on early models, the return hoses by slackening the retaining clips or disconnecting the quick-release fittings **(see illustration)**.

8 Slacken and remove the two bolts securing the fuel rail to the cylinder head, and the nut securing the rail to the manifold. Loosen the bolt securing the fuel rail centre bracket to the inlet manifold, then lift off the bracket (the bracket is slotted to ease removal) **(see illustrations)**.

9 Disconnect the injector wiring harness connector then unclip the connector from the rear of the inlet manifold. Also disconnect the wiring connectors from the throttle housing and position the wiring harness clear of the manifold so that it does not hinder fuel rail removal.

13.5 Undo the retaining screws (arrowed) and remove the accelerator cable bracket – 1.4 litre models

13.7 Depress the retaining clip (arrowed) and disconnect the fuel hose from the fuel rail – 1.4 litre models

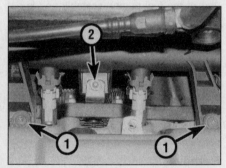

13.8a Unscrew the fuel rail mounting bolts (1) and the nut (2) . . .

Fuel and exhaust systems – petrol models 4A•7

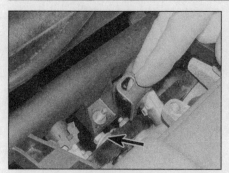

13.8b . . . then loosen the bolt (arrowed) and lift off the centre bracket

13.10 Remove the seal from the end of each injector – 1.4 litre models

13.11a Disconnect the wiring connector . . .

10 Carefully ease the fuel rail and injector assembly out from the cylinder head and manoeuvre it out of position. Remove the seals from the end of each injector and discard them; they must be renewed whenever they are disturbed **(see illustration)**.

11 Disconnect the wiring connector(s) then slide out the retaining clip(s) and remove the relevant injector(s) from the fuel rail. Remove the upper seal from each disturbed injector and discard; all disturbed seals must be renewed **(see illustrations)**.

12 Refitting is a reversal of the removal procedure, noting the following points.
a) *Fit new seals to all disturbed injector unions* **(see illustration)**.
b) *Apply a smear of engine oil to the seals to aid installation, then ease the injectors and fuel rail into position ensuring that none of the seals are displaced.*
c) *On completion, reconnect the battery and pressurise the fuel system as described in Section 7. Start the engine and check for fuel leaks.*

1.6 litre models

13 Remove the inlet manifold as described in Section 14.

14 Undo the two bolts and remove the fuel rail with injectors from the manifold **(see illustration)**.

15 Disconnect the wiring connector(s) then slide out the retaining clip(s) and remove the relevant injector(s) from the fuel rail **(see illustration)**. Remove the seals from each

disturbed injector and discard; all disturbed seals must be renewed.

16 Refitting is a reversal of the removal procedure, noting the following points.
a) *Fit new seals to all disturbed injector unions* **(see illustration)**.
b) *Apply a smear of engine oil to the seals to aid installation, then ease the injectors and fuel rail into position ensuring that none of the seals are displaced.*
c) *On completion, reconnect the battery and pressurise the fuel system as described in Section 7. Start the engine and check for fuel leaks.*

Fuel pressure regulator

Note 1: *The following procedure applies to models with the fuel pressure regulator mounted on the fuel rail. On later models, the*

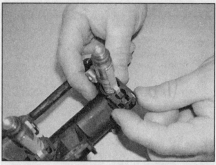

13.11b . . . then slide off the retaining clip and remove the injector from the fuel rail – 1.4 litre models

regulator is mounted on the top of the fuel tank, or is integral with the fuel pump. Access to the tank mounted regulator can be gained with the fuel tank removed (see Section 10). Regulators integral with the fuel pump are not available separately.

Note 2: *Refer to the warning note in Section 1 before proceeding.*

17 Disconnect the battery negative terminal (refer to *Disconnecting the battery* in the Reference Chapter).

18 Disconnect the vacuum pipe from the regulator. Note that on early engines, access to the regulator is poor with the fuel rail in position, if necessary, remove the fuel rail as described earlier, then remove the regulator.

19 Bearing in mind the information given in Section 7, place a wad of rag over the regulator, to catch any fuel spray which may

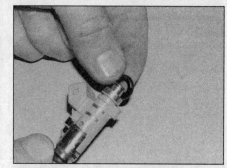

13.12 Renew all injector seals disturbed on removal – 1.4 litre models

13.14 Undo the two bolts (arrowed) and remove the fuel rail from the manifold – 1.6 litre models

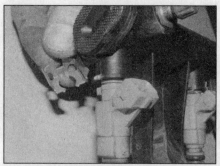

13.15 Slide out the retaining clip(s) and remove the relevant injector(s) from the fuel rail – 1.6 litre models

13.16 Renew all injector seals (arrowed) disturbed on removal – 1.6 litre models

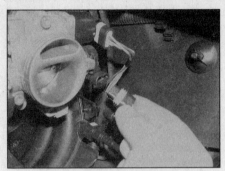

13.22 Disconnect the wiring connector from the throttle potentiometer . . .

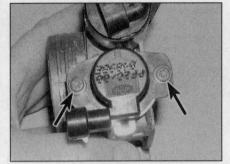

13.23 . . . then undo the retaining screws (arrowed) and remove it from the throttle housing – 1.4 litre models

13.27 Lift the locking catches and disconnect the ECU wiring connectors – early models

be released, then remove the retaining clip and ease the regulator out from the fuel rail.

20 Refitting is a reversal of the removal procedure. Examine the regulator seal for signs of damage or deterioration and renew if necessary.

Throttle potentiometer

Note: On 1.4 litre models with the Sagem S2000 system, and all 1.6 litre models, the throttle potentiometer is an integral part of the throttle housing and cannot be removed.

21 Disconnect the battery negative terminal (refer to *Disconnecting the battery* in the Reference Chapter).

22 Depress the retaining clip and disconnect the wiring connector from the throttle potentiometer **(see illustration)**.

23 Slacken and remove the two retaining screws, then disengage the potentiometer from the throttle valve spindle and remove it from the vehicle **(see illustration)**.

24 Refitting is a reversal of the removal procedure, ensuring that the potentiometer is correctly engaged with the throttle valve spindle.

Electronic Control Unit (ECU)

Note: If a new ECU is to be fitted, this work must be entrusted to a Peugeot/Citroën dealer. It is necessary to initialise the new ECU after installation which requires the use of specialist diagnostic equipment.

Pre-September 2002 models

25 The ECU is located in the plastic box

which forms part of the rear of the battery tray. On some engines, access to the ECU retaining nuts/bolts is poor and it is beneficial to remove the battery mounting tray as described in Chapter 5A, then remove the ECU with the tray on the bench.

26 Disconnect the battery negative terminal (refer to *Disconnecting the battery* in the Reference Chapter).

27 Where fitted, lift up the cover over the ECU, then lift the locking catches and disconnect the ECU wiring connectors **(see illustration)**.

28 Undo the retaining nuts or bolts and lift the ECU mounting plate from the battery tray.

29 Undo the retaining nuts or bolts and separate the ECU from the mounting plate.

30 Refitting is a reverse of the removal procedure ensuring the wiring connectors are securely reconnected.

Post-September 2002 models

31 The ECU is located at the rear left-hand corner of the engine compartment, above the suspension strut upper mounting.

32 Disconnect the battery negative terminal (refer to *Disconnecting the battery* in the Reference Chapter).

33 Undo the retaining nuts and lift off the ECU cover, where fitted **(see illustrations)**.

34 Lift the ECU up and off the mounting bracket, then lift the locking catches and disconnect the wiring connectors **(see illustration)**.

35 If required, the mounting bracket can be removed after undoing the three retaining nuts **(see illustration)**.

36 Refitting is a reverse of the removal procedure ensuring the wiring connectors are securely reconnected.

Idle speed stepper motor

Note: On 1.4 litre models with the Sagem S2000 system, and all 1.6 litre models, the stepper motor is an integral part of the throttle housing and cannot be removed.

37 The idle speed stepper motor is fitted to the rear of the throttle housing.

38 Disconnect the battery negative terminal (refer to *Disconnecting the battery* in the Reference Chapter), then disconnect the

13.33a Undo the retaining nuts (arrowed) . . .

13.33b . . . and lift off the ECU cover – later models

13.34 Lift the ECU off the mounting bracket, then disconnect the wiring connectors – later models

13.35 ECU mounting bracket retaining bolts (arrowed) – later models

13.38 Disconnect the wiring connector from the idle speed stepper motor (arrowed) . . .

13.39 . . . then undo the retaining screws (arrowed) and remove the motor from the throttle housing – 1.4 litre models

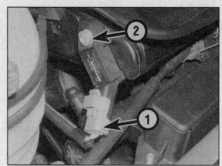

13.43 Disconnect the manifold pressure sensor wiring connector (1), then undo the retaining screw (2) – 1.4 litre model shown

wiring connector from the motor **(see illustration)**.

39 Slacken and remove the retaining screws then remove the motor from the throttle housing **(see illustration)**. If necessary, remove the throttle potentiometer to improve access to the motor lower screw.

40 Refitting is a reversal of the removal procedure ensuring the seal is in good condition.

Manifold pressure sensor

41 The manifold pressure sensor is mounted on the front of the inlet manifold.

42 Disconnect the battery negative terminal (refer to *Disconnecting the battery* in the Reference Chapter).

43 Disconnect the wiring connector then undo the screw and remove the sensor from the manifold **(see illustration)**.

44 Refitting is a reversal of the removal procedure ensuring the sensor seal is in good condition.

Coolant temperature sensor

45 The coolant temperature sensor is screwed into the coolant outlet housing on the left-hand end of the cylinder head. Refer to Chapter 3 for removal and refitting details.

Inlet air temperature sensor

Note: *On 1.4 litre models with the Sagem S2000 system, and all 1.6 litre models, the*

TOOL TIP

The inlet air temperature sensor clips can be released by passing a close-fitting ring spanner over the end of the sensor.

13.47 Disconnect the wiring connector . . .

inlet air temperature sensor is an integral part of the throttle housing and cannot be removed.

46 The inlet air temperature sensor is fitted to the base of the throttle housing. On early models, the sensor is threaded into the underside of the throttle housing, whereas on later models it is clipped in position.

47 Disconnect the battery negative terminal (refer to *Disconnecting the battery* in the Reference Chapter), then disconnect the wiring connector from the sensor **(see illustration)**.

48 Unscrew the sensor, or release the retaining clips **(see Tool Tip)** and ease the sensor out from the throttle housing **(see illustration)**.

49 Refitting is a reversal of the removal procedure ensuring the sensor seal is in good condition.

13.52a Disconnect the wiring connector and undo the retaining screw (arrowed) . . .

13.48 . . . then unclip the inlet air temperature sensor from the throttle housing – 1.4 litre models

Crankshaft sensor

50 The crankshaft sensor is situated on the front face of the transmission clutch housing.

51 Disconnect the battery negative terminal (refer to *Disconnecting the battery* in the Reference Chapter).

52 Disconnect the sensor wiring connector and unclip the wiring. Undo the retaining bolt and remove the sensor and bracket assembly from the transmission unit **(see illustrations)**.

53 Refitting is a reversal of the removal procedure.

Throttle housing heating element

Note: *The heating element is only fitted to aluminium throttle housings. Plastic housings do not need a heater.*

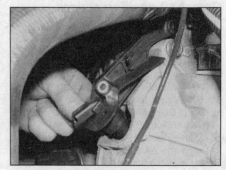

13.52b . . . then remove the crankshaft sensor from the front of the transmission clutch housing

13.56a Disconnect the wiring connector then undo the retaining screw (arrowed) . . .

13.56b . . . and remove the heating element from the throttle housing – 1.4 litre models

13.72 Accelerator pedal position sensor location (arrowed)

54 The heating element is fitted to the top of the throttle housing.
55 Disconnect the battery negative terminal (refer to *Disconnecting the battery* in the Reference Chapter).
56 Disconnect the wiring connector then unscrew the retaining screw and remove the heating element from the throttle housing **(see illustrations)**.
57 Refitting is a reversal of the removal procedure.

Vehicle speed sensor

58 The vehicle speed sensor is an integral part of the speedometer drive. Refer to Chapter 7 for removal and refitting details.

Knock sensor

59 The knock sensor is screwed onto the rear of the cylinder block. Refer to Chapter 5B for removal and refitting details.

Fuel cut-off inertia switch

60 The fuel cut-off inertia switch is located in the right-hand rear corner of the engine compartment.
61 Disconnect the battery negative terminal (refer to *Disconnecting the battery* in the Reference Chapter).
62 Cut the retaining clip (where fitted) then unscrew the retaining nuts and remove the switch from the vehicle, disconnecting it from the wiring connector.
63 Refitting is a reversal of the removal procedure. On completion, reset the switch by firmly depressing its button.

Camshaft position sensor

Note: *The camshaft position sensor is only fitted to 1.4 litre models with Motronic MP7.3 systems.*
64 The camshaft position sensor is fitted to the rear of the coolant outlet housing on the left-hand end of the cylinder head.
65 Disconnect the battery negative terminal (refer to *Disconnecting the battery* in the Reference Chapter).
66 Disconnect the wiring connector then unscrew the retaining bolt and remove the sensor from the housing.
67 Refitting is a reversal of the removal procedure, ensuring the sensor seal is in good condition.

Body accelerometer

Note: *The camshaft position sensor is only fitted to 1.4 litre models with Motronic MP7.3 systems.*
68 The body accelerometer is located in the engine compartment. To remove it, first disconnect the battery negative terminal (refer to *Disconnecting the battery* in the Reference Chapter).
69 Disconnect the wiring connector then unscrew the mounting bolt and remove the sensor from the vehicle.
70 Refitting is a reversal of the removal procedure.

Throttle valve positioner motor

71 The throttle valve positioner motor is fitted to 1.4 litre models with the Sagem S2000 system, and all 1.6 litre models. The unit is integral with the throttle housing, and is not available separately.

Accelerator pedal position sensor

Note: *The accelerator pedal position sensor is fitted to 1.4 litre models with the Sagem S2000 system, and all 1.6 litre models.*
72 The accelerator pedal position sensor is located above the right-hand engine/trans-mission mounting **(see illustration)**.
73 Disconnect the battery negative terminal (refer to *Disconnecting the battery* in the Reference Chapter), then disconnect the wiring connector from the pedal position sensor.
74 Free the accelerator inner cable from the accelerator pedal position sensor cam, then pull the outer cable out from its mounting

bracket rubber grommet. Recover the spring clip from the outer cable.
75 Undo the two mounting bracket retaining bolts and withdraw the pedal position sensor and mounting bracket from the engine compartment.
76 Undo the two nuts and bolts securing the sensor to the mounting bracket and separate the two components.
77 Refitting is a reversal of the removal procedure. On completion, adjust the accelerator cable as described in Section 3.

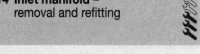

14 Inlet manifold –
removal and refitting

Removal

1.4 litre models

1 Remove the air cleaner assembly as described in Section 2.
2 Remove the fuel rail and injectors as described in Section 13.
3 If not already done, disconnect the wiring connectors from the throttle housing components then unclip the harness and position it clear of the manifold

1.6 litre models

4 Remove the throttle housing as described in Section 12.

All models

5 Release the retaining clips and disconnect the vacuum servo unit pipe and purge valve pipe from the inlet manifold **(see illustrations)**.

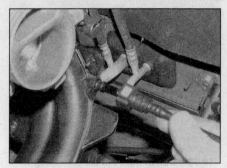

14.5a Disconnect the braking system servo vacuum pipe . . .

14.5b . . . and the purge valve pipe from the inlet manifold – 1.4 litre models shown

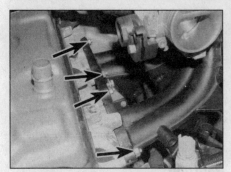

14.9 Inlet manifold upper nuts arrowed – 1.4 litre models shown

14.10 Ensure the new sealing rings are correctly fitted to the manifold prior to refitting

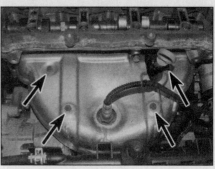

15.4 Slacken and remove the retaining bolts (arrowed) and remove the shroud from the top of the exhaust manifold

6 Disconnect all wiring connectors from the manifold, having first noted their fitted positions. Release the wiring from any retaining clips.

7 Depress the release button and disconnect the fuel pipe and position it clear of the manifold.

8 Where necessary, undo the retaining bolts and remove the support bracket from the underside of the manifold.

9 Undo the manifold retaining nuts and withdraw the manifold from the engine compartment **(see illustration)**. Recover the four manifold seals and discard them; new ones must be used on refitting.

Refitting

10 Refitting is a reverse of the relevant removal procedure, noting the following points:

a) *Ensure that the manifold and cylinder head mating surfaces are clean and dry, then locate the new seals in their recesses in the manifold **(see illustration)**. Refit the manifold and tighten its retaining nuts to the specified torque.*

b) *Ensure that all relevant hoses are reconnected to their original positions and are securely held (where necessary) by the retaining clips.*

c) *Ensure the wiring is correctly routed and all connectors are securely reconnected.*

d) *Adjust the accelerator cable (where applicable) as described in Section 3.*

---

15 Exhaust manifold – removal and refitting

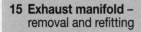

Removal

1 On 1.4 litre models with secondary air injection, remove the secondary air injection valve as described in Part D of this Chapter.

2 Firmly apply the handbrake, then jack up the front of the vehicle and support it on axle stands (see *Jacking and vehicle support*).

3 Trace the lambda (oxygen) sensor(s) wiring back to the connectors and disconnect them.

4 Slacken and remove the retaining bolts and remove the shroud from the top of the exhaust manifold **(see illustration)**. It may be necessary

to remove the engine lifting eye bracket from the left-hand end of the cylinder head, and undo the bolt and remove the oil dipstick tube. Feed the lambda sensor wiring through the hole in the top of the shroud as it is removed.

5 On some models, a second heat shield is fitted on the underside of the manifold, above the oil filter. Undo the bolts and remove the heat shield.

6 Undo the nuts securing the exhaust front pipe/catalytic converter to the manifold, then remove the bolt securing the front pipe to its mounting bracket. Disconnect the front pipe from the manifold, and recover the gasket.

7 Undo the retaining nuts securing the manifold to the cylinder head. Manoeuvre the manifold out of the engine compartment, and discard the manifold gasket(s).

Refitting

8 Refitting is the reverse of the removal procedure, noting the following points:

a) *Examine all the exhaust manifold studs for signs of damage and corrosion; remove all traces of corrosion, and repair or renew any damaged studs.*

b) *Ensure that the manifold and cylinder head sealing faces are clean and flat, and fit the new manifold gasket(s). Tighten the manifold retaining nuts to the specified torque.*

c) *Reconnect the front pipe to the manifold using the information given in Section 16.*

d) *Where necessary, renew the oil dipstick tube O-ring.*

---

16 Exhaust system – general information, removal and refitting

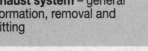

General information

1 On early models, the exhaust system consists of four sections; the front pipe, the catalytic converter, the intermediate pipe and centre silencer, and the tailpipe with rear silencer. All exhaust sections are joined by a flanged joint. The front pipe joints are secured by nuts and bolts, the catalytic converter joint being of the spring-loaded ball type, to allow for movement in the exhaust system. The

catalytic converter-to-intermediate pipe joint and the intermediate pipe-to-silencer joint are secured by a clamping ring.

2 On later models, the exhaust system consists of three sections; the front pipe with integral catalytic converter, the intermediate pipe and centre silencer, and the tailpipe with rear silencer. The front pipe and intermediate pipe sections are joined by flanged joints. All other joints are secured by clamping rings.

3 The system is suspended throughout its entire length by rubber mountings.

Removal

4 Each exhaust section can be removed individually or, alternatively, the complete system can be removed as a unit. Even if only one part of the system needs attention, it is often easier to remove the whole system and separate the sections on the bench.

5 To remove the system or part of the system, first jack up the front or rear of the car and support it on axle stands (see *Jacking and vehicle support*). Alternatively, position the car over an inspection pit or on car ramps.

Front pipe

Note: *On later models, the catalytic converter is integral with the front pipe.*

6 Trace the wiring back from the lambda sensor to its wiring connectors, which are clipped to the transmission housing, and disconnect them from the main harness.

7 Undo the nuts securing the front pipe flange joint to the manifold, and the single bolt securing the front pipe to its mounting bracket **(see illustration)**. Separate the flange joint and collect the gasket.

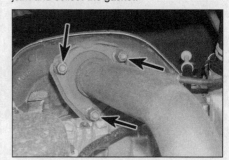

16.7 Front pipe-to-manifold nuts (arrowed) – early models

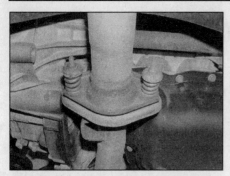

16.12 Front pipe-to-intermediate pipe spring-loaded joint – later models

16.13 Slacken and remove the nut, washer and bolt, then free the clamping ring from the flange joint

8 Slacken and remove the two nuts securing the front pipe flange joint to the catalytic converter or intermediate pipe, and recover the spring cups and springs. Remove the bolts, then withdraw the front pipe from underneath the vehicle, and recover the wire-mesh gasket.

Catalytic converter (early models)

Note: *On later models, the catalytic converter is integral with the front pipe.*

9 Undo the two nuts securing the front pipe flange joint to the catalytic converter. Recover the springs and spring cups, and withdraw the bolts.
10 Slacken the catalytic converter clamping ring bolts and disengage the clamp from the flange joint.
11 Free the converter, then withdraw it from underneath the vehicle, and recover the wire-mesh gasket from the front pipe joint.

Intermediate pipe

12 On later models, slacken and remove the two nuts securing the front pipe flange joint to the intermediate pipe, and recover the spring cups and springs **(see illustration)**. Remove

the bolts, then withdraw the front pipe from underneath the vehicle, and recover the wire-mesh gasket.
13 Slacken the clamping ring bolts and disengage the clamp(s) from the flange joint(s) **(see illustration)**.
14 Unhook the intermediate pipe from its mounting rubber and remove it from underneath the vehicle.

Tailpipe

15 Slacken the tailpipe clamping ring bolts and disengage the clamp from the flange joint.
16 Unhook the tailpipe from its mounting rubbers and remove it from the vehicle.

Complete system

17 Disconnect the lambda sensor wiring connectors from the main wiring harness.
18 Undo the nuts securing the front pipe flange joint to the manifold, and the single bolt securing the front pipe to its mounting bracket. Separate the flange joint and collect the gasket. Free the system from all its mounting rubbers and lower it from under the vehicle.

Heat shield(s)

19 The heat shields are secured to the underside of the body by various nuts and bolts. Each shield can be removed once the relevant exhaust section has been removed. If a shield is being removed to gain access to a component located behind it, it may prove sufficient in some cases to remove the retaining nuts and/or bolts, and simply lower the shield, without disturbing the exhaust system.

Refitting

20 Each section is refitted by reversing the removal sequence, noting the following points:
a) *Ensure that all traces of corrosion have been removed from the flanges and renew all necessary gaskets.*
b) *Inspect the rubber mountings for signs of damage or deterioration, and renew as necessary.*
c) *Prior to assembling the spring-loaded joint, a smear of high-temperature grease should be applied to the joint mating surfaces.*
d) *Where joints are secured together by a clamping ring, apply a smear of exhaust system jointing paste to the flange joint, to ensure a gas-tight seal. Tighten the clamping ring nuts evenly and progressively, so that the clearance between the clamp halves remains equal on either side.*
e) *Prior to tightening the exhaust system fasteners, ensure that all rubber mountings are correctly located, and that there is adequate clearance between the exhaust system and vehicle underbody.*
f) *Ensure that the lambda sensor wiring is reconnected correctly and secured to the underbody by the relevant retaining clips.*

Chapter 4 Part B:
Fuel and exhaust systems –
1.8 and 1.9 litre (XUD series) diesel models

Contents

Degrees of difficulty

Easy, suitable for novice with little experience | **Fairly easy,** suitable for beginner with some experience | **Fairly difficult,** suitable for competent DIY mechanic | **Difficult,** suitable for experienced DIY mechanic | **Very difficult,** suitable for expert DIY or professional

Specifications

General
System type .... Rear-mounted fuel tank, distributor fuel injection pump with integral transfer pump, indirect injection.
Firing order .... 1–3–4–2 (No 1 at flywheel end)

Injection pump
Type .... Bosch or Lucas
Direction of rotation .... Clockwise, viewed from sprocket end
Pump timing*:
  Lucas pump – engine code A9A (XUD7L), D9B (XUD9A) and DJY (XUD9Y):
    Static timing:
      Engine position .... No 4 piston at TDC
      Pump position...................................... Value shown on pump – see text
  Bosch pump – engine code DJY (XUD9Y):
    Static timing:
      Engine position .... No 4 piston at TDC
      Pump timing measurement.......................... 0.66 ± 0.02 mm
Idle speed:
  Without air conditioning .... 800 +0 –50 rpm
  With air conditioning................................... 850 +0 –50 rpm
Anti-stall speed .... 1500 ± 100 rpm
Anti-stall shim thickness*:
  With Lucas pump .... 4.0 mm
  With Bosch pump...................................... 3.0 mm
Fast idle speed.. 950 ± 50 rpm
Maximum speed*:
  Engine codes A9A (XUD7L) and D9B (XUD9A) .... 5150 ± 125 rpm
  Engine code DJY (XUD9Y):
    With Lucas pump .... 5150 ± 125 rpm
    With Bosch pump.................................. 5100 ± 80 rpm

* Refer to Chapter 2B for further information on engine code identification

Injectors

Type . . . . Pintle
Opening pressure:
   With Lucas pump . . . . 140 bars
   With Bosch pump . . . . 130 bars

Torque wrench settings

	Nm	lbf ft
Fuel pipe union nuts	20	15
Injection pump mounting nuts/bolts	20	15
Injection pump sprocket nut	50	37
Injection pump sprocket puller bolts	10	7
Injection pump timing hole blanking plug:		
Lucas pump	6	4
Bosch pump	15	11
Injectors to cylinder head	90	66
No 4 cylinder TDC blanking plug	30	22

1 General information and precautions

General information

1 The fuel system consists of a rear-mounted fuel tank, a fuel filter with integral water separator, a fuel injection pump, injectors and associated components. Before passing through the filter, the fuel is heated by coolant flowing through the base of the fuel filter/ thermostat housing.

2 Fuel is drawn from the fuel tank to the fuel injection pump by a vane-type transfer pump incorporated in the fuel injection pump. Before reaching the pump, the fuel passes through a fuel filter, where foreign matter and water are removed. Excess fuel lubricates the moving components of the pump, and is then returned to the tank.

3 The fuel injection pump is driven at half-crankshaft speed by the timing belt. The high pressure required to inject the fuel into the compressed air in the swirl chambers is achieved by a cam plate acting on a single piston on the Bosch pump, or by two opposed pistons forced together by rollers running in a cam ring on the Lucas (CAV) pump. The fuel passes through a central rotor with a single outlet drilling which aligns with ports leading to the injector pipes.

4 Fuel metering is controlled by a centrifugal governor, which reacts to accelerator pedal position and engine speed. The governor is linked to a metering valve, which increases or decreases the amount of fuel delivered at each pumping stroke.

5 Basic injection timing is determined when the pump is fitted. When the engine is running, it is varied automatically to suit the prevailing engine speed by a mechanism which turns the cam plate or ring.

6 The four fuel injectors produce a homogeneous spray of fuel into the swirl chambers located in the cylinder head. The injectors are calibrated to open and close at critical pressures to provide efficient and even combustion. Each injector needle is lubricated by fuel, which accumulates in the spring chamber and is channelled to the injection pump return hose by leak-off pipes.

7 Bosch or Lucas fuel system components may be fitted, depending on the model. Components from the latter manufacturer are marked either 'CAV', 'Roto-Diesel' or 'Con-Diesel', depending on their date and place of manufacture. With the exception of the fuel filter assembly, new components must be of the same make as those originally fitted.

8 Cold starting is assisted by preheater or 'glow plugs' fitted to each swirl chamber. A thermostatic sensor in the cooling system operates a fast idle lever on the injection pump to increase the idling speed when the engine is cold.

9 A stop solenoid cuts the fuel supply to the injection pump rotor when the ignition is switched off, and there is also a hand-operated stop lever for use in an emergency **(see illustrations)**.

10 Provided that the specified maintenance is carried out, the fuel injection equipment will give long and trouble-free service. The injection pump itself may well outlast the engine. The main potential cause of damage to the injection pump and injectors is dirt or water in the fuel.

11 Servicing of the injection pump and injectors is very limited for the home mechanic, and any dismantling or adjustment other than that described in this Chapter must be entrusted to a Peugeot/Citroën dealer or fuel injection specialist.

Precautions

 Warning: It is necessary to take certain precautions when working on the fuel system components, particularly the fuel injectors. Before carrying out any operations on the fuel system, refer to the precautions given in 'Safety first!' at the beginning of this manual, and to any additional warning notes at the start of the relevant Sections.

2 Fuel system – priming and bleeding

1 After disconnecting part of the fuel supply system or running out of fuel, it is necessary to prime the system and bleed off any air which may have entered the system components.

2 All models are fitted with a hand-operated priming pump, consisting of a rubber bulb,

1.9a Hand-operated stop lever (arrowed) – Lucas pump

1.9b Hand-operated stop lever (arrowed) – Bosch pump

2.2 Hand-operated fuel system priming pump

3.5 Front air distribution housing securing bolt (arrowed)

3.6 Air distribution housing-to-inlet manifold bolts (arrowed)

which is located on the right-hand side of the engine compartment **(see illustration)**.

3 An automatic bleed valve is fitted to certain engines, which bleeds the air from the low pressure circuit when it is primed. On engines without an automatic bleed valve, a bleed screw is fitted to the injection pump fuel inlet pipe union bolt. Where a bleed screw is fitted, slacken the screw half a turn.

4 Pump the priming pump bulb until fuel free from air bubbles emerges from the bleed screw (where fitted), or until resistance is felt. Retighten the bleed screw.

5 Switch on the ignition (to activate the stop solenoid) and continue pumping the priming pump until firm resistance is felt, then pump a few more times.

6 If a large amount of air has entered the pump, place a wad of rag around the fuel return union on the pump (to absorb spilt fuel), then slacken the union. Operate the priming plunger (with the ignition switched on to activate the stop solenoid), or crank the engine on the starter motor in 10 second bursts, until fuel free from air bubbles emerges from the fuel union. Tighten the union and mop-up split fuel.

 Warning: Be prepared to stop the engine if it should fire, to avoid excessive fuel spray and spillage.

7 If air has entered the injector pipes, place wads of rag around the injector pipe unions at the injectors (to absorb spilt fuel), then slacken the unions. Crank the engine on the starter motor until fuel emerges from the unions, then stop cranking the engine and retighten the unions. Mop-up spilt fuel. *Refer to the warning given in the previous paragraph.*

8 Start the engine with the accelerator pedal fully depressed. Additional cranking may be necessary to finally bleed the system before the engine starts.

---

3   Air cleaner and associated components – removal and refitting

Removal

Air cleaner

1 Slacken the retaining clips securing the air cleaner-to-manifold duct in position and undo the duct mounting bolt. Disconnect the duct and remove it from the engine.

2 Slacken and remove the two bolts securing the air intake duct to the front body panel. Slacken the retaining clip then detach the duct from the side of the air cleaner and remove it from the vehicle.

3 Undo the bolt securing the base of the air cleaner housing to the support bracket. Lift up the housing, disengage the front locating pegs and remove it from the vehicle.

Air distribution housing – 1.9 litre models

4 Disconnect the air duct and the crankcase breather hose from the front of the air distribution housing.

5 Unscrew the two bolts securing the housing to the front mounting brackets **(see illustration)**. Recover the spacer plates.

6 Unscrew the four bolts securing the

housing to the inlet manifold. Recover the washers **(see illustration)**.

7 Lift the housing from the inlet manifold, and recover the seals.

Refitting

8 Refitting is the reverse of the relevant removal procedure. Examine the condition of the seals and renew if necessary.

---

4   Fast idle thermostatic sensor – removal, refitting and adjustment

Note: *A new sealing washer must be used when refitting the sensor.*

Removal

1 The thermostatic sensor is located in the side of the thermostat/fuel filter housing.

2 For improved access on 1.9 litre models, remove the air distribution housing as described in Section 3. If necessary, also remove the intake duct, and disconnect the breather hose from the engine oil filler tube. Refer to the relevant Sections of this Chapter for further information.

3 Drain the cooling system as described in Chapter 1B.

4 Loosen the clamp screw or nut (as applicable), and disconnect the fast idle cable end fitting from the inner cable at the fuel injection pump fast idle lever **(see illustrations)**. 5 Slide the cable from the adjustment screw located in the bracket on the fuel injection pump **(see illustration)**.

4.4a Fast idle cable end fitting clamp nut (arrowed) – Lucas pump

4.4b Loosening the fast idle cable end fitting clamp screw (arrowed) – Bosch pump

4.5 Sliding the fast idle cable from the adjustment screw – Bosch pump

4.6 Fast idle thermostatic sensor (arrowed)

5.9a Disconnecting the fuel pump fuel supply banjo union. Note sealing washers (arrowed) – Bosch pump

5.9b Refitting the fuel supply banjo bolt with a small section of fuel hose (arrowed) to prevent dirt entry – Bosch pump

6 Using a suitable open-ended spanner, unscrew the thermostatic sensor from the fuel filter/thermostat housing, and withdraw the sensor complete with the cable (see illustration). Recover the sealing washer, where applicable.

Refitting

7 If sealing compound was originally used to fit the sensor in place of a washer, thoroughly clean all traces of old sealing compound from the sensor and housing. Ensure that no traces of sealant are left in the internal coolant passages of the housing.
8 Fit the sensor, using suitable sealing compound or a new washer as applicable, and tighten it securely.
9 Insert the adjustment screw into the bracket on the fuel injection pump, and screw on the locknut finger-tight.
10 Insert the inner cable through the fast idle lever, and position the end fitting on the cable, but do not tighten the clamp screw or nut (as applicable).
11 Adjust the cable as described in the following paragraphs.

Adjustment

12 With the engine cold, push the fast idle lever fully towards the flywheel end of the engine. Tighten the clamp screw or nut with the cable end fitting touching the lever.
13 Adjust the screw to ensure that the fast idle lever is touching its stop, then tighten the locknut.
14 Measure the exposed length of the inner cable.
15 Refit the components removed for access to the sensor, with reference to the relevant Sections of this Chapter.
16 Refill the cooling system as described in Chapter 1B, and run the engine to its normal operating temperature.
17 Check that the fast idle cable is slack. If not, it is likely that the sensor is faulty.
18 With the engine hot, check that there is approximately 0.5 to 1 mm of free play in the cable on Lucas injection pumps and 5 to 6 mm of free play in the cable on Bosch injection pumps. This indicates that the thermostatic sensor is functioning correctly.

19 Check that the engine speed increases when the fast idle lever is pushed towards the flywheel end of the engine. With the lever against its stop, the fast idle speed should be as specified (see Section 9 for fast idle adjustment details).
20 Stop the engine.

5 Fuel injection pump – removal and refitting

Caution: Be careful not to allow dirt into the injection pump or injector pipes during this procedure. New sealing rings should be used on the fuel pipe banjo unions when refitting.

Removal

1 Disconnect the battery negative terminal (refer to *Disconnecting the battery* in the Reference Chapter).
2 Cover the alternator with a plastic bag, as a precaution against spillage of diesel fuel.
3 For improved access on 1.9 litre models remove the air distribution housing as described in Section 3. If necessary, also remove the intake duct, and disconnect the breather hose from the engine oil filler tube. Refer to the relevant Sections of this Chapter for further information.
4 Chock the rear wheels and release the handbrake. Jack up the front right-hand corner of the vehicle until the wheel is just clear of the ground. Support the vehicle on an

axle stand (see *Jacking and vehicle support*) and engage 4th or 5th gear. This will enable the engine to be turned easily by turning the right-hand wheel.
5 Remove the upper timing belt covers with reference to Chapter 2B.
6 Where necessary, disconnect the hoses from the vacuum converter on the end of the fuel injection pump.
7 Disconnect the accelerator cable from the fuel injection pump, with reference to Section 11.
8 Disconnect the fast idle cable from the fuel injection pump, with reference to Section 4.
9 Loosen the clip, or undo the banjo union, and disconnect the fuel supply hose. Recover the sealing washers from the banjo union, where applicable. Cover the open end of the hose, and refit and cover the banjo bolt to keep dirt out (see illustrations).
10 Disconnect the main fuel return pipe and the injector leak-off return pipe banjo union (see illustration). Recover the sealing washers from the banjo union. Again, cover the open end of the hose and the banjo bolt to keep dirt out. Take care not to get the inlet and outlet banjo unions mixed up.
11 Disconnect all relevant wiring from the pump. Note that on certain Bosch pumps, this can be achieved by simply disconnecting the wiring connectors at the brackets on the pump (see illustration). On some pumps, it will be necessary to disconnect the wiring from the individual components (some connections may be protected by rubber covers).

5.10 Injection pump fuel return pipe banjo union (arrowed) – Bosch pump

5.11 Disconnecting a fuel injection pump wiring plug – Bosch pump

5.12a **Unscrewing a fuel pipe-to-injector union**

5.12b **Cover the open end of the injector to prevent dirt entry**

5.12c **Unscrewing a fuel pipe-to-pump union – Bosch pump**

12 Unscrew the union nuts securing the injector pipes to the fuel injection pump and injectors. Counterhold the unions on the pump, while unscrewing the pipe-to-pump union nuts. Remove the pipes as a set. Cover open unions to keep dirt out, using small plastic bags, or fingers cut from discarded (but clean!) rubber gloves **(see illustrations)**.

13 Turn the crankshaft until the two bolt holes in the fuel injection pump sprocket are aligned with the corresponding holes in the engine front plate.

14 Insert two M8 bolts through the holes, and hand-tighten them. Note that the bolts must retain the sprocket while the fuel injection pump is removed, thereby making it unnecessary to remove the timing belt **(see illustration)**.

15 Mark the fuel injection pump in relation to the mounting bracket, using a scriber or felt tip pen **(see illustration)**. This will ensure the correct pump timing is retained when refitting.

16 Unscrew the three front mounting nuts, and recover the washers. Unscrew and remove the rear mounting nut and bolt, noting the locations of the washers, and support the injection pump on a block of wood **(see illustrations)**.

17 Release the injection pump sprocket from the pump shaft, as described in Chapter 2B. Note that the sprocket can be left engaged with the timing belt as the pump is withdrawn from its mounting bracket. Refit the M8 bolts to retain the sprocket in position while the pump is removed.

18 Carefully withdraw the pump. Recover the

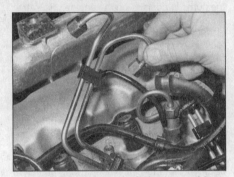

5.12d **Removing a fuel pipe assembly**

Woodruff key from the end of the pump shaft if it is loose, and similarly recover the bush from the rear of the mounting bracket.

Refitting

19 Commence refitting the injection pump by fitting the Woodruff key to the shaft groove (if removed).

20 Offer the pump to the mounting bracket, and support on a block of wood, as during removal.

21 Engage the pump shaft with the sprocket, and refit the sprocket as described in Chapter 2B. Ensure that the Woodruff key does not fall out of the shaft as the sprocket is engaged.

22 Align the marks made on the pump and mounting bracket before removal. If a new pump is being fitted, transfer the mark from the old pump to give an approximate setting.

23 Refit and lightly tighten the pump mounting nuts and bolt.

5.14 **Bolts inserted through timing holes in injection pump sprocket**

24 Set up the injection timing, as described in Sections 6, 7 and 8 (as applicable).

25 Refit and reconnect the injector fuel pipes.

26 Reconnect all relevant wiring to the pump.

27 Reconnect the fuel supply and return hoses, and tighten the unions, as applicable. Use new sealing washers on the banjo unions.

28 Reconnect the fast idle cable, and adjust it as described in Section 4.

29 Reconnect and adjust the accelerator cable with reference to Section 11.

30 Where necessary, reconnect the hoses to the vacuum converter.

31 Refit the upper timing belt covers.

32 Lower the vehicle to the ground.

33 Where applicable, refit the air distribution housing, intake duct, and breather hose

34 Remove the plastic bag used to cover the alternator.

35 Reconnect the battery negative terminal.

5.15 **Mark the injection pump in relation to the mounting bracket (arrowed)**

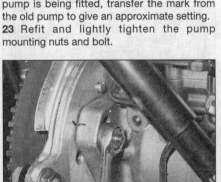

5.16a **Unscrewing an injection pump front mounting nut – Bosch pump**

5.16b **Unscrewing an injection pump rear mounting nut (arrowed) – Bosch pump**

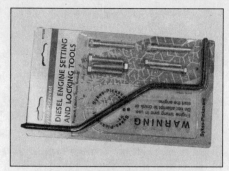

6.3 TDC setting and locking tools for setting injection timing

36 Bleed the fuel system as described in Section 2.

37 Start the engine, and check the fuel injection pump adjustments as described in Section 9.

6 Injection timing – checking methods and adjustment

1 Checking the injection timing is not a routine operation. It is only necessary after the injection pump has been disturbed.

2 Dynamic timing equipment does exist, but it is unlikely to be available to the home mechanic. The equipment works by converting pressure pulses in an injector pipe into electrical signals. If such equipment is available, use it in accordance with its maker's instructions.

3 Static timing as described in this Chapter gives good results if carried out carefully. A dial test indicator will be needed, with probes and adaptors appropriate to the type of injection pump (see illustration). Read through the procedures before starting work, to find out what is involved.

7 Injection timing (Lucas fuel injection pump) – checking and adjustment

Caution: Do not attempt the timing procedure unless accurate instrumentation is available. Suitable special tools

for carrying out pump timing should be available from larger motor factors or your Peugeot/Citroën dealer. Refer to the precautions given in Section 1 of this Chapter before proceeding.

Note: *To check the injection pump timing a dial gauge (Peugeot/Citroën tool No 2437-T) together with a special timing probe and mounting bracket (Peugeot/Citroën tool No 4093-TJ) is required (see illustration 7.4). Without access to this equipment (or suitable alternatives), injection pump timing should be entrusted to a Peugeot/Citroën dealer or other suitably-equipped specialist.*

1 If the injection timing is being checked with the pump in position on the engine unit, rather than as part of the pump refitting procedure, disconnect the battery negative terminal (refer to *Disconnecting the battery* in the Reference Chapter), and cover the alternator with a clean cloth or plastic bag to prevent the possibility of fuel being spilt onto it. Remove the injector pipes as described in paragraph 12 of Section 5.

2 Referring to Chapter 2B, align the engine assembly/valve timing holes to lock the crankshaft in position. Remove the crankshaft locking tool, then turn the crankshaft **backwards** (anti-clockwise) approximately a quarter of a turn.

3 Unscrew the access plug from the guide on the top of the pump body and recover the sealing washer (see illustration). Insert the special timing probe into the guide, making sure it is correctly seated against the guide sealing washer surface.

Note: *The timing probe must be seated against the guide sealing washer surface and not the upper lip of the guide for the measurement to be accurate.*

4 Mount the bracket on the pump guide and securely mount the dial gauge (dial test indicator) in the bracket so that its tip is in contact with the bracket linkage (see illustration). Position the dial gauge so that

its plunger is at the mid-point of its travel and zero the gauge.

5 Rotate the crankshaft slowly in the correct direction of rotation (clockwise) until the crankshaft locking tool can be re-inserted.

6 With the crankshaft locked in position read the dial gauge; the reading should correspond to the value marked on the pump (there is a tolerance of ± 0.04 mm). The timing value may be marked on a plastic disc attached to the front of the pump, or alternatively on a tag attached to the pump control lever (see illustration).

7 If adjustment is necessary, slacken the front pump mounting nuts and the rear mounting bolt, then slowly rotate the pump body until the point is found where the specified reading is obtained on the dial gauge. When the pump is correctly positioned, tighten both its front mounting nuts and the rear bolt to their specified torque settings.

8 Withdraw the timing probe slightly, so that it is positioned clear of the pump rotor dowel, and remove the crankshaft locking pin. Rotate the crankshaft through one and three quarter rotations in the normal direction of rotation.

9 Slide the timing probe back into position ensuring that it is correctly seated against the guide sealing washer surface, not the upper lip, then zero the dial gauge.

10 Rotate the crankshaft slowly in the correct direction of rotation until the crankshaft locking tool can be re-inserted. Recheck the timing measurement.

11 If adjustment is necessary, slacken the pump mounting nuts and bolt and repeat the operations in paragraphs 7 to 10.

12 When the pump timing is correctly set, remove the dial gauge and mounting bracket and withdraw the timing probe.

13 Refit the screw and sealing washer to the guide and tighten it securely.

14 If the procedure is being carried out as part of the pump refitting sequence, proceed as described in Section 5.

15 If the procedure is being carried out with the pump fitted to the engine, refit the injector pipes tightening their union nuts to the specified torque setting. Reconnect the battery, then bleed the fuel system – see Section 2. Start the engine and adjust the idle speed and anti-stall speeds as described in Section 9.

7.3 Removing the injection pump timing inspection plug – Lucas pump

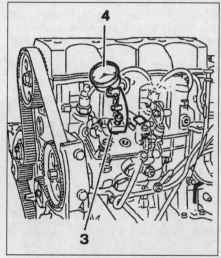

7.4 Injection pump timing dial gauge (4) and mounting bracket (3) in position on the injection pump

7.6 Pump timing values marked on label (1) and tag (2) – Lucas pump

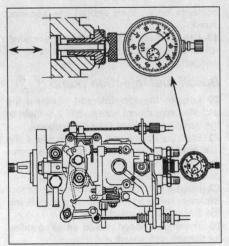

8.8 Dial test indicator, adaptor and timing probe for use with Bosch pump

8 Injection timing (Bosch fuel injection pump) – checking and adjustment

Caution: Do not attempt the timing procedure unless accurate instrumentation is available. Suitable special tools for carrying out pump timing should be available from larger motor factors or your Peugeot/Citroën dealer. Refer to the precautions given in Section 1 of this Chapter before proceeding.

Note: *To check the injection pump timing a dial gauge (Peugeot/Citroën tool No 3089-T) together with a special timing probe (Peugeot/Citroën tool No 5003-TD) and adaptor (Peugeot/Citroën tool No 7010-T) is required. Without access to this equipment (or suitable alternatives), injection pump timing should be entrusted to a Peugeot/Citroën dealer or other suitably-equipped specialist.*

1 If the injection timing is being checked with the pump in position on the engine unit, rather than as part of the pump refitting procedure,

disconnect the battery negative terminal (refer to *Disconnecting the battery* in the Reference Chapter), and cover the alternator with a clean cloth or plastic bag to prevent the possibility of fuel being spilt onto it.

2 Remove the air inlet duct between the air distribution housing and the air cleaner assembly as described in Section 3.

3 Remove the injector pipes as described in paragraph 12 of Section 5.

4 Disconnect the wiring connectors at the rear of the injection pump.

5 Slacken the clamp screw and/or nut (as applicable) and slide the fast idle cable end fitting arrangement along the cable so that it is no longer in contact with the pump fast idle lever (ie, so that the fast idle lever returns to its stop) (see Section 4).

6 Referring to Chapter 2B, align the engine assembly/valve timing holes to lock the crankshaft in position. Remove the crankshaft locking tool, then turn the crankshaft **backwards** (anti-clockwise) approximately a quarter of a turn.

7 Unscrew the access screw, situated in the centre of the four injector pipe unions, from the rear of the injection pump. As the screw is removed, position a suitable container beneath the pump to catch any escaping fuel. Mop-up any spilt fuel with a clean cloth.

8 Screw the adaptor into the rear of the pump and attach the probe to the dial gauge. Mount the dial gauge and probe in the adaptor **(see illustration)**. If access to the special Peugeot/Citroën tools cannot be gained, suitable alternatives can be purchased from most good motor factors. Position the dial gauge so that its plunger is at the mid-point of its travel and securely tighten the adaptor locknut.

9 Slowly rotate the crankshaft back-and-forth whilst observing the dial gauge, to determine when the injection pump piston is at the bottom of its travel (BDC). When the piston is correctly positioned, zero the dial gauge.

10 Rotate the crankshaft slowly in the correct direction until the crankshaft locking tool can be re-inserted.

11 The reading obtained on the dial gauge should be equal to the specified pump timing measurement given in the Specifications at the start of this Chapter. If adjustment is necessary, slacken the front and rear pump mounting nuts and bolts and slowly rotate the pump body until the point is found where the specified reading is obtained. When the pump is correctly positioned, tighten both its front and rear mounting nuts and bolts securely.

12 Rotate the crankshaft through one and three quarter rotations in the normal direction of rotation. Find the injection pump piston BDC as described in paragraph 6 and zero the dial gauge.

13 Rotate the crankshaft slowly in the correct direction of rotation until the crankshaft locking tool can be re-inserted (bringing the engine back to TDC). Recheck the timing measurement.

14 If adjustment is necessary, slacken the pump mounting nuts and bolts and repeat the operations in paragraphs 11 to 13.

15 When the pump timing is correctly set, unscrew the adaptor and remove the dial gauge and probe.

16 Refit the screw and sealing washer to the pump and tighten it securely.

17 If the procedure is being carried out as part of the pump refitting sequence, proceed as described in Section 5.

18 If the procedure is being carried out with the pump fitted to the engine, refit the injector pipes tightening their union nuts to the specified torque setting. Refit the air intake duct, then reconnect the battery and bleed the fuel system as described in Section 2.

19 Start the engine and adjust the idle speed and anti-stall speeds as described in Section 9. Also adjust the fast idle cable as described in Section 4.

9 Fuel injection pump – adjustment

1 The usual type of tachometer (rev counter), which works from ignition system pulses, cannot be used on diesel engines. For the following adjustments to be accurately carried out it will be necessary to purchase or hire an appropriate tachometer, or entrust the work to a Peugeot/Citroën dealer or other suitably-equipped specialist.

2 Before making adjustments, warm-up the engine to normal operating temperature. Make sure that the accelerator cable and fast idle cables are correctly adjusted as described in Sections 11 and 4 respectively.

Lucas fuel injection pump

3 With the engine idling, place a shim of the correct thickness (see Specifications), between the pump control lever and the anti-stall adjustment screw **(see illustration)**.

4 Push the manual stop lever back against its stop, and hold it in position by inserting a

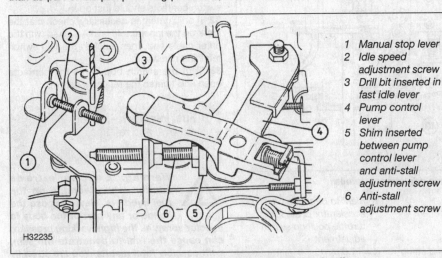

1 Manual stop lever
2 Idle speed adjustment screw
3 Drill bit inserted in fast idle lever
4 Pump control lever
5 Shim inserted between pump control lever and anti-stall adjustment screw
6 Anti-stall adjustment screw

9.3 Lucas fuel injection pump adjustment details

H32235

9.0 mm diameter rod/drill through the hole in the fast idle lever.

5 The engine speed should be as specified for the anti-stall speed.

6 If adjustment is necessary, loosen the locknut, turn the anti-stall adjustment screw as required, then tighten the locknut.

7 Remove the rod/drill and the shim, and check that the engine is idling at the specified idle speed.

8 If adjustment is necessary, loosen the locknut on the idle speed adjustment screw. Turn the screw as required, and retighten the locknut.

9 Move the pump control lever to increase the engine speed to approximately 3000 rpm, then quickly release the lever. The deceleration period should be between 2.5 and 3.5 seconds, and the engine speed should drop to approximately 50 rpm below idle.

10 If the deceleration is too fast and the engine stalls, unscrew the anti-stall adjustment screw a quarter-turn towards the control lever. If the deceleration is too slow, resulting in poor engine braking, turn the screw a quarter-turn away from the lever.

11 Retighten the locknut after making an adjustment. Recheck the idle speed, and adjust if necessary as described previously.

12 With the engine idling, check the operation of the manual stop control by turning the stop lever clockwise **(see illustration 9.3)**. The engine must stop instantly.

13 Where applicable, disconnect the tachometer on completion.

14 With all the previously described

9.17 Throttle position switch operating cam retaining screw (arrowed) – Lucas pump

adjustments completed, check the adjustment of the throttle position switch located on the pump control lever as follows.

15 Working at the fuel injection pump end of the accelerator cable, make a mark on the inner cable, 11.0 mm from the end of the outer cable **(see illustration 9.20)**.

16 Have an assistant depress the accelerator pedal until the mark on the inner cable is aligned with the end of the outer cable. With the cable in this position, the throttle position switch contacts should just open.

17 If adjustment is necessary, check that the mark on the inner cable is still aligned with the outer cable end, then slacken the screw securing the plastic operating cam to the pump control lever **(see illustration)**.

18 Move the operating cam until the switch

contacts open, then tighten the securing screw.

19 Disconnect the tachometer and, where applicable, refit the engine cover on completion.

Bosch fuel injection pump

20 Loosen the locknut, and unscrew the anti-stall adjustment screw until it is clear of the pump control lever **(see illustration)**.

21 Start the engine and allow it to idle. If the idle speed is incorrect, loosen the locknut and turn the idle speed adjustment screw as required, then retighten the locknut.

22 Insert a shim or feeler blade of the correct thickness between the pump control lever and the anti-stall adjustment screw.

23 The engine speed should be as specified for the anti-stall speed.

24 If adjustment is necessary, loosen the locknut and turn the anti-stall adjustment screw as required. Retighten the locknut.

25 Remove the shim or feeler blade and allow the engine to idle.

26 Move the fast idle lever fully towards the flywheel end of the engine, and check that the engine speed increases to the specified fast idle speed. If necessary, loosen the locknut and turn the fast idle adjusting screw as required, then retighten the locknut.

27 With the engine idling, check the operation of the manual stop control by turning the stop lever. The engine must stop instantly.

28 Disconnect the tachometer on completion.

29 With all the previously described adjustments completed, check the adjustment of the throttle position switch located on the pump control lever as follows.

30 Working at the fuel injection pump end of the accelerator cable, make a mark on the inner cable, 11.0 mm from the end of the outer cable.

31 Have an assistant depress the accelerator pedal until the mark on the inner cable is aligned with the end of the outer cable. With the cable in this position, the throttle position switch contacts should just open.

32 If adjustment is necessary, check that the mark on the inner cable is still aligned with the outer cable end, then slacken the two switch retaining screws.

33 Turn the switch body until the contacts open and tighten the retaining screws.

10 Fuel injectors – testing, removal and refitting

⚠️ **Warning: Exercise extreme caution when working on the fuel injectors. Never expose the hands or any part of the body to injector spray, as the high working pressure can cause the fuel to penetrate the skin, with possibly fatal results. You are strongly advised to have any work which involves**

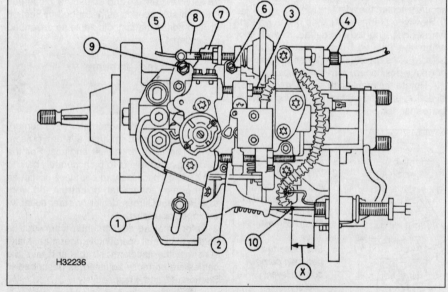

9.20 Bosch fuel injection pump adjustment details

1 Pump control lever
2 Maximum speed adjustment screw
3 Anti-stall adjustment screw
4 Fast idle cable adjustment screw and locknut
5 Fast idle cable
6 Idle speed adjustment screw
7 Fast idle lever
8 Fast idle cable end fitting
9 Fast idle adjustment screw
10 Mark to be made on accelerator cable for throttle position switch adjustment
X = 11.0 mm

H32236

10.5 Pulling a leak-off pipe from a fuel injector

10.7 Unscrewing an injector pipe union nut

10.8 Unscrew the injectors, and remove them from the cylinder head

10.9a Removing a fuel injector copper washer . . .

10.9b . . . fire seal washer . . .

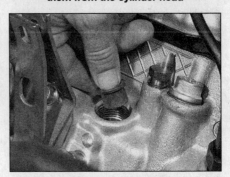

10.9c . . . and sleeve

testing the injectors under pressure carried out by a dealer or fuel injection specialist.

Testing

1 Injectors do deteriorate with prolonged use, and it is reasonable to expect them to need reconditioning or renewal after 60-000 miles (100-000 km) or so. Accurate testing, overhaul and calibration of the injectors must be left to a specialist. A defective injector which is causing knocking or smoking can be located without dismantling as follows.
2 Run the engine at fast idle. Slacken each injector union in turn, placing rag around the union to catch spilt fuel, and being careful not to expose the skin to any spray. When the union on the defective injector is slackened, the knocking or smoking will stop.

Removal

3 For improved access on 1.9 litre models, remove the air distribution housing as described In Section 3. If necessary, also remove the intake duct, and disconnect the breather hose from the engine oil filler tube. Refer to the relevant Sections of this Chapter for further information.
4 Carefully clean around the injectors and injector pipe union nuts.
5 Pull the leak-off pipes from the injectors **(see illustration)**.
6 Unscrew the union nuts securing the injector pipes to the fuel injection pump. Counterhold the unions on the pump when unscrewing the nuts. Cover open unions to keep dirt out, using small plastic bags, or fingers cut from clean rubber gloves.

7 Unscrew the union nuts and disconnect the pipes from the injectors **(see illustration)**. If necessary, the injector pipes may be completely removed. Note carefully the locations of the pipe clamps, for use when refitting. Cover the ends of the injectors, to prevent dirt ingress.
8 Unscrew the injectors using a deep socket or box spanner (27 mm across-flats), and remove them from the cylinder head **(see illustration)**.
9 Recover the copper washers and fire seal washers from the cylinder head. Also recover the sleeves if they are loose **(see illustrations)**.

Refitting

10 Obtain new copper washers and fire seal washers. Also renew the sleeves, if they are damaged.
11 Take care not to drop the injectors, or allow the needles at their tips to become damaged. The injectors are precision-made to fine limits, and must not be handled roughly. In particular, never mount them in a bench vice.
12 Commence refitting by inserting the sleeves (if removed) into the cylinder head, followed by the fire seal washers (convex face uppermost), and copper washers.
13 Insert the injectors and tighten them to the specified torque.
14 Refit the injector pipes and tighten the union nuts. Make sure the pipe clamps are in their previously-noted positions. If the clamps are wrongly positioned or missing, problems

may be experienced with pipes breaking or splitting.
15 Reconnect the leak-off pipes.
16 Refit the components removed for access with reference to the relevant Sections of this Chapter.
17 Start the engine. If difficulty is experienced, bleed the fuel system as described in Section 2.

11 Accelerator cable – removal, refitting and adjustment

Removal

1 Working in the engine compartment, operate the pump control lever on the fuel injection pump, and release the cable inner from the lever **(see illustration)**.

11.1 Releasing the accelerator inner cable from the lever on the injection pump

11.2 Pulling the accelerator outer cable from the bracket

2 Pull the cable outer from the grommet in the fuel injection pump bracket **(see illustration)**.

3 Release the cable from the remaining clips and brackets in the engine compartment, noting its routing.

4 Working inside the car, remove the fusebox cover and the undercover from beneath the facia on the driver's side.

5 Reach up under the facia, depress the ends of the cable end fitting and detach the inner cable from the top of the accelerator pedal. Where fitted, pull out the clip securing the bulkhead grommet.

6 Tie a length of string to the end of the cable.

7 Return to the engine compartment, release the cable grommet from the bulkhead and withdraw the cable. When the end of the cable appears, untie the string and leave it in position – it can then be used to draw the cable back into position on refitting.

Refitting

8 Tie the string to the end of the cable, then use the string to draw the cable into position through the bulkhead. Once the cable end is visible, untie the string, then attach the inner cable to the pedal. Where applicable, refit the bulkhead grommet clip.

9 From within the engine compartment, ensure the outer cable is correctly seated in the bulkhead grommet, then work along the cable, securing it in position with the retaining clips and ties, and ensuring that the cable is correctly routed.

10 Pass the outer cable through its mounting bracket grommet, and reconnect the inner cable to the injection pump lever. Adjust the cable as described below.

Adjustment

11 Remove the spring clip from the accelerator outer cable. Ensuring that the control lever is against its stop, gently pull the cable out of its grommet until all free play is removed from the inner cable.

12 With the cable held in this position, refit the spring clip to the last exposed outer cable groove in front of the rubber grommet and washer. When the clip is refitted and the outer cable is released, there should be only a small amount of free play in the inner cable.

13 Have an assistant depress the accelerator pedal, and check that the control lever opens fully and returns smoothly to its stop.

12 Accelerator pedal – removal and refitting

Refer to Chapter 4A, Section 4, but adjust the accelerator cable as described in Section 11.

13 Fuel gauge sender and pick-up unit – removal and refitting

1 The fuel gauge sender and pick-up unit is located in the same position as the fuel pump on petrol models and the removal and refitting procedures are virtually identical. Refer to Chapter 4A, Section 8.

2 On completion, bleed the fuel system as described in Section 2.

14 Fuel tank – removal and refitting

Refer to Chapter 4A, Section 10.

15 Manifolds – removal and refitting

Note: *Renew the manifold gasket(s) when refitting.*

Inlet manifold

Removal

1 Disconnect the battery negative terminal (refer to *Disconnecting the battery* in the Reference Chapter).

2 Remove the air intake duct and, on 1.9 litre engines, the air distribution housing as described in Section 3.

3 Undo the six nuts securing the manifold flanges to the cylinder head, and the single hexagonal bolt from the centre flange. Recover the washers from the manifold studs, where fitted.

4 Withdraw the manifold from the cylinder head and collect the gaskets.

Refitting

5 Refitting is a reversal of removal, bearing in mind the following points.
   a) Renew the gasket(s) when refitting the manifold.
   b) Refit the air distribution housing and/or air intake duct as described in Section 3.

Exhaust manifold

Removal

6 Remove the inlet manifold as described previously.

7 Disconnect the exhaust front pipe from the manifold, with reference to Section 16.

8 On certain models, it may be necessary to unbolt the resonator chamber from the manifold, to allow sufficient clearance for the manifold to be removed.

9 On DJY (XUD9Y engine) models, remove the exhaust gas recirculation (EGR) valve from the exhaust manifold as described in Part D of this Chapter.

10 Unscrew the six exhaust manifold securing nuts, and recover the spacers from the studs.

11 Lift the exhaust manifold from the cylinder head, and recover the gaskets.

12 It is possible that some of the manifold studs may be unscrewed from the cylinder head when the manifold securing nuts are unscrewed. In this event, the studs should be screwed back into the cylinder head once the manifolds have been removed, using two manifold nuts locked together.

Refitting

13 Refitting is a reversal of removal, bearing in mind the following points.
   a) *Renew the manifold gaskets.*
   b) *Reconnect the exhaust front pipe to the exhaust manifold as described in Section 16.*
   c) *Where applicable, refit the EGR valve as described in Part D of this Chapter.*
   d) *Ensure that all relevant hoses and pipes are correctly reconnected and routed.*

16 Exhaust system – general information and component renewal

General information

1 The exhaust system consists of two sections: the front pipe and the tailpipe. The front pipe to manifold joint is of the spring-loaded ball type, to allow for movement in the exhaust system, and the tailpipe joint is secured by a clamping ring.

2 The system is suspended throughout its entire length by rubber mountings.

Removal

3 Each exhaust section can be removed individually or, alternatively, the complete system can be removed as a unit. Even if only one part of the system needs attention, it is often easier to remove the whole system and separate the sections on the bench.

4 To remove the system or part of the system, first jack up the front or rear of the car, and support it on axle stands (see *Jacking and vehicle support*). Alternatively, position the car over an inspection pit, or on car ramps.

Front pipe

5 Slacken the front pipe clamping ring bolts, and disengage the clamp from the flange joint.

6 Slacken and remove the two nuts securing the front pipe flange joint to the manifold, and recover the spring cups and springs **(see illustration)**. Remove the bolts, then free the front pipe from its mounting rubber(s) and remove it from underneath the vehicle. Recover the wire-mesh gasket from the manifold joint.

Tailpipe

7 Slacken the tailpipe clamping ring bolts, and disengage the clamp from the flange joint.

8 Unhook the tailpipe from its mounting rubbers, and remove it from the vehicle.

Complete system

9 Slacken and remove the two nuts securing the front pipe flange joint to the manifold, and recover the spring cups and springs. Remove the bolts, then free the system from its mounting rubbers and remove it from underneath the vehicle. Recover the wire-mesh gasket from the manifold joint.

Heat shield(s)

10 The heat shields are secured to the underside of the body by various nuts and bolts. Each shield can be removed once the relevant exhaust section has been removed. If a shield is being removed to gain access to a component located behind it, it may prove sufficient in some cases to remove the retaining nuts and/or bolts, and simply lower the shield, without disturbing the exhaust system.

Refitting

11 Each section is refitted by reversing the removal sequence, noting the following points:

a) *Ensure that all traces of corrosion have been removed from the flanges, and renew all necessary gaskets.*

b) *Inspect the rubber mountings for signs of damage or deterioration, and renew as necessary.*

c) *Prior to assembling the spring-loaded joint, a smear of high-temperature grease should be applied to the joint mating surfaces.*

d) *Where joints are secured together by a clamping ring, apply a smear of exhaust system jointing paste to the flange joint, to ensure a gas-tight seal.*

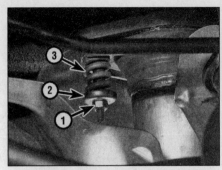

16.6 Exhaust front pipe-to-manifold securing nut (1), spring seat (2) and spring (3) – viewed from underneath vehicle

Tighten the clamping ring nuts evenly and progressively, so that the clearance between the clamp halves remains equal on either side.

e) *Prior to tightening the exhaust system fasteners, ensure that all rubber mountings are correctly located, and that there is adequate clearance between the exhaust system and vehicle underbody.*

Chapter 4 Part C:
Fuel and exhaust systems –
1.6, 1.9 (DW series) and 2.0 litre diesel models

Contents

Degrees of difficulty

Easy, suitable for novice with little experience	**Fairly easy,** suitable for beginner with some experience	**Fairly difficult,** suitable for competent DIY mechanic	**Difficult,** suitable for experienced DIY mechanic	**Very difficult,** suitable for expert DIY or professional

Specifications

General

System type:
1.9 litre models:
 Engine code WJZ . . . . Indirect injection system incorporating a distributor fuel injection pump
 Engine code WJY . . . . Indirect injection system incorporating a semi-electronically controlled distributor fuel injection pump
1.6 and 2.0 litre models . . . . High-pressure Diesel injection (HDi) direct injection 'common-rail' system incorporating an electronically controlled fuel injection pump and injectors

Injection pump type:
1.6 litre models. . . . . Bosch EDC 16 C34
1.9 litre models:
 Engine code WJZ . . . . Bosch VE 4/9 or Lucas DWLP 11
 Engine code WJY . . . . Bosch VE 4/9 or Lucas DWLP12
2.0 litre models. . . . . Bosch EDC 15C2 or Siemens SID 801

Injectors

Opening pressure:
1.9 litre models. . . . . 133 to 138 bars
1.6 and 2.0 litre models . . . . Controlled by ECU

Turbocharger

Type:
1.6 litre models. . . . . MHI
1.9 and 2.0 litre models . . . . KKK K03
Boost pressure (approximate) . . . . 1 bar at 3000 rpm

Adjustment data

Idle speed – 1.9 litre models*:
  Engine code WJZ:
    Lucas injection pump:
      Models without air conditioning . . . . 825 ± 25 rpm
      Models with air conditioning. . . . . 875 ± 25 rpm
    Bosch injection pump:
      Models without air conditioning . . . . 800 ± 25 rpm
      Models with air conditioning. . . . . 875 ± 25 rpm
  Engine code WJY . . . . 850 ± 25 rpm
Idle speed – 1.6 and 2.0 litre models . . . . 800 ± 20 rpm – controlled by ECU
Anti-stall speed – 1.9 litre models:
  Lucas injection pump . . . . 1500 ± 100 rpm
  Bosch injection pump:
    Models without air conditioning . . . . 800 +20 +50 rpm
    Models with air conditioning. . . . . 875 +20 +50 rpm
Anti-stall shim thickness:
  With Lucas injection pump . . . . 3.0 mm
  With Bosch injection pump . . . . 1.0 mm
Fast idle speed – 1.9 litre models*:
  Engine code WJZ . . . . 950 ± 25 rpm
  Engine code WJY . . . . 1150 ± 25 rpm
Maximum speed:
  1.9 litre models . . . . 5350 ± 125 rpm
  1.6 and 2.0 litre models . . . . 5000 rpm – controlled by ECU
*Refer to Chapter 2C for further information on engine code identification

Torque wrench settings

	Nm	lbf ft
1.9 litre models		
Exhaust manifold nuts	30	22
Fuel pipe union nuts	25	18
Inlet manifold:		
Lower section nuts/bolts	20	15
Upper section:		
M6 bolts	8	6
M8 bolts	18	13
Injection pump:		
Front mounting bolts	20	15
Rear mounting bolt	23	17
Mounting bracket-to-cylinder head bolts	20	15
Injection pump sprocket-to-hub bolts	23	17
Injectors to cylinder head	90	66
1.6 and 2.0 litre models		
Camshaft position sensor bolt	5	4
Crankshaft speed/position sensor	5	4
EGR valve bolts	10	7
Exhaust manifold nuts	20	15
Exhaust system:		
Catalytic converter-to-manifold nuts	40	30
Clamping ring nuts	20	15
Fuel filter bracket bolts	18	13
Fuel injector:		
1.6 litre:		
Stage 1	4	3
Stage 2	Angle-tighten a further 65°	
2.0 litre	30	22
Fuel pipe union nuts*:		
Injector end union:		
Stage 1	25	18
Stage 2	27	20
Rail end union:		
Stage 1	24	18
Stage 2	26	19
Fuel pump-to-fuel rail union	25	18
Fuel pressure sensor:		
1.6 litre	45	33
2.0 litre	35	26

Torque wrench settings (continued

	Nm	lbf ft
1.6 and 2.0 litre models (continued)		
Fuel rail mounting bolts	23	17
High-pressure fuel pump (injection pump):		
1.6 litre:		
Front mounting	23	17
Rear mounting bolts/nut (8 mm)	17	13
2.0 litre:		
Front mounting bolts/nut	23	17
Rear bracket bolts	20	15
Mounting bracket-to-cylinder head bolts	20	15
High-pressure fuel pump sprocket nut	50	37
Inlet manifold:		
1.6 litre	10	7
2.0 litre	23	17
Throttle housing (1.6 models)	9	7
Turbocharger:		
Mounting nuts	25	18
Exhaust flange bolts	23	17
Support bracket:		
Bracket-to-cylinder block bolts	23	17
Bracket-to-turbo bolt	30	22
Oil feed pipe:		
Pipe-to-turbo banjo bolt:		
1.6 litre	30	22
2.0 litre	22	16
Pipe-to-cylinder block banjo nut:		
1.6 litre	30	22
2.0 litre	48	35
Oil return hose union bolts	12	9

* These torque settings are using Citroën/Peugeot crow-foot adapters – see Section 2

1 General information

1.9 litre WJZ engine models

1 The fuel system consists of a fuel tank (which is mounted under the rear of the car), a fuel filter with integral water separator, a fuel injection pump, injectors and associated components.

2 The injection pump draws fuel from the tank through the fuel filter, which is mounted on the thermostat housing on the left-hand end of the cylinder head. The fuel filter removes all foreign matter and water, and ensures that the fuel supplied to the injection pump is clean. Excess fuel is returned from the bleed outlet on the filter housing lid to the tank. The filter housing incorporates a thermostat. When the temperature of the fuel in the filter housing is below 15°C, the filter housing thermostat opens and allows the fuel to circulate between the filter housing and thermostat housing which effectively warms the fuel. When the fuel in the filter housing reaches 35°C, the thermostat closes.

3 The fuel injection pump is driven at half-crankshaft speed by the timing belt. The high pressure required to inject the fuel into the compressed air in the swirl chambers is achieved by two opposed pistons forced together by rollers running in a cam ring. The fuel passes through a central rotor with a single outlet drilling which aligns with ports leading to the injector pipes.

4 Fuel metering is controlled by a centrifugal governor, which reacts to accelerator pedal position and engine speed. The governor is linked to a metering valve, which increases or decreases the amount of fuel delivered at each pumping stroke.

5 Basic injection timing is determined when the timing belt is fitted. When the engine is running, it is varied automatically to suit the prevailing engine speed by a mechanism which turns the cam plate or ring.

6 The four fuel injectors produce a homogeneous spray of fuel into the swirl chambers located in the cylinder head. The injectors are calibrated to open and close at critical pressures to provide efficient and even combustion. Each injector needle is lubricated by fuel, which accumulates in the spring chamber and is channelled to the injection pump return hose by leak-off pipes.

7 Cold starting is assisted by preheater or 'glow' plugs fitted to each swirl chamber. A thermostatic sensor in the cooling system operates a fast idle lever on the injection pump to increase the idling speed when the engine is cold.

8 A stop solenoid cuts the fuel supply to the injection pump rotor when the ignition is switched off, and there is also a hand-operated stop lever for use in an emergency **(see illustration)**.

1 Fast idle cable end fitting
2 Fast idle lever
3 Fast idle cable
4 Fast idle cable adjustment screw and locknut
5 Maximum speed adjustment screw
6 Accelerator lever
7 Anti-stall speed adjustment screw
8 Manual stop lever
J Fast idle cable end fitting clearance

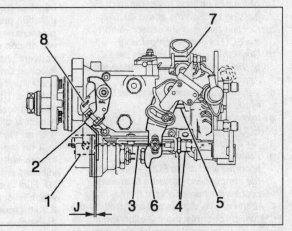

1.8 Lucas injection pump details – 1.9 litre WJZ engine models

9 Provided that the specified maintenance is carried out, the fuel injection equipment will give long and trouble-free service. The injection pump itself may well outlast the engine. The main potential cause of damage to the injection pump and injectors is dirt or water in the fuel.

10 A catalytic converter and exhaust gas recirculation (EGR) system are fitted to the engine to reduce exhaust emissions. Refer to Part D of this Chapter for further information.

11 Servicing of the injection pump and injectors is very limited for the home mechanic, and any dismantling or adjustment other than that described in this Chapter must be entrusted to a Peugeot/Citroën dealer or fuel injection specialist.

 Warning: It is necessary to take certain precautions when working on the fuel system components, particularly the fuel injectors. Before carrying out any operations on the fuel system, refer to the precautions given in 'Safety first!' at the beginning of this manual, and to any additional warning notes at the start of the relevant Sections.

1.9 litre WJY engine models

12 Later 1.9 litre engines (WJY) are fitted with an electronically controlled fuel injection pump to improve emissions in order to meet the next level of emission standards being introduced. The fuel system is very similar to that described in paragraphs 1 to 11, with the following changes to the injection pump.

13 The fuel injection pump electrical control system consists of the ECU, along with the following sensors:

a) *Throttle potentiometer – informs the injection pump accelerator lever position, and the rate of throttle opening/closing. The sensor is remotely located on models with an accelerator cable but integral with the electronic accelerator pedal on models without an accelerator cable.*

b) *Airflow meter (incorporating the intake air temperature sensor – informs the ECU of the amount and temperature of air passing through the intake duct.*

c) *Coolant temperature sensor – informs the ECU of engine temperature.*

d) *Crankshaft sensor – informs the ECU of the crankshaft position and speed of rotation.*

e) *Vehicle speed sensor – informs the ECU of the vehicle speed.*

f) *Injector needle lift sensor – informs the ECU when the start of injection occurs at No 1 injector.*

g) *Atmospheric pressure sensor (incorporated in the ECU) – measures the atmospheric pressure to prevent problems when driving at high-altitude.*

14 All the above signals are analysed by the ECU which controls the injection timing via the advance solenoid valve which is fitted to the injection pump. By opening and closing the solenoid valve, the ECU can advance and retard the injection timing as necessary. When the advance solenoid is open, the hydraulic pressure on the pump piston is reduced which results in the injection timing being retarded. To advance the injection timing, the ECU closes the solenoid valve which increases the pressure on the piston.

15 The ECU also controls the exhaust gas recirculation (EGR) system, described in detail in Part D of this Chapter, and the engine cooling fan.

16 If there is an abnormality in any of the readings obtained from the various sensors, the ECU enters its back-up mode. In this event, it ignores the abnormal sensor signal and assumes a preprogrammed value which will allow the engine to continue running (albeit at reduced efficiency). If the ECU enters this back-up mode, the warning light on the instrument panel will come on, and the relevant fault code will be stored in the ECU memory.

17 If the warning light illuminates, the vehicle should be taken to a Peugeot/Citroën dealer or engine diagnostic specialist at the earliest opportunity. Once there, a complete test of the engine management system can be carried out, using a special electronic diagnostic test unit, which is plugged into the system's diagnostic connector located adjacent to the passenger's compartment fusebox.

 Warning: It is necessary to take certain precautions when working on the fuel system components, particularly the fuel injectors. Before carrying out any operations on the fuel system, refer to the precautions given in 'Safety first!' at the beginning of this manual, and to any additional warning notes at the start of the relevant Sections.

1.6 and 2.0 litre models

18 All 1.6 and 2.0 litre engines are fitted with a high-pressure diesel injection (HDi) system which incorporates the very latest in diesel injection technology. On the HDi system, the injection pump is used purely to provide the pressure required for the injection system and has no control over the injection timing (unlike conventional diesel injection systems). The injection timing is controlled by the electronic control unit (ECU) via the electrically-operated injectors. The system operates as follows.

19 The fuel system consists of a fuel tank (which is mounted under the rear of the car, with an electric fuel supply pump immersed in it on the Bosch system), a fuel filter with integral water separator, a fuel injection pump, injectors and associated components.

20 Fuel is supplied to the fuel filter housing which is located at the front of the engine on 2.0 litre models and on the left-hand end of the engine on 1.6 litre models. After passing through the fuel filter, the fuel reaches the high-pressure pump, which forces it into the fuel rail. Fuel pressure in the fuel rail is monitored by a pressure sensor, and maintained at constant pressure by the engine management ECU which activates a control valve mounted on the high-pressure pump. Excess fuel is returned to the fuel tank via the fuel cooler. The fuel cooler is fitted to the underside of the vehicle and is cooled by the passing airflow to ensure the fuel is cool before it enters the fuel tank.

21 The fuel is heated to ensure no problems occur when the ambient temperature is very low. On early models the filter housing is connected to the coolant outlet housing on the left-hand end of the cylinder head and is fitted with a thermostat. When the temperature of the fuel in the filter housing is below 15ºC, the filter housing thermostat opens and allows the fuel to circulate around the coolant outlet housing which effectively warms the fuel. When the fuel in the filter housing reaches 25ºC, the thermostat closes. On later models an electrically-operated fuel heater is fitted to the fuel feed pipe to the filter housing, the heater is controlled by the ECU.

22 The fuel injection pump is driven by the timing belt. The high pressure required in the system (up to 1350 bar) is produced by the three pistons in the pump. The injection pump supplies high pressure fuel to the fuel rail, which acts as a reservoir for the four injectors. Since the injection pump has no control over the injection timing (unlike conventional diesel injection systems), this means that there is no need to time the injection pump when installing the timing belt.

23 The electrical control system consists of the ECU, along with the following sensors:

a) *Accelerator pedal position sensor – informs the ECU of the accelerator pedal position, and the rate of throttle opening/closing. The sensor is remotely located on models with an accelerator cable but integral with the electronic accelerator pedal on models without an accelerator cable.*

b) *Coolant temperature sensor – informs the ECU of engine temperature.*

c) *Airflow meter (incorporating the intake air temperature sensor – informs the ECU of the amount and temperature of air passing through the intake duct.*

d) *Crankshaft sensor – informs the ECU of the crankshaft position and speed of rotation.*

e) *Camshaft position sensor – informs the ECU of the positions of the pistons.*

f) *Fuel temperature sensor (where fitted) – informs the ECU of the temperature of the fuel in the fuel rail.*

g) *Fuel pressure sensor – informs the ECU of the fuel pressure present in the fuel rail.*

h) *Atmospheric pressure sensor (incorporated in the ECU) – measures the atmospheric pressure to prevent problems when driving at high-altitude.*

i) Vehicle speed sensor – informs the ECU of the vehicle speed.
j) Power steering pressure switch – informs the ECU when the power steering pump is under load.
k) Air conditioning system relay – informs ECU when the air conditioning compressor is under load.
l) Fuel pressure regulator control valve – fitted to the high-pressure pump and returns excess fuel to the fuel tank.
m) Inlet manifold pressure sensor (DV6TED4 only) – informs ECU the air pressure in the inlet manifold.
n) Throttle housing (DV6TED4 only) – controls volume of air supplied to the engine according to engine load and accelerator pedal position.

24 All the above signals are analysed by the ECU which selects the fuelling response appropriate to those values. The ECU controls the fuel injectors (varying the pulse width – the length of time the injectors are held open – to provide a richer or weaker mixture, as appropriate). The mixture is constantly varied by the ECU, to provide the best setting for cranking, starting (with either a hot or cold engine), warm-up, idle, cruising and acceleration. The injectors are operated 'semi-sequentially', injectors No 1 and 4 being operated as one pair and injectors No 2 and 3 as the other.

25 The ECU also has full control over the fuel pressure present in the fuel rail via the high-pressure fuel regulator and third piston deactivator solenoid valve which are fitted to the injection pump. To reduce the pressure, the ECU opens the high-pressure fuel regulator which allows the excess fuel to return direct to the tank from the pump. The third piston deactivator is used mainly to reduce the load on the engine, but can also be used to lower the fuel pressure. The deactivator solenoid valve relieves the fuel pressure from the third piston of the pump which results in only two of the pistons pressurising the fuel system.

26 The ECU also controls the exhaust gas recirculation (EGR) system, described in detail in Part D of this Chapter, and the engine cooling fan.

27 A turbocharger is fitted to increases engine efficiency. It does this by raising the pressure in the inlet manifold above atmospheric pressure. Instead of the air simply being sucked into the cylinders, it is forced in.

28 Energy for the operation of the turbocharger comes from the exhaust gas. The gas flows through a specially-shaped housing (the turbine housing) and in so doing, spins the turbine wheel. The turbine wheel is attached to a shaft, at the end of which is another vaned wheel known as the compressor wheel. The compressor wheel spins in its own housing, and compresses the inlet air on the way to the inlet manifold.

The turbo shaft is pressure-lubricated by an oil feed pipe from the main oil gallery. The shaft 'floats' on a cushion of oil. A drain pipe returns the oil to the sump. Boost pressure (the pressure in the inlet manifold) is limited by a wastegate, which diverts the exhaust gas away from the turbine wheel in response to a pressure-sensitive actuator.

29 If there is an abnormality in any of the readings obtained from the various sensors, the ECU enters its back-up mode. In this event, it ignores the abnormal sensor signal and assumes a preprogrammed value which will allow the engine to continue running (albeit at reduced efficiency). If the ECU enters this back-up mode, the warning light on the instrument panel will come on, and the relevant fault code will be stored in the ECU memory.

30 If the warning light illuminates, the vehicle should be taken to a Peugeot/Citroën dealer or engine diagnostic specialist at the earliest opportunity. Once there, a complete test of the engine management system can be carried out, using a special electronic diagnostic test unit, which is plugged into the system's diagnostic connector located adjacent to the passenger's compartment fusebox.

<table>
<tr><td>2</td><td>**High pressure Diesel injection system** – special information</td></tr>
</table>

Warnings and precautions

1 It is essential to observe strict precautions when working on the fuel system components, particularly the high pressure side of the system. Before carrying out any operations on the fuel system, refer to the precautions given in *Safety first!* at the beginning of this manual, and to the following additional information.

• *Do not carry out any repair work on the high pressure fuel system unless you are competent to do so, have all the necessary tools and equipment required, and are aware of the safety implications involved.*

• *Before starting any repair work on the fuel system, wait at least 30 seconds after switching off the engine to allow the fuel circuit to return to atmospheric pressure.*

• *Never work on the high pressure fuel system with the engine running.*

• *Keep well clear of any possible source of fuel leakage, particularly when starting the engine after carrying out repair work. A leak in the system could cause an extremely high pressure jet of fuel to escape, which could result in severe personal injury.*

• *Never place your hands or any part of your body near to a leak in the high pressure fuel system.*

• *Do not use steam cleaning equipment or compressed air to clean the engine or any of the fuel system components.*

Repair procedures and general information

2 Strict cleanliness must be observed at all times when working on any part of the fuel system. This applies to the working area in general, the person doing the work, and the components being worked on.

3 Before working on the fuel system components, they must be thoroughly cleaned with a suitable degreasing fluid. Peugeot/Citroën recommend the use of a specific product (SODIMAC degreasing fluid – available from Peugeot/Citroën dealers). Alternatively, a suitable brake cleaning fluid may be used. Cleanliness is particularly important when working on the fuel system connections at the following components:
a) Fuel filter.
b) Injection pump.
c) Fuel rail.
d) Fuel injectors.
e) High pressure fuel pipes.

4 After disconnecting any fuel pipes or components, the open union or orifice must be immediately sealed to prevent the entry of dirt or foreign material. Plastic plugs and caps in various sizes are available in packs from motor factors and accessory outlets, and are particularly suitable for this application (**see illustration**). Fingers cut from disposable rubber gloves should be used to protect components such as fuel pipes, fuel injectors and wiring connectors, and can be secured in place using elastic bands. Suitable gloves of this type are available at no cost from most petrol station forecourts.

5 Whenever any of the high pressure fuel pipes are disconnected or removed, a new pipe(s) must be obtained for refitting.

6 On the completion of any repair on the high pressure fuel system, Peugeot/Citroën recommend the use of ARDROX 9D1 BRENT leak-detecting compound. This is a powder which is applied to the fuel pipe unions and connections and turns white when dry. Any leak in the system will cause the product to darken indicating the source of the leak.

7 The torque wrench settings given in the Specifications must be strictly observed when tightening component mountings and connections. This is particularly important when tightening the high pressure fuel pipe

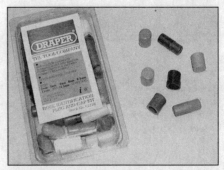

2.4 Typical plastic plug and cap set for sealing disconnected fuel pipes and components

2.7 Two crow-foot adaptors will be necessary for tightening the fuel pipe unions

3.1a Remove the fasteners from the right-hand side . . .

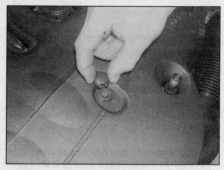

3.1b . . . and top of the engine cover . . .

unions. To enable a torque wrench to be used on the fuel pipe unions, two crow-foot adaptors are required (Peugeot/Citroën special tools (-). 1603-G and (-). 1603-F). Suitable alternatives are available from motor factors and accessory outlets **(see illustration)**.

3 Air cleaner assembly and intake ducts – removal and refitting

Removal – 1.9 litre models

WJZ engine models

1 Release the fasteners from the right-hand side and top of the engine cover then lift off the cover, taking care not to lose its mounting rubbers **(see illustrations)**.

2 Slacken and remove the two bolts securing the air intake duct to the front body panel. Slacken the retaining clip then detach the duct from the side of the air cleaner and remove it from the vehicle.
3 Slacken the retaining clips securing the inlet duct to the air cleaner lid and EGR valve housing. Undo the mounting bolt at the base of the resonator, then disconnect the duct and remove it from the engine.
4 Undo the bolt securing the base of the air cleaner housing to the support bracket. Lift up the housing, disengage the front locating pegs and remove it from the vehicle.

WJY engine models – pre-September 2002

5 Release the fasteners from the right-hand side and top of the engine cover then lift off

the cover, taking care not to lose its mounting rubbers **(see illustrations 3.1a to 3.1c)**.
6 Disconnect the battery negative terminal (refer to *Disconnecting the battery* in the Reference Chapter).
7 Slacken the retaining clips securing the inlet duct to the airflow meter on the air cleaner lid, and to the EGR valve housing. Undo the mounting bolt at the base of the resonator, then disconnect the duct and remove it from the engine **(see illustrations)**.
8 Disconnect the wiring connector from the airflow meter, mounted on the air cleaner lid **(see illustration)**.
9 Undo the screw securing the air intake duct to the front body panel **(see illustration)**. Slide the duct sideways slightly to disengage the additional retaining tab.
10 Undo the bolt securing the air cleaner

3.1c . . . then remove the cover from the engine – 1.9 litre models

3.8 Disconnect the wiring connector from the airflow meter – early 1.9 litre models

3.9 Undo the screw securing the air intake duct to the front body panel – early 1.9 litre models

3.7a Slacken the clip (arrowed) securing the inlet duct to the airflow meter . . .

3.7b . . . and to the EGR valve housing . . .

3.7c . . . then undo the resonator mounting bolt and remove the duct from the engine – early 1.9 litre models

3.10 Undo the bolt (arrowed) securing the air cleaner upper mounting bracket to the body sidemember – early 1.9 litre models

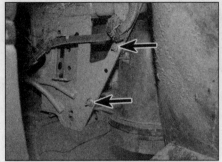

3.13 Air cleaner lower retaining nuts (arrowed) – early 1.9 litre models

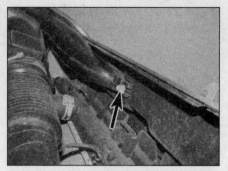

3.15 Undo the nut (arrowed) securing the air intake duct to the front body panel – later 1.9 litre models

upper mounting bracket to the body sidemember **(see illustration)**.

11 Firmly apply the handbrake, then jack up the front of the car and support it securely on axle stands (see *Jacking and vehicle support*).

12 Remove the left-hand roadwheel and undo the screws securing the front of the wheel arch liner to the bumper and front wing.

13 Ease the wheel arch liner from its location, then undo the two air cleaner lower retaining nuts **(see illustration)**. Lift the air cleaner and air intake duct upwards and out of the engine compartment. If necessary, slacken the retaining clip and separate the intake duct from the air cleaner housing.

WJY engine models – post-September 2002

14 Release the fasteners from the right-hand

side and top of the engine cover then lift off the cover, taking care not to lose its mounting rubbers **(see illustrations 3.1a to 3.1c)**.

15 Undo the nut securing the air intake duct to the front body panel **(see illustration)**. Lift the duct off the mounting stud and slide it sideways slightly to disengage the additional retaining tab.

16 Withdraw the duct from the base of the air cleaner and remove it from the vehicle **(see illustration)**.

17 Disconnect the wiring connector from the airflow meter, mounted on the side of the air cleaner lid **(see illustration)**.

18 Slacken the retaining clip securing the inlet duct to the EGR valve housing and undo the mounting bolt at the base of the resonator.

19 Withdraw the duct from the EGR valve housing, and disengage the air cleaner housing from its mounting bracket. Lift the duct and air cleaner housing out of the engine compartment as an assembly **(see illustration)**.

Removal – 2.0 litre models

Pre-September 2002 models

20 Remove the fasteners (rotate them 90° to release them) and remove the engine cover **(see illustrations)**.

21 Slacken the retaining clips and free the flexible duct from the airflow meter and turbocharger rigid inlet duct **(see illustration)**. Suitably plug or cover the turbocharger rigid inlet duct, using clean rag to prevent any dirt or foreign material from entering.

3.16 Withdraw the duct from the base of the air cleaner and remove it from the vehicle – later 1.9 litre models

3.17 Disconnect the wiring connector from the airflow meter – later 1.9 litre models

3.19 Lift the duct and air cleaner housing out of the engine compartment as an assembly – later 1.9 litre models

3.20a Rotate each fastener 90° to release it . . .

3.20b . . . then lift off the engine cover – 2.0 litre models

3.21 Disconnect the flexible air inlet duct from the airflow meter and turbocharger rigid inlet duct – early 2.0 litre models

3.23a Disconnect the wiring connector from the airflow meter . . .

3.23b . . . then lift the air cleaner housing upward at the rear and disengage the front locating lugs – early 2.0 litre models

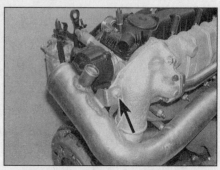

3.27 Undo the upper mounting bolt (arrowed) securing the rigid inlet duct to the inlet manifold – early 2.0 litre models

22 Unscrew the two bolts and free the accelerator pedal position sensor bracket from the side of the air cleaner housing.

23 Disconnect the wiring connector from the airflow meter on the side of the air cleaner lid. Lift the air cleaner housing assembly off of its mounting bracket and remove it from the engine compartment **(see illustrations)**.

24 To remove the air intake duct, slacken the retaining clip and disconnect the duct from the intake sleeve on the front body panel. Undo the bolts securing the duct to the air cleaner mounting bracket and remove the duct from the engine compartment.

25 The rigid ducts at the rear of the engine, connecting the turbocharger to the flexible air inlet duct and to the inlet manifold, are inaccessible with the engine in the car. To gain access it will be necessary to either remove the engine/transmission unit as described in Chapter 2E, or remove the front suspension subframe as described in Chapter 10.

26 Once access has been gained, begin removal of the turbocharger rigid inlet duct by disconnecting the crankcase ventilation hose at the top of the duct.

27 Undo the bolt securing the duct to the inlet manifold elbow **(see illustration)**.

28 At the lower end, undo the bolt securing the duct to the turbocharger **(see illustration)**. Lift off the duct and recover the seal from the lower end.

29 To remove the turbocharger-to-inlet manifold rigid plastic duct, slacken the retaining clip and release the connecting hose from the inlet manifold elbow.

30 Slacken the clip securing the connecting hose at the lower end of the duct to the turbocharger. Release the attachment strap from the lug on the turbocharger and withdraw the duct from the engine.

Post-September 2002 models

31 Remove the fasteners (rotate them 90° to release them) and remove the engine cover **(see illustrations 3.20a and 3.20b)**.

32 Undo the nut securing the air intake duct to the front body panel **(see illustration)**. Lift the duct off the mounting stud and slide it sideways slightly to disengage the additional retaining tab.

33 Disconnect the wiring connector from the airflow meter at the rear of the air cleaner lid **(see illustration)**.

34 Slacken the retaining clip and disconnect the flexible air inlet duct from the airflow meter **(see illustration)**.

35 Disengage the air cleaner housing from its mounting bracket, then lift the air cleaner housing and air intake duct out of the engine compartment as an assembly **(see illustrations)**.

36 To remove the rigid ducts at the rear of the engine, proceed as described in paragraphs 25 to 30 above.

3.28 Undo the bolt securing the rigid inlet duct to the turbocharger and remove the duct – early 2.0 litre models

3.32 Undo the nut securing the air intake duct to the front body panel – later 2.0 litre models

3.33 Disconnect the wiring connector from the airflow meter – later 2.0 litre models

3.34 Slacken the retaining clip and disconnect the flexible air inlet duct from the airflow meter – later 2.0 litre models

3.35a Disengage the air cleaner housing from its mounting bracket . . .

3.35b . . . then remove the air cleaner housing and intake duct as an assembly – later 2.0 litre models

3.40 Disconnect the air duct from the turbocharger and release the breather tube from the oil trap housing

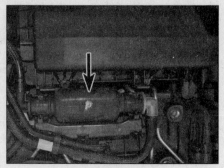

3.41 Manual priming pump and mounting clips

Removal – 1.6 litre models

37 Remove the engine top cover.

38 Disconnect the two air ducts leading from the left-hand end of the air filter housing to the air inlet duct on the front of the engine compartment.

39 Undo the screw and remove the air inlet duct from the front of the engine compartment.

40 Loosen the clip and disconnect the air duct from the left-hand side of the turbocharger, at the same time releasing the breather tube from the oil trap housing (**see illustration**).

41 Without disconnecting the fuel lines, remove the manual priming pump from its mounting clips and position to one side (**see illustration**).

42 Disconnect the wiring plug from the airflow meter (**see illustration**).

43 Loosen the clip and disconnect the air duct from the airflow meter.

44 Lift the air cleaner assembly from its mounting rubbers and remove from the engine (**see illustration**).

Refitting

45 Refitting is a reversal of the removal procedure, ensuring that all hoses and ducts are properly reconnected and correctly seated and are securely held by their retaining clips/bolts.

3.42 Disconnect the wiring from the airflow meter

3.44 Removing the air filter

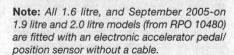

4 Accelerator cable – removal, refitting and adjustment

Note: *All 1.6 litre, and September 2005-on 1.9 litre and 2.0 litre models (from RPO 10480) are fitted with an electronic accelerator pedal/position sensor without a cable.*

Removal

1.9 litre models

1 Remove the air inlet duct as described in Section 3. Free the accelerator inner cable from the injection pump accelerator lever, then

pull the outer cable out from the mounting bracket, complete with its spring clip. Whilst the cable is disconnected, remove the cable locating collar from the mounting bracket for safe-keeping (**see illustrations**).

2.0 litre models – pre-September 2002

Note: *Later 2.0 litre (from RPO 10480) models are not fitted with an accelerator cable.*

2 Remove the fasteners (rotate them 90° to release them) and remove the engine cover (**see illustrations 3.20a and 3.20b**).

3 Unscrew the two bolts and free the accelerator pedal position sensor bracket from the side of the air cleaner housing.

4.1a Free the accelerator inner cable from the lever . . .

4.1b . . . then withdraw the outer cable from the pump bracket, complete with spring clip – 1.9 litre models

4.1c Remove the cable locating collar from the pump whilst the cable is removed – 1.9 litre models

4.3 Detach the accelerator inner cable from the pedal position sensor – early 2.0 litre models

4.4 Detach the accelerator inner cable from the pedal position sensor (arrowed) – later 2.0 litre models to September 2005 (to RPO 10479)

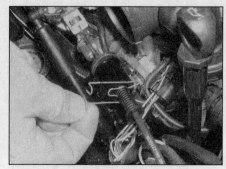

4.15 Slide off the spring clip and adjust the accelerator cable as described in text – 1.9 litre model shown

Detach the accelerator inner cable from the sensor, then pull the outer cable out from sensor bracket, complete with the spring clip **(see illustration)**.

2.0 litre models – post-September 2002 to September 2005 (to RPO 10479)

4 Detach the accelerator inner cable from the pedal position sensor, located above the right-hand engine transmission mounting **(see illustration)**.
5 Withdraw the outer cable from the rubber grommet on the sensor bracket, complete with the spring clip.

All models

6 Working back along the length of the cable, free it from any retaining clips or ties, noting its correct routing.
7 Working inside the car, remove the fusebox cover and the undercover from beneath the facia on the driver's side.
8 Reach up under the facia, depress the ends of the cable end fitting and detach the inner cable from the top of the accelerator pedal. Where fitted, pull out the clip securing the bulkhead grommet.
9 Tie a length of string to the end of the cable.
10 Return to the engine compartment, release the cable grommet from the bulkhead and withdraw the cable. When the end of the cable appears – untie the string and leave it in position – it can then be used to draw the cable back into position on refitting.

Refitting

11 Tie the string to the end of the cable, then use the string to draw the cable into position through the bulkhead. Once the cable end is visible, untie the string, then attach the inner cable to the pedal. Where applicable, refit the bulkhead grommet clip.
12 From within the engine compartment, ensure the outer cable is correctly seated in the bulkhead grommet, then work along the cable, securing it in position with the retaining clips and ties, and ensuring that the cable is correctly routed.
13 On 1.9 litre models, fit the locating collar

to the mounting bracket then pass the cable through the collar and reconnect the inner cable to the accelerator lever. Adjust the cable as described below, then refit the facia trim panels.
14 On 2.0 litre models, pass the outer cable through the sensor bracket grommet and reconnect the inner cable to the accelerator pedal position sensor. Where applicable, refit the sensor bracket to the side of the air cleaner housing, tightening its retaining bolts securely. Adjust the cable as described below, then refit the facia trim panels.

Adjustment

15 On all models, remove the spring clip from the accelerator outer cable **(see illustration)**. Ensuring that the injection pump lever/ accelerator pedal position sensor is fully against its stop, gently pull the cable out of its grommet until all free play is removed from the inner cable.
16 With the cable held in this position, refit the spring clip to the last exposed outer cable groove in front of the rubber grommet and washer. When the clip is refitted and the outer cable is released, there should be only a small amount of free play in the inner cable.
17 Have an assistant depress the accelerator pedal, and check that the accelerator lever/ pedal position sensor opens fully and returns smoothly to its stop.
18 On completion, refit the engine cover, securing it in position with the fasteners.

5 Accelerator pedal – removal and refitting

Note: *No accelerator cable is fitted to 1.6 litre, and September 2005-on 1.9 and 2.0 litre models (from RPO 10480). On these models, an accelerator pedal position sensor (which informs the ECU of the pedal position and rate of change) forms part of the accelerator pedal.*

Removal

1 Disconnect the accelerator cable (where fitted) from the pedal as described in

Section 4, or disconnect the wiring plug from the accelerator pedal position sensor **(see illustration)**.

Right-hand drive models

2 Unscrew the nut from the end of the pedal pivot shaft, whilst retaining the pivot shaft with an open-ended spanner on the flats provided.
3 Withdraw the pedal and pivot shaft assembly from the support bracket.
4 Examine the pivot shaft for signs of wear or damage and, if necessary, renew it. The pivot shaft is a screw fit in the pedal.

Left-hand drive models

5 Unscrew the two nuts and lift off the pedal pivot housing cover and upper bearing.
6 Withdraw the pedal from the lower bearing.
7 Examine the pivot bushes and shaft for signs of wear and renew as necessary.

Refitting

8 Refitting is a reversal of the removal procedure, applying a little multi-purpose grease to the pedal pivot point. On completion, adjust the accelerator cable as described in Section 4 (where applicable).

6 Fuel system – priming and bleeding

1 After disconnecting part of the fuel supply system or running out of fuel, it is necessary to prime the fuel system and bleed off any

5.1 Electronic accelerator pedal and position sensor

**6.3 Priming the fuel system –
1.9 litre models**

**6.9 Priming pump location (arrowed) on
2.0 litre models with Siemens injection
pump**

6.14 Hand-operated priming pump

air which may have entered the system
components, as follows.

1.9 litre models

2 All models are fitted with a hand-operated
priming pump which is built into the fuel filter
housing. To gain access to the pump, release
the fasteners from the right-hand side and
top of the engine cover then lift off the cover,
taking care not to lose its mounting rubbers
(see illustrations 3.1a to 3.1c).
3 Pump the priming pump until resistance
is felt then pump a few more times **(see
illustration)**. This will prime the fuel system
components and remove all air from the
system.
4 Start the engine as normal. If difficulty is
encountered, pump the priming pump a few
times with the ignition switched on.
5 Once the engine has started, ensure the
mounting rubbers are all correctly fitted then
install the engine cover, securing it in position
with the fasteners.

2.0 litre models

Bosch injection pump

Note: *A new fuel filter drain plug and O-ring
will be required for this operation.*
6 Remove the fasteners (rotate them 90° to
release them) and remove the engine cover
(see illustrations 3.20a and 3.20b).
7 On completion of work on the fuel system
slacken, or leave loose (as appropriate), the
new fuel filter drain plug. Operate the low
pressure pump 4 or 5 times by switching
on the ignition each time for a period
of 5 seconds. Switch off the ignition and
wait for a period of 5 to 10 seconds to allow
the pressure to fall in the fuel supply circuit.
Tighten the drain plug and wipe away all spilt
fuel. Start the engine and check that there is
no sign whatever of fuel seepage from the
filter drain plug once the engine is running.

Siemens injection pump

8 Remove the fasteners (rotate them 90° to
release them) and remove the engine cover
(see illustrations 3.20a and 3.20b).
9 A hand-operated priming pump is located
on the front right-hand side of the engine **(see
illustration)**.

10 Pump the priming pump until resistance
is felt then pump a few more times. This
will prime the fuel system components and
remove all air from the system.
11 Start the engine as normal. If difficulty is
encountered, pump the priming pump a few
times with the ignition switched on.
12 Once the engine has started, refit the
engine cover, securing it in position with the
fasteners.

1.6 litre models

13 Remove the engine cover.
14 A hand-operated priming pump is located
on top of the engine, in front of the air cleaner
(see illustration).
15 If the fuel filter has not been renewed, it is
sufficient to operate the hand priming pump
for approximately 2 minutes, then start the
engine normally.
16 If the fuel filter has been renewed, priming
is achieved by connecting a suitable hose (if
necessary, a special Citroën/Peugeot hose
No 4244-T may be available) from the fuel
filter outlet to the fuel return pipe and forcing
fuel though the filter, into the return system. If
the suitable hose is not available, it will suffice
to connect a length of hose to the filter outlet,
with the other end of the hose in a suitable
container. With the system primed, reconnect
the hoses, then operate the starter until the
engine starts.
17 If starting the engine after a major
overhaul or after refitting the turbocharger, it is
recommended that the wiring connectors are
temporarily disconnected from the injectors
and the engine turned over on the starter
motor for 15 seconds to ensure the engine
oil circuit is fully primed. Reconnect the
wiring and operate the starter until the engine
starts.

**7 Fuel supply pump
    (1.6 and 2.0 litre models) –
    removal and refitting**

1 On models with a Bosch injection pump,
the diesel fuel supply pump is located in the
same position as the conventional fuel pump
on petrol engine models, and the removal

and refitting procedures are virtually identical.
Refer to Chapter 4A, Section 8.
2 A fuel supply pump is not fitted to models
with a Siemens injection pump.

**8 Fuel gauge sender unit –
    removal and refitting**

1 The fuel gauge sender unit can be removed
as described in Chapter 4A, Section 8. **Note:**
*On 1.9 litre models, and 2.0 litre models with
a Siemens injection pump, the fuel gauge
sender unit does not have the fuel pump
as part of the assembly. On 1.6 and 2.0
litre models with a Bosch injection pump,
the fuel gauge sender unit is an integral
part of the fuel pump and is not available
separately.*
2 On completion, bleed the fuel system as
described in Section 6.

**9 Fuel tank –
    removal and refitting**

Refer to Chapter 4A, Section 10.

**10 Fast idle thermostatic sensor
     (1.9 litre models) – removal,
     refitting and adjustment**

Removal

Note: *A new sealing washer must be used
when refitting the sensor.*
1 The thermostatic sensor is located in the
side of the thermostat/fuel filter housing.
2 To gain access to the sensor, remove the
relevant air intake duct(s) as described in
Section 3.
3 Drain the cooling system as described in
Chapter 1B.
4 Loosen the clamp screw or nut (as
applicable), and disconnect the fast idle
cable end fitting from the inner cable at

10.4 Slacken the retaining screw (arrowed) then slide the end fitting off the fast idle cable – 1.9 litre models

10.13 Fast idle cable adjustment screw and locknut – 1.9 litre models

the fuel injection pump fast idle lever **(see illustration)**.

5 Slide the cable from the adjustment screw located in the bracket on the fuel injection pump.

6 Using a suitable open-ended spanner, unscrew the thermostatic sensor from the fuel filter/thermostat housing, and withdraw the sensor complete with the cable. Recover the sealing washer and discard it; a new one should be used on refitting.

Refitting

7 Fit the sensor, complete with a new sealing washer, and tighten it securely.

8 Ensure the cable is correctly routed then pass it through the adjustment screw on the bracket.

9 Insert the inner cable through the fast idle lever, and position the end fitting on the cable, but do not tighten the clamp screw or nut (as applicable).

10 Adjust the cable as described in the following paragraphs.

Adjustment

11 If not already done, release the fasteners

from the right-hand side and top of the engine cover then lift off the cover, taking care not to lose its mounting rubbers **(see illustrations 3.1a to 3.1c)**.

12 With the engine cold, slacken the fast idle cable end fitting clamp screw/nut. Push the fast idle lever fully towards the flywheel end of the engine then remove all slack from the cable. With the fast idle lever against its stop and the end fitting firmly against the lever, securely tighten the clamp screw or nut.

13 Check the fast idle lever is firmly against its stop. If necessary, adjust the cable using the screw and locknut arrangement fitted to the injection pump bracket **(see illustration)**.

14 Ensure the end fitting clamp screw/nut and adjuster locknut are securely tightened then measure the exposed length of the fast idle inner cable.

15 Refit the intake duct assembly (where removed – see Section 3).

16 Refill the cooling system as described in Chapter 1B, and run the engine to its normal operating temperature.

17 With the engine at its normal operating temperature, the thermostatic sensor cable should be slack with approximately 0.5 to

1.0 mm of freeplay present. If no freeplay is present in the cable, it is likely that the sensor is faulty. If the thermostatic sensor is functioning correctly, the cable travel should be at least 6 mm from cold to hot.

18 Check that the engine speed increases when the fast idle lever is pushed towards the flywheel end of the engine.

19 If all is well, stop the engine and refit the relevant air intake ducts.

20 Ensure the mounting rubbers are all correctly fitted then install the engine cover, securing it in position with the fasteners.

---

11 Fuel injection pump (1.9 litre models) – adjustment

1 The usual type of tachometer (rev counter), which works from ignition system pulses, cannot be used on diesel engines. For the following adjustments to be accurately carried out, it will be necessary to purchase or hire an appropriate tachometer, or entrust the work to a Peugeot/Citroën dealer or other suitably-equipped specialist.

2 Before making adjustments, warm-up the engine to normal operating temperature. Make sure that the accelerator cable and fast idle cable are correctly adjusted as described in Sections 4 and 10 respectively.

3 Release the fasteners from the right-hand side and top of the engine cover then lift off the cover, taking care not to lose its mounting rubbers **(see illustrations 3.1a to 3.1c)**.

Lucas fuel injection pump

4 With the engine idling, place a shim of the correct thickness (see Specifications), between the pump control lever and the anti-stall adjustment screw **(see illustration)**.

5 Push the manual stop lever back against its stop, and hold it in position by inserting a 3.0 mm diameter rod/drill through the hole in the fast idle lever.

6 The engine speed should be as specified for the anti-stall speed.

7 If adjustment is necessary, loosen the locknut, turn the anti-stall adjustment screw as required, then tighten the locknut.

8 Remove the rod/drill and the shim, and check that the engine is idling at the specified idle speed.

9 If adjustment is necessary, loosen the locknut on the idle speed adjustment screw. Turn the screw as required, and retighten the locknut.

10 Move the pump control lever to increase the engine speed to approximately 3000 rpm, then quickly release the lever. The deceleration period should be between 2.5 and 3.5 seconds, and the engine speed should drop to approximately 50 rpm below idle.

11 If the deceleration is too fast and the engine stalls, unscrew the anti-stall

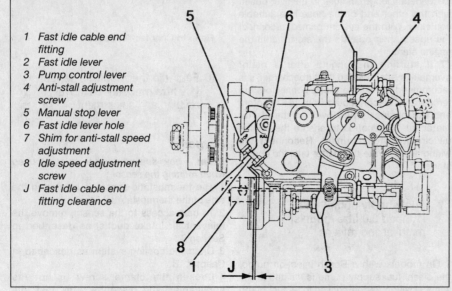

1 Fast idle cable end fitting
2 Fast idle lever
3 Pump control lever
4 Anti-stall adjustment screw
5 Manual stop lever
6 Fast idle lever hole
7 Shim for anti-stall speed adjustment
8 Idle speed adjustment screw
J Fast idle cable end fitting clearance

11.4 Lucas fuel injection pump adjustment points – 1.9 litre models

adjustment screw a quarter-turn towards the control lever. If the deceleration is too slow, resulting in poor engine braking, turn the screw a quarter-turn away from the lever.

12 Retighten the locknut after making an adjustment. Recheck the idle speed, and adjust if necessary as described previously.

13 With the engine idling, check the operation of the manual stop control by turning the stop lever clockwise **(see illustration 11.4)**. The engine must stop instantly.

14 Disconnect the tachometer on completion and refit the engine cover.

Bosch fuel injection pump

15 Loosen the locknut, and unscrew the anti-stall adjustment screw until it is clear of the pump control lever **(see illustration)**.

16 Start the engine and allow it to idle. If the idle speed is incorrect, loosen the locknut and turn the idle speed adjustment screw as required, then retighten the locknut.

17 Insert a shim or feeler blade of the correct thickness between the pump control lever and the anti-stall adjustment screw.

18 The engine speed should be as specified for the anti-stall speed.

19 If adjustment is necessary, loosen the locknut and turn the anti-stall adjustment screw as required. Retighten the locknut.

20 Remove the shim or feeler blade and allow the engine to idle.

21 Slacken the locknut and unscrew the control lever damper adjustment screw, located on the rear of the lever, and insert a 2.0 mm shim or feeler blade between the damper rod and adjustment screw. Make sure the pump control lever is in the idle position then turn the adjustment screw so that the feeler blade/shim is a light, sliding fit between the screw and damper rod. Hold the screw in this position, and tighten its locknut.

22 Move the fast idle lever fully towards the flywheel end of the engine, and check that the engine speed increases to the specified fast idle speed. If necessary, loosen the locknut and turn the fast idle adjusting screw as required, then retighten the locknut.

23 With the engine idling, check the operation of the manual stop control by turning the stop lever. The engine must stop instantly.

24 Disconnect the tachometer on completion.

25 With all the previously described adjustments completed, check the adjustment of the throttle position switch located on the pump control lever as follows.

26 Working at the fuel injection pump end of the accelerator cable, make a mark on the inner cable, 11.0 mm from the end of the outer cable.

27 Have an assistant depress the accelerator pedal until the mark on the inner cable is aligned with the end of the outer cable. With the cable in this position, the throttle position switch contacts should just open.

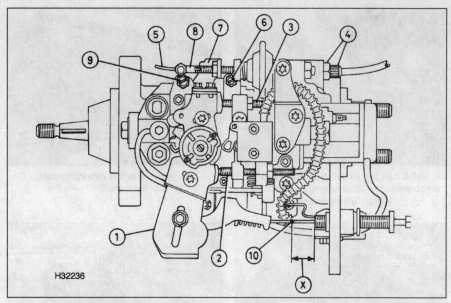

11.15 Bosch fuel injection pump adjustment points – 1.9 litre models

1 *Pump control lever*	5 *Fast idle cable*	10 *Mark to be made on*
2 *Maximum speed*	6 *Idle speed adjustment*	*accelerator cable for*
adjustment screw	*screw*	*throttle position switch*
3 *Anti-stall adjustment screw*	7 *Fast idle lever*	*adjustment*
4 *Fast idle cable adjustment*	8 *Fast idle cable end fitting*	X = 11.0 mm
screw and locknut	9 *Fast idle adjustment screw*	

28 If adjustment is necessary, check that the mark on the inner cable is still aligned with the outer cable end, then slacken the two switch retaining screws.

29 Turn the switch body until the contacts open and tighten the retaining screws.

30 Refit the engine cover on completion.

12 Injection system electrical components – removal and refitting

1.9 litre WJZ engine models

Stop solenoid

1 The stop solenoid is part of the immobiliser unit which is located on the top of the fuel injection pump, its purpose being to cut the fuel supply when the ignition is switched off. Renewal of the immobiliser/solenoid unit is a complex operation which should be entrusted to a Peugeot/Citroën dealer or diesel injection specialist. The immobiliser unit is secured in position with shear bolts which have to be drilled out (a high-risk operation which could lead to damage if carried out carelessly) and the new unit will have to be initialised on refitting.

Fuel cut-off inertia switch

Note: *A fuel cut-off inertia switch is not fitted to all models.*

2 The fuel cut-off inertia switch is located in the right-hand rear corner of the engine compartment. To remove it, first disconnect the battery negative terminal (refer to *Disconnecting the battery* in the Reference Chapter).

3 Unscrew the retaining bolts then disconnect the wiring connector and remove the switch from the vehicle.

4 Refitting is the reverse of removal. On completion, reset the switch by firmly depressing its button.

1.9 litre WJY engine models

Stop solenoid

5 See paragraph 1.

Electronic control unit – pre-September 2002 models

Note: *If a new ECU is to be fitted, this work must be entrusted to a Citroën/Peugeot dealer or suitably-equipped specialist. It is necessary to initialise the new ECU after installation, which requires the use of dedicated diagnostic equipment.*

6 The ECU is located in the plastic box which forms part of the rear of the battery tray. On some engines, access to the ECU retaining nuts/bolts is poor and it is beneficial to remove the battery mounting tray as described in Chapter 5A, then remove the ECU with the tray on the bench.

7 Disconnect the battery negative terminal (refer to *Disconnecting the battery* in the Reference Chapter).

8 Where fitted, lift up the cover over the ECU, then lift the locking catches and

12.8 Lift the locking catches and disconnect the ECU wiring connectors – early 1.9 litre models

12.14a Undo the retaining nuts (arrowed) . . .

12.14b . . . and lift off the ECU cover – later 1.9 litre models

12.15 Lift the ECU off the mounting bracket, then disconnect the wiring connectors – later 1.9 litre models

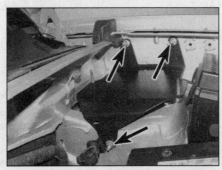

12.16 ECU mounting bracket retaining bolts (arrowed) – later 1.9 litre models

disconnect the ECU wiring connectors **(see illustration)**.

9 Undo the retaining nuts or bolts and lift the ECU mounting plate from the battery tray.

10 Undo the retaining nuts or bolts and separate the ECU from the mounting plate.

11 Refitting is a reverse of the removal procedure ensuring the wiring connectors are securely reconnected.

Electronic control unit – post-September 2002 models

Note: *If a new ECU is to be fitted, this work must be entrusted to a Citroën/Peugeot dealer or suitably-equipped specialist. It is necessary to initialise the new ECU*

after installation, which requires the use of dedicated diagnostic equipment.

12 The ECU is located at the rear left-hand corner of the engine compartment, above the suspension strut upper mounting.

13 Disconnect the battery negative terminal (refer to *Disconnecting the battery* in the Reference Chapter).

14 Undo the retaining nuts and lift off the ECU cover, where fitted **(see illustrations)**.

15 Lift the ECU up and off the mounting bracket, then lift the locking catches and disconnect the wiring connectors **(see illustration)**.

16 If required, the mounting bracket can be removed after undoing the three retaining nuts **(see illustration)**.

17 Refitting is a reverse of the removal procedure ensuring the wiring connectors are securely reconnected.

Airflow meter – pre-September 2002 models

18 Disconnect the battery negative terminal (refer to *Disconnecting the battery* in the Reference Chapter).

19 Slacken the retaining clip securing the air inlet duct to the airflow meter on the air cleaner lid. Detach the duct from the airflow meter.

20 Disconnect the airflow meter wiring connector **(see illustration)**.

21 Slacken the retaining clip securing the airflow meter to the air cleaner lid and lift off the meter **(see illustration)**.

22 Refitting is a reverse of the removal procedure ensuring the wiring connector is securely reconnected.

Airflow meter – post-September 2002 models

23 Disconnect the battery negative terminal (refer to *Disconnecting the battery* in the Reference Chapter).

24 Slacken the retaining clip securing the air inlet duct to the airflow meter on the air cleaner lid.

25 Disconnect the airflow meter wiring connector **(see illustration)**.

26 Undo the four screws securing the lid to

12.20 Disconnect the airflow meter wiring connector – early 1.9 litre models

12.21 Slacken the retaining clip and lift off the airflow meter – early 1.9 litre models

12.25 Disconnect the airflow meter wiring connector – later 1.9 litre models

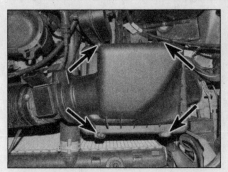

12.26 Undo the four screws (arrowed) securing the lid to the air cleaner housing – later 1.9 litre models

12.27 Undo the two screws (arrowed) and withdraw the airflow meter from the air cleaner lid – later 1.9 litre models

the air cleaner housing **(see illustration)**. Lift off the lid and detach the air inlet duct.

27 Undo the two screws securing the airflow meter to the air cleaner lid and withdraw the meter from the lid **(see illustration)**.

28 Refitting is a reverse of the removal procedure ensuring the wiring connector is securely reconnected.

Crankshaft sensor

29 The crankshaft sensor is situated on the top of the transmission unit.

30 To remove the sensor, first disconnect the battery negative terminal (refer to *Disconnecting the battery* in the Reference Chapter).

31 Disconnect the wiring connector from the sensor then slacken the mounting bolt and remove the sensor from the transmission unit (the sensor is slotted to ease removal) **(see illustrations)**.

32 Refitting is reverse of the removal procedure.

Vehicle speed sensor

33 The vehicle speed sensor is an integral part of the speedometer drive. Refer to Chapter 7 for removal and refitting details.

Injector needle lift sensor

34 The needle lift sensor is an integral part of No 1 cylinder injector. See Section 15 for removal and refitting details.

Coolant temperature sensor

35 The coolant temperature sensor is screwed into the thermostat/fuel filter

housing. Refer to Chapter 3 for removal and refitting information.

Throttle potentiometer and advance solenoid

36 These components are both fitted to the injection pump. If either of the above are faulty, renewal should be entrusted to a Peugeot/Citroën dealer who will have the necessary special equipment to adjust and calibrate the components.

Fuel cut-off inertia switch

Note: *A fuel cut-off inertia switch is not fitted to all models.*

37 Proceed as described in paragraphs 2 to 4.

2.0 litre models

Electronic control unit

Note: *If a new ECU is to be fitted, this work must be entrusted to a Citroën/Peugeot*

12.31a Slacken the mounting bolt . . .

dealer or suitably-equipped specialist. It is necessary to initialise the new ECU after installation, which requires the use of dedicated diagnostic equipment.

38 Proceed as described in paragraphs 6 to 17.

Crankshaft sensor

39 Proceed as described in paragraphs 29 to 32. Access to the sensor is poor; remove the battery and battery tray to improve access (see Chapter 5A)

Vehicle speed sensor

40 The vehicle speed sensor is an integral part of the speedometer drive. Refer to Chapter 7 for removal and refitting details.

Coolant temperature sensor

41 The coolant temperature sensor is fitted to the side of the coolant outlet/thermostat housing on the left-hand end of the cylinder head. Refer to Chapter 3 for removal and refitting information.

Airflow meter

42 Disconnect the battery negative terminal (refer to *Disconnecting the battery* in the Reference Chapter).

43 Disconnect the wiring connector from the airflow meter, located on the air cleaner lid **(see illustration)**.

44 Slacken the retaining clip and disconnect the air inlet duct from the airflow meter.

45 Undo the two screws securing the lid to the air cleaner housing. Lift up the right-hand side of the lid and disengage the two left-hand retaining lugs from the air cleaner housing **(see illustrations)**.

12.31b . . . then free the crankshaft sensor from the bolt and manoeuvre it out of position

12.43 Disconnect the wiring connector from the airflow meter – 2.0 litre models

12.45a Undo the air cleaner lid retaining screws . . .

12.45b . . . disengage the two retaining lugs and lift the lid from the air cleaner housing – 2.0 litre models

46 Undo the two screws securing the airflow meter to the air cleaner lid and withdraw the meter from the lid.

47 Refitting is a reverse of the removal procedure ensuring the wiring connector is securely reconnected.

Camshaft position sensor

48 The camshaft position sensor is fitted to the top of the cylinder head cover right-hand end. Prior to removal, disconnect the battery negative terminal (refer to *Disconnecting the battery* in the Reference Chapter). Remove the fasteners (rotate them 90° to release them) and remove the engine cover (see illustrations 3.20a and 3.20b).

49 Remove the timing belt upper cover (see Chapter 2C).

50 Disconnect the camshaft sensor wiring connector.

51 Unscrew the retaining bolt and remove the sensor from the engine.

52 On refitting, align the camshaft hub timing hole with the cylinder head hole (see Chapter 2C, Section 3). Insert the flywheel locking tool to ensure the camshaft is correctly positioned.

53 Fit the sensor to its mounting bracket and lightly tighten its bolt.

54 If a new sensor is being fitted, position the sensor so its fitting lug is in contact with the rear of the camshaft hub then securely tighten the sensor bolt. The lug automatically sets the sensor air gap to the correct distance and will be knocked off the first time the engine is started.

55 If the original sensor is being refitted, using feeler gauges, set the gap between the sensor tip and camshaft hub to 1.2 mm. Ensure the sensor is correctly positioned then securely tighten its retaining bolt (see illustration). Check the air gap and, if necessary, readjust.

56 Once the sensor is correctly positioned, refit the timing belt cover and remove the flywheel locking tool (where fitted).

57 Reconnect the sensor wiring connector and battery negative terminal, then refit the engine cover.

Fuel temperature sensor

 Warning: Refer to the precautionary information contained in Section 2 before proceeding.

Note: *Do not remove the sensor from the fuel rail unless there is a valid reason to do so. At the time of writing there was no information as to the availability of the sensor seal as a separate item. Consult a Peugeot/Citroën parts stockist for the latest information before proceeding.*

58 The fuel temperature sensor is located towards the right-hand end of the fuel rail (see illustration). Prior to removal, disconnect the battery negative terminal (refer to *Disconnecting the battery* in the Reference Chapter).

59 Remove the fasteners (rotate them 90° to

12.55 Adjust the camshaft sensor air gap as described in the text – 2.0 litre models

release them) and remove the engine cover (see illustrations 3.20a and 3.20b).

60 Disconnect the fuel temperature sensor wiring connector.

61 Thoroughly clean the area around the sensor and its location on the fuel rail.

62 Suitably protect the components below the sensor and have plenty of clean rags handy. Be prepared for considerable fuel spillage.

63 Undo the retaining bolt and withdraw the sensor from the fuel rail. Plug the opening in the fuel rail as soon as the sensor is withdrawn.

64 Prior to refitting, if the original sensor is to be refitted, renew the sensor seal, where applicable (see the note at the start of this sub-Section).

65 Locate the sensor in the fuel rail and refit the retaining bolt, tightened securely.

66 Refit the sensor wiring connector and reconnect the battery.

67 Observing the precautions listed in Section 2, prime the fuel system as described in Section 6, then start the engine and allow it to idle. Check for leaks at the fuel temperature sensor with the engine idling. If satisfactory, increase the engine speed to 4000 rpm and check again for leaks. Take the car for a short road test and check for leaks once again on return. If any leaks are detected, obtain and fit a new sensor.

68 Refit the engine cover on completion.

Fuel pressure sensor

 Warning: Refer to the precautionary information contained in Section 2 before proceeding.

Note: *A 27 mm forked adaptor and a new sensor sealing ring will be required for this operation.*

69 The fuel pressure sensor is located centrally on the underside of the fuel rail (see illustration 12.58).

70 Disconnect the battery negative terminal (refer to *Disconnecting the battery* in the Reference Chapter), then release the fasteners (rotate them 90° to release them) and remove the engine cover (see illustrations 3.20a and 3.20b).

71 Release the retaining clip and disconnect the crankcase ventilation hose from the cylinder head cover.

72 Disconnect the fuel supply and return

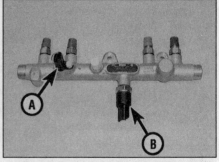

12.58 Fuel temperature sensor (A) and fuel pressure sensor (B) locations on the fuel rail (shown removed for clarity) – 2.0 litre models

hose quick-release fittings at the fuel filter, using a small screwdriver to release the locking clip. Suitably plug or cover the open unions to prevent dirt entry. Release the fuel hoses from the relevant retaining clips.

73 Disconnect the fuel pressure sensor wiring connector.

74 Thoroughly clean the area around the sensor and its location on the fuel rail.

75 Suitably protect the components below the sensor and have plenty of clean rags handy. Be prepared for considerable fuel spillage.

76 Using the 27 mm forked adaptor and a socket bar, unscrew the fuel pressure sensor from the base of the fuel rail.

77 Obtain and fit a new sealing ring to the sensor prior to refitting.

78 Locate the sensor in the fuel rail and tighten it to the specified torque.

79 Reconnect the sensor wiring connector, fuel hoses, crankcase ventilation hose and battery.

80 Observing the precautions listed in Section 2, prime the fuel system as described in Section 6, then start the engine and allow it to idle. Check for leaks at the fuel pressure sensor with the engine idling. If satisfactory, increase the engine speed to 4000 rpm and check again for leaks. Take the car for a short road test and check for leaks once again on return. If any leaks are detected, obtain and fit another new sensor sealing ring.

81 Refit the engine cover on completion.

Third piston deactivator solenoid valve

82 The solenoid valve is mounted on the top of the injection pump; it is an integral part of the pump and cannot be renewed. If the valve is faulty the injection pump will have to be renewed or repaired. Never attempt to remove the solenoid from the pump.

High-pressure fuel regulator

83 The high-pressure fuel regulator is mounted on the rear of the injection pump; it is an integral part of the pump and cannot be renewed. If the regulator is faulty the injection pump will have to be renewed or repaired. Never attempt to remove the regulator from the pump.

12.85 Fuel heater assembly – 2.0 litre models

12.93 Disconnect the wiring connector (arrowed) . . .

12.94 . . . then detach the cable and remove the accelerator pedal position sensor from the vehicle – early 2.0 litre models

Fuel cut-off inertia switch

84 Refer to paragraphs 2 to 4.

Electrically-operated fuel heater

 Warning: Refer to the precautionary information contained in Section 2 before proceeding.

85 The fuel heater is fitted to the fuel feed pipe to the filter housing (see illustration).

86 Disconnect the battery negative terminal (refer to *Disconnecting the battery* in the Reference Chapter), then release the fasteners (rotate them 90° to release them) and remove the engine cover (see illustrations 3.20a and 3.20b).

87 Disconnect the wiring connector from the heater.

88 Remove all traces of dirt from around the heater; the heater and its surrounding area must be clean and dry before proceeding. Position a wad of rag beneath the heater to catch any spilt fuel.

89 Release the clips and disconnect the fuel pipes from the heater. Plug the fuel pipes to prevent the entry of dirt into the fuel system.

90 Unscrew the retaining bolt and remove the fuel heater from the engine.

91 Refitting is the reverse of removal. On completion, prime the fuel system as described in Section 5.

Accelerator pedal position sensor – pre-September 2002 models

92 Working in the engine compartment, unscrew the two bolts and free the accelerator

pedal position sensor bracket from the side of the air cleaner housing.

93 Disconnect the sensor wiring connector (see illustration).

94 Free the accelerator inner cable from the sensor cam then free the outer cable from sensor bracket, complete with the spring clip, and remove the sensor from the vehicle (see illustration).

95 Refitting is the reverse of removal, adjusting the accelerator cable as described in Section 4.

Accelerator pedal position sensor – September 2002 to September 2005 (to RPO 10479) models

96 The accelerator pedal position sensor is located above the right-hand engine/transmission mounting.

97 Disconnect the battery negative terminal (refer to *Disconnecting the battery* in the Reference Chapter), then disconnect the wiring connector from the pedal position sensor (see illustration).

98 Free the accelerator inner cable from the sensor cam, then pull the outer cable out from its mounting bracket rubber grommet, complete with spring clip.

99 Undo the two mounting bracket retaining bolts and withdraw the pedal position sensor and mounting bracket from the engine compartment.

100 Undo the two nuts and bolts securing the sensor to the mounting bracket and separate the two components.

101 Refitting is a reversal of the removal

procedure. On completion, adjust the accelerator cable as described in Section 4.

Accelerator pedal position sensor – September 2005-on (from RPO 10480) models

102 The accelerator pedal position sensor is integral with the electronic accelerator pedal.

1.6 litre models

Note: *Procedures as for paragraphs 38 to 102 in preceding sub-Section, except for the following.*

Airflow meter

103 The airflow meter is located in the intake ducting from the air cleaner housing.

104 Disconnect the meter wiring plug (see illustration).

105 Slacken the retaining clips and disconnect the air intake ducting from either side of the airflow meter. Suitably plug or cover the turbocharger intake duct, using clean rag to prevent any dirt or foreign material from entering. The airflow meter is bolted to the air cleaner cover.

106 Refitting is reverse of the removal procedure.

Camshaft position sensor

107 The camshaft position sensor is mounted on the right-hand end of the cylinder head cover, directly behind the camshaft sprocket.

108 Remove the upper timing belt cover, as described in Chapter 2B.

109 Unplug the sensor wiring connector.

110 Undo the bolt and pull the sensor from position (see illustration).

12.97 Disconnect the wiring connector (arrowed) from the accelerator pedal position sensor – later 2.0 litre models

12.104 Airflow meter wiring plug (arrowed) – 1.6 litre models

12.110 Undo the camshaft sensor retaining bolt (arrowed) – 1.6 litre models

12.111a The gap between the sensor and the signal wheel (arrowed) . . .

12.111b . . . must be 1.2 mm measured with a feeler gauge – 1.6 litre models

12.116 Unscrew the bolts securing the noise attenuator to the turbocharger . . .

12.117a . . . then release the clip . . .

12.117b . . . and remove the noise attenuator

12.118a Disconnect the wiring from the position sensor . . .

111 Upon refitting, position the sensor so that the air gap between the sensor end and the webs of the signal wheel is 1.2 mm, measured with feeler gauges **(see illustrations)**. If a new sensor is being fitted, position it so the nipple of the sensor is just in contact with the camshaft signal wheel. Tighten the sensor retaining bolt to the specified torque.
112 The remainder of refitting is a reversal of removal.

Fuel temperature sensor

113 No fuel temperature sensor is fitted to later models

Fuel pressure sensor

Note: *Citroën/Peugeot insist that the fuel pressure sensor must not be removed during the vehicle warranty period.*
114 The fuel pressure sensor is located in the end of the fuel common rail at the left-hand rear of the engine. Access is gained by removing the battery and its mounting bracket, the air cleaner assembly, and the fuel filter (without disconnecting the fuel lines). The remaining removal and refitting procedure is as given in paragraphs 73 to 80 in this Section. Finally, refit the fuel filter, air cleaner assembly and battery.

Throttle housing

115 Disconnect the battery negative terminal (refer to *Disconnecting the battery* in the Reference Chapter). Remove the engine top cover.
116 Unscrew the bolts securing the noise attenuator to the turbocharger outlet flange **(see illustration)**.
117 Loosen the clip and disconnect the intercooler hose, then remove the noise attenuator **(see illustrations)**.
118 Unclip the wiring from the top of the throttle housing and disconnect the three wiring plugs, noting where they are located **(see illustrations)**.
119 Loosen the clips and disconnect the intercooler and inlet manifold hoses from the throttle housing **(see illustrations)**.

12.118b . . . pressure sensor . . .

12.118.c . . . and temperature sensor

12.119b . . . and inlet manifold hose

12.119a Disconnect the intercooler hose . . .

12.120a Unscrew the mounting bracket bolts . . .

12.120b . . . remove the throttle housing and bracket . . .

12.120c . . . then unscrew the bolts and separate the housing from the bracket

120 Unscrew the mounting bolts and withdraw the throttle housing together with mounting bracket from the engine, then undo the screws and separate the housing from the bracket **(see illustrations).**
121 Refitting is a reversal of removal.

13 Fuel injection pump – removal and refitting

Caution: Be careful not to allow dirt into the injection pump or injector pipes during this procedure.

1.9 litre models

Note: If the injection pump is being taken to a injection specialist for repair, unlock the immobiliser module as follows before disconnecting the battery. Switch on the ignition and lower the driver's door window. Get out of the vehicle and close all the doors then switch off the ignition. Reach in through the window and switch on the ignition again, wait at least ten seconds then switch the ignition off. Immediately disconnect the battery negative terminal (refer to 'Disconnecting the battery' in the Reference Chapter) then disconnect the wiring connectors from the injection pump (the pump must be disconnected within ten minutes of the ignition being switched off). If the immobiliser module is not unlocked it will not be possible for the pump repairers to test the pump.

Removal

1 Disconnect the battery negative terminal (refer to *Disconnecting the battery* in the Reference Chapter).
2 Release the fasteners from the right-hand side and top of the engine cover then lift off the cover, taking care not to lose its mounting rubbers **(see illustrations 3.1a to 3.1c).**
3 Remove the inlet duct connecting the air cleaner to the EGR valve housing (see Section 3).
4 Cover the components beneath the injection pump with a plastic bag, as a precaution against fuel spillage.
5 Remove the injection pump sprocket as described in Chapter 2C, Section 9.

6 Remove the upper section of the inlet manifold (see Section 17).
7 Disconnect the accelerator cable from the fuel injection pump (see Section 4).
8 Disconnect the fast idle cable from the fuel injection pump (see Section 10).
9 Trace the injection pump fuel feed pipe back to the filter. Wipe clean the pipe end fitting then release and disconnect the pipe from the filter. Plug the pipe end and filter housing union to minimise fuel loss and prevent the entry of dirt into the system.
10 Wipe clean the area around the injection pump fuel return metal pipe unions. Disconnect the return pipe and hose from the metal pipe and plug the pipe and union ends to minimise fuel loss and prevent the entry of dirt into the system.
11 Disconnect the wiring connectors from the injection pump **(see illustration).**
12 Remove all traces of dirt from all the injector pipe unions. Unscrew the union nuts securing the injector pipes to the fuel injection pump and injectors. Counterhold the adaptors on the pump, while unscrewing the pipe-to-pump union nuts. Remove the pipes as a set. Plug the injection pump/injector unions to prevent the entry of dirt.
13 Slacken the pump rear mounting bolt.
14 Unscrew the three front mounting bolts securing the pump to the mounting bracket then manoeuvre the pump out of position.
15 If necessary, unbolt the pump mounting bracket and remove it from the cylinder head, taking care not to lose its locating dowels.

Refitting

16 If necessary, ensure the locating dowels are in position, then refit the mounting bracket to the cylinder head. Tighten the bracket bolts to the specified torque.
17 Ensure the pump rear mounting bolt, spacer, washer and nut are correctly fitted to the mounting bracket.
18 Manoeuvre the pump into position and seat it correctly in the mounting bracket.
19 Refit the pump front mounting bolts, tightening them to the specified torque. Once the front mounting bolts have been tightened, tighten the rear mounting bolt to the specified torque.
20 Refit and reconnect the injector fuel pipes.

Loosely tighten all the union nuts to ensure all pipes are correctly seated then go around and tighten them to the specified torque. Counterhold the injection pump adaptors whilst tightening the injection pump end nuts.
21 Reconnect all relevant wiring to the pump.
22 Securely reconnect the feed and return pipes to the injection pump and fuel filter housing.
23 Reconnect and adjust the accelerator cable as described in Section 4.
24 Reconnect and adjust the fast idle cable as described in Section 10.
25 Refit the injection pump sprocket and timing belt as described in Chapter 2C.
26 Refit the inlet manifold as described in Section 17.
27 Prime the fuel system as described in Section 6. Start the engine and check for signs of fuel leaks before refitting the engine cover.

2.0 litre models

Note: A new fuel pump-to-fuel rail high pressure fuel pipe will be required for refitting.

Removal

28 Disconnect the battery negative terminal (refer to *Disconnecting the battery* in the Reference Chapter).
29 Remove the injection pump sprocket as described in Chapter 2C, Section 9.
30 At the connections above the fuel pump, disconnect the fuel supply and return hose quick-release fittings using a small screwdriver

13.11 Disconnect the wiring connectors (arrowed) from the rear of the injection pump – later 1.9 litre models

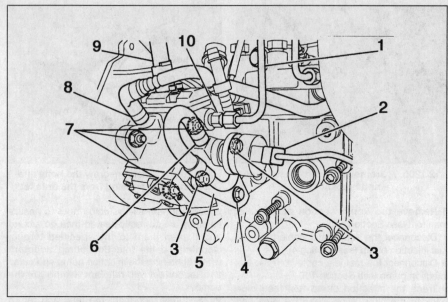

13.36 Injection pump details – 2.0 litre models

1 High-pressure pipe
2 High-pressure fuel regulator wiring connector
3 Rear bracket-to-pump bolts
4 Rear bracket-to-mounting bracket bolt
5 Rear bracket
6 Fuel return hose
7 Pump front mounting nut/ bolts
8 Fuel feed hose
9 Third piston deactivator solenoid valve wiring connector
10 Fuel pipe adaptor

to release the locking clip. Suitably plug or cover the open unions to prevent dirt entry.

31 Similarly disconnect the supply and return hose quick-release fittings at the fuel filter and plug or cover the open unions. Release the fuel hoses (and, on later models, the priming pump) from the relevant retaining clips.

32 Lift the fuel filter out of its mounting bracket and move it slightly to one side, away from the pump.

33 Undo the bolts and remove the filter mounting bracket from the engine.

34 Undo the bolts securing the plastic wiring harness guide to the front of the engine. It will be necessary to lift up the wiring harness as far as possible for access to the rear of the fuel pump. If necessary, disconnect the relevant wiring connectors to enable the harness and guide assembly to be moved further for additional access.

35 Disconnect the wiring connector at the pressure control valve on the rear of the fuel pump, and at the piston de-activator switch on the top of the pump.

36 Thoroughly clean the high pressure fuel pipe unions on the fuel pump and fuel rail. Using an open-ended spanner, unscrew the union nuts securing the high pressure fuel pipe to the fuel pump and fuel rail. Counterhold the unions on the pump and fuel rail with a second spanner, while unscrewing the union nuts. Withdraw the high pressure fuel pipe and plug or cover the open unions to prevent dirt entry **(see illustration)**. Note that a new high pressure fuel pipe will be required for refitting.

37 Undo the nut and bolt securing the fuel pump rear mounting to the mounting bracket.

38 Undo the nut and two bolts securing the front of the fuel pump to the mounting bracket. Withdraw the pump, complete with fuel supply and return hoses, rearwards, and lift it off the engine.

Caution: The high pressure fuel pump is manufactured to extremely close tolerances and must not be dismantled in any way. Do not unscrew the fuel pipe male union on the rear of the pump, or attempt to remove the pressure control valve, piston de-activator switch, or the seal on the pump shaft. No parts for the pump are available separately and if the unit is in any way suspect, it must be renewed.

Refitting

39 Locate the pump on the mounting bracket, and refit the front retaining nut and the two bolts. Refit the nut and bolt securing the fuel pump rear mounting to the mounting bracket, then tighten all the mountings to the specified torque.

40 Remove the blanking plugs from the fuel pipe unions on the pump and fuel rail. Locate a new high pressure fuel pipe over the unions and screw on the union nuts finger tight at this stage.

41 Using a torque wrench and crow-foot adaptor, tighten the fuel pipe union nuts to the specified torque. Counterhold the unions on the pump and fuel rail with an open-ended spanner, while tightening the union nuts **(see illustration)**.

13.41 When refitting the new high-pressure pipe to the pump and fuel rail, counterhold their adapters to tighten the union nuts to the specified torque – 2.0 litre models

42 Reconnect the wiring connector at the pressure control valve on the rear of the fuel pump.

43 Reposition and secure the plastic wiring harness guide to the front of the engine, and reconnect any additional wiring disconnected for access.

44 Refit the filter mounting bracket to the engine and securely tighten the retaining bolts. Locate the fuel filter back in position in the mounting bracket.

45 Remove the blanking plugs and reconnect the supply and return hose quick-release fittings at the fuel filter, and at the connections above the fuel pump. Secure the hoses with their respective retaining clips.

46 Refit the injection pump sprocket and timing belt as described in Chapter 2C.

47 Observing the precautions listed in Section 2, prime the fuel system as described in Section 6, then start the engine and allow it to idle. Check for leaks at the high pressure fuel pipe unions with the engine idling. If satisfactory, increase the engine speed to 4000 rpm and check again for leaks. Take the car for a short road test and check for leaks once again on return. If any leaks are detected, obtain and fit another new high pressure fuel pipe. **Do not** attempt to cure even the slightest leak by further tightening of the pipe unions.

48 Refit the engine cover on completion.

1.6 litre models

Note: *A new fuel pump-to-fuel rail high-pressure fuel pipe will be required for refitting.*

Removal

49 Disconnect the battery (see Chapter 5A) and remove the timing belt as described in Chapter 2B. After removal of the timing belt, temporarily refit the right-hand engine mounting but do not fully tighten the bolts.

50 Remove the air filter assembly as described in Section 3.

51 Drain the cooling system and remove the EGR cooler as described in Chapter 4D.

52 Undo the bolts/nuts and remove the 3

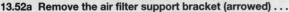

13.52a Remove the air filter support bracket (arrowed) . . .   **13.52b . . . and the brackets around the fuel pump (arrowed)**

support brackets above the fuel common rail and the high-pressure pump **(see illustrations)**.
53 Undo the union nuts and remove the high-pressure fuel pipe between the fuel common rail and the high-pressure pump. Plug the openings to prevent contamination.
54 Disconnect the wiring plug from the high-pressure fuel pump.
55 Depress the release buttons and disconnect the fuel supply and return hoses from the pump. Note that the hoses may have a release button on each side of the fitting. Plug the openings to prevent contamination.
56 Hold the pump sprocket stationary, and loosen the centre nut securing it to the pump shaft **(see Tool Tip)**.
57 The fuel pump sprocket is a taper fit on the pump shaft and it will be necessary to make up a tool to release it from the taper **(see Tool Tip)**. Partially unscrew the sprocket retaining nut, fit the home-made tool, and secure it to the sprocket with two 7.0 mm bolts and nuts. Prevent the sprocket from rotating as before, and screw down the nuts, forcing the sprocket off the shaft taper. Once the taper is released, remove the tool, unscrew the nut fully, and remove the sprocket from the pump shaft.

58 Undo the three bolts, and remove the pump from the mounting bracket.
Caution: The high-pressure fuel pump is manufactured to extremely close tolerances and must not be dismantled in any way. Do not unscrew the fuel pipe male union on the rear of the pump, or attempt to remove the sensor, piston de-activator switch, or the seal on the pump shaft. No parts for the pump are available separately and if the unit is in any way suspect, it must be renewed.

Refitting

59 Refitting is a reversal of removal, noting the following points:
a) *Always renew the pump-to-fuel common rail high-pressure pipe.*
b) *On engines with camshaft driven pumps, renew the drive seal.*
c) *With everything reassembled and reconnected, and observing the precautions listed in Section 2, start the engine and allow it to idle. Check for leaks at the high-pressure fuel pipe unions with the engine idling. If satisfactory, increase the engine speed to 3000 rpm and check again for leaks.*

d) *Take the car for a short road test and check for leaks once again on return. If any leaks are detected, obtain and fit another new high-pressure fuel pipe. Do not attempt to cure even the slightest leak by further tightening of the pipe unions.*

14 Injection timing –
checking and adjustment

1.9 litre models

1 The injection timing is set when the timing belt is installed. If at any time a fault is suspected, referring to Chapter 2C, Section 3, remove the timing belt covers and check that the flywheel, camshaft and injection pump timing holes are all correctly aligned so the locking tools can be inserted. If the timing holes are correctly aligned, the injection pump timing is correct (Peugeot/Citroën do not specify any static or dynamic timing figures for this engine – on the WJY engine the timing is being constantly altered by the ECU anyway). If not, remove and refit the timing belt as described in Chapter 2C.

1.6 and 2.0 litre models

2 On 1.6 and 2.0 litre engines, the injection timing is determined by the ECU using the information from its various sensors. Checking and adjustment can only be carried out using specialist diagnostic equipment (see Section 1).

15 Fuel injectors –
removal and refitting

Sprocket holding tool can be made from two lengths of steel strip bolted together to form a forked end. Bend the ends of the strip through 90° to form the 'prongs'.

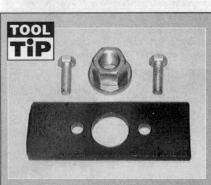

Make a sprocket releasing tool from a short strip of steel. Drill two holes in the strip to correspond with the two holes in the sprocket. Drill a third hole just large enough to accept the flats of the sprocket retaining nut.

⚠ *Warning: Exercise extreme caution when working on the fuel injectors. Never expose the hands or any part of the body to injector spray, as the high working pressure can cause the fuel to penetrate the skin,*

15.2 Disconnecting the leak-off pipe from the injector – 1.9 litre models

15.3 Unscrewing an injector pipe nut – 1.9 litre models

15.14 Retain the adaptors whilst slackening the union nuts then remove and discard the high-pressure pipe linking the injector to the fuel rail – 2.0 litre models

with possibly fatal results. *You are strongly advised to have any work which involves testing the injectors under pressure carried out by a dealer or fuel injection specialist.*

1.9 litre models

Caution: Be careful not to allow dirt into the injection pump or injectors during this procedure.

Removal

1 Remove the upper section of the inlet manifold as described in Section 17.

2 Disconnect the leak-off pipe(s) from the injector to be removed **(see illustration)**.

3 Remove all traces of dirt from all the injector pipe unions. Unscrew the union nuts securing the injector pipes to the fuel injection pump and injectors **(see illustration)**. Counterhold the adaptors on the pump, while unscrewing the pipe-to-pump union nuts. Remove the pipes as a set. Plug the injection pump/injector unions to prevent the entry of dirt.

4 On WJY engines, if No 1 injector is being removed trace the needle lift sensor wiring back from the injector and disconnect its wiring connector from the main harness.

5 Remove all traces of dirt from around the injector then unscrew the injector from the cylinder head. Recover the injector fire seal washer from the cylinder head and discard it; a new one must be used on refitting.

Caution: Take care not to drop the injectors, or allow the needles at their tips to become damaged. The injectors are precision-made to fine limits, and must not be handled

roughly. *In particular, never mount them in a bench vice.*

Refitting

6 Fit the new fire seal washer ensuring its convex surface is facing upwards (towards the injector).

7 Carefully refit the injector to the cylinder head, tightening it to the specified torque.

8 Reconnect the leak-off pipe(s) to the injector. Where necessary, reconnect the needle lift sensor wiring connector.

9 With all the injectors correctly installed, refit and reconnect the injector pipes. Loosely tighten all the union nuts to ensure all pipes are correctly seated then go around and tighten them to the specified torque. Counterhold the injection pump adaptors whilst tightening the injection pump end nuts.

10 Refit the inlet manifold as described in Section 17.

11 Prime the fuel system as described in Section 6. Start the engine and check for signs of fuel leaks before refitting the engine cover.

2.0 litre models

⚠️ *Warning: Refer to the information contained in Section 2 before proceeding.*

Note: *The following procedure describes the removal and refitting of the injectors as a complete set, although each injector may be removed individually if required. New copper washers, upper seals, injector clamp retaining nuts and a high pressure fuel pipe will be required for each disturbed injector when refitting.*

Removal

12 Carry out the operations described in Section 16, paragraphs 1 to 4.

13 At the connections above the fuel pump, disconnect the fuel supply and return hose quick-release fittings using a small screwdriver to release the locking clip. Suitably plug or cover the open unions to prevent dirt entry, then release the fuel hoses (and, on later models, the priming pump) from the relevant retaining clips.

14 Thoroughly clean all the high pressure fuel pipe unions on the fuel injectors and fuel rail. Using two open-ended spanners, unscrew the union nuts securing the high pressure fuel pipes to the fuel injectors and fuel rail **(see illustration)**. Withdraw the high pressure fuel pipes and plug or cover the open unions on the injectors and fuel rail to prevent dirt entry. Note that a new high pressure fuel pipe will be required for each removed injector when refitting.

15 Extract the retaining circlip and disconnect the leak-off pipe from each fuel injector **(see illustration)**.

16 Unscrew the nut and remove the washer securing each injector clamp to its cylinder head stud **(see illustration)**. Note that new clamp nuts will be required for refitting.

17 Withdraw the injectors, together with their clamps, from the cylinder head **(see illustration)**. Slide the clamp off the injector once it is clear of the mounting stud. If the injectors are a tight fit in the cylinder head and

15.15 Remove the retaining clip and disconnect the leak-off pipe connector from the injector – 2.0 litre models

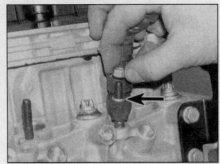

15.16 Slacken and remove the injector retaining nut and lift off the washer (arrowed) – 2.0 litre models

15.17 Remove the injector and retaining clamp from the cylinder head – 2.0 litre models

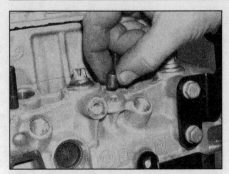

15.18 Recover the injector clamp locating dowel – 2.0 litre models

15.23a Slide the new upper seal onto the injector . . .

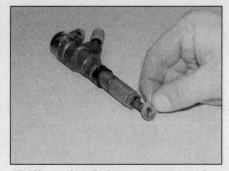

15.23b . . . then fit the new copper washer – 2.0 litre models

cannot be released, unscrew the mounting stud using a stud extractor and slide off the injector clamp. Using an open-ended spanner engaged with the clamp locating slot on the injector body, free the injector by twisting it and at the same time lifting it upwards.

18 Recover the injector clamp locating dowel from the cylinder head **(see illustration)**.

19 Remove the copper washer and the upper seal from each injector, or from the cylinder head if they remained in place during injector removal. New copper washers and upper seals will be required for refitting.

20 Examine each injector visually for any signs of obvious damage or deterioration. If any defects are apparent, renew the injector(s).

Caution: The injectors are manufactured to extremely close tolerances and must not be dismantled in any way. Do not unscrew the fuel pipe union on the side of the injector, or separate any parts of the injector body. Do not attempt to clean carbon deposits from the injector nozzle or carry out any form of ultrasonic or pressure testing.

21 If the injectors are in a satisfactory condition, plug the fuel pipe union (if not already done) and suitably cover the electrical element and the injector nozzle.

22 Prior to refitting, obtain new copper washers, upper seals, injector clamp retaining nuts and high pressure fuel pipes for each removed injector.

Refitting

23 Locate a new upper seal on the body of each injector, and place a new copper washer on the injector nozzle **(see illustrations)**.

24 Refit the injector clamp locating dowels to the cylinder head.

25 Place the injector clamp in the slot on each injector body and refit the injectors to the cylinder head. Guide the clamp over the mounting stud and onto the locating dowel as each injector is inserted.

26 Fit the washer and a new injector clamp retaining nut to each mounting stud. Tighten the nuts finger tight only at this stage.

27 Working on one fuel injector at a time, remove the blanking plugs from the fuel

pipe unions on the fuel rail and the relevant injector. Locate a new high pressure fuel pipe over the unions and screw on the union nuts. Take care not to cross-thread the nuts or strain the fuel pipes as they are fitted. Once the union nut threads have started, tighten the nuts moderately tight only at this stage.

28 When all the fuel pipes are in place, tighten the injector clamp retaining nuts to the specified torque.

29 Using an open-ended spanner, hold each fuel pipe union in turn and tighten the union nut to the specified torque using a torque wrench and crow-foot adaptor. Tighten all the disturbed union nuts in the same way.

30 Connect the leak-off pipes to each fuel injector and secure with the retaining circlips.

31 Remove the blanking plugs and reconnect the supply and return hose quick-release fittings at the connections above the fuel pump. Secure the hoses with their respective retaining clips.

32 Reposition the plastic wiring harness guide over the two mounting studs and secure with the retaining nuts.

33 Reconnect the fuel injector and pump piston de-activator switch wiring connectors, and reconnect any additional wiring disconnected for access.

34 Check that everything has been reconnected and secured with the relevant retaining clips then reconnect the battery negative terminal.

35 Observing the precautions listed in Section 2, prime the fuel system as described in Section 6, then start the engine and allow

it to idle. Check for leaks at the high pressure fuel pipe unions with the engine idling. If satisfactory, increase the engine speed to 4000 rpm and check again for leaks. Take the car for a short road test and check for leaks once again on return. If any leaks are detected, obtain and fit additional new high pressure fuel pipes as required. **Do not** attempt to cure even the slightest leak by further tightening of the pipe unions.

36 Refit the engine cover on completion.

1.6 litre models

 Warning: Refer to the information contained in Section 2 before proceeding.

Note: *The following procedure describes the removal and refitting of the injectors as a complete set, however each injector may be removed individually if required. New copper washers, upper seals, and a high-pressure fuel pipe will be required for each disturbed injector when refitting.*

Removal

37 Remove the plastic cover from the top of the engine, and disconnect the battery negative lead as described in Chapter 5A.

38 Remove the EGR cooler as described in Chapter 4D.

39 Undo the bolts, slacken the clamps and remove the air intake ducting assembly from between the turbocharger and the intake manifold. Note their fitted positions, and disconnect the various wiring plugs as the assembly is withdrawn **(see illustrations)**.

40 Disconnect the injector wiring plugs.

15.39a Intake ducting clamps (arrowed) . . .

15.39b . . . and bolts (arrowed)

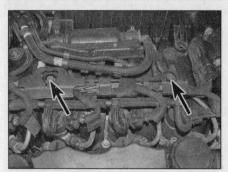

15.41 Wiring harness support bracket bolts (arrowed)

15.43 Prise out the clip and pull the return pipe from each injector

15.44 Use a second spanner to counterhold the high-pressure pipe union nuts

15.45a Injector retaining nuts (arrowed)

15.45b Use a spanner to twist the injector and free it from position

15.47 Note the injector classification number

41 Undo the bolts and move aside the wiring harness support bracket **(see illustration)**.
42 Release the manual fuel priming pump and its support.
43 Extract the retaining circlip and disconnect the leak-off pipe from each fuel injector **(see illustration)**.
44 Clean the area around the high-pressure fuel pipes between the injectors and the fuel common rail, then unscrew the pipe unions. Use a second spanner to counterhold the union screwed in to the injector body **(see illustration)**. The injectors screwed-in unions must not be allowed to move. Remove the bracket above the fuel common rail unions, then remove the pipes. Plug the openings in the fuel common rail and injectors to prevent dirt ingress.
45 Unscrew the injector retaining nuts, and carefully pull or lever the injector from place. If necessary, use an open-ended spanner and twist the injector to free it from position

(see illustrations). Do not lever against or pull on the solenoid housing at the top of the injector. Note down the injectors position – if the injectors are to be refitted, they must be refitted to their original locations. If improved access is required, undo the bolts and remove the oil separator housing from the front of the cylinder head cover.
46 Remove the copper washer and the upper seal from each injector, or from the cylinder head if they remained in place during injector removal. New copper washers and upper seals will be required for refitting. Cover the injector hole in the cylinder head to prevent dirt ingress.
47 Examine each injector visually for any signs of obvious damage or deterioration. If any defects are apparent, renew the injector(s). Note down the 8-digit injector classification number – this may be needed during the refitting procedure if the ECU has been replaced **(see illustration)**.

Caution: The injectors are manufactured to extremely close tolerances and must not be dismantled in any way. Do not unscrew the fuel pipe union on the side of the injector, or separate any parts of the injector body. Do not attempt to clean carbon deposits from the injector nozzle or carry out any form of ultrasonic or pressure testing.

Refitting

48 Locate a new upper seal on the body of each injector, and place a new copper washer on the injector nozzle **(see illustrations)**.
49 Refit the injector clamp locating dowels (where fitted) to the cylinder head.
50 Ensure the injector clamps are in place over their respective circlips on the injector bodies, the fit the injectors into place in the cylinder head. If the original injectors are being refitted, ensure they are fitted into their original positions **(see illustration)**.

15.48a Ensure the circlip (arrowed) is in place on the 1.6 litre engine injectors . . .

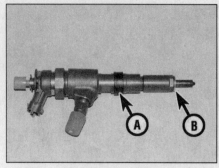

15.48b . . . then fit the upper seal (A) and copper washer (B)

15.50 Fit the injectors into their original locations

15.54 Tighten the high-pressure pipe union nuts using a 'crow-foot' adapter

16.9a Retain the adaptors whilst slackening the union nuts then remove and discard the high-pressure pipes linking the pump and injectors to the fuel rail – 2.0 litre models

16.9b Plug/cap all unions to prevent the entry of dirt into the fuel system – 2.0 litre models

51 Fit the injector retaining bolts/nuts, but only finger-tighten them at this stage. When tightening the nuts/bolts, ensure the clamps stay horizontal.

52 Working on one fuel injector at a time, remove the blanking plugs from the fuel pipe unions on the fuel common rail and the relevant injector. Locate a new high-pressure fuel pipe over the unions and screw on the union nuts. Take care not to cross-thread the nuts or strain the fuel pipes as they are fitted. Once the union nut threads have started, finger-tighten the nuts only at this stage, to the ends of the threads.

53 When all the fuel pipes are in place, tighten the injector clamp retaining nuts/bolts to the specified torque (and angle where applicable).

54 Using an open-ended spanner, hold each fuel pipe union in turn and tighten the union nut to the specified torque using a torque wrench and crow-foot adapter **(see illustration)**. Tighten all the disturbed union nuts in the same way.

55 If new injectors have been fitted, their classification numbers must be programmed into the engine management ECM using dedicated diagnostic equipment/scanner. If this equipment is not available, entrust this task to a Citroën/Peugeot dealer or suitably-equipped repairer. Note that it should be possible to drive the vehicle, albeit with reduced performance/increased emissions, to a repairer for the numbers to be programmed.

56 The remainder of refitting is a reversal of removal, following the points listed in Paragraph 40 of the previous Section.

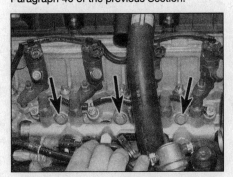

16.11a Undo the mounting bolts (arrowed) . . .

16 Fuel rail (1.6 and 2.0 litre models) – removal and refitting

⚠ **Warning: Refer to the infor-mation contained in Section 2 before proceeding.**
Note: *A complete new set of high pressure fuel pipes will be required for refitting.*

2.0 litre models
Removal

1 Disconnect the battery negative terminal (refer to *Disconnecting the battery* in the Reference Section of this manual).

2 Undo the four plastic nuts and lift off the engine cover **(see illustrations 3.20a and 3.20b)**.

3 Disconnect the wiring connectors at the fuel injectors and at the piston de-activator switch on the top of the fuel pump.

4 Undo the two nuts securing the plastic wiring harness guide to the cylinder head. Lift the guide off the two mounting studs and move it clear of the fuel rail. Disconnect any additional wiring connectors as necessary to enable the harness and guide assembly to be moved further for increased access.

5 Release the retaining clip and disconnect the crankcase ventilation hose from the cylinder head cover.

6 At the connections above the fuel pump,

16.11b . . . and manoeuvre the fuel rail out of position – 2.0 litre models

disconnect the fuel supply and return hose quick-release fittings using a small screwdriver to release the locking clip. Suitably plug or cover the open unions to prevent dirt entry.

7 Similarly disconnect the supply and return hose quick-release fittings at the fuel filter and plug or cover the open unions. Release the fuel hoses (and, on later models, the priming pump) from the relevant retaining clips.

8 Thoroughly clean all the high pressure fuel pipe unions on the fuel rail, fuel pump and injectors. Using an open-ended spanner, unscrew the union nuts securing the high pressure fuel pipe to the fuel pump and fuel rail. Counterhold the unions on the pump and fuel rail with a second spanner, while unscrewing the union nuts. Withdraw the high pressure fuel pipe and plug or cover the open unions to prevent dirt entry.

9 Again using two spanners, hold the unions and unscrew the union nuts securing the high pressure fuel pipes to the fuel injectors and fuel rail. Withdraw the high pressure fuel pipes and plug or cover the open unions to prevent dirt entry **(see illustrations)**.

10 Disconnect the wiring connectors at the fuel temperature sensor and fuel pressure sensor on the fuel rail.

11 Undo the three bolts securing the fuel rail to the cylinder head and withdraw the rail from its location **(see illustrations)**.
Caution: Do not attempt to remove the four high pressure fuel pipe male unions from the fuel rail. These parts are not available separately and if disturbed are likely to result in fuel leakage on reassembly.

12 Obtain a complete new set of high pressure fuel pipes for refitting.

Refitting

13 Locate the fuel rail in position, refit the three securing bolts and tighten to the specified torque.

14 Working on one fuel injector at a time, remove the blanking plugs from the fuel pipe unions on the fuel rail and the relevant injector. Locate a new high pressure fuel pipe over the unions and screw on the union nuts finger tight at this stage.

15 When all four fuel pipes are in place, hold the unions with a spanner and tighten the union nuts to the specified torque using

16.15 Using a torque wrench and crow-foot adaptor, tighten the fuel pipe union nuts – 2.0 litre models

a torque wrench and crow-foot adaptor **(see illustration)**.

16 Similarly, fit a new high pressure fuel pipe to the fuel pump and fuel rail, and tighten the union nuts to the specified torque.

17 Reconnect the fuel temperature sensor and fuel pressure sensor wiring connectors.

18 Remove the blanking plugs and reconnect the supply and return hose quick-release fittings at the fuel filter, and at the connections above the fuel pump. Secure the hoses with their respective retaining clips.

19 Reconnect the crankcase ventilation hose to the cylinder head cover.

20 Reposition the plastic wiring harness guide over the two mounting studs and secure with the retaining nuts.

21 Reconnect the fuel injector and pump piston de-activator switch wiring connectors, and reconnect any additional wiring disconnected for access.

22 Check that everything has been reconnected and secured with the relevant retaining clips then reconnect the battery negative terminal.

23 Observing the precautions listed in Section 2, prime the fuel system as described in Section 6, then start the engine and allow it to idle. Check for leaks at the high pressure fuel pipe unions with the engine idling. If satisfactory, increase the engine speed to 4000 rpm and check again for leaks. Take the car for a short road test and check for leaks once again on return. If any leaks are

detected, obtain and fit additional new high pressure fuel pipes as required. **Do not** attempt to cure even the slightest leak by further tightening of the pipe unions.

24 Refit the engine cover on completion.

1.6 litre models

Removal

25 Disconnect the battery (refer to Chapter 5A).

26 Remove the plastic cover from the top of the engine.

27 Drain the cooling system as described in Chapter 1B.

28 Remove the air cleaner assembly and air inlet ducts as described in Section 3.

29 Unbolt the EGR pipe from the cylinder head cover/intake manifold.

30 Disconnect the wiring from the fuel injectors and the airflow meter, then unbolt the wiring loom conduit from the cylinder head cover/intake manifold and position to one side.

31 Unbolt the intercooler air pipe from the turbocharger.

32 Remove the hand primer pump and its support.

33 Disconnect and plug the fuel feed and return pipes from the top right-hand side of the engine.

34 Unbolt the oil separator and cover from the top of the engine. Cover the aperture with a cloth rag.

35 Clean around the injector high-pressure pipes then unscrew the union nuts while counter-holding the injector adapters, and disconnect the pipes.

36 Undo the 2 mounting bolts, slacken the clamps, and move aside the coolant pump outlet assembly **(see illustration)**.

37 Remove the EGR cooler and mounting bracket as described in Chapter 4D. Also, remove the bracket from the base of the high-pressure pump.

38 Clean around the pipe, then undo the unions and remove the high-pressure pipe from the fuel common rail to the high pressure pump. Similarly, undo the unions and remove the injector high-pressure pipes from the fuel common rail. Plug the openings to prevent contamination.

39 Disconnect the pressure sensor wiring plug from the fuel common rail **(see illustration)**.

40 Unscrew the two rail mounting bolts and manoeuvre it from place **(see illustration)**. If necessary, unscrew and remove the fuel pressure sensor. **Note:** *Citroën/Peugeot insist that the fuel pressure sensor must not be removed during the vehicle warranty period.* ***Caution: Do not attempt to remove the four high-pressure fuel pipe male unions from the fuel common rail. These parts are not available separately and if disturbed are likely to result in fuel leakage on reassembly.***

Refitting

41 Locate the fuel common rail in position, refit and finger-tighten the mounting bolts/nuts.

42 Reconnect the fuel common rail wiring plug.

43 Fit the new pump-to-rail high pressure pipe, and only finger-tighten the unions at first, then tighten the unions to the Stage 1 torque setting, followed by the Stage 2 torque setting. Use a second spanner to counterhold the union screwed into the pump body.

44 Fit the new set of rail-to-injector high pressure pipes, and finger tighten the unions. If it's not possible to fit the new pipes to the injector unions, remove and refit the injectors as described in Section 12. and try again.

45 Tighten the fuel common rail mounting bolts/nuts to the specified torque.

46 Tighten the rail-to-injector pipe unions to the Stage 1 torque setting, followed by the Stage 2 setting. Use a second spanner to counterhold the injector unions.

47 The remainder of refitting is a reversal of removal, noting the following points:

a) Ensure all wiring connectors and harnesses are correctly refitting and secured.

b) Reconnect the battery as described in Chapter 5A.

c) Observing the precautions listed in Section 2, start the engine and allow it to idle. Check for leaks at the high-pressure fuel pipe unions with the engine idling. If satisfactory, increase the engine speed to 3000 rpm and check again for leaks.

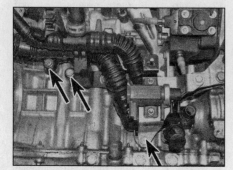

16.36 Undo the bolts (arrowed) and move aside the coolant pump outlet assembly

16.39 The pressure sensor is located at the end of the common rail (arrowed)

16.40 Common rail mounting bolt/stud (arrowed)

*Take the car for a short road test and check for leaks once again on return. If any leaks are detected, obtain and fit additional new high-pressure fuel pipes as required. **Do not** attempt to cure even the slightest leak by further tightening of the pipe unions.*

17 Inlet manifold – removal and refitting

1.9 litre models

Removal

1 The intake manifold is located on the rear of the cylinder head together with the exhaust manifold. First, remove the exhaust manifold as described in Section 18.

2 Slacken the retaining clip and detach the intake duct from the EGR valve.

3 Disconnect the breather hose from the left-hand end of the manifold upper section.

4 Unscrew the bolts securing the manifold upper section to the cylinder head and lower section.

5 Remove the manifold upper section, complete with EGR valve, disconnecting the wiring connector and vacuum hose from the EGR valve solenoid. Recover the four seals fitted between the upper and lower sections.

6 To remove the lower section of the manifold, unscrew the bolts securing the EGR pipe to the top of the exhaust manifold and the cylinder head cover. Free the pipe from the manifold and recover its gasket. Discard the gasket; a new one should be used on refitting.

7 Slacken and remove the nuts and bolt securing the inlet manifold to the cylinder head.

8 Remove the manifold and EGR pipe as an assembly. Recover the manifold gaskets and discard them; new ones must be used on refitting.

Refitting

9 Examine all the manifold studs for signs of damage and corrosion; remove all traces of corrosion, and repair or renew any damaged studs.

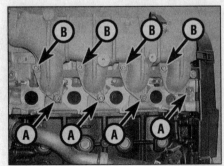

17.17 Inlet manifold retaining nuts (A) and bolts (B) – 2.0 litre models

10 Ensure that the mating surfaces are clean and flat, and fit the new manifold gaskets.

11 Route the EGR pipe through the lower section of the manifold then install both as an assembly. Tighten the manifold retaining nuts and bolt to the specified torque.

12 Fit a new gasket to the exhaust manifold then reconnect the EGR pipe, tightening its retaining bolts securely.

13 Fit a new seal to each of the upper manifold section joints then refit the upper section of the manifold, reconnecting the wiring connector and vacuum hose to the EGR solenoid valve. Refit the retaining bolts, tightening them to the specified torque, and reconnect the breather hose.

14 Reconnect the intake duct and EGR pipe to the manifold upper section, secure them in position with their retaining clips.

15 Ensure the mounting rubbers are all correctly fitted then install the engine cover, securing it in position with the fasteners. Reconnect the battery negative terminal.

2.0 litre models

Removal

16 Remove the exhaust manifold as described in Section 18.

17 Slacken and remove the nuts and bolts securing the inlet manifold to the cylinder head (**see illustration**). Remove the manifold and recover the manifold gasket. Discard the gasket; a new one must be used on refitting.

Refitting

18 Examine all the manifold studs for signs of damage and corrosion; remove all traces of corrosion, and repair or renew any damaged studs.

19 Ensure that the mating surfaces are clean and flat, and fit the new manifold gasket.

20 Refit the manifold and tighten its retaining nuts and bolts to the specified torque.

21 Refit the exhaust manifold as described in Section 18.

1.6 litre models

22 The inlet manifold is integral with the cylinder head cover. Refer to Chapter 2B.

18 Exhaust manifold – removal and refitting

1.9 litre models

Removal

1 Disconnect the battery negative terminal (refer to *Disconnecting the battery* in the Reference Chapter).

2 Release the fasteners from the right-hand side and top of the engine cover then lift off the cover, taking care not to lose its mounting rubbers (**see illustrations 3.1a to 3.1c**).

3 Release the retaining clip and detach the EGR pipe from the side of the EGR valve.

Note: *If the pipe is secured in position with a crimped-type clip, discard the clip and obtain a new one for use on refitting*

4 Unscrew the bolts securing the EGR pipe to the top of the exhaust manifold and the cylinder head cover. Free the pipe from the manifold and recover its gasket. Discard the gasket; a new one should be used on refitting.

5 Disconnect the exhaust front pipe from the manifold as described in Section 21.

6 Unscrew the exhaust manifold retaining nuts and remove the spacers from the manifold studs.

7 Remove the exhaust manifold and recover the manifold gaskets. Discard the gaskets; new ones must be used on refitting.

Refitting

8 Examine all the manifold studs for signs of damage and corrosion; remove all traces of corrosion, and repair or renew any damaged studs.

9 Ensure that the mating surfaces are clean and flat, and fit the new manifold gaskets.

10 Refit the manifold then fit the spacers to the mounting studs and screw on the retaining nuts. Tighten the nuts evenly and progressively to the specified torque.

11 Fit a new gasket then reconnect the EGR pipe to the manifold, tightening its retaining bolts securely. Reconnect the pipe to the EGR valve, securing it in position with the retaining clip, and refit the bolt securing the pipe to the cylinder head cover.

12 Reconnect the exhaust front pipe as described in Section 21.

13 Refit the engine cover then reconnect the battery.

2.0 litre models

Note: *The exhaust manifold is removed complete with the turbocharger and there is insufficient clearance to gain access to all the relevant attachments from either above or below with the engine in the car. Two alternatives are possible; either remove the complete engine/transmission unit from the car as described in Chapter 2F, or remove the front suspension subframe as described in Chapter 10. Both are involved operations and the course of action taken is largely dependent on the tools, equipment, skill and patience available.*

Removal

14 The following procedure is based on the assumption that the engine/transmission unit has been removed from the car. If the front suspension subframe has been removed instead, the operations are basically the same, but it may be necessary to disconnect and move aside certain additional items, and to be prepared for considerable manipulation to withdraw the components from the engine compartment.

15 If the engine is in the car, disconnect the battery negative terminal (refer to *Disconnecting the battery* in the Reference Chapter).

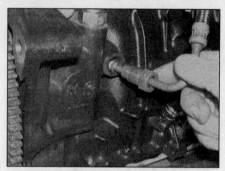

18.18 Unscrew the turbocharger oil feed pipe union nut – 2.0 litre models

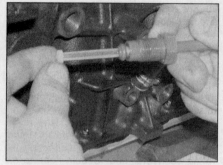

18.19 Withdraw the oil feed pipe and remove the filter – 2.0 litre models

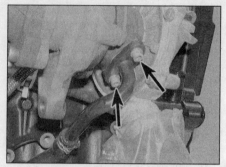

18.20a Undo the oil return pipe flange securing bolts (arrowed) . . .

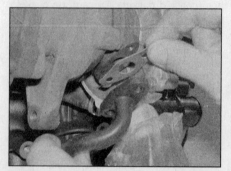

18.20b . . . separate the flange and recover the gasket – 2.0 litre models

18.22a Undo the exhaust manifold retaining nuts (arrowed) . . .

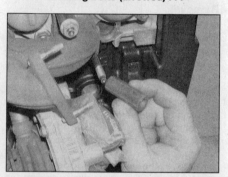

18.22b . . . and recover the spacers – 2.0 litre models

16 If the engine is in the car, remove the exhaust system as described in Section 21.

17 Remove the turbocharger rear inlet and outlet ducts as described in Section 3.

18 Unscrew the union nut securing the turbocharger oil feed pipe to the cylinder block, then withdraw the pipe from its location **(see illustration)**.

19 Remove the filter from the end of the oil feed pipe, and examine it for contamination **(see illustration)**. Clean or renew if necessary.

20 Undo the two bolts securing the oil return pipe flange to the turbocharger. Separate the flange and recover the gasket **(see illustrations)**.

21 Remove the exhaust gas recirculation (EGR) valve and connecting pipe from the exhaust manifold as described in Chapter 4D, Section 3.

22 Undo the eight exhaust manifold retaining nuts and recover the spacers from the studs **(see illustrations)**.

23 Undo the nut and bolt securing the base of the turbocharger to the support bracket on the cylinder block.

24 Withdraw the turbocharger and exhaust manifold off the mounting studs and remove the assembly from the engine. Recover the manifold gasket **(see illustrations)**.

Refitting

25 Refitting is a reverse of the removal procedure, bearing in mind the following points:

a) Ensure that the manifold and cylinder head mating faces are clean, with all traces of old gasket removed.

b) Use new gaskets when refitting the manifold to the cylinder head and the oil return pipe flange to the turbocharger.

c) Tighten the exhaust manifold retaining nuts to the specified torque.

d) Refit the EGR valve and connecting pipe as described in Chapter 4D, Section 3.

e) Refit the turbocharger rear inlet and outlet ducts as described in Section 3.

f) If the engine is in the car, refit the exhaust system as described in Section 21.

g) Refit the engine/transmission unit or the front suspension subframe with reference to Chapter 2E or 10 as applicable.

1.6 litre models

Removal

26 Remove the turbocharger as described in Section 20.

27 Undo the retaining nuts, recover the spacers (where fitted), and remove the manifold. Recover the gasket **(see illustration)**.

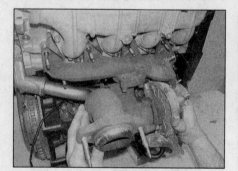

18.24a Withdraw the turbocharger and manifold . . .

18.24b . . . and recover the gasket – 2.0 litre models

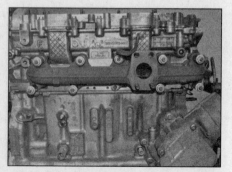

18.27 Exhaust manifold – 1.6 litre engine

Refitting

28 Refitting is a reverse of the removal procedure, bearing in mind the following points:

a) *Ensure that the manifold and cylinder head mating faces are clean, with all traces of old gasket removed.*

b) *Use new gaskets when refitting the manifold to the cylinder head.*

c) *Tighten the exhaust manifold retaining nuts to the specified torque.*

19 Turbocharger (1.6 and 2.0 litre models) – description and precautions

Description

1 A turbocharger is fitted to all 1.6 and 2.0 litre models. It increases engine efficiency by raising the pressure in the inlet manifold above atmospheric pressure. Instead of the air simply being sucked into the cylinders, it is forced in.

2 Energy for the operation of the turbocharger comes from the exhaust gas. The gas flows through a specially-shaped housing (the turbine housing) and, in so doing, spins the turbine wheel. The turbine wheel is attached to a shaft, at the end of which is another vaned wheel known as the compressor wheel. The compressor wheel spins in its own housing, and compresses the inlet air on the way to the inlet manifold.

3 Boost pressure (the pressure in the inlet manifold) is limited by a wastegate, which diverts the exhaust gas away from the turbine wheel in response to a pressure-sensitive actuator. On the 1.6 litre engine, the turbocharger incorporates a variable intake nozzle to improve boost pressure at low engine speeds.

4 The turbo shaft is pressure-lubricated by an oil feed pipe from the main oil gallery. The shaft 'floats' on a cushion of oil. A drain pipe returns the oil to the sump.

Precautions

5 The turbocharger operates at extremely high speeds and temperatures. Certain precautions must be observed, to avoid premature failure of the turbo, or injury to the operator.

6 Do not operate the turbo with any of its

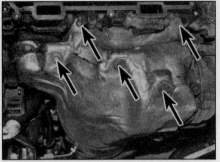

20.5 Undo the bolts and remove the turbocharger heat shield (arrowed)

parts exposed, or with any of its hoses removed. Foreign objects falling onto the rotating vanes could cause excessive damage, and (if ejected) personal injury.

7 Do not race the engine immediately after start-up, especially if it is cold. Give the oil a few seconds to circulate.

8 Always allow the engine to return to idle speed before switching it off – do not blip the throttle and switch off, as this will leave the turbo spinning without lubrication.

9 Allow the engine to idle for several minutes before switching off after a high-speed run.

10 Observe the recommended intervals for oil and filter changing, and use a reputable oil of the specified quality. Neglect of oil changing, or use of inferior oil, can cause carbon formation on the turbo shaft, leading to subsequent failure.

20 Turbocharger (1.6 and 2.0 litre models) – removal, inspection and refitting

Removal

1.6 litre models

1 Apply the handbrake, then jack up the front of the vehicle and support it on axle stands (see *Jacking and vehicle support*). Remove the engine top cover and undershield.

2 Disconnect the battery negative lead as described in Chapter 5A.

3 Place a sheet of thick cardboard over the rear of the radiator to protect it from accidental damage, then remove the catalytic converter as described in Section 21.

20.6 Disconnect the vacuum pipe from the wastegate control assembly (arrowed)

4 Slacken the clamp and disconnect the air inlet duct from the side of the turbocharger, then unbolt the noise attenuator from the top of the turbocharger. Cover the open apertures to prevent entry of dust and dirt and recover the O-ring and seal from the turbocharger.

5 Unbolt the heatshield from the top of the exhaust manifold and turbocharger **(see illustration)**.

6 Disconnect the vacuum hose from the turbocharger wastegate control assembly **(see illustration)**.

7 Loosen the clip and disconnect the oil return pipe from the bottom of the turbocharger.

8 Unscrew the oil supply pipe banjo bolts, remove the pipe and recover the sealing washers **(see illustration)**. Check that the bolt securing the pipe to the cylinder block does not have a strainer inside its end, and if necessary hook out the strainer with a screwdriver.

9 Unscrew the four nuts, and remove the turbocharger from the exhaust manifold **(see illustration)**.

2.0 litre models

10 Remove the exhaust manifold as described in Section 18. The turbocharger and exhaust manifold are removed from the engine as a complete assembly. The turbocharger can then be separated from the manifold on the bench as follows.

11 Undo the four bolts securing the exhaust outlet elbow to the turbocharger body and separate the elbow from the turbocharger.

12 Undo the three retaining nuts and lift the turbocharger off the manifold studs **(see illustration)**.

20.8 Turbocharger oil supply and return pipes (arrowed)

20.9 Undo the 3 nuts (arrowed – one hidden) and remove the support bracket (arrowed)

20.12 Turbocharger-to-exhaust manifold retaining nuts (arrowed)

Inspection

13 With the turbocharger removed, inspect the housing for cracks or other visible damage.

14 Spin the turbine or the compressor wheel, to verify that the shaft is intact and to feel for excessive shake or roughness. Some play is normal, since in use, the shaft is 'floating' on a film of oil. Check that the wheel vanes are undamaged.

15 If oil contamination of the exhaust or induction passages is apparent, it is likely that turbo shaft oil seals have failed.

16 No DIY repair of the turbo is possible and none of the internal or external parts are available separately. If the turbocharger is suspect in any way a complete new unit must be obtained.

Refitting

17 Refitting is a reverse of the removal procedure, bearing in mind the following points:

a) *If a new turbocharger is being fitted, change the engine oil and filter. Also renew the filter in the oil feed pipe.*

b) *Prime the turbocharger by injecting clean engine oil through the oil feed pipe union before reconnecting the union.*

c) *On 1.6 litre models the manufacturers recommend that the oil supply pipe is supported by suitable diameter metal rods while tightening the upper and lower banjo bolts. This is to prevent distortion of the pipe. A 20.5 mm diameter rod is required for the upper banjo and a 7.5 mm diameter rod for the lower banjo.*

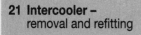

21 Intercooler – removal and refitting

Note: *The intercooler is only fitted to 1.6 litre models.*

Removal

1 The intercooler is located at the front of the engine compartment, on the right-hand side of the radiator.

2 In the engine compartment, loosen the clips and disconnect the inlet and outlet air hoses from the top of the intercooler and from the air ducts **(see illustration)**.

3 Unscrew the top mounting nut and move the top of the intercooler rearwards **(see illustration)**.

4 Lift the intercooler from its lower mounting rubbers and remove from the vehicle taking care not to damage the intercooler core on the mounting stud **(see illustrations)**.

Refitting

5 Refitting is a reversal of removal.

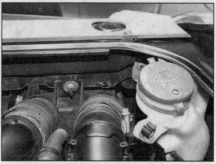

21.2 Intercooler inlet and outlet air hoses and ducts

21.4a Removing the intercooler

22 Exhaust system – general information, removal and refitting

General information

1 According to model, the exhaust system consists of either two, three or four sections. Two section systems consist of a front pipe and tailpipe, and three section systems consist of a front pipe, intermediate pipe and tail pipe. Three section systems also incorporate a catalytic converter which is integral with either the front pipe or intermediate pipe. Four section systems consist of a catalytic converter, front pipe and flexible hose, intermediate pipe, and silencer/ tail pipe.

2 The exhaust system joints are either of the spring-loaded ball type, to allow for movement in the exhaust system, or clamp-ring type.

3 The system is suspended throughout its entire length by rubber mountings.

4 Each exhaust section can be removed individually or, alternatively, the complete system can be removed as a unit. Even if only one part of the system needs attention, it is often easier to remove the whole system and separate the sections on the bench.

5 To remove the system or part of the system, first jack up the front or rear of the car and support it on axle stands (see *Jacking and vehicle support*). Alternatively, position the car over an inspection pit or on car ramps.

21.3 Intercooler top mounting nut

21.4b Intercooler lower mounting rubbers

Front pipe

6 On 1.9 litre models and early 2.0 litre models, undo the nuts securing the flange joint to the manifold, and recover the spring cups and springs. Remove the bolts and recover the wire-mesh gasket. On later 2.0 litre models, slacken and remove the nut washer and bolt from the clamping ring and disengage the clamp from the turbocharger flange joint. On 1.6 litre models, loosen the clips securing the pipe to the catalytic converter and intermediate pipe.

7 Have an assistant support the front end of the pipe, then, where necessary, slacken and remove the nut, washer and bolt from the clamping ring and disengage the clamp from the flange joint.

8 Free the pipe from its mounting rubber(s) and remove it from underneath the vehicle.

Intermediate pipe

9 Slacken the nuts and remove the clamping ring nuts, washers and bolts, and disengage both clamps from the flange joints.

10 Release the pipe from its mounting rubber and remove it from underneath the vehicle.

Tailpipe

11 Slacken and remove the nut, washer and bolt from the tailpipe clamping ring and disengage the clamp from the flange joint.

12 Unhook the tailpipe from its mounting rubbers and remove it from the vehicle.

Catalytic converter – 1.6 litre models

13 Apply the handbrake, then jack up the front of the vehicle and support it on axle

22.19 View of the catalytic converter from under the car

stands (see *Jacking and vehicle support*). Remove the engine top cover and undertray.

14 Disconnect the battery negative lead as described in Chapter 5A.

15 Loosen the clips and remove the intercooler air inlet and outlet hoses.

16 Unbolt the air resonator from the turbocharger and remove it from the front of the engine.

17 Unclip and remove the turbocharger air inlet hose and disconnect it from the airflow meter. Also remove the air inlet duct from the front left-hand side of the engine compartment.

18 Place a sheet of thick cardboard over the rear of the radiator to protect it from accidental damage.

19 Unbolt and remove the heatshield from the catalytic converter **(see illustration)**.

20 Loosen the lower clamp bolt and release the exhaust front pipe from the catalytic converter.

21 Loosen the upper clamp bolt then support the catalytic converter and unscrew the mounting nuts securing it to the cylinder block. Lower it and withdraw from underneath the car.

Complete system

22 Separate the front pipe from the manifold/ turbocharger /catalytic converter as described previously.

23 With the aid of an assistant, free the system from all its mounting rubbers and lower it from under the vehicle. Recover the wire-mesh gasket from the manifold joint (where applicable).

Heat shield(s)

24 The heat shields are secured to the underside of the body by various nuts and fasteners. If a shield is being removed to gain access to a component located behind

it, remove the retaining nuts and/or fastener (unscrew the centre screw then pull out the complete fastener), and manoeuvre the shield out of position. On some models it may be necessary to free the exhaust system from its mountings to gain the clearance necessary to remove the larger heat shield.

Refitting

25 Each section is refitted by reversing the removal sequence, noting the following points:

a) Ensure that all traces of corrosion have been removed from the flanges and renew all necessary gaskets.

b) Inspect the rubber mountings for signs of damage or deterioration, and renew as necessary.

c) Where joints are secured together by a clamping ring, apply a smear of exhaust system jointing paste to the flange joint to ensure a gas-tight seal.

d) Prior to tightening the exhaust system fasteners, ensure that all rubber mountings are correctly located, and that there is adequate clearance between the exhaust system and vehicle underbody.

Chapter 4 Part D:
Emission control systems

Contents

Degrees of difficulty

Easy, suitable for novice with little experience	**Fairly easy,** suitable for beginner with some experience	**Fairly difficult,** suitable for competent DIY mechanic	**Difficult,** suitable for experienced DIY mechanic	**Very difficult,** suitable for expert DIY or professional

Specifications

Torque wrench settings	Nm	lbf ft
Air injection valve – 1.4 litre engine with secondary air injection:		
Valve-to-cylinder head bolts	8	6
Valve-to-adaptor nuts	7	5
Valve adaptor-to-exhaust manifold bolts	7	5

1 General information

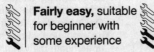

All petrol engines have the ability to use unleaded petrol and also have various other features built into the fuel system to help minimise harmful emissions. In addition, all engines are equipped with the crankcase emission control system described below. All petrol engines are equipped with a catalytic converter and an evaporative emission control system. Certain later engines to emission standard L4, also utilise a secondary air injection system to quickly bring the catalytic converter up to normal working temperature.

All diesel engines are also designed to meet the strict emission requirements and are also equipped with a crankcase emission control system. To further reduce exhaust emissions, a catalytic converter and an exhaust gas recirculation (EGR) system are fitted to the majority of engines.

The emission control systems function as follows.

Petrol engines

Crankcase emission control

To reduce the emission of unburned hydrocarbons from the crankcase into the atmosphere, the engine is sealed and the blow-by gases and oil vapour are drawn from inside the crankcase, through a wire mesh oil separator, into the inlet tract to be burned by the engine during normal combustion.

Under conditions of high manifold depression (idling, deceleration) the gases will be sucked positively out of the crankcase. Under conditions of low manifold depression (acceleration, full-throttle running) the gases are forced out of the crankcase by the (relatively) higher crankcase pressure; if the engine is worn, the raised crankcase pressure (due to increased blow-by) will cause some of the flow to return under all manifold conditions.

Exhaust emission control

To minimise the amount of pollutants which escape into the atmosphere, a catalytic converter is fitted in the exhaust system. The system is of the closed-loop type, in which one or two lambda sensors in the exhaust system provides the engine management ECU with constant feedback, enabling the ECU to adjust the air/fuel mixture ratio to provide the best possible conditions for the converter to operate.

The lambda sensor has a heating element built-in that is controlled by the ECU through the lambda sensor relay to quickly bring the sensor's tip to an efficient operating temperature. The sensor's tip is sensitive to oxygen and sends the ECU a varying voltage depending on the amount of oxygen in the exhaust gases; if the intake air/fuel mixture is too rich, the exhaust gases are low in oxygen so the sensor sends a low-voltage signal, the voltage rising as the mixture weakens and the amount of oxygen rises in the exhaust gases. Peak conversion efficiency of all major pollutants occurs if the intake air/fuel mixture is maintained at the chemically-correct ratio for the complete combustion of petrol of 14.7 parts (by weight) of air to 1 part of fuel (the 'stoichiometric' ratio). The sensor output voltage alters in a large step at this point, the

ECU using the signal change as a reference point and correcting the intake air/fuel mixture accordingly by altering the fuel injector pulse width.

Evaporative emission control

To minimise the escape into the atmosphere of unburned hydrocarbons, an evaporative emission control system is fitted. The fuel tank filler cap is sealed and a charcoal canister is mounted underneath the right-hand front wing to collect the petrol vapours generated in the tank when the car is parked. It stores them until they can be cleared from the canister (under the control of the engine management ECU) via the purge valve into the inlet tract to be burned by the engine during normal combustion.

To ensure that the engine runs correctly when it is cold and/or idling and to protect the catalytic converter from the effects of an over-rich mixture, the purge control valve(s) is/are not opened by the ECU until the engine has warmed-up, and the engine is under load; the valve solenoid is then modulated on and off to allow the stored vapour to pass into the inlet tract.

Secondary air injection

Certain later engines to emission standard L4 are also equipped with a secondary air injection system. This system is designed to reduce exhaust emissions in the period between first starting the engine, and until the catalytic converter reaches operating (functioning) temperature. Introduction of air into the exhaust system during the initial start-up period, creates an 'afterburner' effect which quickly increases the temperature in the exhaust system front pipe, thus bringing the catalytic converter up to normal operating temperatures very quickly.

The system consists of an air pump, an air injection valve, and interconnecting air hoses.

The system operates for between 10 and 45 seconds after engine start-up, dependant on coolant temperature.

Diesel engines

Crankcase emission control

Refer to paragraphs 4 and 5.

Exhaust emission control

To minimise the level of exhaust pollutants released into the atmosphere, a catalytic converter is fitted in the exhaust system of later models.

The catalytic converter consists of a canister containing a fine mesh impregnated with a catalyst material, over which the hot exhaust gases pass. The catalyst speeds up the oxidation of harmful carbon monoxide, unburnt hydrocarbons and soot, effectively reducing the quantity of harmful products released into the atmosphere via the exhaust gases.

Exhaust gas recirculation system

This system is designed to recirculate small quantities of exhaust gas into the inlet tract, and therefore into the combustion process.

This process reduces the level of oxides of nitrogen present in the final exhaust gas which is released into the atmosphere.

The volume of exhaust gas recirculated is controlled by vacuum supplied from the brake servo vacuum pump, via a solenoid valve controlled by the glow plug preheating system, or by an electronic control unit.

A vacuum-operated valve is fitted to the exhaust manifold, to regulate the quantity of exhaust gas recirculated. The valve is operated by the vacuum supplied via the solenoid valve.

Additionally, on certain models, a butterfly valve mounted on the inlet manifold allows the ratio of air-to-recirculated exhaust gas to be controlled. The butterfly valve also enables the exhaust gases to be drawn into the inlet manifold at idle or under light load, when the valve on the exhaust manifold is fully open.

The system is controlled by an electronic control unit, which receives information on coolant temperature, engine load, and engine speed, via the coolant temperature switch/sensor, throttle position switch/sensor and crankshaft sensor respectively.

2 Emission control systems (petrol engines) – testing and component renewal

Crankcase emission control

1 The components of this system require no attention other than to check that the hose(s) are clear and undamaged at regular intervals.

Evaporative emission control system

Testing

2 If the system is thought to be faulty, disconnect the hoses from the charcoal canister and purge control valve and check that they are clear by blowing through them. If the purge control valve(s) or charcoal canister are thought to be faulty, they must be renewed.

Charcoal canister renewal

3 The charcoal canister is located behind the right-hand front wing. To gain access to the

2.4 Lower the charcoal canister out from underneath the right-hand wing

canister, firmly apply the handbrake, then jack up the front of the car and support it securely on axle stands (see *Jacking and vehicle support*). Remove the roadwheel, then undo the retaining screws from the base of the wheel arch liner. Prise out the retaining clips and remove the liner from underneath the wing.

4 On early models, slacken and remove the retaining bolt then free the canister from its mounting clamp and lower it out from underneath the wing **(see illustration)**. On later models, free the canister from its retaining clips, and lower it out from underneath the wing. On all models, mark the hoses for identification purposes.

5 Slacken the retaining clips then disconnect both hoses and remove the canister from the vehicle. Where the crimped-type hose clips are fitted, cut the clips and discard them, use standard worm-drive hose clips on refitting. Where the hoses are equipped with quick-release fittings depress the centre collar of the fitting with a small flat-bladed screwdriver then detach the hose from the canister **(see illustration)**. On later models, also disconnect the purge valve wiring connector.

6 Refitting is a reverse of the removal procedure ensuring the hoses are correctly reconnected.

Purge valve(s) renewal

7 On early models, the purge valve is located on the right-hand side of the engine compartment **(see illustration)**. On later models, the purge valve is integral with the

2.5 To release the quick-release hose connectors, depress their centre collars with a small flat-bladed screwdriver

2.7 On early models, the purge valve (arrowed) is located on the right-hand side of the engine compartment

charcoal canister and cannot be renewed separately.

8 To renew the purge valve on early models, first disconnect the battery negative terminal (refer to *Disconnecting the battery* in the Reference Chapter).

9 Depress the retaining clip and disconnect the wiring connector from the valve. Disconnect the hoses from either end of the valve then release the valve from its retaining clip or strap and remove it from the engine compartment, noting which way around it is fitted.

10 Refitting is a reversal of the removal procedure ensuring the valve is fitted the correct way around and the hoses are securely connected.

Exhaust emission control

Testing

11 The performance of the catalytic converter can only be checked by measuring the exhaust gases using a good-quality, carefully-calibrated exhaust gas analyser. If access to such equipment can be gained, it should be connected and used according with the maker's instructions.

12 If the CO level at the tailpipe is too high, the vehicle should be taken to a Peugeot/Citroën dealer or engine diagnostic specialist so that the complete engine management system can be thoroughly checked using the special diagnostic equipment. Once these have been checked and are known to be free from faults, the fault must be in the catalytic converter, which must be renewed as described in Chapter 4A.

Catalytic converter renewal

13 Refer to Chapter 4A.

Lambda sensor(s) renewal

Note 1: *The lambda sensor is delicate and will not work if it is dropped or knocked, if its power supply is disrupted, or if any cleaning materials are used on it.*

Note 2: *Later engines to emission standard L4 are fitted with a 'downstream' lambda sensor located after the catalytic converter. Removal and refitting procedures are the same for both sensors.*

14 Trace the wiring back from the lambda sensor (which is screwed into the top of the exhaust front pipe or into the exhaust manifold) to the top of the transmission unit. Disconnect both wiring connectors and free the wiring from any relevant retaining clips or ties **(see illustration)**.

15 Unscrew the sensor from the exhaust system front pipe or manifold and remove it along with its sealing washer.

16 Refitting is a reverse of the removal procedure using a new sealing washer. Prior to installing the sensor apply a smear of high-temperature grease to the sensor threads. Ensure the sensor is securely tightened and that the wiring is correctly routed and in no danger of contacting either the exhaust system or engine.

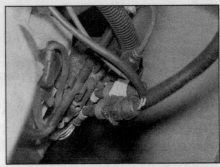

2.14 On early models the lambda sensor wiring connectors are clipped onto the front of the transmission

Secondary air injection

Testing

17 If the air injection pump is thought not to be operating correctly, the vehicle should be taken to a Peugeot/Citroën dealer or engine diagnostic specialist so that the complete engine management system, including the pump, can be thoroughly checked using the special diagnostic equipment (see Chapter 4A).

18 The air injection valve can be checked once it has been removed. The valve should flow air only in one direction; when blown through from the valve (pump) union. If not, it is faulty and should be renewed.

Air pump renewal

19 The air pump is located on the left-hand side of the engine compartment.

20 To gain access to the pump, remove the air cleaner housing as described in Chapter 4A.

21 Unscrew the mounting bolts then disconnect the vacuum hoses and wiring

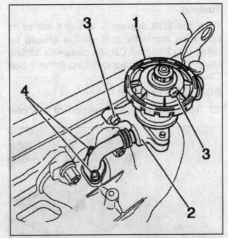

2.25 Secondary air injection valve – later 1.4 litre models

1 Air injection valve
2 Valve adaptor
3 Valve-to-cylinder head bolts
4 Adaptor-to-manifold bolts

connector and remove the pump from the vehicle.

22 Refitting is the reverse of removal.

Air injection valve renewal

23 The air injection valve is mounted on the front of the cylinder head.

24 Disconnect the air hose from the valve.

25 Unscrew the bolts securing the valve adaptor to the top of the exhaust manifold **(see illustration)**.

26 Unscrew the bolts securing the valve to the front of the cylinder head then remove the valve and adaptor assembly from the engine.

27 If necessary, unscrew the retaining nuts and separate the valve and adaptor. Recover the gasket and discard it; a new one should be used on refitting.

28 Refitting is the reverse of removal, using a new gasket (where necessary) and tighten the fixings to the specified torque.

3 Emission control systems (diesel engines) – testing and component renewal

Note: *Numerous variations of emission control systems have been fitted during the course of production. The following information is a guide to the systems most commonly encountered.*

Crankcase emission control

1 The components of this system require no attention other than to check that the hose(s) are clear and undamaged at regular intervals.

Exhaust emission control

Testing

2 The performance of the catalytic converter can only be checked by measuring the exhaust gases using a good-quality, carefully-calibrated exhaust gas analyser. If access to such equipment can be gained, it should be connected and used according with the maker's instructions.

3 If the exhaust emissions are excessive, before assuming the catalytic converter is faulty, it is worth checking the problem is not due to a faulty injector(s), or other diesel fuel system fault. Refer to your Peugeot/Citroën dealer for further information.

Catalytic converter renewal

4 Refer to Chapter 4B or 4C as applicable.

EGR system – 1.9 litre DJY engine models

Testing

5 If the EGR system is thought not to be operating correctly, the vehicle should be taken to a Peugeot/Citroën dealer for testing.

EGR valve renewal

6 Disconnect the battery negative terminal (refer to *Disconnecting the battery* in the Reference Section of this manual).

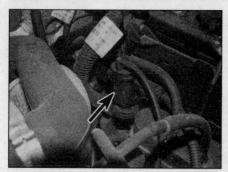

3.22 The EGR solenoid valve (arrowed) is located on the battery mounting plate – 1.9 litre models

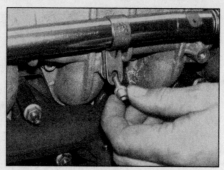

3.27 Undo the bolts securing the EGR pipe support clips to the inlet manifold . . .

3.28 . . . and the two nuts securing the EGR valve to the exhaust manifold – 2.0 litre models

7 Remove the air inlet duct and air distribution housing as described in Chapter 4B.

8 Remove the cylinder head cover as described in Chapter 2B.

9 Remove the clip securing the lower flexible portion of the EGR pipe to the EGR valve. If the original crimped clip is still in place, cut it off; new clips are supplied by Peugeot/Citroën parts stockists with a screw clamp fixing. If a screw clamp type clip is fitted, undo the screw and manipulate the clip off the pipe.

10 Disconnect the vacuum hose from the top of the EGR valve.

11 Undo the two bolts securing the EGR valve to the exhaust manifold. Lift off the valve and recover the gasket.

12 Refitting is a reverse of the removal procedure, bearing in mind the following points:

 a) *Ensure that the EGR valve and exhaust manifold mating faces are clean and use a new gasket.*

 b) *Secure the EGR pipe with new screw clamp type clips, if crimped type clips were initially fitted.*

 c) *Refit the cylinder head cover as described in Chapter 2B.*

 d) *Refit the air inlet duct and air distribution housing as described in Chapter 4B.*

EGR solenoid valve renewal

13 To remove the EGR solenoid valve, disconnect the two vacuum hoses and the

wiring connector. Undo the mounting nuts and remove the valve from the mounting bracket.

14 Refitting is the reverse of removal.

EGR system – 1.9 litre WJZ engine models

Testing

15 If the EGR system is thought not to be operating correctly, the vehicle should be taken to a Peugeot/Citroën dealer for testing.

EGR valve renewal

16 Remove the upper section of the inlet manifold as described in Chapter 4C. The EGR valve can then be removed from the manifold.

17 Refitting is the reverse of removal.

Accelerator lever switch renewal

18 The switch is fitted to the top of the injection pump. If the switch is faulty, renewal should be entrusted to a Peugeot/Citroën dealer who will have the necessary special equipment to adjust it.

EGR system – 1.9 litre WJY engine models

Testing

19 If the EGR system is thought not to be operating correctly, the vehicle should be taken to a Peugeot/Citroën dealer for testing using the special diagnostic equipment (see Chapter 4C).

EGR valve renewal

20 Remove the upper section of the inlet

manifold as described in Chapter 4C. The EGR valve can then be removed from the manifold.

21 Refitting is the reverse of removal.

Solenoid valve renewal

22 The EGR solenoid valve is located on the battery mounting plate **(see illustration)**.

23 To remove the EGR solenoid valve, disconnect the two vacuum hoses and the wiring connector. Undo the mounting bracket bolts and remove the valve from the engine compartment.

24 Refitting is the reverse of removal.

EGR system – 2.0 litre models

Testing

25 Testing of the system should be entrusted to a Peugeot/Citroën dealer.

EGR valve renewal

26 Disconnect the battery negative terminal (refer to *Disconnecting the battery* in the Reference Chapter).

27 Undo the bolts securing the EGR pipe support clips to the inlet manifold **(see illustration)**.

28 Disconnect the vacuum hose, then undo the two nuts securing the EGR valve to the exhaust manifold **(see illustration)**.

29 Undo the two bolts securing the EGR pipe to the inlet manifold elbow. Withdraw the EGR valve and pipe assembly from the manifold and recover the gasket at the EGR pipe-to-inlet manifold flange **(see illustrations)**.

30 To separate the EGR pipe from the valve, remove the clip securing the upper flexible portion of the pipe to the valve. If the original crimped clip is still in place, cut it off; new clips are supplied by Peugeot/Citroën parts stockists with a screw clamp fixing. If a screw clamp type clip is fitted, undo the screw and manipulate the clip off the pipe.

31 Refitting is a reverse of the removal procedure, bearing in mind the following points:

 a) *Ensure that the EGR valve and exhaust manifold mating faces are clean.*

 b) *Secure the EGR pipe with new screw clamp type clips, if crimped type clips were initially fitted.*

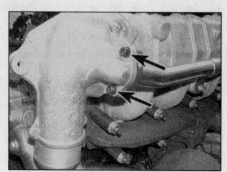

3.29a Undo the two bolts (arrowed) securing the EGR pipe to the inlet manifold elbow . . .

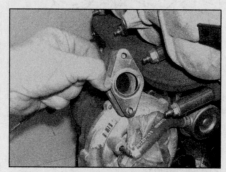

3.29b . . . then withdraw the valve and pipe assembly and recover the gasket at the EGR pipe flange – 2.0 litre models

3.32 EGR solenoid valve location
(arrowed) on the battery mounting plate –
2.0 litre models

3.38a EGR cooler-to-valve clamp
(arrowed) . . .

3.38b . . . EGR cooler-to-pipe clamp
(arrowed)

Solenoid valve renewal

32 The EGR solenoid valve is located on the battery mounting plate **(see illustration)**. To gain access, remove the air cleaner assembly as described in Chapter 4C.

33 To remove the EGR solenoid valve, disconnect the two vacuum hoses and the wiring connector. Undo the mounting bracket bolts and remove the valve from the engine compartment.

34 Refitting is the reverse of removal.

3.40 EGR valve mounting bolts (arrowed –
one hidden)

3.45 EGR cooler on the rear of the engine

EGR system – 1.6 litre models

EGR valve renewal

35 Disconnect the battery negative lead as described in Chapter 5A.

36 Remove the air cleaner housing as described in Chapter 4C.

37 Unscrew the bolts securing the EGR pipe to the right-hand side of the inlet manifold/cylinder head cover. Recover the O-ring.

38 On the rear of the engine, release the clamps securing the EGR pipe to the EGR cooler, and the EGR cooler to the EGR valve **(see illustrations)**.

39 Disconnect the EGR valve wiring plug.

40 Undo the 2 EGR valve mounting bolts, move the EGR cooler to one side without disconnecting the coolant hoses, and manoeuvre the valve from position **(see illustration)**.

41 Recover the gasket/seal. If required, the 'CLIC' type clamps can be replaced by normal worm drive clips.

42 Refitting is a reversal of removal.

EGR heat exchanger (cooler) renewal

43 Disconnect the battery negative lead as described in Chapter 5A.

44 Remove the air cleaner housing as described in Chapter 4C.

45 Fit hose clamps to the hoses connected to the EGR heat exchanger/cooler on the rear of the engine **(see illustration)**, then release the clips and disconnect the hoses.

46 Release the clamps securing the EGR pipe to the EGR cooler, and the EGR cooler to the EGR valve.

47 Unscrew the mounting bolt and manoeuvre the heat exchanger/cooler from the rear of the engine.

48 Refitting is a reversal of removal.

---

4   Catalytic converter – general
    information and precautions

---

1 The catalytic converter is a reliable and simple device which needs no maintenance in itself, but there are some facts of which an owner should be aware if the converter is to function properly for its full service life.

Petrol engines

a) DO NOT use leaded petrol or LRP in a car equipped with a catalytic converter – the lead will coat the precious metals, reducing their converting efficiency and will eventually destroy the converter.

b) Always keep the ignition and fuel systems well-maintained in accordance with the manufacturer's schedule.

c) If the engine develops a misfire, do not drive the car at all (or at least as little as possible) until the fault is cured.

d) DO NOT push- or tow-start the car – this will soak the catalytic converter in

unburned fuel, causing it to overheat when the engine does start.

e) DO NOT switch off the ignition at high engine speeds.

f) DO NOT use fuel or engine oil additives – these may contain substances harmful to the catalytic converter.

g) DO NOT continue to use the car if the engine burns oil to the extent of leaving a visible trail of blue smoke.

h) Remember that the catalytic converter operates at very high temperatures. DO NOT, therefore, park the car in dry undergrowth, over long grass or piles of dead leaves after a long run.

i) Remember that the catalytic converter is FRAGILE – do not strike it with tools during servicing work.

j) In some cases a sulphurous smell (like that of rotten eggs) may be noticed from the exhaust. This is common to many catalytic converter-equipped cars and once the car has covered a few thousand miles the problem should disappear.

k) The catalytic converter, used on a well-maintained and well-driven car, should last for between 50 000 and 100 000 miles – if the converter is no longer effective it must be renewed.

Diesel engines

2 Refer to parts f, g, h and i of the petrol engine information given above.

Chapter 5 Part A:
Starting and charging systems

Contents

Degrees of difficulty

Easy, suitable for novice with little experience | **Fairly easy,** suitable for beginner with some experience | **Fairly difficult,** suitable for competent DIY mechanic | **Difficult,** suitable for experienced DIY mechanic | **Very difficult,** suitable for expert DIY or professional

Specifications

System type . . . . 12 volt, negative earth

Battery
Type . . . . Low maintenance or 'maintenance-free' sealed for life
Charge condition:
  Poor . . . . 12.5 volts
  Normal . . . . 12.6 volts
  Good . . . . 12.7 volts

Alternator
Type . . . . Denso, Valeo, Bosch, Magneti Marelli or Mitsubishi (depending on model)
Rating:
  Petrol engines. . . . . 70, 80 or 90 amp
  Diesel engines . . . . 70, 80, 90, 120 or 150 amp

Starter motor
Type . . . . Mitsubishi, Valeo, Paris Rhone or Bosch (depending on model)

1 General information and precautions

General information

The engine electrical system consists mainly of the charging and starting systems. Because of their engine-related functions, these components are covered separately from the body electrical devices such as the lights, instruments, etc (which are covered in Chapter 12). On petrol engine models refer to Part B for information on the ignition system, and on diesel models refer to Part C for information on the pre/post-heating system.

The electrical system is of the 12 volt negative earth type.

The battery is of the low maintenance or 'maintenance-free' (sealed for life) type and is charged by the alternator, which is belt-driven from the crankshaft pulley.

The starter motor is of the pre-engaged type incorporating an integral solenoid. On starting, the solenoid moves the drive pinion into engagement with the flywheel ring gear before the starter motor is energised. Once the engine has started, a one-way clutch prevents the motor armature being driven by the engine until the pinion disengages from the flywheel.

Precautions

Further details of the various systems are given in the relevant Sections of this Chapter. While some repair procedures are given, the usual course of action is to renew the component concerned. The owner whose interest extends beyond mere component renewal should obtain a copy of the *Automotive Electrical & Electronic Systems Manual*, available from the publishers of this manual.

It is necessary to take extra care when working on the electrical system to avoid damage to semi-conductor devices (diodes and transistors), and to avoid the risk of personal injury. In addition to the precautions given in *Safety first!* at the beginning of this manual, observe the following when working on the system:

• *Always remove rings, watches, etc, before working on the electrical system. Even with the battery disconnected, capacitive discharge could occur if a component's live terminal is earthed through a metal object. This could cause a shock or nasty burn.*

• *Do not reverse the battery connections. Components such as the alternator, electronic control units, or any other components having semi-conductor circuitry could be irreparably damaged.*

• *If the engine is being started using jump leads and a slave battery, connect the batteries positive-to-positive and negative-to-negative (see 'Jump starting'). This also applies when connecting a battery charger.*

• *Never disconnect the battery terminals,*

the alternator, any electrical wiring or any test instruments when the engine is running.

• *Do not allow the engine to turn the alternator when the alternator is not connected.*

• *Never 'test' for alternator output by 'flashing' the output lead to earth.*

• *Never use an ohmmeter of the type incorporating a hand-cranked generator for circuit or continuity testing.*

• *Always ensure that the battery negative lead is disconnected when working on the electrical system.*

• *Before using electric-arc welding equipment on the car, disconnect the battery, alternator and components such as the various vehicle electronic control units to protect them from the risk of damage.*

2 Electrical fault finding – general information

Refer to Chapter 12.

3 Battery – testing and charging

Testing

Standard and low maintenance battery

1 If the vehicle covers a small annual mileage, it is worthwhile checking the specific gravity of the electrolyte every three months to determine the state of charge of the battery. Use a hydrometer to make the check and compare the results with the following table. Note that the specific gravity readings assume an electrolyte temperature of 15°C (60°F); for every 10°C (18°F) below 15°C (60°F) subtract 0.007. For every 10°C (18°F) above 15°C (60°F) add 0.007.

	Above 25°C	Below 25°C
Fully-charged	1.210 to 1.230	1.270 to 1.290
70% charged	1.170 to 1.190	1.230 to 1.250
Discharged	1.050 to 1.070	1.110 to 1.130

2 If the battery condition is suspect, first check the specific gravity of electrolyte in each cell. A variation of 0.040 or more between any cells indicates loss of electrolyte or deterioration of the internal plates.

3 If the specific gravity variation is 0.040 or more, the battery should be renewed. If the cell variation is satisfactory but the battery is discharged, it should be charged as described later in this Section.

Maintenance-free battery

4 In cases where a 'sealed for life' maintenance-free battery is fitted, topping-up and testing of the electrolyte in each cell is not possible. The condition of the battery can therefore only be tested using a battery condition indicator or a voltmeter.

5 Certain models may be fitted with a 'Delco' type maintenance-free battery, with a built-in charge condition indicator. The indicator is located in the top of the battery casing, and indicates the condition of the battery from its colour. If the indicator shows green, then the battery is in a good state of charge. If the indicator shows black, then the battery requires charging, as described later in this Section. If the indicator shows blue, then the electrolyte level in the battery is too low to allow further use, and the battery should be renewed.

Caution: Do not attempt to charge, load or jump start a battery when the indicator shows clear/yellow.

6 If testing the battery using a voltmeter, connect the voltmeter across the battery and compare the result with those given in the Specifications under 'charge condition'. The test is only accurate if the battery has not been subjected to any kind of charge for the previous six hours. If this is not the case, switch on the headlights for 30 seconds, then wait four to five minutes before testing the battery after switching off the headlights. All other electrical circuits must be switched off, so check that the doors and tailgate are fully shut when making the test.

7 If the voltage reading is less than 12.2 volts, then the battery is discharged, whilst a reading of 12.2 to 12.4 volts indicates a partially-discharged condition.

8 If the battery is to be charged, remove it from the vehicle (Section 4) and charge it as described later in this Section.

Charging

Note: *The following is intended as a guide only. Always refer to the manufacturer's recommendations (often printed on a label attached to the battery) before charging a battery.*

Standard and low maintenance battery

9 Charge the battery at a rate of 3.5 to 4 amps and continue to charge the battery at this rate until no further rise in specific gravity is noted over a four hour period.

10 Alternatively, a trickle charger charging at the rate of 1.5 amps can safely be used overnight.

11 Specially rapid 'boost' charges which are claimed to restore the power of the battery in 1 to 2 hours are not recommended, as they can cause serious damage to the battery plates through overheating.

12 While charging the battery, note that the temperature of the electrolyte should never exceed 37.8°C (100°F).

Maintenance-free battery

13 This battery type takes considerably longer to fully recharge than the standard type, the time taken being dependent on the extent of discharge, but it can take anything up to three days.

14 A constant voltage type charger is required to be set, when connected, to 13.9

to 14.9 volts with a charger current below 25 amps. Using this method, the battery should be usable within three hours, giving a voltage reading of 12.5 volts, but this is for a partially-discharged battery and, as mentioned, full charging can take considerably longer.

15 If the battery is to be charged from a fully discharged state (condition reading less than 12.2 volts), have it recharged by your Peugeot/Citroën dealer or local automotive electrician, as the charge rate is higher and constant supervision during charging is necessary.

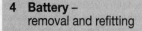

4 Battery – removal and refitting

Note: *Refer to 'Disconnecting the battery' in the Reference Chapter before proceeding.*

Removal

1 The battery is located on the left-hand side of the engine compartment.
2 Slacken the clamp bolt and disconnect the clamp from the battery negative (–) terminal **(see illustration)**.
3 Disconnect the battery positive terminal (+) lead. The positive terminal attachment will either be of the clamp bolt type described in paragraph 2, or of the quick release type, whereby lifting the plastic insulation cover automatically releases the terminal clamp **(see illustration)**.
4 On early models, undo the nut and bolt and lift the battery clamp off the retaining stud **(see illustration)**. Lift the battery out of the engine compartment.
5 On later models, undo the nut securing the battery clamp to the battery tray stud and lift out the clamp **(see illustration)**. Move the battery towards the engine slightly to disengage the lip on the battery case from the battery tray, then lift the battery out of the engine compartment.

Refitting

6 Refitting is a reversal of removal, but smear petroleum jelly on the terminals after reconnecting the leads, and always reconnect the positive lead first, and the negative lead last.

4.2 Slacken the clamp bolt nut and disconnect the negative lead from the battery terminal

4.4 Battery clamp retaining nut and bolt (arrowed) on early models . . .

5 Battery tray and mounting plate – removal and refitting

Note: *The battery tray and mounting plate arrangement varies considerably according to model and year of manufacture. The following procedures describe typical arrangements that may be encountered.*

Removal

1 Remove the battery as described in Section 4.
2 Referring to the relevant Part of Chapter 4, remove the air cleaner and air intake duct components as necessary for access to the battery tray.
3 On models where the engine management electronic control unit (ECU) is housed in the

4.3 Lift the plastic insulation cover to disconnect the quick-release positive lead clamp from the battery terminal

4.5 . . . and clamp retaining nut (arrowed) on later models

end of the battery tray, lift off the cover and disconnect the wiring connector(s) from the ECU. Alternatively, undo the ECU support plate bolts and separate the support plate from the battery tray.
4 Release all the relevant clips securing the wiring to the tray and remove the battery tray from the engine compartment.
5 To remove the mounting plate, undo the bolts securing the mounting plate to the top of the left-hand engine/transmission mounting **(see illustration)**.
6 On diesel engine models, undo the retaining nuts and bolts and remove the vacuum reservoir and solenoid valves from the side of the mounting plate **(see illustration)**.
7 On later 2.0 litre diesel models, unclip the relay box from the front of the mounting plate **(see illustration)**.

5.5 Undo the bolts (arrowed) securing the mounting plate to the top of the engine/transmission mounting

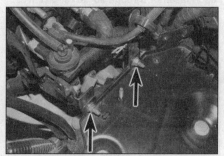

5.6 On diesel models, undo the nuts and bolts (arrowed) and remove the vacuum reservoir and solenoid valves from the mounting plate

5.7 On later 2.0 litre diesel models, unclip the relay box (arrowed) from the front of the mounting plate

8 Release any additional wiring retaining clips and withdraw the mounting plate from the engine compartment.

Refitting

9 Refitting is a reversal of removal, ensuring that the mounting plate retaining bolts are securely tightened.

6 Charging system – testing

Note: *Refer to the warnings given in 'Safety first!' and in Section 1 of this Chapter before starting work.*

1 If the ignition warning light fails to illuminate when the ignition is switched on, first check the alternator wiring connections for security.

If satisfactory, check that the warning light bulb has not blown, and that the bulbholder is secure in its location in the instrument panel. If the light still fails to illuminate, check the continuity of the warning light feed wire from the alternator to the bulbholder. If all is satisfactory, the alternator is at fault and should be renewed or taken to an auto-electrician for testing and repair.

2 If the ignition warning light illuminates when the engine is running, stop the engine and check that the drivebelt is correctly fitted and tensioned (see Chapter 1A or 1B) and that the alternator connections are secure. If all is so far satisfactory, have the alternator checked by an auto-electrician for testing and repair.

3 If the alternator output is suspect even though the warning light functions correctly, the regulated voltage may be checked as follows.

4 Connect a voltmeter across the battery terminals and start the engine.

5 Increase the engine speed until the voltmeter reading remains steady; the reading should be approximately 12 to 13 volts, and no more than 14 volts.

6 Switch on as many electrical accessories (eg, the headlights, heated rear window and heater blower) as possible, and check that the alternator maintains the regulated voltage of around 13 to 14 volts.

7 If the regulated voltage is not as stated, the fault may be due to worn brushes, weak brush springs, a faulty voltage regulator, a faulty diode, a severed phase winding or worn or damaged slip-rings. The alternator should be renewed or taken to an auto-electrician for testing and repair.

7 Alternator drivebelt – removal, refitting and tensioning

Refer to the procedure given for the auxiliary drivebelt in Chapter 1A or 1B.

8 Alternator – removal and refitting

Removal

1 Disconnect the battery negative terminal (refer to *Disconnecting the battery* in the Reference Chapter).

2 Remove the auxiliary drivebelt as described in Chapter 1A or 1B.

3 On 1.9 litre DW series diesel engines, release the clip in the centre of the engine cover and undo the retaining screw on the right-hand side. Lift off the engine cover. On 2.0 litre diesel engines, turn the four plastic fasteners through 90° and lift off the engine cover **(see illustrations)**.

4 For improved access to the alternator on models with power steering, refer to Chapter 10 and unbolt the power steering pump from its location. Move the pump to one side, taking care not to lose the spacer (where fitted) from the rear mounting **(see illustrations)**. Support

8.3a On 1.9 litre DW series diesel engines, remove the fasteners from the right-hand side . . .

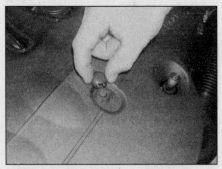

8.3b . . . and top of the engine cover . . .

8.3c . . . then remove the cover from the engine

8.3d On 2.0 litre diesel engines, rotate each fastener through 90° to release it . . .

8.3e . . . then lift off the engine cover

8.4a Slacken and remove the power steering pump front mounting bolts . . .

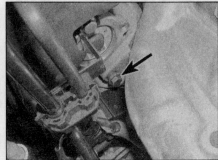

8.4b . . . and rear mounting bolt (arrowed) . . .

8.4c . . . then move the power steering pump to one side – petrol engine shown

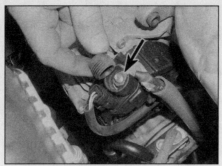

8.6a Remove the rubber cover then unscrew the nut (arrowed) . . .

8.6b . . . and disconnect the wiring from the alternator – petrol engine shown

the weight of the pump by tying it to the vehicle body/engine to prevent any excess strain being placed on the hydraulic pipes/ hoses. **Note:** *There is no need to disconnect the pipes/hoses from the pump. Release the pipes/hoses from any necessary clips to prevent them being strained.*

5 Depending on engine and equipment fitted, either undo the three bolts and remove the auxiliary drivebelt tensioner assembly, or undo the bolts and remove the auxiliary drivebelt idler pulley bracket.

6 Remove the rubber cover(s) from the alternator terminal(s), then unscrew the retaining nut(s) and disconnect the wiring from the rear of the alternator **(see illustrations)**.

7 Unscrew the alternator mounting bolts and, where applicable, the bolt securing the adjuster bolt bracket to the alternator **(see illustration)**. Note that on some models, the left-hand bolt(s) act as centralisers and incorporate a spacer and cone. To access the left-hand lower mounting bolt, unbolt the air conditioning compressor (where fitted) and move it to one side. **Do not** disconnect the refrigerant pipes.

8 Manoeuvre the alternator away from its mounting brackets and out from the engine compartment.

Refitting

9 Refitting is a reversal of removal, tightening the left-hand (centraliser) bolts first, followed by the right-hand bolts. Refit and tension the auxiliary drivebelt as described in Chapter 1A or 1B.

8.7 Alternator front mounting bolts (arrowed) – petrol engine shown

9 Alternator – testing and overhaul

If the alternator is thought to be suspect, it should be removed from the vehicle and taken to an auto-electrician for testing. Most auto-electricians will be able to supply and fit brushes at a reasonable cost. However, check on the cost of repairs before proceeding as it may prove more economical to obtain a new or exchange alternator.

10 Starting system – testing

Note: *Refer to the precautions given in 'Safety first!' and in Section 1 of this Chapter before starting work.*

1 If the starter motor fails to operate when the ignition key is turned to the appropriate position, the following possible causes may be to blame.
a) *The engine immobiliser is faulty.*
b) *The battery is faulty.*
c) *The electrical connections between the switch, solenoid, battery and starter motor are somewhere failing to pass the necessary current from the battery through the starter to earth.*
d) *The solenoid is faulty.*
e) *The starter motor is mechanically or electrically defective.*

10.3 Engine/transmission earth strap connection (arrowed)

2 To check the battery, switch on the headlights. If they dim after a few seconds, this indicates that the battery is discharged – recharge (see Section 3) or renew the battery. If the headlights glow brightly, operate the ignition switch and observe the lights. If they dim, then this indicates that current is reaching the starter motor, therefore the fault must lie in the starter motor. If the lights continue to glow brightly (and no clicking sound can be heard from the starter motor solenoid), this indicates that there is a fault in the circuit or solenoid – see following paragraphs. If the starter motor turns slowly when operated, but the battery is in good condition, then this indicates that either the starter motor is faulty, or there is considerable resistance somewhere in the circuit.

3 If a fault in the circuit is suspected, disconnect the battery leads (including the earth connection to the body), the starter/ solenoid wiring and the engine/ trans-mission earth strap(s) – located on the transmission housing **(see illustration)**. Thoroughly clean the connections and reconnect the leads and wiring, then use a voltmeter or test lamp to check that full battery voltage is available at the battery positive lead connection to the solenoid, and that the earth is sound. Smear petroleum jelly around the battery terminals to prevent corrosion – corroded connections are amongst the most frequent causes of electrical system faults.

4 If the battery and all connections are in good condition, check the circuit by disconnecting the ignition switch supply wire from the solenoid terminal. Connect a voltmeter or test lamp between the wire end and a good earth (such as the battery negative terminal), and check that the wire is live when the ignition switch is turned to the 'start' position. If it is, then the circuit is sound – if not the circuit wiring can be checked as described in Chapter 12.

5 The solenoid contacts can be checked by connecting a voltmeter or test lamp between the battery positive feed connection on the starter side of the solenoid, and earth. When the ignition switch is turned to the 'start' position, there should be a reading or lighted bulb, as applicable. If there is no reading or

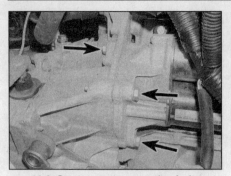

11.6 Starter motor mounting bolts (arrowed) – petrol engine shown

11.7 Remove the starter motor and recover the locating dowel (arrowed) – diesel engine shown

lighted bulb, the solenoid is faulty and should be renewed.

6 If the circuit and solenoid are proved sound, the fault must lie in the starter motor. In this event, it may be possible to have the starter motor overhauled by a specialist, but check on the cost of spares before proceeding, as it may prove more economical to obtain a new or exchange motor.

11 Starter motor – removal and refitting

Removal

1 Disconnect the battery negative terminal (refer to *Disconnecting the battery* in the Reference Chapter).

2 On 1.9 litre DW series diesel engines, release the clip in the centre of the engine cover and undo the retaining screw on the right-hand side. Lift off the engine cover. On 2.0 litre diesel engines, turn the four plastic fasteners through 90° and lift off the engine cover **(see illustrations 8.3a to 8.3e)**.

3 So that access to the motor can be gained both from above and below, apply the handbrake then jack up the front of the vehicle and support it on axle stands (see *Jacking and vehicle support*). Release the screws and remove the engine undershield (where fitted).

4 Remove the air cleaner assembly and air

intake ducts as described in Chapter 4A or 4B.

5 Slacken and remove the two retaining nuts and disconnect the wiring from the starter motor solenoid. Recover the washers under the nuts.

6 Undo the three mounting bolts (two at the rear of the motor, and one which comes through from the top of the transmission housing), supporting the motor as the bolts are withdrawn **(see illustration)**. Recover the washers from under the bolt heads and note the locations of any wiring or hose brackets secured by the bolts.

7 Manoeuvre the starter motor out from underneath the engine and recover the locating dowel(s) from the motor/transmission (as applicable) **(see illustration)**.

Refitting

8 Refitting is a reversal of removal, ensuring that the locating dowel(s) are correctly positioned. Also make sure that any wiring or hose brackets are in place under the bolt heads as noted prior to removal.

12 Starter motor – testing and overhaul

If the starter motor is thought to be suspect, it should be removed from the vehicle and taken to an auto-electrician for testing. Most auto-electricians will be able to supply and fit

brushes at a reasonable cost. However, check on the cost of repairs before proceeding as it may prove more economical to obtain a new or exchange motor.

13 Ignition switch – removal and refitting

The ignition switch is integral with the steering column lock, and can be removed as described in Chapter 10.

14 Oil pressure warning light switch – removal and refitting

Removal

1 The switch is fitted at the front of the cylinder block, above the oil filter mounting or screwed into the oil filter housing. Note that on some models access to the switch may be improved if the vehicle is jacked up and supported on axle stands, and the engine undershield removed (where fitted), so that the switch can be reached from underneath (see *Jacking and vehicle support*).

2 Disconnect the battery negative terminal (refer to *Disconnecting the battery* in the Reference Chapter).

3 Remove the protective sleeve from the wiring plug (where applicable), then disconnect the wiring from the switch **(see illustration)**.

4 Unscrew the switch from the cylinder block, and recover the sealing washer. Be prepared for oil spillage, and if the switch is to be left removed from the engine for any length of time, plug the hole in the cylinder block.

Refitting

5 Examine the sealing washer for signs of damage or deterioration and if necessary renew.

6 Refit the switch, complete with washer, and tighten it securely. Reconnect the wiring connector and reconnect the battery.

7 Lower the vehicle to the ground then check and, if necessary, top-up the engine oil as described in *Weekly checks*.

15 Oil level sensor – removal and refitting

1 On petrol engines the sensor is located on the front side of the cylinder block adjacent to the oil filter housing. On diesel engines, it is fitted to the rear of the cylinder block on the left-hand end **(see illustration)**.

2 The removal and refitting procedure is as described for the oil pressure switch in Section 14. Access is most easily obtained from underneath the vehicle.

14.3 Disconnect the wiring connector (arrowed) from the oil pressure switch

15.1 Oil level sensor (arrowed) – diesel engine shown

Chapter 5 Part B:
Ignition system – petrol models

Contents

Degrees of difficulty

Easy, suitable for novice with little experience	Fairly easy, suitable for beginner with some experience	Fairly difficult, suitable for competent DIY mechanic	Difficult, suitable for experienced DIY mechanic	Very difficult, suitable for expert DIY or professional

Specifications

General

System type	Static (distributorless) ignition system controlled by engine management ECU
Firing order.	1-3-4-2 (No 1 cylinder at transmission end)
Spark plugs	See Chapter 1A Specifications
Ignition timing.	Controlled by engine management ECU

Torque wrench setting

	Nm	lbf ft
Knock sensor securing bolt	20	15

1 Ignition system – general information

The ignition system is integrated with the fuel injection system, to form a combined engine management system under the control of one ECU (see Chapter 4A for further information).

The ignition side of the system is of the static (distributorless) type, consisting only of two twin-output ignition coils. On early models, the ignition coils are housed in a single unit, mounted on the left hand end of the cylinder head; four HT leads connect the coil output terminals to the spark plugs. On later models, the ignition coils are housed in a single unit, which is mounted directly above the spark plugs – no HT leads are fitted.

Each ignition coil serves two cylinders each (one coil supplies cylinders 1 and 4, and the other cylinders 2 and 3).

Under the control of the ECU, the ignition coil operates on the 'wasted spark' principle. The spark plugs are fired in two pairs, twice for each complete cycle of the engine. One plug of each pair will fire on a compression stroke and one on an exhaust stroke; the spark on the exhaust stroke has no effect on the running of the engine and is therefore 'wasted'. The ECU uses inputs from various sensors to calculate the required ignition advance setting and coil charging time.

On certain models, a knock sensor is incorporated into the ignition system. The sensor is mounted on the cylinder block and prevents the engine 'pinking' under load. The sensor is sensitive to vibration and detects the knocking which occurs when the engine starts to 'pink' (pre-ignite). The knock sensor sends an electrical signal to the ECU, which in turn retards the ignition advance setting until the 'pinking' ceases.

2 Ignition system – testing

 Warning: Due to the high voltages produced by the electronic ignition system, extreme care must be taken when working on the system with the ignition switched on. Persons with surgically-implanted cardiac pacemaker devices should keep well clear of the ignition circuits, components and test equipment.

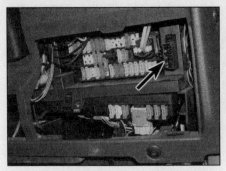

2.2 The diagnostic socket (arrowed) is located adjacent to the passenger's compartment fusebox

3.2 Disconnect the wiring connector from the HT coil

3.3 Disconnect the HT leads from the coil terminals

1 If a fault appears in the engine management system, first ensure that all the system wiring connectors are securely connected and free of corrosion. Ensure that the fault is not due to poor maintenance; ie, check that the air cleaner filter element is clean, the spark plugs are in good condition and correctly gapped, the cylinder compression pressures are correct and that the engine breather hoses are clear and undamaged, referring to Chapters 1A and 2A for further information.

2 If these checks fail to reveal the cause of the problem, the vehicle should be taken to a suitably-equipped Peugeot/Citroën dealer or engine management diagnostic specialist for testing. A diagnostic socket is located adjacent to the passenger's compartment fusebox, to which a fault code reader or other suitable test equipment can be connected **(see illustration)**. By using the code reader or test equipment, the engine management ECU (and the various other vehicle system ECUs) can be interrogated, and any stored fault codes can be retrieved. This will allow the fault to be quickly and simply traced, alleviating the need to test all the system components individually, which is a time-consuming operation that carries a risk of damaging the ECU.

3 The only ignition system checks which can be carried out by the home mechanic are those described in Chapter 1A relating to the spark plugs.

3 Ignition coil unit – removal, testing and refitting

Removal – 1.4 litre engines

Cylinder head mounted coil

1 The ignition HT coil is mounted on the left-hand end of the cylinder head.

2 Disconnect the battery negative terminal (refer to *Disconnecting the battery* in the Reference Chapter), then depress the retaining clip and disconnect the wiring connector from the HT coil **(see illustration)**.

3 Make a note of the correct fitted positions of the HT leads then disconnect them from the coil terminals **(see illustration)**.

4 Undo the four retaining screws securing the coil to its mounting bracket and remove it from the engine compartment **(see illustration)**.

Spark plug mounted coil module

5 Disconnect the battery negative terminal (refer to *Disconnecting the battery* in the Reference Chapter).

6 Disconnect the engine breather hose at the quick-release connections on the air cleaner air intake duct, cylinder head cover and inlet manifold **(see illustrations)**. Move the hose to one side.

7 Unplug the wiring connector from the top of the ignition coil unit **(see illustration)**.

3.4 Undo the four retaining screws and remove the ignition HT coil from the mounting bracket

3.6a Disconnect the engine breather hose at the air cleaner air intake duct . . .

3.6b . . . cylinder head cover (arrowed) . . .

3.6c . . . and inlet manifold (arrowed)

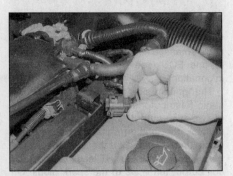

3.7 Unplug the wiring connector from the top of the ignition coil unit

3.8a Remove radio suppresser from the right-hand end of the coil unit . . .

3.8b . . . together with its mounting bracket

3.10 Lift the ignition coil unit from the mounting studs

8 Where applicable, unscrew the securing nut and remove the radio suppresser from the right-hand end of the coil unit, together with its mounting bracket **(see illustrations)**.
9 Undo the nut securing each end of the ignition coil unit to the mounting studs. Note that it is quite likely that the stud will be released with the nut.
10 Lift the ignition coil unit upwards off the mounting studs and at the same time carefully ease the HT extension pillars away from the tops of the spark plugs. Lift the unit off the plugs and withdraw it from the engine **(see illustration)**.

Removal – 1.6 litre engines

11 Undo the six screws and remove the plastic coil unit cover from the top of the engine between the two camshaft covers.
12 Disconnect the wiring plug from the left-hand end of the ignition coil unit **(see illustration)**.
13 Depress the clips and remove the two breather pipes from between the camshaft covers **(see illustration)**.
14 Undo the four mounting screws securing the coil unit **(see illustration)**.
15 Lift the ignition coil unit upwards and at the same time carefully ease the HT extension pillars away from the tops of the spark plugs.

Lift the unit off the plugs and withdraw it from the engine.

Testing

16 The circuitry arrangement of the ignition coil unit on these engines is such that testing of an individual coil in isolation from the remainder of the engine management system is unlikely to prove effective in diagnosing a particular fault. Should there be any reason to suspect a faulty individual coil, the engine management system should be tested by a Peugeot/Citroën dealer or specialist using diagnostic test equipment (see Section 2).

Refitting

17 Refitting is a reversal of the relevant removal procedure ensuring the wiring connectors are securely reconnected.

4   Ignition timing – checking and adjustment

1 There are no timing marks on the flywheel or crankshaft pulley. The timing is constantly being monitored and adjusted by the engine management ECU, and nominal values cannot be given. Therefore, it is not possible

for the home mechanic to check the ignition timing.
2 The only way in which the ignition timing can be checked is using special electronic test equipment, connected to the engine management system diagnostic connector (refer to Chapter 4A for further information).

5   Knock sensor – removal and refitting

Removal

1 The knock sensor is screwed into the rear face of the cylinder block.
2 Firmly apply the handbrake, then jack up the front of the vehicle and support it securely on axle stands (see *Jacking and vehicle support*).
3 Trace the wiring back from the sensor to its wiring connector, and disconnect it from the main loom.
4 Undo the sensor securing bolt and remove the sensor from the cylinder block.

Refitting

5 Refitting is a reversal of the removal procedure, ensuring that the sensor securing bolt is tightened to the specified torque.

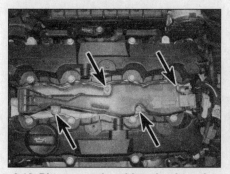

3.12 Disconnect the wiring plug from the HT coils (arrowed)

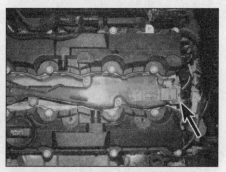

3.13 Depress the clips and disconnect the breather pipes

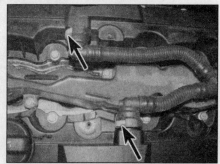

3.14 Undo the coil unit retaining screws

Chapter 5 Part C:
Pre/post-heating system – diesel models

Contents

Degrees of difficulty

Easy, suitable for novice with little experience	**Fairly easy,** suitable for beginner with some experience	**Fairly difficult,** suitable for competent DIY mechanic	**Difficult,** suitable for experienced DIY mechanic	**Very difficult,** suitable for expert DIY or professional

Specifications

Glow plugs

Resistance (typical) . . . . Less than 1 ohm

Torque wrench setting	**Nm**	**lbf ft**
Glow plugs:		
1.6 litre engine	10	7
1.9 and 2.0 litre engines.	22	16

1 Preheating system – description and testing

Description

1 Each swirl chamber has a heater plug (commonly called a glow plug) screwed into it. The plugs are electrically-operated before and during start-up when the engine is cold.
2 The electrical feed to the glow plugs is controlled by the preheating system control unit. With the exception of later 1.9 litre (WJY) engines and all 1.6 and 2.0 litre engines, the control unit operates using signals received from the coolant temperature sensor and accelerator switch on the injection pump. On later 1.9 litre (WJY) engines and all 1.6 and 2.0 litre engines, the control unit is operated by the injection system ECU (see Chapter 4C).
3 On certain models, the glow plugs provide a 'post-heating' function, whereby the glow plugs remain switched on for a period after the engine has started. Once the starter has been switched off, the glow plugs begin a timed 'post-heating' cycle. Post-heating only takes place if the engine is cold (coolant temperature below 60° on 1.8 and 1.9 litre engines, and below 20° on 1.6 and 2.0 litre engines) and the supply to the glow plugs will be interrupted if the engine is placed under load.
4 A warning light in the instrument panel tells the driver that preheating is taking place. When the light goes out, the engine is ready to be started. The voltage supply to the glow plugs continues for several seconds after the light goes out. If no attempt is made to start, the timer then cuts off the supply, in order to avoid draining the battery and overheating the glow plugs.

Testing

1.8 and 1.9 litre engines

5 If the system malfunctions, testing is ultimately by substitution of known good units, but some preliminary checks may be made as follows.
6 Where applicable, release the fasteners from the right-hand side and top of the engine cover, then lift off the cover, taking care not to lose its mounting rubbers.
7 Connect a voltmeter or 12 volt test lamp between the glow plug supply cable and earth (engine or vehicle metal). Make sure that the live connection is kept clear of the engine and bodywork.
8 Have an assistant switch on the ignition, and check that voltage is applied to the glow plugs. Note the time for which the warning light is lit, and the total time for which voltage is applied before the system cuts out. Switch off the ignition.
9 At a coolant temperature of 20°C, typical times noted should be 5 or 6 seconds for warning light operation, followed by a further 10 seconds supply after the light goes out. Warning light time will increase with lower temperatures and decrease with higher temperatures.
10 If there is no supply at all, the control unit or associated wiring is at fault.
11 To locate a defective glow plug, on 1.9 litre models with the D9B engine remove the air distribution housing. If necessary, also remove the inlet duct, and disconnect the breather hose from the engine oil filler tube. Refer to Chapter 4B for further information. Disconnect the main supply cable and the interconnecting wire or strap from the top of the glow plugs. Be careful not to drop the nuts and washers.

12 Use a continuity tester, or a 12 volt test lamp connected to the battery positive terminal, to check for continuity between each glow plug terminal and earth. The resistance of a glow plug in good condition is very low (less than 1 ohm), so if the test lamp does not light or the continuity tester shows a high resistance, the glow plug is certainly defective.

13 If an ammeter is available, the current draw of each glow plug can be checked. After an initial surge of 15 to 20 amps, each plug should draw 12 amps. Any plug which draws much more or less than this is probably defective.

14 As a final check, the glow plugs can be removed and inspected as described in the following Section.

1.6 and 2.0 litre engines

15 The system can be checked as described in paragraphs 7 to 14. However testing will be difficult due to the temperatures at which the preheating system functions; at coolant temperatures above 0°C, preheating is virtually unnecessary. Approximate times for preheating duration are as follows:

Coolant temperature	Preheating time
–30°C	20 seconds
–10°C	5 seconds
0°C	0.5 seconds
18°C	No preheating necessary

2 Glow plugs – removal, inspection and refitting

Removal

Caution: If the preheating system has just been energised, or if the engine has been running, the glow plugs will be very hot.

1 Disconnect the battery negative terminal (refer to *Disconnecting the battery* in the Reference Chapter).

2 On 1.6 litre models, remove the engine top cover, then remove the air cleaner assembly and relevant intake ducts from the rear of the engine with reference to Chapter 4C.

3 On 1.9 litre models with the D9B engine remove the air distribution housing. If necessary, also remove the inlet duct, and disconnect the breather hose from the engine oil filler tube. Refer to Chapter 4B for further information.

4 On 1.9 litre models with an engine cover, release the fasteners from the right-hand side and top of the engine cover, then lift off the cover, taking care not to lose its mounting rubbers. On 2.0 litre models, release the fasteners (rotate them through 90° to release them) and remove the engine cover.

5 Unscrew the nut from the relevant glow plug terminal(s), and recover the washer(s) **(see illustration)**. Note that the main supply cable is connected to No 1 cylinder glow plug and an inter-connecting wire is fitted between the four plugs.

6 Where applicable, carefully move any

obstructing pipes or wires to one side to enable access to the relevant glow plug(s).

7 Unscrew the glow plug(s) and remove from the cylinder head **(see illustration)**.

Inspection

8 Inspect each glow plug for physical damage. Burnt or eroded glow plug tips can be caused by a bad injector spray pattern. Have the injectors checked if this sort of damage is found.

9 If the glow plugs are in good physical condition, check them electrically using a 12 volt test lamp or continuity tester as described in the previous Section.

10 The glow plugs can be energised by applying 12 volts to them to verify that they heat up evenly and in the required time. Observe the following precautions.

    a) Support the glow plug by clamping it carefully in a vice or self-locking pliers. Remember it will become red-hot.

    b) Make sure that the power supply or test lead incorporates a fuse or overload trip to protect against damage from a short-circuit.

    c) After testing, allow the glow plug to cool for several minutes before attempting to handle it.

11 A glow plug in good condition will start to glow red at the tip after drawing current for 5 seconds or so. Any plug which takes much longer to start glowing, or which starts glowing in the middle instead of at the tip, is defective.

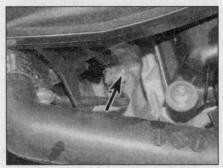

2.5 Unscrew the nut (arrowed) and disconnect the wiring from the glow plug terminal (later 1.9 litre engine shown)

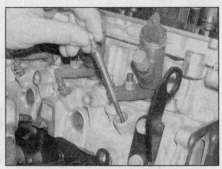

2.7 Unscrew the glow plug(s) and remove them from the cylinder head (2.0 litre engine shown with fuel rail removed)

Refitting

12 Refit by reversing the removal operations. Apply a smear of copper-based anti-seize compound to the plug threads and tighten the glow plugs to the specified torque. Do not overtighten, as this can damage the glow plug element.

3 Preheating system control unit – removal and refitting

Removal

1 The unit is located on the left-hand side of the engine compartment on the inner wing panel, or on the front body panel adjacent to the radiator.

2 Disconnect the battery negative terminal (refer to *Disconnecting the battery* in the Reference Chapter).

3 Unscrew the retaining nut securing the unit to its mounting **(see illustration)**.

4 Disconnect the wiring connector from the base of the unit then unscrew the two retaining nuts and free the main feed and supply wires from the unit **(see illustration)**. Remove the unit from the engine compartment.

Refitting

5 Refitting is a reversal of removal, ensuring that the wiring connectors are correctly connected.

3.3 Unscrew the retaining nut (arrowed) securing the preheating system unit to its mounting

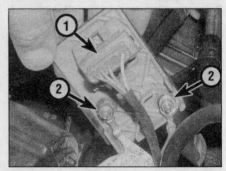

3.4 Disconnect the wiring connector (1) then unscrew the nuts (2) and disconnect the feed and supply wires from the control unit

Chapter 6
Clutch

Contents

Degrees of difficulty

Easy, suitable for novice with little experience	**Fairly easy,** suitable for beginner with some experience	**Fairly difficult,** suitable for competent DIY mechanic	**Difficult,** suitable for experienced DIY mechanic	**Very difficult,** suitable for expert DIY or professional

Specifications

Type .... Single dry plate with diaphragm spring, cable-operated

Friction disc diameter .... 200 mm

Torque wrench settings

	Nm	lbf ft
Pressure plate retaining bolts:		
Petrol models	15	11
Diesel models	20	15

1 General information

The clutch consists of a friction disc, a pressure plate assembly, a release bearing and the release mechanism; all of these components are contained in the large cast-aluminium alloy bellhousing, sandwiched between the engine and the transmission. The release mechanism is mechanical, being operated by a cable on all except later 1.6 litre diesel models (RPO 10557-on) where it is operated hydraulically by means of a master and slave cylinder together with interconnecting hydraulic pipework.

The friction disc is fitted between the engine flywheel and the clutch pressure plate, and is allowed to slide on the transmission input shaft splines.

The pressure plate assembly is bolted to the engine flywheel. When the engine is running, drive is transmitted from the crankshaft, via the flywheel, to the friction disc (these components being clamped securely together by the pressure plate assembly) and from the friction disc to the transmission input shaft.

To interrupt the drive, the spring pressure must be relaxed. At the transmission end of the clutch cable, the outer cable is retained by a fixed mounting bracket, and the inner cable is attached to the release fork lever. Depressing the clutch pedal pulls the control cable inner wire, and this rotates the release fork by acting on the lever at the fork's upper end. The release fork then presses the release bearing against the pressure plate spring fingers. This causes the springs to deform and releases the clamping force on the pressure plate.

On all models the clutch cable has an automatic adjuster built into the cable, and no manual adjustment is required.

2 Clutch cable – removal and refitting

Note: *This Section is not applicable to later 1.6 litre diesel models (RPO 10557-on) which are fitted with a hydraulic clutch release system.*

Removal

1 The clutch cable attachment at the transmission varies according to the transmission type fitted. On MA5 and BE3/5 transmissions, the outer cable is secured to the engine/transmission left-hand mounting bracket and the inner cable end fitting is connected to the release fork lever on the top of the transmission. On BE4/5 transmissions, the outer cable is attached to a support bracket and the inner cable end fitting is connected to the release fork on the forward

2.3a On MA5 and BE3/5 transmissions, release the clutch inner cable end fitting from the release fork lever . . .

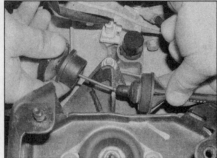

2.3b . . . then depress the tabs and release the outer cable from the transmission mounting bracket

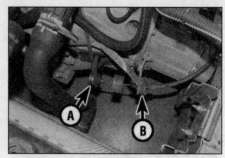

2.3c On BE4/5 transmissions, release the clutch inner cable end fitting (A) from the release fork and the outer cable (B) from the support bracket

facing side of the transmission. Refer to Chapter 7 for transmission type identification.

2 Remove the battery, battery tray and mounting plate as described in Chapter 5A. Depending on model and clearance available, remove any remaining air cleaner and air intake duct components as described in the relevant Part of Chapter 4, to gain access to the cable run over the top of the transmission.

3 Working in the engine compartment, release the inner cable end fitting from the release fork/lever, then depress the tabs and unclip the outer cable end fitting from transmission bracket **(see illustrations)**.

4 Working inside the car, remove the fusebox cover and the under cover from beneath the facia on the driver's side. Note that access to the clutch pedal inside the car is still very limited and it is recommended that the facia be removed first, although this is a major operation.

5 Reach up and release the retaining clip then unhook the inner cable from the upper end of the clutch pedal.

6 Return to the engine compartment, then release the cable guide from the bulkhead and withdraw the cable forwards, releasing it from any relevant retaining clips and guides.

7 Firmly apply the handbrake, then jack up the front of the car and support it securely on axle stands (see *Jacking and vehicle support*). Where fitted, remove the engine undertray.

8 Release the cable from the retaining clips on the subframe and remove it from the car, noting its correct routing.

9 Examine the cable, looking for worn end fittings or a damaged outer casing, and for signs of fraying of the inner cable. Check the cable's operation; the inner cable should move smoothly and easily through the outer casing. Remember that a cable that appears serviceable when tested off the car may well be much heavier in operation when in its working position. Renew the cable if it shows signs of excessive wear or any damage.

Refitting

10 Apply a thin smear of multi-purpose grease to the cable end fittings, then pass the cable through the engine compartment bulkhead.

11 Hold the clutch pedal in its raised position by wedging a suitable tool beneath it.

12 Guide the end of the cable onto the pedal and secure with the retaining clip.

13 From within the engine compartment, lubricate the cable guide and locate it into position on the bulkhead.

14 Ensuring that the cable is correctly routed, secure the cable to the subframe, and engine compartment retaining clips then lay the cable over the transmission.

15 Attach the outer cable to the transmission bracket and connect the inner cable to the clutch release fork/lever. Ensure that the cable spacers and washers are correctly positioned against the lever/support bracket.

16 Depress the clutch pedal two or three times to settle the cable and operate the automatic adjuster.

17 Refit the battery mounting plate, battery tray and battery, referring to Chapter 5A if necessary.

18 Refit the air cleaner and air intake duct components as described in the relevant Part of Chapter 4.

19 Refit the fusebox cover and the under cover beneath the facia. Where applicable, refit the engine undertray then lower the car to the ground.

3 Clutch pedal –
removal and refitting

Removal

1 Remove the battery, battery tray and mounting plate as described in Chapter 5A. Depending on model and clearance available, remove any remaining air cleaner and air intake duct components as described in the relevant Part of Chapter 4, to gain access to the clutch cable run over the top of the transmission (where fitted).

2 Only on models with a clutch cable, working in the engine compartment release the inner cable end fitting from the release fork/lever with reference to Section 2.

3 Working inside the car, remove the fusebox cover and the under cover from beneath the facia on the driver's side. Note that access to the clutch pedal inside the car is still very limited and it is recommended that the facia be removed first, although this is a major operation.

4 On models with a clutch cable, reach up and release the retaining clip then unhook the inner cable from the upper end of the clutch pedal. On models with a hydraulic clutch release system, remove the clip and disconnect the master cylinder pushrod from the pedal. **Note:** *On models with a hydraulic clutch release system, improved access may be gained by first removing the brake pedal.*

5 Detach the clutch pedal helper spring end piece and release the helper spring from the pedal.

6 Undo the nut from the clutch pedal pivot bolt and withdraw the bolt.

7 Remove the clutch pedal from the pedal bracket and stop-plate. Recover the bush from the pedal pivot.

8 Check the condition of the pedal, pivot bush and helper spring assembly and renew any components as necessary.

Refitting

9 Lubricate the pedal pivot bolt with multi-purpose grease, then locate the pedal in the bracket and insert the pivot bolt. Refit the pivot bolt nut but do not fully tighten it at this stage.

10 Reconnect the helper spring to the pedal.

11 On models with a clutch cable, raise the pedal fully and guide the end of the cable onto the pedal. Secure the cable with the retaining clip, then reconnect the clutch inner cable end fitting to the release fork/lever.

12 On models with a hydraulic clutch release system, reconnect the master cylinder pushrod to the pedal and retain with the clip. If removed, refit the brake pedal.

13 Slacken the nut and bolt securing the pedal stop-plate to the pedal bracket.

14 Using a lever, raise the stop-plate fully so that there is a considerable amount of free play at the pedal.

15 Lower the stop-plate until there is between 1.0 and 3.0 mm free play at the pedal. Hold the stop-plate in this position and tighten the retaining nut and bolt and the pedal pivot bolt nut.

16 Depress the pedal two or three times and check the operation of the clutch release mechanism.

17 Refit the remaining components removed for access.

4 Clutch assembly – removal, inspection and refitting

Note: *Although some friction materials may no longer contain asbestos, it is safest to assume they do, and to take precautions accordingly.*

⚠️ **Warning: Dust created by clutch wear and deposited on the clutch components may contain asbestos, which is a health hazard. DON'T blow it out with compressed air, nor inhale any of it. DO NOT use petrol or petroleum-based solvents to clean off the dust. Brake system cleaner or methylated spirit should be used to flush the dust into a suitable receptacle. After the clutch components are wiped clean with rags, dispose of the contaminated rags and cleaner in a sealed, marked container.**

Removal

1 Unless the complete engine/transmission is to be removed from the car and separated for major overhaul (see the relevant Part of Chapter 2), the clutch can be reached by removing the transmission as described in Chapter 7.

2 Before disturbing the clutch, use chalk or a marker pen to mark the relationship of the pressure plate assembly to the flywheel.

3 Working in a diagonal sequence, slacken the pressure plate bolts by half a turn at a time, until spring pressure is released and the bolts can be unscrewed by hand.

4 Prise the pressure plate assembly off its locating dowels, and collect the friction disc, noting which way round the disc is fitted **(see illustrations)**.

Inspection

Note: *Due to the amount of work necessary to remove and refit clutch components, it is considered good practice to renew the clutch friction disc, pressure plate assembly and release bearing as a matched set, even if only one of these is worn enough to require renewal. It is worth considering the renewal of the clutch components on a preventive basis if the engine and/or transmission have been removed for some other reason.*

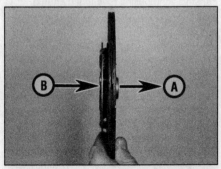

4.14 Fit the friction disc so that its spring hub assembly (B) faces away from the flywheel side (A)

4.4a Free the pressure plate from its locating dowels . . .

5 Remove the clutch assembly.

6 When cleaning clutch components, read first the warning at the beginning of this Section; remove dust using a clean, dry cloth, and working in a well-ventilated atmosphere.

7 Check the friction disc facings for signs of wear, damage or oil contamination. If the friction material is cracked, burnt, scored or damaged, or if it is contaminated with oil or grease (shown by shiny black patches), the friction disc must be renewed.

8 If the friction material is still serviceable, check that the centre boss splines are unworn, that the torsion springs are in good condition and securely fastened, and that all the rivets are tight. If any wear or damage is found, the friction disc must be renewed.

9 If the friction material is fouled with oil, this must be due to an oil leak from the crankshaft left-hand oil seal, from the sump-to-cylinder block joint, or from the transmission input shaft. Renew the seal or repair the joint, as appropriate, as described in the relevant Part of Chapter 2 or 7, before installing the new friction disc.

10 Check the pressure plate assembly for obvious signs of wear or damage; shake it to check for loose rivets or worn or damaged fulcrum rings, and check that the drive straps securing the pressure plate to the cover do not show signs (such as a deep yellow or blue discoloration) of overheating. If the diaphragm spring is worn or damaged, or if its pressure is in any way suspect, the pressure plate assembly should be renewed.

11 Examine the machined bearing surfaces of the pressure plate and of the flywheel; they

4.17 Using a clutch-aligning tool to centralise the friction disc

4.4b . . . then remove the friction disc, noting which way round it is fitted

should be clean, completely flat, and free from scratches or scoring. If either is discoloured from excessive heat, or shows signs of cracks, it should be renewed – although minor damage of this nature can sometimes be polished away using emery paper.

12 Check that the release bearing contact surface rotates smoothly and easily, with no sign of noise or roughness. Also check that the surface itself is smooth and unworn, with no signs of cracks, pitting or scoring. If there is any doubt about its condition, the bearing must be renewed.

Refitting

13 On reassembly, ensure that the bearing surfaces of the flywheel and pressure plate are completely clean, smooth, and free from oil or grease. Use solvent to remove any protective grease from new components.

14 Fit the friction disc so that its spring hub assembly faces away from the flywheel; there may be a marking showing which way round the disc is to be refitted **(see illustration)**.

15 Refit the pressure plate assembly, aligning the marks made on dismantling (if the original pressure plate is re-used), and locating the pressure plate on its three locating dowels. Fit the pressure plate bolts, but tighten them only finger-tight, so that the friction disc can still be moved.

16 The friction disc must now be centralised, so that when the transmission is refitted, its input shaft will pass through the splines at the centre of the friction disc.

17 Centralisation can be achieved by passing a screwdriver or other long bar through the friction disc and into the hole in the crankshaft; the friction disc can then be moved around until it is centred on the crankshaft hole. Alternatively, a clutch aligning tool can be used to eliminate the guesswork; these can be obtained from most accessory shops **(see illustration)**.

 HAYNES HINT *A home-made aligning tool can be fabricated from a length of metal rod or wooden dowel which fits closely inside the crankshaft hole, and has insulating tape wound around it to match the diameter of the friction disc splined hole.*

5.3 Unhook the release bearing from the fork, and slide it off the input shaft – MA5 and BE3/5 transmissions

5.4a Drive out the roll-pin using a suitable punch . . .

5.4b . . . and remove the release lever from the top of the release fork shaft – MA5 and BE3/5 transmissions

18 When the friction disc is centralised, tighten the pressure plate bolts evenly and in a diagonal sequence to the specified torque setting.

19 Apply a thin smear of molybdenum disulphide grease (Peugeot/Citroën recommend the use of Molykote BR2 Plus – available from your dealer) to the splines of the friction disc and the transmission input shaft, and also to the release bearing bore and release fork shaft.

20 Refit the transmission as described in Chapter 7.

5.5a Unclip the upper bush from the transmission housing and slide it off the shaft . . .

5.5b . . . then free the shaft from its lower bush (arrowed) and manoeuvre it out of position – MA5 and BE3/5 transmissions

5 Clutch release mechanism – removal, inspection and refitting

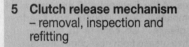

Note: *Refer to the warning concerning the dangers of asbestos dust at the beginning of Section 4.*

Removal

1 Unless the complete engine/transmission is to be removed from the car and separated for major overhaul (see the relevant Part of Chapter 2), the clutch release mechanism can be reached by removing the transmission only, as described in Chapter 7.

2 Different release mechanisms are fitted, depending on transmission type. Refer to Chapter 7 for transmission type identification, then proceed as follows under the relevant sub-heading.

MA5 and BE3/5 transmissions

3 Unhook the release bearing from the fork, and slide it off the input shaft guide tube **(see illustration)**.

4 The release lever must now be removed from the top of the release fork shaft. This is done in one of two ways, depending on transmission type and year of manufacture. Observe the method of attachment of the release lever to the release fork shaft and proceed as follows according to type:

a) *If the release lever is secured to the shaft by a roll-pin, drive out the roll-pin using a suitable punch, and remove the release lever from the top of the release fork shaft* **(see illustrations)**. *Obtain a new roll-pin for refitting.*

b) *If the release lever is secured to the shaft by a retaining pin with a protruding*

threaded end, screw a nut onto the threaded end of the retaining pin. Tighten the nut to draw the pin from the lever then remove the release lever from the top of the release fork shaft. Obtain a new retaining pin for refitting.

5 Depress the retaining tabs, then free the upper bush from the housing and slide it off the release fork shaft. Disengage the shaft from its lower bush, and manoeuvre it out from the transmission **(see illustrations)**. The lower pivot bush can then be removed from the transmission housing.

BE4/5 transmissions

6 Squeeze together the tabs of the retaining clip and pull the release fork off the pivot ball-stud. Recover the shim where fitted. The mounting stud unscrews from the transmission housing **(see illustrations)**.

5.6a Squeeze the tabs of the retaining clip together and remove the release fork . . .

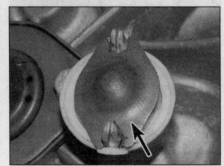

5.6b . . . recover the shim (arrowed) . . .

5.6c . . . then unscrew the pivot ball-stud – BE4/5 transmissions

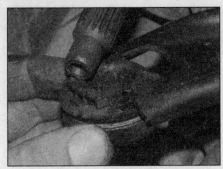

5.7 Disengage the release bearing from the release fork – BE4/5 transmissions

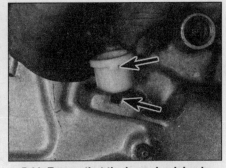

5.11 Ensure that the lower bush lug is correctly located in the transmission housing – MA5 and BE3/5 transmissions

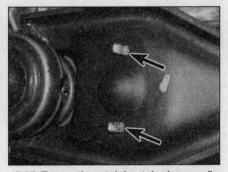

5.17 Ensure the retaining tabs (arrowed) engage correctly with the release fork – BE4/5 transmissions

7 Slide the release bearing off the input shaft guide tube and disengage the arms of the release fork (see illustration).

Inspection

8 Check the release mechanism, renewing any component which is worn or damaged. Carefully check all bearing surfaces and points of contact.

9 When checking the release bearing itself, note that it is often considered worthwhile to renew it as a matter of course. Check that the contact surface rotates smoothly and easily, with no sign of noise or roughness, and that the surface itself is smooth and unworn, with no signs of cracks, pitting or scoring. If there is any doubt about its condition, the bearing must be renewed.

Refitting

MA5 and BE3/5 transmissions

10 Apply a smear of molybdenum disulphide grease to the shaft pivot bushes and the contact surfaces of the release fork.

11 Locate the lower pivot bush in the transmission, ensuring it is securely retained by its locating tangs, and refit the release fork shaft (see illustration). Slide the upper bush down the shaft, and clip it into position in the transmission housing.

12 Refit the release lever to the shaft. Align the lever with the shaft hole, and secure it in position by tapping a new roll-pin or retaining pin fully into position. Slide the release bearing onto the input shaft guide tube, and engage it with the release fork.

13 Refit the transmission as described in Chapter 7.

BE4/5 transmissions

14 Apply a smear of molybdenum disulphide grease to the pivot ball-stud.

15 Insert the outer end of the release fork through the rubber boot in the side of the transmission bellhousing.

16 Engage the arms of the release fork with the release bearing collar, then slide the release bearing onto the input shaft guide tube.

17 Position the shim over the tabs of the pivot ball-stud clip, then push the fork over the stud, ensuring the tabs of the retaining clip engage correctly with the fork (see illustration).

18 Refit the transmission as described in Chapter 7.

6 Clutch hydraulic system components – removal and refitting

Note: This Section is only applicable to later 1.6 litre diesel models (RPO 10557-on).

Clutch master cylinder

Removal

1 Remove the sound insulation material/ heatshield from the right-hand side of the engine compartment.

2 Disconnect the clutch master cylinder pushrod from the pedal as described in the previous Section.

3 Working in the engine compartment, syphon out the hydraulic fluid from the brake/ clutch fluid reservoir. Disconnect the clutch hydraulic fluid supply hose from the master cylinder then tape over or plug the hose and aperture (see illustration).

4 Unclip the slave cylinder hydraulic line from the clutch master cylinder (see illustration).

5 Turn the clutch master cylinder clock-wise to release it from the bulkhead attachment. If

necessary, make up a tool from metal tube to engage the master cylinder, so that it can be turned easily.

Refitting

6 Locate the master cylinder in position. Push and turn the cylinder anti-clockwise to secure.

7 Refit the slave cylinder hydraulic line to the clutch master cylinder.

8 On right-hand drive models, lower the car to the ground. On left-hand drive models, refit the brake vacuum servo unit and the master cylinder with reference to Chapter 9.

9 Reconnect the clutch hydraulic supply hose to the fluid reservoir.

10 Working inside the car, lubricate the master cylinder pushrod balljoint, then lift the clutch pedal and connect the pushrod.

11 Top-up the hydraulic fluid in the reservoir, then bleed the clutch hydraulic system as described in Section 4.

12 Refit the lower facia panels.

13 Refit the air cleaner housing.

Clutch slave cylinder

Removal

14 Remove the air cleaner housing and intake duct components as described in the relevant Part of Chapter 4.

15 Place a clamp on the slave cylinder fluid pressure hose, or plug/seal the hose once it's been disconnected.

16 Unclip the hydraulic pipe from the clutch

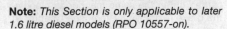

6.3 Disconnect the clutch fluid supply hose (arrowed)

6.4 Prise out the clip (arrowed)

6.16 Prise out the pipe clip

6.17 Slave cylinder retaining Allen bolts (arrowed)

7.3 Prise off the rubber cap (arrowed) and attach a bleed tube

slave cylinder and move it to one side **(see illustration)**. Be prepared for fluid spillage, and plug/seal the openings to prevent contamination.

17 The slave cylinder is retained by 2 bolts. Undo the two bolts and pull the cylinder from position **(see illustration)**.

Refitting

Note: *On a new assembly, the slave cylinder pushrod is retained in the cylinder by a plastic collar which will automatically break off when the clutch pedal is depressed for the first time. Do not attempt to release this collar manually prior to fitting or the pushrod may be ejected.*

18 Lubricate the end of the slave cylinder pushrod with molybdenum disulphide grease then locate the slave cylinder on the transmission and secure with the retaining bolts.

19 Reconnect the hydraulic pipe to the slave cylinder.

20 Top-up the hydraulic fluid in the reservoir, then bleed the clutch hydraulic system as described in Section 7.

21 Refit the air cleaner housing with reference to the relevant Part of Chapter 4.

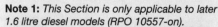

7 Clutch hydraulic system – bleeding

Note 1: *This Section is only applicable to later 1.6 litre diesel models (RPO 10557-on).*

Note 2: *The manufacturers do not recommend the use of an automatic bleeding kit, as there is the risk of foaming in the hydraulic circuit.*

1 Bleeding of the clutch hydraulic system is carried out in the same manner as bleeding the brake hydraulic system (see Chapter 9). First top up the brake/clutch fluid reservoir.

2 Remove the air cleaner housing and intake duct components as described in the relevant Part of Chapter 4.

3 Connect a bleed tube to the bleed screw on the clutch slave cylinder, and place the free end of the tube in a suitable jar with sufficient hydraulic fluid to cover the end of the tube **(see illustration)**.

4 Loosen the bleed screw, then have an assistant depress and release the clutch pedal fully 7 times. On the last stroke, have the assistant hold the pedal depressed. Tighten the bleed screw and have the pedal released.

5 Top-up the hydraulic fluid, then repeat the procedure described in paragraph 4.

6 Top-up the fluid again, then operate the clutch pedal 40 times at the rate of 1 forward and backward movement per second.

7 With the handbrake applied, start the engine and engage a gear. Check that the start of friction of the clutch pedal occurs at a distance of at least 35 mm from the floor. If it occurs at less than 35 mm from the floor, air must still be present in the hydraulic system and it will be necessary to bleed the system again. An alternative method of checking the operation of the clutch pedal is to place a 35 mm thick spacer beneath the pedal on the floor, and check that all gears can be engaged normally when the pedal is depressed onto the spacer.

8 On completion, refit the air cleaner housing.

Chapter 7
Manual transmission

Contents

Degrees of difficulty

Easy, suitable for novice with little experience		**Fairly easy,** suitable for beginner with some experience		**Fairly difficult,** suitable for competent DIY mechanic		**Difficult,** suitable for experienced DIY mechanic		**Very difficult,** suitable for expert DIY or professional	

Specifications

General
Type . . . Manual, five forward speeds and reverse. Synchromesh on all forward speeds

Designation
Petrol models:

1.4 litre engines	MA5
1.6 litre engines	BE4/5

Diesel models:

1.6 litre engines	BE4/5
1.8 litre engines	BE3/5

1.9 litre:

XUD series engines	BE3/5

DW series engines:

Up to September 2002	BE3/5
September 2002 onward	BE4/5

2.0 litre engines:

Up to September 2002	BE3/5
September 2002 onward	BE4/5

Lubrication
Capacity:

MA5 transmission	2.0 litres
BE3/5 transmission	1.8 litres
BE4/5 transmission	1.9 litres

Torque wrench settings

	Nm	lbf ft
MA5 transmission		
Clutch release bearing guide sleeve bolts	6	4
Engine-to-transmission fixing bolts	40	30
Gearchange lever mounting nuts	8	6
Left-hand engine/transmission mounting	Refer to Chapter 2A	
Oil drain plug	25	18
Oil filler/level plug	25	18
Rear mounting link	Refer to Chapter 2A	
Reversing light switch	25	18
Roadwheel bolts	90	66
BE3/5 and BE4/5 transmission		
Clutch release bearing guide sleeve bolts	12	9
Engine-to-transmission fixing bolts	50	37
Gearchange lever mounting nuts	8	6
Left-hand engine/transmission mounting	Refer to Chapter 2A, 2B or 2C	
Oil drain plug	30	22
Oil filler/level plug	20	15
Rear mounting link	Refer to Chapter 2A, 2B or 2C	
Reversing light switch	25	18
Roadwheel bolts	90	66
Speedometer drive housing bolts	20	15

1 General information

1 The transmission is contained in a cast-aluminium alloy casing bolted to the engine's left-hand end, and consists of the gearbox and final drive differential – often called a transaxle.

2 Drive is transmitted from the crankshaft via the clutch to the input shaft, which has a splined extension to accept the clutch friction disc, and rotates in sealed ball-bearings. From the input shaft, drive is transmitted to the output shaft, which rotates in a roller bearing at its right-hand end, and a sealed ball-bearing at its left-hand end. From the output shaft, the drive is transmitted to the differential crownwheel, which rotates with the differential case and planetary gears, thus driving the sun gears and driveshafts. The rotation of the planetary gears on their shaft allows the inner roadwheel to rotate at a slower speed than the outer roadwheel when the car is cornering.

3 The input and output shafts are arranged side-by-side, parallel to the crankshaft and driveshafts, so that their gear pinion teeth are in constant mesh. In the neutral position, the output shaft gear pinions rotate freely, so that drive cannot be transmitted to the crownwheel.

4 Gear selection is via a floor-mounted lever and selector rod mechanism. The selector rod causes the appropriate selector fork to move its respective synchro-sleeve along the shaft, to lock the gear pinion to the synchro-hub. Since the synchro-hubs are splined to the output shaft, this locks the pinion to the shaft, so that drive can be transmitted. To ensure that gearchanging can be made quickly and quietly, a synchromesh system is fitted to all forward gears, consisting of baulk rings and spring-loaded fingers, as well as the gear pinions and synchro-hubs. The synchromesh cones are formed on the mating faces of the baulk rings and gear pinions.

5 Three different manual transmissions are used on the models covered in this manual, however all are similar in construction and operation. Any differences which affect the procedures covered in this Chapter are described in the Section concerned.

2 Manual transmission – draining and refilling

Note: *A suitable square section wrench may be required to undo the transmission filler/level and drain plugs on some models. These wrenches can be obtained from most motor factors or your Peugeot/Citroën dealer.*

1 This operation is much quicker and more efficient if the car is first taken on a journey of sufficient length to warm the engine/transmission up to normal operating temperature.

2 Park the car on level ground, switch off the ignition and apply the handbrake firmly. For improved access, jack up the front of the car and support it securely on axle stands (see *Jacking and vehicle support*). Note that the car must be level to ensure accuracy when refilling and checking the oil level. Undo the screws and remove the engine undertray (where fitted).

3 Remove the engine undertray (where fitted) and the left-hand front roadwheel. Remove the plastic wheel arch liner as described in Chapter 11.

4 Wipe clean the area around the filler/level plug, which is situated on the left-hand end of the transmission, next to the end cover. Unscrew the filler/level plug from the transmission and recover the sealing washer **(see illustrations)**.

5 Position a suitable container under

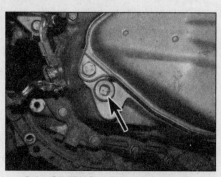

2.4a Oil filler/level plug (arrowed) – MA5 transmission

2.4b Oil filler/level plug (arrowed) – BE3/5 and BE4/5 transmissions

the drain plug (situated at the rear of the transmission) and unscrew the plug. On MA5 transmissions, the plug is on the left-hand side of the differential housing; on BE3/5 and BE4/5 transmissions, it is on the base of the differential housing **(see illustrations)**.

6 Allow the oil to drain completely into the container. If the oil is hot, take precautions against scalding. Clean both the filler/level and the drain plugs, being especially careful to wipe any metallic particles off the magnetic inserts. Discard the original sealing washers; they should be renewed whenever they are disturbed.

7 When the oil has finished draining, clean the drain plug threads and those of the transmission casing, fit a new sealing washer and refit the drain plug, tightening it to the specified torque.

8 Refill the transmission slowly, through the filler/level plug orifice, until the oil begins to trickle out of the orifice. Use only good-quality oil of the specified type (refer to *Lubricants and fluids*). To ensure that a correct level is established, wait until the initial trickle has stopped and allow the oil to settle within the transmission. Add a little more oil until a new trickle emerges; the level will be correct when the new flow ceases.

9 When the level is correct, fit a new sealing washer to the filler/level plug, refit the plug and tighten it to the specified torque.

10 Refit the wheel arch liner, engine undertray (where applicable) and roadwheel, then lower the car to the ground. Tighten the roadwheel bolts to the specified torque.

3 Gearchange linkage –
removal and refitting

Note: *The gearchange linkage is not adjustable. If difficulty is experienced in gear selection, or if there is excess free play at the gearchange lever, dismantle the linkage and check the condition of the link rod balljoints and pivot bushes as described below.*

Removal

1 Firmly apply the handbrake, then jack up the front of the vehicle and support it on axle stands (see *Jacking and vehicle support*). Remove the engine undertray (where fitted).

2 Remove the battery, battery tray and mounting plate as described in Chapter 5A. Depending on model and clearance available, remove any remaining air cleaner and air intake duct components as described in the relevant Part of Chapter 4, to gain access to the top of the transmission.

MA5 transmission – pre-1998 models

3 Slacken and remove the nut and washer, then withdraw the pivot bolt from each end of the selector rod **(see illustration)**. Disengage the rod from the gearchange lever and selector lever, and remove it from

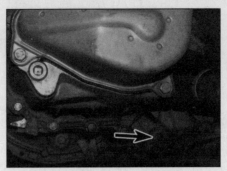
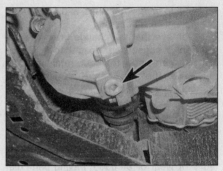

2.5a Oil drain plug (arrowed) –
MA5 transmission (up to RPO 9785)

Note: From RPO 9786-on the drain plug is located approx. 2.0 cm further to the rear of the casing

underneath the vehicle. Recover the spacers and pivot bushes from the gearchange lever and transmission selector lever.

2.5b Oil drain plug (arrowed) –
BE3/5 and BE4/5 transmissions

4 Undo the two nuts securing the selector lever mounting bracket to the transmission housing, then remove the bracket and lever assembly from the transmission.

5 Inspect all the linkage components for signs of wear or damage, paying particular

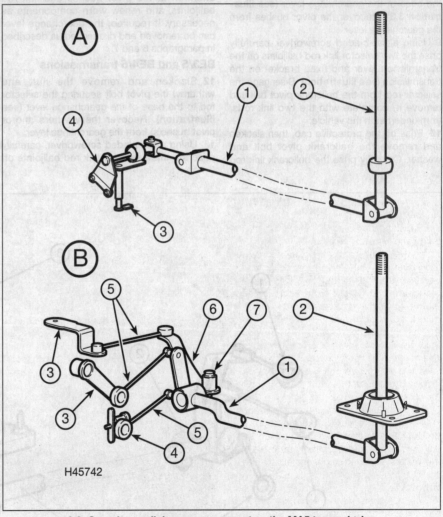

3.3 Gearchange linkage arrangement on the MA5 transmission

A Pre-1998 models	3 Transmission selector	5 Link rods
B 1998 models onward	lever	6 Bellcrank
1 Selector rod	4 Fixed mounting	7 Bellcrank pivot
2 Gearchange lever	bracket	bolt

attention to the pivot bushes, and renew worn components as necessary.

6 To remove the gearchange lever, remove the centre console as described in Chapter 11, then undo the four retaining nuts and lower the gearchange lever out from underneath the vehicle.

7 Peel back the lower gaiter from the base of the gearchange lever, then disengage the lever mounting plate. Slide the upper gaiter up the lever to gain access to the gearchange lever pivot ball. Examine the lever components for signs of wear or damage, paying particular attention to the rubber gaiters, and renew components as necessary. The lever can be separated from its baseplate after the retaining ring has been unclipped.

MA5 transmission – 1998 models onward

8 Slacken and remove the nut, and withdraw the pivot bolt securing the selector rod to the base of the gearchange lever **(see illustration 3.3)**. Recover the pivot bushes from the gearchange lever.

9 Using a flat-bladed screwdriver, carefully prise the two selector link rod balljoints off the transmission lever and fixed bracket on the transmission **(see illustration)**. Disengage the selector rod from the bellcrank pivot ball and remove it, complete with the two link rods, from underneath the vehicle.

10 Prise off the protective cap, then slacken and remove the bellcrank pivot bolt and washer. Carefully prise the bellcrank link rod

3.9 Carefully lever the link rods off their balljoints on the transmission unit

balljoint off the transmission lever and remove the bellcrank and link rod assembly.

11 Inspect all the linkage components for signs of wear or damage, paying particular attention to the pivot bushes and link rod balljoints, and renew worn components as necessary. If required, the gearchange lever can be removed and dismantled as described in paragraphs 6 and 7.

BE3/5 and BE4/5 transmissions

12 Slacken and remove the nut, and withdraw the pivot bolt securing the selector rod to the base of the gearchange lever **(see illustration)**. Recover the washers and/or pivot bushe(s) from the gearchange lever.

13 Using a flat-bladed screwdriver, carefully prise the three selector link rod balljoints off

the two transmission levers and the fixed bracket. Disengage the selector rod from the bellcrank pivot ball and remove it, with the two link rods, from underneath the vehicle.

14 Where fitted, carefully prise the plastic cap off the pivot bolt securing the gearchange linkage bellcrank to the subframe.

15 Slacken and remove the bellcrank pivot bolt and washer, or the nut and washer from the bellcrank shaft, then manoeuvre the bellcrank and the remaining link rod out from under the vehicle. Where applicable, recover the spacer and pivot bushes from the centre of the bellcrank.

16 Inspect all the linkage components for signs of wear or damage, paying particular attention to the pivot bushes and link rod balljoints, and renew worn components as necessary. If required, the gearchange lever can be removed and dismantled as described above in paragraphs 6 and 7.

Refitting

17 Refitting is a reversal of the removal procedure, noting the following points:

a) *Apply a smear of multi-purpose grease to the bellcrank pivot ball. Do not grease the link rod balljoints or the pivot bushes.*

b) *Ensure that all link rods are securely pressed onto their balljoints.*

c) *Where applicable, refit the air cleaner components (Chapter 4A, 4B or 4C), the mounting plate, battery tray and battery (Chapter 5A) and the centre console (Chapter 11).*

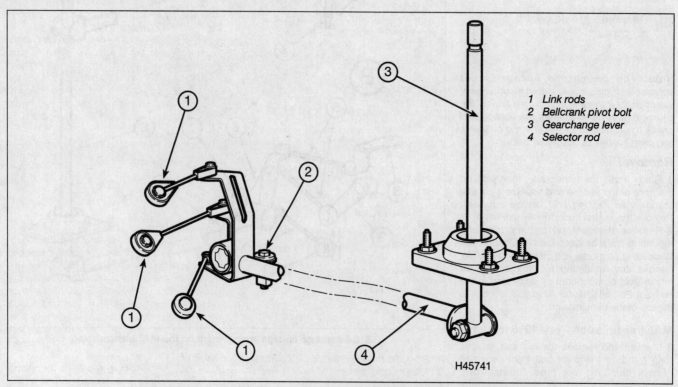

1 Link rods
2 Bellcrank pivot bolt
3 Gearchange lever
4 Selector rod

H45741

3.12 Gearchange linkage arrangement on the BE3/5 and BE4/5 transmissions

4.2 Using a large flat-bladed screwdriver to lever the right-hand oil seal out of position – BE3/5 transmission shown

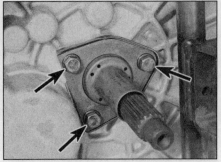

4.7a Clutch release bearing guide sleeve retaining bolts (arrowed) on the MA5 and BE3/5 transmissions . . .

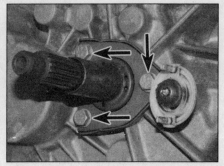

4.7b . . . and on the BE4/5 transmission

4 Oil seals – renewal

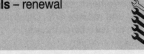

Driveshaft oil seals

1 Remove the appropriate driveshaft as described in Chapter 8.

2 Carefully prise the oil seal out of the transmission, using a large flat-bladed screwdriver **(see illustration)**.

3 Remove all traces of dirt from the area around the oil seal aperture, then apply a smear of grease to the outer lip of the new oil seal. Fit the new seal into its aperture, and drive it squarely into position using a suitable tubular drift (such as a socket) which bears only on the hard outer edge of the seal, until it abuts its locating shoulder.

4 Apply a thin film of grease to the oil seal lip.

5 Refit the driveshaft as described in Chapter 8.

Input shaft oil seal

6 Remove the transmission as described in Section 7, and the clutch release mechanism as described in Chapter 6.

7 Undo the three bolts securing the clutch release bearing guide sleeve in position, and slide the guide off the input shaft, along with its sealing ring or gasket (as applicable) **(see illustrations)**. Recover any shims or thrustwashers which have stuck to the rear of the guide sleeve, and refit them to the input shaft.

8 Carefully lever the oil seal out of the guide sleeve using a suitable flat-bladed screwdriver **(see illustration)**.

9 Before fitting a new seal, check the input shaft's seal rubbing surface for signs of burrs, scratches or other damage, which may have caused the seal to fail in the first place. It may be possible to polish away minor faults of this sort using fine abrasive paper; however, more serious defects will require the renewal of the input shaft. Ensure that the input shaft is clean and greased, to protect the seal lips on refitting.

10 Dip the new seal in clean oil, and fit it to the guide sleeve.

11 Fit a new sealing ring or gasket (as applicable) to the rear of the guide sleeve, then carefully slide the sleeve into position over the input shaft **(see illustration)**. Refit the retaining bolts and tighten them to the specified torque setting.

12 Take the opportunity to inspect the clutch components if not already done (Chapter 6). Finally, refit the transmission as described in Section 7.

Selector shaft oil seal

MA5 transmissions

13 On these models, to renew the selector shaft seal, the transmission must be dismantled. This task should therefore be entrusted to a Peugeot/Citroën dealer or transmission specialist.

BE3/5 and BE4/5 transmissions

14 Park the car on level ground, apply the handbrake, slacken the left-hand front roadwheel bolts, then jack up the front of the vehicle and support it on axle stands (see *Jacking and vehicle support*). Remove the left-hand front roadwheel.

15 Using a large flat-bladed screwdriver, lever the link rod balljoint off the transmission selector shaft, and disconnect the link rod.

16 Using a large flat-bladed screwdriver, carefully prise the selector shaft seal out of the housing, and slide it off the end of the shaft.

17 Before fitting a new seal, check the selector shaft's seal rubbing surface for signs of burrs, scratches or other damage, which may have caused the seal to fail in the first place. It may be possible to polish away minor faults of this sort using fine abrasive paper; however, more serious defects will require the renewal of the selector shaft.

18 Apply a smear of grease to the new seal's outer edge and sealing lip, then carefully slide the seal along the selector rod. Press the seal fully into position in the transmission housing.

19 Refit the link rod to the selector shaft, ensuring that its balljoint is pressed firmly onto the shaft. Lower the car to the ground.

5 Reversing light switch – testing, removal and refitting

Testing

1 The reversing light circuit is controlled by a plunger-type switch screwed into the top of the transmission casing. If a fault develops, first ensure that the circuit fuse has not blown.

2 To gain access to the switch, remove the battery, battery tray and mounting plate as described in Chapter 5A. Depending on model and clearance available, remove any remaining air cleaner and air intake duct components as described in the relevant Part of Chapter 4.

3 To test the switch, disconnect the wiring connector, and use a multimeter (set to the resistance function) or a battery-and-bulb

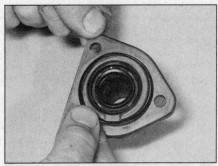

4.8 Carefully lever the oil seal out of the guide sleeve, noting which way round it is fitted

4.11 Fit a new sealing ring or gasket (as applicable) to the rear of the guide sleeve

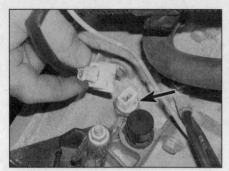

5.5a Reversing light switch location (arrowed) on the MA5 transmission . . .

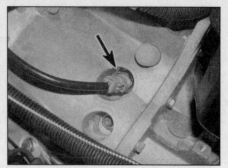

5.5b . . . and on the BE4/5 transmission

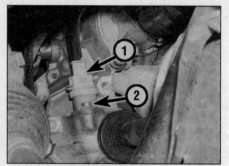

6.2 Speedometer drive wiring connector (1) and retaining bolt (2)

test circuit to check that there is continuity between the switch terminals only when reverse gear is selected. If this is not the case, and there are no obvious breaks or other damage to the wires, the switch is faulty, and must be renewed.

Removal

4 To gain access to the switch, remove the battery, battery tray and mounting plate as described in Chapter 5A. Depending on model and clearance available, remove any remaining air cleaner and air intake duct components as described in the relevant Part of Chapter 4.

5 Disconnect the wiring connector, then unscrew the switch from the transmission casing along with its sealing washer **(see illustrations)**.

Refitting

6 Fit a new sealing washer to the switch, then screw it back into position in the top of the transmission housing and tighten it to the specified torque setting. Refit the wiring plug, and test the operation of the circuit. Refit the components removed for access.

---

6 Speedometer drive – removal and refitting

Removal

1 Chock the rear wheels, firmly apply the handbrake, then jack up the front of the car and support it on axle stands (see *Jacking and vehicle support*). The speedometer drive is on the rear of the transmission housing, next to the inner end of the right-hand driveshaft. Undo the screws and remove the engine undertray (where fitted).

2 Disconnect the wiring connector from the speedometer drive **(see illustration)**.

3 Slacken and remove the retaining bolt and remove the heat shield (where fitted). Withdraw the speedometer drive and driven pinion assembly from the transmission housing, along with its sealing ring.

4 If necessary, the pinion can be slid out of the housing, and the oil seal removed from the top of the housing. Examine the pinion for signs of damage, and renew if necessary. Renew the housing sealing ring as a matter of course.

5 If the driven pinion is worn or damaged, also examine the drive pinion in the transmission housing for similar signs.

6 To renew the drive pinion on MA5 transmissions, the transmission must be dismantled and the differential gear removed. This task should therefore be entrusted to a Peugeot/Citroën dealer or a transmission specialist.

7 To remove the drive pinion on BE3/5 and BE4/5 transmissions, first remove the right-hand driveshaft as described in Chapter 8. Undo the three retaining bolts and remove the speedometer drive housing from the transmission, along with its sealing ring. Remove the drive pinion from the differential gear, and recover any adjustment shims from the gear **(see illustrations)**.

Refitting

8 On BE3/5 and BE4/5 transmissions, where the drive pinion has been removed, refit the adjustment shims to the differential gear, then locate the speedometer drive on the gear, ensuring it is correctly engaged in the gear slots **(see illustration)**. Fit a new sealing ring to the rear of the speedometer drive housing, then refit the housing to the transmission and tighten its retaining bolts to the specified torque. Inspect the driveshaft oil seal for signs of wear, and renew if necessary. Refit the driveshaft as described in Chapter 8.

9 On all transmissions, apply a smear of grease to the lips of the seal and to the driven pinion shaft, and slide the pinion into position in the speedometer drive.

10 Fit a new sealing ring to the speedometer drive and refit it to the transmission, ensuring that the drive and driven pinions are correctly engaged. Refit the drive retaining bolt, complete with heat shield (where fitted), and tighten securely.

11 Reconnect the wiring connector to the speedometer drive, refit the engine undertray (where applicable), then lower the vehicle to the ground.

6.7a On BE3/5 and BE4/5 transmissions, unscrew the housing retaining bolts . . .

6.7b . . . and remove the housing, sealing ring and drive pinion from the transmission

6.8 On BE3/5 and BE4/5 transmissions, ensure the drive pinion dogs are correctly engaged with the gear slots (arrowed) when refitting

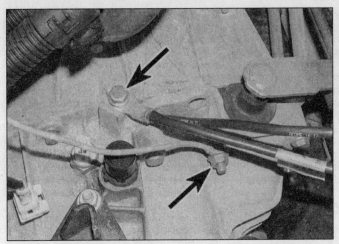

7.8a Unscrew the nut and bolt and detach the earth leads (arrowed) from the transmission – MA5 transmission

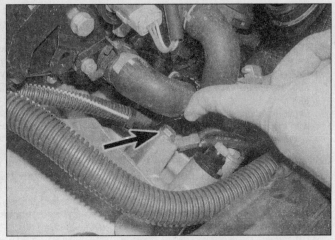

7.8b Unscrew the bolt (arrowed) and disconnect the earth lead from the transmission – BE3/5 and BE4/5 transmissions

7 Manual transmission – removal and refitting

Removal

1 Firmly apply the handbrake, then jack up the front of the car and support it securely on axle stands (see *Jacking and vehicle support*).
2 Drain the transmission oil as described in Section 2, then refit the drain and filler plugs, tightening them to the specified torque.
3 Remove the air cleaner and air intake duct(s) as described in the relevant Part of Chapter 4. On D9B diesel engines, also remove the air distribution housing as described in Chapter 4B.
4 Remove the battery, battery tray and mounting plate as described in Chapter 5A.
5 Remove both driveshafts as described in Chapter 8.
6 Remove the starter motor as described in Chapter 5A.
7 On models with a clutch cable, refer to Chapter 6 and release the clutch inner cable end fitting from the release fork/lever, then depress the retaining tabs and release the outer cable from the transmission bracket. On models with a hydraulic clutch release system, remove the clutch slave cylinder as described in Chapter 6, and support to one side without disconnecting the hydraulic line.
8 Disconnect the wiring connector from the reversing light switch, TDC sensor and speedometer drive. Undo the retaining nuts/bolts, and disconnect the earth straps from the transmission housing **(see illustrations)**. Disconnect the wiring from any additional switches/sensors as necessary, free the wiring loom from the retaining clips, and position it clear of the transmission.
9 On the MA5 transmission, undo the bolt securing the exhaust front pipe to its transmission mounting bracket.
10 On pre-1998 MA5 transmissions,

slacken and remove the nut and washer, then withdraw the pivot bolt securing the selector rod to the transmission selector lever. Disengage the rod from the selector lever. On all other transmissions, using a flat-bladed screwdriver, carefully prise the gearchange mechanism link rod balljoints off their respective levers on the transmission. Position the rods clear of the transmission.
11 On models with power steering, undo the retaining nuts and bolts and release the power steering pipe support brackets from the transmission. Position the pipe clear of the unit so that it will not be damaged during the removal procedure.
12 Undo the retaining bolt(s), and remove the flywheel lower cover plate (where fitted) from the transmission.
13 On the BE3/5 and BE4/5 transmissions, remove the speedometer drive housing from the transmission as described in Section 6.
14 Place a jack with a block of wood beneath the engine, to take the weight of the engine. Alternatively, attach a couple of lifting eyes to the engine, and fit a hoist or support bar to take the engine weight.
15 Place a jack and block of wood beneath the transmission, and raise the jack to take the weight of the transmission.
16 Undo the nut and bolt securing the engine/transmission rear mounting connecting link to the bracket on the subframe.
17 Slacken and remove the centre nut and washer from the left-hand engine/trans-mission mounting. Undo the two bolts/nuts securing the mounting to the support bracket, and remove the rubber mounting.
18 On the MA5 transmission, undo the three retaining nuts and remove the mounting plate from the top of the transmission.
19 On the BE3/5 and BE4/5 transmission, remove the washer and spacer from the mounting stud, then unscrew the stud from the top of the transmission housing. Collect the large spacer plate from the mounting stud.

20 With the jack positioned beneath the transmission taking the weight, slacken and remove the remaining bolts securing the transmission housing to the engine. Note the correct fitted positions of each bolt, and the necessary brackets, as they are removed to use as a reference on refitting. Make a final check that all components have been disconnected, and are positioned clear of the transmission so that they will not hinder the removal procedure.
21 With the bolts removed, move the trolley jack and transmission to the left, to free it from its locating dowels then pivot the differential end of the transmission upwards (to disengage it from the subframe).
Caution: Take great care not to place any excess strain on the exhaust system, or damage the radiator if the engine is moved. On models equipped with air conditioning, care must also be taken to ensure the auxiliary drivebelt pulleys do not damage the air conditioning pipes on the right-hand side of the engine compartment.
22 Once the transmission is free, lower the jack and manoeuvre the unit out from under the car. Remove the locating dowels from the transmission or engine if they are loose, and keep them in a safe place.

Refitting

23 The transmission is refitted by a reversal of the removal procedure, bearing in mind the following points:
a) *Apply a little high melting-point grease (Peugeot/Citroën recommend the use of Molykote BR2 plus – available from your dealer) to the splines of the transmission input shaft. Do not apply too much, otherwise there is a possibility of the grease contaminating the clutch friction disc.*
b) *Ensure that the locating dowels are correctly positioned prior to installation.*
c) *On the BE3/5 and BE4/5 transmissions, apply thread-locking fluid to the left-hand engine/transmission mounting*

stud threads, prior to refitting it to the transmission. Tighten the stud to the specified torque.
d) *Tighten all nuts and bolts to the specified torque (where given).*
e) *Renew the driveshaft oil seals (Section 5), then refit the driveshafts (see Chapter 8).*
f) *On completion, refill the transmission with the specified type and quantity of lubricant, as described in Section 2.*

8 Manual transmission overhaul – general information

1 Overhauling a manual transmission is a difficult and involved job for the DIY home mechanic. In addition to dismantling and reassembling many small parts, clearances must be precisely measured and, if necessary, changed by selecting shims and spacers. Internal transmission components are also often difficult to obtain, and in many instances, extremely expensive. Because of this, if the transmission develops a fault or becomes noisy, the best course of action is to have the unit overhauled by a specialist repairer, or to obtain an exchange reconditioned unit.

2 Nevertheless, it is not impossible for the more experienced mechanic to overhaul the transmission, provided the special tools are available, and the job is done in a deliberate step-by-step manner, so that nothing is overlooked.

3 The tools necessary for an overhaul include internal and external circlip pliers, bearing pullers, a slide hammer, a set of pin punches, a dial test indicator, and possibly a hydraulic press. In addition, a large, sturdy workbench and a vice will be required.

4 During dismantling of the transmission, make careful notes of how each component is fitted, to make reassembly easier and more accurate.

5 Before dismantling the transmission, it will help if you have some idea what area is malfunctioning. Certain problems can be closely related to specific areas in the transmission, which can make component examination and renewal easier. Refer to the *Fault finding* Section for more information.

Chapter 8
Driveshafts

Contents

Degrees of difficulty

Easy, suitable for novice with little experience	**Fairly easy,** suitable for beginner with some experience	**Fairly difficult,** suitable for competent DIY mechanic	**Difficult,** suitable for experienced DIY mechanic	**Very difficult,** suitable for expert DIY or professional

Specifications

Lubrication (overhaul only – see text)

Lubricant type/specification . . . .   Use only special grease supplied in sachets with gaiter kits – joints are otherwise pre-packed with grease and sealed

Torque wrench settings

	Nm	lbf ft
Anti-roll bar connecting link retaining nut*	40	30
Driveshaft retaining nut*	320	236
Lower suspension arm balljoint retaining nuts*	40	30
Right-hand driveshaft intermediate bearing retaining bolt nuts*	17	13
Roadwheel bolts	90	66

* New nuts must be used

1 General information

Drive is transmitted from the differential to the front wheels by means of two unequal-length driveshafts.

Both driveshafts are splined at their outer ends, to accept the wheel hubs, and are threaded so that each hub can be fastened by a large nut. The inner end of each driveshaft is splined, to accept the differential sun gear.

Constant velocity (CV) joints are fitted to each end of the driveshafts, to ensure the smooth and efficient transmission of power at all suspension and steering angles.

Driveshafts from two different manu-facturers may be encountered. On the GKN type driveshaft, the outer constant velocity joints are of the spider-and-yoke type and the inner constant velocity joints are of the tripod type. On the PSA type driveshaft, the outer constant velocity joints are of the ball-and-cage type, with the inner constant velocity joints being of the tripod type. The constant velocity joints are visually different on the two driveshaft types, and the photos accompanying Sections 3 and 4 can be used to aid identification.

Due to the length of the right-hand driveshaft, the inner constant velocity joint on all models is situated approximately halfway along the shaft's length, and an intermediate support bearing is mounted in the engine/transmission rear mounting bracket. The inner end of the driveshaft passes through the bearing (which prevents any lateral movement of the driveshaft inner end) and the inner constant velocity joint outer member.

2 Driveshafts – removal and refitting

Note: *Do not allow the vehicle to rest on its wheels with one or both driveshafts removed, as damage to the wheel bearing(s) may result. If moving the vehicle is unavoidable, temporarily insert the outer end of the driveshaft(s) in the hub(s) and tighten the hub nut(s): in this case, the inner end(s) of the driveshaft(s) must be supported, for example by suspending with string from the vehicle underbody. Do not allow the driveshaft to hang down under its own weight. A new driveshaft retaining nut, lower arm balljoint clamp bolt nut and anti-roll bar connecting link nut must be used on refitting.*

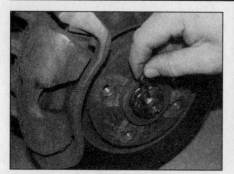

2.4a Withdraw the R-clip . . .

2.4b . . . and remove the locking cap from the driveshaft retaining nut

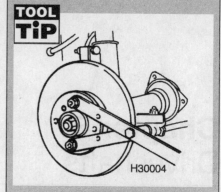

TOOL TiP

H30004

A tool to hold the front hub stationary whilst the driveshaft retaining nut is slackened can be fabricated from two lengths of steel strip (one long, one short) and a nut and bolt; the nut and bolt forming the pivot of a forked tool.

Removal

1 Firmly apply the handbrake, then jack up the front of the car and support it securely on axle stands (see *Jacking and vehicle support*). Remove the appropriate front roadwheel.

2 Remove the appropriate front roadwheel.

3 Drain the transmission oil as described in Chapter 7.

4 Withdraw the R-clip and remove the locking cap from the driveshaft retaining nut **(see illustrations)**.

5 To prevent rotation of the wheel hub as the driveshaft retaining nut is slackened, make up a holding tool and bolt the tool to the wheel hub using two wheel bolts **(see Tool Tip)**.

6 With the holding tool in place, slacken and remove the driveshaft retaining nut using a socket and long bar **(see illustration)**. Where necessary, support the socket on an axle

stand to prevent it slipping off the nut. This nut is very tight; make sure that there is no risk of pulling the car off the axle stands as the nut is slackened.

7 Undo the nut and remove the washer securing the connecting link to the anti-roll bar. Swivel the connecting link to one side.

8 Slacken and remove the nut, then withdraw the lower suspension arm balljoint clamp bolt from the swivel hub. Discard the nut – a new one must be used on refitting **(see illustration)**.

9 Tap a small chisel into the split on the swivel hub, to spread the hub slightly and allow the balljoint shank to be withdrawn **(see illustration)**. Pull the lower suspension arm downwards to release the balljoint shank from the swivel hub. To do this it will be necessary to use a long bar and block of wood which will engage under the front subframe. Attach

the bar to the suspension arm, preferably with a chain, or alternatively with a stout strap or rope. Lever down on the bar to release the balljoint from the swivel hub **(see illustration)**.

10 Once the balljoint is free, remove the protector plate which is fitted to the balljoint shank **(see illustration)**.

Left-hand driveshaft

11 Carefully pull the swivel hub assembly outwards, and withdraw the driveshaft outer constant velocity joint from the hub assembly **(see illustration)**. If necessary, the shaft can

2.6 With the holding tool in place, slacken and remove the driveshaft retaining nut using a socket and long bar

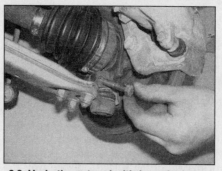

2.8 Undo the nut and withdraw the lower suspension arm balljoint clamp bolt from the swivel hub

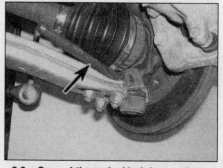

2.9a Spread the swivel hub by tapping a small chisel (arrowed) into the split . . .

2.9b . . . then pull the lower suspension arm downwards using a bar and chain or similar arrangement, pivoting on the subframe

2.10 When the balljoint is released, remove the protector plate from the balljoint shank

2.11 Pull the swivel hub outwards, and withdraw the driveshaft outer constant velocity joint from the hub

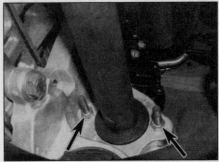

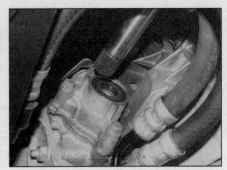

2.12 Support the driveshaft, then withdraw the inner constant velocity joint from the transmission

2.13 On the right-hand driveshaft, slacken the intermediate bearing retaining bolt nuts (arrowed), then turn the bolts through 90°

2.15 Free the shaft inner end from the transmission, and the intermediate bearing from its mounting bracket

be tapped out of the hub using a soft-faced mallet. Take care not to strain the brake hydraulic hose or, where fitted, the ABS wheel speed sensor wiring as the swivel hub is pulled outwards.

12 Support the driveshaft, then withdraw the inner constant velocity joint from the transmission, taking care not to damage the driveshaft oil seal **(see illustration)**. Remove the driveshaft from the vehicle.

Right-hand driveshaft

13 Loosen the two intermediate bearing retaining bolt nuts, then rotate the bolts through 90°, so that their offset heads are clear of the bearing outer race **(see illustration)**.

14 Carefully pull the swivel hub assembly outwards, and withdraw the driveshaft outer constant velocity joint from the hub assembly. If necessary, the shaft can be tapped out of the hub using a soft-faced mallet. Take care not to strain the brake hydraulic hose or, where fitted, the ABS wheel speed sensor wiring as the swivel hub is pulled outwards.

15 Support the outer end of the driveshaft, then pull on the inner end of the shaft to free the shaft from the transmission, and the intermediate bearing from its mounting bracket **(see illustration)**. Remove the driveshaft from the vehicle.

Refitting

16 Before installing the driveshaft, examine the driveshaft oil seal in the transmission for signs of damage or deterioration and, if necessary, renew it as described in Chapter 7. (Having got this far it is worth renewing the seal as a matter of course.)

17 Thoroughly clean the driveshaft splines, and the apertures in the transmission and hub assembly. Apply a thin film of grease to the oil seal lips, and to the driveshaft splines and shoulders. Check that all gaiter clips are securely fastened.

Left-hand driveshaft

18 Offer up the driveshaft, and locate the joint splines with those of the differential sun gear, taking great care not to damage the oil seal. Push the joint fully into position.

19 Locate the outer constant velocity joint splines with those of the swivel hub, and slide the joint back into position in the hub.

20 Refit the protector plate to the lower arm balljoint then, using the method employed on removal, locate the balljoint shank in the swivel hub, ensuring that the lug on the protector plate is correctly located in the clamp split. Insert the balljoint clamp bolt, then fit the new retaining nut and tighten it to the specified torque.

21 Lubricate the inner face and threads of the new driveshaft retaining nut with clean engine oil, and refit it to the end of the driveshaft. Use the method employed on removal to prevent the hub from rotating, and tighten the driveshaft retaining nut to the specified torque. Check that the hub rotates freely.

22 Engage the locking cap with the driveshaft nut so that one of its cut-outs is aligned with the driveshaft hole. Secure the cap in position with the R-clip.

23 Locate the connecting link on the anti-roll bar and refit the washer and a new retaining nut. Tighten the nut to the specified torque.

24 Where necessary, reconnect the ABS wheel sensor wiring connector, ensuring that the wiring is correctly routed and retained by all the necessary clips and ties.

25 Refill the transmission with the specified type and quantity of oil as described in Chapter 7.

26 On completion, refit the roadwheel, then lower the vehicle to the ground and tighten the roadwheel bolts to the specified torque.

Right-hand driveshaft

27 Check that the intermediate bearing rotates smoothly, without any sign of roughness or undue free play between its inner and outer races. If necessary, renew the bearing as described in Section 5.

28 Apply a smear of grease to the outer race of the intermediate bearing, then pass the inner end of the driveshaft through the bearing mounting bracket.

29 Carefully locate the inner driveshaft splines with those of the differential sun gear, taking care not to damage the oil seal. Align

the intermediate bearing with its mounting bracket, and push the driveshaft fully into position. If necessary, use a soft-faced mallet to tap the outer race of the bearing into position in the mounting bracket.

30 Locate the outer constant velocity joint splines with those of the swivel hub, and slide the joint back into position in the hub.

31 Ensure that the intermediate bearing is correctly seated, then rotate its retaining bolts back through 90°, so that their offset heads are resting against the bearing outer race. Tighten the retaining nuts to the specified torque.

32 Carry out the operations described above in paragraphs 20 to 26.

3 Driveshaft rubber gaiters (GKN type driveshaft) – renewal

Outer joint

1 Remove the driveshaft as described in Section 2.

2 Remove the inner constant velocity joint and gaiter as described in paragraphs 13 to 18. It is recommended that the inner gaiter is also renewed, regardless of its apparent condition.

3 Release the two outer gaiter retaining clips, then slide the gaiter off the inner end of the driveshaft.

4 Wipe away as much of the old grease as possible (do not use any solvent) to allow the joint components to be inspected.

5 Check the driveshaft spider and outer member yoke for signs of wear, pitting or scuffing on their bearing surfaces. Also check that the outer member pivots smoothly and easily, with no traces of roughness.

6 If, on inspection, the spider or outer member reveal signs of wear or damage, it will be necessary to renew the complete driveshaft as an assembly, since no components are available separately. If the joint components are in satisfactory condition, obtain a repair kit from your Peugeot/Citroën dealer, consisting of a new gaiter, retaining

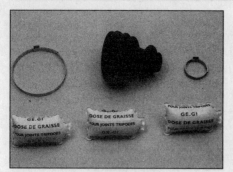

3.6 Driveshaft outer joint gaiter repair kit components

3.7 Sliding the outer joint gaiter onto the driveshaft

3.8 Pack the joint with the grease supplied in the repair kit

clips, and the correct type and quantity of grease **(see illustration)**.

7 Tape over the splines on the inner end of the driveshaft, then carefully slide the outer gaiter onto the shaft **(see illustration)**.

8 Pack the joint with the grease supplied in the repair kit **(see illustration)**. Work the grease well into the bearing tracks whilst twisting the joint, and fill the rubber gaiter with any excess.

9 Ease the gaiter over the joint, and ensure that the gaiter lips are correctly located in the grooves on both the driveshaft and constant velocity joint. Lift the outer sealing lip of the gaiter, to equalise air pressure within the gaiter.

10 Fit the large metal retaining clip to the gaiter. Remove any slack in the gaiter retaining clip by carefully compressing the raised section of the clip. In the absence of the special tool, a pair of side-cutters may be

used. Secure the small retaining clip using the same procedure **(see illustration)**. Check that the constant velocity joint moves freely in all directions before proceeding further.

11 Refit the inner constant velocity joint as described in paragraphs 21 to 28.

Inner joint

12 Remove the driveshaft as described in Section 2.

13 Secure the driveshaft in a vice equipped with soft jaws then, using a suitable pair of pliers, carefully bend back the lip around the circumference of the constant velocity joint outer member cover **(see illustration)**.

14 Once the lip of the cover is fully released, pull the joint outer member out from the cover, and recover the spring and thrust cap from the end of the shaft. Remove the O-ring from the outside of the outer member, and discard it.

15 Fold the gaiter back, and wipe away

the excess grease from the tripod joint. If the rollers are not secured to the joint with circlips, wrap adhesive tape around the joint to hold them in position.

16 Using a dab of paint, or a hammer and punch, mark the relative position of the tripod joint in relation to the driveshaft. Using circlip pliers, extract the circlip securing the joint to the driveshaft **(see illustration)**.

17 The tripod joint can now be removed. If it is tight, draw the joint off the driveshaft end, using a two- or three-legged bearing puller. Ensure that the legs of the puller are located behind the joint inner member, and do not contact the joint rollers **(see illustrations)**. Alternatively, support the inner member of the tripod joint, and press the shaft out of the joint using a hydraulic press, ensuring that no load is applied to the joint rollers.

18 With the tripod joint removed, slide the gaiter and inner retaining collar off the end of the driveshaft.

19 Wipe away as much of the old grease as possible (do not use any solvent) to allow the joint components to be inspected. Take great care not to remove the alignment marks made on dismantling, especially if paint was used.

20 Examine the tripod joint, rollers and outer member for any signs of scoring or wear, and for smoothness of movement of the rollers on the tripod stems. If any component is worn, the complete driveshaft assembly must be renewed; no joint components are available separately. If the joint components are in good condition, obtain a repair kit from your Peugeot/

3.10 Securing a gaiter securing clip using side-cutters

3.13 Peeling back the lip of the joint outer member cover

3.16 Removing the inner tripod joint securing circlip

3.17a Using a three-legged puller to remove the inner tripod joint

3.17b Withdrawing the inner tripod joint. Note the alignment marks (made in the previous paragraph)

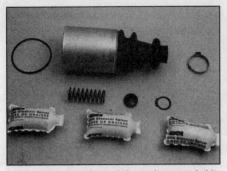

3.20 Driveshaft inner joint gaiter repair kit components

3.21a Slide on the inner retaining collar . . .

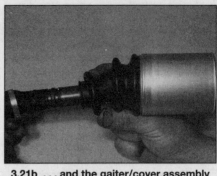

3.21b . . . and the gaiter/cover assembly

Citroën dealer, consisting of a new rubber gaiter and outer cover assembly, circlip, thrust cap, spring, O-ring, and the correct quantity of the special grease **(see illustration)**.

21 Tape over the splines on the end of the driveshaft, and carefully slide the inner retaining collar and gaiter/cover assembly onto the shaft **(see illustrations)**.

22 Remove the tape, then aligning the marks made on dismantling, engage the tripod joint with the driveshaft splines. Use a hammer and soft metal drift (or a suitable tube or socket) to tap the joint onto the shaft, taking great care not to damage the driveshaft splines or joint rollers **(see illustration)**.

23 Secure the tripod joint in position with the new circlip, ensuring that it is correctly located in the driveshaft groove.

24 Remove the tape, and evenly distribute the special grease contained in the repair kit around the tripod joint and outer member **(see illustration)**. Pack the gaiter/cover with more

grease, then draw the cover over the tripod joint. Leave one sachet of grease to lubricate the outer member as the joint is fitted.

25 Fit the new spring, thrust cap and O-ring to the joint outer member **(see illustrations)**.

26 Position the outer member assembly over the tripod joint, and locate the thrust cap

3.22 Using a hammer and a socket to tap the joint onto the driveshaft

against the end of the driveshaft. Apply the remainder of the grease to the joint, then push the outer member onto the shaft, compressing the spring, and locate it inside the outer cover. Secure the outer member in position by peening the end of the cover evenly over the joint outer edge **(see illustrations)**.

3.24 Pack the joint and gaiter/cover with grease

3.25a Fit the new spring . . .

3.25b . . . thrust cap . . .

3.25c . . . and O-ring

3.26a Position the outer member over the tripod joint . . .

3.26b . . . then apply the remainder of the grease . . .

3.26c . . . and peen over the end of the cover

3.27 Securing the inner gaiter clip in position

27 Briefly lift the inner gaiter clip, using a blunt instrument such as a knitting needle, to equalise the air pressure within the gaiter. Secure the inner clip in position **(see illustration)**.

28 Check that the constant velocity joint moves freely in all directions, then refit the driveshaft to the vehicle as described in Section 2.

4 Driveshaft rubber gaiters (PSA type driveshaft) – renewal

Outer joint

1 Remove the driveshaft as described in Section 2.

2 Release the rubber gaiter outer retaining clip by cutting through it using a junior

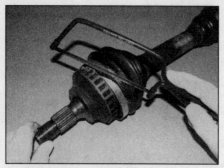

4.2 Release the rubber gaiter outer retaining clip by cutting through it with a hacksaw

hacksaw **(see illustration)**. Spread the clip and remove it from the gaiter.

3 Release the rubber gaiter inner retaining clip using a screwdriver, then mark the position of the end of the gaiter on the driveshaft, using quick-drying paint **(see illustrations)**.

4 Slide the rubber gaiter down the shaft, to expose the outer constant velocity joint then scoop out the excess grease **(see illustration)**. It is advisable to wear disposable rubber gloves during this operation.

5 Hold the driveshaft and, using a mallet, sharply strike the edge of the outer joint to drive it off the end of the shaft **(see illustration)**. The joint is retained on the driveshaft by a circlip, and striking the joint in this manner forces the circlip into its groove, so allowing the joint to slide off.

6 Once the joint assembly has been removed, remove the circlip from the groove

4.3a Release the inner retaining clip using a screwdriver . . .

in the driveshaft splines, and discard it **(see illustration)**. A new circlip must be fitted on reassembly.

7 Withdraw the rubber gaiter from the driveshaft, and slide off the inner retaining clip.

8 With the constant velocity joint removed from the driveshaft, wipe away as much of the old grease as possible (do not use any solvent) to allow the joint components to be inspected.

9 Move the inner splined driving member from side-to-side, to expose each ball in turn at the top of its track. Examine the balls for cracks, flat spots, or signs of surface pitting.

10 Inspect the ball tracks on the inner and outer members. If the tracks have widened, the balls will no longer be a tight fit. At the same time, check the ball cage windows for wear or cracking between the windows.

11 If any of the constant velocity joint components are found to be worn or damaged, it will be necessary to renew the complete joint assembly (where available), or even the complete driveshaft (where no joint components are available separately). Refer to your Peugeot/Citroën dealer for further information on parts availability. If the joint is in satisfactory condition, obtain a repair kit consisting of a new gaiter, circlip, retaining clips, and the correct type and quantity of grease.

12 To install the new gaiter, perform the operations shown **(see illustrations)**. Be sure to stay in order, and follow the captions carefully. Note that different types of gaiter retaining clips may be encountered, but the fitting procedures will be similar to those shown.

4.3b . . . then mark the position of the end of the gaiter on the driveshaft

4.4 Slide the gaiter down the shaft, then scoop out the excess grease

4.5 Sharply strike the edge of the outer joint to drive it off the end of the shaft

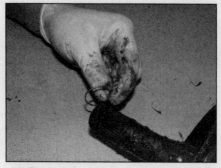

4.6 Remove the circlip from the groove in the driveshaft splines

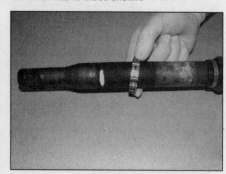

4.12a Slide the new gaiter inner retaining clip on the driveshaft . . .

4.12b . . . followed by the new gaiter with the outer retaining clip in place

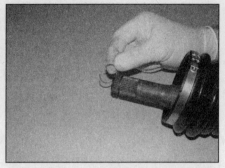

4.12c Locate a new circlip in the driveshaft groove . . .

4.12d . . . then compress the circlip using a cable tie

4.12e Use side-cutters to pull the cable tie as tight as possible, then cut off the end

4.12f Slide the CV joint onto the splines, and position the inner member up against the cable tie

4.12g Strike the end of the joint sharply to displace the cable tie and force the inner member over the circlip

4.12h With the joint in place, cut off the cable tie

4.12i Pack the joint with half the recommended quantity of grease . . .

4.12j . . . working it well into the ball tracks while twisting the joint

4.12k Fill the gaiter with the remaining grease . . .

4.12l . . . then slide the gaiter over the joint outer member, engaging it with the locating groove

4.12m Locate the gaiter inner end in the shaft groove or against the mark made on removal, slide the clip in place and compress the raised portion using pincers or side-cutters

4.12n Secure the gaiter outer retaining clip in the same way

4.15 Measure and record the distance between the inner edges of the driveshaft inner and outer gaiters

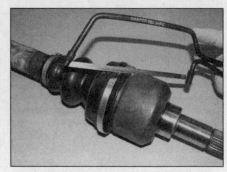

4.16 Release the gaiter retaining clips by cutting through them with a hacksaw

13 Check that the constant velocity joint moves freely in all directions, then refit the driveshaft as described in Section 2.

Inner joint

14 Remove the driveshaft as described in Section 2.

15 Measure the distance between the inner edges of the driveshaft inner and outer rubber gaiters and record this dimension for use when refitting **(see illustration)**.

16 Release the rubber gaiter inner and outer retaining clips by cutting through them using

a junior hacksaw **(see illustration)**. Spread the clips and remove them from the gaiter.

17 Withdraw the joint outer member from the tripod, and recover the spring and thrust cap from inside the outer member **(see illustrations)**. As the outer member is withdrawn, check whether the tripod bearing rollers are staked to the tripod, or secured by circlips. If the rollers are not secured to the tripod, wrap adhesive tape around the rollers to hold them in position.

18 Wipe away as much of the excess grease as possible from the tripod and bearing

rollers **(see illustration)**. It is advisable to wear disposable rubber gloves during this operation.

19 The tripod joint can now be removed using a two- or three-legged hydraulic bearing puller or a press. If a puller is being used, ensure that the legs of the puller are located behind the tripod, and not in contact with the joint rollers. If a press is being used, support the underside of the tripod, and press the driveshaft out of the joint **(see illustration)**.

20 With the tripod removed, slide the gaiter off the end of the driveshaft.

4.17a Withdraw the joint outer member from the tripod . . .

4.17b . . . and recover the spring and thrust cap from inside the outer member

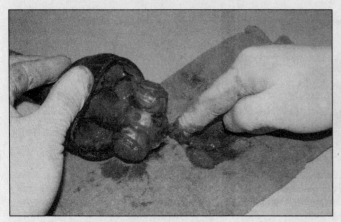

4.18 Wipe away as much grease as possible from the tripod and bearing rollers

4.19 Remove the tripod using a two- or three-legged hydraulic bearing puller or a press

4.22a Slide the new inner retaining clip and the gaiter onto the driveshaft

4.22b Mount the driveshaft in a vice, engage the tripod over the splines and tap it fully into position

4.22c Using a small punch, stake the tripod to the driveshaft in three places

21 Wipe away as much of the old grease as possible (do not use any solvent) to allow the joint components to be inspected. Examine the tripod, bearing rollers and outer member for any signs of scoring or wear, and for smoothness of movement of the rollers on the tripod stems. If any of the components are found to be worn or damaged, it will be necessary to renew the complete joint assembly (where available), or even the complete driveshaft (where no joint components are available separately). Refer to your Peugeot/Citroën dealer for further information on parts availability. If the joint is in satisfactory condition, obtain a repair kit consisting of a new gaiter, retaining clips, and the correct type and quantity of grease.

22 To install the new gaiter, perform the operations shown **(see illustrations)**. Be

sure to stay in order, and follow the captions carefully. Note that different types of gaiter retaining clips may be encountered, but the

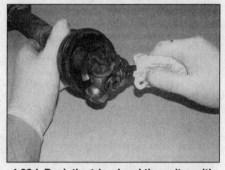

4.22d Pack the tripod and the gaiter with half the recommended quantity of the grease . . .

fitting procedures will be similar to those shown.

23 Check that the constant velocity joint

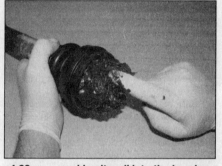

4.22e . . . working it well into the bearing rollers

4.22f Refit the spring and thrust cap to the outer member . . .

4.22g . . . then pack the outer member with the remaining grease

4.22h Locate the outer member over the tripod and engage the gaiter with the outer member groove

4.22i Push the outer member fully into position over the tripod, while lifting the gaiter inner end to expel trapped air

4.22j Position the outer retaining clip over the gaiter and compress the raised portion using pincers or side-cutters

4.22k Position the gaiter inner end at the dimension recorded during removal, slip on the clip and compress the raised portion

moves freely in all directions, then refit the driveshaft to the car as described in Section 2.

5 Driveshaft overhaul – general information

1 If any of the checks described in *Road test* in Chapter 1A or 1B reveal possible wear in any driveshaft joint, carry out the following procedures to identify the source of the problem.
2 Firmly apply the handbrake, then jack up the front of the vehicle and support it securely on axle stands (see *Jacking and vehicle support*).
3 Referring to the information contained in Section 2, make up a tool to hold the wheel hub, and bolt the tool to the hub. Remove the R-clip and locking cap from the driveshaft retaining nut and use a torque wrench to check that the nut is securely fastened. Once tightened, refit the locking cap and R-clip. Repeat this check on the remaining driveshaft nut.
4 Road test the vehicle, and listen for a metallic clicking from the front as the vehicle is driven slowly in a circle on full-lock. If a clicking noise is heard, this indicates wear in the outer constant velocity joint. This means

that the joint must be renewed; reconditioning is not possible.
5 If vibration, consistent with road speed, is felt through the car when accelerating, there is a possibility of wear in the inner constant velocity joints.
6 To check the joints for wear, remove the driveshafts, then dismantle them; if any wear or free play is found, the affected joint must be renewed. In most cases this will mean that the complete driveshaft assembly must be renewed, if the joints are not available separately. Refer to your Peugeot/Citroën dealer for information on the availability of driveshaft components.

6 Right-hand driveshaft intermediate bearing – renewal

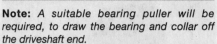

Note: *A suitable bearing puller will be required, to draw the bearing and collar off the driveshaft end.*
1 Remove the right-hand driveshaft as described in Section 2.
2 Check that the bearing outer race rotates smoothly and easily, without any signs of roughness or undue free play between the inner and outer races. If necessary, renew the bearing as follows.

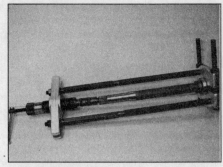

6.3 Using a long-reach bearing puller to remove the intermediate bearing from the right-hand driveshaft

3 Using a long-reach universal bearing puller, carefully draw the collar and intermediate bearing off the driveshaft inner end **(see illustration)**. Apply a smear of grease to the inner race of the new bearing, then fit the bearing over the end of the driveshaft. Using a hammer and suitable piece of tubing which bears only on the bearing inner race, tap the new bearing into position on the driveshaft, until it abuts the constant velocity joint outer member. Once the bearing is correctly positioned, tap the bearing collar onto the shaft until it contacts the bearing inner race.
4 Check that the bearing rotates freely, then refit the driveshaft as described in Section 2.

Chapter 9
Braking system

Contents

Degrees of difficulty

Easy, suitable for novice with little experience	**Fairly easy,** suitable for beginner with some experience	**Fairly difficult,** suitable for competent DIY mechanic	**Difficult,** suitable for experienced DIY mechanic	**Very difficult,** suitable for expert DIY or professional

Specifications

Front disc brakes

Caliper type:
Up to 2002	Lucas C54
2002 onward	Bosch ZOH 54

Disc diameter:
Models without ESP	266.0 mm
Models with ESP	283.0 mm

Disc thickness:

Solid disc:
New	13.0 mm
Minimum thickness	11.0 mm

Ventilated disc:

Up to 2002:
New	20.4 mm
Minimum thickness	18.4 mm

2002 onward:

Models without ESP:
New	22.0 mm
Minimum thickness	20.0 mm

Models with ESP:
New	26.0 mm
Minimum thickness	24.0 mm

Maximum disc run-out:
Models without ESP	0.1 mm
Models with ESP	0.05 mm
Brake pad minimum thickness	2.0 mm

Rear drum brakes

Drum internal diameter:
New	228.0 mm
Maximum after machining	230.0 mm
Brake shoe minimum thickness	1.5 mm

Rear disc brakes

Disc diameter	247.0 mm (solid)
Disc thickness:	
New	9.0 mm
Minimum thickness.	7.0 mm
Maximum variation in thickness between sides.	0.01 mm
Maximum disc run-out	0.05 mm
Minimum disc pad friction material thickness	2.5 mm
ABS sensor air gap (non-adjustable)	0.15 to 1.5 mm

Torque wrench settings

	Nm	lbf ft
ABS hydraulic modulator retaining nuts.	15	11
ABS wheel sensor retaining bolts*	11	8
Front brake caliper guide pin bolts*	27	20
Front brake caliper mounting bracket-to-swivel hub bolts*	105	77
Master cylinder-to-servo unit nuts	20	15
Rear brake pressure-regulating valve mounting bolt	30	22
Rear caliper guide pin bolts*	38	28
Roadwheel bolts.	90	66
Vacuum pump retaining nuts/bolts (diesel engine models)	25	18
Vacuum servo unit mounting nuts	23	17

Use thread-locking compound

1 General information

The braking system is of the servo-assisted, dual-circuit hydraulic type. The arrangement of the hydraulic system is such that each circuit operates one front and one rear brake from a tandem master cylinder. Under normal circumstances, both circuits operate in unison. However, in the event of hydraulic failure in one circuit, full braking force will still be available at two wheels.

All models are fitted with either solid or ventilated front disc brakes and either self-adjusting drum or solid disc rear brakes. An Anti-lock Braking System (ABS) is fitted as standard or available as an option, according to model (refer to Section 19 for further information on ABS operation).

The front disc brakes are actuated by single-piston sliding type calipers, which ensure that equal pressure is applied to each disc pad. The rear disc brakes (models with ESP only) are of twin-piston fixed type, operating on solid discs.

The rear drum brakes incorporate leading and trailing shoes, which are actuated by twin-piston wheel cylinders. A self-adjusting mechanism is incorporated, to automatically compensate for brake shoe wear. As the brake shoe linings wear, the footbrake operation automatically operates the adjuster mechanism, which effectively lengthens the shoe strut and repositions the brake shoes, to reduce the lining-to-drum clearance.

To prevent rear wheel lock-up during emergency braking, a load-sensitive pressure-regulating valve assembly is fitted into the hydraulic circuit to each rear brake. The valve is mounted on the underside of the vehicle at the rear and is attached to the rear suspension by means of an operating rod and spring. The valve measures the load on the rear of the vehicle via the movement of the rear suspension and regulates the hydraulic pressure applied to the rear brakes accordingly. On later models (approximately 2001 onward) equipped with ABS, the hydraulic pressure applied to the rear brakes is regulated by the ABS hydraulic modulator under all braking conditions. On these models, the separate mechanical pressure-regulating valve assembly is not used.

Later 1.6 litre petrol and 2.0 litre diesel models (RPO 9856 onwards) are available with ESP (Electronic Stability Program). This system is designed to maintain the stability of the vehicle during extreme braking manoeuvres by operating the wheel brakes independently of each other. The system utilises the same wheel speed sensor/brake operating components as the ABS system, with the addition of a lateral acceleration sensor (Yaw rate) and a steering angle sensor.

On all models, the handbrake provides an independent mechanical means of rear brake application.

On diesel engine models, there is insufficient vacuum in the inlet manifold to operate the braking system servo effectively at all times. To overcome this problem, a vacuum pump is fitted to the engine, to provide sufficient vacuum to operate the servo unit. The vacuum pump is mounted on the left-hand end of the cylinder head, and driven directly off the end of the camshaft.

Note: *When servicing any part of the system, work carefully and methodically; also observe scrupulous cleanliness when overhauling any part of the hydraulic system. Always renew components (in axle sets, where applicable) if in doubt about their condition, and use only genuine Peugeot/Citroën parts, or at least those of known good quality. Note the warnings given in 'Safety first!' and at relevant points in this Chapter concerning the dangers of asbestos dust and brake hydraulic fluid.*

2 Hydraulic system – bleeding

 Warning: Brake hydraulic fluid is poisonous; wash off immediately and thoroughly in the case of skin contact, and seek immediate medical advice if any fluid is swallowed or gets into the eyes. Certain types of hydraulic fluid are inflammable, and may ignite when allowed into contact with hot components; when servicing any hydraulic system, it is safest to assume that the fluid is inflammable, and to take precautions against the risk of fire as though it is petrol that is being handled. Hydraulic fluid is also an effective paint stripper, and will attack plastics; if any is spilt, it should be washed off immediately, using copious quantities of fresh water. Finally, it is hygroscopic (it absorbs moisture from the air) – old fluid may be contaminated and unfit for further use. When topping-up or renewing the fluid, always use the recommended type, and ensure that it comes from a freshly-opened sealed container.

Models without ABS
General

1 The correct operation of any hydraulic system is only possible after removing all air from the components and circuit; this is achieved by bleeding the system.

2 During the bleeding procedure, add only clean, unused hydraulic fluid of the recommended type (see *Lubricants and fluids*); never re-use fluid that has already been bled from the system. Ensure that sufficient fluid is available before starting work.

3 If there is any possibility of incorrect fluid being already in the system, the brake components and circuit must be flushed completely with uncontaminated, correct fluid, and new seals should be fitted to the various components.

4 If hydraulic fluid has been lost from the system, or air has entered because of a leak, ensure that the fault is cured before proceeding further.

5 Park the vehicle on level ground, switch off the engine and select first or reverse gear, then chock the wheels and release the handbrake.

6 Check that all pipes and hoses are secure, unions tight and bleed screws closed. Clean any dirt from around the bleed screws.

7 Unscrew the master cylinder reservoir cap, and top the master cylinder reservoir up to the MAX level line; refit the cap loosely, and remember to maintain the fluid level above the MIN level line throughout the procedure, or there is a risk of further air entering the system.

8 There is a number of one-man, do-it-yourself brake bleeding kits currently available from motor accessory shops. It is recommended that one of these kits is used whenever possible, as they greatly simplify the bleeding operation, and also reduce the risk of expelled air and fluid being drawn back into the system. If such a kit is not available, the basic (two-man) method must be used, which is described in detail below.

9 If a kit is to be used, prepare the vehicle as described previously, and follow the kit manufacturer's instructions, as the procedure may vary slightly according to the type being used; generally, they are as outlined below in the relevant sub-section.

10 Whichever method is used, the same sequence must be followed (paragraphs 11 and 12) to ensure the removal of all air from the system.

Bleeding sequence

11 If the system has been only partially disconnected, and suitable precautions were taken to minimise fluid loss, it should be necessary only to bleed that part of the system (ie, the primary or secondary circuit).

12 If the complete system is to be bled, then it should be done working in the following sequence:

   a) *Right-hand rear brake.*
   b) *Left-hand rear brake.*
   c) *Right-hand front brake.*
   d) *Left-hand front brake.*

Basic (two-man) method

13 Collect a clean glass jar, a suitable length of plastic or rubber tubing which is a tight fit over the bleed screw, and a ring spanner to fit the screw. The help of an assistant will also be required.

14 Remove the dust cap from the first screw in the sequence. Fit the spanner and tube to the screw, place the other end of the tube in the jar, and pour in sufficient fluid to cover the end of the tube.

15 Ensure that the master cylinder reservoir fluid level is maintained above the MIN level line throughout the procedure.

16 Have the assistant fully depress the brake pedal several times to build-up pressure, then maintain it on the final downstroke.

17 While pedal pressure is maintained, unscrew the bleed screw (approximately one turn) and allow the compressed fluid and air to flow into the jar. The assistant should maintain pedal pressure, following it down to the floor if necessary, and should not release it until instructed to do so. When the flow stops, tighten the bleed screw again, have the assistant release the pedal slowly, and recheck the reservoir fluid level.

18 Repeat the steps given in paragraphs 16 and 17 until the fluid emerging from the bleed screw is free from air bubbles. If the master cylinder has been drained and refilled, and air is being bled from the first screw in the sequence, allow approximately five seconds between cycles for the master cylinder passages to refill.

19 When no more air bubbles appear, tighten the bleed screw securely, remove the tube and spanner, and refit the dust cap. Do not overtighten the bleed screw.

20 Repeat the procedure on the remaining screws in the sequence, until all air is removed from the system and the brake pedal feels firm again.

Using a one-way valve kit

21 As their name implies, these kits consist of a length of tubing with a one-way valve fitted, to prevent expelled air and fluid being drawn back into the system; some kits include a translucent container, which can be positioned so that the air bubbles can be more easily seen flowing from the end of the tube.

22 The kit is connected to the bleed screw, which is then opened. The user returns to the driver's seat, depresses the brake pedal with a smooth, steady stroke, and slowly releases it; this is repeated until the expelled fluid is clear of air bubbles.

23 Note that these kits simplify work so much that it is easy to forget the master cylinder reservoir fluid level; ensure that this is maintained above the MIN level line at all times.

Using a pressure-bleeding kit

24 These kits are usually operated by the reservoir of pressurised air contained in the spare tyre. However, note that it will probably be necessary to reduce the pressure to a lower level than normal; refer to the instructions supplied with the kit.

25 By connecting a pressurised, fluid-filled container to the master cylinder reservoir, bleeding can be carried out simply by opening each screw in turn (in the specified sequence), and allowing the fluid to flow out until no more air bubbles can be seen in the expelled fluid.

26 This method has the advantage that the large reservoir of fluid provides an additional safeguard against air being drawn into the system during bleeding.

27 Pressure-bleeding is particularly effective

when bleeding 'difficult' systems, or when bleeding the complete system at the time of routine fluid renewal.

All methods

28 When bleeding is complete, and firm pedal feel is restored, wash off any spilt fluid, tighten the bleed screws, and refit their dust caps.

29 Check the hydraulic fluid level in the master cylinder reservoir, and top-up if necessary.

30 Discard any fluid that has been bled from the system; it will not be fit for re-use.

31 Check the feel of the brake pedal. If it feels at all spongy, air must still be present in the system, and further bleeding is required. Failure to bleed properly after a reasonable repetition of the bleeding procedure may be due to worn master cylinder seals.

Models with ABS

 Warning: On models equipped with ABS, ensure that the ignition is switched off before starting the bleeding procedure, to avoid any possibility of voltage being applied to the hydraulic modulator before the bleeding procedure is completed. Ideally, the battery should be disconnected. If voltage is applied to the modulator before the bleeding procedure is complete, this will effectively drain the hydraulic fluid in the modulator, rendering the unit unserviceable. Do not, therefore, attempt to 'run' the modulator in order to bleed the brakes.

32 A pressure-bleeding kit must be used for bleeding the hydraulic system on ABS models – see paragraphs 24 to 27.

33 Following the sequence given in paragraph 12, bleed each brake in turn until clean fluid, free of air bubbles, is seen to emerge. Pause between bleeding each brake to ensure that the fluid level in the reservoir is above the MIN level.

34 When bleeding is complete, and firm pedal feel is restored, wash off any spilt fluid, tighten the bleed screws, and refit their dust caps.

35 Check the hydraulic fluid level in the master cylinder reservoir, and top-up if necessary.

36 Discard any fluid that has been bled from the system; it will not be fit for re-use.

37 Check the feel of the brake pedal. If it feels at all spongy, air must still be present in the system, and further bleeding is required.

Warning: Do not operate the vehicle if you are in doubt about the effectiveness of the braking system. If considerable air was present in the system prior to bleeding, it is possible for some of this air to remain trapped in the hydraulic modulator assembly. If the pedal continues to feel spongy after repeated bleedings, or if any of the brake system warning lights remain on, have the vehicle towed to a Peugeot/Citroën dealer to be bled with the use of Peugeot/Citroën diagnostic equipment.

3 Hydraulic pipes and hoses – renewal

Note: *Before starting work, refer to the note at the beginning of Section 2 concerning the dangers of hydraulic fluid.*

1 If any pipe or hose is to be renewed, minimise fluid loss by first removing the master cylinder reservoir cap, then tightening it down onto a piece of polythene to obtain an airtight seal. Alternatively, flexible hoses can be sealed, if required, using a proprietary brake hose clamp; metal brake pipe unions can be plugged (if care is taken not to allow dirt into the system) or capped immediately they are disconnected. Place a wad of rag under any union that is to be disconnected, to catch any spilt fluid.

2 If a flexible hose is to be disconnected, unscrew the brake pipe union nut before removing the spring clip which secures the hose to its mounting bracket.

3 To unscrew the union nuts, it is preferable to obtain a brake pipe spanner of the correct size; these are available from most large motor accessory shops. Failing this, a close-fitting open-ended spanner will be required, though if the nuts are tight or corroded, their flats may be rounded-off if the spanner slips. In such a case, a self-locking wrench is often the only way to unscrew a stubborn union, but it follows that the pipe and the damaged nuts must be renewed on reassembly. Always clean a union and surrounding area before disconnecting it. If disconnecting a component with more than one union, make a careful note of the connections before disturbing any of them.

4 If a brake pipe is to be renewed, it can be obtained, cut to length and with the union nuts and end flares in place, from Peugeot/Citroën dealers. All that is then necessary is to bend it to shape, following the line of the original, before fitting it to the car. Alternatively, most motor accessory shops can make up brake pipes from kits, but this requires very careful measurement of the original, to ensure that the new one is of the correct length. The safest answer is usually to take the original to the shop as a pattern.

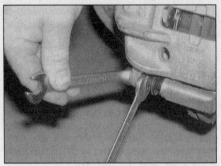
4.4 Retain the guide pin with a spanner while undoing the lower guide pin bolt

5 On refitting, do not overtighten the union nuts. It is not necessary to exercise brute force to obtain a sound joint.

6 Ensure that the pipes and hoses are correctly routed, with no kinks, and that they are secured in the clips or brackets provided. After fitting, remove the polythene from the reservoir, and bleed the hydraulic system as described in Section 2. Wash off any spilt fluid, and check carefully for fluid leaks.

4 Front brake pads – renewal

Warning: Renew BOTH sets of front brake pads at the same time – NEVER renew the pads on only one wheel, as uneven braking may result. Note that the dust created by wear of the pads may contain asbestos, which is a health hazard. Never blow it out with compressed air, and don't inhale any of it. An approved filtering mask should be worn when working on the brakes. DO NOT use petrol or petroleum-based solvents to clean brake parts; use brake cleaner or methylated spirit only.

Note: *New guide pin bolts must be used on refitting.*

Lucas caliper

1 Apply the handbrake, then jack up the front of the vehicle and support it on axle stands (see *Jacking and vehicle support*). Remove the front roadwheels.

4.5 Slacken the upper guide pin bolt, and pivot the caliper upwards off the brake pads

2 Disconnect the brake pad wear sensor wiring at the connector on the swivel hub. Note the routing of the wires, and free them from any relevant retaining clips.

3 Push the piston into its bore by pulling the caliper outwards.

4 Undo and remove the lower caliper guide pin bolt, using a second, slim, open-ended spanner to prevent the guide pin itself from rotating **(see illustration)**. Discard the guide pin bolt – new bolts must be used on refitting.

5 Slacken the upper guide pin bolt, while holding the guide pin with the open-ended spanner as before. Pivot the caliper upwards off the brake pads, and tie the caliper to the suspension strut to hold it in this position **(see illustration)**.

6 Withdraw the two brake pads from the caliper mounting bracket noting their fitted positions if they are to be re-used (ie, inner and outer) **(see illustration)**.

7 First measure the thickness of each brake pad's friction material. If either pad is worn at any point to the specified minimum thickness or less, all four pads must be renewed **(see illustration)**. Also, the pads should be renewed if any are fouled with oil or grease; there is no satisfactory way of degreasing friction material, once contaminated. If any of the brake pads are worn unevenly, or are fouled with oil or grease, trace and rectify the cause before reassembly. New brake pads and repair kits are available from Peugeot/Citroën dealers.

8 If the brake pads are still serviceable, carefully clean them using a clean, fine wire brush or similar, paying particular attention to the sides and back of the metal backing. Clean out the grooves in the friction material, and pick out any large embedded particles of dirt or debris. Carefully clean the pad locations in the caliper mounting bracket.

9 Prior to fitting the pads, check that the guide pins are free to slide easily in the caliper body/ mounting bracket, and check that the rubber guide pin gaiters are undamaged. Brush the dust and dirt from the caliper and piston, but do not inhale it, as it is injurious to health. Inspect the dust seal around the piston for damage, and the piston for evidence of fluid leaks, corrosion or damage. If attention to any of these components is necessary, refer to Section 8.

10 If new brake pads are to be fitted, the caliper piston must be pushed back into the

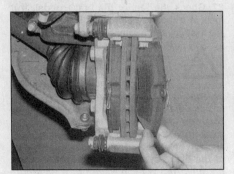
4.6 Withdraw the two brake pads from the caliper mounting bracket

4.7 Measuring brake pad friction material thickness

4.10a Use a suitable tool to retract the caliper piston . . .

4.10b . . . and with the bleed nipple open, collect the expelled fluid in a container

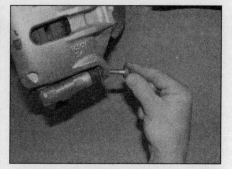

4.20 Undo and remove the lower caliper guide pin bolt . . .

4.21 . . . then pivot the caliper upwards off the brake pads

4.22a Withdraw the brake pads from the caliper mounting bracket . . .

4.22b . . . then recover the top and bottom shims

cylinder to make room for them; either use a G-clamp or similar tool, or use suitable pieces of wood as levers. Clamp off the flexible brake hose leading to the caliper then connect a brake bleeding kit to the caliper bleed nipple. Open the bleed nipple as the piston is retracted, the surplus brake fluid will then be collected in the bleed kit vessel **(see illustrations)**. Close the bleed nipple just before the caliper piston is pushed fully into the caliper. This should ensure no air enters the hydraulic system. **Note:** *The ABS modulator contains hydraulic components that are very sensitive to impurities in the brake fluid. Even the smallest particles can cause the system to fail through blockage. The pad retraction method described here prevents any debris in the brake fluid expelled from the caliper from being passed back to the ABS modulator, as well as preventing any chance of damage to the master cylinder seals.*

11 Install the pads in the caliper mounting bracket, ensuring that the friction material of each pad is against the brake disc, and that the pads are in their correct locations if the original pads are being re-used. Where new pads are being fitted, the pad with the white wear sensor wire should be on the outside.

12 Pivot the caliper down over the pads, and pass the pad wear sensor wiring through the caliper aperture.

13 If not already precoated, apply suitable thread locking compound to the threads of the two new guide pin bolts. Insert the lower bolt and tighten it to the specified torque. Hold the guide pin with the open-ended spanner as the guide pin bolt is tightened.

14 Remove the original upper guide pin bolt and fit the new bolt, tightening it to the specified torque.

15 Reconnect the brake pad wear sensor wiring connectors, ensuring that the wiring is correctly routed through the loop of the caliper bleed screw cap.

16 Depress the brake pedal repeatedly, until the pads are pressed into firm contact with the brake disc, and normal (non-assisted) pedal pressure is restored.

17 Repeat the above procedure on the remaining front brake caliper.

Bosch caliper

18 Apply the handbrake, then jack up the front of the vehicle and support it on axle stands (see *Jacking and vehicle support*). Remove the front roadwheels.

19 Push the piston into its bore by pulling the caliper outwards.

20 Undo and remove the lower caliper guide pin bolt **(see illustration)**. Discard the guide pin bolt – a new bolt must be used on refitting.

21 Pivot the caliper upwards off the brake pads, and tie the caliper to the suspension strut to hold it in this position **(see illustration)**.

22 Withdraw the two brake pads from the caliper mounting bracket noting their fitted positions if they are to be re-used (ie, inner and outer). Recover the shims from the top and bottom of the caliper mounting bracket **(see illustrations)**.

23 Proceed as described in paragraphs 7 to 10.

24 Refit the shims to the top and bottom of

the caliper mounting bracket, ensuring they are correctly located.

25 Install the pads in the caliper mounting bracket, ensuring that the friction material of each pad is against the brake disc, and that the pads are in their correct locations if the original pads are being re-used.

26 Untie the caliper piston and carefully pivot it back down over the pads. Position the flat on the lower guide pin horizontally to allow the machined face on the caliper mounting lug to correctly engage **(see illustration)**.

27 If not precoated, apply suitable thread locking compound to the threads of the new lower guide pin bolt. Insert the bolt and tighten it to the specified torque.

28 Depress the brake pedal repeatedly, until the pads are pressed into firm contact with the brake disc, and normal (non-assisted) pedal pressure is restored.

4.26 Position the flat (arrowed) on the guide pin horizontally to allow the caliper mounting lug to correctly engage

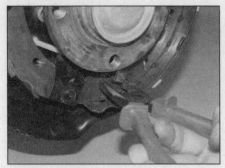

5.6 Disengage the lower return spring from the trailing shoe, unhook it from the leading shoe and lift out the spring

5.7a Depress the retainer spring cup and turn it through 90°, while holding the retainer pin from the rear of the backplate

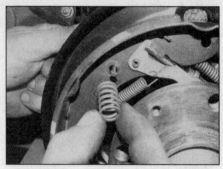

5.7b With the cup removed, lift off the spring, then withdraw the retainer pin

29 Repeat the above procedure on the remaining front brake caliper.

All calipers

30 Refit the roadwheels, then lower the vehicle to the ground and tighten the roadwheel bolts to the specified torque.
31 Finally, check the hydraulic fluid level in the master cylinder reservoir as described in *Weekly checks*.
32 Note that new pads will not give full braking efficiency until they have bedded-in. Be prepared for this, and avoid hard braking as far as possible for the first hundred miles or so after pad renewal.

5 Rear brake shoes – renewal

⚠️ *Warning: Brake shoes must be renewed on BOTH rear wheels at the same time – NEVER renew the shoes on only one wheel, as uneven braking may result. Also, the dust created by wear of the shoes may contain asbestos, which is a health hazard. Never blow it out with compressed air, and don't inhale any of it. An approved filtering mask should be worn when working on the brakes. DO NOT use petrol or petroleum-based solvents to clean brake parts; use brake cleaner or methylated spirit only.*

1 Remove the brake drum as described in Section 7.
2 Working carefully, and taking the necessary precautions, remove all traces of brake dust from the brake drum, backplate and shoes.
3 Measure the thickness of the friction material of each brake shoe at several points; if either shoe is worn at any point to the specified minimum thickness or less, all four shoes must be renewed as a set. The shoes should also be renewed if any are fouled with oil or grease; there is no satisfactory way of degreasing friction material, once contaminated.
4 If any of the brake shoes are worn unevenly, or fouled with oil or grease, trace and rectify the cause before reassembly.
5 Make a note of the correct fitted positions of the springs and adjuster strut, to use as a guide on reassembly.
6 Disengage the end of the lower return spring from the trailing shoe, unhook it from the leading shoe and lift out the spring **(see illustration)**.
7 Using pliers, depress the leading shoe retainer spring cup and turn it through 90°, while holding the retainer pin with your finger from the rear of the backplate. With the cup removed, lift off the spring, then withdraw the retainer pin **(see illustrations)**. Repeat this procedure for the retainer on the trailing shoe.
8 Detach the handbrake cable end from the lever on the trailing shoe **(see illustration)**.
9 Disconnect the adjuster lever spring

from the leading shoe and adjuster lever, then withdraw the adjuster lever **(see illustrations)**.
10 Lift the brake shoes off the lower pivot post and off the wheel cylinder pistons. Spread the shoes apart at the bottom and remove the adjuster strut, upper return spring and then the two brake shoes.
11 With the brake shoes removed, retain the wheel cylinder pistons in the wheel cylinder using a cable tie or a strong elastic band. Do not depress the brake pedal until the brakes are reassembled.
12 Withdraw the forked end from the adjuster strut, and carefully examine the assembly for signs of wear or damage. Pay particular attention to the threads and the knurled adjuster wheel, and renew if necessary.
13 Check the condition of all return springs and renew any that show signs of distortion or other damage.
14 Peel back the rubber protective caps, and check the wheel cylinder for fluid leaks or other damage; check that both cylinder pistons are free to move easily. Refer to Section 9, if necessary, for information on wheel cylinder renewal.
15 Prior to installation, clean the backplate, and apply a thin smear of high-temperature brake grease or anti-seize compound to all those surfaces of the backplate which bear on the shoes, particularly the wheel cylinder pistons and lower pivot point. Do not allow the lubricant to foul the friction material.
16 Ensure that the handbrake lever stop-peg

5.8 Detach the handbrake cable end from the lever on the trailing shoe

5.9a Disconnect the adjuster lever spring (arrowed) . . .

5.9b . . . then withdraw the adjuster lever

5.17 Fit the upper return spring to the leading and trailing brake shoes

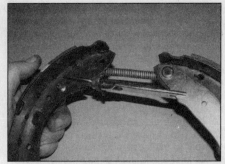

5.18 Engage the adjuster strut with the leading shoe and handbrake lever

5.20 Manoeuvre the partially assembled brake shoe assembly into position on the backplate

is correctly located against the edge of the trailing shoe, and that the return spring is in position.

17 Fit the upper return spring to its location in the leading and trailing brake shoes **(see illustration)**.

18 Screw in the adjuster wheel until the minimum strut length is obtained, then engage the strut with the leading shoe and handbrake lever **(see illustration)**.

19 Undo the two bolts securing the wheel cylinder to the brake backplate. Carefully ease the cylinder from its location until the bleed screw is clear of the backplate. Move the cylinder upwards as far as the hydraulic pipe will allow, to provide as much clearance between the cylinder and wheel hub as possible.

20 Manoeuvre the partially assembled brake shoe assembly into position on the backplate, and engage the brake shoes with the wheel cylinder pistons **(see illustration)**.

21 Feed the lower return spring behind the lower pivot post and connect one end to the leading brake shoe **(see illustration)**.

22 Hold the spring in place on the leading shoe and engage a screwdriver with the other end of the spring **(see illustration)**.

23 Pull the spring by means of the screwdriver until it just catches on the edge of its locating hole in the trailing shoe. Now engage the tip of the screwdriver with the end of the spring and pull it fully into place **(see illustration)**. Be prepared to have several attempts at this as there is very little working

5.21 Feed the lower return spring behind the pivot post and connect one end to the leading shoe

clearance behind the trailing shoe. Extreme patience is necessary!

24 Once the lower spring is connected, locate the brake shoes on the lower pivot post and at the same time ease the wheel cylinder back into its location. Refit the wheel cylinder retaining bolts and tighten them securely **(see illustration)**.

25 Position the adjuster lever on the leading shoe, ensuring that it locates behind the forked end of the adjuster strut. Reconnect the adjuster lever spring to the lever and leading shoe **(see illustration)**.

26 Reconnect the handbrake cable end to the handbrake lever on the trailing shoe.

27 Insert the leading brake shoe retainer pin through the backplate and place the spring on the pin. Hold the pin from behind, refit the cup

5.22 Hold the spring on the leading shoe and engage a screwdriver with the other end of the spring

and turn it through 90°. Repeat this procedure for the retainer on the trailing shoe, then tap the shoes to centralise them with the backplate.

28 Using a screwdriver, turn the strut adjuster wheel to expand the shoes until the brake drum just slides over the shoes.

29 Refit the brake drum as described in Section 7.

30 Repeat the above procedure on the remaining rear brake.

31 Once both sets of rear shoes have been renewed, adjust the lining-to-drum clearance by repeatedly depressing the brake pedal. Whilst depressing the pedal, have an assistant listen to the rear drums, to check that the adjuster strut is functioning correctly; if so, a clicking sound will be emitted by the strut as the pedal is depressed.

5.23 Pull the spring until it catches on its locating hole, then pull it fully into place with the tip of a screwdriver

5.24 Locate the brake shoes on the lower pivot post and ease the wheel cylinder back into its location

5.25 Position the adjuster lever on the leading shoe and reconnect the spring

32 Check and, if necessary, adjust the handbrake as described in Section 13.

33 On completion, check the hydraulic fluid level in the master cylinder as described in *Weekly checks*.

34 Note that new shoes will not give full braking efficiency until they have bedded-in. Be prepared for this, and avoid hard braking as far as possible for the first hundred miles or so after shoe renewal.

6 Rear brake pads – renewal

⚠ *Warning: Renew both sets of rear brake pads at the same time – never renew the pads on only one wheel, as uneven braking may result. Note that the dust created by wear of the pads may contain asbestos, which is a health hazard. Never blow it out with compressed air, and don't inhale any of it. An approved filtering mask should be worn when working on the brakes. DO NOT use petrol or petroleum-based solvents to clean brake parts; use brake cleaner or methylated spirit only.*

1 Chock the front wheels, slacken the rear roadwheel bolts, then jack up the rear of the vehicle and support it on axle stands (see *Jacking and vehicle support*). Remove the rear wheels.

2 With the handbrake fully released, unhook the handbrake cable end from the lever on the rear caliper.

3 Push the piston into its bore by pulling the caliper outwards.

4 Undo and remove the upper and lower caliper guide pin bolts, using a second, slim, open-ended spanner to prevent the guide pin itself from rotating. Discard the guide pin bolts – new bolts must be used on refitting.

5 Slide the caliper off of the brake pads and support to one side.

6 Withdraw the two brake pads from the caliper mounting bracket noting their fitted positions if they are to be re-used (ie inner and outer).

7 First measure the thickness of each brake pad's friction material. If either pad is worn at any point to the specified minimum thickness or less, all four rear pads must be renewed. Also, the pads should be renewed if any are fouled with oil or grease; there is no satisfactory way of degreasing friction material once contaminated. If any of the brake pads are worn unevenly, or are fouled with oil or grease, trace the rectify the cause before reassembly.

8 If the brake pads are still serviceable, carefully clean them using a clean, fine wire brush or similar, paying particular attention to the sides and back of the metal backing. Clean out the grooves in the friction material, and pick out any large embedded particles of dirt or debris. Carefully clean the pad locations in the caliper mounting bracket.

9 Prior to fitting the pads, check that the guide pins are free to slide easily in the caliper

body/mounting bracket, and check that the rubber guide pin gaiters are undamaged. Brush the dust and dirt from the caliper and piston, but do not inhale it, as it is injurious to health. Inspect the dust seal around the piston for damage, and the piston for evidence of fluid leaks, corrosion or damage. If attention to any of these components is necessary, refer to Section 12.

10 If new brake pads are to be fitted, the caliper piston must be pushed back into the cylinder to make room for them; either use a G-clamp or similar tool, or use suitable pieces of wood as levers. Clamp off the flexible brake hose leading to the caliper then connect a brake bleeding kit to the caliper bleed nipple. Open the bleed nipple as the piston is retracted; the surplus brake fluid will then be collected in the bleed kit vessel. Close the bleed nipple just before the caliper piston is pushed fully into the caliper. This should ensure no air enters the hydraulic system. **Note:** *The ABS modulator contains hydraulic components that are very sensitive to impurities in the brake fluid. Even the smallest particles can cause the system to fail through blockage. The pad retraction method described here prevents any debris in the brake fluid expelled from caliper from being passed back to the ABS modulator, as well as preventing any chance of damage to the master cylinder seals.*

11 Install the pads in the caliper mounting bracket, ensuring that the friction material of each pad is against the brake disc, and that the pads are in their correct locations if the original pads are being re-used.

12 If not already precoated, apply suitable thread locking compound to the threads of the two new guide pin bolts, then slide the caliper into position over the brake pads, insert the bolts and tighten to the specified torque.

13 Hook the handbrake cable end onto the lever on the rear caliper.

14 Depress the brake pedal repeatedly, until the pads are pressed into firm contact with the brake disc, and normal (non-assisted) pedal pressure is restored, then apply the handbrake fully several times to restore correct handbrake action.

15 Repeat the above procedure on the remaining rear brake caliper.

16 Refit the roadwheels, then lower the

vehicle to the ground and tighten the roadwheel bolts to the specified torque.

17 Check the hydraulic fluid level as described in *Weekly checks*.

Caution: New pads will not give full braking efficiency until they have bedded-in. Be prepared for this, and avoid hard braking as far as possible for the first hundred miles or so after pad renewal.

7 Front brake disc – inspection, removal and refitting

Note: *Before starting work, refer to the note at the beginning of Section 4 concerning the dangers of asbestos dust.*

Inspection

Note: *If either disc requires renewal, BOTH should be renewed at the same time, to ensure even and consistent braking. New brake pads should also be fitted.*

1 Apply the handbrake, then jack up the front of the car and support it on axle stands (see *Jacking and vehicle support*). Remove the appropriate front roadwheel.

2 Slowly rotate the brake disc so that the full area of both sides can be checked; remove the brake pads if better access is required to the inboard surface. Light scoring is normal in the area swept by the brake pads, but if heavy scoring or cracks are found, the disc must be renewed.

3 It is normal to find a lip of rust and brake dust around the disc's perimeter; this can be scraped off if required. If, however, a lip has formed due to excessive wear of the brake pad swept area, then the disc's thickness must be measured using a micrometer (see illustration). Take measurements at several places around the disc, at the inside and outside of the pad swept area; if the disc has worn at any point to the specified minimum thickness or less, the disc must be renewed.

4 If the disc is thought to be warped, it can be checked for run-out. Either use a dial gauge mounted on any convenient fixed point while the disc is slowly rotated, or use feeler blades to measure (at several points all around the disc) the clearance between the disc and a fixed point, such as the caliper mounting bracket (see

7.3 Using a micrometer to measure disc thickness

7.4 Checking disc run-out using a dial gauge

7.7 Front caliper mounting bracket retaining bolts (arrowed)

7.8a Undo the two retaining screws . . .

7.8b . . . and remove the front brake disc

illustration). If the measure-ments obtained are at the specified maximum or beyond, the disc is excessively warped, and must be renewed; however, it is worth checking first that the hub bearing is in good condition (Chapter 1A or 1B and/or 10). Also try the effect of removing the disc and turning it through 180° to reposition it on the hub; if the run-out is still excessive, the disc must be renewed.

5 Check the disc for cracks, especially around the wheel bolt holes, and any other wear or damage, and renew if necessary.

Removal

6 Remove the brake pads as described in Section 4.

7 Undo the two bolts securing the caliper mounting bracket to the swivel hub **(see illustration)**. Withdraw the mounting bracket, complete with caliper, from the disc and swivel hub, and tie it to the front suspension coil spring, to avoid placing any strain on the fluid hose.

8 Use chalk or paint to mark the relationship of the disc to the hub, then remove the screws securing the brake disc to the hub, and remove the disc **(see illustrations)**. If it is tight, lightly tap its rear face with a hide or plastic mallet.

Refitting

9 Refitting is the reverse of the removal procedure, noting the following points:

a) *Ensure that the mating surfaces of the disc and hub are clean and flat.*

b) *Align (if applicable) the marks made on removal, and securely tighten the disc retaining screws.*

c) *If a new disc has been fitted, use a suitable solvent to wipe any preservative coating from the disc before refitting the caliper.*

d) *Apply suitable thread locking compound to the threads of the caliper mounting bracket retaining bolts and tighten the bolts to the specified torque.*

e) *Refit the brake pads as described in Section 4.*

f) *Refit the roadwheel, then lower the vehicle to the ground and tighten the roadwheel bolts to the specified torque. On completion, repeatedly depress the*

brake pedal until normal (non-assisted) pedal pressure returns.

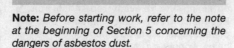

8 Rear brake drum – removal, inspection and refitting

Note: *Before starting work, refer to the note at the beginning of Section 5 concerning the dangers of asbestos dust.*

Removal

1 Chock the front wheels, then jack up the rear of the vehicle and support it on axle stands (see *Jacking and vehicle support*). Remove the appropriate rear roadwheel and release the handbrake.

2 Remove the drum retaining screw(s).

3 It should now be possible to withdraw the brake drum by hand. It may be difficult to remove the drum due to the brake shoes binding on the inner circumference of the drum. If the brake shoes are binding, first check that the handbrake is fully released, then proceed as follows.

4 Turn the drum until one of the wheel bolt holes is positioned over the handbrake operating lever on the trailing shoe. This will be at approximately the 5 o'clock position on the left-hand rear brake, and the 7 o'clock position on the right-hand rear brake. Insert a screwdriver through the wheel bolt hole and move the handbrake operating lever towards the rear of the vehicle allowing the brake shoes to retract fully. It will be necessary to lift the lever slightly with the screwdriver so that the lever stop-peg can pass over the brake shoe web. The brake drum can now be withdrawn.

Inspection

Note: *If either drum requires renewal, BOTH should be renewed at the same time, to ensure even and consistent braking. New brake shoes should also be fitted.*

5 Working carefully, remove all traces of brake dust from the drum, but *avoid inhaling the dust, as it is injurious to health.*

6 Clean the outside of the drum, and check it for obvious signs of wear or damage, such as cracks around the roadwheel bolt holes; renew the drum if necessary.

7 Examine carefully the inside of the drum. Light scoring of the friction surface is normal, but if heavy scoring is found, the drum must be renewed. It is usual to find a lip on the drum's inboard edge which consists of a mixture of rust and brake dust; this should be scraped away, to leave a smooth surface which can be polished with fine (120- to 150-grade) emery paper. If, however, the lip is due to the friction surface being recessed by excessive wear, then the drum must be renewed.

8 If the drum is thought to be excessively worn, or oval, its internal diameter must be measured at several points using an internal micrometer. Take measurements in pairs, the second at right-angles to the first, and compare the two, to check for signs of ovality. Provided that it does not enlarge the drum to beyond the specified maximum diameter, it may be possible to have the drum refinished by skimming or grinding; if this is not possible, the drums on both sides must be renewed. Note that if the drum is to be skimmed, BOTH drums must be refinished, to maintain a consistent internal diameter on both sides.

Refitting

9 If a new brake drum is to be installed, use a suitable solvent to remove any preservative coating that may have been applied to its interior. Note that it may also be necessary to shorten the adjuster strut length, by rotating the strut wheel, to allow the drum to pass over the brake shoes.

10 Ensure that the handbrake lever stop-peg is correctly repositioned against the edge of the brake shoe web, then locate the brake drum on the stub axle.

11 Refit and tighten the drum retaining screw(s).

12 Depress the footbrake several times to operate the self-adjusting mechanism.

13 Repeat the above procedure on the remaining rear brake assembly (where necessary), then check and, if necessary, adjust the handbrake cable as described in Section 13.

14 On completion, refit the roadwheel(s), then lower the vehicle to the ground and tighten the wheel bolts to the specified torque.

9 Rear brake disc – inspection, removal and refitting

Note: *Before starting work, refer to the warning at the beginning of Section 6 concerning the dangers of asbestos dust.*

Inspection

Note: *If either disc requires renewal, BOTH should be renewed at the same time, to ensure even and consistent braking. New brake pads should also be fitted.*

1 With the rear brake pads removed (Section 6), the inspection procedures are the same as for the front brake disc, and reference should be made to Section 7, paragraphs 2 to 5 inclusive.

Removal

2 If not already done, remove the rear brake pads as described in Section 6. Suitably support the caliper, or suspend it using string or wire tied to a convenient suspension component.
3 Undo the two caliper mounting bracket bolts, and withdraw the bracket.
4 Unscrew the disc retaining screws.
5 Mark the position of the disc in relation to the hub, then pull off the disc. Tap it with a soft-faced mallet if necessary to free it.

Refitting

6 Ensure that the hub and disc mating faces are spotlessly clean. Clean any rust-proofing compound off a new disc with de-greaser and a rag.
7 Locate the disc on the hub with the orientation marks aligned, and refit the retaining screws.
8 Refit the brake caliper mounting bracket, apply a little thread-locking compound and tighten the bolts to the specified torque.
9 Refit the brake pads as described in Section 6.
10 Check and if necessary, adjust the handbrake as described in Section 16.

10 Front brake caliper – removal, overhaul and refitting

Note 1: *Before starting work, refer to the note at the beginning of Section 2 concerning the dangers of hydraulic fluid, and to the warning at the beginning of Section 4 concerning the dangers of asbestos dust.*
Note 2: *New guide pin bolts must be used on refitting.*

Removal

1 Apply the handbrake, then jack up the front of the vehicle and support it on axle stands (see *Jacking and vehicle support*). Remove the appropriate roadwheel.
2 Minimise fluid loss by first removing the master cylinder reservoir filler cap, and then tightening it down onto a piece of polythene, to obtain an airtight seal. Alternatively, use a brake hose clamp, a G-clamp or a similar tool to clamp the flexible hose.
3 Clean the area around the hydraulic fluid hose union on the caliper, then loosen the fluid hose union nut by half a turn.
4 With reference to Section 4, slacken and remove the upper and lower caliper guide pin bolts. If working on the Lucas caliper, use a slim open-ended spanner to prevent the guide pin itself from rotating. Discard the guide pin bolts – new bolts must be used on refitting. With the guide pin bolts removed, lift the caliper away from the brake disc, then unscrew the caliper from the end of the brake hose. Note that the brake pads need not be disturbed, and can be left in position in the caliper mounting bracket.

Overhaul

5 The caliper can be overhauled after obtaining the relevant repair kit from a Peugeot/Citroën dealer. Ensure that the correct repair kit is obtained for the caliper being worked on. Note the locations of all components to ensure correct refitting, and lubricate the new seals using clean brake fluid. Follow the assembly instructions supplied with the repair kit.

Refitting

6 Screw the caliper body fully onto the flexible hydraulic fluid hose union, then check that the brake pads are still correctly fitted in the caliper mounting bracket.
7 Position the caliper over the brake pads. If the threads of the new guide pin bolts are not precoated with locking compound, apply a suitable locking compound to them. Fit the new lower guide pin bolt, then press the caliper into position and fit the new upper guide pin bolt. If working on the Bosch caliper, position the flat on the guide pins horizontally to allow the machined face on the caliper mounting lugs to correctly engage Tighten both the guide pin bolts to the specified torque, while retaining the guide pin with an open-ended spanner (where necessary).
8 Tighten the hydraulic fluid hose union securely, then remove the brake hose clamp or polythene, where fitted, and bleed the hydraulic system as described in Section 2. Providing the precautions described were taken to minimise brake fluid loss, it should only be necessary to bleed the relevant front brake.
9 Depress the brake pedal repeatedly, until the pads are pressed into firm contact with the brake disc, and normal (non-assisted) pedal pressure is restored.
10 Refit the roadwheel, then lower the vehicle to the ground and tighten the roadwheel bolts to the specified torque.

11 Rear wheel cylinder – removal and refitting

Note: *Before starting work, refer to the note at the beginning of Section 2 concerning the dangers of hydraulic fluid, and to the warning at the beginning of Section 5 concerning the dangers of asbestos dust.*

Removal

1 Remove the rear brake shoes as described in Section 5.
2 Minimise fluid loss by first removing the master cylinder reservoir filler cap, and then tightening it down onto a piece of polythene, to obtain an airtight seal. Alternatively, use a brake hose clamp, a G-clamp or a similar tool to clamp the flexible hose at the nearest convenient point to the wheel cylinder **(see illustration)**.
3 Wipe away all traces of dirt around the brake pipe union at the rear of the wheel cylinder, and unscrew the union nut **(see illustration)**. Carefully ease the pipe out of the wheel cylinder, and plug or tape over its end to prevent dirt entry. Wipe off any spilt fluid immediately.
4 Unscrew the two wheel cylinder retaining bolts from the rear of the backplate, and remove the cylinder, taking great care not to allow surplus hydraulic fluid to contaminate the brake shoe linings.
5 Note that it is not possible to overhaul the cylinder, since no components are available separately. If faulty, the complete wheel cylinder assembly must be renewed.

Refitting

6 The arrangement of the brake shoe components is such that the wheel cylinder

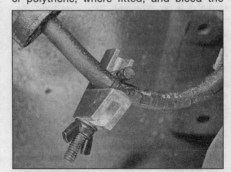

11.2 To minimise fluid loss, fit a brake hose clamp to the flexible hose

11.3 Using a brake pipe spanner to unscrew the wheel cylinder union nut

must be released from the backplate to allow the shoes to be refitted. Follow the brake shoe refitting procedures contained in Section 5 then, with the wheel cylinder in position, proceed as follows.

7 Engage the brake pipe, and screw in the union nut two or three turns to ensure that the thread has started.

8 Insert the two wheel cylinder retaining bolts, and tighten them securely. Now fully tighten the brake pipe union nut.

9 Remove the clamp from the flexible brake hose, or the polythene from the master cylinder reservoir (as applicable).

10 Bleed the brake hydraulic system as described in Section 2. Providing suitable precautions were taken to minimise loss of fluid, it should only be necessary to bleed the relevant rear brake.

12 Rear brake caliper – removal, overhaul and refitting

Note 1: *Before starting work, refer to the warning at the beginning of Section 2 concerning the dangers of hydraulic fluid, and to the warning at the beginning of Section 6 concerning the dangers of asbestos dust.*
Note 2: *New guide pin bolts must be used on refitting.*

Removal

1 To minimise fluid loss, unscrew the master cylinder reservoir filler cap, and place a piece of polythene over the filler neck. Secure the polythene with an elastic band, ensuring that an airtight seal is obtained. Preferably, use a brake hose clamp, a G-clamp, or a similar tool with protected jaws, to clamp the rear flexible hydraulic hose.

2 Clean around the hydraulic union on the caliper, then slacken the pipe union half a turn.

3 Remove the rear brake pads as described in Section 6, then disconnect the handbrake cable as described in Section 18.

4 Undo the caliper from the flexible pipe union. Be prepared for fluid spillage, and plug or cap the open unions.

Overhaul

5 It would appear that overhaul kits for the rear calipers are not available. However, it may be that reconditioned/exchange calipers are available from Citroën/Peugeot dealers/ parts specialists. If faulty, the caliper must be replaced.

Refitting

6 Refit the brake pipe to the caliper, and tighten the union securely.

7 Refit the brake pads as described in Section 6, then refit the handbrake cable as described in Section 18.

8 Remove the brake hose clamp or polythene, where fitted, and bleed the hydraulic system as described in Section 2.

9 Apply the footbrake two or three times to settle the pads, then refit the roadwheel and lower the car. Tighten the wheel bolts to the specified torque. If necessary, adjust the handbrake cable as described in Section 16.

13 Master cylinder – removal, overhaul and refitting

Note: *Before starting, refer to the warning in Section 2 on the dangers of hydraulic fluid.*

Removal

1 On left-hand drive models, remove the battery and battery tray as described in Chapter 5A. Depending on model and clearance available, remove any remaining air cleaner and air intake duct components as described in the relevant Part of Chapter 4, to gain access to the master cylinder.

2 Unscrew the master cylinder fluid reservoir filler cap and empty the brake fluid from the reservoir by syphoning it out using a syringe or pipette. **Note:** *Do not syphon the fluid by mouth, as it is poisonous.*

3 Disconnect the wiring connector at the fluid level sensor on the side of the reservoir, and release the wiring from its cable clip.

4 Suitably cover the area below the master cylinder with absorbent rags and be prepared for escaping hydraulic fluid.

5 Wipe clean the area around the brake hydraulic pipe unions on the side of the master cylinder. Make a note of the correct fitted positions of the unions, then unscrew the union nuts/bolts and carefully withdraw the pipes. Where banjo unions are fitted, recover the copper washers located on each side of the union and obtain new washers for refitting. Plug or tape over the pipe ends and master cylinder orifices, to minimise fluid loss, and to prevent the entry of dirt into the system.

6 Slacken and remove the two nuts securing the master cylinder to the vacuum servo unit, then withdraw the unit from the servo. If the sealing ring fitted to the rear of the master cylinder shows signs of damage or deterioration, it must be renewed.

7 If required, the fluid reservoir can be removed from the master cylinder. Various methods are used to secure the reservoir in position, depending on master cylinder type. These will be either a nut, bolt and retaining clamp located under the master cylinder, a roll-pin, or a retaining pin and clip. Remove the relevant attachment, then pull the reservoir upwards and off its two seals in the master cylinder.

Overhaul

8 Check that spare parts are available before deciding to overhaul the master cylinder. Although Peugeot/Citroën dealers supply internal parts for some (but not all) of the master cylinders fitted, it may be possible to obtain a repair kit from specialist motor factors.

Ensure that the correct repair kit is obtained for the master cylinder being worked on. Note the locations of all components to ensure correct refitting, and lubricate the new seals using clean brake fluid. Follow the assembly instructions supplied with the repair kit.

Refitting

9 If removed, carefully ease the fluid reservoir back into position, ensuring that it is fully seated on the rubber seals. Refit the relevant retaining components to secure the reservoir to the master cylinder.

10 Fit the master cylinder to the servo unit, ensuring that the servo unit pushrod enters the master cylinder bore centrally. Refit the master cylinder mounting nuts, and tighten them to the specified torque.

11 Wipe clean the brake pipe unions, refit them to the master cylinder ports and tighten them securely. Where banjo unions are used, ensure that a new copper washer is fitted on each side of the union.

12 Reconnect the fluid level sensor wiring connector and retain the wiring with the cable clip.

13 On left-hand drive models, refit the battery tray and battery, referring to Chapter 5A if necessary. Refit the air cleaner and air intake duct components removed for access, as described in the relevant Part of Chapter 4.

14 Refill the master cylinder reservoir with new fluid, and bleed the complete hydraulic system as described in Section 2.

14 Vacuum servo unit – testing, removal and refitting

Testing

1 To test the operation of the servo unit, depress the footbrake several times to exhaust the vacuum, then start the engine whilst keeping the pedal firmly depressed. As the engine starts, there should be a noticeable 'give' in the brake pedal as the vacuum builds-up. Allow the engine to run for at least two minutes, then switch it off. If the brake pedal is now depressed it should feel normal, but further applications should result in the pedal feeling firmer, with the pedal stroke decreasing with each application.

2 If the servo does not operate as described, first inspect the servo unit check valve as described in Section 12. On diesel engine models, also check the operation of the vacuum pump as described in Section 22.

3 If the servo unit still fails to operate satisfactorily, the fault lies within the unit itself. Repairs to the unit are not possible – if faulty, the servo unit must be renewed.

Removal

4 Disconnect the battery negative terminal (refer to *Disconnecting the battery* in the Reference Chapter).

5 On left-hand drive models, remove the battery and battery tray as described in Chapter 5A. Depending on model and clearance available, remove any remaining air cleaner and air intake duct components as described in the relevant Part of Chapter 4, to gain access to the servo unit.

6 Remove the master cylinder as described in Section 10.

7 Slacken the retaining clip, or depress the tabs on the side of the quick-release fitting, and disconnect the vacuum pipe from the servo unit check valve.

8 Working inside the car, remove the fusebox cover and the undercover from beneath the facia on the driver's side.

9 Prise off the spring clip, then withdraw the clevis pin securing the servo unit pushrod to the brake pedal. Note that a new spring clip will be required for refitting.

10 Slacken and remove the four nuts securing the servo unit to the bulkhead.

11 Manoeuvre the servo unit out of position, along with its gasket which is fitted between the servo and housing. Renew the gasket if it shows signs of damage.

Refitting

12 Locate the servo unit in position from within the engine compartment.

13 From inside the car, refit the servo retaining nuts and tighten them to the specified torque.

14 Refit the servo unit pushrod-to-brake pedal clevis pin, and secure it in position with a new spring clip.

15 Refit the fusebox cover and the undercover from beneath the facia.

16 Reconnect the vacuum pipe to the servo unit check valve.

17 Refit the master cylinder as described in Section 10, then bleed the complete hydraulic system as described in Section 2.

18 On left-hand drive models, refit the battery tray and battery, referring to Chapter 5A if necessary. Refit the air cleaner and air intake duct components removed for access, as described in the relevant Part of Chapter 4.

19 On completion, reconnect the battery, start the engine, and check for air leaks at the servo unit check valve.

15 Vacuum servo unit check valve – removal, testing and refitting

Removal

1 On left-hand drive models, remove the battery and battery tray as described in Chapter 5A. Depending on model and clearance available, remove any remaining air cleaner and air intake duct components as described in the relevant Part of Chapter 4, to gain access to the servo unit.

2 Slacken the retaining clip, or depress the tabs on the side of the quick-release fitting,

and disconnect the vacuum pipe from the check valve.

3 Withdraw the valve from its rubber sealing grommet in the servo unit, using a pulling and twisting motion. Remove the grommet from the servo.

Testing

4 Examine the check valve for signs of damage, and renew if necessary. The valve may be tested by blowing through it in both directions. Air should flow through the valve in one direction only – when blown through from the servo unit end of the valve. Renew the valve if this is not the case.

5 Examine the rubber sealing grommet and flexible vacuum hose for signs of damage or deterioration, and renew as necessary.

Refitting

6 Fit the sealing grommet into the servo unit.

7 Ease the check valve into position, taking care not to displace or damage the grommet.

8 Reconnect the vacuum pipe to the check valve.

9 On left-hand drive models, refit the battery tray and battery, referring to Chapter 5A if necessary. Refit the air cleaner and air intake duct components removed for access, as described in the relevant Part of Chapter 4.

10 On completion, reconnect the battery, start the engine and check for air leaks at the check valve.

16 Handbrake – adjustment

1 To check the handbrake adjustment, first apply the footbrake firmly several times to establish correct shoe-to-drum clearance, then apply and release the handbrake several times to ensure that the self-adjust mechanism is fully adjusted. Applying normal moderate pressure, pull the handbrake lever to the fully-applied position, counting the number of clicks emitted from the handbrake ratchet mechanism. If adjustment is correct, there should be 5 clicks before the handbrake is fully applied. If this is not the case, adjust as follows.

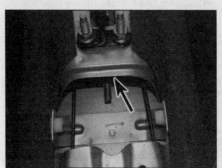

16.5 Handbrake adjusting nut location (arrowed)

2 Remove the rear section of the centre console as described in Chapter 11 for access to the handbrake adjuster nut.

3 Chock the front wheels then jack up the rear of the vehicle and support it securely on axle stands (see *Jacking and vehicle support*).

4 Apply and release the handbrake four times.

5 With the handbrake set on the fifth notch of the ratchet mechanism, check that both rear wheels are locked. If not, tighten the handbrake adjusting nut until both rear wheels are locked **(see illustration)**. Once this is so, fully release the handbrake lever, and check that the rear wheels rotate freely. Check the adjustment by applying the handbrake fully, counting the clicks from the handbrake ratchet and, if necessary, re-adjust.

6 When the adjustment is correct, refit the centre console, then lower the vehicle to the ground.

17 Handbrake lever – removal and refitting

Removal

1 Remove the rear section of the centre console as described in Chapter 11 for access to the handbrake adjuster nut.

2 Chock the front wheels then jack up the rear of the vehicle and support it securely on axle stands (see *Jacking and vehicle support*).

3 Ensure that the handbrake is released, then unscrew the handbrake adjuster nut to allow the adjuster rod to be withdrawn from the equaliser plate **(see illustration 13.5)**.

4 Disconnect the wiring connector from the handbrake warning light switch, and release the cable from its retaining clip.

5 Undo and remove the three retaining nuts and lift the lever from its mounting studs **(see illustration)**. Withdraw the adjuster rod from the equaliser plate and remove the lever assembly from the car.

Refitting

6 Refitting is a reversal of removal. Prior to refitting the centre console, adjust the handbrake as described in Section 13.

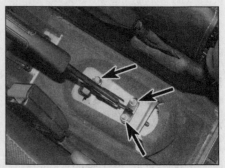

17.5 Handbrake lever retaining nuts (arrowed)

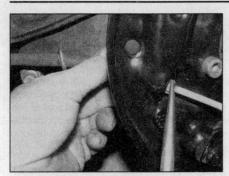

18.7 Release the handbrake outer cable from the brake backplate

18 Handbrake cables – removal and refitting

Removal

1 The handbrake cable consists of two sections, a right- and a left-hand section, which are linked to the lever by an equaliser plate. Each section can be removed individually.

2 Remove the rear section of the centre console as described in Chapter 11 for access to the handbrake adjuster nut.

3 Chock the front wheels then jack up the rear of the vehicle and support it securely on axle stands (see *Jacking and vehicle support*).

4 Ensure that the handbrake is released, then unscrew the handbrake adjuster nut **(see illustration 13.5)**. Slide the equaliser plate off the adjuster rod and slip the relevant handbrake inner cable end out of the equaliser plate.

5 Where necessary, slacken and remove the retaining nuts, then release the exhaust system heat shield(s) from the vehicle underbody, to gain access to the front of the relevant handbrake cable. Free the front end of the outer cable from the body, and withdraw the cable from its support guide.

6 Working back along the length of the cable, free it from the fuel tank plastic clip and the wire support hooks on the underbody and trailing arm.

Drum brake models

7 Remove the rear brake shoes from the relevant side as described in Section 5. Using pliers, carefully release the outer cable from the brake backplate, and remove it from underneath the vehicle **(see illustration)**.

Disc brake models

8 Use a pair of pliers to disengage the inner cable end fitting from the lever on the caliper, then squeeze together the sides of the clips and pull the outer cable from the support bracket.

Refitting

9 Refitting is a reversal of removal. Prior to refitting the centre console, adjust the handbrake as described in Section 13.

19 Rear brake pressure-regulating valve – removal and refitting

Note 1: *Before starting work, refer to the warning at the beginning of Section 2 concerning the dangers of hydraulic fluid.*
Note 2: *The rear brake pressure-regulating valve is not fitted to later models with ABS.*

Removal

1 Firmly chock the front wheels, then jack up the rear of the vehicle and support it on axle stands (see *Jacking and vehicle support*). Remove the right-hand rear roadwheel.

2 Minimise fluid loss by first removing the master cylinder reservoir filler cap, and tightening it down onto a piece of polythene, to obtain an airtight seal.

3 Disconnect the regulating valve operating spring from the bracket on the rear suspension.

4 Wipe clean the area around the brake pipe unions on the valve, and place absorbent rags beneath the pipe unions to catch any surplus fluid.

5 Unscrew the union nuts and carefully withdraw the brake pipes from the pressure-regulating valve. Plug or tape over the pipe ends and valve orifices, to minimise the loss of brake fluid, and to prevent the entry of dirt into the system.

6 Undo the bolt securing the valve to the mounting bracket and remove the assembly from under the car.

Refitting

7 Refitting is a reverse of the removal procedure, ensuring that the brake pipe union nuts are securely tightened. On completion, bleed the complete braking system as described in Section 2. If a new valve has been fitted, or if the adjusting nuts on the operating rod have been disturbed, the vehicle should be taken to a Peugeot/Citroën dealer for adjustment of the valve pressure settings.

20 Stop-light switch – removal, refitting and adjustment

Removal

1 The stop-light switch is located on the brake pedal bracket under the facia.

2 Remove the fusebox cover and the undercover from beneath the facia on the driver's side.

3 Disconnect the wiring connector, then loosen the locking ring and unscrew the switch from the pedal bracket.

Refitting and adjustment

4 Screw the switch back into position in the mounting bracket, until the gap between the end of the main body of the switch and the lug on the brake pedal is 2.0 to 3.0 mm.

5 Once the stop-light switch is correctly positioned, reconnect the wiring connector, and check the operation of the stop-lights. The stop-lights should illuminate after the brake pedal has travelled approximately 5.0 mm.

6 When the adjustment is correct, secure the switch with the locking ring and refit the fusebox cover and the undercover from beneath the facia.

21 Handbrake 'on' warning light switch – removal and refitting

Removal

1 Remove the rear section of the centre console as described in Chapter 11 for access to the handbrake lever assembly.

2 Disconnect the wiring connector and remove the switch from the frame of the handbrake lever.

Refitting

3 Refitting is a reverse of the removal procedure.

22 Anti-lock braking system (ABS) – general information

ABS is fitted as standard or optional equipment, according to model and year of manufacture. The system comprises a hydraulic modulator unit and the four wheel speed sensors. The modulator unit contains the electronic control unit (ECU), the hydraulic solenoid valves and the electrically-driven return pump. The purpose of the system is to prevent the wheel(s) locking during heavy braking. This is achieved by automatic release of the brake on the relevant wheel, followed by re-application of the brake.

The solenoid valves are controlled by the ECU, which itself receives signals from the four wheel speed sensors which monitor the speed of rotation of each wheel. By comparing these signals, the ECU can determine the speed at which the vehicle is travelling. It can then use this speed to determine when a wheel is decelerating at an abnormal rate, compared to the speed of the vehicle, and therefore predicts when a wheel is about to lock. During normal operation, the system functions in the same way as a non-ABS braking system.

If the ECU senses that a wheel is about to lock, it closes the relevant outlet solenoid valves in the hydraulic unit, which then isolates the relevant brake(s) on the wheel(s) which is/are about to lock from the master cylinder, effectively sealing-in the hydraulic pressure.

If the speed of rotation of the wheel continues to decrease at an abnormal rate, the ECU opens the inlet solenoid valves on the relevant brake(s), and operates the electrically-driven return pump which pumps the hydraulic fluid back into the master cylinder, releasing the brake. Once the speed of rotation of the wheel returns to an acceptable rate, the pump stops; the solenoid valves switch again, allowing the hydraulic master cylinder pressure to return to the caliper or wheel cylinder, which then re-applies the brake. This cycle can be carried out many times a second.

The action of the solenoid valves and return pump creates pulses in the hydraulic circuit. When the ABS system is functioning, these pulses can be felt through the brake pedal.

The operation of the ABS system is entirely dependent on electrical signals. To prevent the system responding to any inaccurate signals, a built-in safety circuit monitors all signals received by the ECU. If an inaccurate signal or low battery voltage is detected, the ABS system is automatically shut-down, and the warning light on the instrument panel is illuminated, to inform the driver that the ABS system is not operational. Normal braking should still be available, however.

Later models, from approximately 2001 onward are also equipped with additional safety features built around the ABS system. These systems are EBFD (Electronic Brake Force Distribution), which automatically apportions braking effort between the front and rear wheels, and (on some models) ESP (Electronic Stability Program) which monitors the vehicles cornering forces and steering wheel angle, then applies the braking force to the appropriate roadwheel to enhance the stability of the vehicle.

If a fault does develop in the any of these systems, the vehicle must be taken to a Peugeot/Citroën dealer or suitably-equipped specialist for fault diagnosis and repair.

23 Anti-lock braking system (ABS) components – removal and refitting

Modulator assembly

Note: *Before starting, refer to the note in Section 2 on the dangers of hydraulic fluid.*

Removal

1 Remove the battery and battery tray as described in Chapter 5A. Depending on model and clearance available, remove any remaining air cleaner and air intake duct components as described in the relevant Part of Chapter 4, to gain access to the modulator assembly.
2 Release the locking clip and disconnect the ECU wiring harness connector.
3 Minimise hydraulic fluid loss by first removing the master cylinder reservoir filler cap, then tightening it down onto a piece of polythene, to obtain an airtight seal.
4 Wipe clean the area around the brake pipe unions on the side of the modulator, and place absorbent rags beneath the pipe unions to catch any surplus fluid. Make a note of the correct fitted positions of the unions, then unscrew the union nuts and carefully withdraw the pipes. Plug or tape over the pipe ends and modulator orifices to minimise the loss of fluid, and to prevent the entry of dirt into the system.
5 Undo the retaining nuts, and lift the modulator from its location. When sufficient clearance exists, undo the nut and disconnect the earth lead (where fitted) from the end of the modulator return pump casing.

Refitting

6 If a new modulator assembly is being fitted, it will be supplied prefilled with hydraulic fluid, and sealed with blanking plugs. Leave the plugs in position until just before connecting the brake pipes.
7 Locate the modulator in position and refit the earth lead and its retaining nut. Engage the unit over the mounting studs and secure with the retaining nuts, tightened to the specified torque.
8 Reconnect the brake pipes to their correct locations as noted during removal and tighten the union nuts securely.
9 Reconnect the ECU wiring connector.
10 Refit the battery tray and battery, referring to Chapter 5A if necessary. Refit the air cleaner and air intake duct components removed for access, as described in the relevant Part of Chapter 4.
11 Remove the polythene from the

master cylinder reservoir and bleed the complete hydraulic system as described in Section 2.

Electronic control unit

12 The electronic control unit is removed with the modulator assembly as described previously. The ECU is an integral part of the modulator and the two components cannot be separated.

Front wheel speed sensor

Note: *Thread locking compound must be applied to the sensor securing stud on refitting.*

Removal

13 Disconnect the battery negative terminal (refer to *Disconnecting the battery* in the Reference Chapter).
14 Firmly apply the handbrake, then jack up the front of the car and support it securely on axle stands (see *Jacking and vehicle support*). Remove the relevant front roadwheel.
15 Unclip the wheel speed sensor wiring from the brackets on the suspension strut and inner wheelarch.
16 Trace the wiring back from the sensor, and separate the two halves of the wiring connector. Note the routing of the wiring to aid correct refitting.
17 Unscrew the retaining nut and lift off the wheel speed sensor protective cover **(see illustration)**.
18 Unscrew the securing stud, and withdraw the sensor from the swivel hub **(see illustrations)**.

Refitting

19 Refitting is a reversal of removal, noting the following points:
  a) Ensure that the mating faces of the sensor and the swivel hub are clean, and apply a smear of high melting-point brake grease to the sensor location in the swivel hub before refitting.
  b) Ensure that the end face of the sensor is clean.
  c) Coat the threads of the sensor securing stud with thread-locking compound and tighten the stud to the specified torque.
  d) Route the wiring as noted before removal.

23.17 Unscrew the nut and lift off the wheel sensor protective cover

23.18a Unscrew the securing stud . . .

23.18b . . . and withdraw the front wheel sensor from the swivel hub

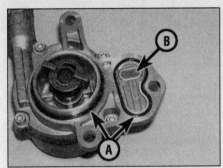

24.5 Vacuum pump O-ring locations (A) and gauze filter (B) – 2.0 litre

Rear wheel speed sensor

Note: *Thread-locking compound must be applied to the sensor securing stud on refitting.*

Removal

20 Chock the front wheels, then jack up the rear of the vehicle and support it on axle stands (see *Jacking and vehicle support*). Remove the appropriate roadwheel.
21 Trace the wiring back from the sensor to its wiring connector, then free the connector from its retaining clip, and disconnect the wiring from the main wiring loom.
22 Work back along the sensor wiring, and free it from the retaining clips. Note the routing of the wiring to aid correct refitting.
23 Slacken and remove the bolt securing the sensor unit to the trailing arm, and remove the sensor and lead assembly.

Refitting

24 Refitting is a reversal of removal, bearing in mind the following points:
 a) Ensure that the mating faces of the sensor and the trailing arm are clean, and apply a smear of high melting-point brake grease to the sensor location in the trailing arm before refitting.
 b) Ensure that the end face of the sensor is clean.
 c) Coat the threads of the sensor securing bolt with thread-locking compound and tighten the stud to the specified torque.
 d) Route the wiring as noted before removal.

24 Vacuum pump (diesel engine models) – removal and refitting

Note: *New O-rings must be used on refitting.*

Removal

1 Disconnect the battery negative terminal (refer to *Disconnecting the battery* in the Reference Chapter).
2 Remove the air cleaner assembly and air intake ducts as described in Chapter 4B or 4C.
3 Release the retaining clip and disconnect the vacuum hose from the pump.
4 Slacken and remove the three bolts/nuts and washers securing the pump to the left-hand end of the cylinder head, then remove the pump, along with its two O-rings. Discard the O-rings – new ones must be used on refitting. On 2.0 litre models, check the condition of the gauze filter at the rear of the pump and renew if necessary.

Refitting

5 Fit new O-rings to the pump recesses, then align the drive dog with the slot in the end of the camshaft, and refit the pump to the cylinder head, ensuring that the O-rings remain correctly seated **(see illustration)**.
6 Refit the pump mounting bolts/nuts and washers, and tighten them to the specified torque.
7 Reconnect the vacuum hose to the pump, and tighten its securing clip.
8 Refit the air cleaner assembly and air intake ducts as described in Chapter 4B or 4C, then reconnect the battery

25 Vacuum pump (diesel engine models) – testing and overhaul

Testing

1 The operation of the braking system vacuum pump can be checked using a vacuum gauge.
2 Disconnect the vacuum pipe from the pump, and connect the gauge to the pump union using a suitable length of hose.
3 Start the engine and allow it to idle, then measure the vacuum created by the pump. As a guide, after one minute, a minimum of approximately 500 mm Hg should be recorded. If the vacuum registered is significantly less than this, it is likely that the pump is faulty. However, seek the advice of a Peugeot/Citroën dealer before condemning the pump.

Overhaul

4 Overhaul of the vacuum pump is not possible, since no components are available separately for it. If faulty, the complete pump assembly must be renewed.

Chapter 10
Suspension and steering

Contents

Degrees of difficulty

| **Easy,** suitable for novice with little experience | | **Fairly easy,** suitable for beginner with some experience | | **Fairly difficult,** suitable for competent DIY mechanic | | **Difficult,** suitable for experienced DIY mechanic | | **Very difficult,** suitable for expert DIY or professional | |

Specifications

Front wheel alignment

Front wheel toe setting:
  Up to September 2002:
    With manual steering . . . .   1.0 to 3.0 mm toe-out
    With power-assisted steering . . . .   1.0 to 3.0 mm toe-in
  September 2002 onward . . . .   1.0 ± 1.0 mm toe-in

Roadwheels

Type . . . .   Pressed-steel or aluminium alloy (depending on model)

Torque wrench settings

	Nm	lbf ft
Front suspension		
Anti-roll bar:		
Mounting clamp bolts	65	48
Connecting link securing nuts	40	30
Lower arm balljoint clamp bolt nut	40	30
Lower arm balljoint retaining nuts	50	37
Lower arm front pivot bolt	80	59
Lower arm rear pivot bush mounting bolts:		
8 mm bolt	35	26
10 mm bolt	65	48
Strut upper mounting bolts	25	18
Strut piston rod retaining nut	45	33
Subframe mounting bolts	85	63
Swivel hub-to-strut bolt	45	33
Rear suspension		
Rear axle mountings:		
Front mounting-to-body bolts	40	30
Rear mounting nuts	55	41
Rear hub nut:		
Nut with separate thrustwasher	275	203
Nut with integral thrustwasher	250	185
Shock absorber mounting nuts	110	81
Steering		
Power steering pump mounting bolts	22	16
Steering column mounting bolts	23	17
Steering column shaft-to-intermediate shaft universal joint pinch-bolt	23	17
Steering gear mounting bolts	70	52
Steering intermediate shaft-to-steering gear pinion universal joint pinch-bolt nut	23	17
Steering wheel bolt:		
Up to September 2002	33	24
September 2002 onward	20	15
Track rod balljoint-to-swivel hub nut	35	26
Roadwheels		
Wheel bolts	90	66

1 General information

The independent front suspension is of the MacPherson strut type, incorporating coil springs and integral telescopic shock absorbers. The MacPherson struts are located by transverse lower suspension arms, which utilise rubber inner mounting bushes, and incorporate a balljoint at the outer ends. The front swivel hubs, which carry the wheel bearings, brake calipers and the hub/disc assemblies, are clamped to the MacPherson struts, and connected to the lower arms via the balljoints. A front anti-roll bar is fitted to all models. The anti-roll bar is rubber-mounted onto the subframe, and is attached to the front suspension struts by a connecting link on each side.

The rear suspension is of the semi-independent trailing arm type, which consists of two trailing arms, linked by a tubular crossmember. A torsion bar is fitted transversely between each trailing arm and the opposite suspension side member. An anti-roll bar is fitted between the trailing arms. The complete rear axle assembly is mounted onto the vehicle underbody by four rubber mountings.

The steering column has a universal joint fitted in the centre of its length, which is connected to an intermediate shaft having a second universal joint at its lower end. The lower universal joint is clamped to the steering gear pinion by means of a pinch-bolt.

The steering gear is mounted onto the front subframe, and is connected by two track rods, with balljoints at their outer ends, to the steering arms projecting rearwards from the swivel hubs. The track rods and balljoints are threaded, to facilitate toe setting adjustment.

Power-assisted steering was optionally available on early models and is fitted as standard on all models from September 2002 onwards. Hydraulic power for the steering system is provided by a pump, which is driven off the crankshaft pulley by the auxiliary drivebelt. On later models, the hydraulic fluid from the pump is passed through a cooler pipe located on the front valance, below the radiator.

2 Front swivel hub assembly – removal and refitting

Note: *All nuts disturbed on removal must be renewed as a matter of course. These nuts have threads which are precoated with locking compound (this is only effective once), and include the track rod balljoint nut, lower suspension arm balljoint clamp bolt nut, and the swivel hub clamp bolt nut. The driveshaft retaining nut must also be renewed, and suitable thread-locking compound will also be required for the brake caliper mounting bracket bolts.*

Removal

Caution: Do not allow the vehicle to rest on its wheels with one or both driveshafts disconnected from the swivel hubs, as damage to the wheel bearing(s) may result. If moving the vehicle is unavoidable, temporarily insert the outer end of the driveshaft(s) in the hub(s) and tighten the hub nut(s).

2.2a Withdraw the R-clip . . .

2.2b . . . and remove the locking cap from
the driveshaft retaining nut

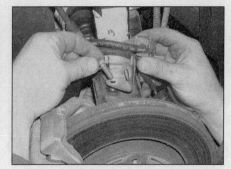

2.5 Remove the bolt securing the wiring
retaining bracket to the swivel hub

1 Chock the rear wheels, then firmly apply the handbrake. Jack up the front of the vehicle, and support it on axle stands (see *Jacking and vehicle support*). Remove the appropriate front roadwheel.

2 Withdraw the R-clip, and remove the locking cap from the driveshaft retaining nut **(see illustrations)**.

3 To prevent rotation of the wheel hub as the driveshaft retaining nut is slackened, make up a holding tool and bolt the tool to the wheel hub using two wheel bolts as described in Chapter 8, Section 2.

4 With the holding tool in place, slacken and remove the driveshaft retaining nut using a socket and long bar. Where necessary, support the socket on an axle stand to prevent it slipping off the nut. This nut is very tight; make sure that there is no risk of pulling the car off the axle stands as the nut is slackened.

5 Where applicable, disconnect the brake pad wear sensor wiring at the connector on the swivel hub. Slacken and remove the bolt securing the wiring retaining bracket to the top of the swivel hub **(see illustration)**.

6 On models with ABS, remove the wheel speed sensor from the swivel hub as described in Chapter 9.

7 If the hub bearings are to be disturbed, remove the brake disc as described in Chapter 9. If not, unscrew the two bolts securing the brake caliper mounting bracket assembly to the swivel hub, and slide the caliper assembly off the disc. Using a piece of wire or string, tie the caliper to the front suspension coil spring, to avoid placing any strain on the hydraulic brake hose.

8 On all models, slacken and remove the nut securing the steering gear track rod balljoint to the swivel hub, and release the balljoint tapered shank using a balljoint separator.

9 Slacken and remove the nut, then withdraw the lower suspension arm balljoint clamp bolt from the swivel hub **(see illustration)**. Discard the nut – a new one must be used on refitting.

10 Tap a small chisel into the split on the swivel hub to spread the hub slightly, and allow the balljoint shank to be withdrawn **(see illustration)**. Pull the lower suspension arm downwards to release the balljoint shank from the swivel hub. To do this it will be necessary

to use a long bar and block of wood which will engage under the front subframe. Attach the bar to the suspension arm, preferably with a chain, or alternatively with a stout strap or rope. Lever down on the bar to release the balljoint from the swivel hub **(see illustration)**.

11 Once the balljoint is free, remove the protector plate which is fitted to the balljoint shank **(see illustration)**.

12 Undo the nut and withdraw the swivel hub-to-suspension strut clamp bolt.

13 Tap a small chisel into the split on the swivel hub to spread the hub slightly. Free the swivel hub assembly from the end of the strut, then release it from the outer constant velocity joint splines, and remove it from the vehicle.

2.9 Undo the nut and withdraw the lower
suspension arm balljoint clamp bolt from
the swivel hub

2.10b . . . then pull the lower suspension
arm downwards using a bar and chain
or similar arrangement, pivoting on the
subframe

Refitting

14 Note that all nuts disturbed on removal must be renewed as a matter of course. These nuts have threads which are precoated with locking compound (this is only effective once), and include the track rod balljoint nut, lower suspension arm balljoint clamp bolt nut, and the swivel hub clamp bolt nut.

15 Ensure that the driveshaft outer constant velocity joint and hub splines are clean, then slide the hub fully onto the driveshaft splines.

16 Slide the hub assembly fully onto the suspension strut, aligning the split in the hub clamp with the lug on the base of the strut. Also ensure that the stop bosses on the strut are in contact with the top surface

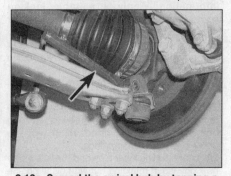

2.10a Spread the swivel hub by tapping a
small chisel (arrowed) into the split . . .

2.11 When the balljoint is released,
remove the protector plate from the
balljoint shank

2.16 Ensure the swivel hub clamp is aligned with the lug (arrowed) on the strut prior to inserting the clamp bolt

of the swivel hub. Insert the swivel hub-to-suspension strut clamp bolt, then fit a new nut to the clamp bolt, and tighten it to the specified torque **(see illustration)**.

17 Refit the protector plate to the lower arm balljoint then, using the method employed on removal, locate the balljoint shank in the swivel hub, ensuring that the lug on the protector plate is correctly located in the clamp split. Insert the balljoint clamp bolt, then fit the new retaining nut and tighten it to the specified torque.

18 Engage the track rod balljoint in the swivel hub, then fit a new retaining nut and tighten it to the specified torque.

19 Where necessary, refit the brake disc to the hub, referring to Chapter 9 for further information. Apply a suitable locking compound to the threads of the caliper mounting bracket bolts. Slide the caliper assembly into position over the disc, then fit the mounting bolts and tighten them to the specified torque (see Chapter 9).

20 Where applicable, refit the ABS wheel sensor as described in Chapter 9.

21 Refit the wiring retaining bracket to the top of the swivel hub, and tighten its retaining bolt securely. Where fitted, reconnect the brake pad wear sensor wiring.

22 Lubricate the inner face and threads of the new driveshaft retaining nut with clean engine oil, and refit it to the end of the driveshaft. Use the method employed on removal to prevent the hub from rotating, and tighten the driveshaft retaining nut to the specified torque

(see Chapter 8). Check that the hub rotates freely.

23 Engage the locking cap with the driveshaft nut so that one of its cut-outs is aligned with the driveshaft hole. Secure the cap with the R-clip.

24 Refit the roadwheel, then lower the vehicle to the ground and tighten the roadwheel bolts to the specified torque.

3 Front hub bearings – renewal

Note 1: *The bearing is a sealed, pre-adjusted and prelubricated, double-row roller type, and is intended to last the car's entire service life without maintenance or attention. Never overtighten the driveshaft nut beyond the specified torque wrench setting in an attempt to 'adjust' the bearing.*

Note 2: *A press will be required to dismantle and rebuild the assembly; if such a tool is not available, a large bench vice and spacers (such as large sockets) will serve as an adequate substitute. The bearing's inner races are an interference fit on the hub; if the inner race remains on the hub when it is pressed out of the hub carrier, a knife-edged bearing puller will be required to remove it. A new bearing retaining circlip must be used on refitting.*

1 Remove the swivel hub assembly as described in Section 2.

2 Support the swivel hub securely on blocks or in a vice. Using a tubular spacer which bears only on the inner end of the hub flange, press the hub flange out of the bearing. If the bearing's outboard inner race remains on the hub, remove it using a bearing puller (see note above).

3 Extract the bearing retaining circlip from the inner end of the swivel hub assembly **(see illustration)**.

4 Where necessary, refit the inner race back in position over the ball cage, and securely support the inner face of the swivel hub. Using a tubular spacer which bears only on the inner race, press the complete bearing assembly out of the swivel hub.

5 Thoroughly clean the hub and swivel hub, removing all traces of dirt and grease, and polish away any burrs or raised edges which might hinder reassembly. Check both for cracks or any other signs of wear or damage, and renew them if necessary. Renew the circlip, regardless of its apparent condition.

6 On reassembly, apply a light film of oil to the bearing outer race and hub flange shaft, to aid installation of the bearing.

7 Securely support the swivel hub, and locate the bearing in the hub. Press the bearing fully into position, ensuring that it enters the hub squarely, using a tubular spacer which bears only on the bearing outer race. Note that on September 2002 models onward with ABS, the bearing is equipped with a magnetic encoder on its inboard face. When fitting the bearing ensure this face is inboard adjacent to the ABS wheel speed sensor **(see illustration)**. Take care not to damage this encoder, or place it adjacent to a magnetic source. Ensure the encoder face is clean.

8 Once the bearing is correctly seated, secure the bearing in position with the new circlip, ensuring that it is correctly located in the groove in the swivel hub. **Note:** *On September 2002 models onward with ABS, align the gap between the ends of the circlip with the gap for the ABS wheel speed sensor.*

9 Securely support the outer face of the hub flange, and locate the swivel hub bearing inner race over the end of the hub flange. Press the bearing onto the hub, using a tubular spacer which bears only on the inner race of the hub bearing, until it seats against the hub shoulder. Check that the hub flange rotates freely, and wipe off any excess oil or grease.

10 Refit the swivel hub assembly as described in Section 2.

4 Front suspension strut – removal and refitting

Note: *All nuts disturbed on removal must be renewed as a matter of course. These nuts have threads which are precoated with locking compound (this is only effective once), and include the swivel hub clamp bolt nut, and the anti-roll bar connecting link nut. Suitable spring compressor tools will be required for this operation.*

Removal

1 Chock the rear wheels, apply the handbrake, then jack up the front of the vehicle and support it on axle stands (see *Jacking and vehicle support*). Remove the appropriate roadwheel.

2 If the left-hand suspension strut is to be removed on September 2002 models onward, remove the engine management ECU and its mounting bracket as described in the relevant part of Chapter 4, for access to the strut upper mounting.

3.3 Front hub bearing retaining circlip (arrowed)

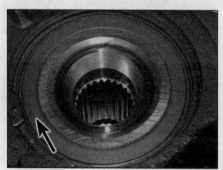

3.7 On later models, take care not to damage the seal in the bearing (arrowed) – it contains the encoder for the wheel speed sensor

4.5 Unscrew the nut securing the anti-roll bar connecting link to the strut

4.6 Unscrew the nut and remove the swivel hub-to-suspension strut clamp bolt

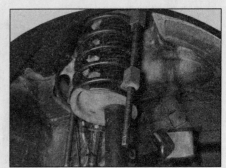

4.7 Coil spring compressors fitted to strut spring

3 Slacken and remove the bolt securing the wiring retaining bracket to the top of the swivel hub.

4 Unclip the brake flexible hydraulic hose and any wiring from the strut.

5 Unscrew the nut (and recover the washer) securing the anti-roll bar connecting link to the strut, and position the link clear of the strut. Counterhold the link with an Allen key to prevent rotation as the nut is undone **(see illustration)**. Discard the nut – a new one must be used on refitting.

6 Undo the nut and withdraw the swivel hub-to-suspension strut clamp bolt. Discard the nut – a new one must be used on refitting **(see illustration)**.

7 The coil spring must now be compressed to enable the strut to be removed. Working under the wheel arch, fit suitable spring compressors to the spring and compress the spring sufficiently to enable the lower end of the strut to be disconnected from the swivel hub **(see illustration)**. Ensure that the compressors used are of a type that incorporate a method for positively locking them to the spring (usually by a small clamp bolt). Any other type may slip off or slide round the spring as they are tightened.

8 Tap a small chisel into the split on the swivel hub to spread the hub slightly, and allow the end of the strut to be withdrawn **(see illustration)**.

9 Slacken and remove the three suspension strut upper mounting bolts, then withdraw the strut from under the wheel arch **(see illustration)**.

Refitting

10 With the coil spring compressors in place, as during removal, manoeuvre the strut assembly into position. Ensure that the top mounting plate locating pin is correctly located in the corresponding hole in the body and that the mounting plate is correctly orientated. On models with manual steering, the orientation lug on the mounting rubber must be toward the rear of the vehicle. On models with power steering, the orientation lug must be toward the front of the vehicle **(see illustration 4.9)**.

11 Engage the lower end of the strut with the swivel hub, aligning the split in the hub with the lug on the base of the strut. Also ensure that the stop bosses on the strut are in contact with the top surface of the swivel hub.

12 Insert the strut upper mounting bolts, and tighten them to the specified torque.

13 Insert the swivel hub-to-suspension strut clamp bolt, fit a new nut to the clamp bolt, and tighten it to the specified torque.

14 Carefully slacken and then remove the spring compressors.

15 Where applicable, refit the engine management ECU and mounting bracket as described in the relevant Part of Chapter 4.

16 Reconnect the anti-roll bar connecting link to the strut. Fit a new nut to the connecting link, and tighten it to the specified torque.

17 Refit the wiring retaining bracket to the top of the swivel hub, and clip the flexible hose and wiring to their locations on the strut.

18 Refit the roadwheel, then lower the vehicle to the ground and tighten the roadwheel bolts to the specified torque.

5 Front suspension strut – overhaul

> **Warning:** *Before attempting to dismantle the suspension strut, a suitable tool to hold the coil spring in compression must be obtained. Adjustable coil spring compressors which can be positively secured to the spring coils are readily available, and are recommended for this operation. Any attempt to dismantle the strut without such a tool is likely to result in damage or personal injury.*

1 With the strut removed from the car as described in Section 4, clean away all external dirt then mount the unit upright in a vice.

2 If not already in place, fit the spring compressors to the coils of the spring. Ensure that the compressors used are of a type that incorporate a method for positively locking them to the spring (usually by a small clamp bolt). Any other type may slip off or slide round the spring as they are tightened. Tighten the compressors until the load is taken off the spring seats.

3 Remove the protective cap then unscrew the piston rod nut, counterholding the piston rod with a suitable Allen key **(see illustration)**. Note that a new nut will be required for reassembly.

4.8 Tap a small chisel (arrowed) into the split in the swivel hub to spread the hub

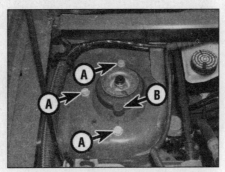

4.9 Suspension strut upper mounting bolts (A) and orientation lug (B)

5.3 Unscrew the strut piston rod nut while counterholding the piston rod with a suitable Allen key

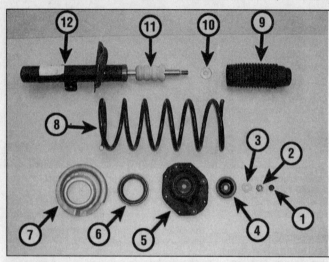

1 Protective cap
2 Piston rod nut
3 Washer
4 Collar
5 Mounting plate
6 Bearing
7 Upper spring seat
8 Coil spring
9 Piston dust cover
10 Flat washer
11 Damper stop
12 Strut body

5.4 Front suspension strut components

4 Remove the nut and washer, then lift off the collar, mounting plate, bearing, upper spring seat and flat washer. Remove the coil spring, then slide off the piston dust cover and rubber damper stop **(see illustration)**. The spring may remain in the compressed state ready for refitting to the strut. If the spring is to be renewed, release the compressors very gently and evenly until they can be removed and fitted to the new spring.

5 With the strut assembly now completely dismantled, examine all the components for wear, damage or deformation, and check the bearing for smoothness of operation. Renew any components as necessary.

6 Examine the strut body for signs of fluid leakage or damage, and the piston for signs of pitting or scoring. Test the operation of the strut, while holding it in an upright position, by moving the piston through a full stroke and then through short strokes of 50 to 100 mm. In both cases, the resistance felt should be smooth and continuous. If the resistance is jerky, or uneven, or if there is any visible sign of wear or damage, renewal is necessary.

7 If any doubt exists about the condition of the coil spring, carefully remove the spring compressors, and check the spring for distortion and signs of cracking. Renew the spring if it is damaged or distorted.

8 To reassemble the strut, follow the accompanying photos. Be sure to stay in order, and carefully read the captions **(see illustrations)**.

9 Refit the strut to the car as described in Section 4 on completion of reassembly.

5.8a Pull the piston rod out as far as it will go and fit the damper stop

5.8b Fit the piston dust cover . . .

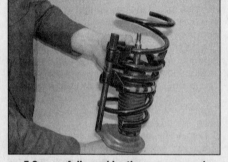

5.8c . . . followed by the compressed spring . . .

5.8d . . . ensuring that the end of the lower coil is located correctly in the lower seat

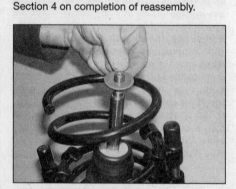

5.8e Place the flat washer in position . . .

5.8f . . . followed by the upper spring seat . . .

5.8g . . . bearing . . .

5.8h . . . and mounting plate

5.8i Locate the collar over the mounting plate . . .

5.8j . . . fit the upper washer . . .

5.8k . . . then fit and tighten the piston rod nut

6 Front suspension lower arm – removal, overhaul and refitting

Note 1: *All nuts disturbed on removal must be renewed as a matter of course. These nuts have threads which are precoated with locking compound (this is only effective once), and include the lower arm balljoint clamp bolt nut.*
Note 2: *Two different types of lower suspension arm may be encountered; type 1 being a steel pressing with a removable lower arm balljoint, and type 2 being a steel forging with fixed lower arm balljoint. The photos in this Section depict the type 1 suspension arm.*

Removal

1 Chock the rear wheels then jack up the front of the vehicle and support it on axle stands (see *Jacking and vehicle support*). Remove the appropriate front roadwheel.
2 Slacken and remove the nut, then withdraw the lower arm balljoint clamp bolt from the swivel hub. Discard the nut – a new one must be used on refitting.
3 Slacken and remove the lower arm front pivot bolt and nut. Recover the nut from its housing if it is loose **(see illustration)**.
4 Unscrew the two bolts securing the lower arm rear mounting bush to the subframe, noting that the larger bolt also secures the anti-roll bar mounting clamp (counterhold the nut if necessary) **(see illustration)**. Recover the nut from the top of the anti-roll bar mounting clamp.

5 Tap a small chisel into the split on the swivel hub to spread the hub slightly, and allow the balljoint shank to be withdrawn. Withdraw the inner end of the arm from the subframe and release the balljoint from the swivel hub. Remove the protector plate which is fitted to the balljoint shank.
6 Manoeuvre the lower arm assembly out from underneath the vehicle **(see illustration)**.

Overhaul

Note: *If the lower arm balljoint on the type 1 suspension arm is to be renewed, new retaining nuts must be used on refitting.*
7 Thoroughly clean the lower arm and the area around the arm mountings, removing all traces of dirt and underseal if necessary, then check carefully for cracks, distortion or any other signs of wear or damage, paying particular attention to the pivot bushes, and renew components as necessary. Due to the number of special tools required (including a press), pivot bush renewal should be entrusted to a dealer or suitably-equipped garage.
8 Check that the lower arm balljoint moves freely, without any sign of roughness; check also that the balljoint dust cover shows no sign of deterioration, and is free from cracks and splits. If renewal is necessary (which is only possible on the type 1 suspension arm), slacken and remove its retaining bolts, and remove the balljoint from the arm. Fit the new balljoint, and insert its retaining bolts. Fit new nuts to the bolts, and tighten them to the specified torque.

9 Examine the shank of the lower arm pivot bolt for signs of wear or scoring, and renew if necessary.

Refitting

10 Manoeuvre the lower arm assembly into position, refit the protector plate to the lower arm balljoint, then locate the balljoint shank in the swivel hub. Ensure that the lug on the protector plate is correctly located in the clamp split.
11 Insert the balljoint clamp bolt, then fit the new retaining nut and tighten it to the specified torque.
12 Refit the front pivot bolt, tightening it finger-tight only. Ensure that the nut is located in its housing.
13 Refit the rear pivot bush retaining bolts and nut, ensuring that the bush bracket is located between the subframe and the anti-roll bar clamp. Tighten the fixings to the specified torque.
14 Refit the roadwheel, then lower the vehicle and tighten the roadwheel bolts to the specified torque. Rock the vehicle to settle the disturbed components, then tighten the lower arm front pivot bolt to the specified torque.

7 Front suspension lower arm balljoint – removal and refitting

Note 1: *Two different types of lower suspension arm may be encountered; type 1 being a steel pressing with a removable lower*

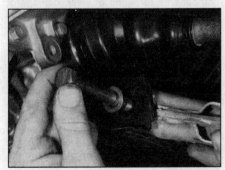

6.3 Remove the lower arm front pivot bolt . . .

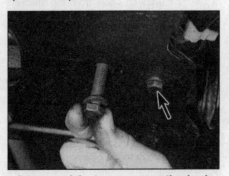
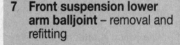

6.4 . . . and the two rear mounting bush bolts (second bolt arrowed) . . .

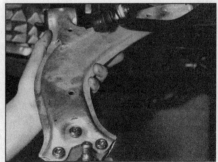

6.6 . . . then remove the lower arm from the vehicle

7.5a Remove the three retaining bolts . . .

7.5b . . . and remove the lower arm balljoint

8.2 Undo the nut and washer (arrowed) securing the left-hand connecting link to the anti-roll bar

arm balljoint, and type 2 being a steel forging with fixed lower arm balljoint. The following procedures are applicable only to the type 1 lower suspension arm.

Note 2: *A new balljoint clamp bolt nut, and new balljoint securing nuts must be used on refitting.*

Removal

1 Chock the rear wheels then jack up the front of the vehicle and support it on axle stands (see *Jacking and vehicle support*). Remove the appropriate front roadwheel.
2 Slacken and remove the nut, then withdraw the lower suspension arm balljoint clamp bolt from the swivel hub. Discard the nut – a new one must be used on refitting.
3 Tap a small chisel into the split on the swivel hub to spread the hub slightly, and allow the balljoint shank to be withdrawn. Pull the lower suspension arm downwards to release the balljoint shank from the swivel hub. To do this it will be necessary to use a long bar and block of wood which will engage under the front subframe. Attach the bar to the suspension arm, preferably with a chain, or alternatively with a stout strap or rope. Lever down on the bar to release the balljoint from the swivel hub **(see illustration 2.10b)**.
4 Once the balljoint is free, remove the protector plate which is fitted to the balljoint shank.
5 Slacken and remove the three nuts, then withdraw the balljoint retaining bolts and remove the balljoint from the lower arm **(see illustrations)**. Discard the nuts – new ones must be used on refitting.
6 Check that the lower arm balljoint moves freely, without any sign of roughness. Check also that the balljoint dust cover shows no sign of deterioration, and is free from cracks and splits. Renew worn or damaged components as necessary.

Refitting

7 Locate the balljoint in the end of the suspension arm, and insert the three retaining bolts. Fit new nuts to the bolts, and tighten them to the specified torque.
8 Refit the protector plate to the lower arm balljoint then, using the method employed

on removal, locate the balljoint shank in the swivel hub, ensuring that the lug on the protector plate is correctly located in the clamp split. Insert the balljoint clamp bolt (from the rear of the swivel hub), then fit the new retaining nut and tighten it to the specified torque.
9 Refit the roadwheel, then lower the vehicle and tighten the roadwheel bolts to the specified torque.

8 Front suspension anti-roll bar – removal and refitting

Note: *All nuts disturbed on removal must be renewed as a matter of course. These nuts have threads which are precoated with locking compound (this is only effective once), and include the anti-roll bar connecting link nuts and the intermediate shaft pinch-bolt nut (and pinch-bolt).*

Removal

1 Firmly apply the handbrake, then jack up the front of the car and support it securely on axle stands (see *Jacking and vehicle support*). Position the roadwheels in the straight-ahead position, then remove both front roadwheels.
2 Undo the nut and washer securing the left-hand connecting link to the anti-roll bar, and position the link clear of the bar **(see illustration)**. Repeat the procedure on the right-hand side.
3 Unclip the clutch cable from the brackets on the subframe.
4 Where fitted, release the power steering fluid pipe support clips from the engine and transmission.
5 Working in the engine compartment, unscrew the securing nut from the intermediate shaft-to-steering gear pinion pinch-bolt, then carefully tap the pinch-bolt from the universal joint – discard the pinch-bolt and nut, new ones must be used on refitting. Pull off the metal clip securing the intermediate shaft to the pinion.
6 Make alignment marks on the universal joint and the steering gear pinion, then push the universal joint upwards to separate it

from the pinion. Engage the steering lock to prevent the steering wheel from turning while the shaft is disconnected.
7 Unscrew the nut and remove the bolt securing the engine/transmission rear mounting connecting link to the mounting on the rear of the cylinder block.
8 Make a final check to ensure that all relevant pipes, hoses and wiring harnesses have been released and moved clear of the subframe to allow the rear of the subframe to be lowered.
9 Accurately measure and record the position of the subframe, both laterally and horizontally with respect to the chassis members and underbody. In practice, there will be marks made on the subframe by the retaining bolts and these can be used as a very accurate guide to correct location when refitting.
10 Slacken and remove the four subframe rear mounting bolts. Loosen the two subframe front mounting bolts by a few turns, until it is possible to lower the rear edge of the subframe approximately 65.0 mm. Wedge a block of wood between the rear of the subframe and the vehicle underbody to hold the subframe in this position.
11 Slacken the two anti-roll bar mounting clamp retaining bolts, and recover the nuts from the top of the clamps. Remove both clamps from the subframe.
12 Manoeuvre the anti-roll bar out from underneath the vehicle, and remove the mounting bushes from the bar.
13 Carefully examine the anti-roll bar components for signs of wear, damage or deterioration, paying particular attention to the mounting bushes. Renew worn components as necessary.

Refitting

14 Fit the rubber mounting bushes to the anti-roll bar, ensuring that the lugs on the inside of each bush engage with the corresponding cut-outs in the anti-roll bar. The bushes are correctly positioned when the alignment marks on the edges of the bushes are aligned with the paint marks on the anti-roll bar.
15 Offer up the anti-roll bar, and manoeuvre it into position on the subframe. Refit the

10.2 Rear engine/transmission mounting connecting link attachments (arrowed)

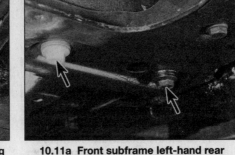

10.11a Front subframe left-hand rear mounting bolts (arrowed) . . .

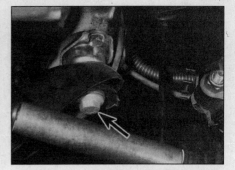

10.11b . . . and front mounting bolt (arrowed)

mounting clamps, ensuring that their ends are correctly located in the hooks on the subframe, and refit the retaining bolts and nuts. Ensure that the bush markings are still aligned with the paint marks on the bar, then tighten the mounting clamp retaining bolts to the specified torque.

16 The remainder of the refitting is a reversal of the removal procedure, noting the following points:

a) All nuts disturbed on removal must be renewed as a matter of course. These nuts have threads which are precoated with locking compound (this is only effective once), and include the anti-roll bar connecting link nuts and the intermediate shaft pinch-bolt nut (and pinch-bolt).

b) Ensure that the subframe is correctly positioned by using the measurements made during removal, or with reference to the marks made by the retaining bolts.

c) Tighten all nuts and bolts to the specified torque settings (where given).

d) Ensure that the metal clip is correctly refitted to the steering intermediate shaft universal joint and that the marks made on removal are aligned.

e) Fit a new intermediate shaft pinch-bolt and nut, ensuring that the lugs on the bolt engage with the cut-outs in the universal joint.

f) On completion have the front wheel alignment checked and where necessary adjusted (see Section 24).

9 Front suspension anti-roll bar connecting link – removal and refitting

Note: *New connecting link securing nuts must be used on refitting.*

Removal

1 Firmly apply the handbrake, then jack up the front of the car and support it securely on axle stands (see *Jacking and vehicle support*). Remove the appropriate front roadwheel.

2 Slacken and remove the upper and lower connecting link retaining nuts and washers, and remove the link from the vehicle.

3 Examine the connecting link for signs of damage, paying particular attention to the mounting bushes or balljoints (as applicable), and renew the link if necessary. It is not possible to renew the bushes or balljoints separately. Note that the connecting link retaining nuts must be renewed as a matter of course.

Refitting

4 Refitting is a reversal of the removal procedure, using new retaining nuts and tightening them to the specified torque.

10 Front suspension subframe – removal and refitting

Note: *All nuts disturbed on removal must be renewed as a matter of course. These nuts have threads which are precoated with locking compound (this is only effective once), and include the steering gear bolt nuts.*

Removal

1 Firmly apply the handbrake, then jack up the front of the car and support it securely on axle stands (see *Jacking and vehicle support*). Remove both front roadwheels.

2 Unscrew and remove the bolt securing the engine/transmission rear mounting connecting link to the mounting on the rear of the cylinder block. Remove the bolt securing the rear mounting link to the bracket on the subframe and withdraw the link **(see illustration)**.

3 On models with power steering, undo the bolt(s) securing the power steering fluid pipe(s) to the mounting bracket(s) on the subframe, and free the pipe(s) from any subframe retaining clips. Unclip the clutch cable from the brackets on the subframe.

4 Where applicable, carefully prise the plastic cap, then undo the pivot bolt securing the gearchange linkage bellcrank to the subframe.

5 Slacken and remove the steering gear mounting bolts, and recover the nuts. Withdraw the mounting bolts, and recover the spacers from the subframe apertures. Secure the steering gear to the exhaust front pipe using a large cable tie or similar.

6 Slacken and remove the suspension lower arm front pivot bolt and nut on both sides. Recover the nut from its housing if it is loose.

7 Unscrew the two bolts securing the suspension lower arm rear mounting bush to the subframe on each side, noting that the larger bolt also secures the anti-roll bar mounting clamp (counterhold the nut if necessary). Recover the nut from the top of each anti-roll bar mounting clamp.

8 Release the inner ends of both suspension lower arms from their locations in the subframe.

9 Place a jack and a suitable block of wood under the subframe to support the subframe as it is lowered.

10 Accurately measure and record the position of the subframe, both laterally and horizontally with respect to the chassis members and underbody. In practice, there will be marks made on the subframe by the retaining bolts and these can be used as a very accurate guide to correct location when refitting.

11 Slacken and remove the four rear subframe mounting bolts, and the two front bolts, then carefully lower the subframe assembly out of position and remove it from underneath the vehicle **(see illustrations)**. Ensure that the subframe assembly does not catch the power steering pipes as it is lowered out of position.

Refitting

12 Refitting is a reversal of the removal procedure, noting the following points:

a) Ensure that the subframe is correctly positioned by using the measurements made during removal, or with reference to the marks made by the retaining bolts.

b) All nuts disturbed on removal must be renewed as a matter of course. These nuts have threads which are precoated with locking compound (this is only effective once) and include the steering gear mounting bolt nuts.

c) Tighten all nuts and bolts to the specified torque settings (where given).

d) On completion have the front wheel alignment checked and where necessary adjusted (see Section 24).

11 Rear hub assembly – removal and refitting

Note: *Do not remove the hub assembly unless it is absolutely necessary. A puller will be required to draw the hub assembly off the stub axle, and the hub bearing will be damaged by the removal procedure. A complete new hub assembly, hub nut, and a new hub cap must be used on refitting.*

Removal

1 Remove the relevant rear brake drum and, on models with ABS, the rear wheel speed sensor as described in Chapter 9.

2 Using a hammer and a large flat-bladed screwdriver, carefully tap and prise the cap out of the centre of the hub. Discard the cap – a new one must be used on refitting. Using a hammer and a chisel-nosed tool, tap up the staking securing the hub retaining nut to the groove in the stub axle.

3 Using a socket and long bar, slacken and remove the rear hub nut, and withdraw the thrustwasher (where fitted). Discard the hub nut – a new nut must used on refitting.

4 Using a puller, draw the hub assembly off the stub axle, along with the outer bearing. With the hub removed, use a bearing puller to draw the inner bearing inner race off the stub axle, then remove the flanged hub spacer, noting which way around it is fitted. On later models a plain spacer is used which can be fitted either way round.

5 With the hub removed, examine the stub axle shaft for signs of wear or damage. If stub axle shaft is worn, it will be necessary to renew the complete trailing arm, as the shaft is not available separately. Trailing arm renewal entails the use of numerous special tools and must be entrusted to a Peugeot/Citroën dealer.

6 Obtain a new hub assembly, hub nut and hub cap for refitting. Note that there are two different types of hub nut, one with a separate thrustwasher, and one with an integral thrustwasher. The two types are inter-changeable, but there is a different torque setting for each type.

Refitting

7 Lubricate the stub axle shaft with clean engine oil, then slide on the spacer, ensuring it is fitted the correct way round on early versions.

8 Slide the hub assembly onto the stub axle and tap it into position using a tubular drift.

9 Fit the thrustwasher (where applicable) then screw on the new nub nut. Do not use the separate thrustwasher if the new nut is of the type with an integral thrustwasher. Lubricate the threads and contact faces of the hub nut and tighten the nut to the specified torque according to type. Stake the nut firmly into the groove on the stub axle to secure it in position, then tap the new hub cap into place in the centre of the hub **(see illustrations)**.

11.9a Fit the thrustwasher (where applicable) and new hub nut, and tighten to the specified torque

11.9c . . . stake the hub nut firmly into the stub axle groove . . .

10 On completion, refit the brake drum and ABS wheel sensor (where applicable) as described in Chapter 9.

12 Rear hub bearings – renewal

Note: *The bearing is intended to last the car's entire service life without maintenance or attention. Never overtighten the hub nut beyond the specified torque setting in an attempt to 'adjust' the bearings.*

1 The rear hub bearing is integral with the rear hub, and it is not possible to renew the hub bearing separately. If the bearing is worn, the complete rear hub assembly must be renewed. See Section 11 for hub removal and refitting procedures.

13 Rear suspension components – general

Although it is possible to remove the rear suspension torsion bars, trailing arms and anti-roll bar independently of the complete rear axle assembly, it is essential to have certain special tools available to complete the work successfully.

Due to the complexity of the tasks, and the requirement for special tools to accurately set the suspension geometry on refitting, the removal and refitting of individual rear suspension components is considered to be

11.9b Using a hammer and suitable punch . . .

11.9d . . . then fit the new hub cap

beyond the scope of DIY work, and should be entrusted to a Peugeot/Citroën dealer.

Procedures for removal and refitting of the rear shock absorbers, and the complete rear suspension assembly are given in Sections 14 and 15 respectively.

14 Rear shock absorber – removal, testing and refitting

Note: *New shock absorber mounting nuts must be used on refitting.*

Removal

1 Drive the rear of the vehicle onto ramps, then apply the handbrake and chock the front wheels.

2 Do not support the vehicle with the trailing arms hanging unsupported.

3 Counterhold the bolts, and unscrew the

14.3a Slacken and remove the shock absorber upper mounting nut (arrowed) . . .

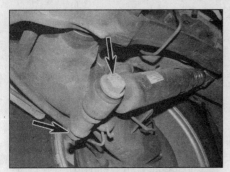

14.3b . . . and lower mounting nut and bolt (arrowed)

shock absorber upper and lower securing nuts **(see illustrations)**. Recover the washers.
4 Tap the bolts from the mountings to free the shock absorber, then withdraw the unit from under the vehicle.

Testing

5 Examine the shock absorber for signs of fluid leakage or damage. Test the operation of the shock absorber, while holding it in an upright position, by moving the piston through a full stroke and then through short strokes of 50 to 100 mm. In both cases, the resistance felt should be smooth and continuous. If the resistance is jerky, or uneven, or if there is any visible sign of wear or damage, renewal is necessary.
6 Also check the rubber mounting bushes for damage and deterioration. New bushes can be fitted using a long bolt, nut and spacers to draw the bush into position. Lubricate the new bush with soapy water to aid fitting.
7 Inspect the shanks of the mounting bolts for signs of wear or damage, and renew as necessary.

Refitting

8 Prior to refitting the shock absorber, mount it upright in the vice, and operate it fully through several strokes in order to prime it. Apply a smear of multi-purpose grease to both the shock absorber mounting bolts.
9 Manoeuvre the shock absorber into position, and insert its mounting bolts (with washers in place). Note that the bolts fit from

15.8 Unscrew the two brake inlet pipe union nuts at the brake pipe connecting block

the inside of the vehicle, ie, the nuts fit on the roadwheel side of the shock absorber.
10 Fit the washers and new nuts to the mounting bolts, but do not tighten the fixings at this stage.
11 Measure the distance between the shock absorber bolt centres, and load the vehicle (by adding weight to the luggage compartment) until a distance of approximately 315.0 mm (Van models), or 340.0 mm (Multispace and Combi models) is obtained between the bolt centres. Tighten the shock absorber mounting nuts and bolts to the specified torque.
12 Drive the vehicle off the ramps.

15 Rear axle assembly – removal and refitting

Removal

1 Disconnect the battery negative terminal (refer to *Disconnecting the battery* in the Reference Chapter).
2 Firmly chock the front wheels, then jack up the rear of the vehicle and support it on axle stands (see *Jacking and vehicle support*). Remove both rear roadwheels.
3 Remove the relevant exhaust system components and heat shield(s) as described in the relevant Part of Chapter 4.
4 Referring to Chapter 9, disconnect the handbrake cables from the equaliser plate at the handbrake lever.
5 From underneath the vehicle, work along the length of each handbrake cable, and free them from the retaining clips which secure them to the vehicle underbody. Note the routing of the cables to ensure correct refitting.
6 On vehicles equipped with ABS, disconnect the ABS wheel speed sensors at the wiring connectors located just forward of the rear axle assembly. Free the cables from the retaining clips on the underbody.
7 To minimise brake hydraulic fluid loss, remove the master cylinder reservoir filler cap, and then tighten it down onto a piece of polythene, to obtain an airtight seal.
8 Wipe clean the area around the brake pipe connecting block or pressure regulating valve and unscrew the union nuts of the two brake inlet pipes **(see illustration)**. Carefully withdraw the brake pipes from the connecting block or regulating valve and plug or cap the pipe ends and the orifices. Release the brake pipe leading to the left-hand rear brake from its clips on the underbody.
9 Make a final check that all necessary components have been disconnected and positioned so that they will not hinder the removal procedure, then position a trolley jack beneath the centre of the rear axle assembly. Raise the jack until it is supporting the weight of the axle.
10 Using a long-reach Torx bit, slacken and remove the rear axle rear mounting bolt on each side, accessible through the hole in the

axle side-member just in front of the shock absorber upper mounting.
11 Slacken and remove the two retaining bolts securing each front mounting assembly to the underbody.
12 Lower the jack and axle assembly out of position, and remove it from underneath the car.
13 Examine the rear axle mountings for signs of damage or deterioration of the mounting rubber, and renew if necessary. Note that all four mountings should be renewed as a set; do not renew the mountings individually.

Refitting

14 Refitting is a reversal of the removal procedure, bearing in mind the following points:
  a) Take care not to crush the brake pipes when positioning the axle assembly under the body.
  b) Raise the rear axle assembly into position, and tighten the mounting retaining bolts to their specified torque settings.
  c) Ensure that the brake pipes, handbrake cables and wiring (as applicable) are correctly routed, and retained by all the necessary retaining clips.
  d) Tighten the brake pipe union nuts.
  e) Reconnect and adjust the handbrake cables as described in Chapter 9.
  f) Bleed the braking system hydraulic circuit as described in Chapter 9.

16 Vehicle ride height – checking

Checking of the vehicle ride height requires the use of special tools to accurately compress the suspension in a suspension checking bay.
The operation should be entrusted to a Peugeot/Citroën dealer, as it not possible to carry out checking accurately without the use of the appropriate tools.

17 Steering wheel – removal and refitting

Models without an airbag
Removal

1 Set the front wheels in the straight-ahead position, and release the steering lock by inserting the ignition key.
2 Carefully ease off the steering wheel centre pad.
3 Slacken the steering wheel retaining bolt. Do not fully remove the bolt at this stage.
4 Tap the wheel upwards near the centre, using the palm of your hand, or twist it from side-to-side, whilst pulling to release it from the shaft splines.

17.9 Separate the two halves of the horn wiring connector

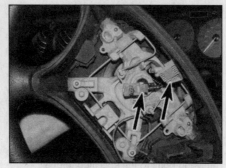

17.13 Feed the wiring harness (arrowed) through the steering wheel as it is withdrawn

5 Once the wheel is released, remove the bolt then mark the steering wheel and steering column shaft in relation to each other. Withdraw the steering wheel from the column shaft.

Refitting

6 Refitting is a reversal of removal, noting the following points:
a) Ensure that the indicator switch stem is in its central position (failure to do this could lead to the steering wheel lug breaking the switch tab) then engage the wheel with the column splines, aligning the mark made on removal.
b) Tighten the steering wheel retaining bolt to the specified torque.

Models with an airbag

Removal

7 Remove the airbag unit as described in Chapter 12.
8 Set the front wheels in the straight-ahead position, and release the steering lock by inserting the ignition key.

9 On later models, lift the horn wiring connector from the slot on the side of the steering wheel and separate the two halves of the connector **(see illustration)**.
10 Slacken the steering wheel retaining bolt. Do not fully remove the bolt at this stage.
11 Tap the wheel upwards near the centre, using the palm of your hand, or twist it from side-to-side, whilst pulling to release it from the shaft splines.
12 Once the wheel is released, remove the bolt then mark the steering wheel and steering column shaft in relation to each other.
13 Carefully withdraw the steering wheel, feeding the wiring harness for the airbag rotary connector and, where applicable, the horn connector through the wheel as it is withdrawn **(see illustration)**.

Refitting

14 Refitting is a reversal of removal, noting the following points:
a) Ensure that the roadwheels are in the straight-ahead position.

b) On early models, align the two arrows on the face of the airbag rotary connector before fitting the steering wheel.
c) Make sure that the wiring is correctly routed through the wheel.
d) Align the marks made on removal, and tighten the retaining bolt to the specified torque.
e) Refit the airbag unit as described in Chapter 12.

18 Steering column – removal, inspection and refitting

Note: Where applicable, a new intermediate shaft-to-steering gear pinion nut and bolt must be used on refitting.

Removal

1 Disconnect the battery negative terminal (refer to Disconnecting the battery in the Reference Chapter).
2 Remove the steering wheel as described in Section 17.
3 Remove the fusebox cover and the undercover from beneath the facia on the driver's side. Remove the steering column upper and lower shrouds as described in Chapter 12.
4 Disconnect the wiring for the airbag (where fitted), and the steering column controls and switches at the connectors on either side of the column **(see illustration)**. Check that any additional wiring connectors leading to the steering column components have been disconnected.
5 Make alignment marks on the universal joint and the intermediate shaft, then unscrew the column-to-intermediate shaft pinch-bolt.
6 Unscrew the two lower steering column securing bolts.
7 Unscrew the two upper steering column securing bolts, and carefully withdraw the column from the vehicle.
8 To remove the intermediate shaft, proceed as follows. Note that on certain models, it will be necessary to jack up the front of the vehicle and support on axle stands (see Jacking and vehicle support) for access to the intermediate shaft-to-steering gear joint. On some models, the joint can be reached through the engine compartment.
a) Unscrew the securing nut from the intermediate shaft-to-steering gear pinion pinch-bolt, then carefully tap the pinch-bolt from the universal joint – discard the pinch-bolt and nut, new ones must be used on refitting.
b) Pull off the metal clip securing the intermediate shaft to the pinion.
c) Make alignment marks on the universal joint and the steering gear pinion, then push the universal joint upwards to separate it from the pinion.
d) Release the shaft from the pinion splines, and remove it from the vehicle.

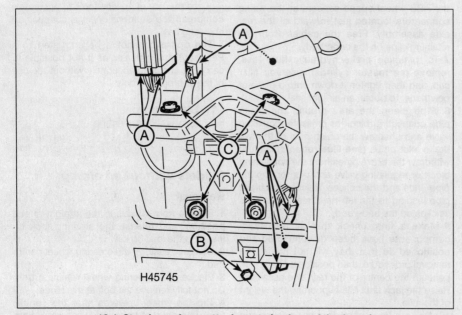

H45745

18.4 Steering column attachments (early models shown)

A Wiring connectors B Universal joint pinch-bolt C Column mounting bolts

Inspection

9 The steering column incorporates a telescopic safety feature. In the event of a front-end crash, the shaft collapses and prevents the steering wheel injuring the driver. Before refitting the steering column, examine the column and mountings for signs of damage and deformation, and renew as necessary.

10 Check the steering shaft for signs of free play in the column bushes, and check the universal joints for signs of damage or roughness in the joint bearings. If any damage or wear is found on the steering column universal joints or shaft bushes, the column must be renewed as an assembly.

11 Where disturbed, the intermediate shaft-to-steering gear pinch-bolt and nut must be renewed as a matter of course.

Refitting

12 Where removed, refit the intermediate shaft, engaging the universal joint with the steering gear drive pinion splines (align the marks made on removal). Ensure that the metal clip is correctly refitted to the intermediate shaft-to-steering gear universal joint, then fit a new pinch-bolt and nut, ensuring that the lugs on the bolt engage with the cut-outs in the universal joint. Tighten the nut to the specified torque.

13 Manoeuvre the steering column assembly into position then, aligning the marks made prior to removal, engage the universal joint with the intermediate shaft splines.

14 Hold the column in position, and refit the steering column upper mounting bolts. Fit the lower mounting bolts and tighten all the bolts to the specified torque.

15 Refit the universal joint pinch-bolt and tighten the bolt to the specified torque.

16 Reconnect the wiring connectors under the facia and secure them in position with the relevant clips.

17 Refit the steering column shrouds as described in Chapter 11, then refit the fusebox cover and the undercover from beneath the facia.

18 Refit the steering wheel as described in Section 17.

19 Ignition switch/steering column lock – removal and refitting

Removal

1 Disconnect the battery negative terminal (refer to *Disconnecting the battery* in the Reference Chapter).

2 Remove the fusebox cover and the undercover from beneath the facia on the driver's side. Remove the steering column upper and lower shrouds as described in Chapter 12.

3 Trace the wiring back from the ignition switch, and disconnect its wiring connectors under the facia. Release the harness from the retaining clips.

4 Disconnect the wiring at the electronic immobiliser receiver on the ignition switch, then unclip and remove the receiver cover from the ignition switch barrel **(see illustration)**.

5 Slacken and remove the lock retaining screw and washer from the side of the lock. On later models the lock is secured by a tamperproof screw. Use a centre punch to mark the centre of the screw, then using a drill and an extractor, remove the screw. Obviously a new screw will be required.

6 With the ignition key inserted, turn the key so that is aligned with the mark positioned between the A and M marks on the barrel.

7 Using a small flat-bladed screwdriver, depress the retaining lug on the side of the lock **(see illustration)**.

8 Withdraw the lock assembly from the steering column, and feed the wiring harness through the column tube.

Refitting

9 Feed the wiring harness through the column tube and locate the lock assembly in position. Check that the ignition key is still aligned with the mark positioned between the A and M marks, then push the lock firmly into place until the retaining lug engages.

10 Secure the lock with the retaining screw and washer, then refit the electronic immobiliser receiver. Reconnect the wiring connector to the immobiliser receiver.

11 Remove the ignition key and check that the steering lock functions correctly.

12 Reconnect the wiring connectors under the facia and secure them in position with the relevant clips.

13 Refit the steering column shrouds as described in Chapter 11, then refit the fusebox cover and the undercover from beneath the facia. Reconnect the battery

20 Steering gear assembly – removal, overhaul and refitting

Note: *All nuts disturbed on removal must be renewed as a matter of course. These nuts have threads which are precoated with locking compound (this is only effective once), and include the track rod balljoint nuts, steering gear mounting bolt nuts, and the intermediate shaft pinch-bolt nut.*

Removal

1 Firmly apply the handbrake, then jack up the front of the vehicle and support on axle stands (see *Jacking and vehicle support*). Remove both front roadwheels.

2 Slacken and remove the nuts securing the steering gear track rod balljoints to the swivel hubs, and release the balljoint tapered shanks using a universal balljoint separator **(see illustration)**.

3 Unscrew the nut from the intermediate shaft-to-steering gear pinion pinch-bolt, then carefully tap the pinch-bolt from the universal joint – discard the pinch-bolt and nut, new ones must be used on refitting. Pull off the metal clip securing the intermediate shaft to the pinion.

4 Make alignment marks on the universal joint and the steering gear pinion, then push the universal joint upwards to separate it from the pinion.

5 Unscrew and remove the bolt securing the engine/transmission rear mounting connecting link to the mounting on the rear of the cylinder block.

6 Unclip the clutch cable from the brackets on the subframe.

7 On models with power steering, undo

19.4 Unclip and remove the immobiliser receiver from the ignition switch barrel

19.7 Depress the lug (arrowed) and withdraw the switch/lock from the steering column

20.2 Releasing a track rod balljoint using a balljoint separator

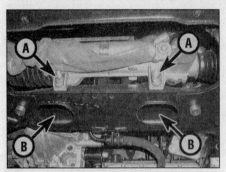

20.13 Undo the steering gear mounting bolts (A), and recover the spacers (B) from the subframe apertures

the bolt(s) securing the power steering fluid pipe(s) to the mounting bracket(s) on the engine/transmission and subframe.

8 Accurately measure and record the position of the subframe, both laterally and horizontally with respect to the chassis members and underbody. In practice, there will be marks made on the subframe by the retaining bolts and these can be used as a very accurate guide to correct location when refitting.

9 Place a jack and a suitable block of wood under the front subframe to support the subframe as it is lowered.

10 Slacken and remove the four rear subframe mounting bolts, and the two front bolts, then carefully lower the subframe slightly.

11 On models with power steering, position a suitable container beneath the power steering gear assembly. On early models, mark the pipe unions to ensure they are correctly positioned on refitting, then unscrew the feed and return pipe union nuts from the steering gear. On later models, undo the bolt securing the fluid pipe flange plate to the rack housing and ease the flange plate from the rack. On all models, allow the power steering fluid to drain into the container. When the fluid has finished draining, suitably cover the pipe ends and the orifices in the rack to prevent dirt ingress. Note that on later models, new O-rings will be required for the pipe ends for refitting.

12 Undo the two retaining screws (where fitted), then unclip the heat shield and remove it from the top of the steering gear assembly.

13 Undo and remove the two steering gear mounting bolts, and recover the spacers from the subframe apertures **(see illustration)**.

14 Manoeuvre the steering gear out from under the right-hand wheel arch (right-hand drive models) or left-hand wheel arch (left-hand drive models).

Overhaul

15 Examine the steering gear assembly for signs of wear or damage, and check that the rack moves freely throughout the full length of its travel, with no signs of roughness or excessive free play between the steering gear pinion and rack. It is possible to overhaul the steering gear assembly housing components,

but this task should be entrusted to a Peugeot/Citroën dealer. The only components which can be renewed easily by the home mechanic are the track rod balljoints (see Section 23).

16 Inspect all the steering gear fluid unions for signs of leakage, and check that all union nuts are securely tightened. Also examine the steering gear hydraulic ram for signs of fluid leakage or damage, and if necessary renew it.

Refitting

17 Note that all nuts disturbed on removal must be renewed as a matter of course. These nuts have threads which are precoated with locking compound (this is only effective once), and include the track rod balljoint nuts, and the steering gear mounting bolt nuts.

18 Manoeuvre the steering gear assembly into position from the right-hand or left-hand side of the vehicle, as applicable.

19 Position the spacers in the subframe apertures, then insert the mounting bolts. Tighten the mounting bolts to the specified torque.

20 Clip the heat shield onto the top of the steering gear, and securely tighten its two retaining screws (where fitted).

21 On models with power steering wipe clean the power steering pipes and the steering gear orifices. On early models, refit the feed and return pipe unions then refit them to their respective positions on the steering gear. Tighten the union nuts securely. On later models, locate new O-rings on the pipe ends. Locate the fluid pipe flange plate on the rack housing and secure with the retaining bolt.

22 Raise the jack and locate the subframe in position. Ensure that the subframe is correctly positioned by using the measurements made during removal, or with reference to the marks made by the retaining bolts. Fit the front and rear subframe retaining bolts and tighten to the specified torque.

23 Where applicable, refit the power steering fluid pipe(s) to the mounting bracket(s) on the engine/transmission and subframe.

24 Secure the clutch cable to the brackets on the subframe.

25 Refit the bolt securing the engine/transmission rear mounting link to the cylinder block and tighten to the specified torque (refer to the relevant Part of Chapter 2).

26 Engage the intermediate shaft universal joint with the steering gear pinion splines (align the marks made before removal). Ensure that the metal clip is correctly refitted to the intermediate shaft-to-steering gear universal joint, then fit a new pinch-bolt and nut, ensuring that the lugs on the bolt engage with the cut-outs in the universal joint. Tighten the nut to the specified torque.

27 Engage the track rod balljoints in the swivel hubs, then fit a new retaining nut to each one. Tighten the nuts to the specified torque.

28 Make a final check that all cables, pipes and hoses are correctly routed, and are

securely held by all the necessary retaining clips.

29 Refit the roadwheels, then lower the vehicle to the ground and tighten the roadwheel bolts to the specified torque.

30 Refill the fluid reservoir and bleed the hydraulic system as described in Section 21.

31 On completion have the front wheel alignment checked and, if necessary, adjusted (see Section 24).

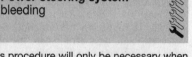

21 Power steering system – bleeding

1 This procedure will only be necessary when any part of the hydraulic system has been disconnected.

2 Referring to *Weekly checks*, remove the fluid reservoir filler cap, and top-up with the specified fluid until the level is up to the MAX mark on the side of the reservoir (early models) or up to the Cold mark on the filler cap dipstick (later models).

3 With the engine stopped, slowly move the steering from lock-to-lock approximately ten times to purge out the trapped air, then top-up the fluid until the level is again up to the MAX or Cold mark as applicable. Repeat this procedure until the fluid level in the reservoir does not drop any further.

4 Start the engine, and allow it to idle for two or three minutes without moving the steering wheel. Switch the engine off and, if necessary, top-up the fluid again, to the MAX or Cold mark.

5 Start the engine and slowly move the steering from lock-to-lock several times to purge out any remaining air in the system. Repeat this procedure until bubbles cease to appear in the fluid reservoir.

6 Once all traces of air have been removed from the power steering hydraulic system, turn the engine off and allow the system to cool. Once cool, check that the fluid level is up to the MAX or Cold mark, topping-up if necessary.

22 Power steering pump – removal and refitting

Removal

1 The power steering pump is mounted on the front facing side of the engine.

2 Remove the auxiliary drivebelt as described in the relevant Part of Chapter 1.

3 On later diesel engine models, release the four plastic fasteners and remove the engine cover from the top of the engine.

4 On later petrol engine models, unbolt and remove the heat shield at the rear of the power steering pump.

5 Unscrew the power steering fluid reservoir filler cap and empty the hydraulic fluid from

22.7a Power steering fluid supply pipe support bracket attachment (arrowed) on 1.4 litre petrol engines . . .

22.7b . . . and on 2.0 litre diesel diesel engines (arrowed)

the reservoir by syphoning it out using a syringe or pipette. **Note:** *Do not syphon the fluid by mouth, as it is poisonous.*

6 Place absorbent rags beneath the fluid supply and return pipe and hose connections on the pump and be prepared for fluid spillage.

7 Undo the nut and bolt securing the fluid supply pipe to the support bracket located either at the rear of the pump, or adjacent to the cylinder head cover **(see illustrations)**.

8 Undo the union nut and disconnect the fluid supply pipe from the top of the pump. Move the pipe to one side and suitably cover the pipe end and the orifice in the pump to prevent dirt ingress.

9 Slacken the retaining clip, and disconnect the fluid return hose from the pump. If the original crimped type clip is still fitted, cut the clip and discard it; use a standard worm-drive hose clip on refitting. Suitably cover the hose end and the orifice in the pump to prevent dirt ingress.

10 Undo the rear mounting bolt and the two front mounting bolts and withdraw the pump from the mounting bracket **(see illustrations)**. Access to the front mounting bolts can be gained through the holes in the pump pulley.

Refitting

11 Manoeuvre the pump into position, refit the pump mounting bolts and tighten them to the specified torque.

12 Reconnect the fluid supply pipe to the pump and securely tighten the union nut. Secure the pipe to the support bracket.

13 Refit the return hose to the pump, and securely tighten its retaining clip.

14 On later diesel engine models, refit the engine cover. On later petrol engine models, refit the heat shield to the rear of the pump.

15 Refit and tension the auxiliary drivebelt as described in Chapter 1A or 1B as applicable.

16 On completion, bleed the hydraulic system as described in Section 21.

23 Track rod balljoint – removal and refitting

Note: *A new track rod balljoint-to-swivel hub nut must be used on refitting.*

Removal

1 Apply the handbrake, then jack up the front of the vehicle and support it on axle stands (see *Jacking and vehicle support*). Remove the appropriate front roadwheel.

2 If the balljoint is to be re-used, use a straight-edge and a scriber, or similar, to mark its relationship to the track rod.

3 Hold the track rod, and unscrew the balljoint locknut by a quarter of a turn **(see illustration)**. Do not move the locknut from this position, as it will serve as a handy reference mark on refitting.

4 Slacken and remove the nut securing the track rod balljoint to the swivel hub, and release the balljoint tapered shank using a universal balljoint separator. Discard the nut – a new one must be used when refitting.

5 Counting the **exact** number of turns necessary to do so, unscrew the balljoint from the track rod.

6 Count the number of exposed threads between the end of the balljoint and the locknut, and record this figure. If a new balljoint is to be fitted, unscrew the locknut from the old balljoint.

7 Carefully clean the balljoint and the threads. Renew the balljoint if its movement is sloppy or too stiff, if excessively worn, or if damaged in any way; carefully check the stud taper and threads. If the balljoint dust cover is damaged, the complete balljoint assembly must be renewed; it is not possible to obtain the dust cover separately.

Refitting

8 If a new balljoint is to be fitted, screw the locknut onto its threads, and position it so that the same number of exposed threads are visible, as was noted prior to removal.

9 Screw the balljoint into the track rod by the number of turns noted on removal. This should bring the balljoint locknut to within a quarter of a turn from the end face of the track rod, with the alignment marks that were made on removal (if applicable) lined up. Hold the track rod and securely tighten the locknut.

10 Refit the balljoint shank to the swivel hub, then fit a new retaining nut and tighten it to the specified torque.

11 Refit the roadwheel, then lower the vehicle to the ground and tighten the roadwheel bolts to the specified torque.

12 On completion have the front wheel alignment checked, and if necessary, adjusted (see Section 24).

24 Wheel alignment and steering angles – general information, checking and adjustment

Definitions

1 A car's steering and suspension geometry is defined in four basic settings – all angles are expressed in degrees (toe settings are also expressed as a measurement); the steering axis is defined as an imaginary line drawn through the axis of the suspension

22.10a Power steering pump rear mounting bolt (arrowed) . . .

22.10b . . . and front mounting bolts (arrowed)

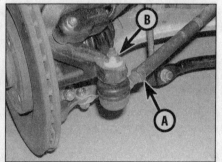

23.3 Track rod balljoint locknut (A) and balljoint-to-swivel hub retaining nut (B)

strut, extended where necessary to contact the ground.

2 Camber is the angle between each roadwheel and a vertical line drawn through its centre and tyre contact patch, when viewed from the front or rear of the car. Positive camber is when the roadwheels are tilted outwards from the vertical at the top; negative camber is when they are tilted inwards. The camber angle is not adjustable.

3 Castor is the angle between the steering axis and a vertical line drawn through each roadwheel's centre and tyre contact patch, when viewed from the side of the car. Positive castor is when the steering axis is tilted so that it contacts the ground ahead of the vertical; negative castor is when it contacts the ground behind the vertical. The castor angle is not adjustable.

4 Toe is the difference, viewed from above, between lines drawn through the roadwheel centres and the car's centre-line. 'Toe-in' is when the roadwheels point inwards, towards each other at the front, while 'toe-out' is when they splay outwards from each other at the front.

5 The front wheel toe setting is adjusted by screwing the track rod in or out of its balljoints, to alter the effective length of the track rod assembly.

6 Rear wheel toe setting is not adjustable.

Checking and adjustment

7 Due to the special measuring equipment necessary to check the wheel alignment and steering angles, and the skill required to use it properly, the checking and adjustment of these settings is best left to a Peugeot/Citroën dealer or similar expert. Note that most tyre-fitting shops now possess sophisticated checking equipment.

Chapter 11
Bodywork and fittings

Contents

Degrees of difficulty

Easy, suitable for novice with little experience	Fairly easy, suitable for beginner with some experience	Fairly difficult, suitable for competent DIY mechanic	Difficult, suitable for experienced DIY mechanic	Very difficult, suitable for expert DIY or professional

Specifications

Torque wrench setting	Nm	lbf ft
Seat belt mountings	25	18
Sliding side door attachments:		
Lower carriage end stop	8	6
Centre carriage bracket	20	15

1 General information

The bodyshell is made of pressed-steel sections, and is available in Van or MPV format. Most components are welded together, but some use is made of structural adhesives. The front wings are bolted on.

The bonnet, doors and some other vulnerable panels are made of zinc-coated metal, and are further protected by being coated with an anti-chip primer prior to being sprayed.

Extensive use is made of plastic materials, mainly in the interior, but also in exterior components. The front and rear bumpers and the front grille are injection-moulded from a synthetic material which is very strong, yet light. Plastic components such as wheel arch liners are fitted to the underside of the vehicle, to improve the body's resistance to corrosion.

2 Maintenance – bodywork and underframe

The general condition of a vehicle's bodywork is the one thing that significantly affects its value. Maintenance is easy, but needs to be regular. Neglect, particularly after minor damage, can lead quickly to further deterioration and costly repair bills. It is important also to keep watch on those parts of the vehicle not immediately visible, for instance the underside, inside all the wheel arches, and the lower part of the engine compartment.

The basic maintenance routine for the bodywork is washing – preferably with a lot of water, from a hose. This will remove all the loose solids which may have stuck to the vehicle. It is important to flush these off in such a way as to prevent grit from scratching the finish. The wheel arches and underframe need washing in the same way, to remove any accumulated mud which will retain moisture and tend to encourage rust. Paradoxically enough, the best time to clean the underframe and wheel arches is in wet weather, when the mud is thoroughly wet and soft. In very wet weather, the underframe is usually cleaned of large accumulations automatically, and this is a good time for inspection.

Periodically, except on vehicles with a wax-based underbody protective coating, it is a good idea to have the whole of the underframe of the vehicle steam-cleaned, engine compartment included, so that a thorough inspection can be carried out to see what minor repairs and renovations are necessary. Steam-cleaning is available at many garages, and is necessary for the removal of the accumulation of oily grime, which sometimes is allowed to become thick in certain areas. If steam-cleaning facilities are not available, there are one or two excellent grease solvents available, which can be brush-applied; the dirt can then be simply hosed off. Note that these methods should not be used on vehicles with wax-based underbody protective coating, or the coating will be removed. Such vehicles should be inspected annually, preferably just prior to winter, when the underbody should be washed down, and any damage to the wax coating repaired using underseal. Ideally, a completely fresh coat should be applied. It would also be worth considering the use of wax-based protection for injection into door panels, sills, box sections, etc, as an additional safeguard against rust damage, where such protection is not provided by the vehicle manufacturer.

After washing paintwork, wipe off with a chamois leather to give an unspotted clear finish. A coat of clear protective wax polish will give added protection against chemical pollutants in the air. If the paintwork sheen has dulled or oxidised, use a cleaner/ polisher combination to restore the brilliance of the shine. This requires a little effort, but such dulling is usually caused because regular washing has been neglected. Care needs to be taken with metallic paintwork, as a special non-abrasive cleaner/polisher is required to avoid damage to the finish. Always check that the door and ventilator opening drain holes and pipes are completely clear, so that water can be drained out. Brightwork should be treated in the same way as paintwork. Windscreens and windows can be kept clear

of the smeary film which often appears, by the use of proprietary glass cleaner. Never use any form of wax or other body or chromium polish on glass.

3 Maintenance – upholstery and carpets

Mats and carpets should be brushed or vacuum-cleaned regularly, to keep them free of grit. If they are badly stained, remove them from the vehicle for scrubbing or sponging, and make quite sure they are dry before refitting. Seats and interior trim panels can be kept clean by wiping with a damp cloth and a proprietary upholstery cleaner. If they do become stained (which can be more apparent on light-coloured upholstery), use a little liquid detergent and a soft nail brush to scour the grime out of the grain of the material. Do not forget to keep the headlining clean in the same way as the upholstery. When using liquid cleaners inside the vehicle, do not over-wet the surfaces being cleaned. Excessive damp could get into the seams and padded interior, causing stains, offensive odours or even rot. If the inside of the vehicle gets wet accidentally, it is worthwhile taking some trouble to dry it out properly, particularly where carpets are involved. *Caution: Do not leave oil or electric heaters inside the vehicle for this purpose.*

4 Minor body damage – repair

Scratches

If the scratch is very superficial, and does not penetrate to the metal of the bodywork, repair is very simple. Lightly rub the area of the scratch with a paintwork renovator, or a very fine cutting paste, to remove loose paint from the scratch, and to clear the surrounding bodywork of wax polish. Rinse the area with clean water.

Apply touch-up paint to the scratch using a fine paint brush; continue to apply fine layers of paint until the surface of the paint in the scratch is level with the surrounding paintwork. Allow the new paint at least two weeks to harden, then blend it into the surrounding paintwork by rubbing the scratch area with a paintwork renovator or a very fine cutting paste. Finally apply wax polish.

Where the scratch has penetrated right through to the metal of the bodywork, causing the metal to rust, a different repair technique is required. Remove any loose rust from the bottom of the scratch with a penknife, then apply rust-inhibiting paint, to prevent the formation of rust in the future. Using a rubber or nylon applicator, fill the scratch with bodystopper paste. If required, this paste can

be mixed with cellulose thinners, to provide a very thin paste which is ideal for filling narrow scratches. Before the stopper-paste in the scratch hardens, wrap a piece of smooth cotton rag around the top of a finger. Dip the finger in cellulose thinners, and quickly sweep it across the surface of the stopper-paste in the scratch; this will ensure that the surface of the stopper-paste is slightly hollowed. The scratch can now be painted over as described earlier in this Section.

Dents

When deep denting of the vehicle's bodywork has taken place, the first task is to pull the dent out, until the affected bodywork almost attains its original shape. There is little point in trying to restore the original shape completely, as the metal in the damaged area will have stretched on impact, and cannot be reshaped fully to its original contour. It is better to bring the level of the dent up to a point which is about 3 mm below the level of the surrounding bodywork. In cases where the dent is very shallow anyway, it is not worth trying to pull it out at all. If the underside of the dent is accessible, it can be hammered out gently from behind, using a mallet with a wooden or plastic head. Whilst doing this, hold a suitable block of wood firmly against the outside of the panel, to absorb the impact from the hammer blows and thus prevent a large area of the bodywork from being 'belled-out'.

Should the dent be in a section of the bodywork which has a double skin, or some other factor making it inaccessible from behind, a different technique is called for. Drill several small holes through the metal inside the area – particularly in the deeper section. Then screw long self-tapping screws into the holes, just sufficiently for them to gain a good purchase in the metal. Now the dent can be pulled out by pulling on the protruding heads of the screws with a pair of pliers.

The next stage of the repair is the removal of the paint from the damaged area, and from an inch or so of the surrounding 'sound' bodywork. This is accomplished most easily by using a wire brush or abrasive pad on a power drill, although it can be done just as effectively by hand, using sheets of abrasive paper. To complete the preparation for filling, score the surface of the bare metal with a screwdriver or the tang of a file, or alternatively, drill small holes in the affected area. This will provide a really good 'key' for the filler paste.

To complete the repair, see the Section on filling and respraying.

Rust holes or gashes

Remove all paint from the affected area, and from an inch or so of the surrounding 'sound' bodywork, using an abrasive pad or a wire brush on a power drill. If these are not available, a few sheets of abrasive paper will do the job most effectively. With the paint removed, you will be able to judge the severity of the corrosion, and therefore decide whether to renew the whole panel (if this is possible) or to repair the affected area. New body panels are not as expensive as most people think, and it is often quicker and more satisfactory to fit a new panel than to attempt to repair large areas of corrosion.

Remove all fittings from the affected area, except those which will act as a guide to the original shape of the damaged bodywork (eg headlight shells etc). Then, using tin snips or a hacksaw blade, remove all loose metal and any other metal badly affected by corrosion. Hammer the edges of the hole inwards, in order to create a slight depression for the filler paste.

Wire-brush the affected area to remove the powdery rust from the surface of the remaining metal. Paint the affected area with rust-inhibiting paint; if the back of the rusted area is accessible, treat this also.

Before filling can take place, it will be necessary to block the hole in some way. This can be achieved by the use of aluminium or plastic mesh, or aluminium tape.

Aluminium or plastic mesh, or glass-fibre matting, is probably the best material to use for a large hole. Cut a piece to the approximate size and shape of the hole to be filled, then position it in the hole so that its edges are below the level of the surrounding bodywork. It can be retained in position by several blobs of filler paste around its periphery.

Aluminium tape should be used for small or very narrow holes. Pull a piece off the roll, trim it to the approximate size and shape required, then pull off the backing paper (if used) and stick the tape over the hole; it can be overlapped if the thickness of one piece is insufficient. Burnish down the edges of the tape with the handle of a screwdriver or similar, to ensure that the tape is securely attached to the metal underneath.

Filling and respraying

Before using this Section, see the Sections on dent, minor scratch, rust holes and gash repairs.

Many types of bodyfiller are available, but generally speaking, those proprietary kits which contain a tin of filler paste and a tube of resin hardener are best for this type of repair; some can be used directly from the tube. A wide, flexible plastic or nylon applicator will be found invaluable for imparting a smooth and well-contoured finish to the surface of the filler.

Mix up a little filler on a clean piece of card or board – measure the hardener carefully (follow the maker's instructions on the pack), otherwise the filler will set too rapidly or too slowly. Using the applicator, apply the filler paste to the prepared area; draw the applicator across the surface of the filler to achieve the correct contour and to level the surface. As soon as a contour that approximates to the correct one is achieved, stop working the paste – if you carry on too

long, the paste will become sticky and begin to 'pick-up' on the applicator. Continue to add thin layers of filler paste at 20-minute intervals, until the level of the filler is just proud of the surrounding bodywork.

Once the filler has hardened, the excess can be removed using a metal plane or file. From then on, progressively-finer grades of abrasive paper should be used, starting with a 40-grade production paper, and finishing with a 400-grade wet-and-dry paper. Always wrap the abrasive paper around a flat rubber, cork, or wooden block – otherwise the surface of the filler will not be completely flat. During the smoothing of the filler surface, the wet-and-dry paper should be periodically rinsed in water. This will ensure that a very smooth finish is imparted to the filler at the final stage.

At this stage, the 'dent' should be surrounded by a ring of bare metal, which in turn should be encircled by the finely 'feathered' edge of the good paintwork. Rinse the repair area with clean water, until all of the dust produced by the rubbing-down operation has gone.

Spray the whole area with a light coat of primer – this will show up any imperfections in the surface of the filler. Repair these imperfections with fresh filler paste or bodystopper, and once more smooth the surface with abrasive paper. If bodystopper is used, it can be mixed with cellulose thinners, to form a really thin paste which is ideal for filling small holes. Repeat this spray-and-repair procedure until you are satisfied that the surface of the filler, and the feathered edge of the paintwork, are perfect. Clean the repair area with clean water, and allow to dry fully.

The repair area is now ready for final spraying. Paint spraying must be carried out in a warm, dry, windless and dust-free atmosphere. This condition can be created artificially if you have access to a large indoor working area, but if you are forced to work in the open, you will have to pick your day very carefully. If you are working indoors, dousing the floor in the work area with water will help to settle the dust which would otherwise be in the atmosphere. If the repair area is confined to one body panel, mask off the surrounding panels; this will help to minimise the effects of a slight mismatch in paint colours. Bodywork fittings (eg chrome strips, door handles etc) will also need to be masked off. Use genuine masking tape, and several thicknesses of newspaper, for the masking operations.

Before commencing to spray, agitate the aerosol can thoroughly, then spray a test area (an old tin, or similar) until the technique is mastered. Cover the repair area with a thick coat of primer; the thickness should be built up using several thin layers of paint, rather than one thick one. Using 400 grade wet-and-dry paper, rub down the surface of the primer until it is really smooth. While doing this, the work area should be thoroughly doused with water, and the wet-and-dry paper periodically rinsed in water. Allow to dry before spraying on more paint.

Spray on the top coat, again building up

the thickness by using several thin layers of paint. Start spraying at the top of the repair area, and then, using a side-to-side motion, work downwards until the whole repair area and about 2 inches of the surrounding original paintwork is covered. Remove all masking material 10 to 15 minutes after spraying on the final coat of paint.

Allow the new paint at least two weeks to harden, then, using a paintwork renovator or a very fine cutting paste, blend the edges of the paint into the existing paintwork. Finally, apply wax polish.

Plastic components

With the use of more and more plastic body components by the vehicle manufacturers (eg bumpers. spoilers, and in some cases major body panels), rectification of more serious damage to such items has become a matter of either entrusting repair work to a specialist in this field, or renewing complete components. Repair of such damage by the DIY owner is not really feasible, owing to the cost of the equipment and materials required for effecting such repairs. The basic technique involves making a groove along the line of the crack in the plastic, using a rotary burr in a power drill. The damaged part is then welded back together, using a hot air gun to heat up and fuse a plastic filler rod into the groove. Any excess plastic is then removed, and the area rubbed down to a smooth finish. It is important that a filler rod of the correct plastic is used, as body components can be made of a variety of different types (eg polycarbonate, ABS, polypropylene).

Damage of a less serious nature (abrasions, minor cracks etc) can be repaired by the DIY owner using a two-part epoxy filler repair material. Once mixed in equal proportions, this is used in similar fashion to the bodywork filler used on metal panels. The filler is usually cured in twenty to thirty minutes, ready for sanding and painting.

If the owner is renewing a complete component himself, or if he has repaired it with epoxy filler, he will be left with the problem of finding a suitable paint for finishing which is compatible with the type of plastic used. At one time, the use of a universal paint was not possible, owing to the complex range of plastics encountered in body component applications. Standard paints, generally speaking, will not bond to plastic or rubber satisfactorily. However, it is now possible to obtain a plastic body parts finishing kit which consists of a pre-primer treatment, a primer and coloured top coat. Full instructions are normally supplied with a kit, but basically, the method of use is to first apply the pre-primer to the component concerned, and allow it to dry for up to 30 minutes. Then the primer is applied, and left to dry for about an hour before finally applying the special-coloured top coat. The result is a correctly-coloured component, where the paint will flex with the plastic or rubber, a property that standard paint does not normally posses.

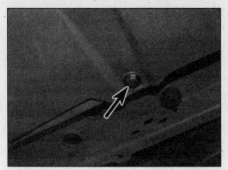

6.4 Undo the bolts (arrowed) securing the lower front part of the bumper to the radiator support platform – early models

5 Major body damage – repair

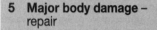

Where serious damage has occurred, or large areas need renewal due to neglect, it means that complete new panels will need welding-in, and this is best left to professionals. If the damage is due to impact, it will also be necessary to check completely the alignment of the bodyshell, and this can only be carried out accurately by a Peugeot/Citroën dealer, or accident repair specialist, using special jigs. If the body is left misaligned, it is primarily dangerous, as the car will not handle properly, and secondly, uneven stresses will be imposed on the steering,

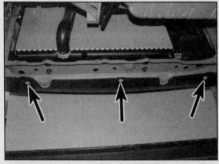

6.10 Undo the bolts (arrowed) securing the bumper to the radiator support platform – later models

6.11 Undo the bolts (arrowed) securing the upper front edge of the bumper to the bumper bracket – later models

6.5 Front bumper attachments under the wheel arch (arrowed) – early models

suspension and possibly transmission, causing abnormal wear, or complete failure, particularly to such items as the tyres.

6 Front bumper – removal and refitting

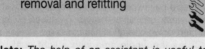

Note: *The help of an assistant is useful to support the bumper during the removal and refitting procedure.*

Pre-September 2002 models

Removal

1 Firmly apply the handbrake, then jack up the front of the vehicle and support it securely on axle stands (see *Jacking and vehicle support*). To improve access to the bumper fasteners, remove both front roadwheels.
2 Remove the radiator grille as described in Section 25.
3 Release the front section of the wheel arch liner on each side as described in Section 23.
4 Undo the two bolts securing the lower front part of the bumper to the radiator support platform **(see illustration)**.
5 Working under the wheel arch on each side, undo the bolt securing the rear edge of the bumper to the front wing **(see illustration)**. Similarly, undo the two bolts securing the bumper to the mounting bracket and inner wing panel.
6 With the help of an assistant, carefully pull the bumper forward and off the car **(see illustration)**.

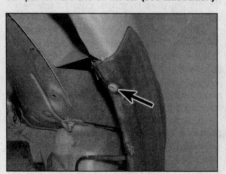

6.13 Undo the bolt (arrowed) securing the rear edge of the bumper to the front wing – later models

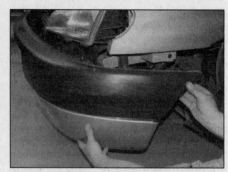

6.6 Carefully pull the bumper forward and off the car – early models

Refitting

7 Refitting is a reversal of removal.

Post-September 2002 models

Removal

8 Firmly apply the handbrake, then jack up the front of the vehicle and support it securely on axle stands (see *Jacking and vehicle support*). To improve access to the bumper fasteners, remove both front roadwheels.
9 Remove the radiator grille as described in Section 25.
10 Undo the three bolts securing the lower front part of the bumper to the radiator support platform **(see illustration)**.
11 Undo the three bolts securing the upper front edge of the bumper to the bumper bracket **(see illustration)**.
12 Release the front section of the wheel arch liner on each side as described in Section 23.
13 Undo the bolt securing the rear edge of the bumper to the front wing each side **(see illustration)**.
14 On models equipped with foglights, disconnect the foglight wiring connectors, and release the wiring from the bumper clips.
15 Working on one side at a time, reach up under the wheel arch and release the catch securing the upper rear section of the bumper to the front wing. To do this, insert a screwdriver through the square hole in the wing and depress the catch while at the same time pulling the rear of the bumper outward **(see illustration)**.
16 With the catch released, pull the bumper

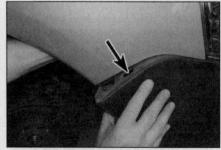

6.15 Using a screwdriver through the square hole (arrowed), depress the internal catch in the wing to release the bumper – later models

outward and sharply forward to release the remaining retaining clip **(see illustration)**.

17 Release the other side of the bumper in the same way then, with the help of an assistant, carefully pull the bumper forward and off the car.

18 To remove the bumper bracket, undo the two bolts each side and lift the bracket from its location.

Refitting

19 Refitting is a reversal of removal, ensuring that the catches each side correctly engage with the front wings as it is located in position.

7 Rear bumper – removal and refitting

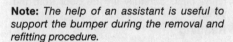

Note: *The help of an assistant is useful to support the bumper during the removal and refitting procedure.*

Removal

1 Chock the front wheels, then jack up the rear of the vehicle and support securely on axle stands (see *Jacking and vehicle support*).

2 Undo the screw securing the wheel arch liner to the lower corner of the bumper on each side **(see illustration)**.

3 Remove the rear light unit on both sides as described in Chapter 12.

4 Ease the wheel arch liner away from the bumper and undo the screw securing the

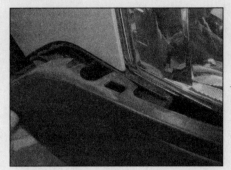

6.16 Pull the bumper outwards and sharply forward to release the remaining retaining clip – later models

upper front corner of the bumper to the rear wing on each side **(see illustration)**.

5 Similarly, from behind the wheel arch liner, undo the bolt securing the side of the bumper to the rear wing **(see illustration)**.

6 Undo the bumper securing screw each side at the base of the rear light unit location **(see illustration)**.

7 Undo the five screws securing the upper edge of the bumper to the bumper bracket **(see illustration)**.

8 Release the two retaining tabs on the lower edge of the bumper from the support brackets **(see illustration)**.

9 With the help of an assistant, carefully pull the bumper rearwards and off the car. At the same time on models fitted with a parking aid system, disconnect the wiring from the

7.2 Undo the screw securing the wheel arch liner to the lower corner of the rear bumper

sensors, and if necessary remove the sensors as described in Chapter 12.

10 To remove the bumper bracket, undo the four bolts and lift the bracket from its location.

Refitting

11 Refitting is a reversal of removal, ensuring that the pegs each side correctly engage with the rear wings as it is located in position **(see illustration)**.

8 Bonnet – removal, refitting and adjustment

Removal

1 Open the bonnet and have an assistant support it then, using a pencil or felt tip pen,

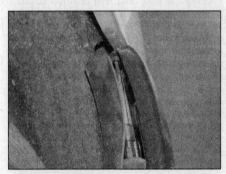

7.4 Undo the screw securing the upper front corner of the bumper to the rear wing

7.5 Undo the bolt securing the side of the bumper to the rear wing

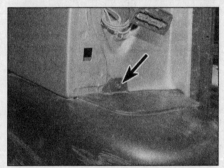

7.6 Undo the securing screw (arrowed) each side, at the base of the rear light unit location

7.7 Undo the screws securing the upper edge of the bumper to the bumper bracket

7.8 Release the retaining tabs on the lower edge of the bumper from the support brackets

7.11 Ensure that the pegs each side correctly engage with the rear wings as the bumper is located in position

9.2 Bonnet lock retaining bolts (arrowed)

9.5 Undo the bolt securing the bonnet release lever

10 Door – removal and refitting

Front door

Removal

1 Disconnect the battery negative terminal (refer to *Disconnecting the battery* in the Reference Chapter).
2 Open the door then release the locking ring and disconnect the door wiring connector from the door socket.
3 Unscrew the two securing bolts, and disconnect the door check strap from the door pillar.
4 Ensure that the door is adequately supported, then unscrew the upper and lower hinge pins. Carefully lift the door from the vehicle.

Refitting

5 Refitting is a reversal of removal, but on completion check the fit of the door in relation to the surrounding body panels. If adjustment is necessary, the door position can be altered by means of the elongated slots in the hinge plates attached to the door.

Sliding side door

Removal

6 Remove the side door upper trim panel as described in Section 28.
7 Open the side door and position suitably protected axle stands below the door. Pack the stands so they are just taking the weight of the door.
8 Remove the end piece from the rear of the door upper guide rail. Undo the retaining screw and remove the end stop plate from the upper guide rail. Note that the end piece and end stop plate are not fitted to all models.
9 Undo the retaining bolt and remove the lower carriage end stop, from the rear end of the lower guide rail **(see illustrations)**.
10 Undo the two bolts securing the centre carriage bracket to the rear of the door.
11 With the help of an assistant, disengage the upper and lower carriages from the guide

mark the outline of each bonnet hinge relative to the bonnet, to use as a guide on refitting.
2 Disconnect the washer jet supply tubing from the right-hand jet and release the supply tubing from the retaining clips.
3 Unscrew the bonnet-to-hinge retaining bolts each side. With the help of the assistant, carefully lift the bonnet from the vehicle. Store the bonnet out of the way in a safe place.
4 Inspect the bonnet hinges for signs of wear and free play at the pivots, and if necessary renew. Each hinge is secured to the body by two bolts. On refitting, apply a smear of multi-purpose grease to the hinges.

Refitting and adjustment

5 With the aid of an assistant, offer up the bonnet, and engage the retaining bolts. Align the hinges with the marks made on removal, then tighten the retaining bolts securely. Reconnect the washer jet tubing.
6 Close the bonnet, and check for alignment with the adjacent panels. If necessary, slacken the hinge bolts and re-align the bonnet to suit. When correctly aligned, tighten the hinge bolts securely.
7 Once the bonnet is correctly aligned, check that the bonnet fastens and releases in a satisfactory manner. If adjustment is necessary, slacken the bonnet lock retaining bolts, and adjust the position of the lock to suit. Once the lock is operating correctly, securely tighten its retaining bolts.

9 Bonnet lock and release cable – removal and refitting

Removal

1 Remove the radiator grille as described in Section 25.
2 Undo the two bolts securing the bonnet lock to the radiator support frame **(see illustration)**. Withdraw the lock and disconnect the release cable.
3 Work along the length of the cable in the engine compartment, note their fitted locations, and release the cable retaining clips.
4 Use a screwdriver to push the cable

bulkhead grommet into the passenger compartment.
5 Working under the facia on the right- or left-hand side (according to model), unscrew the release lever retaining bolt, and withdraw the lever assembly from its location **(see illustration)**.
6 Tie a length of string to the end of the cable in the engine compartment, note its routing, then carefully pull the cable through into the passenger compartment. Untie the string from the end of the cable, and leave it in position to aid refitting.

Refitting

7 Locate the cable in position in the passenger compartment.
8 Tie the end of the new cable to the string, and pull it through into the engine compartment.
9 Check that the bulkhead grommet is securely seated, then remove the string and connect the cable to the bonnet lock lever.
10 Secure the release lever in place, tightening its retaining bolt securely.
11 Reconnect the cable to the bonnet lock then refit the lock, tightening its retaining bolts securely.
12 Secure the cable in place with its retaining clips. Check the operation of the lock and, if necessary, adjust the position of the lock within the elongated bolt holes to achieve satisfactory operation prior to closing the bonnet.
13 Refit the radiator grille as described in Section 25 on completion.

10.9a Undo the retaining bolt . . .

10.9b . . . and remove the side door lower carriage end stop from the rear end of the lower guide rail

10.20 Release the tailgate wiring harness grommet, then withdraw the harness from the door

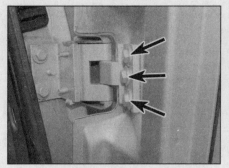

10.21a Undo the three upper bolts (arrowed) . . .

10.21b . . . and three lower bolts (arrowed) securing the hinges to the rear door

rails and carefully remove the door from the vehicle.

Refitting

12 Refitting is a reversal of removal, tightening the retaining bolts to the specified torque.

Hinged rear door

Note: *The following procedure is based on the equipment fitted to high-specification models. Some of the components listed may not be fitted to lower specification models.*

Removal

13 Disconnect the battery negative terminal (refer to *Disconnecting the battery* in the Reference Chapter).
14 Remove the rear door inner trim panel as described in Section 28.
15 Disengage the door check strap from the bracket on the body.

16 Disconnect the washer hose from the rear window wiper motor, and release the hose from its retaining clips.
17 Disconnect the wiring connectors from the following components with reference to the relevant Sections of this Chapter, and Chapter 12:
   a) *Rear window wiper motor.*
   b) *Door lock motor.*
   c) *Rear window demister elements.*
   d) *High-level stop-light.*
   e) *Number plate lights.*
18 Release the wiring harness retaining clips from the door panel.
19 Check that all wiring connectors have been disconnected, then tie a length of string to the high-level stop-light wiring connector. The string can be used to draw the wiring back up through the door when the harness is refitted.

20 Release the wiring harness grommet, then withdraw the harness from the door (**see illustration**). When the string appears, untie it from the wiring connector and leave it in position in the door.
21 With the help of an assistant to support the door, undo the three upper bolts and three lower bolts securing the hinges to the door (**see illustrations**). Carefully lift the door from the vehicle.

Refitting

22 Refitting is a reversal of removal, ensuring all wiring connectors are securely reconnected.

11 Door inner trim panel – removal and refitting

Front door

Removal

1 On models with manual windows, pull the winder handle off the spindle (**see illustration**).
2 Using a small screwdriver, carefully prise off the base of the door pull handle trim. Lift the handle trim off the upper locating lug and remove it from the handle (**see illustrations**).
3 Undo the two retaining screws in the centre of the door pull handle.
4 Carefully prise up the interior door handle surround and disengage it from the handle (**see illustrations**).

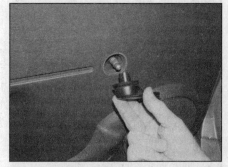

11.1 On models with manual windows, pull the winder handle off the spindle

11.2a Carefully prise off the base of the door pull handle trim . . .

11.2b . . . lift the handle trim off the upper locating lug and remove it from the handle

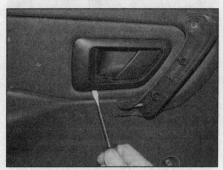

11.4a Carefully prise up the interior door handle surround . . .

11.4b . . . and disengage it from the handle

11.7 Pull the trim panel outwards, lift it up and remove it from the door

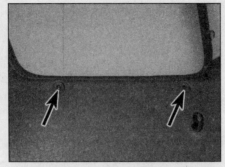

11.10 Undo the screws (arrowed) securing the top of the trim panel to the sliding side door

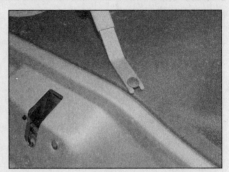

11.11 Work around the edge of the sliding side door trim panel, and release the stud fasteners

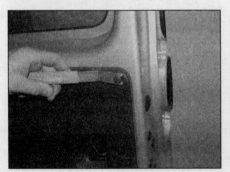

11.14 Work around the edge of the rear door trim panel and release the stud fasteners

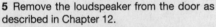

12.2 Slide the front door interior handle assembly towards the front of the door to disengage the locating lug (arrowed)

5 Remove the loudspeaker from the door as described in Chapter 12.

6 Using a suitable forked tool, work around the edge of the trim panel, and release the securing clips.

7 Pull the panel outwards, lift it up and remove it from the door (see illustration).

Refitting

8 Before refitting, check whether any of the trim panel retaining studs were broken on removal. Renew the panel retaining studs as necessary, then refit the panel using a reversal of removal.

Sliding side door

Removal

9 Remove the sliding side door as described in Section 10.

10 Undo the two screws securing the top of the panel to the door (see illustration).

11 Using a suitable forked tool, work around the edge of the trim panel, and release the stud fasteners (see illustration).

12 Remove the panel from the door.

Refitting

13 Refitting is a reversal of removal.

Hinged rear door

Removal

14 Using a suitable forked tool, work around the edge of the trim panel, and release the stud fasteners (see illustration).

15 Remove the panel from the door.

Refitting

16 Refitting is a reversal of removal.

---

12 Front door handle and lock components – removal and refitting

---

Interior door handle

Removal

1 Remove the door inner trim panel, as described in Section 11.

2 Slide the handle assembly towards the front of the door to disengage the locating lug,

12.4 Drill off the rivet heads (arrowed) and withdraw the front door exterior handle from the door

ease it away from the door and disconnect the link rod (see illustration).

Refitting

3 Refitting is a reversal of removal. Refit the inner trim panel as described in Section 11.

Exterior door handle

Note: *The exterior handle is riveted to the door. Ensure that new rivets of the correct size are available for refitting.*

Removal

4 Using a 6.0 mm drill, drill off the rivet heads from the outside and withdraw the handle from the door (see illustration). Disconnect the link rod and remove the handle.

Refitting

5 Refitting is a reversal of removal, using new pop rivets to secure the handle.

Lock cylinder

Note: *A new door sealing sheet may be required on refitting.*

Removal

6 Remove the door inner trim panel, as described in Section 11.

7 Using a sharp knife, carefully release the plastic sealing sheet from the adhesive bead and remove the sheet from the door. If care is taken, it may just be possible to remove the sheet in one piece and re-use it when refitting (see illustration).

8 Working inside the door, disconnect the lock cylinder link rod from the door lock.

12.7 Using a sharp knife, carefully release the plastic sealing sheet from the adhesive bead

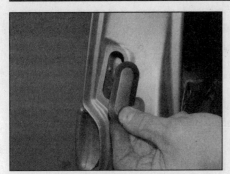

12.9 Carefully prise out the plastic aperture cover from the rear edge of the door

12.10a The lock cylinder retaining clip has a hole (arrowed) in its side to allow a threaded removal tool to be screwed into it

12.10b Using a suitable removable tool, extract the retaining clip from the lock cylinder

9 Using a screwdriver, carefully prise out the plastic aperture cover from the rear edge of the door **(see illustration)**. Note that the cover is made of extremely brittle plastic and is likely to be damaged during removal.

10 Working through the aperture in the edge of the door, extract the large horseshoe-shaped retaining clip from the rear of the lock cylinder. The retaining clip has a hole in its side to allow a threaded removal tool to be screwed into it. A suitable tool can be made from a length of rod with a self-tapping screw brazed to one end **(see illustrations)**.

11 With the retaining clip removed, withdraw the lock cylinder from outside the door **(see illustration)**.

Refitting

12 Refitting is a reversal of removal, but ensure that the lock cylinder retaining clip is securely refitted. Fit a new sealing sheet to the door if the original was damaged in any way during removal. On completion, refit the door inner trim panel as described in Section 11.

Door lock

Note: *A new door sealing sheet may be required on refitting.*

Removal

13 Remove the door inner trim panel, as described in Section 11.

14 Using a sharp knife, carefully release the plastic sealing sheet from the adhesive bead and remove the sheet from the door. If care is taken, it may just be possible to remove the sheet in one piece and re-use it when refitting **(see illustration 12.7)**.

15 Working inside the door, disconnect the link rods from the door lock.

16 Disconnect the wiring connector from the door lock motor.

17 Undo the three screws securing the lock assembly to the edge of the door.

18 Undo the bellcrank retaining screw located above the three door lock screws.

19 Remove the door lock assembly, complete with bellcrank out through the door aperture **(see illustration)**.

Refitting

20 Refitting is a reversal of removal. Fit a new sealing sheet to the door if the original

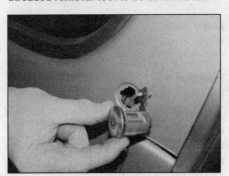

12.11 Withdraw the lock cylinder from outside the door

was damaged in any way during removal. On completion, refit the door inner trim panel as described in Section 11.

13 Sliding side door handle and lock components – removal and refitting

Note: *The sliding side door must be removed from the vehicle for all the following operations (see Section 10).*

Interior door handle

Removal

1 Remove the door inner trim panel, as described in Section 11.

2 Undo the upper and lower interior door handle retaining screws, noting that the

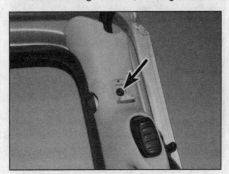

13.2a Undo the upper (arrowed) . . .

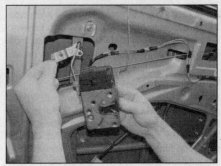

12.19 Remove the door lock assembly, complete with bellcrank out through the door aperture

upper screw is located under a trim cap **(see illustrations)**.

3 Disconnect the operating link rod from the bellcrank and remove the interior handle from the door.

Refitting

4 Refitting is a reversal of removal. On completion, refit the door inner trim panel as described in Section 11.

Exterior door handle

Removal

5 Remove the door inner trim panel, as described in Section 11.

6 Disconnect the two exterior door handle link rods from their respective levers on the lock control unit, noting their fitted positions **(see illustration)**.

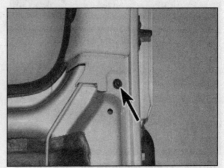

13.2b . . . and lower (arrowed) interior door handle retaining screws

13.6 Disconnect the exterior door handle link rods (arrowed) from their respective levers on the lock control unit

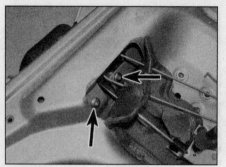

13.7a Peel back the foam sealing panel and undo the two exterior door handle retaining screws (arrowed) . . .

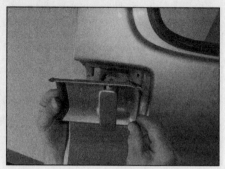

13.7b . . . then remove the handle and link rods from outside the door

7 Peel back the foam sealing panel and undo the two exterior door handle retaining screws. Remove the handle and link rods from outside the door **(see illustrations)**.

Refitting

8 Refitting is a reversal of removal. When connecting the link rod with the adjustable threaded end, engage it in the clips on the lock control unit lever and check for correct operation of the lock mechanism. If necessary, reposition the link rod in the lock control unit lever to achieve satisfactory operation. On completion, relocate the foam sealing panel in position and refit the door inner trim panel as described in Section 11.

Door lock

Note: *A new foam sealing panel may be required on refitting.*

Removal

9 Remove the door inner trim panel, as described in Section 11.

10 Using a sharp knife, carefully release the foam sealing panel adjacent to the door lock, from the adhesive bead and remove the foam panel from the door. If care is taken, it may just be possible to remove the panel in one piece and re-use it when refitting.

11 Disconnect the door lock link rod from the lever on the lock control unit, noting its fitted position **(see illustration)**.

12 Undo the three retaining screws and withdraw the lock and link rod from the door **(see illustrations)**.

Refitting

13 Refitting is a reversal of removal. Fit a new foam sealing panel to the door if the original was damaged in any way during removal. On completion, refit the door inner trim panel as described in Section 11.

Door open holding latch

Removal

14 Undo the three retaining screws and withdraw the latch from the door **(see illustration)**.

15 Slacken the screw securing the operating cable clamp plate to the door and slide the cable out of the clamp. Disconnect the cable end from the operating lever and remove the latch from the door **(see illustration)**.

Refitting

16 Refitting is a reversal of removal, but adjust the operating cable as follows before tightening the operating cable clamp plate screw.

17 Align the adjustment holes in the latch locking lever and mounting bracket and insert a 5.0 mm drill bit through the two holes **(see illustration 13.15)**.

18 Pull the operating cable to take up any slack, then tighten the clamp plate retaining

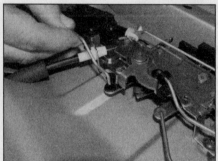

13.11 Disconnect the door lock link rod from the lever on the lock control unit

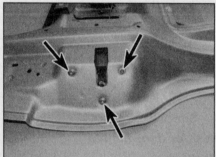

13.12a Undo the three retaining screws (arrowed) . . .

13.12b . . . and withdraw the lock and link rod from the door

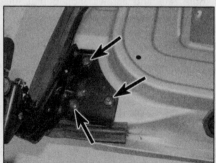

13.14 Undo the three screws (arrowed) and withdraw the door open holding latch from the door

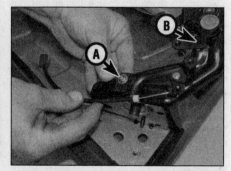

13.15 Slacken the clamp screw (A) and slide the cable out of the clamp. Note the adjustment hole (B) in the latch locking lever

13.20 Release the plastic sealing sheet from the adhesive bead and remove the sheet from the door

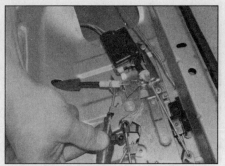

13.21a Release the outer cable sheath from the mounting bracket . . .

13.21b . . . then disconnect the inner cable end fitting from the operating lever

screw. Remove the drill bit and check for correct operation of the latch.

Door open holding latch control cable

Removal

19 Remove the door inner trim panel, as described in Section 11.

20 Using a sharp knife, carefully release the plastic sealing sheet from the adhesive bead and remove the sheet from the door. If care is taken, it may just be possible to remove the sheet in one piece and re-use it when refitting **(see illustration)**.

21 At the upper end of the cable, release the outer cable sheath from the mounting bracket using a small screwdriver. Disconnect the inner cable end fitting from the operating lever **(see illustrations)**.

22 At the lower end of the cable, slacken the screw securing the cable clamp plate to the door and slide the cable out of the clamp. Disconnect the cable end from the operating lever on the latch.

23 Release the rubber grommets and remove the cable from the door.

Refitting

24 Refitting is a reversal of removal, but adjust the cable as described in paragraphs 17 and 18 before tightening the cable clamp plate screw. Fit a new sealing sheet to

the door if the original was damaged in any way during removal. On completion, refit the door inner trim panel as described in Section 11.

Child lock

Removal

25 Remove the exterior door handle as described previously.

26 Working through the exterior door handle aperture, depress the tabs on the side of the child lock using pointed-nose pliers **(see illustration)**.

27 Withdraw the child lock, together with the operating rod, from the outside of the door **(see illustration)**.

Refitting

28 Refitting is a reversal of removal.

Lock control unit

Note: *The lock control unit is riveted to the door. Ensure that new rivets of the correct size are available for refitting.*

Removal

29 Remove the door inner trim panel, as described in Section 11.

30 Remove the child lock as described previously.

31 Disconnect the upper end of the door open holding latch control cable as described in paragraph 21.

32 Note the fitted positions and the correct routing of all the link rods, then disconnect the link rods from the control unit operating levers.

33 Disconnect the wiring connector from the lock control motor **(see illustration)**.

34 Using a 6.0 mm drill, drill off the rivet heads securing the control unit to the door. Undo the remaining retaining screw and remove the unit from the door.

Refitting

35 Refitting is a reversal of removal, ensuring that all link rods are correctly positioned. On completion, refit the door inner trim panel as described in Section 11.

14 Hinged rear door handle and lock components – removal and refitting

Exterior door handle

Note: *The exterior handle is riveted to the door. Ensure that new rivets of the correct size are available for refitting.*

Removal

1 Remove the door inner trim panel, as described in Section 11.

2 Remove the plastic cap from the edge of the door and disconnect the door handle

13.26 Depress the tabs on the side of the child lock using pointed-nose pliers

13.27 Withdraw the child lock, together with the operating rod, from the outside of the door

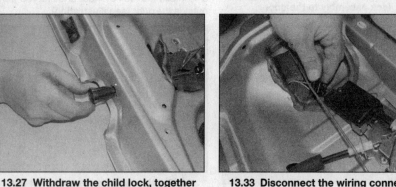

13.33 Disconnect the wiring connector from the lock control motor

14.2a Remove the plastic cap from the edge of the door . . .

14.2b . . . and disconnect the door handle operating rod from the door lock lever

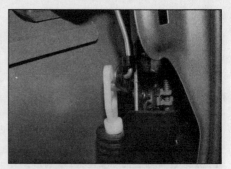

14.6 Disconnect the lock cylinder link rod from the door lock motor

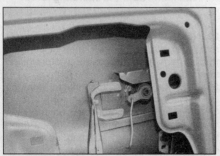

14.7 Extract the large horseshoe-shaped retaining clip from the rear of the lock cylinder

14.8 Remove the lock cylinder and link rod from outside the door

14.11 Disconnect the wiring connector from the door lock motor

operating rod from the door lock lever **(see illustrations)**.

3 Using a 6.0 mm drill, drill off the rivet heads from the outside and remove the handle from the door.

Refitting

4 Refitting is a reversal of removal. Before refitting the inner trim panel, check the operation of the handle mechanism. If necessary adjust by repositioning the operating rod on the door lock lever. On completion, refit the inner trim panel as described in Section 11.

Lock cylinder

Removal

5 Remove the door inner trim panel, as described in Section 11.

6 Working inside the door, disconnect the lock cylinder link rod from the door lock motor **(see illustration)**.

7 Using pliers, extract the large horseshoe-shaped retaining clip from the rear of the lock cylinder **(see illustration)**.

8 Remove the lock cylinder and link rod from outside the door **(see illustration)**.

Refitting

9 Refitting is a reversal of removal. On completion, refit the door inner trim panel as described in Section 11.

Door lock

Removal

10 Remove the door inner trim panel, as described in Section 11.

11 Disconnect the wiring connector from the door lock motor **(see illustration)**.

12 Undo the four bolts securing the lock assembly to the door **(see illustration)**.

13 Manoeuvre the lock from its location and recover the spacer plate **(see illustration)**.

14 Disconnect the lock cylinder link rod from the door lock lever.

15 Note the fitted position of the threaded ends of the upper and lower door latch operating cables. Disconnect the cables from the door lock levers and remove the lock assembly from the door **(see illustrations)**.

14.12 Undo the four bolts securing the lock assembly to the door

14.13 Manoeuvre the lock from its location and recover the spacer plate

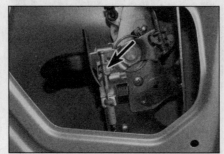

14.15a Note the fitted position of the threaded ends (arrowed) of the latch operating cables . . .

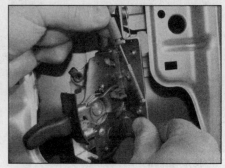

14.15b . . . then disconnect the cables from the door lock levers

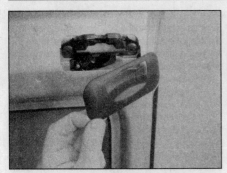

14.18 Carefully prise off the plastic trim from the door latch

14.19 Undo the two door latch retaining screws

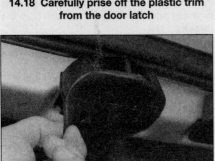

14.22 Ease off the protective rubber cover over the upper striker

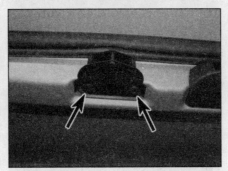

14.23 Striker retaining bolts (arrowed)

the striker should be altered (the securing bolt holes are elongated) until satisfactory lock operation is obtained. Use the marks made prior to removal, if appropriate.

15 Front door window glass and regulator – removal and refitting

Note: *A new door sealing sheet may be required on refitting.*

Window glass

Removal

1 Remove the door inner trim panel, as described in Section 11.
2 Using a sharp knife, carefully release the plastic sealing sheet from the adhesive bead and remove the sheet from the door. If care is taken, it may just be possible to remove the sheet in one piece and re-use it when refitting **(see illustration 12.7)**.
3 Position the window approximately three quarters of the way down.
4 Depress the tab on the window regulator lifting channel, lift the glass slightly and free the glass from the support **(see illustration)**.
5 Lower the glass at the front and remove it from the outside of the door frame **(see illustration)**.

Refitting

6 Refitting is a reversal of removal. Fit a new sealing sheet to the door if the original was damaged in any way during removal. On completion, refit the door inner trim panel as described in Section 11.

Door window regulator

Removal

7 Release the window glass from the regulator lifting channel as described in paragraphs 1 to 4 above.
8 Slide the window glass up to the fully closed position and secure it in this position with masking tape over the top of the door frame.
9 Undo the two lower bolts securing the window glass rear guide channel to the door **(see illustration)**.

Refitting

16 Refitting is a reversal of removal. Before refitting the inner trim panel, check the operation and synchronisation of the upper and lower door latches. If necessary, adjust by repositioning the ends of the operating cables on the door lock levers. On completion, refit the inner trim panel as described in Section 11.

Upper and lower door latches

Removal

17 Remove the door lock as described previously.
18 Carefully prise off the plastic trim from the door latch **(see illustration)**.
19 Undo the two door latch retaining screws and remove the door latch and operating cable from the door **(see illustration)**.

Refitting

20 Refitting is a reversal of removal.

Door lock striker

Removal

21 If working on the lower striker, fold back the floor covering for access to the lock striker cover plate. Undo the three screws and remove the lock striker cover plate from the floor.
22 If working on the upper striker, ease off the protective rubber cover **(see illustration)**.
23 Mark the position of the striker on the body, for use when refitting. Unscrew the two securing bolts, and remove the relevant striker from the body **(see illustration)**.

Refitting

24 Refitting is a reversal of removal. Before tightening the securing bolts, the position of

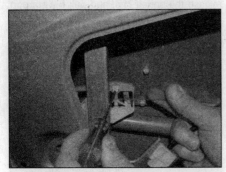

15.4 Depress the tab on the window regulator lifting channel, lift the glass slightly and free the glass from the support

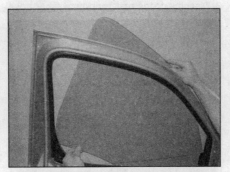

15.5 Lower the glass at the front and remove it from the outside of the door frame

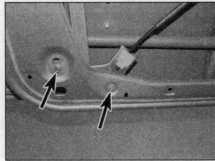

15.9 Undo the two lower bolts (arrowed) securing the window glass rear guide channel to the door

15.10 Undo the upper bolt (arrowed) securing the window glass rear guide channel to the door

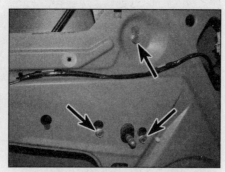

15.11 Slacken the three bolts (arrowed) securing the window regulator to the door

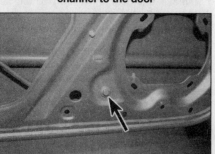

15.12 Undo the lower bolt (arrowed) securing the window regulator to the door

15.14 Remove the regulator assembly out through the door aperture

10 Undo the upper bolt securing the window glass rear guide channel to the door **(see illustration)**.
11 Slacken the three bolts securing the window regulator to the door **(see illustration)**.
12 Undo the lower bolt securing the window regulator to the door **(see illustration)**.
13 On models with electric windows, disconnect the wiring connector from the regulator motor.
14 Lift the regulator assembly upwards slightly to allow the mounting bolts to slip through the elongated bolt holes, then remove the regulator assembly out through the door aperture **(see illustration)**.

Refitting

15 Refitting is a reversal of removal. Fit a new sealing sheet to the door if the original was damaged in any way during removal. On completion, refit the door inner trim panel as described in Section 11.

16 Tailgate and support struts – removal and refitting

Tailgate

Note: *New tailgate aperture sealing sheets may be required on refitting.*

Removal

1 Remove the tailgate trim panel as described in Section 28.
2 Using a sharp knife, carefully release the plastic sealing sheets from the adhesive beads and remove the sheets from the tailgate. If care is taken, it may just be possible to remove the sheets in one piece and re-use them when refitting **(see illustration)**.
3 Disconnect the rear window washer hose

from the wiper motor, and release the hose from its retaining clips.
4 Disconnect the wiring connectors from the following components with reference to the relevant Sections of this Chapter, and Chapter 12:
   a) *Rear window wiper motor.*
   b) *Tailgate lock motor.*
   c) *Rear window demister elements.*
   d) *High-level stop-light.*
   e) *Number plate lights.*
5 Release the wiring harness retaining clips from the tailgate.
6 Check that all wiring connectors have been disconnected, then release the wiring harness grommet and withdraw the harness from the tailgate.
7 Undo the two screws and remove the hinge cover plates each side, from the tailgate **(see illustration)**.
8 With the aid of an assistant, suitably support the tailgate, then prise out the support strut spring clips, and pull the struts from the balljoints on the body.
9 Unscrew the tailgate hinge pin on each side and carefully lift the tailgate from the vehicle **(see illustration)**.

Refitting

10 If a new tailgate is to be fitted, transfer all serviceable components (lock mechanism, wiper motor, etc) to it, with reference to the relevant procedures in this Chapter, and in Chapter 12.
11 Refitting is a reversal of removal, bearing in mind the following points:
   a) *Fit new sealing sheets to the tailgate if the original sheets were damaged in any way during removal.*
   b) *If necessary, adjust the rubber buffers to obtain a good fit when the tailgate is shut.*
   c) *If necessary, adjust the position of the tailgate lock striker to achieve satisfactory lock operation.*
   d) *On completion, refit the tailgate trim panel as described in Section 28.*

Support struts

Removal

12 Support the tailgate in the open position, with the help of an assistant, or using a stout piece of wood.
13 Using a suitable flat-bladed screwdriver, release the spring clip, and pull the support

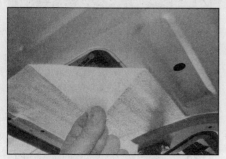

16.2 Carefully release the plastic sealing sheets from the adhesive beads and remove the sheets from the tailgate

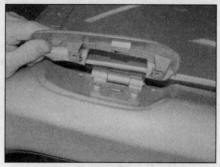

16.7 Undo the two screws and remove the hinge cover plates from the tailgate

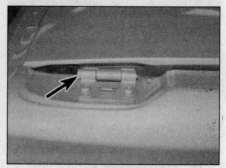

16.9 Unscrew the tailgate hinge pin (arrowed) on each side

16.13 Release the spring clip, and pull the support strut from its balljoint on the body

17.3 Disconnect the link rod from the tailgate lock cylinder and tailgate lock lever

17.4a Undo the nut (arrowed) securing the lock cylinder to the exterior handle . . .

strut from its balljoint on the body **(see illustration)**.

14 Similarly, release the strut from the balljoint on the tailgate, and withdraw the strut from the vehicle.

Refitting

15 Refitting is a reversal of removal, but ensure the spring clips are correctly engaged.

17 Tailgate lock components – removal and refitting

Tailgate lock

Note: *A new tailgate aperture sealing sheet may be required on refitting.*

Removal

1 Remove the tailgate trim panel as described in Section 28.
2 Using a sharp knife, carefully release the centre plastic sealing sheet from the adhesive bead and remove the sheet from the tailgate. If care is taken, it may just be possible to remove the sheet in one piece and re-use it when refitting.
3 Disconnect the link rod from the tailgate lock cylinder and tailgate lock lever **(see illustration)**.
4 Undo the nut securing the lock cylinder to the exterior handle and remove the lock cylinder through the tailgate aperture **(see illustrations)**.
5 Undo the remaining retaining nut securing

the exterior handle to the tailgate. Disengage the operating rod from the tailgate lock and remove the exterior handle from the tailgate **(see illustrations)**.
6 Undo the two screws and withdraw the latch unit from the tailgate. As the latch is

17.4b . . . and remove the lock cylinder through the tailgate aperture

17.5b . . . then disengage the operating rod and remove the exterior handle from the tailgate

withdrawn, disconnect the link rod from the latch lever **(see illustrations)**.
7 Undo the three tailgate lock retaining screws. Withdraw the lock through the tailgate aperture and disconnect the wiring connector **(see illustrations)**.

17.5a Undo the remaining retaining nut (arrowed) . . .

17.6a Undo the two screws (arrowed) . . .

17.6b . . . and withdraw the latch unit from the tailgate

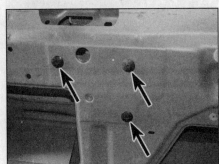

17.7a Undo the three tailgate lock retaining screws (arrowed) . . .

17.7b . . . then withdraw the lock through the tailgate aperture and disconnect the wiring connector

17.10 Undo the three screws and remove the lock striker cover plate from the floor

17.11 Unscrew the two securing bolts (arrowed) and remove the striker from the body

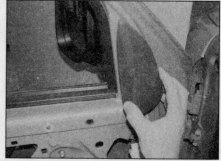

19.2 Carefully prise off the mirror trim panel

Refitting

8 Refitting is a reversal of removal. Fit a new sealing sheet to the tailgate if the original was damaged in any way during removal. If necessary, adjust the position of the tailgate lock striker to achieve satisfactory lock operation. On completion, refit the tailgate trim panel as described in Section 28.

Tailgate lock striker

Removal

9 Fold back the floor covering for access to the lock striker cover plate.
10 Undo the three screws and remove the lock striker cover plate from the floor **(see illustration)**.
11 Mark the position of the striker on the body, for use when refitting. Unscrew the two securing bolts, and remove the striker from the body **(see illustration)**.

Refitting

12 Refitting is a reversal of removal. Before tightening the securing bolts, the position of the striker should be altered (the securing bolt holes are elongated) until satisfactory lock operation is obtained. Use the marks made prior to removal, if appropriate.

18 Central locking components – removal and refitting

Control unit

1 On early models, the central locking system is controlled by an electronic control unit, located in the sill panel to the rear of the front door, on the driver's side.
2 On later models, the central locking system is controlled by the Built-in Systems Interface (BSI) which is the vehicle central computer controlling the main body electrical system functions. The unit is located under the facia on the left-hand side. Refer to Chapter 12 for further information.
3 Should any problems be experienced with

the operation of the central locking system or any of the other functions controlled by the BSI, the vehicle should be taken to a Peugeot/Citroën dealer for diagnostic investigation.

Front door lock motor

4 The motor is integral with the door lock assembly. Removal and refitting of the lock assembly is described in Section 12.

Sliding side door lock motor

5 The motor is integral with the door lock assembly. Removal and refitting of the lock assembly is described in Section 13.

Hinged rear door lock motor

6 The motor is integral with the door lock assembly. Removal and refitting of the lock assembly is described in Section 14.

Tailgate lock motor

7 The motor is integral with the door lock assembly. Removal and refitting of the lock assembly is described in Section 17.

Remote control transmitter

Battery renewal

8 The battery should be renewed with a type CR 2016 (3 volt) battery.
9 Using a small screwdriver, undo the screw, carefully prise the two halves of the transmitter apart, and remove the battery.
10 Fit the new battery and reassemble the transmitter.

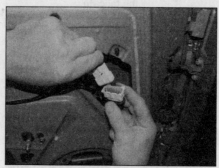

19.3 Disconnect the mirror wiring connector

Initialisation

11 To initialise the unit after renewing the battery, switch off the ignition, then switch on the ignition and immediately press the locking button. Switch off the ignition and remove the key from the ignition lock.

19 Exterior mirrors and mirror glass – removal and refitting

Exterior mirror assembly

Removal

1 Ensure the ignition is turned off.
2 Remove the door inner trim panel as described in Section 11, then carefully prise off the mirror trim panel **(see illustration)**.
3 Disconnect the mirror wiring connector **(see illustration)**.
4 Undo the three retaining screws and remove the mirror from the door frame **(see illustration)**.

Refitting

5 Refitting is a reversal of removal.

Exterior mirror glass

Removal

6 Tilt the glass downward then reach behind and pull the top of the glass away from the

19.4 Undo the three retaining screws (arrowed) and remove the mirror from the door frame

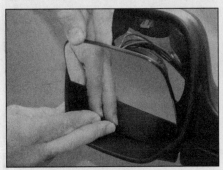

19.6 Tilt the mirror glass downward then reach behind and pull the top of the glass away from the adjuster plate

adjuster plate to release the retaining clips **(see illustration)**.

7 Withdraw the glass, and disconnect the wiring connector, if fitted **(see illustration)**.

Refitting

8 Where applicable, reconnect the wiring connectors, then push the mirror glass into the mirror until it locks into position.

20 Windscreen, tailgate and rear door window glass – general information

These areas of glass are secured by the tight fit of the weatherstrip in the body aperture, and are bonded in position with a special adhesive. Renewal of such fixed glass is a difficult, messy and time-consuming task,

21.1 Undo the three screws securing the side window glass closing catch to the body

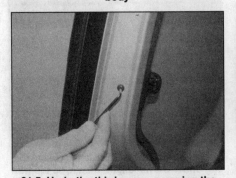

21.5 Undo the third screw, securing the catch to the outer edge of the door frame

19.7 Withdraw the mirror glass, and disconnect the wiring connector

which is considered beyond the scope of the home mechanic. It is difficult, unless one has plenty of practice, to obtain a secure, waterproof fit. Furthermore, the task carries a high risk of breakage; this applies especially to the laminated glass windscreen. In view of this, owners are strongly advised to have this sort of work carried out by one of the many specialist windscreen fitters.

21 Opening side and door window glass – removal and refitting

Side window glass

Removal

1 Undo the three screws securing the window glass closing catch to the body **(see illustration)**.

21.2 Undo the screws (arrowed) securing the window glass hinges to the body

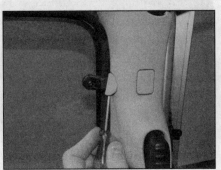

21.6a Lift up the trim caps . . .

2 Support the glass, then undo the upper and lower screws securing the window glass hinges to the body **(see illustrations)**. Lift the glass from its location.

Refitting

3 Refitting is a reversal of removal.

Side door glass

Removal

4 Undo the two screws securing the window glass closing catch to the door **(see illustration)**.

5 Open the door and undo the third screw, securing the catch to the outer edge of the door frame **(see illustration)**.

6 Support the glass, then lift up the trim caps and undo the upper and lower screws securing the window glass hinges to the door **(see illustrations)**. Lift the glass off the door.

Refitting

7 Refitting is a reversal of removal.

22 Sunroof – general information

The factory-fitted sunroof is of the electric tilt/slide type.

Due to the complexity of the sunroof mechanism, considerable expertise is required to repair, renew or adjust the sunroof components successfully. Removal of the roof first requires the headlining to be removed,

21.4 Undo the two screws (arrowed) securing the side door glass closing catch to the door

21.6b . . . and undo the screws (arrowed) securing the window glass hinges to the door

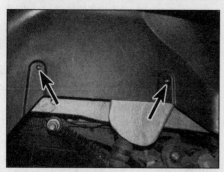

23.5 Undo the two nuts (arrowed) securing the rear wheel arch liner to the body

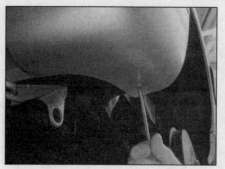

23.6a Undo the screw securing the liner to the rear bumper . . .

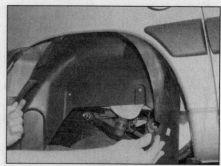

23.6b . . . and remove the liner from under the wheel arch

which is a tedious operation, and not a task to be undertaken lightly. Any problems with the sunroof should be referred to a Peugeot/Citroën dealer.

23 Body exterior fittings – removal and refitting

Wheel arch liners

Front

1 Firmly apply the handbrake, then jack up the front of the car and support it securely on axle stands (see *Jacking and vehicle support*). Remove the relevant front roadwheel.
2 The wheel arch liners are secured by a combination of screws, and push-fit clips. The screws attach the liner to the underside of the front bumper (and on some models, to the front wing).
3 The push-fit clips can be released using a forked-shaped tool, although, in some instances extreme force will be needed.

Rear

4 Chock the front wheels then jack up the rear of the car and securely support it on axle stands (see *Jacking and vehicle support*). Remove the relevant rear roadwheel.
5 Undo the two nuts securing the liner to the body (see illustration).
6 Undo the screw securing the liner to the

rear bumper and remove the liner from under the wheel arch (see illustrations).

Body trim strips and badges

7 The various body trim strips and badges are held in position with a special adhesive membrane. Removal requires the trim/badge to be heated, to soften the adhesive, and then cut away from the surface. Due to the high risk of damage to the vehicle paintwork during this operation, it is recommended that this task should be entrusted to a Peugeot/Citroën dealer.

24 Scuttle grille panel – emoval and refitting

Removal

Pre-September 2002 models

1 Open and support the bonnet.
2 Remove the windscreen wiper arms as described in Chapter 12.
3 Undo the retaining screw securing the right-hand side scuttle panel in position.
4 Using a suitable forked tool, release the securing clip at the right-hand end of the panel.
5 Release the fasteners on the right-hand side grille panel by turning them through 90°, then lift off the right-hand panel.
6 Remove the left-hand panel in a similar fashion.

Post-September 2002 models

7 Open and support the bonnet.
8 Remove the windscreen wiper arms as described in Chapter 12.
9 Undo the retaining screw securing the corner of the panel to the front wing.
10 Release the fasteners on the right-hand side grille panel by turning them through 180°, then lift off the right-hand panel (see illustration).
11 Remove the left-hand panel in a similar fashion (see illustration).

Refitting

12 Refitting is a reversal of removal.

25 Radiator grille – removal and refitting

Removal

Pre-September 2002 models

1 Open and support the bonnet.
2 Remove the direction indicator light units as described in Chapter 12.
3 Release the outer retaining clip securing plastic trim under the direction indictor light unit locations on each side.
4 Pull the trim outwards to release the lug under the headlight, then slide the trim away from the centre of the car to remove (see illustration).

24.10 Release the fasteners on the right-hand side scuttle grille panel, then lift off the right-hand panel

24.11 Remove the left-hand scuttle grille panel in a similar fashion

25.4 Pull the trim outwards to release the lug under the headlight, then slide the trim away from the centre of the car to remove – early models

25.5 Undo the two retaining screws (arrowed) each side – early models

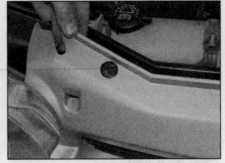

25.6a Lift the grille over the bonnet height adjuster buffers . . .

25.6b . . . and pull it sharply forward to release the central locating tangs (arrowed) – early models

5 Undo the two retaining screws each side (**see illustration**).

6 Lift the grille over the bonnet height adjuster buffers and pull it sharply forward to release the central locating tangs (**see illustrations**). Remove the grille from the car.

Post-September 2002 models

7 Undo the four screws along the top edge, securing the grille in position (**see illustration**).

8 Lift the grille upwards to disengage the centre locating lug and the pegs on each side (**see illustrations**). Remove the grille from the car.

Refitting

9 Refitting is a reversal of removal.

26 Seats – removal and refitting

Front seats

⚠️ *Warning: Depending on model, the front seats may be equipped with seat belt pretensioners, and side airbags may be built into the outer sides of the seats. Where side airbags are fitted, refer to Chapter 12 for the precautions which should be observed when dealing with an airbag system. Do not tamper with the seat belt pretensioner unit in any way, and do not attempt to test the*

unit. Note that the unit is triggered if the mechanism is supplied with an electrical current (including via an ohmmeter), or if the assembly is subjected to a temperature of greater than 100°C.

1 On models with seat belt pretensioners, observe the following precautions before attempting to remove the seat:
   a) *Remove the ignition key.*
   b) *Disconnect the battery negative terminal (refer to 'Disconnecting the battery' in the Reference Chapter), and wait for two minutes before carrying out any further work.*

Removal

2 Where applicable, de-activate the airbag system (see Chapter 12) before attempting to remove the seat.

3 On later models, carefully prise off the plastic panels for access to the seat belt mountings.

4 Move the seat fully forwards.

5 Remove the bolts (one on each side) securing the rear of the seat rails to the vehicle floor.

6 Move the seat fully rearwards.

7 Remove the bolts (one bolt on each side) securing the front of the seat frame to the floor. Note that on some models, the outer bolt may be located under a trim cover.

8 Tip the seat backwards and disconnect the seat wiring connectors. Release the wiring harness from the retaining clips on the seat then remove the seat from the passenger compartment.

Refitting

9 Refitting is a reversal of removal. Where applicable, reactivate the airbag system as described in Chapter 12, before reconnecting the battery.

Rear seats

10 Lift off the trim caps (where fitted) then undo the mounting bolts at the front of the seat cushion.

11 Press the seat back release control and tip the seat back forward to release the floor catches.

12 Pull and tilt the seat towards the front then remove it from the car.

13 With the seat removed, undo the lower pivot bolts and separate the seat back from the cushion.

Refitting

14 Refitting is a reversal of removal.

27 Seat belt components – removal and refitting

Note: *Record the positions of the washers and spacers on the seat belt anchors, and ensure they are refitted in their original positions.*

Front seat belt

Removal

1 On models with a sliding side door, remove

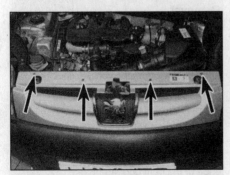

25.7 Undo the four screws (arrowed) along the top edge of the grille

25.8a Lift the grille upwards to disengage the centre locating lug (arrowed) . . .

25.8b . . . and the pegs on each side (arrowed)

the centre pillar trim panels as described in Section 28. On models without a sliding side door, remove the side trim panel as described in Section 28.

2 Prise off the trim cap, then undo the lower belt anchor bolt, and recover the washer.

3 Undo the inertia reel mounting bolt.

4 Using a 3.5 mm drill bit, drill out the pop rivet securing the belt guide to the centre pillar.

5 Withdraw the inertia reel from the door pillar, then withdraw the seat belt assembly from the vehicle.

Refitting

6 Refitting is a reversal of removal, using a new pop rivet to secure the seat belt guide. Ensure that all washers and/or spacers are positioned as noted before removal, and tighten all mounting bolts to the specified torque.

Front seat belt stalk – models without seat belt pretensioners

Removal

7 Remove the securing screws or release the clips, as applicable, and remove the trim panel from the side of the seat.

8 Each stalk is secured to the front seat frame by a bolt and washer.

Refitting

9 Tighten the securing bolt to the specified torque.

Front seat belt stalk – models with seat belt pretensioners

Warning: On models with seat belt pretensioners, observe the following precautions before attempting to remove the seat belt stalk assembly:
a) Remove the ignition key.
b) Disconnect the battery negative terminal (refer to 'Disconnecting the battery' in the Reference Chapter), and wait for two minutes before carrying out any further work.

Warning: Do not tamper with the pretensioner unit in any way, and do not attempt to test the unit. Note that the unit is triggered if the mechanism is supplied with an electrical current (including via an ohmmeter), or if the assembly is subjected to a temperature of greater than 100°C.

Removal

10 The seat belt stalk is an integral part of the seat belt pretensioner mechanism.

11 Remove the front seat as described in Section 26.

12 Undo the securing bolt and remove the clamp from the pretensioner body.

13 Disconnect the pretensioner wiring connector from the tensioner unit.

14 Undo the pretensioner securing bolt and withdraw the pretensioner and seat belt stalk assembly from the seat.

Warning: Do not hold the tensioner by the buckle or by the cable – only hold the unit around the tensioner body.

Refitting

15 Refitting is a reversal of removal, but observe the following precautions:
a) *Before refitting, ensure that the battery negative terminal is disconnected, and that the ignition is switched off.*
b) *Do not touch the seat belt buckle when the ignition is first switched on.*

Rear seat belt

Removal

16 Remove the luggage compartment side trim panel as described in Section 28.

17 Unclip the trim plate, then unbolt the upper seat belt anchor bolt.

18 Undo the anchor bolt securing the seat belt inertia reel to the vehicle body and remove the reel and seat belt from the car.

19 To remove the seat belt buckles, fold forward the rear seats forward and undo the bolt securing the buckles to the rear seat mounting.

20 To remove the centre seat belt inertia reel, the seat must be partially dismantled. This work should be entrusted to a Peugeot/Citroën dealer.

Refitting

21 Refitting is a reversal of removal. Tighten the seat belt mounting bolts to the specified torque.

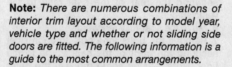

28 Interior trim – removal and refitting

Note: There are numerous combinations of interior trim layout according to model year, vehicle type and whether or not sliding side doors are fitted. The following information is a guide to the most common arrangements.

Door inner trim panel

1 Refer to Section 11.

Front pillar trim panel

Removal

2 Prise the weatherstrip from the front door aperture in the vicinity of the door pillar.

3 Starting at the top, carefully pull the trim away from the pillar to release the internal retaining lugs.

4 Lift the trim up to disengage it from the side of the facia and remove it from the vehicle.

Refitting

5 Refitting is a reversal of removal, but ensure that all retaining clips are fully engaged and that the weatherstrip is fully seated.

Centre pillar upper trim panel

Removal

6 Open the front door and, where applicable,

the sliding side door, and prise the weatherstrips from the centre pillar.

7 Unclip the trim plate, then unbolt the upper seat belt anchor bolt.

8 Undo the screw securing the lower edge of the upper trim panel to the door pillar.

9 Pull the upper panel from the pillar to release the securing clips, disengage it from the lower panel and remove it from the car.

Refitting

10 Refitting is a reversal of removal. Tighten the seat belt anchor bolt to the specified torque.

Centre pillar lower trim panel – models with a sliding side door

Removal

11 Remove the centre pillar upper trim panel as described previously.

12 Remove the trim cap, then unscrew the front seat belt lower anchor bolt.

13 Undo the retaining screw and carefully lift the rear edge of the front sill trim upwards.

14 Carefully prise the lower trim panel away from the pillar, to release the internal clips, then disengage the seat belt and remove the trim panel.

Refitting

15 Refitting is a reversal of removal. Tighten the seat belt anchor bolt to the specified torque.

Side trim panel – models without a sliding side door

Removal

16 Remove the centre pillar upper trim panel as described previously.

17 Undo the four retaining screws and remove the lower section of the panel.

18 Using a small screwdriver, carefully prise off the outer part of the grab handle. Undo the two retaining bolts and disengage the inner part of the handle from the body.

19 Undo the remaining retaining screws and carefully prise the trim panel away from the body, to release the internal clips.

Refitting

20 Refitting is a reversal of removal.

Sliding side door upper trim panel

Removal

21 Undo the four screws securing the panel to the roof above the sliding side door aperture.

22 Carefully pull the panel from its location and remove it from the vehicle.

Refitting

23 Refitting is a reversal of removal.

Front door sill trim panel

Removal

24 Prise the weatherstrip from the lower edge of the front door aperture.

25 Undo the retaining screw at the rear of the panel.

28.36 Carefully prise the cover(s) off the tailgate grab handle(s)

28.37 Pull the trim panel sharply away from the tailgate to release the internal retaining clips

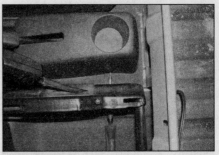

29.2 Undo the screw each side securing the rear console section to the mounting brackets

26 Carefully prise the front door sill trim away from the sill to release its retaining clips and remove it from the vehicle.

Refitting

27 Refitting is a reversal of removal, but ensure that all retaining clips are fully engaged and that the weatherstrip is fully seated.

Luggage compartment side trim panel

Removal

28 Prise the weatherstrip from the load compartment aperture in the vicinity of the side panel.

29 Remove the trim cap, then unscrew the rear seat belt lower mounting bolt.

30 On models with hinged rear doors, undo the bolts and remove the door check strap bracket.

31 Release the seat belt guide trim from the panel and slide the seat belt through the slit in the guide.

32 If removing the right hand-side panel, remove the jack and tool storage access cover from the centre of the panel, then undo the retaining screws around the periphery of the aperture.

33 Working around the panel, undo all the retaining screws and visible attachments.

34 Carefully prise the side panel away from the body, to release the internal clips, then remove the trim panel.

Refitting

35 Refitting is a reversal of removal, but ensure that all retaining clips are fully engaged and that the weatherstrip is fully seated.

Tailgate trim panel

Removal

36 Using a small screwdriver, carefully prise the cover(s) off the tailgate grab handle(s) **(see illustration)**. Undo the two grab handle retaining screws now exposed.

37 Starting at the lower corner, pull the trim panel sharply away from the tailgate to release the internal retaining clips **(see illustration)**. When all the clips have been released, remove the panel.

Refitting

38 Refitting is a reversal of removal, but ensure that all retaining clips are fully engaged.

Headlining

Note: *Headlining removal requires considerable skill and experience if it is to be carried out without damage, and is therefore best entrusted to a Peugeot/Citroën dealer or bodywork specialist. A general overview of the procedure is given below for those with the expertise to attempt the operation on a DIY basis.*

39 The headlining is clipped and glued to the roof, and can be withdrawn only once all fittings such as the grab handles, courtesy lights, sunvisors, sunroof (if fitted), pillar trim panels, and associated additional panels have been removed. The door, tailgate and sunroof aperture weatherstrips will also have to be prised clear and any additional screws and clips removed. Once the headlining attachments are released,

the adhesive bonding in the centre panels must be broken using a hot air gun and spatula, starting at the front and working rearwards.

40 When refitting, a coat of neoprene adhesive (available from Peugeot/Citroën dealers) must be applied to the centre panels in the locations noted during removal. Position the headlining carefully and refit all components disturbed during removal. Clean the headlining with soap and water or white spirit on completion.

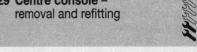

29 Centre console – removal and refitting

Removal

1 Tip up the front seats, or slide the front seats forward as far as possible.

2 Undo the screw each side securing the rear console section to the mounting brackets **(see illustration)**.

3 Undo the two screws, one on each side of the handbrake lever **(see illustration)**.

4 Pull the rear console section rearwards, to disengage the front locating pegs. Lift the console up at the rear, slide it up and over the handbrake lever and remove the rear section from the car **(see illustration)**. Where applicable, disconnect the wiring from the parking aid switch and if necessary remove the switch as described in Chapter 12.

5 Twist and remove the gear lever knob off the gear lever **(see illustration)**.

6 Unclip the gear lever gaiter from the front

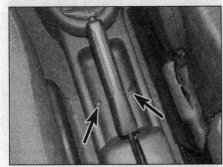

29.3 Undo the two screws (arrowed) on each side of the handbrake lever

29.4 Lift the console up at the rear, slide it up and over the handbrake lever and remove the rear section from the car

29.5 Twist and remove the gear lever knob off the gear lever

29.6 Unclip the gear lever gaiter from the front console and slide it up and off the gear lever

29.7a Undo the two screws (arrowed) at the rear of the console front section . . .

29.7b . . . and the central screw (arrowed) below the heater/ventilation controls

console and slide it up and off the gear lever **(see illustration)**.

7 Undo the two screws at the rear of the console front section, and the central screw below the heater/ventilation controls **(see illustrations)**.

8 Undo the retaining screw and detach the side ventilation panel, on each side, from the centre console and facia **(see illustration)**.

9 Disengage the centre console front section from the facia, and lift it up at the rear to clear the gear lever **(see illustration)**. Disconnect the wiring connectors and remove the console front section from the car.

Refitting

10 Refitting is a reversal of removal.

30 Facia panel components (pre-September 2002 models) – removal and refitting

Steering column shrouds

Removal

1 Undo the four screws securing the lower shroud in position **(see illustration)**.

2 Remove the lower shroud, then lift up and remove the upper shroud from its location **(see illustration)**.

Refitting

3 Refitting is a reversal of removal.

Facia upper panel

Removal

4 Remove the steering column lower and upper shrouds as described previously.

5 Undo the three screws and remove the centre vent unit from the facia **(see illustrations)**.

29.8 Detach the side ventilation panel, on each side, from the centre console and facia

29.9 Disengage the centre console front section from the facia, and lift it up at the rear to clear the gear lever

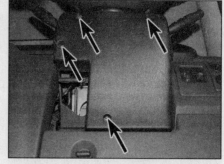

30.1 Undo the four screws (arrowed) securing the steering column lower shroud in position

30.2 Remove the lower shroud, then lift up and remove the upper shroud from its location

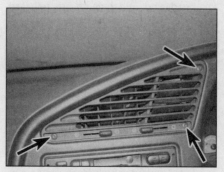

30.5a Undo the three screws (arrowed) . . .

30.5b . . . and remove the centre vent unit from the facia

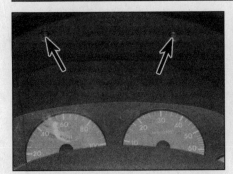

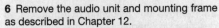

30.7 Undo the two facia upper panel retaining screws above the instrument panel (arrowed)

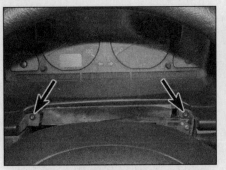

30.8a Undo the upper panel retaining screws below the instrument panel (arrowed) . . .

30.8b . . . and in the audio unit aperture (arrowed)

6 Remove the audio unit and mounting frame as described in Chapter 12.

7 Undo the two facia upper panel retaining screws located above the instrument panel **(see illustration)**.

8 Similarly, undo the upper panel retaining screws located below the instrument panel and in the audio unit aperture **(see illustrations)**.

9 Pull the facia upper panel from its location to release the retaining clips and remove it from the car **(see illustration)**.

Refitting

10 Refitting is a reversal of removal.

Instrument panel

11 Refer to Chapter 12.

Complete facia assembly

Note: *This is an involved operation entailing the removal of numerous components and assemblies, and the disconnection of a multitude of wiring connectors. Make notes of the location of all disconnected wiring, or attach labels to the connectors, to avoid confusion when refitting.*

Removal

12 Disconnect the battery negative terminal (refer to 'Disconnecting the battery' in the Reference Chapter).

13 Remove the scuttle grille panel as described in Section 24.

14 Remove the windscreen wiper motor and linkage as described in Chapter 12.

15 Working in the scuttle aperture, undo the three nuts securing the facia to the bulkhead.

16 Move the front seats as far back as possible. Set the steering wheel in the straight-ahead position, and engage the steering lock.

17 Remove the steering column shrouds and the facia upper panel as described previously in this Section.

18 Remove the centre console as described in Section 29.

19 Remove the steering wheel as described in Chapter 10.

20 Remove the following components as described in Chapter 12:
 a) Instrument panel.
 b) Audio unit.
 c) Passenger's airbag.
 d) Steering column switches.

21 Remove all the facia panel switches as described in Chapter 12.

22 On the passenger's side of the facia, remove the loudspeaker, then undo the bolt in the loudspeaker aperture.

23 Remove the front pillar trim panels as described in Section 28.

24 Undo the two upper retaining screws at each corner of the heater/ventilation control unit.

25 Using a small screwdriver, release the retaining lug at the lower centre of the control unit and withdraw the unit from the facia.

26 Pivot the control unit upwards, as far as clearance will allow, then release the securing

clips and disconnect the control cables from the unit. Note the locations of the cables to ensure correct refitting.

27 Disconnect the wiring plug from the rear of the control unit, then withdraw the unit.

28 Remove the stowage box above the heater ventilation/control unit and undo the four centre panel retaining screws.

29 Remove the ashtray and undo the two screws in the ashtray aperture.

30 Undo the bolt at the base of the facia above the centre console location.

31 Remove the fusebox cover panel and release the fuse/relay box from its facia attachments.

32 Undo the retaining bolt and release the bonnet opening handle from its location.

33 Undo the bolt each side on the outer sides of the facia.

34 Disconnect or release all the remaining facia attachments

35 With the help of an assistant, lift the facia from its location and move it rearward. As soon as sufficient clearance exists, disconnect all the facia wiring connectors, noting their fitted positions. Note the wiring harness routing and release it from the various retaining clips.

36 Check that everything is disconnected and moved clear, then remove the facia from the vehicle.

Refitting

37 Refitting is a reversal of removal ensuring that all wiring is correctly reconnected and all mountings securely tightened.

30.9 Pull the upper panel from its location to release the retaining clips

31.2 Remove the steering column lower shroud, then lift up and remove the upper shroud

31 Facia panel components (post-September 2002 models) – removal and refitting

Steering column shrouds

Removal

1 Undo the three screws securing the lower shroud in position.

2 Remove the lower shroud, then lift up and remove the upper shroud from its location **(see illustration)**.

31.6 Carefully prise the multi-function display surround from the facia

31.7 Carefully prise the centre switch panel from the facia to release the upper retaining clips

31.9 Undo the two screws (arrowed) above the audio unit aperture

Refitting

3 Refitting is a reversal of removal.

Instrument panel

4 Refer to Chapter 12.

Multi-function display

5 Refer to Chapter 12.

Facia centre panels

Removal

6 Carefully prise the multi-function display surround from the facia **(see illustration)**.

7 Carefully prise the centre switch panel from the facia to release the upper retaining clips **(see illustration)**.

8 Remove the audio unit as described in Chapter 12.

9 Undo the two screws above the audio unit aperture **(see illustration)**.

10 Undo the two screws in the multi-function display aperture **(see illustration)**.

11 Carefully prise the centre panel away from the facia to release the side retaining clips, and remove the panel from the car **(see illustration)**.

Refitting

12 Refitting is a reversal of removal.

Complete facia assembly

Note: *This is an involved operation entailing*

the removal of numerous components and assemblies, and the disconnection of a multitude of wiring connectors. Make notes of the location of all disconnected wiring, or attach labels to the connectors, to avoid confusion when refitting.

Removal

13 Disconnect the battery negative terminal (refer to 'Disconnecting the battery' in the Reference Chapter).

14 Remove the scuttle grille panel as described in Section 24.

15 Remove the windscreen wiper motor and linkage as described in Chapter 12.

16 Working in the scuttle aperture, undo the three nuts securing the facia to the bulkhead.

17 Move the front seats as far back as possible. Set the steering wheel in the straight-ahead position, and engage the steering lock.

18 Remove the steering column shrouds, and the facia centre panels as described previously in this Section.

19 Remove the front pillar trim panels as described in Section 28.

20 Remove the centre console as described in Section 29.

21 Remove the undercovers from beneath the facia both sides.

22 Remove the steering wheel as described in Chapter 10.

23 Remove the following components as described in Chapter 12:
   a) *Instrument panel.*
   b) *Audio unit.*
   c) *Passenger's airbag.*
   d) *Steering column switches.*
   e) *Multi-function display unit.*

24 Remove all the facia panel switches as described in Chapter 12.

25 Remove the tweeter speakers from the top of the facia as described in Chapter 12.

26 Undo the bolt each side on the outer sides of the facia.

27 Undo the two upper retaining screws at each corner of the heater/ventilation control unit.

28 Using a small screwdriver, release the retaining lug at the lower centre of the control unit and withdraw the unit from the facia.

29 Pivot the control unit upwards, as far as clearance will allow, then release the securing clips and disconnect the control cables from the unit. Note the locations of the cables to ensure correct refitting.

30 Disconnect the wiring plug from the rear of the control unit, then withdraw the unit.

31 Undo all the facia retaining screws/bolts.

32 Remove the fusebox cover panel and release the fuse/relay box from its facia attachments.

33 Undo the retaining bolt and release the bonnet opening handle from its location.

34 Disconnect or release all the remaining facia attachments

35 With the help of an assistant, lift the facia from its location and move it rearward. As soon as sufficient clearance exists, disconnect all the facia wiring connectors, noting their fitted positions. Note the wiring harness routing and release it from the various retaining clips.

36 Check that everything is disconnected and moved clear, then remove the facia from the vehicle.

Refitting

37 Refitting is a reversal of removal ensuring that all wiring is correctly reconnected and all mountings securely tightened.

31.10 Undo the two screws (arrowed) in the multi-function display aperture

31.11 Carefully prise the centre panel away from the facia to release the side retaining clips

Chapter 12
Body electrical systems

Contents

Degrees of difficulty

Easy, suitable for novice with little experience	Fairly easy, suitable for beginner with some experience	Fairly difficult, suitable for competent DIY mechanic	Difficult, suitable for experienced DIY mechanic	Very difficult, suitable for expert DIY or professional

Specifications

General

System type .... 12 volt negative earth

Bulbs

	Type	Wattage
Direction indicator light	Bayonet	21
Direction indicator side repeater	Push-fit	5
Front foglight	H1	55
Front sidelights..............................	Push-fit	5
Headlights	H4	60/55
High-level stop-light.........................	Push-fit	5
Interior/courtesy lights	Push-fit	5
Number plate light...........................	Push-fit	5
Rear foglight................................	Bayonet	21
Reversing light..............................	Bayonet	21
Stop/tail light	Bayonet	21/5

Torque wrench setting

	Nm	lbf ft
Airbag control unit retaining nuts..................	8	6

1 General information

Warning: Before carrying out any work on the electrical system, read through the precautions given in 'Safety first!' at the beginning of this manual, and in Chapter 5A.

The electrical system is of 12 volt negative earth type. Power for the lights and all electrical accessories is supplied by a lead-acid type battery, which is charged by the alternator.

From the 2001 model year onwards, many of the body electrical systems are controlled by individual electronic control units (ECUs) and these are in turn controlled by a main ECU known as a Built-in Systems Interface (BSI). The various ECUs and the BSI

exchange data with each other via a multiplex network. The multiplex network is a two-wire system linking the BSI with the system ECUs and is termed by Peugeot/Citroën as CAN (controlled area network) and VAN (vehicle area network). Essentially this means that the BSI and the ECUs controlling the 'comfort' systems, safety systems, security systems, and entertainment systems in the vehicle, are all inter-connected via the two networks.

An ECU connected to the multiplex network

only receives some of the data needed for it to operate directly, with the remaining data being supplied by the other ECUs on the network. Because the ECUs share information via the network, several ECUs can control the operation of the same system. Also, one ECU can control several systems in an autonomous manner. The BSI is the manager of this information interchange as well as also being responsible for the control of certain vehicle systems itself. The BSI has a full diagnostic capability whereby any fault in any of the ECUs on the multiplex network can be traced using diagnostic equipment connected to the vehicle diagnostic connector. Should any fault develop with a system on the network, have the self-diagnosis facility interrogated by a Peugeot/Citroën dealer or suitably-equipped specialist.

This Chapter covers repair and service procedures for the various electrical components not associated with the engine. Information on the battery, alternator and starter motor can be found in Chapter 5A.

It should be noted that, prior to working on any component in the electrical system, the battery should first be disconnected, to prevent the possibility of electrical short-circuits (refer to *Disconnecting the battery* in the Reference Chapter).

2 Electrical fault finding – general information

Note: *Refer to the precautions given in 'Safety first!' and in Chapter 5A before starting work. The following tests relate to testing of the main electrical circuits, and should not be used to test delicate electronic circuits (such as anti-lock braking systems), particularly where an electronic control unit (ECU) or multiplexing is used (see Section 1).*

General

1 A typical electrical circuit consists of an electrical component, any switches, relays, motors, fuses, fusible links or circuit breakers related to that component, and the wiring and connectors which link the component to both the battery and the chassis. To help to pinpoint a problem in an electrical circuit, wiring diagrams are included at the end of this Chapter.
2 Before attempting to diagnose an electrical fault, first study the appropriate wiring diagram, to obtain a more complete understanding of the components included in the particular circuit concerned. The possible sources of a fault can be narrowed down by noting whether other components related to the circuit are operating properly. If several components or circuits fail at one time, the problem is likely to be related to a shared fuse or earth connection.
3 Electrical problems usually stem from simple causes, such as loose or corroded connections, a faulty earth connection, a blown fuse, a melted fusible link, or a faulty

relay (refer to Section 3 for details of testing relays). Visually inspect the condition of all fuses, wires and connections in a problem circuit before testing the components. Use the wiring diagrams to determine which terminal connections will need to be checked, in order to pinpoint the trouble-spot.
4 The basic tools required for electrical fault finding include a circuit tester or voltmeter; an ohmmeter (to measure resistance); a battery and set of test leads; and a jumper wire, preferably with a circuit breaker or fuse incorporated, which can be used to bypass suspect wires or electrical components. Before attempting to locate a problem with test instruments, use the wiring diagram to determine where to make the connections.
5 To find the source of an intermittent wiring fault (usually due to a poor or dirty connection, or damaged wiring insulation), a 'wiggle' test can be performed on the wiring. This involves wiggling the wiring by hand, to see if the fault occurs as the wiring is moved. It should be possible to narrow down the source of the fault to a particular section of wiring. This method of testing can be used in conjunction with any of the tests described in the following sub-Sections.
6 Apart from problems due to poor connections, two basic types of fault can occur in an electrical circuit – open-circuit, or short-circuit.
7 Open-circuit faults are caused by a break somewhere in the circuit, which prevents current from flowing. An open-circuit fault will prevent a component from working, but will not cause the relevant circuit fuse to blow.
8 Short-circuit faults are caused by a 'short' somewhere in the circuit, which allows the current flowing in the circuit to 'escape' along an alternative route, usually to earth. Short-circuit faults are normally caused by a breakdown in wiring insulation, which allows a feed wire to touch either another wire, or an earthed component such as the bodyshell. A short-circuit fault will normally cause the relevant circuit fuse to blow. **Note:** *On models equipped with a multiplex network (2001 model year onwards) as an aid to economy and to prevent battery discharge, certain functions of the electrical system can only be used for 30 minutes after the engine has been stopped. Bear this in mind when tracing power supply faults on these systems.*

Functions affected
Windscreen wipers.
Electric windows.
Sunroof.
Courtesy lights.
Audio equipment.
After this period the BSI (Built-in Systems Interface) cuts the power to these circuits. To restore power, start the engine.
It is also possible for the BSI to turn off certain functions (heater blower, heated rear window) depending on the state of charge of the battery. When tracing a fault, ensure the battery is in a good state of charge.

Finding an open-circuit

9 To check for an open-circuit, connect one lead of a voltmeter to either the negative battery terminal or a known good earth.
10 Connect the other lead to a connector in the circuit being tested, preferably nearest to the battery or fuse.
11 Switch on the circuit, bearing in mind that some circuits are live only when the ignition switch is moved to a particular position.
12 If voltage is present (indicated either by the tester bulb lighting or a voltmeter reading, as applicable), this means that the section of the circuit between the relevant connector and the battery is problem-free.
13 Continue to check the remainder of the circuit in the same fashion.
14 When a point is reached at which no voltage is present, the problem must lie between that point and the previous test point with voltage. Most problems can be traced to a broken, corroded or loose connection.

Finding a short-circuit

15 To check for a short-circuit, first disconnect the load(s) from the circuit (loads are the components which draw current from a circuit, such as bulbs, motors, heating elements, etc).
16 Remove the relevant fuse from the circuit, and connect a circuit tester or voltmeter to the fuse connections.
17 Switch on the circuit, bearing in mind that some circuits are live only when the ignition switch is moved to a particular position.
18 If voltage is present (indicated either by the tester bulb lighting or a voltmeter reading, as applicable), this means that there is a short-circuit.
19 If no voltage is present, but the fuse still blows with the load(s) connected, this indicates an internal fault in the load(s).

Finding an earth fault

20 The battery negative terminal is connected to 'earth' – the metal of the engine/transmission and the car body – and most systems are wired so that they only receive a positive feed, the current returning via the metal of the car body. This means that the component mounting and the body form part of that circuit. Loose or corroded mountings can therefore cause a range of electrical faults, ranging from total failure of a circuit, to a puzzling partial fault. In particular, lights may shine dimly (especially when another circuit sharing the same earth point is in operation), motors (eg, wiper motors or the radiator cooling fan motor) may run slowly, and the operation of one circuit may have an apparently-unrelated effect on another. Note that on many vehicles, earth straps are used between certain components, such as the engine/transmission and the body, usually where there is no metal-to-metal contact between components, due to flexible rubber mountings, etc.
21 To check whether a component is properly earthed, disconnect the battery, and connect one lead of an ohmmeter to a known

good earth point. Connect the other lead to the wire or earth connection being tested. The resistance reading should be zero; if not, check the connection as follows.

22 If an earth connection is thought to be faulty, dismantle the connection, and clean back to bare metal both the bodyshell and the wire terminal or the component earth connection mating surface. Be careful to remove all traces of dirt and corrosion, then use a knife to trim away any paint, so that a clean metal-to-metal joint is made. On reassembly, tighten the joint fasteners securely; if a wire terminal is being refitted, use serrated washers between the terminal and the bodyshell, to ensure a clean and secure connection. When the connection is remade, prevent the onset of corrosion in the future by applying a coat of petroleum jelly or silicone-based grease, or by spraying on (at regular intervals) a proprietary ignition sealer or water-dispersant lubricant.

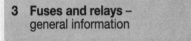

3 Fuses and relays – general information

Fuses

1 Fuses are designed to break a circuit when a predetermined current is reached, in order to protect the components and wiring which could be damaged by excessive current flow. Any excessive current flow will be due to a fault in the circuit, usually a short-circuit (see Section 2).

2 The majority of fuses are located on the driver's side of the facia, behind a detachable panel. Additional fuses (including the larger, higher-rated maxi-fuses) are located in the fuse/relay box on the left-hand side of the engine compartment **(see illustrations)**.

3 To gain access to the facia fuses, remove the lower facia panel (turn the retaining knobs 90° and remove the panel). To gain access to the fuses in the engine compartment, simply unclip the cover from the fuse/relay box. The main fuses and relays are in the upper part of the box, with the maxi-fuses located below.

4 To remove a fuse, first switch off the circuit concerned (or the ignition), then pull the fuse out of its terminals. The wire within the fuse

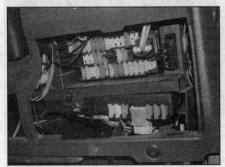

3.2a The majority of fuses are located in the facia fusebox . . .

should be visible; if the fuse has blown it will be broken or melted.

5 Always renew a fuse with one of the correct rating, never use a fuse with a different rating from that specified. The fuse rating is stamped on the top of the fuse, the fuses are also colour-coded as follows. Refer to the wiring diagrams for details of the fuse ratings and the circuits protected.

Colour	Rating
Orange	5A
Red	10A
Blue	15A
Yellow	20A
Clear or white	25A
Green	30A

6 Never renew a fuse more than once without tracing the source of the trouble. If the new fuse blows immediately, find the cause before renewing it again; a short to earth as a result of faulty insulation is most likely. Where a fuse protects more than one circuit, try to isolate the fault by switching on each circuit in turn (where possible) until the fuse blows again. Always carry a supply of spare fuses of each relevant rating on the vehicle; a spare of each rating should be clipped into the fusebox.

Relays

7 A relay is an electrically-operated switch, which is used for the following reasons:
a) A relay can switch a heavy current remotely from the circuit in which the current is flowing, allowing the use of lighter-gauge wiring and switch contacts.
b) A relay can receive more than one control input, unlike a mechanical switch.
c) A relay can have a timer function – for example, the intermittent wiper relay.

8 On models so equipped, the majority of relay functions are incorporated into the built-in system interface (BSI) unit (see Section 22). Other relays are located in the fuse/relay box in the engine compartment. Additional relays for the engine electric cooling fans are located in the fan shroud in front of the radiator (refer to Chapter 3 for details). Other relays may be encountered according to model, equipment specification, and year of manufacture. Refer to the wiring diagrams in Chapter 12 for specific details

9 If a circuit or system controlled by a relay

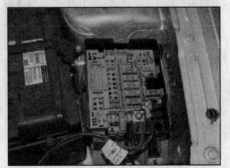

3.2b . . . and in the engine compartment fuse/relay box

develops a fault and the relay is suspect, operate the system. If the relay is functioning, it should be possible to hear it 'click' as it is energised. If this is the case, the fault lies with the components or wiring of the system. If the relay is not being energised, then either the relay is not receiving a main supply or a switching voltage, or the relay itself is faulty. Testing is by the substitution of a known good unit, but be careful – while some relays are identical in appearance and in operation, others look similar but perform different functions.

10 To remove a relay, first ensure that the relevant circuit is switched off. The relay can then simply be pulled out from the socket, and pushed back into position. Note, however, that with the ever increasing standardisation of vehicle wiring and electrical system components, many relays are now 'welded' in position in their relevant circuit boards for ease of manufacture. This means that the relays are soldered in place and cannot be individually removed. If faulty, the complete circuit board or relay housing must be renewed as an assembly. Changes of this nature occur regularly during the course of vehicle production and are not normally documented by the vehicle manufacturer. Therefore, if a relay appears reluctant to come free from its location, consider that it may be of the welded type and consult a Peugeot/Citroën dealer for the latest information.

4 Switches – removal and refitting

Note: *Disconnect the battery negative terminal before removing any switch, and reconnect the terminal after refitting the switch. Refer to 'Disconnecting the battery' in the Reference Chapter.*

Ignition switch

1 Refer to Chapter 10.

Steering column switches

Pre-September 2002 models

2 Remove the steering wheel as described in Chapter 10.

3 Remove the steering column lower and upper shrouds as described in Chapter 11.

4 On models equipped with an airbag, remove the airbag rotary connector as described in Section 21.

5 Disconnect the wiring connectors at the rear of the steering column switches.

6 Undo the three screws securing the switch housing to the steering column and remove the housing from the column.

7 The relevant switch can now be removed from the housing after unscrewing the two retaining screws.

8 Refitting is a reversal of removal.

Post-September 2002 models

9 Remove the steering wheel as described in Chapter 10.

4.11a Slacken the switch assembly retaining clamp (arrowed) . . .

4.11b . . . carefully prise the retaining catches (arrowed) away from the column . . .

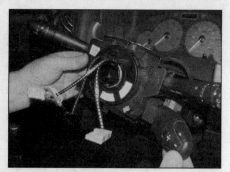

4.11c . . . and lift off the switch assembly – later models

4.11d Turn the unit over and disconnect the wiring connectors – later models

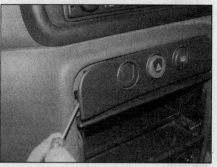

4.14 Carefully prise off the trim panel for access to the switches – early models

4.15a Depress the retaining lugs on the side of the switch body . . .

10 Remove the steering column lower and upper shrouds as described in Chapter 11.

11 Slacken the switch assembly retaining clamp, then using a small screwdriver, carefully prise the retaining catches away from the column and lift off the switch assembly. Disconnect the wiring connectors as the assembly is withdrawn **(see illustrations)**. *Caution: Take great care not damage the switch assembly retaining catches.*

12 If required, the audio unit remote control switch can be unclipped from the main switch assembly.

13 Refitting is a reversal of removal.

Note: *If a new switch assembly is fitted the unit must be initialised using dedicated test equipment. Entrust this task to a Peugeot/ Citroën dealer or suitably-equipped specialist.*

Facia centre-mounted switches

Pre-September 2002 models

14 Using a small screwdriver, carefully prise off the trim panel for access to the switches **(see illustration)**.

15 Depress the retaining lugs on the side of the switch body and withdraw the relevant switch from its location **(see illustrations)**. Disconnect the wiring connector and remove the switch.

16 Refitting is the reverse of removal.

Post-September 2002 models

17 Remove the trim panels in the centre of the facia, for access to the switches, as described in Chapter 11.

18 To remove the lower switches, reach in through the audio unit aperture, or through

the opening at the side of the switch, and push the relevant switch out from behind the facia **(see illustration)**. Disconnect the wiring connector and remove the switch.

19 To remove the upper switches, depress the retaining lugs on the top of the switch body and withdraw the switch from the facia **(see illustration)**. Disconnect the wiring connector and remove the switch.

20 Refitting is the reverse of removal.

Facia side-mounted switches

21 On pre-September 2002 models, additional switches are located above the fusebox on the driver's side.

22 Using a small screwdriver, carefully prise out the trim cover around the switch unit. Undo the retaining screw(s) and withdraw

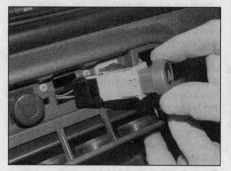

4.15b . . . and withdraw the relevant switch from its location – early models

4.18 To remove the lower switches, reach in through the facia aperture and push the switch out from behind – later models

4.19 To remove the upper switches, depress the retaining lugs and withdraw the switch – later models

the switch unit from the facia. Disconnect the wiring connectors and remove the unit. The switch(es) can then be pushed out from the rear of the panel.

23 On post-September 2002 models, additional switches are located in the facia adjacent to the heater/ventilation air vents. Using a small screwdriver, carefully prise the relevant switch from its location. Disconnect the wiring connector and remove the switch.

24 Refitting is the reverse of removal.

Heating/ventilation control

25 The switches are an integral part of the heater/ventilation control panel, and cannot be renewed separately. If any switch is faulty, the complete control panel must be renewed – refer to Chapter 3 for details.

Stop-light switch

26 Refer to Chapter 9.

Handbrake warning light switch

27 Refer to Chapter 9.

Courtesy light switch

28 The courtesy light switches are an integral part of the door lock assemblies. Refer to Chapter 11 for door lock removal and refitting details.

Parking aid de-activation switch

29 The parking aid de-activation switch is located on the centre console rear section. Using a small screwdriver, carefully prise the switch from the console, then disconnect the wiring and tie to one side to prevent loosing it inside the console.

30 Refitting is a reversal of removal.

---

5 Bulbs (exterior lights) – renewal

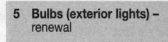

General

1 Whenever a bulb is renewed, note the following points:
  a) Remember that, if the light has just been in use, the bulb may be extremely hot.
  b) Always check the bulb contacts and holder, ensuring that there is clean metal-to-metal contact between the bulb and its

5.2 Remove the protective rubber cover from the headlight unit – early models

5.3b . . . and withdraw the headlight bulb – early models

live(s) and earth. Clean off any corrosion or dirt before fitting a new bulb.
  c) Wherever bayonet-type bulbs are fitted (see Specifications), ensure that the live contact(s) bear firmly against the bulb contact.
  d) Always ensure that the new bulb is of the correct rating, and that it is completely clean before fitting it; this applies particularly to headlight/foglight bulbs (see below).

Headlight

Pre-September 2002 models

2 Working in the engine compartment, disconnect the wiring connector from the rear of the headlight bulb, then remove the protective rubber cover from the headlight unit **(see illustration)**.

3 Release the spring clip and withdraw the bulb **(see illustrations)**.

4 When handling the new bulb, use a tissue

5.3a Release the spring clip . . .

5.7 Remove the plastic cover from the light unit – later models

or clean cloth to avoid touching the glass with the fingers; moisture and grease from the skin can cause blackening and rapid failure of this type of bulb. If the glass is accidentally touched, wipe it clean using methylated spirit.

5 Install the new bulb, ensuring that its locating tabs are correctly seated in the light unit cut-outs. Secure the bulb in position with the spring clip.

6 Refit the protective rubber cover, ensuring that it is correctly seated, then reconnect the wiring connector.

Post-September 2002 models

7 Working in the engine compartment, turn the large plastic cover anti-clockwise and remove it from the rear of the headlight unit **(see illustration)**.

8 Disconnect the wiring connector from the rear of the headlight bulb **(see illustration)**.

9 Release the spring clip and withdraw the bulb **(see illustrations)**.

5.8 Disconnect the wiring connector from the headlight bulb – later models

5.9a Release the spring clip . . .

5.9b . . . and withdraw the headlight bulb – later models

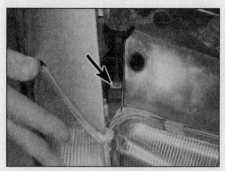

5.13 Depress the tab (arrowed), and withdraw the direction indicator light unit – early models

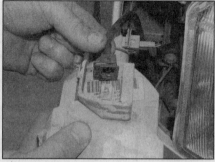

5.14 Disconnect the wiring connector from the sidelight bulbholder – early models

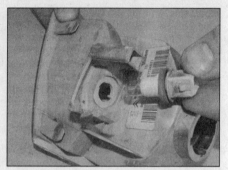

5.15a Rotate the sidelight bulbholder anti-clockwise to release it . . .

10 When handling the new bulb, use a tissue or clean cloth to avoid touching the glass with the fingers; moisture and grease from the skin can cause blackening and rapid failure of this type of bulb. If the glass is accidentally touched, wipe it clean using methylated spirit.
11 Install the new bulb, ensuring that its locating tabs are correctly seated in the light unit cut-outs. Secure the bulb in position with the spring clip.
12 Reconnect the wiring connector then refit the plastic cover, turning it clockwise to lock it in place.

Front sidelight

Pre-September 2002 models

13 Open the bonnet and depress the tab located at the top of the direction indicator light unit, using a screwdriver (see

illustration). Withdraw the direction indicator light unit from its location.
14 Disconnect the wiring connector from the sidelight bulbholder (see illustration).
15 Rotate the bulbholder anti-clockwise, and free it from the rear of the direction indicator light unit. The bulb is a push-fit in the bulbholder (see illustrations).
16 Refit the bulbholder and turn it clockwise to secure, then reconnect the wiring connector.
17 Refit the direction indicator light unit, ensuring that the upper and lower guides are correctly engaged.

Post-September 2002 models

18 Working in the engine compartment, turn the large plastic cover anti-clockwise and remove it from the rear of the headlight unit (see illustration 5.7). The sidelight bulbholder

is located above the headlight bulb. For improved access remove the headlight bulb as described previously.
19 Pull the sidelight bulbholder from its location in the headlight unit (see illustration). The bulb is a push-fit in the bulbholder.
20 Refit the bulbholder and, where removed, the headlight bulb.
21 Refit the plastic cover, turning it clockwise to lock it in place.

Front direction indicator

Pre-September 2002 models

22 Open the bonnet and depress the tab located at the top of the direction indicator light unit, using a screwdriver (see illustration 5.13). Withdraw the direction indicator light unit from its location.
23 Rotate the bulbholder anti-clockwise, and free it from the rear of the light unit. The bulb is a bayonet fit in the bulbholder (see illustrations).
24 Refit the direction indicator light unit, ensuring that the upper and lower guides are correctly engaged.

Post-September 2002 models

25 Working in the engine compartment, turn the direction indicator bulbholder anti-clockwise and remove it from the rear of the headlight unit. The bulb is a bayonet fit in the bulbholder (see illustrations).
26 Refitting is a reversal of the removal procedure.

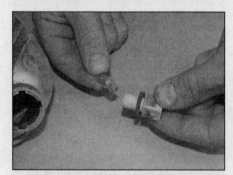

5.15b . . . the bulb is a push-fit in the bulbholder – early models

5.19 Pull the sidelight bulbholder from its location in the headlight unit – later models

5.23a Rotate the direction indicator bulbholder anti-clockwise to release it . . .

5.23b . . . the bulb is a bayonet fit in the bulbholder – early models

5.25a Rotate the direction indicator bulbholder anti-clockwise to release it . . .

5.25b . . . the bulb is a bayonet fit in the bulbholder – later models

5.27 Push the side repeater light unit forward, then ease it out from the wing

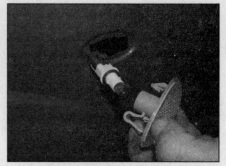

5.28a Rotate the bulbholder anti-clockwise to release it . . .

Direction indicator side repeater

27 Push the light unit forward to free its rear retaining clip, then ease it out from the front wing (see illustration).
28 Rotate the bulbholder anti-clockwise and free it from the rear of the light unit. The bulb is a push-fit in the bulbholder (see illustrations).
29 Refitting is a reversal of the removal procedure.

Front foglight

30 Undo the retaining screws and partially withdraw the front wheel arch liner for access to the foglight unit.
31 Reach up under the front bumper and disconnect the foglight wiring connector.
32 Turn the bulbholder a quarter turn and withdraw it from the light unit.

33 Release the spring clip, and remove the bulb from the bulbholder.
34 When handling the new bulb, use a tissue or clean cloth to avoid touching the glass with the fingers; moisture and grease from the skin can cause blackening and rapid failure of this type of bulb. If the glass is accidentally touched, wipe it clean using methylated spirit.
35 Install the new bulb, ensuring that its locating tabs are correctly located. Secure the bulb in position with the clip, and refit the bulbholder.
36 Reconnect the foglight wiring connector and refit the wheel arch liner.

Rear light cluster

37 Open the tailgate, or the rear door on the relevant side.
38 Undo the plastic retaining nut securing the light unit to the body (see illustration).

39 Push the light unit toward the centre of the car, to release the two outer retaining lugs and gently pull it away from the body (see illustrations).
40 Depress the tabs on the side of the bulbholder and withdraw the bulbholder from the light unit (see illustration).
41 All the bulbs have bayonet fittings. The relevant bulb can be removed by pressing it in and rotating it anti-clockwise (see illustration).
42 Refitting is the reverse of removal, ensuring the light unit and bulbholder seals are in good condition.

High-level stop-light

Models with a tailgate

43 Open the tailgate and undo the two nuts securing the light unit in position.
44 Withdraw the light unit, then depress

5.28b . . . the bulb is a push-fit in the bulbholder

5.38 Undo the plastic retaining nut securing the rear light unit to the body

5.39a Push the light unit toward the centre of the car . . .

5.39b . . . to release the two outer retaining lugs (arrowed)

5.40 Depress the tabs and withdraw the bulbholder from the light unit . . .

5.41 . . . all the bulbs are a bayonet fit in the bulbholder

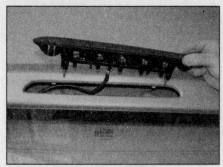

5.44a Withdraw the high-level stop-light unit . . .

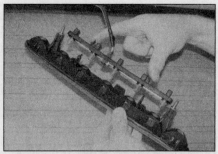

5.44b . . . then depress the two tabs to release the bulbholder – models with a tailgate

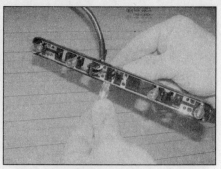

5.45 All the bulbs are a push-fit in the bulbholder – models with a tailgate

the two tabs to release the bulbholder **(see illustrations)**.

45 All the bulbs are a push-fit in the bulbholder **(see illustration)**.

46 Refitting is a reversal of the removal procedure.

Models with hinged rear doors

47 Open the relevant rear door and carefully

prise off the stop light inner trim panel using a screwdriver **(see illustration)**.

48 Depress the two tabs to release the bulbholder **(see illustration)**.

49 All the bulbs are a push-fit in the bulbholder **(see illustration)**.

50 Refitting is a reversal of the removal procedure.

Number plate light

Models with a tailgate

51 There is very little clearance between the number plate light unit and the plastic exterior moulding above, to allow removal of the light unit lens. In practice it was found necessary to remove the tailgate trim panel (see Chapter 11) then unscrew the three nuts and remove the exterior moulding **(see illustration)**. The nuts are accessible through apertures inside the tailgate.

52 Unclip the lens from the number plate light unit. The bulb is a push-fit in the bulbholder **(see illustrations)**.

53 Clip the lens into position then refit the exterior moulding.

54 Refit the tailgate trim panel (Chapter 11).

Models with hinged rear doors

55 There is very little clearance between the number plate light unit and the plastic exterior moulding above, to allow removal of the light unit lens. In practice it was found necessary to first remove the rear door trim panel (see Chapter 11), then proceed as follows.

56 Reach in through the aperture in the rear door and disconnect the number plate light wiring connector **(see illustration)**.

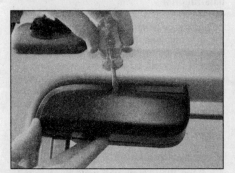

5.47 Prise off the high-level stop-light inner trim panel . . .

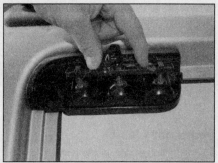

5.48 . . . then depress the two tabs to release the bulbholder – models with hinged rear doors

5.49 All the bulbs are a push-fit in the bulbholder – models with hinged rear doors

5.51 Remove the exterior moulding above the number plate lights – models with a tailgate

5.52a Unclip the lens from the number plate light unit . . .

5.52b . . . the bulb is a push-fit in the bulbholder – models with a tailgate

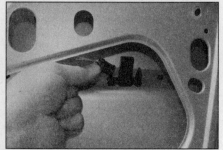

5.56 Disconnect the number plate light wiring connector – models with hinged rear doors

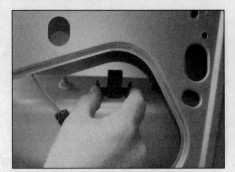

5.57a Depress the tabs . . .

5.57b . . . and push the light unit out of the door – models with hinged rear doors

5.58 Unclip the lens from the number plate light unit. The bulb is a push-fit in the bulbholder – models with hinged rear doors

57 Depress the tabs and push the light unit out of the door **(see illustrations)**.
58 Unclip the lens from the number plate light unit **(see illustration)**. The bulb is a push-fit in the bulbholder.
59 Clip the lens into position then refit the light unit to the door. Reconnect the wiring and refit the door trim panel (Chapter 11).

---

6 Bulbs (interior lights) – renewal

General

1 Refer to Section 5, paragraph 1.

Courtesy lights

2 Using a small screwdriver, carefully prise the light unit from its location **(see illustration)**.
3 Depress the tabs and withdraw the bulbholder from the light unit. The bulb is a push-fit in the bulbholder **(see illustrations)**.
4 Refitting is the reverse of the removal procedure.

Instrument panel illumination and warning light bulbs

Note: *Renewal of the instrument panel bulbs is only possible on pre-2001 model year vehicles. On later models, the instrument panel and warning lights are illuminated by integral LEDs. It is not possible to renew them independently of the panel.*
5 Remove the instrument panel as described in Section 9.
6 Twist the relevant bulbholder anti-clockwise to remove it from the rear of the panel.
7 The bulbs are integral with the bulbholders.
8 On completion, refit the instrument panel with reference to Section 9.

Heater/ventilation control illumination

9 Remove the heater/ventilation control unit as described in Chapter 3.
10 Rotate the bulbholders anti-clockwise to

remove them. The capless bulbs simply pull from the bulbholders.
11 Refitting is the reverse of the removal procedure.

Multi-function display illumination

12 Remove the multi-function display as described in Section 10.
13 Rotate the bulbholders anti-clockwise and remove them **(see illustration)**. The capless bulbs simply pull from the bulbholder.

Switch illumination

14 All of the switches that are illuminated, are done so by LEDs. These LEDs are an integral part of the switch and cannot be renewed separately. Renewal will therefore require

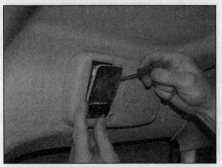

6.2 Carefully prise the courtesy light unit from its location

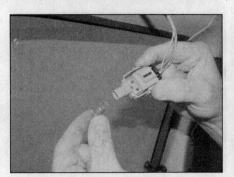

6.3b The bulb is a push-fit in the bulbholder

renewal of the complete switch assembly (see Section 4).

---

7 Exterior light units – removal and refitting

Headlight

Pre-September 2002 models

1 Remove the radiator grille as described in Chapter 11.
2 Remove the direction indicator light unit as described later in this Section.
3 Undo the three retaining bolts and

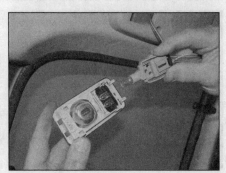

6.3a Depress the tabs and withdraw the bulbholder from the light unit

6.13 Remove the multi-function display bulbholders. The bulbs are a push-fit in the bulbholders

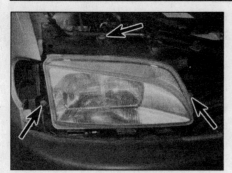

7.3 Undo the three retaining bolts (arrowed) and withdraw the headlight unit

7.4 Disconnect the wiring connectors and remove the light unit – early models

7.5a To remove the headlight adjuster motor, lift the tag and turn the motor through 90° . . .

withdraw the light unit from its location **(see illustration)**.

4 Disconnect the wiring connectors at the headlight beam adjuster motor and headlight bulb, and remove the light unit from the car **(see illustration)**.

5 If desired, the electric adjuster motor can be removed from the light unit after lifting the tag and turning the adjuster motor through 90° to release it. Once the motor is released, pull the adjuster rod balljoint from the socket in the rear of the headlight **(see illustrations)**.

6 To refit the electric adjuster motor, turn the manual height control adjuster using an Allen key to fully extend the adjuster rod. To enable the initial position to be reset after refitting, count the number of turns of the adjuster needed to fully extend the adjuster rod. Engage the balljoint with the socket on the headlight, then fit and secure the adjuster

motor. Reset the manual height adjuster to the position noted before removal.

7 Reconnect the wiring connectors and locate the headlight unit in position. Refit the headlight mounting bolts and tighten securely.

8 The remainder of refitting is a reversal of removal, but on completion have the headlight beam alignment checked at the earliest opportunity.

Post-September 2002 models

9 Remove the front bumper as described in Chapter 11.

10 Undo the lower inner and outer headlight unit retaining screws and the upper retaining screw **(see illustrations)**.

11 Using a small screwdriver, lift the upper mounting arm slightly to disengage the retaining lug, and withdraw the headlight from its location **(see illustration)**.

12 Disconnect the wiring connector and remove the headlight unit from the car.

13 Refitting is the reverse of the removal procedure, but on completion have the headlight beam alignment checked at the earliest opportunity.

Front direction indicator

14 The procedure is described as part of the bulb renewal procedure in Section 5.

Direction indicator side repeater

15 The procedure is described as part of the bulb renewal procedure in Section 5.

Front foglight

16 Firmly apply the handbrake, then jack up the front of the car and support it securely on axle stands (see *Jacking and vehicle support*).

17 Undo the retaining screws and partially withdraw the front wheel arch liner for access to the foglight unit.

18 Disconnect the foglight wiring connector.

19 Undo the three foglight retaining bolts and remove the unit from the front bumper.

20 Refitting is a reversal of removal.

Rear light unit

21 The procedure is described as part of the rear light cluster bulb renewal procedure in Section 5.

High-level stop-light

Models with a tailgate

22 The procedure is described as part of the bulb renewal procedure in Section 5.

7.5b . . . then pull the adjuster rod balljoint from the headlight socket – early models

7.10a Undo the headlight lower inner (arrowed) . . .

7.10b . . . lower outer (arrowed) . . .

7.10c . . . and upper (arrowed) retaining screws – later models

7.11 Lift the upper mounting arm slightly to disengage the retaining lug, and withdraw the headlight – later models

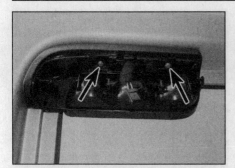

7.24 Undo the two screws (arrowed) and remove the high-level stop-light unit – models with hinged rear doors

Models with hinged rear doors

23 Remove the bulbholder as described in the bulb renewal procedure in Section 5.
24 Undo the two screws and remove the light unit from the door **(see illustration)**.
25 Refitting is a reversal of removal.

Number plate light

Models with a tailgate

26 There is very little clearance between the number plate light unit and the plastic exterior moulding above to allow removal of the light unit lens. In practice it was found necessary to remove the tailgate trim panel (see Chapter 11) then unscrew the three nuts and remove the exterior moulding **(see illustration 5.51)**. The nuts are accessible through apertures inside the tailgate.
27 Reach in through the tailgate aperture,

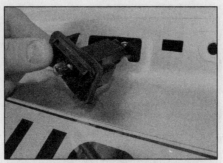

7.27 Depress the tabs and push out the number plate light unit – models with a tailgate

depress the tabs and push the light unit out of the tailgate **(see illustration)**. Disconnect the wiring connector and remove the light unit.
28 Reconnect the wiring connector and push the unit back into its location.
29 Refit the exterior moulding and the tailgate trim panel.

Models with hinged rear doors

30 The procedure is described as part of the bulb renewal procedure in Section 5.

---

8 Headlight beam alignment – general information

1 Accurate adjustment of the headlight beam is only possible using optical beam-setting equipment, and this work should therefore

be carried out by a Peugeot/Citroën dealer or suitably-equipped workshop.
2 Each headlight unit is equipped with a five-position vertical beam adjuster unit – this can be used to adjust the headlight beam to compensate for the relevant load which the vehicle is carrying. The adjuster units are operated by a switch on the facia. The adjusters should be positioned as follows according to the load being carried in the vehicle:

Position 0	Front seats occupied (1 or 2 people)
Position -	Front or rear seats occupied (3 people)
Position 1	Front and rear seats occupied (5 people)
Position 2	Front and rear seats occupied and luggage compartment fully-loaded
Position 3	Driver's seat occupied and luggage compartment fully-loaded

3 Be sure to reset the adjustment if the vehicle load is altered.

---

9 Instrument panel – removal and refitting

Removal

Pre-September 2002 models

1 Disconnect the battery negative terminal (refer to *Disconnecting the battery* in the Reference Chapter).
2 Remove the steering column lower and upper shrouds as described in Chapter 11.
3 Undo the three screws and remove the centre vent unit from the facia **(see illustrations)**.
4 Remove the audio unit and mounting frame as described in Section 17.
5 Undo the two facia upper panel retaining screws located above the instrument panel **(see illustration)**.
6 Similarly, undo the upper panel retaining screws located below the instrument panel and in the audio unit aperture **(see illustrations)**.
7 Pull the facia upper panel from its location

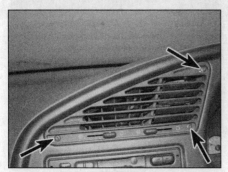

9.3a Undo the three screws (arrowed) . . .

9.3b . . . and remove the centre vent unit from the facia – early models

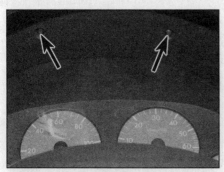

9.5 Undo the two facia upper panel retaining screws above the instrument panel (arrowed) – early models

9.6a Undo the upper panel retaining screws below the instrument panel (arrowed) . . .

9.6b . . . and in the audio unit aperture (arrowed) – early models

9.7 Pull the upper panel from its location to release the retaining clips – early models

9.8a Undo the two instrument panel retaining screws each side (arrowed) . . .

9.8b . . . and withdraw the panel from the facia – early models

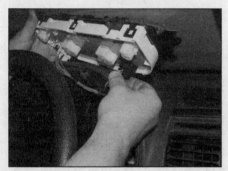

9.9 Turn the instrument panel over and disconnect the wiring connectors – early models

9.10a Pull the instrument panel upper trim upwards and towards the steering wheel to release the retaining clips – later models

9.10b Disengage the front locating lugs from the facia and lift off the panel – later models

9.11a Undo the retaining screw at the top of the instrument panel . . .

9.11b . . . then lift the panel up and withdraw it from its location – later models

9.12 Turn the instrument panel over and disconnect the wiring connectors – later models

to release the retaining clips and remove it from the car **(see illustration)**.
8 Undo the two instrument panel retaining screws each side and withdraw the panel from the facia **(see illustrations)**.
9 Turn the panel over and disconnect the wiring connectors at the rear **(see illustration)**.

Post-September 2002 models

10 Pull the top of the instrument panel upper trim panel upwards and towards the steering wheel to release the retaining clips. Disengage the front locating lugs from the facia and lift off the panel **(see illustrations)**.
11 Undo the retaining screw at the top of the instrument panel. Lift the panel up and

withdraw it from its location **(see illustrations)**.
12 Turn the panel over and disconnect the wiring connectors at the rear **(see illustration)**.

Refitting

13 Refitting is a reversal of removal.

10 Multi-function display unit – removal and refitting

Removal

1 Carefully prise the multi-function display surround from the facia **(see illustration)**.

10.1 Carefully prise the multi-function display surround from the facia

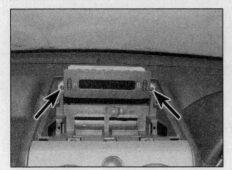

10.2a Undo the two screws (arrowed) . . .

10.2b . . . then withdraw the multi-function display and disconnect the wiring connector

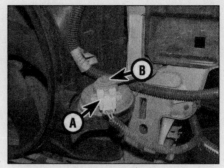

12.3 Horn wiring connector (A) and mounting nut (B)

2 Undo the two screws and withdraw the unit from the facia. Disconnect the wiring connector and remove the unit from the car (see illustrations).

Refitting

3 Refitting is a reversal of removal.

11 Cigarette lighter/accessory socket – removal and refitting

Removal

1 Remove the centre console as described in Chapter 11.
2 Carefully release the retaining clips and slide the illumination light assembly off the base of the lighter, taking great care not to break its electrical contacts.
3 Pull out the lighter element then release the tangs and push out the metal insert/accessory socket. The plastic outer section can then be removed from the console.

Refitting

4 Align the plastic outer section tab with the cut-out then insert it into the console.
5 Align the bulbholder contact on the metal insert with the holder tangs on the plastic outer then clip the insert into position.
6 Slide the illumination light assembly onto the metal insert and clip it securely onto the plastic outer.

7 Ensure the cigarette lighter is correctly assembled then refit the centre console.

12 Horn – removal and refitting

Removal

1 The horn is located behind the front bumper, on the left-hand side.
2 Remove the front bumper as described in Chapter 11.
3 Disconnect the wiring connector(s) then undo the mounting nut and remove the horn from the vehicle (see illustration).

Refitting

4 Refitting is a reversal of removal.

13 Wiper arm – removal and refitting

Note: The wiper arms are a very tight fit on their spindles and it is likely that a puller will be needed to remove them safely and without damage.

Removal

1 Operate the wiper motor, then switch it off so that the wiper arm returns to the at-rest

position. Stick tape to the screen alongside the wiper blade to ensure correct refitment. There is also an alignment mark provided on the windscreen.
2 Remove the wiper arm spindle nut cover then slacken and remove the spindle nut.
3 Lift the blade off the glass, and pull the wiper arm off its spindle. If the arm is very tight, free it from the spindle using a suitable puller.

Refitting

4 Ensure that the wiper arm and spindle splines are clean and dry, then refit the arm to the spindle, aligning the wiper blade with the tape fitted on removal, or the alignment marks provided.
5 Refit the spindle nut, tightening it securely, and clip the nut cover (where fitted) back into position.

14 Windscreen wiper motor and linkage – removal and refitting

Removal

1 Remove the scuttle grille panel as described in Chapter 11.

Wiper motor

2 Using a suitable screwdriver, prise the linkage off the balljoint on the motor crank arm (see illustration).
3 Undo the three nuts and withdraw the motor mounting plate from the scuttle (see illustration). Disconnect the wiring connector and remove the motor and mounting plate.
4 To remove the motor from the mounting plate, note the position of the crank arm with the motor in the parked position.
5 Undo the retaining nut and remove the crank arm from the motor spindle. Undo the three bolts and separate the motor from the mounting plate.

Wiper linkage

6 Remove the wiper motor as described previously.
7 Undo the bolts/nuts securing the outer

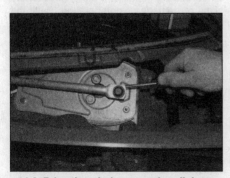

14.2 Prise the windscreen wiper linkage off the balljoint on the motor crank arm

14.3 Undo the three nuts and withdraw the motor mounting plate from the scuttle

14.7a Undo the bolts/nuts (arrowed) securing the outer spindle assembly . . .

14.7b . . . and centre spindle assembly to the scuttle

15.4 Tailgate wiper motor attachment rivets (arrowed)

spindle assembly and centre spindle assembly to the scuttle **(see illustrations)**. Manipulate the linkage assembly out from its location.

Refitting

8 Refitting is a reversal of removal. Ensure that the motor is in the parked position before refitting the crank arm in the position noted during removal.

15 Tailgate window wiper motor – removal and refitting

Note: *On later models, a pop rivet gun and suitable rivets will be required on refitting.*

Removal

1 Remove the wiper arm (see Section 13).
2 Remove the tailgate trim panel as described in Chapter 11.
3 On early models, unscrew the three nuts securing the wiper motor bracket to the tailgate.
4 On later models, using a 8 mm drill bit, carefully drill the heads off the pop rivets securing the wiper motor bracket to the tailgate **(see illustration)**.
Caution: Take care not to damage the motor and tailgate when drilling out the rivets.
5 With the three nuts or three rivets removed, disconnect the wiring connector and the washer fluid hose and remove the wiper

motor from the tailgate. Take care not to lose the collars from the motor mounting rubbers.
6 Remove the wiper motor sealing grommet from the tailgate glass.
7 Where applicable, recover the remnants of each rivet from the motor bracket/tailgate. Ensure all traces of rivet are removed.

Refitting

8 Prior to refitting check the sealing grommet and rubber mountings for signs of damage or deterioration and renew as necessary.
9 Ensure the rubber grommet is correctly fitted to the tailgate glass, and the rubber mountings and collars are correctly fitted to the motor mounting bracket.
10 Manoeuvre the wiper motor into position and secure it in position with the nuts or new pop rivets.
11 Reconnect the wiring connector and washer hose to the motor then refit the trim panel to the tailgate. Turn on the ignition, then operate the wiper and allow it to stop in the park position.
12 Refit the wiper arm as described in Section 13.

16 Washer system components – removal and refitting

1 The washer reservoir is located behind the right-hand front wing and supplies the windscreen and tailgate washers via single or multiple pumps fitted to the reservoir.

Washer fluid reservoir

2 Slacken the right-hand front roadwheel bolts. Jack up the front of the vehicle, and support it securely on axle stands (see *Jacking and vehicle support*). Remove the right-hand roadwheel.
3 From underneath the front wing, undo the screws, prise out the retaining clips, and remove the wheel arch liner from the wing valance.
4 Note the correct fitted location of the washer hoses (if necessary, mark them for identification purposes) then disconnect the hoses from the washer pump(s).
5 Disconnect the wiring connector(s) from the washer pump(s).
6 Slacken and remove the upper and lower retaining nuts, then manoeuvre the reservoir out from underneath the wing **(see illustrations)**.
7 Refitting is the reverse of removal, ensuring that the hoses are securely reconnected. Refill the reservoir and check for leaks.

Washer pump

8 Proceed as described in paragraphs 2 to 5 and disconnect the hose(s) and wiring connector from the pump.
9 Position a container beneath the reservoir to catch the washer fluid as the pump is removed.
10 Carefully ease the pump out from the reservoir, and recover its sealing grommet. Wash off any spilt fluid with cold water.
11 Refitting is the reverse of removal, using a new sealing grommet if the original shows signs of damage or deterioration. Refill the reservoir and check the pump grommet for leaks on completion.

Windscreen washer jet

12 Open and support the bonnet
13 Disconnect the washer hose(s) from the relevant jet, then depress the retaining clips and ease the jet out of position.
14 On refitting, clip the jet into the bonnet and reconnect the hose. The aim of the washer jets is not adjustable.

Tailgate washer jet

15 The tailgate washer jet is integral with the wiper assembly.

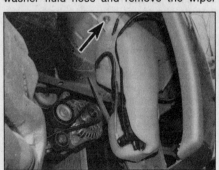

16.6a Washer reservoir upper retaining nut (arrowed) . . .

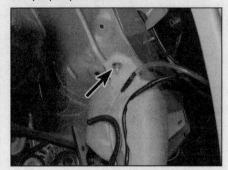

16.6b . . . and lower retaining nut (arrowed)

17.3 Insert the removal tools into the holes on the audio unit and withdraw the unit from the facia

17 Audio unit – removal and refitting

Note: *The following procedure is for the range of equipment fitted by Peugeot/Citroën.*

Removal

1 Ensure the audio unit and ignition is switched off.
2 The audio units fitted by Peugeot/Citroën have DIN standard fixings. Two special tools, obtainable from most car accessory retailers, are required for removal. Alternatively, suitable tools can be fabricated from 3 mm diameter wire, such as welding rod.
3 Insert the tools into the holes on each side of the audio unit and push them in until they snap into place. The audio unit can be slid out of the facia **(see illustration)**.
4 Once the unit has been withdrawn from the facia, disconnect the wiring connections and aerial lead from the rear, and remove the unit from the vehicle.
5 To remove the mounting frame on pre-September 2002 models, use a small screwdriver to release the locating lugs on each side of the unit **(see illustration)**. Note that the frame will be slightly distorted by this procedure, but can be aligned after removal.
6 Once the locating lugs have been released, withdraw the frame from the facia **(see illustration)**.

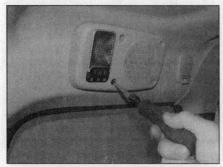

18.3 Undo the four screws securing the speaker housing in position

17.5 On early models, use a small screwdriver to release the mounting frame lugs . . .

Refitting

7 Where applicable, clip the mounting frame back into position.
8 Securely reconnect the aerial lead and wiring connectors then slide the unit back into position, taking care not to trap the wiring.

18 Loudspeakers – removal and refitting

Removal

Door speakers

1 Turn the speaker grille a quarter turn anti-clockwise and remove it from the door trim panel.

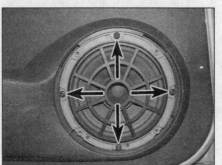

18.2a Undo the four screws (arrowed) and withdraw the speaker from the door panel

18.4a Disconnect the speaker wiring . . .

17.6 . . . then remove the mounting frame from the facia

2 Undo the four screws and withdraw the speaker from the panel. Disconnect the wiring connector and remove the speaker **(see illustrations)**.

Rear speakers

3 Undo the four screws securing the speaker housing in position **(see illustration)**.
4 Withdraw the housing and disconnect the speaker wiring. Undo the two screws and remove the speaker from the housing **(see illustrations)**.

Facia-mounted tweeters

5 Prise the tweeter from its location on the top of the facia, disconnect the wiring connector and remove the tweeter.

Refitting

6 Refitting is a reversal of removal.

18.2b Disconnect the wiring connector and remove the speaker

18.4b . . . then undo the two screws (arrowed) and remove the speaker from the housing

19 Engine immobiliser and anti-theft alarm system – general information

Note: *This information is applicable only to the later systems fitted by Peugeot/Citroën as standard equipment. Early models utilised a keypad to de-activate the engine immobiliser. At the time of writing, information on the early keypad system was not available.*

Engine immobiliser

1 An engine immobiliser system is fitted as standard to most models and the system is operated automatically every time the ignition key is inserted/removed.

2 The immobiliser system ensures the vehicle can only be started using the original Peugeot/Citroën ignition key. The key contains an electronic chip (transponder) which is programmed with a code. When the key is inserted into the ignition switch it uses the current present in the sensor ring (which is fitted to the ignition switch housing) to send a signal to the immobiliser electronic control unit (ECU). On pre-2001 model year vehicles, the control unit is located under the facia, on the driver's side. On post-2001 model year vehicles, the ECU is incorporated into the built-in systems interface (BSI) unit (see Section 22). The ECU checks this code every time the ignition is switched on. If the key code does not match the ECU code, the ECU will disable the starter, fuel and ignition (as applicable) to prevent the engine being started.

3 When the vehicle is new, a confidential security card is supplied along with the other vehicle documentation. This card contains the security code which your Peugeot/Citroën dealer requires when carrying out any work on the immobiliser system. Keep this card in a safe place at home; never store it in the vehicle. If the ignition key is lost, a new one can be obtained from a Peugeot/Citroën dealer. Take the confidential security card and all the existing keys along to your Peugeot/Citroën dealer who will supply a new key and reprogramme all the keys with a new security code; this will render the lost key useless.

Caution: Without the confidential security card, it will not be possible to have the keys and immobiliser system reprogrammed.

If you have purchased the vehicle second-hand, as a precaution have all the keys and the immobiliser system reprogrammed with a new security code. This will ensure the keys in your possession are the only ones able to start the vehicle and render all other keys useless.

4 Any problems with the engine immobiliser system should be referred to a Peugeot/Citroën dealer.

Anti-theft alarm system

5 Most models covered in this manual were equipped with an anti-theft alarm system as standard equipment. The system was available as a option on all other models. The alarm is automatically armed when the deadlocking is set using the remote central locking transmitter and is disarmed when the doors are unlocked using the remote transmitter. The alarm system has switches on the bonnet, tailgate and each of the doors and, on some models, also has ultrasonic sensing, which detects movement inside the vehicle, via sensors mounted on either side of the vehicle interior.

6 Details of the alarm system operation, according to model, are given in the Owner's handbook. For obvious security reasons, they are not given here.

7 Should the alarm system become faulty, the vehicle should be taken to a Peugeot/Citroën dealer for examination.

20 Airbag system – general information, precautions and system de-activation

General information

1 According to model and year of manufacture, a driver's airbag, passenger's airbag, side airbags, and side curtain airbags may be fitted.

2 The driver's and passenger's airbag system is triggered in the event of a heavy frontal impact above a predetermined force, depending on the point of impact. The airbag is then inflated within milliseconds, and forms a safety cushion between the cabin occupants and the vehicle interior. This prevents contact between the upper body and vehicle interior, and therefore greatly reduces the risk of injury. The airbag then deflates almost immediately. The control unit also operates the front seat belt tensioner mechanisms at the same time (see Chapter 11).

3 The side airbags are fitted to the seat back of each front seat. Each airbag unit has its own lateral acceleration sensor which is mounted onto the vehicle body. The side airbags are not linked in any way and operate individually.

4 The curtain airbags are fitted behind the windscreen pillars and headlining on each side of the passenger cabin.

5 Every time the ignition is switched on, the airbag control unit performs a self-test. The self-test takes approximately six seconds and during this time the warning light in the instrument panel will be illuminated. After the self-test is complete, the warning light will go out (unless the passenger airbag unit has been deactivated – see paragraph 6). If the warning light fails to come on, remains illuminated after the self-test period, or comes on at any time when the vehicle is being

driven, there is a fault in the airbag system. The vehicle should be taken to a Peugeot/Citroën dealer for examination at the earliest possible opportunity.

6 Vehicles with a passenger airbag are equipped with a disabling switch fitted to the facia. The switch is operated using the ignition key and switches off the passenger airbag (it is not possible to disable the driver's or side/curtain airbags) to enable a rear-facing child seat to be installed in the passenger seat.

Precautions

 Warning: The following precautions must be observed when working on vehicles equipped with an airbag system, to prevent the possibility of personal injury.

General precautions

7 The following precautions **must** be observed when carrying out work on a vehicle equipped with an airbag:

a) *Do not disconnect the battery with the engine running.*
b) *Before carrying out any work in the vicinity of the airbag, removal of any of the airbag components, or any welding work on the vehicle, de-activate the system as described in the following sub-Section.*
c) *Do not attempt to test any of the airbag system circuits using test meters or any other test equipment.*
d) *If the airbag warning light comes on, or any fault in the system is suspected, consult a Peugeot/Citroën dealer without delay. Do not attempt to carry out fault diagnosis, or any dismantling of the components.*

When handling an airbag

a) *Transport the airbag by itself, bag upward.*
b) *Do not put your arms around the airbag.*
c) *Carry the airbag close to the body, bag outward.*
d) *Do not drop the airbag or expose it to impacts.*
e) *Do not attempt to dismantle the airbag unit.*
f) *Do not connect any form of electrical equipment to any part of the airbag circuit.*

When storing an airbag unit

a) *Store the unit in a cupboard with the airbag upward.*
b) *Do not expose the airbag to temperatures above 80°C.*
c) *Do not expose the airbag to flames.*
d) *Do not attempt to dispose of the airbag – consult a Peugeot/Citroën dealer.*
e) *Never refit an airbag which is known to be faulty or damaged.*

De-activation of airbag system

8 The system must be de-activated before carrying out any work on the airbag components or surrounding area:

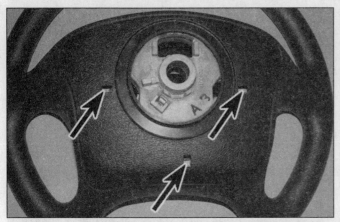

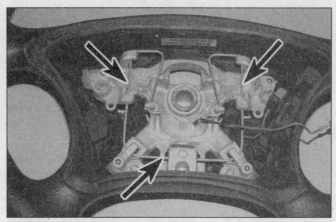

21.8a Insert a screwdriver into the three holes (arrowed) on the underside of the steering wheel . . .

21.8b . . . and push the internal retaining spring wire (arrowed) sideways to release the airbag lugs (shown with airbag removed)

a) Switch on the ignition and check the operation of the airbag warning light on the instrument panel. The light should illuminate when the ignition is switched on, then extinguish.
b) Switch off the ignition.
c) Remove the ignition key.
d) Switch off all electrical equipment.
e) Disconnect the battery negative terminal (refer to 'Disconnecting the battery' in the Reference Chapter).
f) Insulate the battery negative terminal and the end of the battery negative lead to prevent any possibility of contact.
g) Wait for at least two minutes before carrying out any further work. Wait at least ten minutes if the airbag warning light did not operate correctly.

Activation of airbag system

9 To activate the system on completion of any work, proceed as follows:
a) Ensure that there are no occupants in the vehicle, and that there are no loose objects around the vicinity of the steering wheel. Close the vehicle doors and windows.
b) Ensure that the ignition is switched off then reconnect the battery negative terminal.
c) Open the driver's door and switch on the ignition, without reaching in front of the steering wheel. Check that the airbag

warning light illuminates briefly then extinguishes.
d) Switch off the ignition.
e) If the airbag warning light does not operate as described in paragraph c), consult a Peugeot/Citroën dealer before driving the vehicle.

21 Airbag system components – removal and refitting

⚠️ **Warning: Refer to the precautions given in Section 20 before carrying out the following operations.**

Driver's airbag – removal

Pre-September 2002 models

1 De-activate the airbag system as described in Section 20.
2 Move the steering wheel as necessary for access to the two airbag unit securing screws. The screws are located at the rear of the steering wheel boss.
3 Remove the two airbag unit securing screws.
4 Gently pull the airbag unit from the centre of the steering wheel.
5 Carefully unclip the wiring connector from the airbag unit (use the fingers only, and pull

the connector upward from the airbag unit).
6 If the airbag unit is to be stored for any length of time, refer to the storage precautions given in Section 20.

Post-September 2002 models

7 De-activate the airbag system as described in Section 20.
8 Insert a screwdriver into the three holes on the underside of the steering wheel, one at a time, and push the internal retaining spring wire sideways to release the airbag retaining lugs. At the same time pull the airbag unit away from the steering wheel to release it **(see illustrations)**.
9 Disconnect the horn push earth connector, then release the locking clip and disconnect the airbag wiring connector **(see illustrations)**. Remove the airbag unit.
10 If the airbag unit is to be stored for any length of time, refer to the storage precautions given in Section 20.

Driver's airbag – refitting

11 Refitting is a reversal of removal, bearing in mind the following points:
a) Do not strike the airbag unit, or expose it to impacts during refitting.
b) Securely reconnect the wiring connectors then seat the airbag unit in the steering wheel, ensuring the wiring does not become trapped.
c) Where the airbag is retained by screws, tighten the screws securely.
d) Where the airbag is retained by a spring wire, press it into place until the retaining clips engage.
e) On completion of refitting, activate the airbag system as described in Section 20.

Passenger airbag – removal

Pre-September 2002 models

12 De-activate the airbag system as described in Section 20.
13 Remove the glovebox.
14 Working in the glovebox aperture, undo the five airbag retaining bolts, located at the base of the airbag unit.

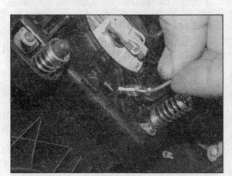

21.9a Disconnect the horn push earth connector . . .

21.9b . . . then release the locking clip and disconnect the airbag wiring connector

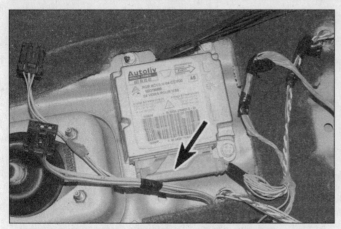

21.34 Release the retaining clip and disconnect the wiring connector (arrowed) from the airbag control unit

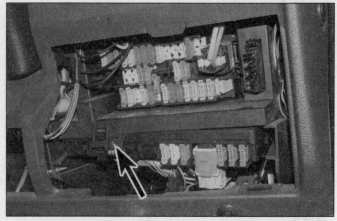

22.5 On early models, undo the retaining screw (arrowed) then release the clip and pivot the BSI unit downwards

15 Release the locking clip, disconnect the airbag wiring connector, then remove the airbag unit from the facia.

16 If the airbag unit is to be stored for any length of time, refer to the storage precautions given in Section 20.

Post-September 2002 models

17 De-activate the airbag system as described in Section 20.

18 Remove the complete facia assembly as described in Chapter 11.

19 Remove the air duct located over the top of the airbag unit.

20 Undo the four nuts securing the airbag unit in position. Detach the airbag cover retaining clips around the periphery of the cover, and withdraw the airbag from its location.

21 Release the locking clip, disconnect the airbag wiring connector, then remove the airbag unit from the car.

22 If the airbag unit is to be stored for any length of time, refer to the storage precautions given in Section 20.

Passenger airbag – refitting

23 Refitting is a reversal of removal, bearing in mind the following points:

a) Do not strike the airbag unit, or expose it to impacts during refitting.

b) Securely reconnect the wiring connector then seat the airbag unit in position, ensuring the wiring does not become trapped.

c) Securely tighten the airbag retaining nuts/bolts.

d) Refit the facia, or glovebox, as applicable, as described in Chapter 11.

e) On completion of refitting, activate the airbag system as described in Section 20.

Side airbag

24 Removal and refitting of the side airbag units should be entrusted to a Peugeot/Citroën dealer. The seat must be dismantled to enable the airbag unit to removed/refitted.

Curtain airbag

25 Removal and refitting of the curtain airbag units should be entrusted to a Peugeot/Citroën dealer. The headlining must be partially removed to enable the airbag unit to removed/refitted.

Rotary connector – removal

Pre-September 2002 models

26 Remove the airbag unit, as described previously in this Section.

27 Remove the steering wheel as described in Chapter 10.

28 Remove the steering column lower and upper shrouds as described in Chapter 11.

29 Trace the rotary connector wiring back to the connectors below the steering column and disconnect the wiring.

30 Unscrew the three securing screws, and withdraw the rotary connector from the steering column, feeding the wiring harness through the stalk switch bracket. Note the routing of the wiring harness.

Post-September 2002 models

31 The airbag rotary connector is an integral part of the steering column switch assembly, located below the steering wheel. Refer to Section 4 for removal and refitting details.

Rotary connector – refitting

32 Refitting is a reversal of removal, bearing in mind the following points on pre-September 2002 models:

a) Ensure that the rotary connector is centralised by aligning the marks on the rotary connector body and the rotating centre part prior to refitting. Instructions for centralising the unit are also provided on a label on the face of the unit.

b) Ensure that the roadwheels are in the straight-ahead position before refitting the rotary connector and steering wheel.

c) Before refitting the steering column shrouds, ensure that the rotary connector wiring harness is correctly routed as noted before removal.

d) Refit the steering wheel as described in Chapter 10, and refit the airbag unit as described previously in this Section.

Airbag control unit

Removal

33 De-activate the airbag system as described in Section 20.

34 Remove the centre console as described in Chapter 11, then release the retaining clip and disconnect the wiring connector from the airbag control unit **(see illustration)**.

35 Unscrew the retaining bolts then remove the control unit from the vehicle.

Refitting

36 Refitting is a reversal of removal, bearing in mind the following points:

a) Make sure the arrow on the top of the unit is pointing towards the front of the vehicle.

b) Refit the control unit retaining bolts and tighten them securely.

c) Refit the centre console as described in Chapter 11.

d) On completion of refitting, activate the airbag system as described in Section 20.

22 Built-in systems interface (BSI) unit/fusebox – general, removal and refitting

General information

1 The built-in systems interface (BSI) unit is an electronic control unit which controls a variety of functions, normally controlled by individual control units and relays (refer to Section 1 for additional information). The BSI unit is located in the left-hand side of the facia where it is situated directly beneath the fusebox. The BSI unit controls the following functions (not all functions are fitted to all models).

a) Direction indicator/hazard warning lights.

b) Windscreen/tailgate wiper motors.

c) Rear screen heating element.

d) Immobiliser system.

e) Anti-theft alarm system.
f) Lights-on/ignition key warning buzzer.
g) Central locking/deadlocking, including the remote central locking receiver.
h) Door open indicator.
i) Courtesy light delay timer.

2 Should any of the above functions become faulty, first check the condition of the fuses. If this fails to locate the problem, take the vehicle to a Peugeot/Citroën dealer for testing.

Removal

3 Disconnect the battery negative terminal (refer to Disconnecting the battery in the Reference Chapter).
4 Remove the lower facia panel on the driver's side (turn the retaining knobs 90° and remove the panel).
5 On early models, undo the retaining screw (where fitted) then release the retaining clip and pivot the BSI unit downwards to free it from the base of the fusebox (see illustration).
6 On later models, rotate the two white plastic fasteners 90 degrees anti-clockwise, and prise the fusebox outwards slightly. Lower the rear edge of the unit, then lift up the front edge and slide it from place.
7 On all models, note their fitted positions, then release the retaining clips then disconnect all the wiring connectors and remove the BSI unit from the vehicle. Note that there are several different designs of locking catches for the various connectors. Take your time to study the wiring connectors, and release them without using excessive force as they are easily damaged.

Refitting

8 Refitting is the reverse of removal, ensuring the wiring connectors are all securely reconnected. Note that the connector colours are listed adjacent to their respective sockets on the BSI.

23 Parking aid components – general information, removal and refitting

General information

1 The parking aid system is available as an option on certain models from RPO 10557. Four ultrasound sensors located in the rear bumper measure the distance to the closest object behind the car, and inform the driver using acoustic signals from a buzzer located under the rear trim. The nearer the object, the more frequent the acoustic signals. A switch located on the centre console allows the driver to switch the system on or off.
2 The system includes a control unit and self-diagnosis program, and therefore, in the event of a fault, the vehicle should be taken to a Citroën/Peugeot dealer for investigation.

Control unit

3 Remove the left-hand rear panel trim with reference to Chapter 11.
4 Unscrew the nut and remove the unit from the box bracket, then disconnect the wiring. The bracket is secured with rivets.
5 Refitting is a reversal of removal. If a new unit is being fitted, it will be necessary to have a Citroën/Peugeot dealer program the unit using a specialist diagnostic tool.

Range/distance sensor

6 Remove the rear bumper as described in Chapter 11.
7 If only one sensor is being removed, disconnect the wiring at the sensor then release the clips and remove the sensor from the rear bumper. Recover the tripod support. Take care not to scratch or damage the sensor as it is fragile.
8 Refitting is a reversal of removal.

Warning buzzer

9 Remove the left-hand rear panel trim with reference to Chapter 11.
10 The warning buzzer is clipped to the body inner panel; disconnect the wiring then release and remove the unit.
11 Refitting is a reversal of removal.

PARTNER/BERLINGO (early models)

Diagram 1

Typical fuse table

Engine fuse box

Fuses	Rating	Circuit protected
F1	20A	Headlight washer
F2	-	Not used
F3	30A	Engine cooling fan
F4	-	Not used
F5	-	Not used
F6	30A	ABS
F7	-	Not used
F8	-	Not used
F9	10A	Fuel pump
F10	5A	Oxygen sensor
F11	-	Not used
F12	10A	RH main beam
F13	10A	LH main beam
F14	10A	RH dipped beam
F15	10A	LH dipped beam

Maxi fuses A to H should only be changed by a main dealer

Passenger fuse box

Fuses	Rating	Circuit protected
F1	10A	Radio
F2	5A	Engine control unit, instrument panel
F3	15A	ABS
F4	5A	LH front side light, RH rear side light
F5	-	Not used
F6	10A	Air conditioning
F7	20A	Horn, diagnostic connector
F8	-	Shunt
F9	5A	RH front side light, LH rear side light, number plate lights
F10	20A	Electric windows
F11	20A	Passenger's electric window
F12	20A	Reversing light, engine cooling fan brake lights
F13	5A	Driver's electric window
F14	10A	Central locking
F15	15A	Central locking

Fuses	Rating	Circuit protected
F16	15A	Cigarette lighter
F17	-	Not used
F18	5A	Rear fog light
F19	5A	Interior illumination
F20	25A	Heater blower
F21	5A	Heated rear window, air conditioning
F22	20A	Rear wiper motor
F23	-	Shunt
F24	20A	Front wiper motor
F25	5A	Interior lighting, clock, air conditioning engine control unit
F26	15A	Direction indicators, central locking
F27	30A	Heated rear window
F28	15A	Electric windows, electric mirrors
F29	30A	Air conditioning, heated seats
F30	10A	Direction indicators, instrument panel, interior lights, central locking

Key to circuits

Diagram 1	Information for wiring diagrams
Diagram 2	Typical starting and charging, radio, horn, cigarette lighter, heated rear window, reversing lights
Diagram 3	Typical fog, side, number plate, brake, headlights, tail lights, direction indicators and hazard lights
Diagram 4	Typical ABS, airbag, electric windows, headlight adjustment
Diagram 5	Typical wash/wipe, central locking with deadlocking
Diagram 6	Typical heater blower, typical engine cooling, air conditioning
Diagram 7	Typical instrument panel, interior lights, electric mirrors

Earth points

E1	Battery earth	E8	Inside RH front wing
E2	RH lower 'A' pillar above E10	E9	Behind centre of the dashboard
E3	Behind battery	E10	RH lower 'A' pillar
E4	LH wing	E11	LH lower 'A' pillar above E5
E5	LH lower 'A' pillar	E12	Engine earth, front of the engine
E6	LH under tail light		
E7	RH under tail light		

Key to symbols

Bulb

Switch

Fuse/fusible link and current rating — F5 10A

Multiple contact switch (ganged)

Resistor

Variable resistor

Heater

Item no. — 2

Pump/motor — M

Earth point and location — E12

Solenoid actuator

Diode

Light emitting diode (LED)

Speaker

Connecting wires

Wire joint

Wire colour (brown with black tracer) — Mr/Nr

Screened cable

Dashed outline denotes part of a larger item, containing in this case an electronic or solid state device. Pin types:

2 - Unspecified colour connector, pin 2.

2Mr 1 - Brown two pin connector, pin 1.

— 2Mr

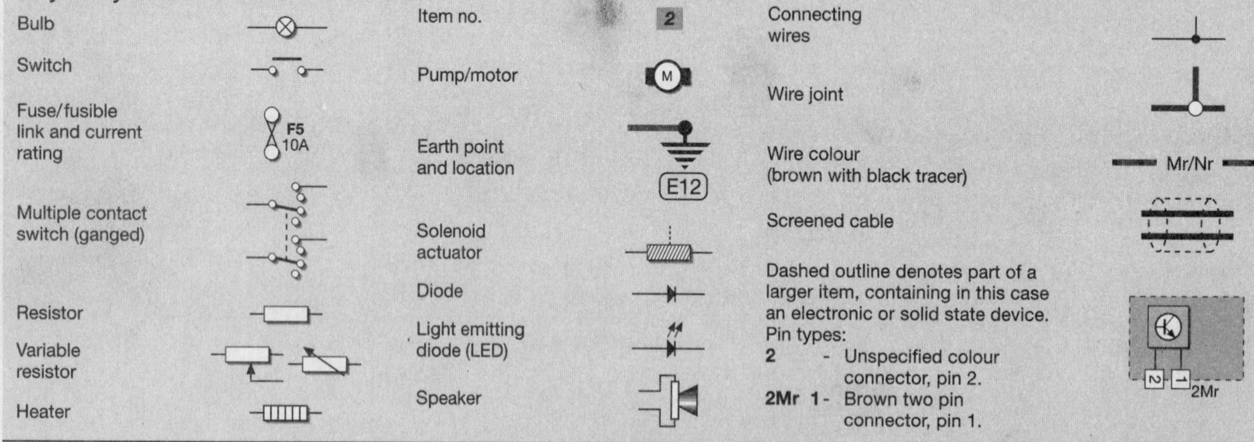

Please Note

The prime method of wire identification is by using the terminal pin numbers (moulded into each component or connector and shown in the diagrams) together with the number code printed on each wire. To relate each diagram to the vehicle wiring, locate the relevant component or connector illustrated and find the wire(s) connected to the terminal pin(s) as shown in the diagram.

Caution: Whilst a number (indicating the function of that wire) may be printed on each wire, this is not always the case, and in such instances, this is reflected by the absence of such wire numbering on our diagrams. Similarly, numbering of the connector/component terminal pins is not always available from the manufacturers' source information and may also be missing from our diagrams. In these cases, it may be necessary to refer to your local dealer for further information.

Note that the conventional method of using colour coding does not apply – whilst the wires on the vehicle will be coloured, the wire colour has no relevance.

Connector colours

Nr	Black	Or	Orange
Be	Blue	Rg	Red
Mr	Brown	Ba	White
Gr	Grey	Jn	Yellow
Ve	Green		

Key to items

1 Battery
2 Ignition switch
3 Engine fuse box
4 Passenger fuse box
5 Alternator
6 Starter motor
7 Engine running relay
8 Diagnostic connector
9 Radio
10 Aerial
11 RH speaker
12 LH speaker
13 Horn switch
14 Horn
15 Cigarette lighter
16 Ashtray illumination
17 Heated rear window relay
18 Heated rear window switch
19 RH rear window heater
20 LH rear window heater
21 Reversing light switch
22 LH tail light
a) reversing light

Diagram 2

MTS
H33268

Starting and charging

Radio

Cigarette lighter

Horn

Heated rear window

Reversing lights

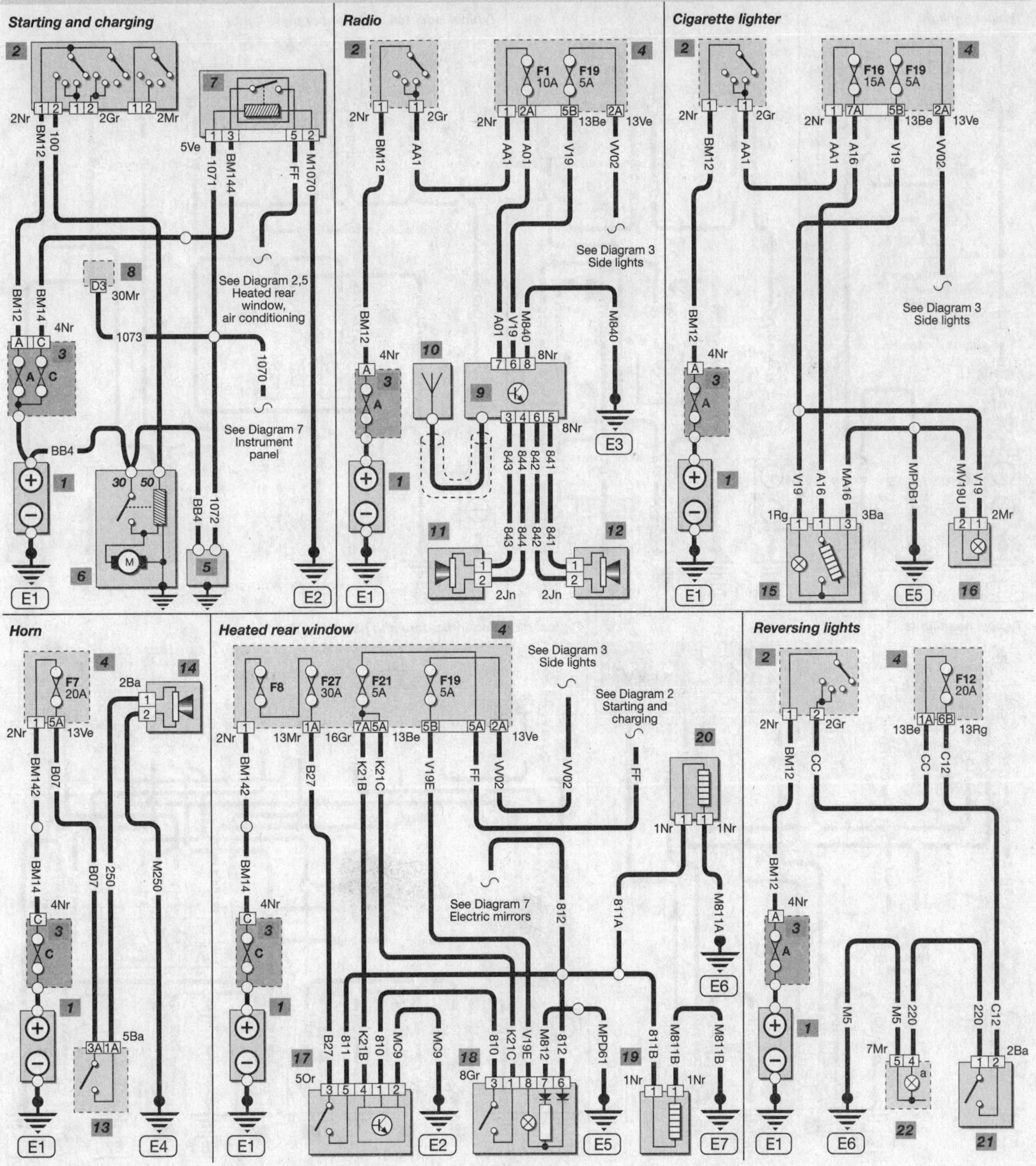

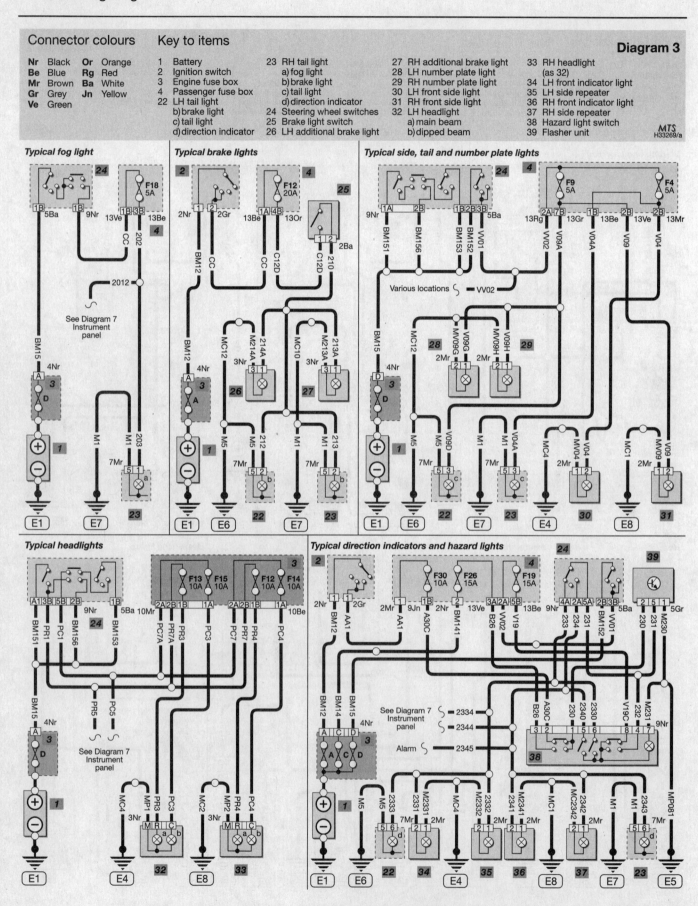

Connector colours

Nr	Black	Or	Orange
Be	Blue	Rg	Red
Mr	Brown	Ba	White
Gr	Grey	Jn	Yellow
Ve	Green		

Key to items

1 Battery
2 Ignition switch
3 Engine fuse box
4 Passenger fuse box
22 LH tail light
  b) brake light
  c) tail light
  d) direction indicator

23 RH tail light
  a) fog light
  b) brake light
  c) tail light
  d) direction indicator
24 Steering wheel switches
25 Brake light switch
26 LH additional brake light

27 RH additional brake light
28 LH number plate light
29 RH number plate light
30 LH front side light
31 RH front side light
32 LH headlight
  a) main beam
  b) dipped beam

33 RH headlight
  (as 32)
34 LH front indicator light
35 LH side repeater
36 RH front indicator light
37 RH side repeater
38 Hazard light switch
39 Flasher unit

Diagram 3

MTS
H33269/a

Typical fog light

Typical brake lights

Typical side, tail and number plate lights

Typical headlights

Typical direction indicators and hazard lights

Connector colours

Nr	Black	**Or**	Orange
Be	Blue	**Rg**	Red
Mr	Brown	**Ba**	White
Gr	Grey	**Jn**	Yellow
Ve	Green		

Key to items

1	Battery	42	Driver's seatbelt pretensionner
2	Ignition switch	43	Passenger's airbag
3	Engine fuse box	44	Driver's airbag
4	Passenger fuse box	45	Clock spring
8	Diagnostic connector	46	ABS module
24	Steering wheel switches	47	LH front wheel sensor
25	Brake light switch	48	RH front wheel sensor
40	Airbag module	49	LH rear wheel sensor
41	Passenger's seatbelt pretensionner	50	RH rear wheel sensor

51	Headlight adjustment switch
52	LH headlight adjustment motor
53	RH headlight adjustment motor
54	Electric window relay
55	LH window switch
56	RH window switch
57	Electric window module
58	LH window motor
59	RH window motor

Diagram 4

MTS
H33270/a

Typical airbag

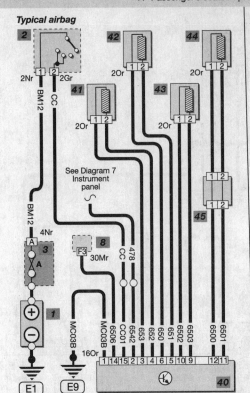

Typical ABS

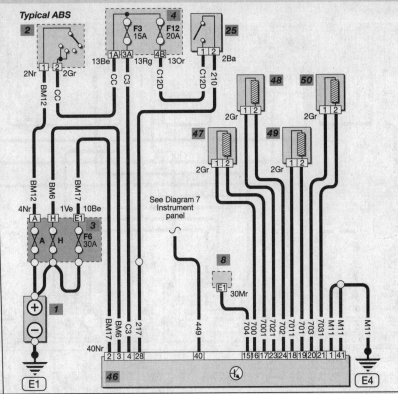

Typical headlight adjustment

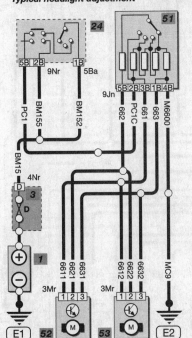

Typical electric windows

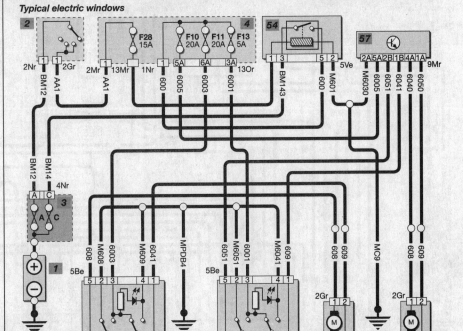

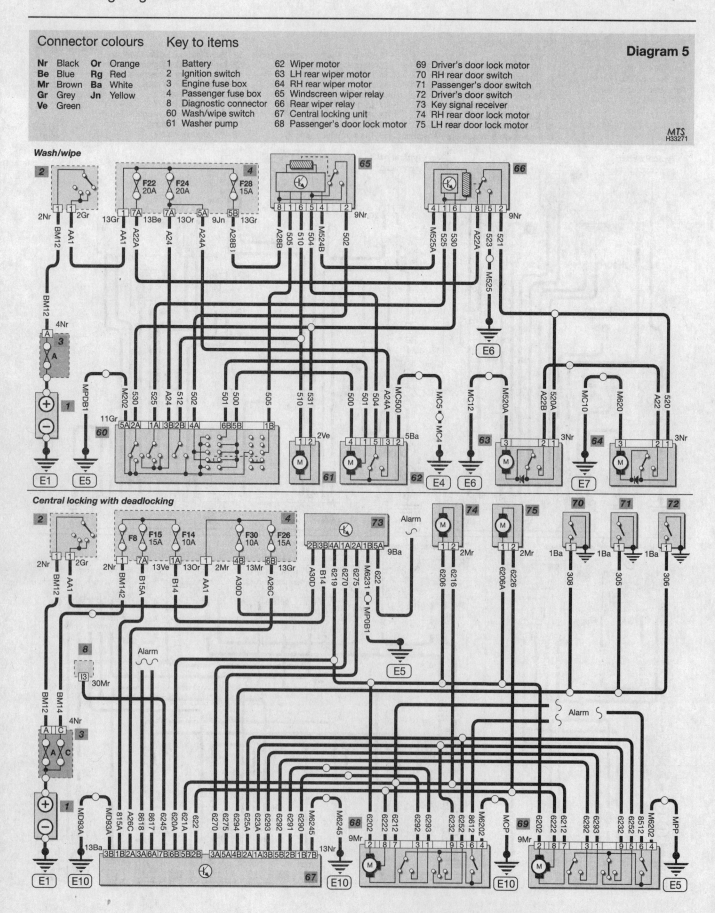

Connector colours

Nr	Black	Or	Orange
Be	Blue	Rg	Red
Mr	Brown	Ba	White
Gr	Grey	Jn	Yellow
Ve	Green		

Key to items

1 Battery
2 Ignition switch
3 Engine fuse box
4 Passenger fuse box
8 Diagnostic connector
60 Wash/wipe switch
61 Washer pump
62 Wiper motor
63 LH rear wiper motor
64 RH rear wiper motor
65 Windscreen wiper relay
66 Rear wiper relay
67 Central locking unit
68 Passenger's door lock motor
69 Driver's door lock motor
70 RH rear door switch
71 Passenger's door switch
72 Driver's door switch
73 Key signal receiver
74 RH rear door lock motor
75 LH rear door lock motor

Diagram 5

MTS
H33271

Wash/wipe

Central locking with deadlocking

Connector colours

Nr	Black	Or	Orange
Be	Blue	Rg	Red
Mr	Brown	Ba	White
Gr	Grey	Jn	Yellow
Ve	Green		

Key to items

1 Battery
2 Ignition switch
3 Engine fuse box
4 Passenger fuse box
76 Heater blower panel
77 Heater blower switches
78 Heater blower resistor pack
79 A/C heating controls
80 Blower motor
81 A/C panel
82 Passenger compartment thermostat
83 Evaporator temperature sensor
84 A/C switches
85 Blower motor relay
86 A/C compressor relay
87 A/C compressor
88 A/C cut-off relay
89 Pressostat
90 A/C control unit
91 Engine coolant temperature sensor
92 Engine cooling relay
93 Cooling fan switch
94 RH cooling fan
95 LH cooling fan

Diagram 6

MTS
H33272/a

Typical heater blower

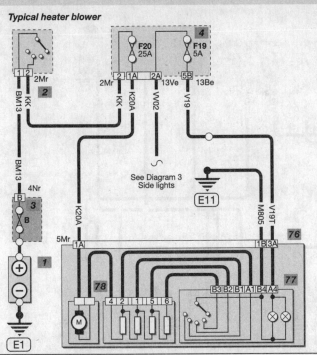

Typical engine cooling

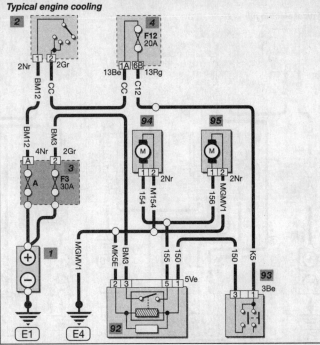

Typical air conditioning

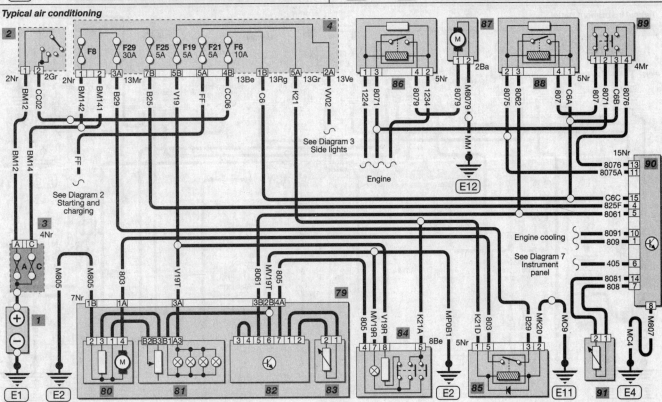

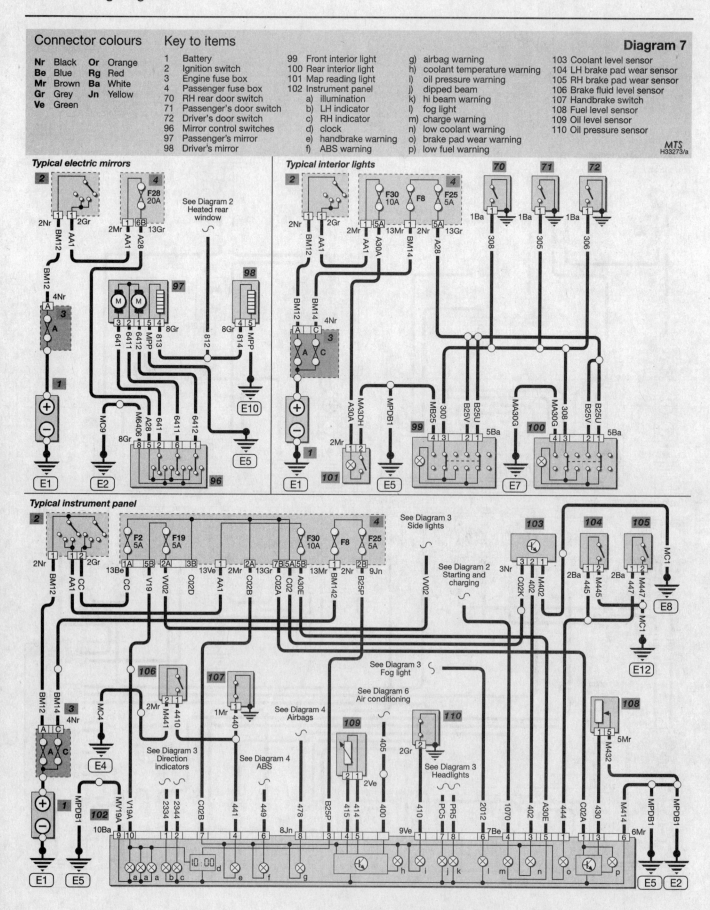

Connector colours

Nr	Black	**Or**	Orange
Be	Blue	**Rg**	Red
Mr	Brown	**Ba**	White
Gr	Grey	**Jn**	Yellow
Ve	Green		

Key to items

1 Battery
2 Ignition switch
3 Engine fuse box
4 Passenger fuse box
70 RH rear door switch
71 Passenger's door switch
72 Driver's door switch
96 Mirror control switches
97 Passenger's mirror
98 Driver's mirror

99 Front interior light
100 Rear interior light
101 Map reading light
102 Instrument panel
   a) illumination
   b) LH indicator
   c) RH indicator
   d) clock
   e) handbrake warning
   f) ABS warning

   g) airbag warning
   h) coolant temperature warning
   i) oil pressure warning
   j) dipped beam
   k) hi beam warning
   l) fog light
   m) charge warning
   n) low coolant warning
   o) brake pad wear warning
   p) low fuel warning

103 Coolant level sensor
104 LH brake pad wear sensor
105 RH brake pad wear sensor
106 Brake fluid level sensor
107 Handbrake switch
108 Fuel level sensor
109 Oil level sensor
110 Oil pressure sensor

Diagram 7

MTS H33273/a

Typical electric mirrors

Typical interior lights

Typical instrument panel

PARTNER/BERLINGO (later models)

Diagram 1

Typical fuse table

Engine fuse box

Fuses	Rating	Circuit protected
F1	70A	Built-in systems interface
F5	20A	Built-in systems interface
F7	20A	Additional heater
F8	70A	Passenger fuse box
F9	50A	Built-in systems interface
F10	40A	Rear wipers, lights
F11	60A	Passenger fuse box
F12	50A	Ignition switch
F14	20A	Injection relay
F15	50A	ABS
F16	20A	Engine fan
F17	20A	Engine fan
F18	10A	RH main beam
F19	10A	LH main beam
F20	10A	ABS
F21	5A	Alarm
F22	20A	Carburettor heater
F23	15A	Diesel heater
F25	15A	Fuel pump
F26	40A	Double relay
F28	10A	Diesel injection pump
F29	30A	Air pump
F30	10A	Front fog lights
F32	10A	Engine ECU
F33	15A	Reversing light, engine ECU, cooling fan
F34	5A	Oxygen sensor

Passenger fuse box

Fuses	Rating	Circuit protected
F1	Shunt	Airbag
F2	5A	Instrument panel
F4	5A	Built-in systems interface
F5	10A	Brake light switch
F6	5A	Dipped beam, clock
F7	10A	Engine ECU
F8	10A	Radio, interior lights, navigation
F9	5A	Built-in systems interface
F11	5A	Built-in systems interface, radio, heating
F12	5A	Fog lights
F13	15A	Heated seats
F14	30A	Headlight washer
F15	20A	12V socket
F16	30A	Air conditioning
F17	15A	Horn
F18	5A	LH front sidelight, RH rear tail light
F19	5A	RH front sidelight, LH rear tail light, number plate lights
F20	10A	LH dipped beam
F21	10A	RH dipped beam
F22	20A	Electric mirrors, interior lights, navigation
F23	20A	Cigarette lighter
F24	15A	Radio
F25	20A	Rear wiper
F27	10A	Built-in system interface

Built-in systems interface fuse box

Fuses	Rating	Circuit protected
FA	20A	Central locking
FB	25A	Wipe/wash
FC	30A	Heated rear windscreen and mirrors
FD	15A	Air conditioning, rear wiper
FE	30A	Electric windows, sunroof
FF	15A	Built-in systems interface

Key to circuits

Diagram 1	Information for wiring diagrams
Diagram 2	Typical wash/wipe, central locking with deadlocking
Diagram 3	Typical headlights, tail lights, side lights, number plate lights
Diagram 4	Typical brake lights, reversing lights, direction indicators
Diagram 5	Typical fog lights, cigarette lighter, electric windows and sunroof

Earth points

E1	Battery earth	E7	Inside RH front wing
E2	LH wing	E8	RH lower 'A' pillar above E3
E3	RH lower 'A' pillar		
E4	LH lower 'A' pillar	E9	LH lower 'A' pillar above E4
E5	RH under tail light		
E6	LH under tail light		

Key to symbols

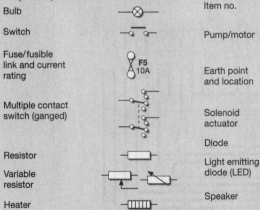

Bulb

Switch

Fuse/fusible link and current rating — F5 10A

Multiple contact switch (ganged)

Resistor

Variable resistor

Heater

Item no. — 2

Pump/motor

Earth point and location — E12

Solenoid actuator

Diode

Light emitting diode (LED)

Speaker

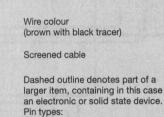

Connecting wires

Wire joint

Wire colour (brown with black tracer)

Screened cable

Dashed outline denotes part of a larger item, containing in this case an electronic or solid state device. Pin types:
2   - Unspecified colour connector, pin 2.
2Mr 1- Brown two pin connector, pin 1.

Mr/Nr

Please Note

The prime method of wire identification is by using the terminal pin numbers (moulded into each component or connector and shown in the diagrams) together with the number code printed on each wire. To relate each diagram to the vehicle wiring, locate the relevant component or connector illustrated and find the wire(s) connected to the terminal pin(s) as shown in the diagram.

Caution: Whilst a number (indicating the function of that wire) may be printed on each wire, this is not always the case, and in such instances, this is reflected by the absence of such wire numbering on our diagrams. Similarly, numbering of the connector/component terminal pins is not always available from the manufacturers' source information and may also be missing from our diagrams. In these cases, it may be necessary to refer to your local dealer for further information.

Note that the conventional method of using colour coding does not apply – whilst the wires on the vehicle will be coloured, the wire colour has no relevance.

H33274/a

Connector colours

Nr	Black	Or	Orange
Be	Blue	Rg	Red
Mr	Brown	Ba	White
Gr	Grey	Jn	Yellow
Ve	Green		

Key to items

1 Battery
2 Ignition switch
3 Engine fuse box
4 Passenger fuse box
5 Built-in system interface
6 Steering wheel switches
7 Washer pump
8 Wiper motor
9 LH rear wiper motor
10 RH rear wiper motor
11 Passenger's door lock motor
12 Driver's door lock motor
13 LH rear door lock motor
14 Tailgate lock motor
15 RH rear door lock motor

Diagram 2

MTS
H33275/a

Typical wash/wipe

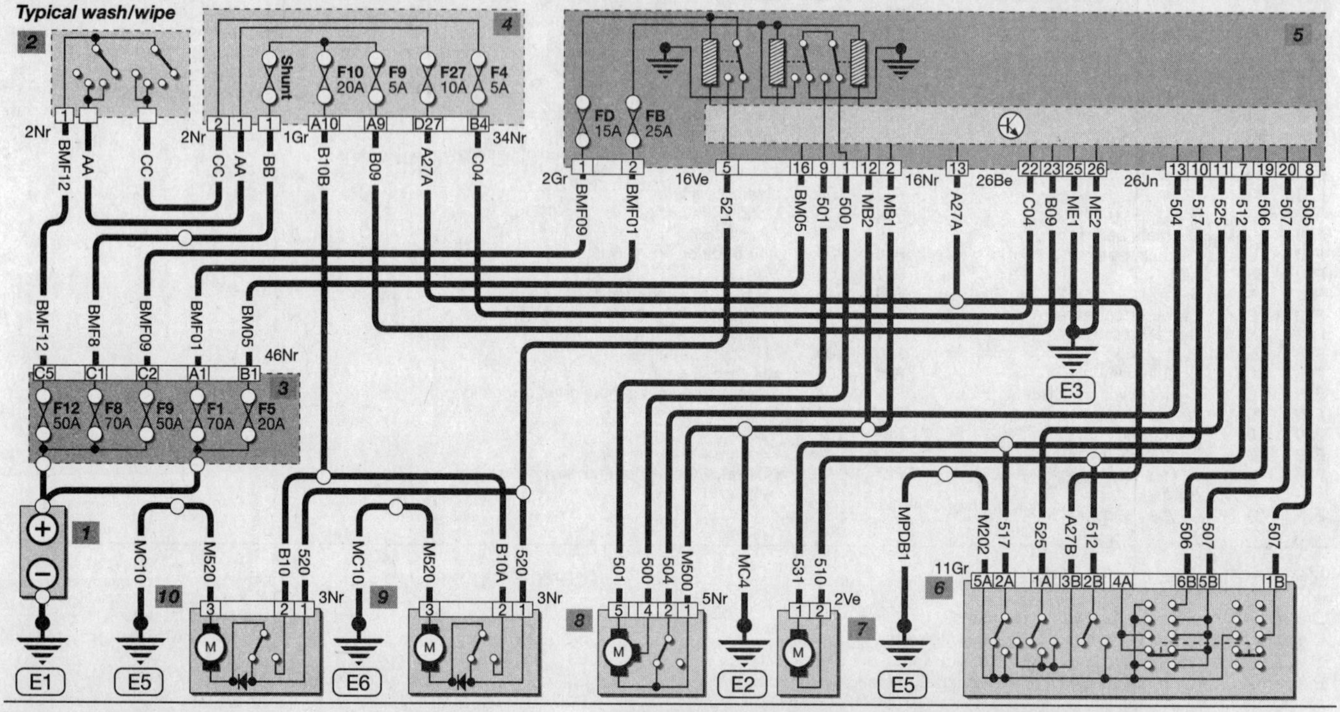

Typical central locking

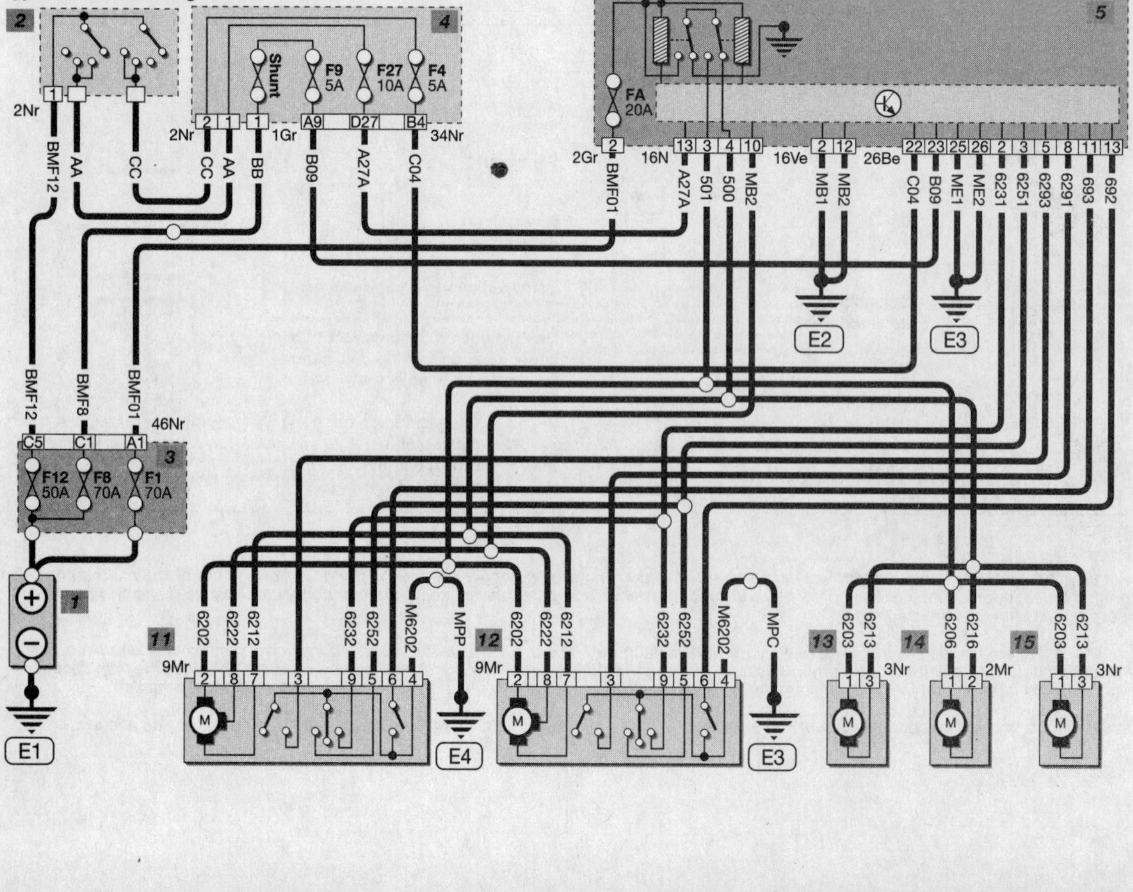

Connector colours

Nr	Black	Or	Orange
Be	Blue	Rg	Red
Mr	Brown	Ba	White
Gr	Grey	Jn	Yellow
Ve	Green		

Key to items

1. Battery
2. Ignition switch
3. Engine fuse box
4. Passenger fuse box
5. Built-in system interface
6. Steering wheel switches
16. LH headlight
    a) main beam
    b) dipped beam
17. RH headlight
    (as 16)
18. Dipped beam relay
19. LH tail light
    a) tail light
20. RH tail light
    (as 19)
21. LH number plate light
22. RH number plate light
23. RH front side light
24. LH front side light

Diagram 3

MTS
H33276/a

Typical headlights

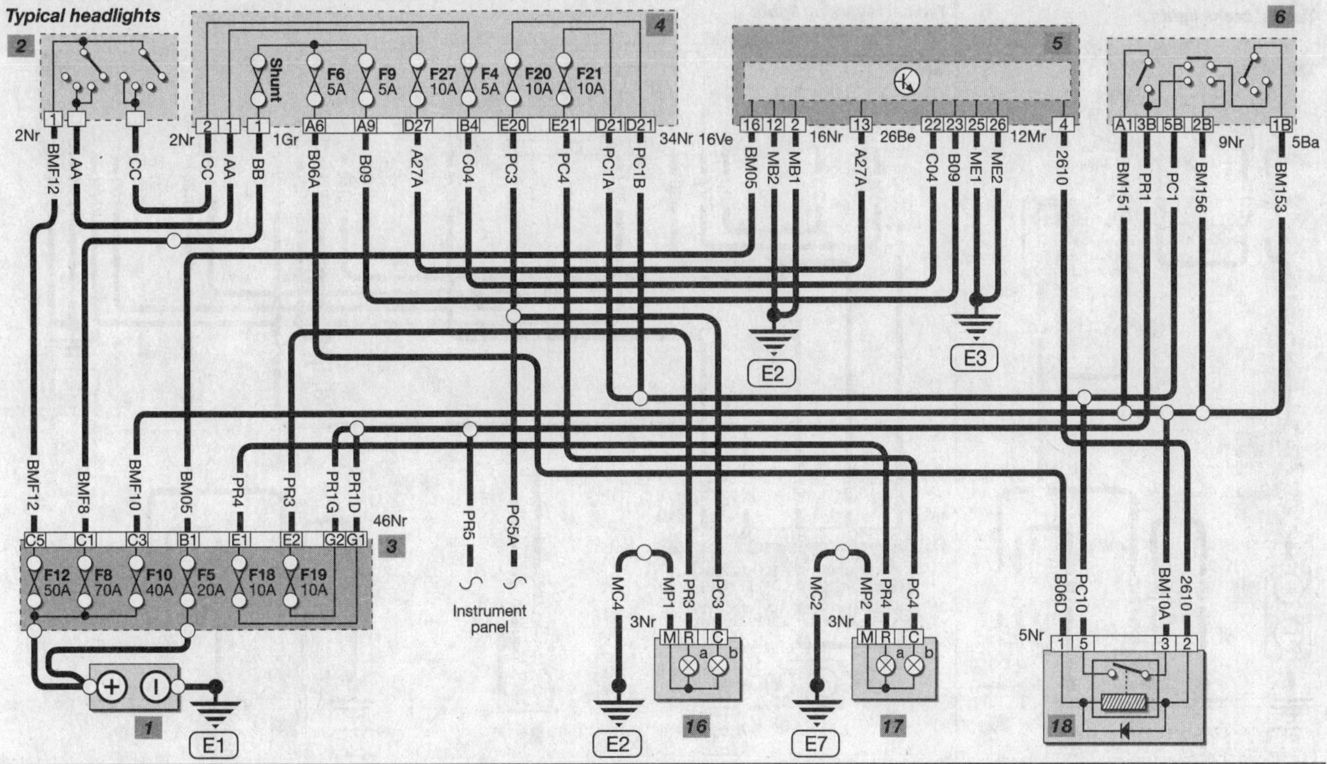

Typical side, tail and number plate lights

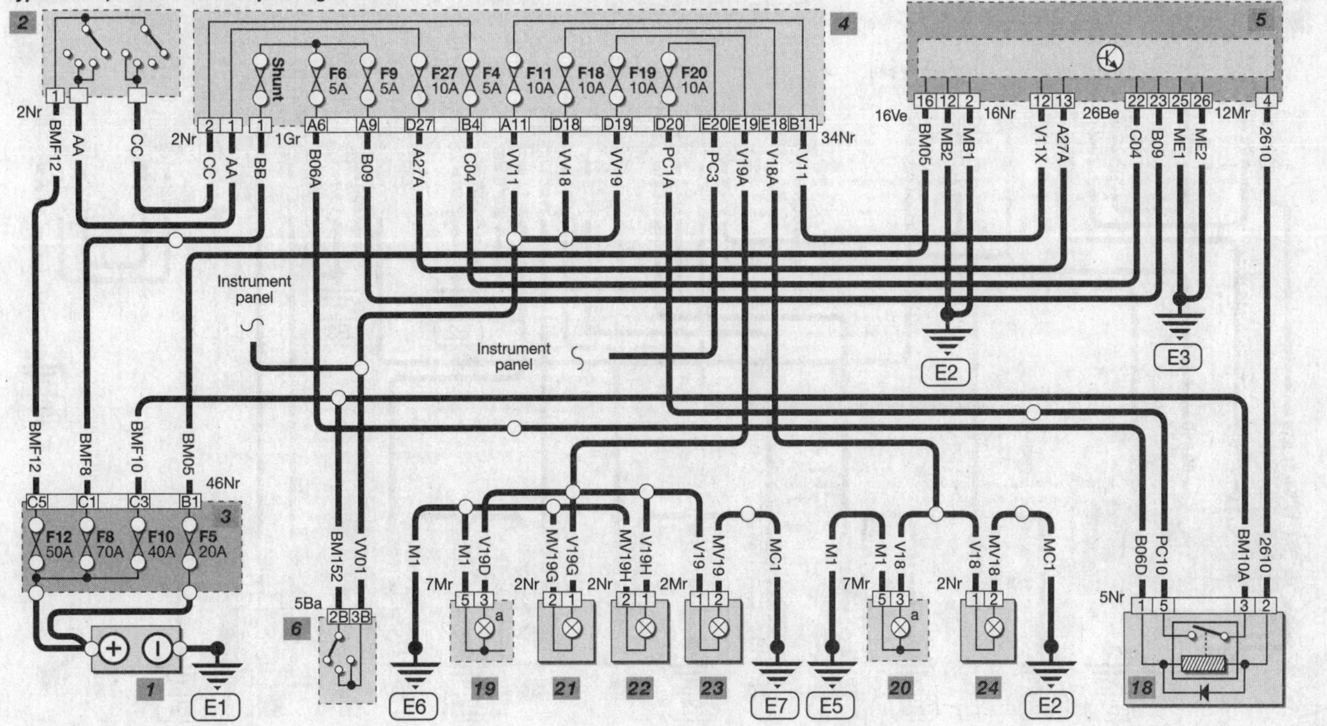

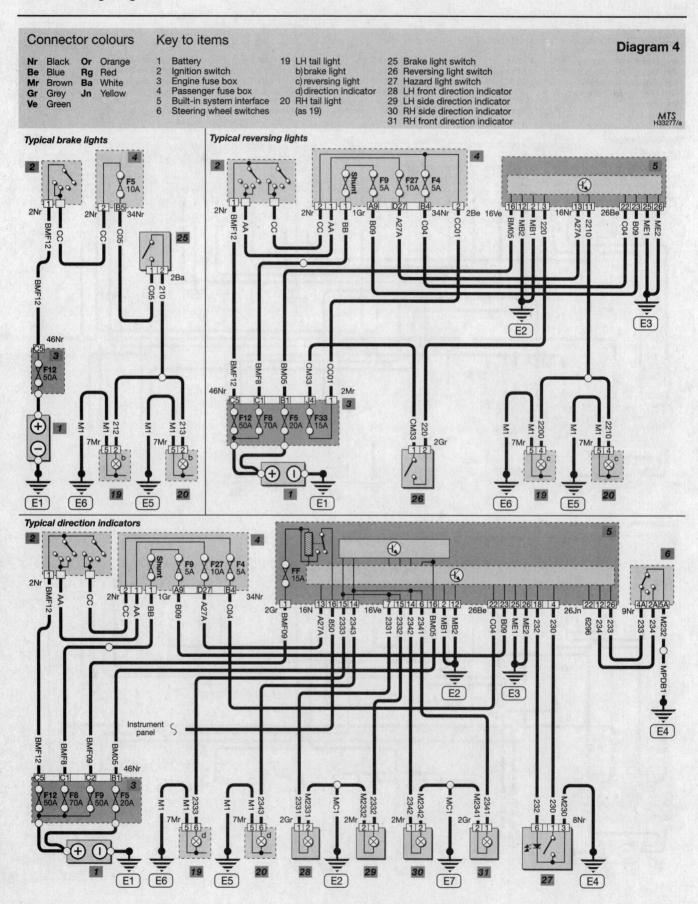

Connector colours

Nr	Black	Or	Orange
Be	Blue	Rg	Red
Mr	Brown	Ba	White
Gr	Grey	Jn	Yellow
Ve	Green		

Key to items

1 Battery
2 Ignition switch
3 Engine fuse box
4 Passenger fuse box
5 Built-in system interface
6 Steering wheel switches
19 LH tail light
b) brake light
c) reversing light
d) direction indicator
20 RH tail light
(as 19)
25 Brake light switch
26 Reversing light switch
27 Hazard light switch
28 LH front direction indicator
29 LH side direction indicator
30 RH side direction indicator
31 RH front direction indicator

Diagram 4

MTS
H33277/a

Typical brake lights

Typical reversing lights

Typical direction indicators

Connector colours

Nr	Black	Or	Orange
Be	Blue	Rg	Red
Mr	Brown	Ba	White
Gr	Grey	Jn	Yellow
Ve	Green		

Key to items

1 Battery
2 Ignition switch
3 Engine fuse box
4 Passenger fuse box
5 Built-in system interface
6 Steering wheel switches
20 RH tail light
   e) fog light
32 Cigarette lighter
33 Ashtray illumination
34 Horn
35 Sunroof motor
36 Sunroof switch
37 Sunroof limit switch
38 LH window motor
39 LH window switch
40 RH window switch
41 RH window motor
42 Electric window control unit

Diagram 5

MTS
H33278/a

Typical fog light

Typical cigarette lighter

See diagram 3
Side lights

Typical horn

Typical electric windows and sunroof

Instrument panel

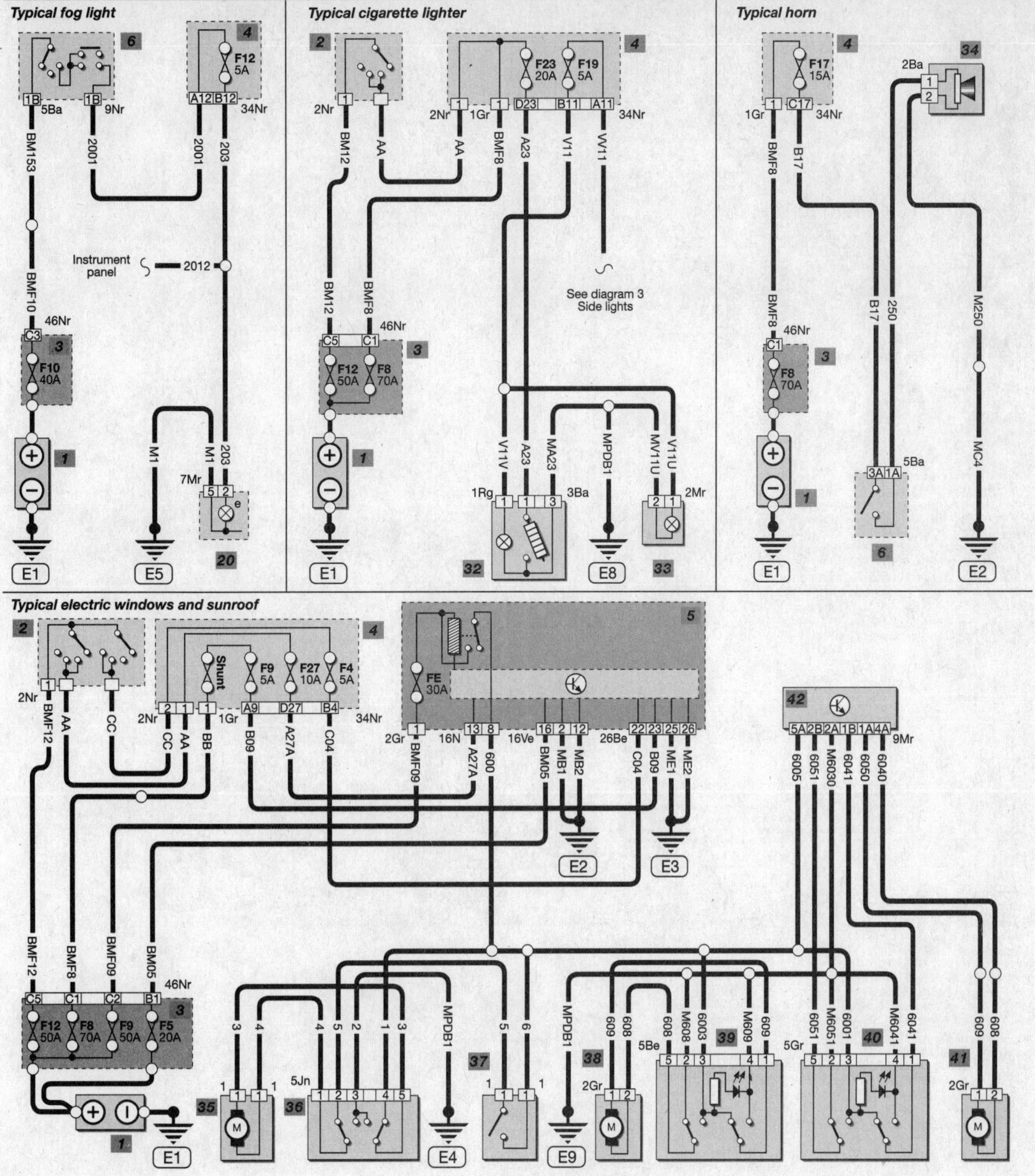

Notes

Reference REF•1

Dimensions and weights

Note: *All figures are approximate, and may vary according to model. Refer to manufacturer's data for exact figures.*

Dimensions

Overall length	4137 mm
Overall width (including mirrors)	1960 mm
Overall height (unladen)	1796 to 1834 mm
Wheelbase	2693 mm
Front track	1420 mm
Rear track	1440 mm

Weights

Kerb weight*	1055 to 1206 kg
Maximum gross vehicle weight*	1655 to 1990 kg
Maximum roof rack load	100 kg
Maximum towing weight:**	
Unbraked trailer	500 kg
Braked trailer:	
1.4 litre petrol engine models	900 kg
All other models	1100 kg
Maximum trailer nose weight	70 kg

* Depending on model and specification.
** Refer to a Peugeot/Citroën dealer for exact recommendations.
Note: *All figures are approximate, and may vary according to model. Refer to manufacturer's data for exact figures.*

Conversion factors

Length (distance)

Inches (in)	x 25.4	= Millimetres (mm)	x 0.0394	=	Inches (in)
Feet (ft)	x 0.305	= Metres (m)	x 3.281	=	Feet (ft)
Miles	x 1.609	= Kilometres (km)	x 0.621	=	Miles

Volume (capacity)

Cubic inches (cu in; in³)	x 16.387	= Cubic centimetres (cc; cm³)	x 0.061	=	Cubic inches (cu in; in³)
Imperial pints (Imp pt)	x 0.568	= Litres (l)	x 1.76	=	Imperial pints (Imp pt)
Imperial quarts (Imp qt)	x 1.137	= Litres (l)	x 0.88	=	Imperial quarts (Imp qt)
Imperial quarts (Imp qt)	x 1.201	= US quarts (US qt)	x 0.833	=	Imperial quarts (Imp qt)
US quarts (US qt)	x 0.946	= Litres (l)	x 1.057	=	US quarts (US qt)
Imperial gallons (Imp gal)	x 4.546	= Litres (l)	x 0.22	=	Imperial gallons (Imp gal)
Imperial gallons (Imp gal)	x 1.201	= US gallons (US gal)	x 0.833	=	Imperial gallons (Imp gal)
US gallons (US gal)	x 3.785	= Litres (l)	x 0.264	=	US gallons (US gal)

Mass (weight)

Ounces (oz)	x 28.35	= Grams (g)	x 0.035	=	Ounces (oz)
Pounds (lb)	x 0.454	= Kilograms (kg)	x 2.205	=	Pounds (lb)

Force

Ounces-force (ozf; oz)	x 0.278	= Newtons (N)	x 3.6	=	Ounces-force (ozf; oz)
Pounds-force (lbf; lb)	x 4.448	= Newtons (N)	x 0.225	=	Pounds-force (lbf; lb)
Newtons (N)	x 0.1	= Kilograms-force (kgf; kg)	x 9.81	=	Newtons (N)

Pressure

Pounds-force per square inch (psi; lbf/in²; lb/in²)	x 0.070	= Kilograms-force per square centimetre (kgf/cm²; kg/cm²)	x 14.223	=	Pounds-force per square inch (psi; lbf/in²; lb/in²)
Pounds-force per square inch (psi; lbf/in²; lb/in²)	x 0.068	= Atmospheres (atm)	x 14.696	=	Pounds-force per square inch (psi; lbf/in²; lb/in²)
Pounds-force per square inch (psi; lbf/in²; lb/in²)	x 0.069	= Bars	x 14.5	=	Pounds-force per square inch (psi; lbf/in²; lb/in²)
Pounds-force per square inch (psi; lbf/in²; lb/in²)	x 6.895	= Kilopascals (kPa)	x 0.145	=	Pounds-force per square inch (psi; lbf/in²; lb/in²)
Kilopascals (kPa)	x 0.01	= Kilograms-force per square centimetre (kgf/cm²; kg/cm²)	x 98.1	=	Kilopascals (kPa)
Millibar (mbar)	x 100	= Pascals (Pa)	x 0.01	=	Millibar (mbar)
Millibar (mbar)	x 0.0145	= Pounds-force per square inch (psi; lbf/in²; lb/in²)	x 68.947	=	Millibar (mbar)
Millibar (mbar)	x 0.75	= Millimetres of mercury (mmHg)	x 1.333	=	Millibar (mbar)
Millibar (mbar)	x 0.401	= Inches of water (inH₂O)	x 2.491	=	Millibar (mbar)
Millimetres of mercury (mmHg)	x 0.535	= Inches of water (inH₂O)	x 1.868	=	Millimetres of mercury (mmHg)
Inches of water (inH₂O)	x 0.036	= Pounds-force per square inch (psi; lbf/in²; lb/in²)	x 27.68	=	Inches of water (inH₂O)

Torque (moment of force)

Pounds-force inches (lbf in; lb in)	x 1.152	= Kilograms-force centimetre (kgf cm; kg cm)	x 0.868	=	Pounds-force inches (lbf in; lb in)
Pounds-force inches (lbf in; lb in)	x 0.113	= Newton metres (Nm)	x 8.85	=	Pounds-force inches (lbf in; lb in)
Pounds-force inches (lbf in; lb in)	x 0.083	= Pounds-force feet (lbf ft; lb ft)	x 12	=	Pounds-force inches (lbf in; lb in)
Pounds-force feet (lbf ft; lb ft)	x 0.138	= Kilograms-force metres (kgf m; kg m)	x 7.233	=	Pounds-force feet (lbf ft; lb ft)
Pounds-force feet (lbf ft; lb ft)	x 1.356	= Newton metres (Nm)	x 0.738	=	Pounds-force feet (lbf ft; lb ft)
Newton metres (Nm)	x 0.102	= Kilograms-force metres (kgf m; kg m)	x 9.804	=	Newton metres (Nm)

Power

Horsepower (hp)	x 745.7	= Watts (W)	x 0.0013	=	Horsepower (hp)

Velocity (speed)

Miles per hour (miles/hr; mph)	x 1.609	= Kilometres per hour (km/hr; kph)	x 0.621	=	Miles per hour (miles/hr; mph)

Fuel consumption*

Miles per gallon, Imperial (mpg)	x 0.354	= Kilometres per litre (km/l)	x 2.825	=	Miles per gallon, Imperial (mpg)
Miles per gallon, US (mpg)	x 0.425	= Kilometres per litre (km/l)	x 2.352	=	Miles per gallon, US (mpg)

Temperature

Degrees Fahrenheit = (°C x 1.8) + 32   Degrees Celsius (Degrees Centigrade; °C) = (°F - 32) x 0.56

It is common practice to convert from miles per gallon (mpg) to litres/100 kilometres (l/100km), where mpg x l/100 km = 282

Spare parts are available from many sources, including maker's appointed garages, accessory shops, and motor factors. To be sure of obtaining the correct parts, it may sometimes be necessary to quote the vehicle identification number. If possible, it can also be useful to take the old parts along for positive identification. Items such as starter motors and alternators maybe available under a service exchange scheme – any parts returned should be clean.

Our advice regarding spare part sources is as follows.

Officially-appointed garages

This is the best source of parts which are peculiar to your car, and are not otherwise generally available (eg, badges, interior trim, certain body panels, etc). It is also the only place at which you should buy parts if the vehicle is still under warranty.

Accessory shops

These are very good places to buy materials and components needed for the maintenance of your car (oil, air and fuel filters, spark plugs, light bulbs, drivebelts, oils and greases, brake pads, touch-up paint, etc). Components of this nature sold by a reputable shop are of the same standard as those used by the car manufacturer.

Besides components, these shops will also sell tools and general accessories, usually have convenient opening hours. charge lower prices, and can often be found close to home. Some accessory shops also have parts counters where components needed for almost any repair job can be purchased or ordered.

Motor factors

Good factors will stock all the more important components which wear out comparatively quickly and can sometimes supply individual components needed for the overhaul of a larger assembly. They may also handle work such as cylinder block reboring, crankshaft regrinding and balancing, etc.

Tyre and exhaust specialists

These outlets may be independent or members of a local or national chain. They frequently offer competitive prices when compared with a main dealer or local garage, but it will pay to obtain several quotes before making a decision. Also ask what 'extras' may be added to the quote – for instance, fitting a new valve and balancing the wheel are both often charged on top of the price of a new tyre.

Other sources

Beware of parts or materials obtained from market stalls, car boot sales or similar outlets. Such items are not invariably sub-standard, but there is little chance of compensation if they do prove unsatisfactory. In the case of safety-critical components such as brake pads there is the risk not only of financial loss but also of an accident causing injury or death.

Vehicle identification

Modifications are a continuing and unpublicised process in vehicle manufacture, quite apart from major model changes. Spare parts manuals and lists are compiled upon a numerical basis, the individual vehicle identification numbers being essential for correct identification of the part concerned.

When ordering spare parts, always give as much information as possible. Quote the car model, year of manufacture, VIN and engine numbers, as appropriate.

The *vehicle identification (chassis) number* is stamped into the body, along the top edge of the right-hand wing, and can be viewed with the bonnet open.

The *manufacturer's chassis plate* (which also carries the vehicle identification number) is located on the right-hand side of the engine compartment adjacent to the suspension strut turret. Additional identification numbers for weight information and paint codes are located on, or adjacent to this plate.

The *engine number* is situated on the front face of the cylinder block, and can be found in the following locations:

a) *On petrol engines the engine number is located on the left-hand side of the cylinder block. The number is either stamped directly onto the block or is stamped onto a plate which is riveted to the block.*

b) *On diesel engines the engine number is stamped on the base of the cylinder block on the flat surface located on the right- hand side of the oil filter/cooler.*

Note: *The first part of the engine number gives the engine code, eg KFW.*

Jacking and vehicle support

The jack supplied with the vehicle should only be used for changing the roadwheels – see *Wheel changing* at the front of this manual. When carrying out any other kind of work, raise the vehicle using a hydraulic (or 'trolley') jack, and always supplement the jack with axle stands at the vehicle jacking points.

When using a hydraulic jack or axle stands, always position the jack head or axle stand head under one of the relevant jacking points in the ridge on the underside of the sill **(see illustration).**

To raise the front of the vehicle, position the jack with an interposed block of wood underneath the centre of the front subframe. **Do not** jack the vehicle under the sump, or any of the steering or suspension components.

To raise the rear of the vehicle, position the jack head underneath the centre of the rear axle tubular crossmember. **Do not** attempt to raise the vehicle with the jack positioned underneath the spare wheel, as the vehicle floor will almost certainly be damaged.

The jack supplied with the vehicle locates in the jacking points in the ridge on the underside of the sill. Ensure that the jack head is correctly engaged before attempting to raise the vehicle.

Never work under, around, or near a raised vehicle, unless it is adequately supported in at least two places.

The jacking and supporting point is indicated by a triangle (arrowed on the sill)

Whenever servicing, repair or overhaul work is carried out on the car or its components, observe the following procedures and instructions. This will assist in carrying out the operation efficiently and to a professional standard of workmanship.

Joint mating faces and gaskets

When separating components at their mating faces, never insert screwdrivers or similar implements into the joint between the faces in order to prise them apart. This can cause severe damage which results in oil leaks, coolant leaks, etc upon reassembly. Separation is usually achieved by tapping along the joint with a soft-faced hammer in order to break the seal. However, note that this method may not be suitable where dowels are used for component location.

Where a gasket is used between the mating faces of two components, a new one must be fitted on reassembly; fit it dry unless otherwise stated in the repair procedure. Make sure that the mating faces are clean and dry, with all traces of old gasket removed. When cleaning a joint face, use a tool which is unlikely to score or damage the face, and remove any burrs or nicks with an oilstone or fine file.

Make sure that tapped holes are cleaned with a pipe cleaner, and keep them free of jointing compound, if this is being used, unless specifically instructed otherwise.

Ensure that all orifices, channels or pipes are clear, and blow through them, preferably using compressed air.

Oil seals

Oil seals can be removed by levering them out with a wide flat-bladed screwdriver or similar implement. Alternatively, a number of self-tapping screws may be screwed into the seal, and these used as a purchase for pliers or some similar device in order to pull the seal free.

Whenever an oil seal is removed from its working location, either individually or as part of an assembly, it should be renewed.

The very fine sealing lip of the seal is easily damaged, and will not seal if the surface it contacts is not completely clean and free from scratches, nicks or grooves. If the original sealing surface of the component cannot be restored, and the manufacturer has not made provision for slight relocation of the seal relative to the sealing surface, the component should be renewed.

Protect the lips of the seal from any surface which may damage them in the course of fitting. Use tape or a conical sleeve where possible. Where indicated, lubricate the seal lips with oil before fitting and, on dual-lipped seals, fill the space between the lips with grease.

Unless otherwise stated, oil seals must be fitted with their sealing lips toward the lubricant to be sealed.

Use a tubular drift or block of wood of the appropriate size to install the seal and, if the seal housing is shouldered, drive the seal down to the shoulder. If the seal housing is unshouldered, the seal should be fitted with its face flush with the housing top face (unless otherwise instructed).

Screw threads and fastenings

Seized nuts, bolts and screws are quite a common occurrence where corrosion has set in, and the use of penetrating oil or releasing fluid will often overcome this problem if the offending item is soaked for a while before attempting to release it. The use of an impact driver may also provide a means of releasing such stubborn fastening devices, when used in conjunction with the appropriate screwdriver bit or socket. If none of these methods works, it may be necessary to resort to the careful application of heat, or the use of a hacksaw or nut splitter device. Before resorting to extreme methods, check that you are not dealing with a left-hand thread!

Studs are usually removed by locking two nuts together on the threaded part, and then using a spanner on the lower nut to unscrew the stud. Studs or bolts which have broken off below the surface of the component in which they are mounted can sometimes be removed using a stud extractor.

Always ensure that a blind tapped hole is completely free from oil, grease, water or other fluid before installing the bolt or stud. Failure to do this could cause the housing to crack due to the hydraulic action of the bolt or stud as it is screwed in.

For some screw fastenings, notably cylinder head bolts or nuts, torque wrench settings are no longer specified for the latter stages of tightening, "angle-tightening" being called up instead. Typically, a fairly low torque wrench setting will be applied to the bolts/nuts in the correct sequence, followed by one or more stages of tightening through specified angles.

When checking or retightening a nut or bolt to a specified torque setting, slacken the nut or bolt by a quarter of a turn, and then retighten to the specified setting. However, this should not be attempted where angular tightening has been used.

Locknuts, locktabs and washers

Any fastening which will rotate against a component or housing during tightening should always have a washer between it and the relevant component or housing.

Spring or split washers should always be renewed when they are used to lock a critical component such as a big-end bearing retaining bolt or nut. Locktabs which are folded over to retain a nut or bolt should always be renewed.

Self-locking nuts can be re-used in non-critical areas, providing resistance can be felt when the locking portion passes over the bolt or stud thread. However, it should be noted that self-locking stiffnuts tend to lose their effectiveness after long periods of use, and should then be renewed as a matter of course.

Split pins must always be replaced with new ones of the correct size for the hole.

When thread-locking compound is found on the threads of a fastener which is to be re-used, it should be cleaned off with a wire brush and solvent, and fresh compound applied on reassembly.

Special tools

Some repair procedures in this manual entail the use of special tools such as a press, two or three-legged pullers, spring compressors, etc. Wherever possible, suitable readily-available alternatives to the manufacturer's special tools are described, and are shown in use. In some instances, where no alternative is possible, it has been necessary to resort to the use of a manufacturer's tool, and this has been done for reasons of safety as well as the efficient completion of the repair operation. Unless you are highly-skilled and have a thorough understanding of the procedures described, never attempt to bypass the use of any special tool when the procedure described specifies its use. Not only is there a very great risk of personal injury, but expensive damage could be caused to the components involved.

Environmental considerations

When disposing of used engine oil, brake fluid, antifreeze, etc, give due consideration to any detrimental environmental effects. Do not, for instance, pour any of the above liquids down drains into the general sewage system, or onto the ground to soak away. Many local council refuse tips provide a facility for waste oil disposal, as do some garages. You can find your nearest disposal point by calling the Environment Agency on 08708 506 506 or by visiting www.oilbankline.org.uk.

Note: It is illegal and anti-social to dump oil down the drain. To find the location of your local oil recycling bank, call 08708 506 506 or visit www.oilbankline.org.uk.

Numerous systems fitted to the vehicle require battery power to be available at all times, either to ensure their continued operation (such as the clock) or to maintain control unit memories which would be erased if the battery were to be disconnected. Whenever the battery is to be disconnected therefore, first note the following, to ensure that there are no unforeseen consequences of this action:

a) *First, on any vehicle with central locking, it is a wise precaution to remove the key from the ignition, and to keep it with you, so that it does not get locked in if the central locking should engage accidentally when the battery is reconnected.*

b) *The majority of models covered in this manual are equipped with a Peugeot/ Citroën anti-theft alarm system. When reconnecting the battery after disconnection, the alarm may be automatically activated. If so, use the remote transmitter to turn off the alarm, or turn off the alarm manually by switching on the ignition. To fully reactivate the system once the battery is reconnected, lock then unlock the vehicle using the remote transmitter; the alarm will be functional again the next time the vehicle is locked with the remote transmitter.*

c) *If a security-coded audio unit is fitted, and the unit and/or the battery is disconnected, the unit will not function again on reconnection until the correct security code is entered. Details of this procedure, which varies according to the unit fitted, are given in the vehicle owner's handbook. Ensure you have the correct code before you disconnect the battery. If you do not have the code or details of the correct procedure, but can supply proof of ownership and a legitimate reason for wanting this information, a Peugeot/ Citroën dealer may be able to help.*

d) *On all petrol engines, later 1.9 litre diesel engines and all 2.0 litre diesel engines, the engine management electronic control unit is of the 'self-learning' type, meaning that as it operates, it also monitors and stores the settings which give optimum engine performance under all operating conditions. When the battery is disconnected, these settings are lost and the ECU reverts to the base settings programmed into its memory at the factory. On restarting, this may lead to the engine running/idling roughly for a short while, until the ECU has re-learned the optimum settings. This process is best accomplished by taking the vehicle*

on a road test (for approximately 15 minutes), covering all engine speeds and loads, concentrating mainly in the 2500 to 3500 rpm region.

e) *On all models, when reconnecting the battery after disconnection, switch on the ignition and wait 10 seconds to allow the electronic vehicle systems to stabilise and re-initialise.*

Devices known as 'memory-savers' (or 'code-savers') can be used to avoid some of the above problems. Precise details vary according to the device used. Typically, it is plugged into the cigarette lighter, and is connected by its own wires to a spare battery; the vehicle's own battery is then disconnected from the electrical system, leaving the 'memory-saver' to pass sufficient current to maintain audio unit security codes and any other memory values, and also to run permanently-live circuits such as the clock.

 Warning: Some of these devices allow a considerable amount of current to pass, which can mean that many of the vehicle's systems are still operational when the main battery is disconnected. If a 'memory saver' is used, ensure that the circuit concerned is actually 'dead' before carrying out any work on it!

Introduction

A selection of good tools is a fundamental requirement for anyone contemplating the maintenance and repair of a motor vehicle. For the owner who does not possess any, their purchase will prove a considerable expense, offsetting some of the savings made by doing-it-yourself. However, provided that the tools purchased meet the relevant national safety standards and are of good quality, they will last for many years and prove an extremely worthwhile investment.

To help the average owner to decide which tools are needed to carry out the various tasks detailed in this manual, we have compiled three lists of tools under the following headings: *Maintenance and minor repair, Repair and overhaul,* and *Special.* Newcomers to practical mechanics should start off with the *Maintenance and minor repair* tool kit, and confine themselves to the simpler jobs around the vehicle. Then, as confidence and experience grow, more difficult tasks can be undertaken, with extra tools being purchased as, and when, they are needed. In this way, a *Maintenance and minor repair* tool kit can be built up into a *Repair and overhaul* tool kit over a considerable period of time, without any major cash outlays. The experienced do-it-yourselfer will have a tool kit good enough for most repair and overhaul procedures, and will add tools from the *Special* category when it is felt that the expense is justified by the amount of use to which these tools will be put.

Maintenance and minor repair tool kit

The tools given in this list should be considered as a minimum requirement if routine maintenance, servicing and minor repair operations are to be undertaken. We recommend the purchase of combination spanners (ring one end, open-ended the other); although more expensive than open-ended ones, they do give the advantages of both types of spanner.

☐ *Combination spanners:*
    Metric - 8 to 19 mm inclusive
☐ *Adjustable spanner - 35 mm jaw (approx.)*
☐ *Spark plug spanner (with rubber insert) - petrol models*
☐ *Spark plug gap adjustment tool - petrol models*
☐ *Set of feeler gauges*
☐ *Brake bleed nipple spanner*
☐ *Screwdrivers:*
    Flat blade - 100 mm long x 6 mm dia
    Cross blade - 100 mm long x 6 mm dia
    Torx - various sizes (not all vehicles)
☐ *Combination pliers*
☐ *Hacksaw (junior)*
☐ *Tyre pump*
☐ *Tyre pressure gauge*
☐ *Oil can*
☐ *Oil filter removal tool (if applicable)*
☐ *Fine emery cloth*
☐ *Wire brush (small)*
☐ *Funnel (medium size)*
☐ *Sump drain plug key (not all vehicles)*

Repair and overhaul tool kit

These tools are virtually essential for anyone undertaking any major repairs to a motor vehicle, and are additional to those given in the *Maintenance and minor repair* list. Included in this list is a comprehensive set of sockets. Although these are expensive, they will be found invaluable as they are so versatile - particularly if various drives are included in the set. We recommend the half-inch square-drive type, as this can be used with most proprietary torque wrenches.

The tools in this list will sometimes need to be supplemented by tools from the *Special* list:

☐ *Sockets to cover range in previous list (including Torx sockets)*
☐ *Reversible ratchet drive (for use with sockets)*
☐ *Extension piece, 250 mm (for use with sockets)*
☐ *Universal joint (for use with sockets)*
☐ *Flexible handle or sliding T "breaker bar" (for use with sockets)*
☐ *Torque wrench (for use with sockets)*
☐ *Self-locking grips*
☐ *Ball pein hammer*
☐ *Soft-faced mallet (plastic or rubber)*
☐ *Screwdrivers:*
    Flat blade - long & sturdy, short (chubby), and narrow (electrician's) types
    Cross blade – long & sturdy, and short (chubby) types
☐ *Pliers:*
    Long-nosed
    Side cutters (electrician's)
    Circlip (internal and external)
☐ *Cold chisel - 25 mm*
☐ *Scriber*
☐ *Scraper*
☐ *Centre-punch*
☐ *Pin punch*
☐ *Hacksaw*
☐ *Brake hose clamp*
☐ *Brake/clutch bleeding kit*
☐ *Selection of twist drills*
☐ *Steel rule/straight-edge*
☐ *Allen keys (inc. splined/Torx type)*
☐ *Selection of files*
☐ *Wire brush*
☐ *Axle stands*
☐ *Jack (strong trolley or hydraulic type)*
☐ *Light with extension lead*
☐ *Universal electrical multi-meter*

Sockets and reversible ratchet drive

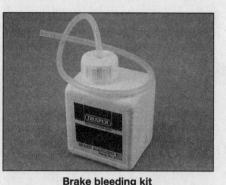

Brake bleeding kit

Torx key, socket and bit

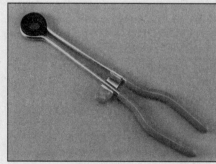

Hose clamp

Angular-tightening gauge

Special tools

The tools in this list are those which are not used regularly, are expensive to buy, or which need to be used in accordance with their manufacturers' instructions. Unless relatively difficult mechanical jobs are undertaken frequently, it will not be economic to buy many of these tools. Where this is the case, you could consider clubbing together with friends (or joining a motorists' club) to make a joint purchase, or borrowing the tools against a deposit from a local garage or tool hire specialist.

The following list contains only those tools and instruments freely available to the public, and not those special tools produced by the vehicle manufacturer specifically for its dealer network. You will find occasional references to these manufacturers' special tools in the text of this manual. Generally, an alternative method of doing the job without the vehicle manufacturers' special tool is given. However, sometimes there is no alternative to using them. Where this is the case and the relevant tool cannot be bought or borrowed, you will have to entrust the work to a dealer.

☐ Angular-tightening gauge
☐ Valve spring compressor
☐ Valve grinding tool
☐ Piston ring compressor
☐ Piston ring removal/installation tool
☐ Cylinder bore hone
☐ Balljoint separator
☐ Coil spring compressors (where applicable)
☐ Two/three-legged hub and bearing puller
☐ Impact screwdriver
☐ Micrometer and/or vernier calipers
☐ Dial gauge
☐ Tachometer
☐ Fault code reader
☐ Cylinder compression gauge
☐ Hand-operated vacuum pump and gauge
☐ Clutch plate alignment set
☐ Brake shoe steady spring cup removal tool
☐ Bush and bearing removal/installation set
☐ Stud extractors
☐ Tap and die set
☐ Lifting tackle

Buying tools

Reputable motor accessory shops and superstores often offer excellent quality tools at discount prices, so it pays to shop around.

Remember, you don't have to buy the most expensive items on the shelf, but it is always advisable to steer clear of the very cheap tools. Beware of 'bargains' offered on market stalls, on-line or at car boot sales. There are plenty of good tools around at reasonable prices, but always aim to purchase items which meet the relevant national safety standards. If in doubt, ask the proprietor or manager of the shop for advice before making a purchase.

Care and maintenance of tools

Having purchased a reasonable tool kit, it is necessary to keep the tools in a clean and serviceable condition. After use, always wipe off any dirt, grease and metal particles using a clean, dry cloth, before putting the tools away. Never leave them lying around after they have been used. A simple tool rack on the garage or workshop wall for items such as screwdrivers and pliers is a good idea. Store all normal spanners and sockets in a metal box. Any measuring instruments, gauges, meters, etc, must be carefully stored where they cannot be damaged or become rusty.

Take a little care when tools are used. Hammer heads inevitably become marked, and screwdrivers lose the keen edge on their blades from time to time. A little timely attention with emery cloth or a file will soon restore items like this to a good finish.

Working facilities

Not to be forgotten when discussing tools is the workshop itself. If anything more than routine maintenance is to be carried out, a suitable working area becomes essential.

It is appreciated that many an owner-mechanic is forced by circumstances to remove an engine or similar item without the benefit of a garage or workshop. Having done this, any repairs should always be done under the cover of a roof.

Wherever possible, any dismantling should be done on a clean, flat workbench or table at a suitable working height.

Any workbench needs a vice; one with a jaw opening of 100 mm is suitable for most jobs. As mentioned previously, some clean dry storage space is also required for tools, as well as for any lubricants, cleaning fluids, touch-up paints etc, which become necessary.

Another item which may be required, and which has a much more general usage, is an electric drill with a chuck capacity of at least 8 mm. This, together with a good range of twist drills, is virtually essential for fitting accessories.

Last, but not least, always keep a supply of old newspapers and clean, lint-free rags available, and try to keep any working area as clean as possible.

Micrometers

Dial test indicator ("dial gauge")

Oil filter removal tool (strap wrench type)

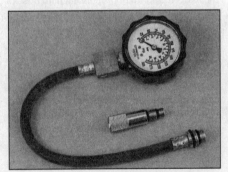

Compression tester

Fault code reader

This is a guide to getting your vehicle through the MOT test. Obviously it will not be possible to examine the vehicle to the same standard as the professional MOT tester. However, working through the following checks will enable you to identify any problem areas before submitting the vehicle for the test.

It has only been possible to summarise the test requirements here, based on the regulations in force at the time of printing. Test standards are becoming increasingly stringent, although there are some exemptions for older vehicles.

An assistant will be needed to help carry out some of these checks.

The checks have been sub-divided into four categories, as follows:

1 Checks carried out **FROM THE DRIVER'S SEAT**

2 Checks carried out **WITH THE VEHICLE ON THE GROUND**

3 Checks carried out **WITH THE VEHICLE RAISED AND THE WHEELS FREE TO TURN**

4 Checks carried out on **YOUR VEHICLE'S EXHAUST EMISSION SYSTEM**

---

1 Checks carried out **FROM THE DRIVER'S SEAT**

Handbrake

☐ Test the operation of the handbrake. Excessive travel (too many clicks) indicates incorrect brake or cable adjustment.
☐ Check that the handbrake cannot be released by tapping the lever sideways. Check the security of the lever mountings.

Footbrake

☐ Depress the brake pedal and check that it does not creep down to the floor, indicating a master cylinder fault. Release the pedal, wait a few seconds, then depress it again. If the pedal travels nearly to the floor before firm resistance is felt, brake adjustment or repair is necessary. If the pedal feels spongy, there is air in the hydraulic system which must be removed by bleeding.

☐ Check that the brake pedal is secure and in good condition. Check also for signs of fluid leaks on the pedal, floor or carpets, which would indicate failed seals in the brake master cylinder.
☐ Check the servo unit (when applicable) by operating the brake pedal several times, then keeping the pedal depressed and starting the engine. As the engine starts, the pedal will move down slightly. If not, the vacuum hose or the servo itself may be faulty.

Steering wheel and column

☐ Examine the steering wheel for fractures or looseness of the hub, spokes or rim.
☐ Move the steering wheel from side to side and then up and down. Check that the steering wheel is not loose on the column, indicating wear or a loose retaining nut. Continue moving the steering wheel as before, but also turn it slightly from left to right.
☐ Check that the steering wheel is not loose on the column, and that there is no abnormal movement of the steering wheel, indicating

wear in the column support bearings or couplings.

Windscreen, mirrors and sunvisor

☐ The windscreen must be free of cracks or other significant damage within the driver's field of view. (Small stone chips are acceptable.) Rear view mirrors must be secure, intact, and capable of being adjusted.

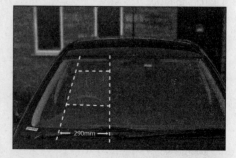

☐ The driver's sunvisor must be capable of being stored in the "up" position.

Seat belts and seats

Note: *The following checks are applicable to all seat belts, front and rear.*

☐ Examine the webbing of all the belts (including rear belts if fitted) for cuts, serious fraying or deterioration. Fasten and unfasten each belt to check the buckles. If applicable, check the retracting mechanism. Check the security of all seat belt mountings accessible from inside the vehicle.

☐ Seat belts with pre-tensioners, once activated, have a "flag" or similar showing on the seat belt stalk. This, in itself, is not a reason for test failure.

☐ The front seats themselves must be securely attached and the backrests must lock in the upright position.

Doors

☐ Both front doors must be able to be opened and closed from outside and inside, and must latch securely when closed.

2 Checks carried out WITH THE VEHICLE ON THE GROUND

Vehicle identification

☐ Number plates must be in good condition, secure and legible, with letters and numbers correctly spaced – spacing at (A) should be 33 mm and at (B) 11 mm.

☐ The VIN plate and/or homologation plate must be legible.

Electrical equipment

☐ Switch on the ignition and check the operation of the horn.

☐ Check the windscreen washers and wipers, examining the wiper blades; renew damaged or perished blades. Also check the operation of the stop-lights.

☐ Check the operation of the sidelights and number plate lights. The lenses and reflectors must be secure, clean and undamaged.

☐ Check the operation and alignment of the headlights. The headlight reflectors must not be tarnished and the lenses must be undamaged.

☐ Switch on the ignition and check the operation of the direction indicators (including the instrument panel tell-tale) and the hazard warning lights. Operation of the sidelights and stop-lights must not affect the indicators - if it does, the cause is usually a bad earth at the rear light cluster.

☐ Check the operation of the rear foglight(s), including the warning light on the instrument panel or in the switch.

☐ The ABS warning light must illuminate in accordance with the manufacturers' design. For most vehicles, the ABS warning light should illuminate when the ignition is switched on, and (if the system is operating properly) extinguish after a few seconds. Refer to the owner's handbook.

Footbrake

☐ Examine the master cylinder, brake pipes and servo unit for leaks, loose mountings, corrosion or other damage.

☐ The fluid reservoir must be secure and the fluid level must be between the upper (**A**) and lower (**B**) markings.

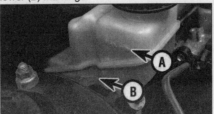

☐ Inspect both front brake flexible hoses for cracks or deterioration of the rubber. Turn the steering from lock to lock, and ensure that the hoses do not contact the wheel, tyre, or any part of the steering or suspension mechanism. With the brake pedal firmly depressed, check the hoses for bulges or leaks under pressure.

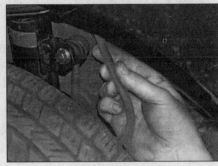

Steering and suspension

☐ Have your assistant turn the steering wheel from side to side slightly, up to the point where the steering gear just begins to transmit this movement to the roadwheels. Check for excessive free play between the steering wheel and the steering gear, indicating wear or insecurity of the steering column joints, the column-to-steering gear coupling, or the steering gear itself.

☐ Have your assistant turn the steering wheel more vigorously in each direction, so that the roadwheels just begin to turn. As this is done, examine all the steering joints, linkages, fittings and attachments. Renew any component that shows signs of wear or damage. On vehicles with power steering, check the security and condition of the steering pump, drivebelt and hoses.

☐ Check that the vehicle is standing level, and at approximately the correct ride height.

Shock absorbers

☐ Depress each corner of the vehicle in turn, then release it. The vehicle should rise and then settle in its normal position. If the vehicle continues to rise and fall, the shock absorber is defective. A shock absorber which has seized will also cause the vehicle to fail.

Exhaust system

☐ Start the engine. With your assistant holding a rag over the tailpipe, check the entire system for leaks. Repair or renew leaking sections.

3 Checks carried out **WITH THE VEHICLE RAISED AND THE WHEELS FREE TO TURN**

Jack up the front and rear of the vehicle, and securely support it on axle stands. Position the stands clear of the suspension assemblies. Ensure that the wheels are clear of the ground and that the steering can be turned from lock to lock.

Steering mechanism

☐ Have your assistant turn the steering from lock to lock. Check that the steering turns smoothly, and that no part of the steering mechanism, including a wheel or tyre, fouls any brake hose or pipe or any part of the body structure.
☐ Examine the steering rack rubber gaiters for damage or insecurity of the retaining clips. If power steering is fitted, check for signs of damage or leakage of the fluid hoses, pipes or connections. Also check for excessive stiffness or binding of the steering, a missing split pin or locking device, or severe corrosion of the body structure within 30 cm of any steering component attachment point.

Front and rear suspension and wheel bearings

☐ Starting at the front right-hand side, grasp the roadwheel at the 3 o'clock and 9 o'clock positions and rock gently but firmly. Check for free play or insecurity at the wheel bearings, suspension balljoints, or suspension mount-ings, pivots and attachments.
☐ Now grasp the wheel at the 12 o'clock and 6 o'clock positions and repeat the previous inspection. Spin the wheel, and check for roughness or tightness of the front wheel bearing.

☐ If excess free play is suspected at a component pivot point, this can be confirmed by using a large screwdriver or similar tool and levering between the mounting and the component attachment. This will confirm whether the wear is in the pivot bush, its retaining bolt, or in the mounting itself (the bolt holes can often become elongated).

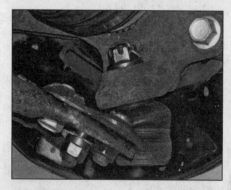

☐ Carry out all the above checks at the other front wheel, and then at both rear wheels.

Springs and shock absorbers

☐ Examine the suspension struts (when applicable) for serious fluid leakage, corrosion, or damage to the casing. Also check the security of the mounting points.
☐ If coil springs are fitted, check that the spring ends locate in their seats, and that the spring is not corroded, cracked or broken.
☐ If leaf springs are fitted, check that all leaves are intact, that the axle is securely attached to each spring, and that there is no deterioration of the spring eye mountings, bushes, and shackles.

☐ The same general checks apply to vehicles fitted with other suspension types, such as torsion bars, hydraulic displacer units, etc. Ensure that all mountings and attachments are secure, that there are no signs of excessive wear, corrosion or damage, and (on hydraulic types) that there are no fluid leaks or damaged pipes.
☐ Inspect the shock absorbers for signs of serious fluid leakage. Check for wear of the mounting bushes or attachments, or damage to the body of the unit.

Driveshafts (fwd vehicles only)

☐ Rotate each front wheel in turn and inspect the constant velocity joint gaiters for splits or damage. Also check that each driveshaft is straight and undamaged.

Braking system

☐ If possible without dismantling, check brake pad wear and disc condition. Ensure that the friction lining material has not worn excessively, (A) and that the discs are not fractured, pitted, scored or badly worn (B).

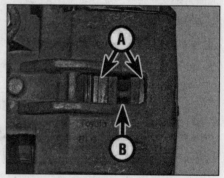

☐ Examine all the rigid brake pipes underneath the vehicle, and the flexible hose(s) at the rear. Look for corrosion, chafing or insecurity of the pipes, and for signs of bulging under pressure, chafing, splits or deterioration of the flexible hoses.
☐ Look for signs of fluid leaks at the brake calipers or on the brake backplates. Repair or renew leaking components.
☐ Slowly spin each wheel, while your assistant depresses and releases the footbrake. Ensure that each brake is operating and does not bind when the pedal is released.

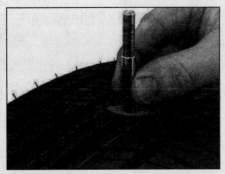

□ Examine the handbrake mechanism, checking for frayed or broken cables, excessive corrosion, or wear or insecurity of the linkage. Check that the mechanism works on each relevant wheel, and releases fully, without binding.

□ It is not possible to test brake efficiency without special equipment, but a road test can be carried out later to check that the vehicle pulls up in a straight line.

Fuel and exhaust systems

□ Inspect the fuel tank (including the filler cap), fuel pipes, hoses and unions. All components must be secure and free from leaks.

□ Examine the exhaust system over its entire length, checking for any damaged, broken or missing mountings, security of the retaining clamps and rust or corrosion.

Wheels and tyres

□ Examine the sidewalls and tread area of each tyre in turn. Check for cuts, tears, lumps, bulges, separation of the tread, and exposure of the ply or cord due to wear or damage. Check that the tyre bead is correctly seated on the wheel rim, that the valve is sound and properly seated, and that the wheel is not distorted or damaged.

□ Check that the tyres are of the correct size for the vehicle, that they are of the same size

and type on each axle, and that the pressures are correct.

□ Check the tyre tread depth. The legal minimum at the time of writing is 1.6 mm over at least three-quarters of the tread width. Abnormal tread wear may indicate incorrect front wheel alignment.

Body corrosion

□ Check the condition of the entire vehicle structure for signs of corrosion in load-bearing areas. (These include chassis box sections, side sills, cross-members, pillars, and all suspension, steering, braking system and seat belt mountings and anchorages.) Any corrosion which has seriously reduced the thickness of a load-bearing area is likely to cause the vehicle to fail. In this case professional repairs are likely to be needed.

□ Damage or corrosion which causes sharp or otherwise dangerous edges to be exposed will also cause the vehicle to fail.

4 Checks carried out on YOUR VEHICLE'S EXHAUST EMISSION SYSTEM

Petrol models

□ The engine should be warmed up, and running well (ignition system in good order, air filter element clean, etc).

□ Before testing, run the engine at around 2500 rpm for 20 seconds. Let the engine drop to idle, and watch for smoke from the exhaust. If the idle speed is too high, or if dense blue or black smoke emerges for more than 5 seconds, the vehicle will fail. Typically, blue smoke signifies oil burning (engine wear); black smoke means unburnt fuel (dirty air cleaner element, or other fuel system fault).

□ An exhaust gas analyser for measuring carbon monoxide (CO) and hydrocarbons (HC) is now needed. If one cannot be hired or borrowed, have a local garage perform the check.

CO emissions (mixture)

□ The MOT tester has access to the CO limits for all vehicles. The CO level is measured at idle speed, and at 'fast idle' (2500 to 3000 rpm). The following limits are given as a general guide:

At idle speed – Less than 0.5% CO
At 'fast idle' – Less than 0.3% CO
Lambda reading – 0.97 to 1.03

□ If the CO level is too high, this may point to poor maintenance, a fuel injection system problem, faulty lambda (oxygen) sensor or catalytic converter. Try an injector cleaning treatment, and check the vehicle's ECU for fault codes.

HC emissions

□ The MOT tester has access to HC limits for all vehicles. The HC level is measured at 'fast idle' (2500 to 3000 rpm). The following limits are given as a general guide:

At 'fast idle' – Less then 200 ppm

□ Excessive HC emissions are typically caused by oil being burnt (worn engine), or by a blocked crankcase ventilation system ('breather'). If the engine oil is old and thin, an oil change may help. If the engine is running badly, check the vehicle's ECU for fault codes.

Diesel models

□ The only emission test for diesel engines is measuring exhaust smoke density, using a calibrated smoke meter. The test involves accelerating the engine at least 3 times to its maximum unloaded speed.

Note: *On engines with a timing belt, it is VITAL that the belt is in good condition before the test is carried out.*

□ With the engine warmed up, it is first purged by running at around 2500 rpm for 20 seconds. A governor check is then carried out, by slowly accelerating the engine to its maximum speed. After this, the smoke meter is connected, and the engine is accelerated quickly to maximum speed three times. If the smoke density is less than the limits given below, the vehicle will pass:

Non-turbo vehicles: 2.5m-1
Turbocharged vehicles: 3.0m-1

□ If excess smoke is produced, try fitting a new air cleaner element, or using an injector cleaning treatment. If the engine is running badly, where applicable, check the vehicle's ECU for fault codes. Also check the vehicle's EGR system, where applicable. At high mileages, the injectors may require professional attention.

Engine

- ☐ Engine fails to rotate when attempting to start
- ☐ Engine rotates, but will not start
- ☐ Engine difficult to start when cold
- ☐ Engine difficult to start when hot
- ☐ Starter motor noisy or excessively-rough in engagement
- ☐ Engine starts, but stops immediately
- ☐ Engine idles erratically
- ☐ Engine misfires at idle speed
- ☐ Engine misfires throughout the driving speed range
- ☐ Engine hesitates on acceleration
- ☐ Engine stalls
- ☐ Engine lacks power
- ☐ Engine backfires
- ☐ Oil pressure warning light on with engine running
- ☐ Engine runs-on after switching off
- ☐ Engine noises

Cooling system

- ☐ Overheating
- ☐ Overcooling
- ☐ External coolant leakage
- ☐ Internal coolant leakage
- ☐ Corrosion

Fuel and exhaust systems

- ☐ Excessive fuel consumption
- ☐ Fuel leakage and/or fuel odour
- ☐ Excessive noise or fumes from exhaust system

Clutch

- ☐ Pedal travels to floor – no pressure or very little resistance
- ☐ Clutch fails to disengage (unable to select gears)
- ☐ Clutch slips (engine speed rises, with no increase in vehicle speed)
- ☐ Judder as clutch is engaged
- ☐ Noise when depressing or releasing clutch pedal

Transmission

- ☐ Noisy in neutral with engine running
- ☐ Noisy in one particular gear
- ☐ Difficulty engaging gears
- ☐ Jumps out of gear
- ☐ Vibration
- ☐ Lubricant leaks

Driveshafts

- ☐ Clicking or knocking noise on turns (at slow speed on full-lock)
- ☐ Vibration when accelerating or decelerating

Braking system

- ☐ Vehicle pulls to one side under braking
- ☐ Noise (grinding or high-pitched squeal) when brakes applied
- ☐ Excessive brake pedal travel
- ☐ Brake pedal feels spongy when depressed
- ☐ Excessive brake pedal effort required to stop vehicle
- ☐ Judder felt through brake pedal or steering wheel when braking
- ☐ Brakes binding
- ☐ Rear wheels locking under normal braking

Suspension and steering systems

- ☐ Vehicle pulls to one side
- ☐ Wheel wobble and vibration
- ☐ Excessive pitching and/or rolling around corners, or during braking
- ☐ Wandering or general instability
- ☐ Excessively-stiff steering
- ☐ Excessive play in steering
- ☐ Lack of power assistance
- ☐ Tyre wear excessive

Electrical system

- ☐ Battery will not hold a charge for more than a few days
- ☐ Ignition/no-charge warning light stays on with engine running
- ☐ Ignition/no-charge warning light fails to come on
- ☐ Lights inoperative
- ☐ Instrument readings inaccurate or erratic
- ☐ Horn inoperative, or unsatisfactory in operation
- ☐ Windscreen/tailgate wipers failed, or unsatisfactory in operation
- ☐ Windscreen/tailgate washers failed, or unsatisfactory in operation
- ☐ Electric windows inoperative, or unsatisfactory in operation
- ☐ Central locking system inoperative, or unsatisfactory in operation

Introduction

The vehicle owner who does his or her own maintenance according to the recommended service schedules should not have to use this section of the manual very often. Modern component reliability is such that, provided those items subject to wear or deterioration are inspected or renewed at the specified intervals, sudden failure is comparatively rare. Faults do not usually just happen as a result of sudden failure, but develop over a period of time. Major mechanical failures in particular are usually preceded by characteristic symptoms over hundreds or even thousands of miles. Those components which do occasionally fail without warning are often small and easily carried in the vehicle.

With any fault-finding, the first step is to decide where to begin investigations. Sometimes this is obvious, but on other occasions, a little detective work will be necessary. The owner who makes half a dozen haphazard adjustments or replacements may be successful in curing a fault (or its symptoms), but will be none the wiser if the fault recurs, and ultimately may have spent more time and money than was necessary. A calm and logical approach will be found to be more satisfactory in the long run. Always take into account any warning signs or abnormalities that may have been noticed in the period preceding the fault – power loss, high or low gauge readings, unusual smells, etc – and remember that failure of components such as fuses or spark plugs may only be pointers to some underlying fault.

The pages which follow provide an easy-reference guide to the more common problems which may occur during the operation of the vehicle. These problems and their possible causes are grouped under headings denoting various components or systems, such as Engine, Cooling system, etc. The general Chapter which deals with the problem is also shown in brackets; refer to the relevant part of that Chapter for system-specific information. Whatever the fault, certain basic principles apply. These are as follows:

□ *Verify the fault*. This is simply a matter of being sure that you know what the symptoms are before starting work. This is particularly important if you are investigating a fault for someone else, who may not have described it very accurately.

□ *Don't overlook the obvious*. For example, if the vehicle won't start, is there fuel in the tank? (Don't take anyone else's word on this particular point, and don't trust the fuel gauge either!) If an electrical fault is indicated, look for loose or broken wires before digging out the test gear.

□ *Cure the disease, not the symptom*. Substituting a flat battery with a fully-charged one will get you off the hard shoulder, but if the underlying cause is not attended to, the new battery will go the same way. Similarly, changing oil-fouled spark plugs (petrol models) for a new set will get you moving again, but remember that the reason for the fouling (if it wasn't simply an incorrect grade of plug) will have to be found and corrected.

□ *Don't take anything for granted*. Particularly, don't forget that a 'new' component may itself be defective (especially if it's been rattling around in the boot for months), and don't leave components out of a fault diagnosis sequence just because they are new or recently-fitted. When you do finally diagnose a difficult fault, you'll probably realise that all the evidence was there from the start.

Engine

Engine fails to rotate when attempting to start

□ Battery terminal connections loose or corroded (*Weekly checks*).
□ Battery discharged or faulty (Chapter 5).
□ Broken, loose or disconnected wiring in the starting circuit (Chapter 5).
□ Defective starter motor (Chapter 5).
□ Starter pinion or flywheel ring gear teeth loose or broken (Chapter 2 and 5).
□ Engine earth strap broken or disconnected (Chapter 5 and 12).

Engine rotates, but will not start

□ Fuel tank empty.
□ Battery discharged (engine rotates slowly) (Chapter 5).
□ Battery terminal connections loose or corroded (*Weekly checks*).
□ Worn, faulty or incorrectly-gapped spark plugs – petrol models (Chapter 1).
□ Pre/post-heating system faulty – diesel models (Chapter 5).
□ Engine management system fault (Chapter 4).
□ Air in fuel system – diesel models (Chapter 4).
□ High pressure fuel system fault – diesel models (Chapter 4).
□ Low cylinder compressions (Chapter 2).
□ Major mechanical failure (eg camshaft drive) (Chapter 2).

Engine difficult to start when cold

□ Battery discharged (Chapter 5).
□ Battery terminal connections loose or corroded (*Weekly checks*).
□ Worn, faulty or incorrectly-gapped spark plugs – petrol models (Chapter 1).
□ Pre/post-heating system faulty – diesel models (Chapter 5).
□ Engine management system fault (Chapter 4).
□ High pressure fuel system fault – diesel models (Chapter 4).
□ Low cylinder compressions (Chapter 2).

Engine difficult to start when hot

□ Engine management system fault (Chapter 4).
□ High pressure fuel system fault – diesel models (Chapter 4).
□ Low cylinder compressions (Chapter 2).

Starter motor noisy or excessively-rough in engagement

□ Starter pinion or flywheel ring gear teeth loose or broken (Chapter 2 and 5).
□ Starter motor mounting bolts loose or missing (Chapter 5).
□ Defective starter motor (Chapter 5).

Engine starts, but stops immediately

□ Vacuum leak at the throttle housing/inlet manifold – petrol models (Chapter 4).
□ Engine management system fault (Chapter 4).
□ Air in fuel system – diesel models (Chapter 4).
□ High pressure fuel system fault – diesel models (Chapter 4).

Engine idles erratically

□ Vacuum leak at the throttle housing/inlet manifold – petrol models (Chapter 4).
□ Worn, faulty or incorrectly-gapped spark plugs – petrol models (Chapter 1).
□ Engine management system fault (Chapter 4).
□ Air in fuel system – diesel models (Chapter 4).
□ High pressure fuel system fault – diesel models (Chapter 4).
□ Uneven or low cylinder compressions (Chapter 2).
□ Camshaft lobes worn (Chapter 2).
□ Timing belt incorrectly fitted (Chapter 2).

Engine misfires at idle speed

□ Worn, faulty or incorrectly-gapped spark plugs – petrol models (Chapter 1).
□ Vacuum leak at the throttle housing/inlet manifold – petrol models (Chapter 4).
□ Engine management system fault (Chapter 4).
□ High pressure fuel system fault – diesel models (Chapter 4).
□ Uneven or low cylinder compressions (Chapter 2).
□ Disconnected, leaking, or perished crankcase ventilation hoses (Chapter 4).

Engine misfires throughout the driving speed range

□ Fuel filter blocked (Chapter 1).
□ Fuel pump faulty – petrol models (Chapter 4).
□ Fuel tank vent blocked, or fuel pipes restricted (Chapter 4).
□ Worn, faulty or incorrectly-gapped spark plugs – petrol models (Chapter 1).
□ Vacuum leak at the throttle housing/inlet manifold – petrol models (Chapter 4).
□ Engine management system fault (Chapter 4).
□ High pressure fuel system fault – diesel models (Chapter 4).
□ Faulty ignition HT coil – petrol models (Chapter 5).
□ Uneven or low cylinder compressions (Chapter 2).

Engine (continued)

Engine hesitates on acceleration

☐ Worn, faulty or incorrectly-gapped spark plugs – petrol models (Chapter 1).
☐ Vacuum leak at the throttle housing/inlet manifold – petrol models (Chapter 4).
☐ Engine management system fault (Chapter 4).
☐ High pressure fuel system fault – diesel models (Chapter 4).

Engine stalls

☐ Fuel filter blocked (Chapter 1).
☐ Fuel pump faulty – petrol models (Chapter 4).
☐ Fuel tank vent blocked, or fuel pipes restricted (Chapter 4).
☐ Worn, faulty or incorrectly-gapped spark plugs – petrol models (Chapter 1).
☐ Vacuum leak at the throttle housing/inlet manifold – petrol models (Chapter 4).
☐ Engine management system fault (Chapter 4).
☐ High pressure fuel system fault – diesel models (Chapter 4).

Engine lacks power

☐ Timing belt incorrectly fitted (Chapter 2).
☐ Fuel filter blocked (Chapter 1).
☐ Fuel pump faulty – petrol models (Chapter 4).
☐ Uneven or low cylinder compressions (Chapter 2).
☐ Worn, faulty or incorrectly-gapped spark plugs – petrol models (Chapter 1).
☐ Vacuum leak at the throttle housing/inlet manifold – petrol models (Chapter 4).
☐ Engine management system fault (Chapter 4).
☐ High pressure fuel system fault – diesel models (Chapter 4).
☐ Brakes binding (Chapter 1 and 9).
☐ Clutch slipping (Chapter 6).

Engine backfires

☐ Timing belt incorrectly fitted (Chapter 2).
☐ Vacuum leak at the throttle housing/inlet manifold – petrol models (Chapter 4).
☐ Engine management system fault (Chapter 4).

Oil pressure warning light on with engine running

☐ Low oil level, or incorrect oil grade (*Weekly checks*).

☐ Faulty oil pressure warning light switch (Chapter 5).
☐ Worn engine bearings and/or oil pump (Chapter 2).
☐ High engine operating temperature (Chapter 3).
☐ Oil pressure relief valve defective (Chapter 2).
☐ Oil pick-up strainer clogged (Chapter 2).

Engine runs-on after switching off

☐ Excessive carbon build-up in engine (Chapter 2).
☐ High engine operating temperature (Chapter 3).
☐ Engine management system fault (Chapter 4).
☐ High pressure fuel system fault – diesel models (Chapter 4).

Engine noises

Pre-ignition (pinking) or knocking during acceleration or under load

☐ Engine management system fault (Chapter 4).
☐ Incorrect grade of spark plug – petrol models (Chapter 1).
☐ Incorrect grade of fuel – petrol models (Chapter 4).
☐ Vacuum leak at the throttle housing/inlet manifold – petrol models (Chapter 4).
☐ Excessive carbon build-up in engine (Chapter 2).

Whistling or wheezing noises

☐ Leaking inlet manifold or throttle housing gasket – petrol models (Chapter 4).
☐ Leaking vacuum hose (Chapter 4 and 9).
☐ Blowing cylinder head gasket (Chapter 2).

Tapping or rattling noises

☐ Worn valve gear or camshaft (Chapter 2).
☐ Ancillary component fault (coolant pump, alternator, etc) (Chapters 3, 5, etc).

Knocking or thumping noises

☐ Worn big-end bearings (regular heavy knocking, perhaps less under load) (Chapter 2).
☐ Worn main bearings (rumbling and knocking, perhaps worsening under load) (Chapter 2).
☐ Piston slap (most noticeable when cold) (Chapter 2).
☐ Ancillary component fault (coolant pump, alternator, etc) (Chapters 3, 5, etc).

Cooling system

Overheating

☐ Insufficient coolant in system (*Weekly checks*).
☐ Thermostat faulty (stuck closed) (Chapter 3).
☐ Radiator core blocked, or grille restricted (Chapter 3).
☐ Electric cooling fan or sensor faulty (Chapter 3).
☐ Pressure cap faulty (Chapter 3).
☐ Inaccurate temperature gauge/sensor (Chapter 3).
☐ Airlock in cooling system (Chapter 1).
☐ Engine management system fault (Chapter 4).

Overcooling

☐ Thermostat faulty (stuck open) (Chapter 3).
☐ Inaccurate temperature gauge/sensor (Chapter 3).

External coolant leakage

☐ Deteriorated or damaged hoses or hose clips (Chapter 1).
☐ Radiator core or heater matrix leaking (Chapter 3).
☐ Pressure cap faulty (Chapter 3).
☐ Coolant pump leaking (Chapter 3).
☐ Boiling due to overheating (Chapter 3).
☐ Core plug leaking (Chapter 2).

Internal coolant leakage

☐ Leaking cylinder head gasket (Chapter 2).
☐ Cracked cylinder head or cylinder bore (Chapter 2).

Corrosion

☐ Infrequent draining and flushing (Chapter 1).
☐ Incorrect coolant mixture or inappropriate coolant type (Chapter 1).

Fuel and exhaust systems

Excessive fuel consumption

☐ Air filter element dirty or clogged (Chapter 1).
☐ Engine management system fault (Chapter 4).
☐ High pressure fuel system fault – diesel models (Chapter 4).
☐ Tyres under-inflated (*Weekly checks*).
☐ Brakes binding (Chapters 1 and 9).

Fuel leakage and/or fuel odour

☐ Damaged or corroded fuel tank, pipes or connections (Chapter 4).

Excessive noise or fumes from exhaust system

☐ Leaking exhaust system or manifold joints (Chapters 1 and 4).
☐ Leaking, corroded or damaged silencers or pipe (Chapters 1 and 4).
☐ Broken mountings causing body or suspension contact (Chapters 1 and 4).

Clutch

Pedal travels to floor – no pressure or very little resistance

☐ Broken clutch cable (Chapter 6).
☐ Broken clutch release bearing or fork (Chapter 6).
☐ Broken diaphragm spring in clutch pressure plate (Chapter 6).

Clutch fails to disengage (unable to select gears)

☐ Clutch disc sticking on gearbox input shaft splines (Chapter 6).
☐ Clutch disc sticking to flywheel or pressure plate (Chapter 6).
☐ Faulty pressure plate assembly (Chapter 6).
☐ Clutch release mechanism worn or incorrectly assembled (Chapter 6).

Clutch slips (engine speed rises, with no increase in vehicle speed)

☐ Clutch disc linings excessively worn (Chapter 6).
☐ Clutch disc linings contaminated with oil or grease (Chapter 6).
☐ Faulty pressure plate or weak diaphragm spring (Chapter 6).

Judder as clutch is engaged

☐ Clutch disc linings contaminated with oil or grease (Chapter 6).
☐ Clutch disc linings excessively worn (Chapter 6).
☐ Faulty or distorted pressure plate or diaphragm spring (Chapter 6).
☐ Worn or loose engine or gearbox mountings (Chapter 2 or).
☐ Clutch disc hub or gearbox input shaft splines worn (Chapter 6).

Noise when depressing or releasing clutch pedal

☐ Worn clutch release bearing (Chapter 6).
☐ Worn or dry clutch pedal bushes (Chapter 6).
☐ Faulty pressure plate assembly (Chapter 6).
☐ Pressure plate diaphragm spring broken (Chapter 6).
☐ Broken clutch disc cushioning springs (Chapter 6).

Transmission

Noisy in neutral with engine running

☐ Input shaft bearings worn (noise apparent with clutch pedal released, but not when depressed) (Chapter 7).*
☐ Clutch release bearing worn (noise apparent with clutch pedal depressed, possibly less when released) (Chapter 6).

Noisy in one particular gear

☐ Worn, damaged or chipped gear teeth (Chapter 7).*

Difficulty engaging gears

☐ Clutch fault (Chapter 6).
☐ Worn or damaged gear selector mechanism (Chapter 7).
☐ Worn synchroniser units (Chapter 7).*

Jumps out of gear

☐ Worn or damaged gear selector mechanism (Chapter 7).
☐ Worn synchroniser units (Chapter 7).*
☐ Worn selector forks (Chapter 7).*

Vibration

☐ Lack of oil (Chapter 1 and 7).
☐ Worn bearings (Chapter 7).*

Lubricant leaks

☐ Leaking differential output oil seal (Chapter 7).
☐ Leaking housing joint (Chapter 7).*
☐ Leaking input shaft oil seal (Chapter 7).

Although the corrective action necessary to remedy the symptoms described is beyond the scope of the home mechanic, the above information should be helpful in isolating the cause of the condition, so that the owner can communicate clearly with a professional mechanic.

Driveshafts

Clicking or knocking noise on turns (at slow speed on full-lock)

- [ ] Lack of constant velocity joint lubricant, possibly due to damaged gaiter (Chapter 8).
- [ ] Worn outer constant velocity joint (Chapter 8).

Vibration when accelerating or decelerating

- [ ] Worn inner constant velocity joint (Chapter 8).
- [ ] Bent or distorted driveshaft (Chapter 8).
- [ ] Worn intermediate bearing (where fitted) (Chapter 8).

Braking system

Note: *Before assuming that a brake problem exists, make sure that the tyres are in good condition and correctly inflated, that the front wheel alignment is correct, and that the vehicle is not loaded with weight in an unequal manner. Apart from checking the condition of all pipe and hose connections, any faults occurring on the anti-lock braking system should be referred to a Peugeot/Citroën dealer for diagnosis.*

Vehicle pulls to one side under braking

- [ ] Worn, defective, damaged or contaminated brake pads/shoes on one side (Chapter 9).
- [ ] Seized or partially-seized front brake caliper (Chapter 9).
- [ ] A mixture of brake pad/shoe materials fitted between sides (Chapter 9).
- [ ] Brake caliper mounting bolts loose (Chapter 9).
- [ ] Worn or damaged steering or suspension components (Chapter 1 and 10).

Noise (grinding or high-pitched squeal) when brakes applied

- [ ] Brake pad/shoe material worn down to metal backing (Chapter 1 and 9).
- [ ] Excessive corrosion of brake disc/drum. May be apparent after the vehicle has been standing for some time (Chapter 9).
- [ ] Foreign object (stone chipping, etc) trapped between brake disc and shield (Chapter 9).

Excessive brake pedal travel

- [ ] Faulty master cylinder (Chapter 9).
- [ ] Air in hydraulic system (Chapter 9).
- [ ] Faulty vacuum servo unit (Chapter 9).

Brake pedal feels spongy when depressed

- [ ] Air in hydraulic system (Chapter 9).

- [ ] Deteriorated flexible rubber brake hoses (Chapter 1 and 9).
- [ ] Master cylinder mounting nuts loose (Chapter 9).
- [ ] Faulty master cylinder (Chapter 9).

Excessive brake pedal effort required to stop vehicle

- [ ] Faulty vacuum servo unit (Chapter 9).
- [ ] Disconnected, damaged or insecure brake servo vacuum hose (Chapter 9).
- [ ] Primary or secondary hydraulic circuit failure (Chapter 9).
- [ ] Seized brake caliper or wheel cylinder (Chapter 9).
- [ ] Brake pads/shoes incorrectly fitted (Chapter 9).
- [ ] Incorrect grade of brake pads/shoes fitted (Chapter 9).
- [ ] Brake pads/shoes contaminated (Chapter 9).

Judder felt through brake pedal or steering wheel when braking

- [ ] Excessive run-out or distortion of discs or drums (Chapters 9).
- [ ] Brake pads/shoes worn (Chapters 1 or and 9).
- [ ] Brake caliper mounting bolts loose (Chapter 9).
- [ ] Wear in suspension or steering components or mountings (Chapter 1 and 10).

Brakes binding

- [ ] Seized brake caliper or wheel cylinder (Chapter 9).
- [ ] Incorrectly-adjusted handbrake mechanism (Chapter 9).
- [ ] Faulty master cylinder (Chapter 9).

Rear wheels locking under normal braking

- [ ] Rear brake shoes contaminated (Chapter 1 and 9).
- [ ] Faulty or incorrectly adjusted rear brake pressure-regulating valve – models without ABS (Chapter 9).
- [ ] ABS system fault (Chapter 9).

Suspension and steering

Note: *Before diagnosing suspension or steering faults, be sure that the trouble is not due to incorrect tyre pressures, mixtures of tyre types, or binding brakes.*

Vehicle pulls to one side

☐ Defective tyre (*Weekly checks*).
☐ Excessive wear in suspension or steering components (Chapter 1 and 10).
☐ Incorrect front wheel alignment (Chapter 10).
☐ Damage to steering or suspension components (Chapter 1 and 10).

Wheel wobble and vibration

☐ Front roadwheels out of balance (vibration felt mainly through the steering wheel) (*Weekly checks*).
☐ Rear roadwheels out of balance (vibration felt throughout the vehicle) (*Weekly checks*).
☐ Roadwheels damaged or distorted (*Weekly checks*).
☐ Faulty or damaged tyre (*Weekly checks*).
☐ Worn steering or suspension joints, bushes or components (Chapter 1 and 10).
☐ Wheel bolts loose (Chapter 1 and 10).

Excessive pitching and/or rolling around corners, or during braking

☐ Defective shock absorbers (Chapter 1 and 10).
☐ Broken or weak spring and/or suspension part (Chapter 1 and 10).
☐ Worn or damaged anti-roll bar or mountings (Chapter 10).

Wandering or general instability

☐ Incorrect front wheel alignment (Chapter 10).
☐ Worn steering or suspension joints, bushes or components (Chapter 1 and 10).
☐ Roadwheels out of balance (*Weekly checks*).
☐ Faulty or damaged tyre (*Weekly checks*).
☐ Wheel bolts loose (Chapter 1 and 10).
☐ Defective shock absorbers (Chapter 1 and 10).

Excessively-stiff steering

☐ Broken or incorrectly-adjusted auxiliary drivebelt (Chapter 1).
☐ Faulty power steering pump (Chapter 10).

☐ Seized track rod end balljoint or suspension balljoint (Chapter 1 and 10).
☐ Incorrect front wheel alignment (Chapter 10).
☐ Steering rack or column bent or damaged (Chapter 10).

Excessive play in steering

☐ Worn steering column universal joint (Chapter 10).
☐ Worn steering track rod end balljoints (Chapter 1 and 10).
☐ Worn steering rack (Chapter 10).
☐ Worn steering or suspension joints, bushes or components (Chapter 1 and 10).

Lack of power assistance

☐ Broken or incorrectly-adjusted auxiliary drivebelt (Chapter 1).
☐ Faulty power steering pump (Chapter 10).
☐ Restriction in power steering fluid hoses (Chapter 1).
☐ Faulty steering rack (Chapter 10).

Tyre wear excessive

Tyre treads exhibit feathered edges

☐ Incorrect toe setting (Chapter 10).

Tyres worn in centre of tread

☐ Tyres over-inflated (*Weekly checks*).

Tyres worn on inside and outside edges

☐ Tyres under-inflated (*Weekly checks*).

Tyres worn on inside or outside edges

☐ Incorrect camber/castor angles (wear on one edge only) (Chapter 10).
☐ Worn steering or suspension joints, bushes or components (Chapter 1 and 10).
☐ Excessively-hard cornering.
☐ Accident damage.

Tyres worn unevenly

☐ Tyres/wheels out of balance (*Weekly checks*).
☐ Excessive wheel or tyre run-out (Chapter 1).
☐ Worn shock absorbers (Chapter 1 and 10).
☐ Faulty tyre (*Weekly checks*).

Electrical system

Note: *For problems associated with the starting system, refer to the faults listed under 'Engine' earlier in this Section.*

Battery won't hold a charge for more than a few days

- ☐ Battery defective internally (Chapter 5).
- ☐ Battery terminal connections loose or corroded (*Weekly checks*).
- ☐ Auxiliary drivebelt broken, worn or incorrectly adjusted (Chapter 1).
- ☐ Alternator not charging at correct output (Chapter 5).
- ☐ Alternator or voltage regulator faulty (Chapter 5).
- ☐ Short-circuit causing continual battery drain (Chapter 5 and 12).

Ignition/no-charge warning light stays on with engine running

- ☐ Auxiliary drivebelt broken, worn, or incorrectly adjusted (Chapter 1).
- ☐ Internal fault in alternator or voltage regulator (Chapter 5).
- ☐ Broken, disconnected, or loose wiring in charging circuit (Chapter 5).

Ignition/no-charge warning light fails to come on

- ☐ Warning light bulb blown (Chapter 12).
- ☐ Broken, disconnected, or loose wiring in warning light circuit (Chapter 12).
- ☐ Alternator faulty (Chapter 5).

Lights inoperative

- ☐ Bulb blown (Chapter 12).
- ☐ Corrosion of bulb or bulbholder contacts (Chapter 12).
- ☐ Blown fuse (Chapter 12).
- ☐ Faulty relay (Chapter 12).
- ☐ Broken, loose, or disconnected wiring (Chapter 12).
- ☐ Faulty switch (Chapter 12).

Instrument readings inaccurate or erratic

Fuel or temperature gauges give no reading

- ☐ Faulty gauge sensor/sender unit (Chapter 3 or 4).
- ☐ Wiring open-circuit (Chapter 12).
- ☐ Faulty gauge (Chapter 12).
- ☐ Built-in Systems Interface (BSI) faulty (Chapter 12).

Fuel or temperature gauges give continuous maximum reading

- ☐ Faulty gauge sensor/sender unit (Chapter 3 or 4).
- ☐ Wiring short-circuit (Chapter 12).
- ☐ Faulty gauge (Chapter 12).
- ☐ Built-in Systems Interface (BSI) faulty (Chapter 12).

Horn inoperative, or unsatisfactory in operation

Horn operates all the time

- ☐ Horn push either earthed or stuck down (Chapter 12).
- ☐ Horn cable-to-horn push earthed (Chapter 12).

Horn fails to operate

- ☐ Blown fuse (Chapter 12).
- ☐ Cable or cable connections loose, broken or disconnected (Chapter 12).
- ☐ Faulty horn (Chapter 12).

Horn emits intermittent or unsatisfactory sound

- ☐ Cable connections loose (Chapter 12).
- ☐ Horn mountings loose (Chapter 12).
- ☐ Faulty horn (Chapter 12).

Windscreen/tailgate wipers failed, or unsatisfactory in operation

Wipers fail to operate, or operate very slowly

- ☐ Wiper blades stuck to screen, or linkage seized or binding (Chapter 1 and 12).

- ☐ Blown fuse (Chapter 12).
- ☐ Cable or cable connections loose, broken or disconnected (Chapter 12).
- ☐ Built-in Systems Interface (BSI) faulty (Chapter 12).
- ☐ Faulty wiper motor (Chapter 12).

Wiper blades sweep over too large or too small an area of the glass

- ☐ Wiper arms incorrectly positioned on spindles (Chapter 12).
- ☐ Excessive wear of wiper linkage (Chapter 12).
- ☐ Wiper motor or linkage mountings loose or insecure (Chapter 12).

Wiper blades fail to clean the glass effectively

- ☐ Wiper blade rubbers worn or perished (*Weekly checks*).
- ☐ Wiper arm tension springs broken, or arm pivots seized (Chapter 12).
- ☐ Insufficient windscreen washer additive to adequately remove road film (*Weekly checks*).

Windscreen/tailgate washers failed, or unsatisfactory in operation

One or more washer jets inoperative

- ☐ Blocked washer jet (*Weekly checks*).
- ☐ Disconnected, kinked or restricted fluid hose (Chapter 12).
- ☐ Insufficient fluid in washer reservoir (*Weekly checks*).

Washer pump fails to operate

- ☐ Broken or disconnected wiring or connections (Chapter 12).
- ☐ Blown fuse (Chapter 12).
- ☐ Faulty washer switch (Chapter 12).
- ☐ Faulty washer pump (Chapter 12).

Electric windows inoperative, or unsatisfactory in operation

Window glass will only move in one direction

- ☐ Faulty switch (Chapter 12).

Window glass slow to move

- ☐ Regulator seized or damaged, or in need of lubricant (Chapter 11).
- ☐ Door internal components or trim fouling regulator (Chapter 11).
- ☐ Faulty motor (Chapter 11).

Window glass fails to move

- ☐ Blown fuse (Chapter 12).
- ☐ Broken or disconnected wiring or connections (Chapter 12).
- ☐ Faulty motor (Chapter 11).
- ☐ Built-in Systems Interface (BSI) faulty (Chapter 12).

Central locking system inoperative, or unsatisfactory in operation

Complete system failure

- ☐ Blown fuse (Chapter 12).
- ☐ Broken or disconnected wiring or connections (Chapter 12).
- ☐ Built-in Systems Interface (BSI) faulty (Chapter 12).

Door/tailgate locks but will not unlock, or unlocks but will not lock

- ☐ Broken or disconnected link rod(s) (Chapter 11).
- ☐ Faulty lock motor (Chapter 11).

One lock fails to operate

- ☐ Broken or disconnected wiring or connections (Chapter 12).
- ☐ Faulty lock motor (Chapter 11).
- ☐ Broken, binding or disconnected link rod(s) (Chapter 11).

A

ABS (Anti-lock brake system) A system, usually electronically controlled, that senses incipient wheel lockup during braking and relieves hydraulic pressure at wheels that are about to skid.

Air bag An inflatable bag hidden in the steering wheel (driver's side) or the dash or glovebox (passenger side). In a head-on collision, the bags inflate, preventing the driver and front passenger from being thrown forward into the steering wheel or windscreen.

Air cleaner A metal or plastic housing, containing a filter element, which removes dust and dirt from the air being drawn into the engine.

Air filter element The actual filter in an air cleaner system, usually manufactured from pleated paper and requiring renewal at regular intervals.

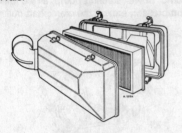

Air filter

Allen key A hexagonal wrench which fits into a recessed hexagonal hole.

Alligator clip A long-nosed spring-loaded metal clip with meshing teeth. Used to make temporary electrical connections.

Alternator A component in the electrical system which converts mechanical energy from a drivebelt into electrical energy to charge the battery and to operate the starting system, ignition system and electrical accessories.

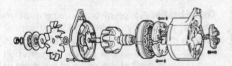

Alternator (exploded view)

Ampere (amp) A unit of measurement for the flow of electric current. One amp is the amount of current produced by one volt acting through a resistance of one ohm.

Anaerobic sealer A substance used to prevent bolts and screws from loosening. Anaerobic means that it does not require oxygen for activation. The Loctite brand is widely used.

Antifreeze A substance (usually ethylene glycol) mixed with water, and added to a vehicle's cooling system, to prevent freezing of the coolant in winter. Antifreeze also contains chemicals to inhibit corrosion and the formation of rust and other deposits that would tend to clog the radiator and coolant passages and reduce cooling efficiency.

Anti-seize compound A coating that reduces the risk of seizing on fasteners that are subjected to high temperatures, such as exhaust manifold bolts and nuts.

Anti-seize compound

Asbestos A natural fibrous mineral with great heat resistance, commonly used in the composition of brake friction materials. Asbestos is a health hazard and the dust created by brake systems should never be inhaled or ingested.

Axle A shaft on which a wheel revolves, or which revolves with a wheel. Also, a solid beam that connects the two wheels at one end of the vehicle. An axle which also transmits power to the wheels is known as a live axle.

Axle assembly

Axleshaft A single rotating shaft, on either side of the differential, which delivers power from the final drive assembly to the drive wheels. Also called a driveshaft or a halfshaft.

B

Ball bearing An anti-friction bearing consisting of a hardened inner and outer race with hardened steel balls between two races.

Bearing

Bearing The curved surface on a shaft or in a bore, or the part assembled into either, that permits relative motion between them with minimum wear and friction.

Big-end bearing The bearing in the end of the connecting rod that's attached to the crankshaft.

Bleed nipple A valve on a brake wheel cylinder, caliper or other hydraulic component that is opened to purge the hydraulic system of air. Also called a bleed screw.

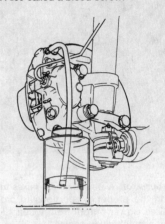

Brake bleeding

Brake bleeding Procedure for removing air from lines of a hydraulic brake system.

Brake disc The component of a disc brake that rotates with the wheels.

Brake drum The component of a drum brake that rotates with the wheels.

Brake linings The friction material which contacts the brake disc or drum to retard the vehicle's speed. The linings are bonded or riveted to the brake pads or shoes.

Brake pads The replaceable friction pads that pinch the brake disc when the brakes are applied. Brake pads consist of a friction material bonded or riveted to a rigid backing plate.

Brake shoe The crescent-shaped carrier to which the brake linings are mounted and which forces the lining against the rotating drum during braking.

Braking systems For more information on braking systems, consult the *Haynes Automotive Brake Manual*.

Breaker bar A long socket wrench handle providing greater leverage.

Bulkhead The insulated partition between the engine and the passenger compartment.

C

Caliper The non-rotating part of a disc-brake assembly that straddles the disc and carries the brake pads. The caliper also contains the hydraulic components that cause the pads to pinch the disc when the brakes are applied. A caliper is also a measuring tool that can be set to measure inside or outside dimensions of an object.

Camshaft A rotating shaft on which a series of cam lobes operate the valve mechanisms. The camshaft may be driven by gears, by sprockets and chain or by sprockets and a belt.

Canister A container in an evaporative emission control system; contains activated charcoal granules to trap vapours from the fuel system.

Canister

Carburettor A device which mixes fuel with air in the proper proportions to provide a desired power output from a spark ignition internal combustion engine.

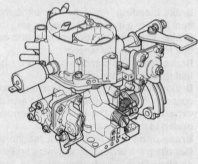

Carburettor

Castellated Resembling the parapets along the top of a castle wall. For example, a castellated balljoint stud nut.

Castellated nut

Castor In wheel alignment, the backward or forward tilt of the steering axis. Castor is positive when the steering axis is inclined rearward at the top.

Catalytic converter A silencer-like device in the exhaust system which converts certain pollutants in the exhaust gases into less harmful substances.

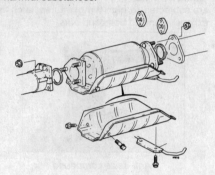

Catalytic converter

Circlip A ring-shaped clip used to prevent endwise movement of cylindrical parts and shafts. An internal circlip is installed in a groove in a housing; an external circlip fits into a groove on the outside of a cylindrical piece such as a shaft.

Clearance The amount of space between two parts. For example, between a piston and a cylinder, between a bearing and a journal, etc.

Coil spring A spiral of elastic steel found in various sizes throughout a vehicle, for example as a springing medium in the suspension and in the valve train.

Compression Reduction in volume, and increase in pressure and temperature, of a gas, caused by squeezing it into a smaller space.

Compression ratio The relationship between cylinder volume when the piston is at top dead centre and cylinder volume when the piston is at bottom dead centre.

Constant velocity (CV) joint A type of universal joint that cancels out vibrations caused by driving power being transmitted through an angle.

Core plug A disc or cup-shaped metal device inserted in a hole in a casting through which core was removed when the casting was formed. Also known as a freeze plug or expansion plug.

Crankcase The lower part of the engine block in which the crankshaft rotates.

Crankshaft The main rotating member, or shaft, running the length of the crankcase, with offset "throws" to which the connecting rods are attached.

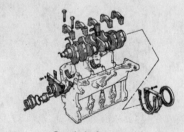

Crankshaft assembly

Crocodile clip See Alligator clip

D

Diagnostic code Code numbers obtained by accessing the diagnostic mode of an engine management computer. This code can be used to determine the area in the system where a malfunction may be located.

Disc brake A brake design incorporating a rotating disc onto which brake pads are squeezed. The resulting friction converts the energy of a moving vehicle into heat.

Double-overhead cam (DOHC) An engine that uses two overhead camshafts, usually one for the intake valves and one for the exhaust valves.

Drivebelt(s) The belt(s) used to drive accessories such as the alternator, water pump, power steering pump, air conditioning compressor, etc. off the crankshaft pulley.

Accessory drivebelts

Driveshaft Any shaft used to transmit motion. Commonly used when referring to the axleshafts on a front wheel drive vehicle.

Driveshaft

Drum brake A type of brake using a drum-shaped metal cylinder attached to the inner surface of the wheel. When the brake pedal is pressed, curved brake shoes with friction linings press against the inside of the drum to slow or stop the vehicle.

Drum brake assembly

E

EGR valve A valve used to introduce exhaust gases into the intake air stream.

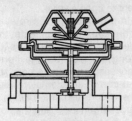

EGR valve

Electronic control unit (ECU) A computer which controls (for instance) ignition and fuel injection systems, or an anti-lock braking system. For more information refer to the *Haynes Automotive Electrical and Electronic Systems Manual.*

Electronic Fuel Injection (EFI) A computer controlled fuel system that distributes fuel through an injector located in each intake port of the engine.

Emergency brake A braking system, independent of the main hydraulic system, that can be used to slow or stop the vehicle if the primary brakes fail, or to hold the vehicle stationary even though the brake pedal isn't depressed. It usually consists of a hand lever that actuates either front or rear brakes mechanically through a series of cables and linkages. Also known as a handbrake or parking brake.

Endfloat The amount of lengthwise movement between two parts. As applied to a crankshaft, the distance that the crankshaft can move forward and back in the cylinder block.

Engine management system (EMS) A computer controlled system which manages the fuel injection and the ignition systems in an integrated fashion.

Exhaust manifold A part with several passages through which exhaust gases leave the engine combustion chambers and enter the exhaust pipe.

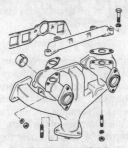

Exhaust manifold

F

Fan clutch A viscous (fluid) drive coupling device which permits variable engine fan speeds in relation to engine speeds.

Feeler blade A thin strip or blade of hardened steel, ground to an exact thickness, used to check or measure clearances between parts.

Feeler blade

Firing order The order in which the engine cylinders fire, or deliver their power strokes, beginning with the number one cylinder.

Flywheel A heavy spinning wheel in which energy is absorbed and stored by means of momentum. On cars, the flywheel is attached to the crankshaft to smooth out firing impulses.

Free play The amount of travel before any action takes place. The "looseness" in a linkage, or an assembly of parts, between the initial application of force and actual movement. For example, the distance the brake pedal moves before the pistons in the master cylinder are actuated.

Fuse An electrical device which protects a circuit against accidental overload. The typical fuse contains a soft piece of metal which is calibrated to melt at a predetermined current flow (expressed as amps) and break the circuit.

Fusible link A circuit protection device consisting of a conductor surrounded by heat-resistant insulation. The conductor is smaller than the wire it protects, so it acts as the weakest link in the circuit. Unlike a blown fuse, a failed fusible link must frequently be cut from the wire for replacement.

G

Gap The distance the spark must travel in jumping from the centre electrode to the side

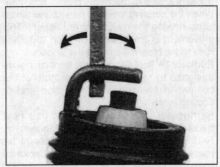

Adjusting spark plug gap

electrode in a spark plug. Also refers to the spacing between the points in a contact breaker assembly in a conventional points-type ignition, or to the distance between the reluctor or rotor and the pickup coil in an electronic ignition.

Gasket Any thin, soft material - usually cork, cardboard, asbestos or soft metal - installed between two metal surfaces to ensure a good seal. For instance, the cylinder head gasket seals the joint between the block and the cylinder head.

Gasket

Gauge An instrument panel display used to monitor engine conditions. A gauge with a movable pointer on a dial or a fixed scale is an analogue gauge. A gauge with a numerical readout is called a digital gauge.

H

Halfshaft A rotating shaft that transmits power from the final drive unit to a drive wheel, usually when referring to a live rear axle.

Harmonic balancer A device designed to reduce torsion or twisting vibration in the crankshaft. May be incorporated in the crankshaft pulley. Also known as a vibration damper.

Hone An abrasive tool for correcting small irregularities or differences in diameter in an engine cylinder, brake cylinder, etc.

Hydraulic tappet A tappet that utilises hydraulic pressure from the engine's lubrication system to maintain zero clearance (constant contact with both camshaft and valve stem). Automatically adjusts to variation in valve stem length. Hydraulic tappets also reduce valve noise.

I

Ignition timing The moment at which the spark plug fires, usually expressed in the number of crankshaft degrees before the piston reaches the top of its stroke.

Inlet manifold A tube or housing with passages through which flows the air-fuel mixture (carburettor vehicles and vehicles with throttle body injection) or air only (port fuel-injected vehicles) to the port openings in the cylinder head.

J

Jump start Starting the engine of a vehicle with a discharged or weak battery by attaching jump leads from the weak battery to a charged or helper battery.

L

Load Sensing Proportioning Valve (LSPV) A brake hydraulic system control valve that works like a proportioning valve, but also takes into consideration the amount of weight carried by the rear axle.

Locknut A nut used to lock an adjustment nut, or other threaded component, in place. For example, a locknut is employed to keep the adjusting nut on the rocker arm in position.

Lockwasher A form of washer designed to prevent an attaching nut from working loose.

M

MacPherson strut A type of front suspension system devised by Earle MacPherson at Ford of England. In its original form, a simple lateral link with the anti-roll bar creates the lower control arm. A long strut - an integral coil spring and shock absorber - is mounted between the body and the steering knuckle. Many modern so-called MacPherson strut systems use a conventional lower A-arm and don't rely on the anti-roll bar for location.

Multimeter An electrical test instrument with the capability to measure voltage, current and resistance.

N

NOx Oxides of Nitrogen. A common toxic pollutant emitted by petrol and diesel engines at higher temperatures.

O

Ohm The unit of electrical resistance. One volt applied to a resistance of one ohm will produce a current of one amp.

Ohmmeter An instrument for measuring electrical resistance.

O-ring A type of sealing ring made of a special rubber-like material; in use, the O-ring is compressed into a groove to provide the sealing action.

O-ring

Overhead cam (ohc) engine An engine with the camshaft(s) located on top of the cylinder head(s).

Overhead valve (ohv) engine An engine with the valves located in the cylinder head, but with the camshaft located in the engine block.

Oxygen sensor A device installed in the engine exhaust manifold, which senses the oxygen content in the exhaust and converts this information into an electric current. Also called a Lambda sensor.

P

Phillips screw A type of screw head having a cross instead of a slot for a corresponding type of screwdriver.

Plastigage A thin strip of plastic thread, available in different sizes, used for measuring clearances. For example, a strip of Plastigage is laid across a bearing journal. The parts are assembled and dismantled; the width of the crushed strip indicates the clearance between journal and bearing.

Plastigage

Propeller shaft The long hollow tube with universal joints at both ends that carries power from the transmission to the differential on front-engined rear wheel drive vehicles.

Proportioning valve A hydraulic control valve which limits the amount of pressure to the rear brakes during panic stops to prevent wheel lock-up.

R

Rack-and-pinion steering A steering system with a pinion gear on the end of the steering shaft that mates with a rack (think of a geared wheel opened up and laid flat). When the steering wheel is turned, the pinion turns, moving the rack to the left or right. This movement is transmitted through the track rods to the steering arms at the wheels.

Radiator A liquid-to-air heat transfer device designed to reduce the temperature of the coolant in an internal combustion engine cooling system.

Refrigerant Any substance used as a heat transfer agent in an air-conditioning system. R-12 has been the principle refrigerant for many years; recently, however, manufacturers have begun using R-134a, a non-CFC substance that is considered less harmful to the ozone in the upper atmosphere.

Rocker arm A lever arm that rocks on a shaft or pivots on a stud. In an overhead valve engine, the rocker arm converts the upward movement of the pushrod into a downward movement to open a valve.

Rotor In a distributor, the rotating device inside the cap that connects the centre electrode and the outer terminals as it turns, distributing the high voltage from the coil secondary winding to the proper spark plug. Also, that part of an alternator which rotates inside the stator. Also, the rotating assembly of a turbocharger, including the compressor wheel, shaft and turbine wheel.

Runout The amount of wobble (in-and-out movement) of a gear or wheel as it's rotated. The amount a shaft rotates "out-of-true." The out-of-round condition of a rotating part.

S

Sealant A liquid or paste used to prevent leakage at a joint. Sometimes used in conjunction with a gasket.

Sealed beam lamp An older headlight design which integrates the reflector, lens and filaments into a hermetically-sealed one-piece unit. When a filament burns out or the lens cracks, the entire unit is simply replaced.

Serpentine drivebelt A single, long, wide accessory drivebelt that's used on some newer vehicles to drive all the accessories, instead of a series of smaller, shorter belts. Serpentine drivebelts are usually tensioned by an automatic tensioner.

Serpentine drivebelt

Shim Thin spacer, commonly used to adjust the clearance or relative positions between two parts. For example, shims inserted into or under bucket tappets control valve clearances. Clearance is adjusted by changing the thickness of the shim.

Slide hammer A special puller that screws into or hooks onto a component such as a shaft or bearing; a heavy sliding handle on the shaft bottoms against the end of the shaft to knock the component free.

Sprocket A tooth or projection on the periphery of a wheel, shaped to engage with a chain or drivebelt. Commonly used to refer to the sprocket wheel itself.

Starter inhibitor switch On vehicles with an automatic transmission, a switch that prevents starting if the vehicle is not in Neutral or Park.

Strut See MacPherson strut.

T

Tappet A cylindrical component which transmits motion from the cam to the valve stem, either directly or via a pushrod and rocker arm. Also called a cam follower.

Thermostat A heat-controlled valve that regulates the flow of coolant between the cylinder block and the radiator, so maintaining optimum engine operating temperature. A thermostat is also used in some air cleaners in which the temperature is regulated.

Thrust bearing The bearing in the clutch assembly that is moved in to the release levers by clutch pedal action to disengage the clutch. Also referred to as a release bearing.

Timing belt A toothed belt which drives the camshaft. Serious engine damage may result if it breaks in service.

Timing chain A chain which drives the camshaft.

Toe-in The amount the front wheels are closer together at the front than at the rear. On rear wheel drive vehicles, a slight amount of toe-in is usually specified to keep the front wheels running parallel on the road by offsetting other forces that tend to spread the wheels apart.

Toe-out The amount the front wheels are closer together at the rear than at the front. On front wheel drive vehicles, a slight amount of toe-out is usually specified.

Tools For full information on choosing and using tools, refer to the *Haynes Automotive Tools Manual*.

Tracer A stripe of a second colour applied to a wire insulator to distinguish that wire from another one with the same colour insulator.

Tune-up A process of accurate and careful adjustments and parts replacement to obtain the best possible engine performance.

Turbocharger A centrifugal device, driven by exhaust gases, that pressurises the intake air. Normally used to increase the power output from a given engine displacement, but can also be used primarily to reduce exhaust emissions (as on VW's "Umwelt" Diesel engine).

U

Universal joint or U-joint A double-pivoted connection for transmitting power from a driving to a driven shaft through an angle. A U-joint consists of two Y-shaped yokes and a cross-shaped member called the spider.

V

Valve A device through which the flow of liquid, gas, vacuum, or loose material in bulk may be started, stopped, or regulated by a movable part that opens, shuts, or partially obstructs one or more ports or passageways. A valve is also the movable part of such a device.

Valve clearance The clearance between the valve tip (the end of the valve stem) and the rocker arm or tappet. The valve clearance is measured when the valve is closed.

Vernier caliper A precision measuring instrument that measures inside and outside dimensions. Not quite as accurate as a micrometer, but more convenient.

Viscosity The thickness of a liquid or its resistance to flow.

Volt A unit for expressing electrical "pressure" in a circuit. One volt that will produce a current of one ampere through a resistance of one ohm.

W

Welding Various processes used to join metal items by heating the areas to be joined to a molten state and fusing them together. For more information refer to the *Haynes Automotive Welding Manual*.

Wiring diagram A drawing portraying the components and wires in a vehicle's electrical system, using standardised symbols. For more information refer to the *Haynes Automotive Electrical and Electronic Systems Manual*.

Note: References throughout this index are in the form "Chapter number" • "Page number". So, for example, 2C•15 refers to page 15 of Chapter 2C.

Haynes Manuals – The Complete UK Car List

Title	Book No.
ALFA ROMEO Alfasud/Sprint (74 – 88) up to F *	0292
Alfa Romeo Alfetta (73 – 87) up to E *	0531
AUDI 80, 90 & Coupe Petrol (79 – Nov 88) up to F	0605
Audi 80, 90 & Coupe Petrol (Oct 86 – 90) D to H	1491
Audi 100 & A6 Petrol & Diesel (May 91 – May 97) H to P	3504
Audi A3 Petrol & Diesel (96 – May 03) P to 03	4253
Audi A3 Petrol & Diesel (June 03 – Mar 08) 03 to 08	4884
Audi A4 Petrol & Diesel (95 – 00) M to X	3575
Audi A4 Petrol & Diesel (01 – 04) X to 54	4609
Audi A4 Petrol & Diesel (Jan 05 – Feb 08) 54 to 57	4885
AUSTIN A35 & A40 (56 – 67) up to F *	0118
Mini (59 – 69) up to H *	0527
Mini (69 – 01) up to X	0646
Austin Healey 100/6 & 3000 (56 – 68) up to G *	0049
BEDFORD/Vauxhall Rascal & Suzuki Supercarry (86 – Oct 94) C to M	3015
BMW 1-Series 4-cyl Petrol & Diesel (04 – Aug 11) 54 to 11	4918
BMW 316, 320 & 320i (4-cyl)(75 – Feb 83) up to Y *	0276
BMW 3- & 5- Series Petrol (81 – 91) up to J	1948
BMW 3-Series Petrol (Apr 91 – 99) H to V	3210
BMW 3-Series Petrol (Sept 98 – 06) S to 56	4067
BMW 3-Series Petrol & Diesel (05 – Sept 08) 54 to 58	4782
BMW 5-Series 6-cyl Petrol (April 96 – Aug 03) N to 03	4151
BMW 5-Series Diesel (Sept 03 – 10) 53 to 10	4901
BMW 1500, 1502, 1600, 1602, 2000 & 2002 (59 – 77) up to S *	0240
CHRYSLER PT Cruiser Petrol (00-09) W to 09	4058
CITROEN 2CV, Ami & Dyane (67 – 90) up to H	0196
Citroen AX Petrol & Diesel (87- 97) D to P	3014
Citroen Berlingo & Peugeot Partner Petrol & Diesel (96 – 10) P to 60	4281
Citroen C1 Petrol (05 – 11) 05 to 11	4922
Citroen C3 Petrol & Diesel (02 – 09) 51 to 59	4890
Citroen C4 Petrol & Diesel (04 – 10) 54 to 60	5576
Citroen C5 Petrol & Diesel (01 – 08) Y to 08	4745
Citroen C15 Van Petrol & Diesel (89 – Oct 98) F to S	3509
Citroen CX Petrol (75 – 88) up to F	0528
Citroen Saxo Petrol & Diesel (96 – 04) N to 54	3506
Citroen Visa Petrol (79 – 88) up to F	0620
Citroen Xantia Petrol & Diesel (93 – 01) K to Y	3082
Citroen XM Petrol & Diesel (89 – 00) G to X	3451
Citroen Xsara Petrol & Diesel (97 – Sept 00) R to W	3751
Citroen Xsara Picasso Petrol & Diesel (00 – 02) W to 52	3944
Citroen Xsara Picasso (Mar 04 – 08) 04 to 58	4784
Citroen ZX Diesel (91 – 98) J to S	1922
Citroen ZX Petrol (91 – 98) H to S	1881
FIAT 126 (73 – 87) up to E *	0305
Fiat 500 (57 – 73) up to M *	0090
Fiat 500 & Panda (04 – 12) 53 to 61	5558
Fiat Bravo & Brava Petrol (95 – 00) N to W	3572
Fiat Cinquecento (93 – 98) K to R	3501
Fiat Panda (81 – 95) up to M	0793
Fiat Punto Petrol & Diesel (94 – Oct 99) L to V	3251
Fiat Punto Petrol (Oct 99 – July 03) V to 03	4066
Fiat Punto Petrol (03 – 07) 03 to 07	4746
Fiat Punto Petrol (Oct 99 – 07) V to 07	5634
Fiat X1/9 (74 – 89) up to G *	0273
FORD Anglia (59 – 68) up to G *	0001
Ford Capri II (& III) 1.6 & 2.0 (74 – 87) up to E *	0283
Ford Capri II (& III) 2.8 & 3.0 V6 (74 – 87) up to E	1309
Ford C-Max Petrol & Diesel (03 – 10) 53 to 60	4900
Ford Escort Mk I 1100 & 1300 (68 – 74) up to N *	0171
Ford Escort Mk I Mexico, RS 1600 & RS 2000 (70 – 74) up to N *	0139
Ford Escort Mk II Mexico, RS 1800 & RS 2000 (75 – 80) up to W *	0735
Ford Escort (75 – Aug 80) up to V *	0280
Ford Escort Petrol (Sept 80 – Sept 90) up to H	0686
Ford Escort & Orion Petrol (Sept 90 – 00) H to X	1737
Ford Escort & Orion Diesel (Sept 90 – 00) H to X	4081
Ford Fiesta Petrol (Feb 89 – Oct 95) F to N	1595
Ford Fiesta Petrol & Diesel (Oct 95 – Mar 02) N to 02	3397
Ford Fiesta Petrol & Diesel (Apr 02 – 08) 02 to 58	4170
Ford Fiesta Petrol & Diesel (08 – 11) 58 to 11	4907
Ford Focus Petrol & Diesel (98 – 01) S to Y	3759
Ford Focus Petrol & Diesel (Oct 01 – 05) 51 to 05	4167
Ford Focus Petrol (05 – 09) 54 to 09	4785
Ford Focus Diesel (05 – 09) 54 to 09	4807
Ford Fusion Petrol & Diesel (02 – 11) 02 to 61	5566
Ford Galaxy Petrol & Diesel (95 – Aug 00) M to W	3984
Ford Galaxy Petrol & Diesel (00 – 06) X to 06	5556
Ford Granada Petrol (Sept 77 – Feb 85) up to B *	0481
Ford Ka (96 – 08) P to 58	5567
Ford Mondeo Petrol (93 – Sept 00) K to X	1923
Ford Mondeo Petrol & Diesel (Oct 00 – Jul 03) X to 03	3990
Ford Mondeo Petrol & Diesel (July 03 – 07) 03 to 56	4619
Ford Mondeo Petrol & Diesel (Apr 07 – 12) 07 to 61	5548
Ford Mondeo Diesel (93 – Sept 00) L to X	3465
Ford Sierra V6 Petrol (82 – 91) up to J	0904
Ford Transit Connect Diesel (02 – 11) 02 to 11	4903
Ford Transit Diesel (Feb 86 – 99) C to T	3019
Ford Transit Diesel (00 – Oct 06) X to 56	4775
Ford 1.6 & 1.8 litre Diesel Engine (84 – 96) A to N	1172
HILLMAN Imp (63 – 76) up to R *	0022
HONDA Civic (Feb 84 – Oct 87) A to E	1226
Honda Civic (Nov 91 – 96) J to N	3199
Honda Civic Petrol (Mar 95 – 00) M to X	4050
Honda Civic Petrol & Diesel (01 – 05) X to 55	4611
Honda CR-V Petrol & Diesel (02 – 06) 51 to 56	4747
Honda Jazz (02 to 08) 51 to 58	4735
JAGUAR E-Type (61 – 72) up to L *	0140
Jaguar Mk I & II, 240 & 340 (55 – 69) up to H *	0098
Jaguar XJ6, XJ & Sovereign, Daimler Sovereign (68 – Oct 86) up to D	0242
Jaguar XJ6 & Sovereign (Oct 86 – Sept 94) D to M	3261
Jaguar XJ12, XJS & Sovereign, Daimler Double Six (72 – 88) up to F	0478
JEEP Cherokee Petrol (93 – 96) K to N	1943
LAND ROVER 90, 110 & Defender Diesel (83 – 07) up to 56	3017
Land Rover Discovery Petrol & Diesel (89 – 98) G to S	3016
Land Rover Discovery Diesel (Nov 98 – Jul 04) S to 04	4606
Land Rover Discovery Diesel (Aug 04 – Apr 09) 04 to 09	5562
Land Rover Freelander Petrol & Diesel (97 – Sept 03) R to 53	3929
Land Rover Freelander (97 – Oct 06) R to 56	5571
Land Rover Series II, IIA & III 4-cyl Petrol (58 – 85) up to C	0314
Land Rover Series II, IIA & III Petrol & Diesel (58 – 85) up to C	5568
MAZDA 323 (Mar 81 – Oct 89) up to G	1608
Mazda 323 (Oct 89 – 98) G to R	3455
Mazda B1600, B1800 & B2000 Pick-up Petrol (72 – 88) up to F	0267
Mazda MX-5 (89 – 05) G to 05	5565
Mazda RX-7 (79 – 85) up to C *	0460
MERCEDES-BENZ 190, 190E & 190D Petrol & Diesel (83 – 93) A to L	3450
Mercedes-Benz 200D, 240D, 240TD, 300D & 300TD 123 Series Diesel (Oct 76 – 85) up to C	1114
Mercedes-Benz 250 & 280 (68 – 72) up to L *	0346
Mercedes-Benz 250 & 280 123 Series Petrol (Oct 76 – 84) up to B *	0677
Mercedes-Benz 124 Series Petrol & Diesel (85 – Aug 93) C to K	3253
Mercedes-Benz A-Class Petrol & Diesel (98 – 04) S to 54	4748
Mercedes-Benz C-Class Petrol & Diesel (93 – Aug 00) L to W	3511
Mercedes-Benz C-Class (00 – 07) X to 07	4780
Mercedes-Benz Sprinter Diesel (95 – Apr 06) M to 06	4902
MGA (55 – 62)	0475
MGB (62 – 80) up to W	0111
MGB 1962 to 1980 (special edition) *	4894
MG Midget & Austin-Healey Sprite (58 – 80) up to W *	0265
MINI Petrol (July 01 – 06) Y to 56	4273
MINI Petrol & Diesel (Nov 06 – 13) 56 to 13	4904
MITSUBISHI Shogun & L200 Pick-ups Petrol (83 – 94) up to M	1944
MORRIS Minor 1000 (56 – 71) up to K	0024
NISSAN Almera Petrol (95 – Feb 00) N to V	4053
Nissan Almera & Tino Petrol (Feb 00 – 07) V to 56	4612
Nissan Micra (83 – Jan 93) up to K	0931
Nissan Micra (93 – 02) K to 52	3254
Nissan Micra Petrol (03 – Oct 10) 52 to 60	4734
Nissan Primera Petrol (90 - Aug 99) H to T	1851
Nissan Qashqai Petrol & Diesel (07 – 12) 56 to 62	5610
OPEL Ascona & Manta (B-Series) (Sept 75 – 88) up to F *	0316
Opel Ascona Petrol (81 – 88)	3215
Opel Ascona Petrol (Oct 91 – Feb 98)	3156
Opel Corsa Petrol (83 – Mar 93)	3160
Opel Corsa Petrol (Mar 93 – 97)	3159
Opel Kadett Petrol (Oct 84 – Oct 91)	3196
Opel Omega & Senator Petrol (Nov 86 – 94)	3157
Opel Vectra Petrol (Oct 88 – Oct 95)	3158
PEUGEOT 106 Petrol & Diesel (91 – 04) J to 53	1882
Peugeot 107 Petrol (05 – 11) 05 to 11	4923
Peugeot 205 Petrol (83 – 97) A to P	0932
Peugeot 206 Petrol & Diesel (98 – 01) S to X	3757

* Classic reprint